Beginning Microsoft® SQL Server® 2008 Administration

Beginning
Microsoft® SQL Server® 2008 Administration

Beginning
Microsoft® SQL Server® 2008 Administration

Chris Leiter
Dan Wood
Albert Boettger
Michael Cierkowski

WILEY

Wiley Publishing, Inc.

Beginning Microsoft® SQL Server® 2008 Administration

Published by
Wiley Publishing, Inc.
10475 Crosspoint Boulevard
Indianapolis, IN 46256
www.wiley.com

Copyright © 2009 by Wiley Publishing, Inc., Indianapolis, Indiana

Published simultaneously in Canada

ISBN: 978-0-470-44091-9

Manufactured in the United States of America

10 9 8 7 6 5 4 3 2 1

Library of Congress Cataloging-in-Publication Data

Beginning Microsoft SQL server 2008 administration / Chris Leiter ... [et al.].
    p. cm.
  Includes index.
  ISBN 978-0-470-44091-9 (paper/website)
 1. SQL server. 2. Database management. 3. Relational databases. I. Leiter,
Chris, 1975-
  QA76.9.D3B4465 2009
  005.4′476--dc22

2009004135

For my wife, Bridget Your patience, love, and support have made everything I have, and everything I am, possible. Thanks for believing in me

— Chris Leiter

I dedicate my contribution of this book to my dad, Reginald Kaaikaula Wood, who lost his battle with cancer while I was writing this book. He was a great encouragement and proud that his son was a published author even though he said, "I don't understand a darn word of it." My dad left an amazing legacy and he will be missed.

— Dan Wood

I dedicate this book to my daughter, Rachel. Watching you grow and re-experiencing the beauty and wonder of the world through your eyes, is and has been the greatest joy in my life. So few years to give you wings to fly.
I love you.

— Albert Boettger

I would like to dedicate this accomplishment to my daughter, Alina. You are the best thing that has ever happened to me and I love you very much.

— Michael Cierkowski

About the Authors

Chris Leiter (Auburn, WA) is a Senior Consultant for Hitachi Consulting. His primary focus is Microsoft's Business Intelligence and Performance Management products. Chris has been a Microsoft Certified Professional since 1997 and a Microsoft Certified Trainer since 2001. He currently holds the MCSE: Security, MCITP: Database Administrator, and ITIL: Foundation certifications. Chris is also co-author of *Beginning SQL Server 2005 Administration* by Dan Wood, Chris Leiter, and Paul Turley from Wrox Press 2006. When not writing about or working with Microsoft SQL Server, he enjoys watching movies from his extensive DVD collection with his wife, Bridget, and their cat, Cosmo. Chris contributed Chapters 1, 2, 3, 6, 7, 8, 12, 13, 15, 16, 17, and 19.

Dan Wood (Silverdale, WA) is the senior database administrator for Avalara, a sales tax compliance company where he both administers and develops database solutions for several enterprise applications that handle global address validation, tax rate calculation, and sales tax remittance for e-commerce and ERP clients. He has been working with SQL Server as a DBA, consultant, and trainer since 1999. Dan was a co-author on *Beginning Transact-SQL with SQL Server 2000 and 2005* by Paul Turley and Dan Wood (2005) and *Beginning T-SQL with Microsoft SQL Server 2005 and 2008* by Paul Turley and Dan Wood (2008) and the lead author of *Beginning SQL Server 2005 Administration*, all from WROX press. Dan contributed Chapters 4 and 9.

Albert Boettger (Federal Way, WA) is the Senior Software Engineer and Database Administrator for Sagem Morpho, Inc. Albert has more than 20 years of experience as a solution developer, database architect, and software engineer. Albert contributed Chapters 10 and 11.

Michael Cierkowski (Maple Valley, WA) currently works as an instructor for Netdesk Corporation, with a primary focus on SQL Server Administration. Michael has been a Microsoft Certified Professional and Trainer since 2000. He currently holds his MCSD, MCDBA, MCAD, MCSA, MCPD: (Windows, Web, and Enterprise), and MCITP: (Database Administrator, Database Developer, BI Developer, Server Administrator, and Enterprise Administrator). Michael contributed Chapters 5, 14, and 18.

Credits

Executive Editor
Bob Elliott

Development Editor
Maureen Spears

Technical Editor
Jim Adams

Senior Production Editor
Debra Banninger

Copy Editor
Cate Caffrey

Editorial Manager
Mary Beth Wakefield

Production Manager
Tim Tate

Vice President and Executive Group Publisher
Richard Swadley

Vice President and Executive Publisher
Barry Pruett

Associate Publisher
Jim Minatel

Project Coordinator, Cover
Lynsey Stanford

Proofreader
Nancy Carrasco

Indexer
J & J Indexing

Acknowledgments

First and foremost, I thank my wife, Bridget, for once again supporting and encouraging me through this process. It'll be nice to have our evenings back. Thanks also to Dan Wood, for letting me take the reins on this one. I'm really glad that you were able to stay on as a Contributing Author. Michael Cierkowski and Albert Boettger also deserve my gratitude for stepping up to the plate and co-authoring this book. Both of you are absolutely brilliant, and I'm lucky to know you. I also thank Lance Baldwin, one of the best people I've had the privilege of working for (twice!), and Paul Turley, who helped Dan and me get introduced to Wiley. And speaking of Wiley, I must also thank Bob Elliott for his support on this project and faith that I could pull it all together; Maureen Spears for having the patience of a saint; and Jim Adams, who never let anything get by him (and provided a huge contribution to Chapter 17!). There are several other people whom I would like to thank for helping me in one way or another during the process of creating this book. They include (in no particular order) Jeff Sparks, for constantly feeding my ego; Rick Kinglsan, for setting the bar and letting me raise it; D.J. Norton, for being as much of a gadget geek as I am; Stephanie Gulick, for being so supportive; everyone at Hitachi Consulting; and, of course, the Banz and Leiter families, who put up with me working through yet another holiday season.

— *Chris Leiter*

A great deal of thanks to Chris Leiter for taking over this book and being an outstanding Project Lead. Special thanks to all the wonderful people at Wrox for their patience for missed deadlines and support when my dad was ill. Lastly, but most importantly, my gratitude and undying love goes to my beautiful wife, Sarah, who supported me through yet another book project and expressed her pride and love while spending many nights and weekends without me. Thank you, my love.

— *Dan Wood*

A special thanks to Chris Leiter for convincing me to join the team and introducing me to Wiley Publishing. You were right. Thank you to Jeff Sparks for being a friend and mentor, and for always pushing me to explore and master new technologies. Your opinions and insights were invaluable. Thanks to everyone at Wiley Publishing who helped to make this book a reality, and especially to Bob Elliot for all his hard work. Thanks, Maureen, for keeping us all on schedule and answering all of our questions (kind of like herding cats), and to Jim for his excellent technical editing. To my loving wife, Elise, and beautiful daughter, Rachel, thank you for your love, patience, and understanding. You mean more to me than words can convey.

— *Albert C. Boettger*

First, I thank both Dan and Chris for considering me for this project. It has been a wonderful experience working with you, and I hope we can do it again sometime. I also thank everyone at Wrox for making the entire process a fairly painless affair. And finally, I thank my wife, Stacy, for dealing with many nights of neglect while I worked on my many projects. I love you more each and every day. A task that I didn't think was possible.

— *Michael Cierkowski*

Contents

Contents

Contents

Contents

Contents

Contents

Contents

Contents

Introduction

Microsoft officially announced SQL Server 2008, codenamed *Katmai*, at the first Microsoft Business Intelligence (BI) conference in May 2007. I suppose I had the same reaction as many others — "Already?" SQL Server 2005 had only been released a year and a half earlier, and I started to wonder if it was too soon. I can't tell you why I thought that. I also knew that it wasn't unusual for Microsoft's product teams to start planning for the next version of a product by the time the current version had been released. I knew that the time between the SQL Server 2000 and the SQL Server 2005 releases was *too* long. And I knew that Microsoft was committed to more frequent and consistent release cycles of two to three years for new versions of SQL Server.

I expected SQL Server 2008 to be more of a product refresh than a full new release. Most of the public material available hinted at that. It was designed to build on the framework laid out by SQL Server 2005, which offered two benefits. First, organizations that had already migrated to SQL Server 2005 would find the transition to SQL Server 2008 to be easier than moving from SQL Server 2000, or other database products. Additionally, Microsoft had solidified itself as a player in the BI market space by bundling Analysis Services, Integration Services, and Reporting Services as part of the SQL platform.

What I didn't expect was that some of the changes made were not incidental, but fairly significant. As you'll read in this book, Notification Services is gone, and Reporting Services no longer uses Internet Information Services to publish access to the Report Server. Having decided to withhold judgment for the time being, I have to admit I was concerned about how existing implementations of both these tools would be affected.

As information about Katmai became available, I tried to absorb as much as I could. I read articles online and in print magazines that outlined new features to make management of the system, and data, much easier. One of the more compelling features for me was FILESTREAM, which allowed files to be stored in an NTFS file system while still being maintained through SQL. I immediately saw how this feature could be leveraged for a product that had been developed by my co-workers for receiving, archiving, and forwarding Electronic Fingerprint Transmission records. Looking beyond that, I could envision how other Microsoft products, like SharePoint, might eventually leverage FILESTREAM for storing extremely large files that, if stored as BLOB data, would cause the database size to quickly become unwieldy and difficult to manage.

In 2007, Microsoft announced that it intended to release Windows Server 2008, SQL Server 2008, and Visual Studio 2008 on February 27, 2008. They had been releasing CTPs on a fairly regular schedule every couple of months or so. However, by the time CTP 6 had come around in February 2008, it was clear that SQL Server 2008 (and Visual Studio 2008) would not be ready by the intended release date. Microsoft has announced that they were targeting Q3 of 2008 for a release. Being somewhat of a cynic, I honestly didn't expect to see a release until November 2008. In fact, I thought it would have been appropriate to release it on November 7, coinciding with the third anniversary of the release of SQL Server 2005.

CTP 6 was considered to be "feature complete," which meant that changes from that point on were likely to be cosmetic, or relatively insignificant. At this point, components such as Data Compression, Policy-Based Management, and the Resource Governor had been through the ringer by beta testers and application developers, and most were happy with what they saw.

SQL Server 2008 was officially released on August 6, 2008 (although MSDN and TechNet subscribers had already been able to access it for a week). By this time, its features, tools, and components had gone through rigorous internal certification processes as well as significant public beta testing through the CTP availability. As I write this, it's been just over five months since the release of SQL Server 2008. I, and my associates, have had a chance to put SQL Server 2008 through its paces in both production and test environments. While, admittedly, there have been some growing pains, I believe that SQL Server 2008 is a solid product. I have worked with a number of people who often state, "I won't install Product X until at least Service Pack 1!" Because SQL Server 2008 is built on a stable SQL Server 2005 platform and improves upon it, I find it hard to justify a statement like that.

A common theme I reiterate with my clients, and also throughout this book, is that SQL Server is much more than a relational database management system. While the heart of SQL Server is, and always will be, the Database Engine, it's the client features, the performance management tools, the data integrity components, and the Business Intelligence solutions that make SQL Server an attractive solution to many people — DBAs and business users alike.

If you're reading this book, then chances are you're responsible for managing a SQL Server 2008 system, or you will be. Several years ago, when I worked for a training company in Seattle, I would find that students would usually (although not always) fit into one of three categories. The most common was IT administrators who have "inherited" a SQL Server. Typically, this would be a new server that was required by a new application or service the business was implementing. These students would have a good working knowledge of Windows system management, but were new to SQL. If you find that you fit in this category, this book is for you.

Another type of student I frequently saw was the developer who was involved in a project that used a SQL Server database for storing application data. These developers understood how the data needed to be stored, but were responsible for configuring and managing the development and test environments. Often, they would have limited (if any) knowledge of systems administration, but they knew what they were trying to accomplish. If you're one of these developers, this book is for you.

A third category of students I sometimes saw, although admittedly less frequently than the first two, were experienced DBAs who were familiar with Oracle, or other database technology, who needed to know how things worked in the Microsoft realm. Although there may be a difference in terminology or implementation, for the most part, the core technology is pretty standard. If you have experience with other database applications and are looking to get a better understanding of how Microsoft SQL Server 2008 can meet your needs, this book is for you.

Some of you may not fit into any of these categories, or you may fit into more than one. Whatever your intent for reading this book is, the subject matter is the same. This book, as the title suggests, is all about database administration. But what is database administration? Database administrators are more and more often being called on to perform duties that are not strictly "administrative" in nature. Along with typical administrative duties such as backups, database maintenance, and user management, database administrators are increasingly being asked to perform tasks such as building complex data transformations for data import, building distributed data solutions, and maintaining the security and integrity of the database while enabling the integration of managed-code into the Database Engine.

In a nutshell, for many organizations, the database administrator has become the one-stop shop for all things related to data storage. This makes the job of being a database administrator much more complicated and difficult than in the past because of the scope and power of each subsequent release.

As a result of the database administrator's increasingly broadening role in the enterprise, it is impossible for one book to adequately cover every facet of this critical skill set. This book lays the foundation by covering in detail the most common database administrative tasks. It will also introduce you to many of the more advanced areas that enterprise database administrators need to be familiar with. Read these pages carefully, and apply what you learn. From here, move on to more complex jobs and tasks. The opportunities for talented and hard-working database administrators are virtually unlimited.

Who This Book Is For

I've already given you an outline of who might be reading the book. When Dan Wood and I originally set out to write a book on SQL Server Administration, we knew our primary audience would be IT professionals (both developers and administrators) who have found themselves responsible for the management and maintenance of a SQL Server database. You may have been responsible for another database application, or even an earlier version of SQL, when you learned that SQL Server 2008 was now going to be part of the business plan.

We wrote this book for you. You may be thinking, "I'm a senior DBA and this book's title is *Beginning Microsoft SQL Server 2008 Administration*. I am not a beginner." I understand. However, we also wrote this book for you. Although SQL Server 2008 is based on SQL Server 2005, there are some key differences that are addressed in this book. SQL Server 2008 is also a dramatic departure from even earlier versions, and, even if you are an expert on SQL Server 2000 or SQL Server 7, you will find a great deal of very useful information in this book. Go ahead, flip through the pages, and check it out for yourself. I believe you will find what you're looking for.

A Note about This Second Edition

This book is technically a second edition of *Beginning SQL Server 2005 Administration*. If you've read through our first book (and we thank you, by the way), you may already be familiar with some of the concepts in this book. However, each chapter has been updated to accommodate new features and tools that are in SQL Server 2008 that were not available in its predecessor.

Assumptions

Even though we made no assumptions about prior SQL Server experience in this book, we did make a couple of other assumptions. This book assumes that you are familiar with relational database concepts. It also assumes that you are comfortable with navigating a Windows Operating System (all of our examples were built using Windows Server 2008). Probably the biggest assumption is that you are at least marginally experienced with the Structured Query Language (SQL). The examples in this book are all clearly defined, but there will be times when you will be required to alter the provided scripts to work in your environment. A basic knowledge of SQL will be invaluable in this case. *Beginning T-SQL with Microsoft SQL Server 2005 and 2008* (Wiley, 2008) is a great resource if you need some help in this area.

What This Book Covers

As much as we would like to have included everything that any database administrator might need for any given circumstance, there just isn't enough time or paper to cover it all. We have made every attempt to cover the main areas of SQL Server 2008 Administration. Inside this book, you will find detailed information about how to maintain and manage your SQL Server 2008 installation. Most of the day-to-day tasks of the DBA are described within the pages of this book. Installation, configuration, backups, restores, security, availability, performance monitoring, and the tools to manage these areas are all covered. Our intent, our goal, and our sincere desire are to provide you with the information necessary to be a competent and successful database administrator.

With this edition, we were also able to add additional material that was not covered in the first edition. This includes new chapters on SQL Server Analysis Services and SQL Server Reporting Services, the two key offerings in the Microsoft SQL Server BI stack. There is also a new chapter on optimizing SQL Server 2008 that beginners and experienced DBAs alike will find useful.

How This Book Is Structured

When putting this book together, we made a conscious effort to cover the material in a logical and sequential order:

❑ The first four chapters (Chapters 1–4) cover the overall structure of SQL Server 2008, as well as the installation process.

❑ Once that foundation is laid, we moved on to the administration process of building and securing databases in the next two chapters (Chapters 5 and 6).

❑ This is followed by seven chapters (Chapters 7–13) on specific administrative tasks and high-availability solutions.

❑ The last six chapters (Chapters 14–19) are dedicated to introducing you to the SQL Server 2008 services, and features including the Common Language Runtime (CLR), SQL Server's Business Intelligence offerings, and the Service Broker.

As mentioned, we tried to follow a logical order in the structure of this book, but like most technical books, it is not absolutely essential to read it in any particular order. However, if you are fairly new to SQL Server, you may want to read through Chapter 1 first to get an overall picture of the product before diving in to the remaining chapters.

What You Need to Use This Book

To take full advantage of this book, you will need to have an edition of SQL Server 2008 installed along with the AdventureWorks2008 sample database. To perform all the steps outlined in the following chapters, the Developer Edition (with its full support of the Enterprise Edition feature set) is highly recommended. In order to duplicate the examples in Chapter 14, "Introduction to the Common Language Runtime," as well as the example on using SOAP endpoints in Chapter 7, you will also need to have either Visual Basic 2008 or Visual C# 2008 installed (Visual Studio 2008 Professional is recommended).

Conventions

To help you get the most from the text and keep track of what's happening, we've used a number of conventions throughout the book.

Examples that you can download and try out for yourself generally appear in a box like this:

Try It Out

The "Try It Out" is an exercise you should work through, following the text in the book.

1. They usually consist of a set of steps.
2. Each step has a number.
3. Follow the steps through with your copy of the database.

> **Boxes like this one hold important, not-to-be forgotten information that is directly relevant to the surrounding text.**

Tips, hints, tricks, and asides to the current discussion are offset and placed in italics like this.

Styles in the text are presented as follows:

❑ We *highlight* new terms and important words when we introduce them.

❑ We show keyboard strokes like this: [Ctrl]+A.

❑ We show URLs and code within the text like so: persistence.properties.

❑ We present code in two different ways:

```
We use a monofont type with no highlighting for most code examples.
We use gray highlighting to emphasize code that's particularly important in the
present context.
```

Source Code

As you work through the examples in this book, you may choose either to type in all the code manually or to use the source code files that accompany the book. All of the source code used in this book is available for download at www.wrox.com. Once at the site, simply locate the book's title (either by using the Search box or by using one of the title lists) and click on the "Download Code" link on the book's detail page to obtain all the source code for the book.

Because many books have similar titles, you may find it easiest to search by ISBN; this book's ISBN is 978-0-470-44091-9.

Once you download the code, just decompress it with your favorite compression tool. Alternatively, you can go to the main Wrox code download page at www.wrox.com/dynamic/books/download.aspx to see the code available for this book and all other Wrox books.

Errata

We make every effort to ensure that there are no errors in the text or in the code. However, no one is perfect, and mistakes do occur. If you find an error in one of our books, like a spelling mistake or faulty piece of code, we would be very grateful for your feedback. By sending in errata, you may save another reader hours of frustration, and at the same time you will be helping us provide even higher quality information.

To find the errata page for this book, go to www.wrox.com and locate the title using the Search box or one of the title lists. Then, on the Book Search Results page, click on the Errata link. On this page, you can view all errata that have been submitted for this book and posted by Wrox editors.

A complete book list including links to errata is also available at www.wrox.com/misc-pages/booklist.shtml.

If you don't spot "your" error on the Errata page, click on the "Errata Form" link and complete the form to send us the error you have found. We'll check the information and, if appropriate, post a message to the book's Errata page and fix the problem in subsequent editions of the book.

p2p.wrox.com

For author and peer discussion, join the P2P forums at p2p.wrox.com. The forums are a web-based system for you to post messages relating to Wrox books and related technologies and interact with other readers and technology users. The forums offer a subscription feature to e-mail you topics of interest of your choosing when new posts are made to the forums. Wrox authors, editors, other industry experts, and your fellow readers are present on these forums.

At http://p2p.wrox.com, you will find a number of different forums that will help you not only as you read this book, but also as you develop your own applications. To join the forums, just follow these steps:

1. Go to p2p.wrox.com and click on the Register link.
2. Read the Terms of Use and click Agree.
3. Complete the required information to join as well as any optional information you wish to provide and click Submit.
4. You will receive an e-mail with information describing how to verify your account and complete the joining process.

You can read messages in the forums without joining P2P, but in order to post your own messages, you must join.

Once you join, you can post new messages and respond to messages other users post. You can read messages at any time on the Web. If you would like to have new messages from a particular forum e-mailed to you, click on the "Subscribe to this Forum" icon by the forum name in the forum listing.

For more information about how to use the Wrox P2P, be sure to read the P2P FAQs for answers to questions about how the forum software works as well as many common questions specific to P2P and Wrox books. To read the FAQs, click the FAQ link on any P2P page.

Introducing SQL Server 2008

Before getting into the meat (or tofu, if you prefer) and potatoes of SQL Server 2008, it's important that you understand what exactly it is that you have on your plate. In this chapter, you will learn about the history of SQL Server, the key components of SQL Server, and the different editions, or *flavors*, of SQL Server. This chapter also covers architecture, database objects, database storage, and server security from a very high level, with more detail to follow in subsequent chapters.

A Condensed History of SQL Server

Now that the world revolves around SQL Server (at least, it feels that way, doesn't it?), it's interesting to trace Microsoft SQL Server 2008 back to its humble origins. While this is by no means a comprehensive history of SQL, it does provide some insight into the evolution of the product, as well as an idea of where it might be headed. And who knows? This bit of trivia may still show up in *Trivial Pursuit: Geek Edition* for a yellow pie slice.

In the Beginning

Microsoft's foray into the enterprise database space came in 1987 when it formed a partnership with Sybase to market Sybase's DataServer product on the Microsoft/IBM OS/2 platform. From that partnership, SQL Server 1.0 emerged, which was essentially the UNIX version of Sybase's DataServer ported to OS/2.

The Evolution of a Database

After several years, the developers at Microsoft were allowed more and more access to the Sybase source code for test and debugging purposes, but the core SQL Server application continued to be a product of Sybase until SQL Server 4.2 was released for Windows NT in March 1992.

SQL Server 4.2 was the first true joint product developed by both Sybase and Microsoft. The Database Engine was still Sybase, but the tools and database libraries were developed by

Microsoft. While SQL Server had been developed to run primarily on the OS/2 platform, the release of Windows NT heralded in a new era. The developers at Microsoft essentially abandoned any OS/2 development and focused on bringing a version of SQL Server to Windows NT.

Microsoft Goes It Alone

With the growing success of Sybase in the UNIX market and Microsoft in Windows, the two companies found themselves competing for market share on a product essentially developed by Sybase. As a result, in 1994, the two companies terminated their joint development agreement, and Sybase granted Microsoft a limited license to use and modify Sybase technology exclusively for systems running on Windows.

A year later, in June 1995, Microsoft released the first version of SQL Server developed exclusively by Microsoft developers — SQL Server 6.0 — but the core technology was still largely Sybase code-base. Less than a year later, more changes were made, and Microsoft released SQL Server 6.5 in April 1996.

With SQL Server 6.5 complete, the developers on the SQL Server team were beginning work on a new database system code-named *Sphinx*. The Sybase code-base was rewritten almost from scratch for Sphinx, and only a handful of code remained to indicate SQL Server's humble beginnings in OS/2.

In December 1998, Sphinx was officially released as SQL Server 7.0. The changes from SQL Server 6.5 were readily apparent from the first second a database administrator launched the new Enterprise Manager. Finally, there was a robust and reliable database system that was easy to manage, easy to learn, and still powerful enough for many businesses.

As SQL Server 7.0 was being released, the next version was already in development. It was code-named *Shiloh*. Shiloh became SQL Server 2000 and was released in August 2000. The changes to the underlying data engine were minimal, but many exciting changes that affected SQL Server's scalability issues were added (such as indexed views and federated database servers), along with improvements like cascading referential integrity. Microsoft's enterprise database server was finally a true contender in the marketplace.

Over the next few years, the SQL team was working on an even more powerful and exciting release code-named *Yukon*, which is now SQL Server 2005. After more than five years in development, a product that some were calling "Yukon the giant (Oracle) killer" was finally released.

BI for the Masses

While calling SQL Server 2005 an "Oracle killer" might have been a bit optimistic, no one can deny the broad appeal of SQL Server 2005 as a great leap forward for Microsoft. Since its release, it has been the core technology behind a great number of Microsoft products, including SharePoint, PerformancePoint, and the System Center family of products. Many third-party vendors have also leveraged SQL for ERP systems and other software products.

Where SQL Server 2005 really stood apart from its competitors was in its Business Intelligence (BI) offerings. These include tools for moving and transforming data (SQL Server Integration Services), analyzing data (SQL Server Analysis Services), and reporting on data (SQL Server Reporting Services). These three components, in addition to Notification Services and the Service Broker, were part of Microsoft's commitment to make SQL Server 2005 stand out as more than just a Database Engine. The inclusion of these technologies made SQL Server 2005 extremely attractive to businesses that were just starting to discover and utilize BI.

2008 . . . and Beyond!

In August 2008, Microsoft SQL Server 2008 was released to manufacturing (RTM). While SQL Server 2008 isn't as much of a paradigm shift from SQL Server 2005 as its predecessor was from SQL Server 2000, it contains many improvements and new features that make it a compelling upgrade (which we will cover throughout this book). SQL Server 2000 reached its end-of-life mainstream support in April 2008, which should also help drive the adoption of SQL Server 2008.

Microsoft has invested heavily in SQL Server as a core technology and key platform, and there doesn't appear to be any slowdown in the near future. Rumors continue to persist that Microsoft Exchange and Active Directory, as well as a new file system, will leverage SQL Server 2008's Database Engine.

What Is SQL Server 2008?

As you most likely know, SQL Server 2008 is primarily thought of as a *Relational Database Management System* (*RDBMS*). It is certainly that, but it is also much more.

SQL Server 2008 can be more accurately described as an *Enterprise Data Platform*. It builds on many of the features that had first been incorporated in SQL Server 2005, while also expanding its offerings to include several improvements and additions. Primarily known for its traditional RDBMS role, SQL Server 2008 also provides rich reporting capabilities, powerful data analysis, and data mining. It also has features that support asynchronous data applications, data-driven Event Notification, and more.

This book is primarily focused on the administration of the Database Engine. However, as mentioned, SQL Server 2008 includes many more features than just the relational engine. In light of that, it is important to start with some point of common reference. This section introduces the features of SQL Server 2008. It is not meant to be all-inclusive, but it will provide the context for the remainder of the book.

Database Engine

The Database Engine is the primary component of SQL Server 2008. It is the Online Transaction Processing (OLTP) engine for SQL Server and has received further enhancements since SQL Server 2005. The Database Engine is a high-performance component responsible for the efficient storage, retrieval, and manipulation of relational and Extensible Markup Language (XML) formatted data.

SQL Server 2008's Database Engine is highly optimized for transaction processing, but offers exceptional performance in complex data retrieval operations. The Database Engine is also responsible for the controlled access and modification of data through its security subsystem. The Relational Database Engine in SQL Server 2008 has many improvements to support scalability, availability, security, and programmability. The following list is by no means a comprehensive list, but just a short overview of what's new in SQL Server 2008:

- ❑ **Hot Add CPU** — If your hardware or software environment supports it, SQL Server 2008 will allow you to dynamically add one or more CPUs to a running system. These CPUs can be physical, logical, or virtual.

- ❑ **Option to Optimize for Ad Hoc Workloads** — SQL Server 2008 includes a new feature that allows administrators to configure the server to improve plan cache efficiency for ad hoc batches. With this feature enabled, the Database Engine no longer needs to store fully compiled plans that will not be reused. Instead, the plan cache stores a stub of the ad hoc workload.

❑ **SQL Server Extended Events** — SQL Server 2005 introduced the ability to associate SQL Profiler traces with Windows Performance Log counters. This was extremely helpful in identifying poorly performing queries or the lack of sufficient resources in the system to handle certain events. SQL Server 2008 takes this a step further by introducing SQL Server Extended Events. Extended events allow database administrators to get a better understanding of the system behavior by correlating SQL Server data to the operating system or database applications. This is handled by directing output from extended events to Event Tracing for Windows (ETW).

❑ **Resource Governor** — The Resource Governor is a new feature that allows administrators to specify configuration options that limit the amount of CPU and memory available to incoming requests. This can help prevent applications or queries from consuming 100 percent of the CPU or all available memory. The Resource Governor uses configurable workload groups, which define what the CPU and memory limits are for any session that is classified as being a member of that group. Classification can be performed based on a number of system functions or user-defined functions.

❑ **Policy-Based Management** — SQL Server 2008 includes features that allow administrators greater control over their server environments by enforcing behaviors or constraints through a policy-based mechanism. In addition to using the included policies, administrators can create their own policies to configure servers to meet compliance requirements and standardize naming conventions, thereby simplifying administration.

❑ **Centralized Management** — Central Management servers are SQL Servers that can be configured to manage multiple servers as part of a group. You can also execute queries against a SQL Server group that can return results to either a combined set or a separate pane per server. A Central Management server can also be used to enforce management policies against multiple target servers simultaneously.

❑ **Query Editor IntelliSense** — SQL Server Management Studio now provides IntelliSense functionality in the Query Editor. The IntelliSense functionality provides auto-completion ability, error underlining, quick info help, syntax pair matching, and parameter help.

❑ **PowerShell Provider** — SQL Server 2008 includes new features that integrate with Windows PowerShell to help administrators automate many SQL Server 2008 tasks. *PowerShell* is an administrative command-line shell and scripting language that can make it easier to perform many common tasks through automation. The PowerShell provider in SQL Server 2008 exposes SQL Server Management Objects (SMO) in a structure similar to file system paths. SQL Server PowerShell also includes several SQL Server cmdlets for running scripts and other common tasks.

❑ **Compressed Indexes and Tables** — Compression is now supported for tables, indexes, and indexed views on either rows or pages. Compression operations will have an effect on performance. Because of this, row and page compression can be configured on a per-partition basis. For example, you could choose to compress a Read Only partition, but leave a Write-intensive partition uncompressed to minimize impact on the CPU.

❑ **FILESTREAM** — FILESTREAM is a new storage mechanism for storing data on the file system, rather than in the database itself. SQL Server 2008 applications can use FILESTREAM to take advantage of the storage and performance benefits of the NTFS file system while maintaining transactional consistency with the files themselves. Developers can leverage FILESTREAM as a mechanism for allowing large files to be maintained by the application database, without causing the database to become unnecessarily bloated. (Although this is just speculation on my part, I would be surprised if future releases of SharePoint didn't leverage FILESTREAM storage.)

- ❑ **Partition Switching** — Simply put, Partition Switching enables you to move data between partitions for a table or index. Data can be transferred between partitions without disrupting the integrity of the table or index.

- ❑ **Spatial Data Types** — Two new data types have been created for storing planar, or "flat-earth" data as well as ellipsoidal, or "round-earth" data. These data types are known as the geometry data type and geography data type, respectively.

- ❑ MERGE **Statement** — Transact-SQL includes a new MERGE statement that, based on the results of a join with a source table, can perform INSERT, UPDATE, or DELETE operations against a target table. For example, you can use MERGE to incrementally update a destination table by comparing the differences from a source table.

Integration Services

SQL Server Integration Services (SSIS) is Microsoft's enterprise class data Extract, Transform, and Load (ETL) tool. SSIS was originally introduced in SQL Server 2005 as a significant re-design of SQL Server 2000's Data Transformation Services (DTS). SSIS offers a much richer feature set and the ability to create much more powerful and flexible data transformations than its predecessor, and this has been further expanded in SQL Server 2008. As another component in SQL Server's BI stack, SSIS provides a rich environment for moving and transforming data from a variety of source and destinations systems. SSIS 2008 includes performance enhancements, new ADO.NET components, and a new script environment that integrates with Visual Studio Tools for Applications (VSTA). SSIS is covered in more detail in Chapter 16.

For a very thorough discussion of this feature of SQL Server 2008, read the book by Brian Knight, Erik Veerman, Grant Dickinson, Douglas Hinson, and Darren Herbold, Professional Microsoft SQL Server 2008 Integration Services (Wiley, 2008).

Analysis Services

Analysis Services delivers Online Analytical Processing (OLAP) and Data Mining functionality for Business Intelligence applications. As its name suggests, Analysis Services provides a very robust environment for the detailed analysis of data. It does this through user-created, multidimensional data structures that contain de-normalized and aggregated data from diverse data sources (such as relational databases, spreadsheets, flat files, and other multidimensional sources). Unlike the OLTP engine, which is optimized for Write performance, the OLAP engine is optimized for Read performance, allowing queries and reports to return results from millions of rows of data in a short period of time, with minimal (if any) impact to the OLTP engine.

The Data Mining component of Analysis Services allows the analysis of large quantities of data. This data can be "mined" for hidden relationships and patterns that may be of interest to an organization's data analyst. In fact, a well-known story about data mining involves Wal-Mart, Pop-Tarts, and hurricanes. Data mining revealed that prior to a hurricane event, sales of Pop-Tarts, particularly strawberry Pop-Tarts, would surge. In fact, they concluded that sales of strawberry Pop-Tarts before a hurricane were seven times that of normal sales. This allowed Wal-Mart to plan their inventory accordingly and meet customer demands. What's interesting about this example is that it seems completely random. Data mining does not attempt to answer the question of why Strawberry Pop-Tarts sell at a much higher rate, and sometimes, it may not even matter. Data mining revealed an absolute and consistent pattern that was used to plan inventory accordingly and paid off for the retailer.

A more detailed introduction to SSAS and Data Mining is in Chapter 17.

Reporting Services

Reporting Services is a Web Service–based solution for designing, deploying, and managing flexible, dynamic web-based reports, as well as traditional paper reports. These reports can contain information from virtually any data source. Although Reporting Services is implemented as a Web Service, it does not depend on Internet Information Services (IIS). In fact, in SQL Server 2008, IIS is no longer used to manage SQL Server Reporting Services. SQL Server Reporting Services (SSRS) can publish reports to a Virtual Directory hosted by the SQL Server itself, or to a SharePoint library. More information about SSRS can be found in Chapter 18.

> *For a detailed description of SQL Server 2008 Reporting Services and information about how to implement and extend SQL Server 2008 reports, check out an excellent book,* Professional Microsoft SQL Server 2008 Reporting Services *(Wiley, 2008), by my friends and co-workers Paul Turley, Thiago Silva, Bryan C. Smith, and Ken Withee.*

Service Broker

Service Broker provides the framework and services to enable the creation of asynchronous, loosely coupled applications. Service Broker implements a Service Oriented Architecture (SOA) in the data tier. It provides more controlled transaction-based communications than traditionally available in other SOA implementations such as Microsoft Message Queuing (MSMQ), without some of the limitations that MSMQ has (e.g., message size). Service Broker allows developers to create database applications that focus on a particular task and allows the asynchronous communication with other applications that perform related (yet disconnected) tasks. For more information, see Chapter 19.

Data Tier Web Services

SQL Server 2008 provides support for creating and publishing data tier objects via HTTP without the use of an Internet Information Services (IIS) server. SQL Server 2008 registers itself with the HTTP.sys listener, allowing it to respond to Web Services requests. Developers can take advantage of this by creating applications that interact with a database across the Internet or through a firewall by using a Web Service. For more information, see Chapter 7.

Replication Services

SQL Server 2008 Replication Services provides the ability to automate and schedule the copying and distribution of data and database objects from one database or server to another, while ensuring data integrity and consistency. Replication has been enhanced in SQL Server 2008 to include a new Peer-to-Peer Topology Wizard, which allows replication nodes to be managed using a topology viewer. The process of adding and removing nodes has also been made easier in this version of SQL Server. More detail about replication can be found in Chapter 13.

Multiple Instances

As with previous versions, SQL Server 2008 provides the capability of installing multiple instances of the database application on a single computer. SQL Server 2008 can also coexist with SQL Server 2000 and SQL Server 2005 instances installed on the same server. Depending on the edition of SQL Server being installed, up to 50 instances can be installed. This feature allows for one high-performance server to host multiple instances of the SQL Server services, each with its own configuration and databases. Each instance can be managed and controlled separately with no dependency on each other.

Database Mail

In the past, SQL Server relied on a Messaging Application Programming Interface (MAPI) mail client configured on the server to facilitate e-mail and pager notification for administrative and programmatic purposes. What this essentially meant was that to fully utilize administrative notifications, the administrator needed to install Outlook (or some other MAPI-compliant client) on the server and then create a mail profile for the service account to use.

Many organizations wanted to take advantage of the SQL Server Agent's ability to send job and Event Notification via e-mail but were unwilling to install unnecessary and potentially risky software on production server assets. The Database Mail feature removes this requirement by supporting Simple Mail Transfer Protocol (SMTP) for all mail traffic. In addition, multiple mail profiles can be created in the database to support different database applications. Configuring Database Mail is covered in Chapter 8.

A Note about Notification Services

In our *Beginning SQL Server 2005 Administration* (Wiley, 2006) book, Notification Services was introduced. If you are familiar with Notification Services and have used it with SQL Server 2000 or SQL Server 2005, you might be dismayed (or overjoyed, depending on your experience) that SQL Server Notification Services *is* no more. Most of the functionality of Notification Services has been absorbed into SQL Server Reporting Services, eliminating the need for Notification Services in SQL Server 2008.

SQL Server 2008 Editions

SQL Server 2008 comes in several different flavors, and each has its specific place in the data management infrastructure with the probable exception of the Enterprise Evaluation Edition, which is only useful for short-term evaluation of the product (180 days). At the top of the list is the Enterprise Edition, which supports absolutely everything that SQL Server 2008 has to offer. On the other end of the spectrum is the Express Edition, which offers very limited (but still exciting) features. Each edition, with the exception of the Compact Edition, has an x64 and x86 version. The Enterprise Edition (and consequently, the Developer Edition) also supports IA64 environments.

The available editions are:

❑ Enterprise Edition

❑ Standard Edition

❑ Workgroup Edition

❑ Web Edition

❑ Express Edition

❑ Express Advanced Edition

❑ Developer Edition

❑ Compact Edition

The following table contrasts the major differences between the four main editions of SQL Server 2008. The Developer Edition includes the same feature set as the Enterprise Edition but is not licensed for production use.

Feature	Enterprise Edition	Standard Edition	Workgroup Edition	Web Edition
Failover Clustering	Yes (limited by OS)	2-node	No	No
Multi-Instance Support	50	16	16	16
Database Mirroring	Yes	Limited	Witness Server Role only	Witness Server Role only
Enhanced Availability Features	Yes	No	No	No
Table and Index Physical Partitioning	Yes	No	No	No
Policy-Based Management	Yes	Yes	Yes	Yes
T-SQL and MDX IntelliSense	Yes	Yes	Yes	No
Spatial and Location Services	Yes	Yes	Yes	Yes
Service Broker	Yes	Yes	Yes	Client only
Analysis Services	Yes	Limited	No	No
Data Mining	Yes	Limited	No	No
Reporting Services	Yes	Limited	Limited	Limited
Integration Services	Yes	Limited	Very limited	Very limited
Replication Services	Yes	Limited	Limited features available to Subscriber only	Limited features available to Subscriber only

For a complete list of supported features, consult SQL Server 2008 Books Online under the topic "Features Supported by the Editions of SQL Server 2008."

SQL Server Compact 3.5 SP1

There have been several iterations of the SQL Server Compact Edition, beginning with SQL Server CE, first offered in SQL Server 2000. When SQL Server 2005 was released, it was rebranded as SQL Server 2005 Mobile Edition, specifically targeting Smartphones and PDAs. The new Compact Edition enables the installation of a small SQL Server database on a mobile device or Windows platform to support a

Windows Embedded CE or Windows Mobile application, as well as supporting desktop applications that require a much smaller feature set than offered in the Express Edition.

This ability creates a world of opportunity for collecting data in a remote scenario and synchronizing that data with a land-based database. For example, consider an overnight delivery service that must maintain a record of a delivery truck's inventory, including packages delivered and picked up. The truck inventory could be uploaded via replication to a mobile device, where a mobile application keeps track of the deliveries and new packages picked up at delivery locations. Once the truck comes back to the delivery center, the mobile device could be synchronized with the central database via replication or data upload.

SQL Server 2008 Express Edition

Back in the old days, when I had to manage database systems (in the snow, uphill both ways), the Microsoft Desktop Edition (MSDE) of SQL Server was the primary client-side Database Engine. It was extremely limited and included almost no management tools (except for the command-line osql utility) but had a compelling price — free. This has since been replaced with the SQL Server 2008 Express Edition. It's still not as robust as the Standard or Enterprise Editions, but for its very low price (you can't beat free), it still contains a great deal of functionality.

What makes this edition compelling is that it is perfect for many organizations that are starting or running small businesses. They have a genuine need for a centralized managed database but aren't ready to pay for a more scalable and robust solution. At the risk of offending my friends in the Open Source community, many small businesses that are not in the tech industry often don't have the benefit of having tech-savvy personnel on staff. Viable Open Source solutions like MySQL running on Linux or Windows is simply not appropriate when a Database Engine with an intuitive and free graphical management tool exists.

One of the most exciting improvements to Microsoft's free version of its database system is that it comes with a graphical management environment, SQL Server Management Studio Basic. It also supports databases up to 4 GB in size and contains much of the same functionality as the other editions. There is even an "advanced" edition of SQL Server 2008 Express that includes full-text search and Reporting Services (still free!).

SQL Express can be installed on any Microsoft desktop or server operating system from Windows 2000 and beyond, so a very small company can still leverage the database technology without making a large investment. Once the company starts to grow, it will inevitably need to make the move to one of the more robust editions, but the upgrade process from SQL Express to its bigger siblings is a piece of cake because the data structures are nearly identical. Even larger organizations can take advantage of the SQL Server Express Edition by using it for smaller, departmental or business unit installations.

SQL Server 2008 Web Edition

SQL Server 2008 Web Edition is the newest entry in the SQL Server product family. The Web Edition is designed around support for Web-facing environments and applications. With support for up to four processors and no limits on memory or database size, the Web Edition positions itself as a cost-efficient means for hosting services that rely on SQL Server databases. The Web Edition is targeted toward service providers, or Select Licensing customers that need to host public data.

The Web Edition has some very specific licensing guidelines and requirements. For example, it is licensed for public-facing web applications, sites, and services. It is not licensed for internal line-of-business applications. Because it is designed around public consumption, Client Access Licenses (CALs) are not applicable to the Web Edition.

The Web Edition is only available to Select Licensing and Service Provider License Agreement Customers. Contact your reseller or licensing representative to find out if the Web Edition is appropriate for your scenario.

SQL Server 2008 Workgroup Edition

The Workgroup Edition contains all the functionality of the SQL Server 2008 Express Edition and then some. This edition is targeted to those small companies that have either outgrown the Express Edition or needed a more flexible solution to begin with and yet do not need all the features of the Standard or Enterprise Editions.

The Workgroup Edition is very flexible and contains many of the features of the more expensive editions. What the Workgroup Edition doesn't provide is support for more advanced Business Intelligence applications, because SQL Server Integration Services and Analysis Services are not included in this edition. The Workgroup Edition also has a reduced feature set in regard to Reporting Services, but the Reporting Services features supported should satisfy most small organizations.

Like the Express Edition, the Workgroup Edition can be installed on both desktop and server operating systems, with the exception of Windows XP Home (which is not supported).

SQL Server 2008 Standard Edition

Most of the capabilities of SQL Server 2008 are supported in the Standard Edition, which makes it the ideal data platform for many organizations. What the Standard Edition does not provide are many of the features designed for the support of large enterprise databases. These features include many of the high-availability and scalability enhancements, such as Partitioned Tables and Parallel index operations. It also lacks some of the more advanced features of the Analysis Services and Integration Services engines.

SQL Server 2008 Enterprise Edition

The Enterprise Edition is the bee's knees. Nothing is held back. Parallel operations, physical table partitioning, complete business intelligence, and data-mining support — you name it, the Enterprise Edition has it.

If you require an easy-to-implement-and-maintain platform that will allow you to dynamically add memory and CPUs, Transparent Data Encryption, and parallel index operations, this release is for you. It is also an appropriate solution if you require only advanced business analytics, and not necessarily the millions of transactions per second that this edition offers.

The Enterprise Edition is about performance and scalability. Although the feature set in the Enterprise Edition may be more than the average company needs, the differences in performance between the Standard and Enterprise editions can have a significant impact on whether their SQL Server is scalable enough to accommodate quick growth within the organization. The Enterprise Edition fully optimizes Read-ahead execution and table scans, which results in a noticeable performance improvement.

The difference in cost between the Standard Edition and the Enterprise Edition can be significant; especially to smaller organizations where budget constraints can limit their purchasing power. However, be aware that some software may depend on certain features of the Enterprise Edition. A good example of this is the Microsoft Office PerformancePoint Server 2007 Planning Server, which relies heavily on proactive caching for Analysis Services cubes. This feature is only available in the Enterprise Edition of SQL Server.

SQL Server 2008 Architecture

It is the job of SQL Server to efficiently store and manage related data in a transaction-intensive environment. The actual theories and principles of a relational database are beyond the scope of this book, and, hopefully, you already have some of that knowledge. What is pertinent to this book is the way SQL Server manages the data and how it communicates with clients to expose the data. The following discussion describes the communication architecture utilized by SQL Server 2008, the services SQL Server 2008 offers, and the types of databases used by SQL Server. This section also introduces at a high level how those databases are stored and accessed, but you can find a detailed description of the SQL Server 2008 storage architecture in Chapter 4.

SQL Server 2008 Communication

To adequately plan for a SQL Server database application, it is important to understand how SQL Server 2008 communicates with clients. As mentioned previously, SQL Server 2008 is more than just a relational database server. Because the SQL Server 2008 platform offers several different data services, it also must provide different ways of accessing that data.

SQL Server 2008 ships with the ability to communicate over different protocols. By default, SQL Server will accept network connections via TCP/IP. The local Shared Memory protocol is also enabled by default to allow local connections without having to incur the overhead of a network protocol. A more complete description of the protocols that can be leveraged by SQL Server 2008 is provided in Chapter 7.

In addition to the TCP/IP, Named Pipes, and Shared Memory protocols, the Virtual Interface Adapter (VIA) protocol is available for VIA Storage Area Network (SAN) implementations.

With the exception of HTTP endpoints, SQL Server uses a communication format called *Tabular Data Stream* (TDS). The TDS packets utilized by SQL Server are encapsulated in the appropriate protocol packets for network communication.

The task of wrapping the TDS packets is the responsibility of the SQL Server Network Interface (SNI) protocol layer. The SNI replaces the Server Net-Libraries and the Microsoft Data Access Components (MDAC) that were used in SQL Server 2000. SQL Server creates separate TDS endpoints for each network protocol.

Although TDS is the primary method for connecting to and manipulating data on a SQL Server, it is not the only method available. In addition to TDS communication, SQL Server 2008 supports native Data

Tier Web services (see Chapter 7). By utilizing SQL Server Web services, connections can be made to SQL Server via any client application that supports HTTP and Simple Object Access Protocol (SOAP).

Supported Languages

SQL Server 2008 supports the following five different languages to enable data manipulation, data retrieval, administrative functions, and database configuration operations:

❑ **Transact-Structured Query Language (T-SQL)** — This is Microsoft's procedural language extension to the Structured Query Language (SQL) standard established by the American National Standards Institute (ANSI). T-SQL is entry-level compliant with the ANSI-99 standard. T-SQL is the primary and most common method for manipulating data. For more information about T-SQL, consult *Beginning T-SQL with Microsoft SQL Server 2005 and 2008* by Paul Turley and Dan Wood (Wiley, 2008).

❑ **Extensible Markup Language (XML)** — This is fully supported in SQL Server 2008 as a data type, as well as language extensions to XML that enable the retrieval and modification of data by using XQuery syntax or native XML methods.

❑ **Multidimensional Expressions (MDX)** — This language is used to query against multidimensional objects in SQL Server 2008 Analysis Services.

❑ **Data Mining Extensions (DMX)** — This is an extension of Transact-SQL that enables the creation of queries against a data-mining model implemented in SQL Server 2008 Analysis Services.

❑ **Extensible Markup Language for Analysis (XMLA)** — This can be used to both discover metadata from an instance of SQL Server 2008 Analysis Services and to execute commands against an instance of SSAS. XMLA commands are generally limited to the creation or modification of SSAS objects. Actual retrieval of SSAS data is done with MDX queries.

SQL Server Programming Object Models

Most of the administrative activity that must be done on SQL Server 2008 can be done using the provided tools, but sometimes it may be necessary to build custom administrative tools, or to be able to programmatically build and manipulate database objects. Three new object models have been created to support this need:

❑ **SQL Management Objects (SMOs)** — SMOs enable developers to create custom applications to manage and configure SQL Server 2008, SQL Server 2005, SQL Server 2000, or SQL Server 7.0 Database Engines. It is an extensive library that provides full support for virtually all aspects of the relational store. The SMO library makes it possible to automate administrative tasks that an administrator must perform through custom applications, or with command-line scripts using the SMO `scripter` class.

❑ **Replication Management Objects (RMOs)** — RMOs can be used along with SMOs to implement and automate all replication activity, or to build custom replication applications.

❑ **Analysis Management Objects (AMOs)** — AMOs, like SMOs and RMOs, represent a complete library of programming objects. AMOs enable the creation of custom applications or automation of Analysis Server management.

❑ **SQL Distributed Management Objects (DMOs)** — SQL-DMO is a legacy set of management objects that have been held over from SQL Server 2000. Although they are available in SQL Server 2005 and SQL Server 2008, they have been deprecated in favor of SQL-SMO. Applications that still use SQL-DMO should be upgraded to support SQL-SMO for SQL Server 2008.

SQL Server 2008 Services

SQL Server runs as a service. In fact, it runs as several services if all the different features of the product are installed. It is important to know what service is responsible for what part of the application so that each service can be configured correctly, and so that unneeded services can be disabled to reduce the overhead on the server and reduce the surface area of SQL Server. These services are identified by their executable names.

MSSQLServer (SQL Server)

The MSSQLServer service is the Database Engine. To connect and transact against a SQL Server 2008 database, the MSSQLServer service must be running. Most of the functionality and storage features of the Database Engine are controlled by this service.

The MSSQLServer service can be configured to run as the local system or as a domain user. If installed on Windows Server 2003 or Windows Server 2008, it can also be configured to run under the Network System account.

SQLServerAgent (SQL Server Agent)

The SQLServerAgent service is responsible for the execution of scheduled jobs such as backups, import/export jobs, and Integration Services packages. If any scheduled tasks require network or file system access, the SQLServerAgent service's credentials are typically used.

The SQLServerAgent service is dependent on the MSSQLServer service. During installation, the option is given to configure both services with the same credentials. Although this is by no means required, it is common practice. A frequent problem encountered by database administrators is when a job that executes perfectly during a manual invocation fails when run by the agent. Often, the reason for the failure is because the account that is used when testing the job manually is the logged-in administrator, but when the job is executed by the agent, the account the agent is running under does not have adequate permissions.

MSSQLServerADHelper100 (SQL Server Active Directory Helper)

Microsoft SQL Server 2008 has the ability to publish itself and its features in Active Directory. This can make it easier for Active Directory–aware services and applications to find the necessary SQL components that they need. Typically, the MSSQLServer service and the SQLServerAgent service are configured to run with a domain account that has local administrative rights on the server that SQL Server is installed on. Although this configuration offers a great deal of flexibility to what the two services can do locally, it doesn't give them any permission to publish objects in Active Directory.

In order for the MSSQLServer service to register its respective instance of SQL Server, it must be either running as the local system account (which significantly reduces the flexibility of the service) or be a member of the domain admin group (which grants it way too much access, violating the principle of least privilege).

To enable SQL Server to register itself in the domain, but not limit its functionality, the MSSQLServerADHelper service was created. The MSSQLServerADHelper service runs under the local system account of the domain computer that SQL Server is installed on and is automatically granted the right to add and remove objects from Active Directory. The MSSQLServerADHelper service only runs when needed to access Active Directory and is started by the MSSQLServer service when required.

Regardless of the number of installed instances, there is only one MSSQLServerADHelper service per computer.

The version information "100" is used to denote that this service is associated with SQL Server 2008, or SQL Server 10.0.

MSSQLServerOLAPService (SQL Server Analysis Services)

MSSQLServerOLAPService is the service that Analysis Services runs under. Analysis Services provides the services and functionality to support all of SQL Server 2008's OLAP needs, as well as the Data Mining engine included with SQL Server 2008.

SQLBrowser (SQL Server Browser)

The SQLBrowser Service is used by SQL Server for named instance name resolution and server name enumeration over TCP/IP and VIA networks.

The default instance of SQL Server is assigned the TCP Port 1433 by default to support client communication. However, because more than one application cannot share a port assignment, any named instances are given a random port number when the service is started. This random port assignment makes it difficult for clients to connect to it, because the client applications don't know what port the server is listening on. To meet this need, the SQLBrowser Service was created.

On start-up, the SQLBrowser Service queries the registry to discover all the names and port numbers of installed servers and reserves UDP Port 1434. It then listens on UDP Port 1434 for SQL Server Resolution Protocol (SSRP) requests and responds to the requests with the list of instances and their respective port assignments so that clients can connect without knowing the port number assignment. There are definite security considerations to this arrangement, so it is very important that no unauthenticated traffic on UDP Port 1434 be allowed on the network, because the service will respond to any request on that port. This creates the potential of exposing more information about the server instances than some organizations find acceptable.

If the SQLBrowser Service is disabled, it will be necessary to specify a static port number for all named instances of the SQL Server Service and to configure all client applications that connect to those instances with the appropriate connection information. For a full list of what features are affected by disabling the SQLBrowser, consult SQL Server 2008 Books Online.

MSSQLFDLauncher (SQL Full-Text Filter Daemon Launcher)

The Microsoft Full-Text Daemon Launcher for SQL Server (MSSQLFDLauncher) is used to support full-text indexing and full-text queries against text data stored in the database. The text data can be of several different data types including char, nchar, varchar, nvarchar, text, and ntext. In addition, full-text indexes can be created on binary formatted text such as Microsoft Word documents.

The chief advantage of the MSSQLFDLauncher service and associated engine is that it allows much more flexible and powerful searches against text data than the Transact-SQL LIKE command, which is limited to exact match searches. The MSSQLFDLauncher engine can perform exact match, proximity, linguistic, and inflectional searches. It will also exponentially outperform comparative Transact-SQL LIKE searches against large (millions of rows) tables. For a more complete discussion on both the Transact-SQL LIKE command and Full-Text search, see *Beginning T-SQL with Microsoft SQL Server 2005 and 2008*.

MSDTSServer100 (SQL Server Integration Services)

The MSDTSServer service provides management and storage support for SSIS. Although this service is not required to create, store, and execute SSIS packages, it does allow for the monitoring of SSIS package execution and displaying of a hierarchical view of SSIS packages and folders that are stored in different physical locations.

ReportingServicesServer (SQL Server Reporting Services)

The ReportingServicesServer service is the process in which Reporting Services runs. The service is accessible as a Web Service and provides for report rendering, creation, management, and deploying. For more information on Reporting Services, see *Professional Microsoft SQL Server 2008 Reporting Services*.

SQLWriter (SQL Server VSS Writer)

The SQLWriter service allows for the volume backup of SQL Server data and log files while the SQL Server service is still running. It does this through the Volume Shadow Copy Service (VSS). SQL Server database backups are typically performed through SQL Server's backup program or through third-party applications that communicate with SQL Server's backup program.

Normal file system backups of volumes containing SQL Server log or data files will typically fail to properly back up those files, because as long as SQL Server is running, the files are open. The SQLWriter service overcomes this limitation by allowing you to perform the backups of a snapshot copy of the files with the VSS service. It is still recommended, however, to perform regular backups through SQL Server's backup program.

MSDTC (Distributed Transaction Coordinator)

The MSDTC service is used to manage transactions that span more than one instance of SQL Server or an instance of SQL Server and another transaction-based system. It uses a protocol known as *two-phased commit (2 PC)* to ensure that all transactions that span systems are committed on all participating systems.

SQL Server 2008 Database Objects

SQL Server 2008 database objects exist within a defined scope and hierarchy. This hierarchy enables more control over security permissions and organization of objects by similar function. SQL Server 2008 objects are defined at the server, database, and schema levels.

Server

The server scope encompasses all the objects that exist on the instance of SQL Server, regardless of their respective database or namespace. The database object resides within the server scope.

One of the more confusing terms when working with SQL Server 2008 is *server*. When you hear the term *server*, you often think of that piece of hardware taking up space on a *server* rack in the *server* room. And let's not even get started on how virtualization mucks up the term. Where the confusion arises is that you can install multiple instances of SQL Server on a single *server* (huh?).

What would probably be clearer is to say that the capability exists to install multiple instances of the SQL Server 2008 Data Platform application on a single computer running a Windows operating system. Although this might be more descriptive, it doesn't make for very interesting marketing material.

What is left is the fact that, when it comes to SQL Server 2008 and you read "server," it is important to check the context to make sure that it means an instance of SQL Server 2008 or the physical computer that SQL Server is installed on.

When it comes to the server scope and SQL Server 2008 database objects, the term *server* actually refers to the SQL Server 2008 *instance*. The default instance is actually SERVERNAME\MSSQLService. However, since it is the *default instance*, appending *MSSQLService* to the server name is unnecessary. For example, we are using a server called *AUGHTEIGHT* that runs the Windows Server 2008 Operating System while writing this book. The default instance of SQL Server is known simply as *AUGHTEIGHT*. If you were to install a second instance, named *SECONDINSTANCE*, the SQL Server name would be *AUGHTEIGHT\SECONDINSTANCE*. From a SQL Server point of view, each instance is considered a separate "server."

Database

The database scope defines all the objects within a database catalog. Schemas exist in the database scope.

The ANSI synonym for *database* is *catalog*. When connecting to an instance of SQL Server 2008, it is generally desired to specify an Initial Catalog, or Initial Database. An instance of SQL Server 2008 can contain many databases. It used to be common for a typical database application to be constrained within one database that contained all the data objects required to provide the functionality for the application. However, now it is not uncommon to see more and more applications requiring multiple databases to manage different components of the application (this tends to increase the scalability of said application). An example of this is SharePoint, which creates databases for managing the SharePoint environment itself, as well as content databases for the various sites and site collections.

Schema

Each database can contain one or more schemas. A schema is a namespace for database objects. All data objects in a SQL Server 2008 database reside in a specific schema.

SQL Server 2008 implements the ANSI schema object. A *database schema* is a defined namespace in which database objects exist. It is also a fully configurable security scope. In previous releases of SQL Server, the namespace was defined by the owner of an object, and it wasn't uncommon to see everything in the database in the dbo schema. In SQL Server 2008, the ownership of an object is separated from an object's namespace. An individual user may be granted ownership of a schema, but the underlying objects belong to the schema itself. This adds greater flexibility and control to the management and securing of database objects. Permissions can be granted to a schema, and those permissions will be inherited by all the objects defined in the schema.

Object Names

Every object in a SQL Server 2008 database is identified by a four-part, fully qualified name. This fully qualified name takes the form of `server.database.schema.object`. However, when referring to objects, the fully qualified name can be abbreviated. By omitting the server name, SQL Server will assume the instance the connection is currently connected to. Likewise, omitting the database name will cause SQL Server to assume the existing connection's database context.

Omitting the schema name will cause SQL Server to assume the namespace of the logged-in user. This is where some confusion can be created. Unless explicitly assigned, new users are assigned the default schema of dbo. (See Chapter 6 for user and login management information.) As a result, all references to database objects not explicitly qualified will be resolved to the dbo schema.

For example, the user Fred logs in to the server AUGHTEIGHT, and his database context is set to AdventureWorks2008. Because Fred was not assigned a user-defined schema, he exists in the default dbo schema. Fred wants to retrieve the contents of the Person table, so he executes the following query:

```
SELECT * FROM Person;
```

Fred's query will resolve to AUGHTEIGHT.AdventureWorks2008.dbo.Person. Unfortunately, that table does not exist. The fully qualified name for the contact table is AUGHTEIGHT.AdventureWorks2008 .Person.Person. In order for Fred's query to work, one of two things will have to happen. The query will have to be rewritten to reference the appropriate schema scope, as in the following example:

```
SELECT * FROM Person.Person;
```

Or, Fred's default schema can be changed to the Person schema so that his query will be properly resolved with the following command:

```
USE AdventureWorks2008;
GO
ALTER USER Fred WITH DEFAULT_SCHEMA=Person;
GO
```

Now, take a look at a different scenario. The user Fred is created and assigned the default schema of Production. Fred wants to retrieve the contents of a table called dbo.DatabaseLog so he executes the following:

```
SELECT * FROM DatabaseLog;
```

SQL Server first resolves this query as AUGHTEIGHT.AdventureWorks2008.Person.DatabaseLog because Fred's default schema is Person and he did not explicitly tell SQL Server what schema to work with. Because the DatabaseLog table does not exist in the Person schema, the initial resolution fails, but SQL Server then falls back to the dbo schema and resolves the name as AUGHTEIGHT.AdventureWorks2008.dbo.DatabaseLog. The resolution succeeds, and Fred is able to retrieve the data he wanted.

SQL Server will always search the assigned schema first, then the dbo schema if the initial resolution fails. Care must be taken when creating objects so that the proper namespace is referenced. It is completely possible to create a table with the same name in two different schemas (e.g., a dbo.HourlyWage and a HumanResources.HourlyWage). When this happens and an application is created to expose the contents of the HourlyWage table, the possibilities for inconsistencies and confusion are endless. If the schema is not referenced in the application's query, some users will invariably get their results from the table in the dbo schema, whereas others will end up getting results from the HumanResources version of the table. As a best practice, all objects should be referenced by (at least) a two-part name to avoid this confusion.

SQL Server 2008 Databases

There are two types of databases in SQL Server: system databases and user databases. The *system databases* are used to store system-wide data and metadata. *User databases* are created by users (sometimes during the process of installing an application) who have the appropriate level of permissions to store application data.

System Databases

The system databases are comprised of `master`, `model`, `msdb`, and `tempdb` databases, as well as the hidden `resource` database. If the server is configured to be a replication distributor, there will also be at least one system distribution database that is named during the replication configuration process.

The `master` *Database*

The `master` database is used to record all server-level objects in SQL Server 2008. This includes Server Logon accounts, Linked Server definitions, and EndPoints. The `master` database also records information about all the other databases on the server (such as their file locations and names). SQL Server 2008 does not store system information in the `master` database but, rather, in the `Resource` database. However, system information is logically presented as the `SYS` schema in the `master` database.

The `model` *Database*

The `model` database is a template database. Whenever a new database is created (including the system database `tempdb`), a copy of the `model` database is created and renamed with the name of the database being created. The advantage of this behavior is that objects can be placed in the `model` database prior to the creation of any new database, and, when the database is created, the objects will appear in the new database. For example, Transact-SQL does not contain a `Trim` function to truncate both leading and trailing spaces from a string of characters. Transact-SQL offers an `RTRIM` function that truncates trailing spaces and an `LTRIM` function that removes leading spaces. The code to successfully implement a traditional trim operation thus becomes the following:

```
LTRIM(RTRIM('character string'))
```

To make it easier to perform this task with the least amount of effort, a custom `TRIM` function can be added to the `model` database with the following code:

```
USE Model
GO
CREATE FUNCTION dbo.Trim (@String varchar(MAX))
RETURNS varchar(MAX)
AS
BEGIN
  SELECT @String = LTRIM(RTRIM(@String))
  RETURN @String
END
```

After creating this function in the `model` database, it will be propagated to all databases created and can be used with the following simplified code:

```
dbo.TRIM('character string')
```

Sure, it's only a small savings, but the open and close parenthesis characters are often the source of annoying syntax errors. By reducing the nested functions, the overall complexity of the function call is also reduced.

Almost any database object can be added to the `model` database so that it will be available in subsequently created databases. This includes database users, roles, tables, stored procedures, functions, and assemblies.

The `msdb` Database

The `msdb` database can be considered the SQL Server Agent's database. That's because the SQL Server Agent uses the `msdb` database extensively for the storage of automated job definitions, job schedules, operator definitions, and alert definitions. The SQL Server Agent is described in greater detail in Chapter 8, but for now, just know that the Agent is responsible for almost all automated and scheduled operations.

The SQL Server Agent is not the only service that makes extensive use of the `msdb` database. Service Broker, Database Mail, and Reporting Services also use the `msdb` database for the storage of scheduling information. In addition to automation and scheduling information, SQL Server Integration Services (SSIS) can also use the `msdb` database for the storage of SSIS packages.

The `tempdb` Database

The `tempdb` database is used by SQL Server to store data — yes, you guessed it, temporarily. The `tempdb` database is used extensively during SQL Server operations, so careful planning and evaluation of its size and placement are critical to ensure efficient SQL Server database operations.

One of the primary functions of this database is to store temporary objects (such as temporary tables, views, cursors, and table-valued variables) that are explicitly created by database programmers. In addition, the `tempdb` database stores work tables containing intermediate results of a query prior to a sort operation or other data manipulation. For example, if you wrote a query that returned 100,000 rows and you wanted the results sorted by a date value in the results, SQL Server could send the unsorted results to a temporary work table, where it would perform the sorting operation and then return the sorted results to you. It is also used extensively to support connection options such as SNAPSHOT ISOLATION or Multiple Active Result Sets (MARS). If online index operations are performed, the `tempdb` database will hold the index during the build or rebuild process.

Another important aspect to keep in mind about the `tempdb` database is that all database users have access to it and have the ability to create and populate temporary objects. This access can potentially create locking and size limitation issues on SQL Server, so it is important to monitor the `tempdb` database just like any other database on SQL Server.

The `resource` Database

The last system database is the `resource` database. The `resource` database is a Read Only database that contains all system objects used by an instance of SQL Server. The `resource` database is not accessible during normal database operations. It is logically presented as the SYS schema in every database. It contains no user data or metadata. Instead, it contains the structure and description of all system objects. This design enables the fast application of service packs by replacing the existing `resource` database with a new one. As an added bonus, to roll back a service pack installation, all you have to do is replace the new `resource` database with the old one. This very elegant design replaces the older method of running many scripts that progressively dropped and added system objects.

User Databases

User databases are simply that — databases created by users. They are created to store data used by data applications and are the primary purpose of having a database server. Unlike previous versions, SQL Server 2008 does not ship with any sample databases. Instead, sample databases are available from Microsoft's Open Source CodePlex site (www.codeplex.com). There you can search for the three sample databases that are available at the time of this writing: AdventureWorks2008, AdventureWorksLT2008, and AdventureWorksDW2008.

The AdventureWorks2008 database is an OLTP database used by the fictitious Adventure Works Cycles Company, which sells mountain bikes and mountain-biking-related merchandise.

The AdventureWorksLT2008 database is an OLTP database that is a subset of the larger AdventureWorks2008 database. It was scaled down to help those who are new to relational databases.

The AdventureWorksDW2008 database is an OLAP database used for data analysis of historical Adventure Works Cycles data.

Distribution Databases

One or more distribution databases can be configured to support replication. Some SQL Server professionals describe the distribution databases as system databases, and yet others describe them as user databases. I don't think it makes much difference. What is important is what the database or databases do.

A distribution database stores metadata and transactional history to support all types of replication on a SQL Server. Typically, one distribution database is created when configuring a SQL Server as a replication Distributor. However, if needed, multiple distribution databases can be configured.

A model distribution database is installed by default and is used in the creation of a distribution database used in replication. It is installed in the same location as the rest of the system databases and is named distmdl.mdf.

SQL Server 2008 Database Storage

All system and user databases (including the resource database) are stored in files. There is always a minimum of two files: one data file and one transaction log file. The default extension for data files is .mdf, and the default for transaction log files is .ldf.

The default location for the system database files is <drive>:\Program Files\Microsoft SQL Server\ MSSQL.X\MSSQL\Data\, where *<drive>* is the installation drive and *X* is the instance number (MSSQL.1 for the first instance of the Database Engine). The following table lists the names and default locations for system database files associated with the first instance of SQL Server:

System Database	Physical Location
master	\<install path>\MSSQL10.MSSQLSERVER\MSSQL\Data\master.mdf \<install path>\MSSQL10.MSSQLSERVER\MSSQL\Data\mastlog.ldf
model	\<install path>\MSSQL10.MSSQLSERVER\MSSQL\Data\model.mdf \<install path>\MSSQL10.MSSQLSERVER\MSSQL\Data\modellog.ldf
msdb	\<install path>\MSSQL10.MSSQLSERVER\MSSQL\Data\msdbdata.mdf \<install path>\MSSQL10.MSSQLSERVER\MSSQL\Data\msdblog.ldf
tempdb	\<install path>\MSSQL10.MSSQLSERVER\MSSQL\Data\tempdb.mdf \<install path>\MSSQL10.MSSQLSERVER\MSSQL\Data\templog.ldf
resource	\<install path>\MSSQL10.MSSQLSERVER\MSSQL\Binn\Mssqlsystemresource.mdf \<install path>\MSSQL10.MSSQLSERVER\MSSQL\Binn\Mssqlsystemresource.ldf

When it comes to the system databases, the following guidance is given: *Don't mess with them*. Your ability to manipulate the system databases in SQL Server 2008 has been extremely limited by the developers at Microsoft. Overall, this is a good thing. Generally speaking, the only thing you are permitted to do with system databases is back them up or move them to faster, more reliable disk arrays if they prove to be a performance bottleneck. The ability to modify the data contained in system tables through ad hoc updates has been almost completely removed from SQL Server 2008. To modify the system catalog, the server must be started in Single-User mode, and even then, activity is restricted and is not supported by Microsoft.

Data Files and Filegroups

When a user database is created, it must contain at least one data file. This first data file is known as the *primary data file*. The primary data file is a member of the default *Primary filegroup*. Every database has one Primary filegroup when created, which consists of at least the primary data file. Additional data files can also be added to the Primary filegroup. More filegroups can also be defined upon initial creation of the database, or added after the database is created. Chapter 4 describes the storage architecture of files in greater detail, and Chapter 5 explains the advantage of filegroups. For now, it is sufficient to know that all of the data objects in a database (such as tables, views, indexes, and stored procedures) are stored within the data files. Data files can be logically grouped to improve performance and allow for more flexible maintenance (see Figure 1-1).

Log Files

Upon initial creation of a database, one transaction log must be defined. The *transaction log* is used to record all modifications to the database to guarantee transactional consistency and recoverability.

Although it is often advantageous to create multiple data files and multiple filegroups, it is rarely necessary to create more than one log file. This is because of how SQL Server accesses the files. Data files can be accessed in parallel, enabling SQL Server to read and write to multiple files and filegroups simultaneously. Log files, on the other hand, are not accessed in this manner. Log files are serialized to maintain transactional consistency. Each transaction is recorded serially in the log, in the sequence it was executed. A second log file will not be accessed until the first log file is completely filled. You can find a complete description of the transaction log and how it is accessed in Chapter 4.

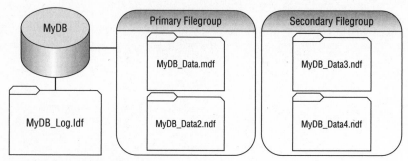

Figure 1-1: Data files and filegroups.

SQL Server Security

Chapter 6 provides a thorough discussion of SQL Server 2008 security features. However, to select the proper authentication model during installation, it is important to have a basic understanding of how SQL Server controls user access.

SQL Server 2008 can be configured to work in either the Windows Authentication Mode or the SQL Server and Windows Authentication Mode, which is frequently called *Mixed Mode*.

Windows Authentication Mode

In Windows Authentication Mode, only logins for valid Windows users are allowed to connect to SQL Server. In this authentication mode, SQL Server "trusts" the Windows or Active Directory security sub-system to have validated the account credentials. No SQL Server accounts are allowed to connect. They can be created, but they cannot be used for login access. This is the default behavior of a fresh installation of SQL Server 2008.

SQL Server and Windows Authentication Mode (Mixed Mode)

In SQL Server Mode and Windows Authentication Mode, or Mixed Mode, valid Windows accounts and standard SQL Server logins are permitted to connect to the server. SQL Server logins are validated by supplying a username and password. Windows accounts are still trusted by SQL Server. The chief advantage of Mixed Mode is the ability of non-Windows accounts (such as UNIX) or Internet clients to connect to SQL Server.

Summary

This chapter introduced the basic structure and purpose of SQL Server 2008, along with a brief explanation of the various features available in this release of Microsoft's database application. Subsequent chapters delve into the technologies and features exposed in this chapter so that the database administrator can better understand and implement each feature introduced.

In Chapter 2, you will learn how to plan and perform a SQL Server 2008 installation. Included in the discussions are prerequisite hardware and software configurations, as well as service and security considerations. A thorough installation plan will always reap enormous benefits when it comes to post-installation modifications. Understanding what to install (and how to install it) is invaluable.

2

Installing SQL Server 2008

Installing SQL Server 2008 is deceptively simple. I say *deceptively* because although SQL Server includes several wizards and tools that make the installation process itself go smoothly, a good database administrator will have devised a thorough plan for installing SQL Server and its requisite components. This chapter will introduce you to the process of installing SQL Server, beginning with an overview of the planning process. Although it would be impossible to document every possible design decision for every possible scenario, the goal of this chapter is to help you understand the installation process, some key design considerations, and the various components and options available prior to and during installation.

SQL Server Installation Planning

"There is never enough time to do it right, but always enough time to do it twice." "Measure twice, cut once." How many times have you heard these sayings? There are a number of these clichés that point out that doing something right the first time means not having to do it over and over again. To avoid having to do it twice (or more!), you need to create a thorough plan. Too often installations are rushed and then must be uninstalled when technical issues arise. The questions that must be asked range from collation settings and named instances to the separation of log and data files. Will SQL Server be installed in a cluster? How about Storage Area Networks (SAN) or Network Attached Storage (NAS)? And virtualization, won't someone *please* think of the virtualization! Although the Installation Wizards will ask you to provide answers to several questions about *how* you want SQL Server installed, before you launch the Wizard you should know the *why* behind your answers.

In addition to the "how" and "why," there are the "who," "what," and "when" questions that must be answered to create an adequate plan.

❑ The "who" is most likely going to be the database administrator (DBA), but other individuals will need to be included in the deployment plan as well. In addition to getting members of the IT department because there are network and storage considerations to account for, other departments or individuals that are considered key stakeholders may need to be involved in the process. Remember that SQL Server 2008 is an enterprise data platform, and users who own or interact with the data that will be managed by SQL Server will need to have their interests represented.

❑ The "what" question can be a bit more complex. The first "what" is "What features will be installed?" However, more "what" questions could include "What constitutes a successful installation?" or "What resources are required?"

❑ The "when" question is also imperative. "When will the installation be started and when will it be complete?"

It would be impossible to cover all the possible variations that could arise during a SQL Server installation, so this chapter covers only the essentials. Remember, when it comes to technology, the answer to almost every question is, "It depends." There are almost always "best practices," but sometimes the best practices are based on various "ivory tower" assumptions. We don't all have 50 billion dollars, 20,000 IT professionals, and unlimited access to hardware and software. Sometimes the "best practices" have to be left behind in favor of practicality and budget.

For example, as a best practice, transaction logs should be placed on a RAID 1 array as opposed to any striped array configuration because of how the transaction log is accessed by SQL Server. However, if the only available fault-tolerant storage is a RAID 5 striped array, then by all means it should be used to store and protect the log data. In many cases, the only storage available because of budget and hardware constraints is a single RAID 5 array where both the transaction log and data files are hosted. In a large enterprise solution, this would be completely unacceptable; but for a small-to-medium business implementation, it may be the only choice. The key point is that it is very important to know what the "best" solution is, but also keep in mind that compromises are often necessary to meet deadlines and budgetary constraints.

Hardware Considerations

Minimum requirements are exactly that: *minimum*. SQL Server will run on a system with minimum hardware, but the performance is not going to be stellar. Even the "recommended" hardware is to be exceeded whenever practical. I tend to think of these as "minimum to install and start the services" and "minimum to run a production system," respectively.

Upgrading almost any hardware object on a server hosting SQL Server 2008 will result in improved performance, but all things being equal, increasing RAM often has the best impact on performance. An underpowered processor or slow disk system will cause just as many performance problems as insufficient RAM, but RAM limitations will often cause processor and disk issues to be exacerbated.

A common scenario for certification exams often presents a series of questions that involve allocating different limited resources across different types of servers such as a file server, domain controller, and database server. Often, you're tasked with determining where to place the faster CPU, the better disk array, and the new RAM. I've been an IT generalist for many years, so I know what the test designers are after, but when I wear my DBA hat, I want to put everything into SQL Server.

This seems kind of self-serving, but based on my experience, SQL Server tends to be the core or underlying technology for a lot of the business applications. A company that I worked at for a number of years relies on a single SQL Server for all financial data, logistics and materials tracking, SharePoint, and several other line-of-business applications. Without exception, these applications used SQL Server as a data store. Optimizing the server running SQL Server would have an immediate positive impact on a majority of the applications used for the key business activities, as well as many support applications.

There are four main subsystems that you need to optimize for SQL Server 2008 to perform optimally. These include the Processor, Memory, Storage, and Network subsystems. Performance of these subsystems will affect SQL Server in a variety of ways, and as part of the pre-installation process, you should have an understanding of what your hardware needs are. One quick note about the network subsystem is that it is often the one the DBA has the least control over, and yet sometimes has the most impact, depending on the number of applications and users that are being supported. You should work with your network administrators and engineers to plan a strategy for concurrent database access by your users.

Processor Considerations

Microsoft sets the minimum processor requirements at 1 GHz Pentium III or a compatible processor for 32-bit installations of SQL Server, and 1.4 GHz for 64-bit systems. However, 2.0 GHz is considered the recommended speed for both platforms. SQL Server uses the processor extensively during the compilation and execution of query plans. Your server can have an extraordinarily fast disk array and plenty of RAM, but if it has an underpowered processor, it is all for naught. As the workload of the server increases and more and more transactions are executed against it, the processor will have to schedule and handle the multitude of query execution plans and programmatic manipulation of data.

Chapter 10 discusses the ways to monitor SQL Server to ensure that the CPU is not a bottleneck, but from the outset, SQL Server should be given plenty of processor power. In addition, SQL Server is very adept at using multiple processors to execute parallel operations, so adding a second processor will often pay larger dividends than upgrading a single processor. However, if your license is per processor, the cost may be prohibitive to add additional processors.

> As of this writing, Microsoft considers multiple logical processors to be covered under a single processor license. This would allow you to buy a quad-core CPU, essentially supplying SQL Server with up to four CPUs for the cost of a single processor license. For example, if you wanted to buy a new server that has two quad-core processors, you would be able to leverage all eight cores, but only have to buy two processor licenses.

Memory Considerations

The minimum amount of RAM, according to Microsoft, is 512 MB. I personally find this minimum requirement a bit on the ridiculous side. I wouldn't set up a Windows server running any multi-user application with only 512 MB of RAM, let alone a RAM-hungry application like SQL Server. Would 512 MB be sufficient for a desktop machine running SQL Server 2008 Developer Edition? Maybe, as long as no serious load was put on the server.

That's not to say that SQL Server wastes memory or that it consumes a bloated footprint. The simple fact is that SQL Server likes memory — *a lot*. It attempts to place as much data as possible in RAM so that the data is readily available for processing. It also tries to keep the data in RAM as long as possible.

SQL Server creates and maintains different memory pools for various database operations. For example, there is a *buffer cache* that is used to store data pages retrieved from the disk; a *procedure cache* that is used to store compiled stored procedures, triggers, functions, views, and query plans; and even a *log cache* for transaction log operations.

Having sufficient RAM on hand allows SQL Server to minimize the amount of page swapping required and enables the data to be pre-fetched for fast processing. If you want to keep SQL Server happy, feed it RAM. What you will get in return is a hard-working database server that efficiently and effectively utilizes that RAM to service your requests as fast as possible. Lack of sufficient RAM can also cause degradation in performance of the storage subsystem, as more data gets paged to disk.

Microsoft recommends just over 2 GB of RAM for both the 32-bit and 64-bit editions. Although Microsoft considers operating system overhead when publishing their recommended values, given the relatively low cost of RAM, I typically recommend this *above* the operating system requirements. For example, if Windows Server 2008 recommends 2 GB of RAM for the OS, I would recommend a total of 4 GB to help optimize performance.

Storage Considerations

An often overlooked hardware aspect of many SQL Server installations is the disk subsystem. I have personally witnessed deployments in which undertrained personnel installed the OS, SQL Server, and all the database files on the system partition. Although this will work, it is less than ideal. The question of how to best place the application and database files is answered with a definite "It depends."

If you're not familiar with the different levels of RAID technology, let me offer a quick primer. *RAID*, first of all, stands for "Redundant Array of Inexpensive Disks" (*inexpensive* being a relative term here). When working with SQL Server, there are four types of RAID implementations that are commonly used:

❑ **RAID 0** — RAID 0 offers no redundancy or fault tolerance, but instead helps improve performance by striping across multiple disks. RAID 0 also allows you to use the combined storage capacity of both disks. RAID 1, also known as *mirroring*, provides fault tolerance by making a bit-for-bit copy of your data on two disks. While this provides basic redundancy and can improve Read performance (by having two separate disks available to read from), you might suffer minor loss of Write performance, since the data will have to be written across both disks. RAID 1 has 50 percent storage overhead.

❑ **RAID 5** — RAID 5 is one of the more common implementation types of RAID, utilizing three or more disks. RAID 5 is also called *striping with parity*, because as it stripes across multiple disks, it writes a parity block on each stripe that allows the data to be rebuilt in case of a disk failure. RAID 5 is considered a good option for most scenarios because it provides fault tolerance and improved Read and Write performance and has a relatively low storage overhead. Because the available capacity on a RAID 5 array is $n - 1$ (n being the total number of disks in the array), the storage overhead decreases as the number of disks in the array increases.

❑ **RAID 10** — RAID 10 (also sometimes known as *RAID 1+0*) is the cat's pajamas of RAID, and is considered the optimal design solution for SQL Server database files. RAID 10 requires a minimum of four disks and essentially stripes data across two mirrored sets. So let's say, for example, that you have four disks: $a, b, c,$ and d. Disks a and b will be used to make one mirrored set, which we'll call ab, and disks c and d will be used to make the cd mirrored set. The two mirrored sets are then part of a new striped set, so when data is written to the array, it is striped across ab and cd.

Now that you know a little bit more about the various RAID levels, it's important to understand that there are several factors that can have an impact on the decision regarding where to install everything. How important is fault tolerance? How much money is the organization willing to spend on the database solution? How much disk space will be needed? How busy is the existing disk system? An optimal installation of SQL Server could look something like Figure 2-1.

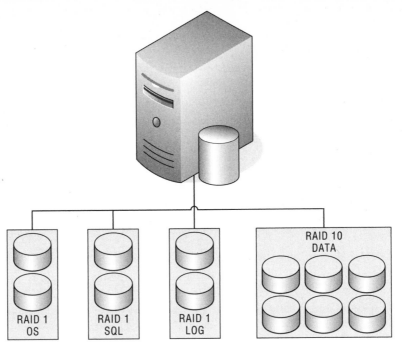

Figure 2-1: Optimal installation.

Notice that the application is installed on a separate set of spindles from the operating system. This reduces contention for disk resources and makes the application more efficient. Notice use of the term *spindle*. This is preferred to *drive* or *disk* because it leaves little room for interpretation. Physical disk drives have one spindle, which is loosely analogous with the center of a spinning top. Granted, the increase in capacity and general availability (as well as decreasing costs) of Solid State Drives, which have no spinning platter, may eventually make the term *spindle* obsolete. For now, let's agree to continue to use that term. In the case of Figure 2-1, the two spindles that host the log file on a RAID 1 array will actually look like a single drive to the operating system, when, in reality, there are two physical *disks*, or *spindles*.

In addition to the application existing on a separate set of spindles, the data files and the log files are on yet another set. The idea here is not to keep the hard disk industry in business, but to maximize efficiency, fault tolerance, and recoverability. Placing the operating system, application, and database all on the same spindle is basically putting all of your eggs in one basket. If the basket is dropped, you will lose all of your eggs. Likewise, if the spindle fails, you will lose your operating system, application, and databases. Your recovery time in this instance is tripled. Even if your server weren't to suffer a catastrophic failure, the amount of contention for resources on the disk subsystem could cause a severe degradation in performance.

Separating the database files from the transaction logs files can also help improve recovery efforts. If the database file is corrupted or damaged, the most recent backup can be used to recover it, and then the existing transaction log can be used to recover all the transactions since the last backup. Likewise, if the transaction log is lost, it can be re-created with minimal data loss from the database. If both data files and the log file are on the same spindle, a catastrophic failure of the spindle will result in all data since the last backup being lost.

Backup and recovery strategies are covered in more detail in Chapter 9.

The separation of the different components of SQL Server is just part of the equation. When choosing a disk system, it is also important to know what type of disk is best for each part of the database. Notice in Figure 2-1 that the operating system is installed on a RAID 1 array. The same goes for the SQL Server application and the database log file, while the data files are placed on a striped array. It is possible to place all the SQL resources on one or more RAID 10 or RAID 5 arrays, and many organizations do just that. However, when it comes to the transaction log, a RAID 1 configuration is more appropriate than a RAID 5 one. A transaction log placed on a striped array will actually decrease the performance of SQL Server. This is because of the inherent hit in Write performance on a RAID 5 array, and also because of the way SQL Server writes serialized data to the log. Log files, by their nature, are mostly written to, which means that often RAID 1 (or RAID 10, if you have the budget) is the best choice for performance. RAID 1 or RAID 10 is also better because of the sequential and serial nature of the transaction log as compared to the parallel friendly nature of data files.

Each transaction is written to the transaction log before it is written to memory. This puts the transaction log in the position to become a possible bottleneck. A fast array will help prevent the log from becoming a performance liability.

SAN and NAS versus Local Disk Storage

Another decision to be made during a SQL Server installation is that of storage architecture. There are many vendors in the marketplace with hundreds of possible configurations for sale. Many larger organizations have placed much of their corporate data on local and remote SANs. At the same time, other organizations have chosen NAS, and still others (mostly smaller organizations) have chosen to place all their data on local attached disk arrays. Although a complete discussion of these different technologies is beyond the scope of this book, a brief explanation is useful in describing the utilization of these technologies in database implementations.

Storage Area Network (SAN)

SANs typically transmit Small Computer Systems Interface (SCSI) block commands over a network (usually either Fibre Channel or iSCSI) in lieu of a SCSI connection for a direct-attached storage array. This option is well-suited to SQL Server because the database application expects block access to data, which is not easily supplied using NAS. Utilizing SAN software, multiple volumes can be created and "presented" to the servers, using the storage space on the SAN, as shown in Figure 2-2.

Network Attached Storage (NAS)

The NAS network interface is usually Gigabit Ethernet or Fast Ethernet, but the storage type is file-based via traditional file sharing protocols. Volumes are not presented to the servers that utilize a NAS; instead, files are accessed through Universal Naming Convention (UNC) shares, as shown in Figure 2-3. File-based access degrades SQL Server performance considerably, which is why NAS storage should be avoided. By default, databases cannot be created with a UNC location, but this behavior can be changed. However, if the database is going to be used for any serious I/O scenarios, you will find that NAS will not be able to provide an adequate response.

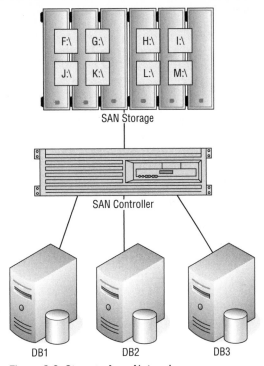

Figure 2-2: Storage Area Network.

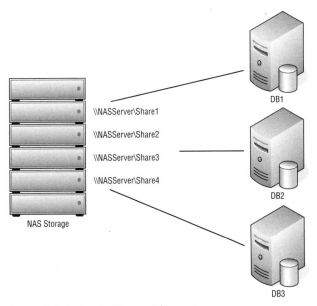

Figure 2-3: Network Attached Storage.

Local Attached Disk Array

There is a lot to be said for sharing storage resources among multiple servers on a high network, but some organizations (for a variety of reasons) have chosen to dedicate local attached storage to their database implementations (see Figure 2-4). In reality, the only differences between local attached disk arrays and SANs are that the volumes created on the local array are only accessible to the server to which the array is attached and that SAN controllers can optimize data transfer. Local arrays are typically connected via a high-speed SCSI cable or Fiber Channel.

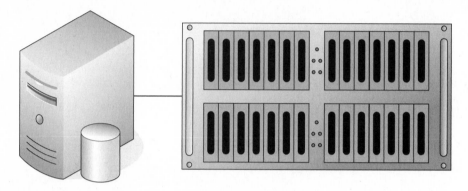

Figure 2-4: Local attached disk array.

Virtualization Considerations

SQL Server 2008 is the first version of SQL Server that is supported in virtual environments; however, there are some limitations. Microsoft will officially only support installations of SQL Server in Hyper-V environments on Windows Server 2008, and clustering of virtual machines is not supported. Because of the continued improvement in virtualization technology, it is becoming a much more attractive option to companies that want to either consolidate hardware or take advantage of some of the recovery and porta-bility options available. It's been my experience that the biggest bottleneck that occurs when running SQL Server in a virtual machine is I/O performance. For this, I strongly recommend using SAN storage for the database and transaction log files to avoid storing database information in a virtual hard drive file.

Software Prerequisites

In addition to the hardware dependencies mentioned above, there are a number of software dependen-cies that exist to support the various features of SQL Server 2008. The System Consistency Checker does a very thorough job of identifying all the requirements and dependencies, and informing you if anything is missing. For example, if a critical component is missing, the installer won't proceed until that component has been installed. If, however, you are running with less than recommended RAM, the SCC will give you a warning, but allow you to proceed with the installation. It is up to the DBA to evaluate the warning to ensure that it is acceptable to continue the installation.

Another critical dependency is the operating system. As you might expect, the IA86 and x64 editions of SQL Server 2008 can only be installed if the operating system is using the same platform. Note that 32-bit versions of SQL can be installed on 64-bit operating systems, but may actually suffer a perfor-mance loss because it will need to run within the WOW64. The following table describes the different operating systems required for each edition of SQL Server 2008. For a complete list of requirements, visit http://technet.microsoft.com/en-us/library/ms143506.aspx.

Operating System	SQL Server Edition					
	Enterprise	Standard	Workgroup	Web	Developer	Express
Windows XP SP2 Pro		X	X	X	X	X
Windows XP Home Edition SP2					X	X
Windows Server 2003 SP2 Web						X
Windows Server 2003 SP2 Standard	X	X	X	X	X	X
Windows Server 2003 SP2 Enterprise	X	X	X	X	X	X
Windows Server 2003 SP2 Datacenter	X	X	X	X	X	X
Windows Vista Ultimate		X	X	X	X	X
Windows Vista Enterprise		X	X	X	X	X
Windows Vista Business		X	X	X	X	X
Windows Vista Home Premium			X		X	X
Windows Vista Home Basic			X		X	X
Windows Vista Starter Edition					X	
Windows Server 2008 Web	X	X	X	X	X	X
Windows Server 2008 Standard	X	X	X	X	X	X
Windows Server 2008 Enterprise	X	X	X	X	X	X
Windows Server 2008 Datacenter	X	X	X	X	X	X
Windows Small Business Server 2003, Standard Edition SP2	X	X	X	X	X	X
Windows Small Business Server 2003, Premium Edition SP2	X	X	X	X	X	X

SQL Server Installation Center

The SQL Server 2008 setup process itself is pretty straightforward. If Autorun is enabled (I usually turn it off), the setup splash screen will launch as soon as you insert the media. If not, the installation can be launched from the SETUP.EXE file located in the root folder of the installation media.

You may also note that there are three folders in the root folder of the SQL Server 2008 installation media. Each folder contains the platform-specific setup files for the x86, x64, and IA64 platforms. When you launch setup from the root folder, it runs a detection script to determine the platform of the current system and launches the installer for that platform. If you have a specific need to install, for example, the 32-bit version on a 64-bit platform, the preferred method is to select the Options page of the SQL Server Installation Center.

Before the setup application launches the SQL Server Installation Center, it checks for several dependencies that are critical to installing SQL Server. This includes an updated version of the Microsoft .NET Framework (version 3.5 SP1), and in some cases, an update to the Windows Installer service may be required as well. Be aware that if these components have not yet been installed, a reboot will be necessary before SQL Server setup can continue.

Once the dependent components can be installed, the SQL Server Installation Center menu pops up. From here, you can navigate through the different pages, to learn more about the planning and installation process. You can choose to run the System Configuration Checker manually, but all of the tests are run as part of the Installation Wizard for SQL Server 2008.

Setup Support Rules (for Setup Support Files)

Prior to installing the SQL Server setup support files, SQL Server checks a series of conditions to ensure that the support files can be installed before the actual setup process begins. The six items shown in Figure 2-5 and described in the following table are checked:

Component	Description
Minimum operating system version	Checks whether the computer meets minimum operating system version requirements.
Setup administrator	Checks whether the account running SQL Server Setup has administrator rights on the computer.
Restart computer	Checks if a pending computer restart is required. A pending restart can cause Setup to fail.
Windows Management Instrumentation (WMI) service	Checks whether the WMI service is started and running on the computer.
Consistency validation for SQL Server registry keys	Checks if the SQL Server registry keys are consistent.
Long path names to files on SQL Server installation media	Checks whether the SQL Server installation media is too long.

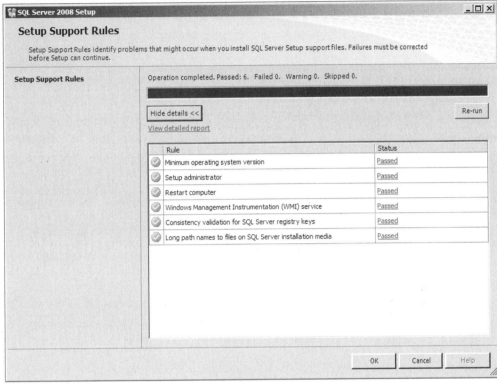

Figure 2-5: Setup Support Rules results for setup files.

Once the initial validation tests have been completed and there are no errors that would halt the installation, the Registration Information screen appears and asks for your 25-character product key. After entering the product key, you will be presented with the License Terms to review and accept.

Before proceeding with installation, you should understand some of the licensing constraints around SQL Server 2008. Many organizations are not aware that the components of SQL Server are licensed as a bundle, and when you purchase a server or processor license for SQL Server, you can install some or all of those components on one machine, and one machine only. For example, if the Database Engine is installed on one server and the Reporting Services engine is installed on a different server, a separate license is required for each installation. This is a major area of confusion for many DBAs. Common sense would say that a purchase of a SQL Server license that included the Database Engine, Reporting Services, Integration Services, and Analysis Services would give an organization the right to spread these services across as many servers as necessary, as long as only one instance of each service was used. Common sense, in this instance, may get you into trouble with the licensing police. If you haven't read the licensing agreement, do so, or have your lawyer read it for you. The license agreement can also be found in the Resources section of the SQL Server Installation Center.

After accepting the terms of the license agreement, you will be prompted to install the SQL Server Setup files. These files are used during the installation process and are usually removed as part of the post-install cleanup.

Setup Support Rules (for Installation)

Another set of validation tests must be performed to verify that the system meets the conditions for installing SQL Server. The tested components are listed in the following table and shown in Figure 2-6:

Component	Description
Fusion Active Template Library (ATL)	Checks if a computer restart is required because of broken fusion ATL. A pending restart can cause SQL Server Setup to fail.
Unsupported SQL Server products	Checks whether SQL Server 7.0 or SQL Server 7.0 OLAP Services is installed. SQL Server 2008 is not supported with SQL Server 7.0.
Performance counter registry hive consistency	Checks if the existing performance counter registry hive is consistent.
Previous releases of SQL Server 2008 Business Intelligence Development Studio	Checks for previous releases of SQL Server 2008 Business Intelligence Development Studio.
Previous CTP installation	Checks whether there is an existing SQL Server 2008 CTP installation.
Consistency validation for SQL Server registry keys	Checks if the SQL Server registry keys are consistent.
Computer domain controller	Checks whether the computer is a domain controller. Installing SQL Server 2008 on a domain controller is not recommended.
Microsoft .NET Application Security	Verifies that the computer is connected to the Internet. When a Microsoft .NET application like Microsoft Management Studio starts, there may be be a slight delay while the .NET security check validates a certificate.
Edition WOW64 platform	Determines whether SQL Server Setup is supported on this operating system platform.
Windows PowerShell	Checks whether Windows PowerShell is installed. Windows PowerShell is a prerequisite of Microsoft SQL Server 2008 Express with Advanced Services.
Windows Firewall	Checks whether the Windows Firewall is enabled. If the Windows Firewall is enabled, a warning event will be generated. This is to inform you that the SQL Server will *not* automatically open the required firewall ports to enable SQL connectivity. The Windows Firewall service must be manually configured to allow incoming connections.

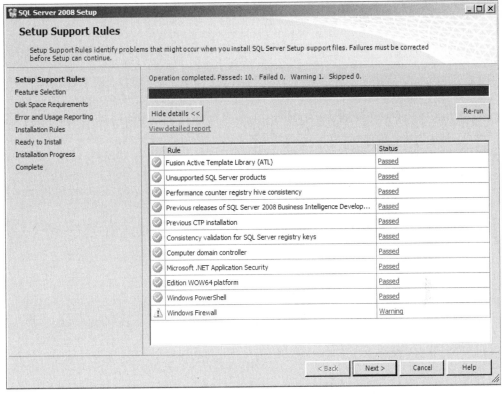

Figure 2-6: Setup Support Rules results for installation.

Feature Selection

The next step in the Installation Wizard is the Feature Selection screen (see Figure 2-7). This is where you will choose what aspects of SQL Server you want to install. If you intend to follow along with the examples in this book, it's recommended that you install all features in your test environment. In a production environment, you should install the features you intend to use, and no more. You can always go back and install additional services and features, but for the sake of efficiency, if you're not going to be using Analysis Services, there's no reason to install it. If you've installed an earlier version of SQL Server, sample databases were often included with the installation media. In the case of SQL Server 2005, installation of the sample databases was disabled, but it was still a feature that you could enable through the advanced installation options. With SQL Server 2008, the sample databases are not included with the media and are available online at www.codeplex.com. More information on installing the sample databases is covered later in this chapter.

Instance Configuration

After choosing what features of SQL Server are to be installed, the setup utility asks for instance information. You can install either a named instance or a default instance. The *default instance* takes on the name of the machine where SQL Server is being installed. There can be only one default instance; however, SQL Server 2008 Enterprise Edition supports installing up to 50 instances of SQL Server on a single machine.

If there is a default instance, a maximum of 49 named instances can be configured. If no default instance is installed, 50 named instances can be configured.

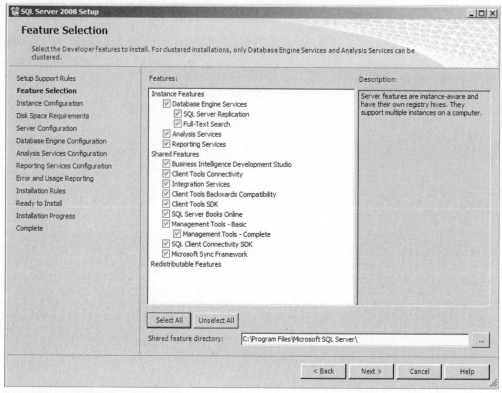

Figure 2-7: Feature Selection screen.

Named instances are referenced by the server name followed by the instance name. For example, the server name used in the examples for this book is *AughtEight*. The default name of the SQL Server 2008 installation is the same as the server name. However, you could install a named instance on AughtEight called *Dagobah*. To connect to the Dagobah instance of SQL Server, it must be referenced as *AughtEight\Dagobah*. In addition to the name, any client accessing a named instance must use the SQL connection objects from SQL Server 2000 or later. Legacy ODBC and old OLEDB drivers will be unable to enumerate a named instance of SQL Server 2008.

The Instance Configuration screen also provides you with the opportunity to change the default location for the SQL Server files. This sets the file location for the SQL binaries as well as the system databases. Best practices recommend that you separate the instance folders from the OS drive.

Server Configuration

After the instance configuration is completed and the Disk Space Requirements have been verified, the service accounts that SQL Server will use must be specified. Chapter 1 describes the various services that SQL Server may need to run depending on what features were installed. When configuring the security credentials for these services, you have a choice to make. Does the service require the ability to authenticate and connect to external resources? If so, the local system account will not be appropriate.

Best-practice security guidelines recommend that the local system account not be used because it grants full administrative access to the computer on which SQL Server is installed. This expands the attack surface of the system by allowing a compromised SQL Server to be used to attack other components on the system. Also, services running as the local system account will have no authenticated access to resources that exist on other servers in your environment.

A very useful feature of SQL Server is the ability to use the SQL Server Agent's scheduling options to run unattended jobs. If the ability to schedule SQL Server jobs that require access to external resources is desired, then at a minimum, the SQL Agent account will need to be configured to use a domain account so that the respective account can be granted permissions to the remote resource.

The ability to configure each installed SQL Server service individually is provided (see Figure 2-8), which is also a security best practice, but it does increase the administrative complexity of the system.

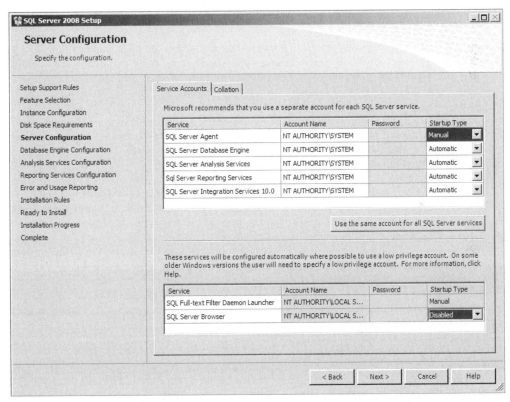

Figure 2-8: Service account screen.

In addition to the security information for each individual service, each service can be configured for automatic or manual startup during installation. By default, the SQL Agent Service is configured to start manually, while other installed components will start automatically. In order for scheduled tasks and jobs to execute, the SQL Agent Service must be running. It is usually a good practice to configure this service to run automatically.

Additionally, the SQL Server Browser Service is disabled by default. The Browser Service is only needed if you have multiple instances of SQL Server installed on the same machine. Although you cannot change the account being used by the Browser Service or the Full-Text Daemon Filter Launcher, these can be changed manually after SQL Server is installed.

Collation Settings

After setting the Authentication mode of SQL Server, you can configure the collation settings of SQL Server 2008 by selecting the Collation tab in the Server Configuration window. The first question many people have is, "What is collation?" The dictionary definition of *collation* is "assembling in proper numerical or logical sequence." Collation settings have two significant effects on your database: the sorting of your character-based data and the searching of your character-based data.

A different collation can be set for both the SQL Server and Analysis Services, but Analysis Services only supports Windows collation, whereas SQL Server can support both Windows and SQL collation. SQL collation support is included for backward compatibility, and it is recommended to configure the server collation with Windows collation (despite the fact that SQL collation is configured as the default).

Choosing Windows collation by selecting the Collation Designator provides a greater level of control and more choices when it comes to customizing the collation settings for the server. The collation setting affects what data will be returned when searching on character data and in what order the data will be returned. It also determines what characters will be supported.

The default collation for an installation is determined by the locale with which Windows was configured. For example, the default collation the SQL Server installation application chooses when being installed on a Windows server configured for the United States is SQL_Latin1_General_CP1_CI_AS. A brief definition of this underscore-delimited name is definitely in order:

❑   SQL_Latin1_General_CP1 indicates that characters from the Latin Code Page One (CP1), which is equivalent to the 1,252-character set, are supported. These characters provide support for the storing, sorting, and searching of character data in any Latin-derived language. These languages include Western European, English, and Latin American languages. However, it is important to note that sort orders can be different among Latin-derived languages. For example, in German the *ö* character comes before *z*, but in Swedish, the opposite is true (*z* comes before *ö*). Therefore, small discrepancies can occur from language to language.

> *The number 1,252 represents the character set identifier as assigned by the International Organizations for Standardization (ISO).*

❑   CI (Case Insensitive) indicates that the character data is to be sorted and searched in dictionary order without regard to capitalization. As this setting infers, there is also a CS (Case Sensitive) setting as well.

❑   AS (Accent Sensitive) indicates that the character data is to be sorted and searched in dictionary order with preference to accent marks. As a result, a search for a German "spatlese" wine will not return the correct spelling of this sweet late-harvest wine, which is *spätlese* if it is stored with the umlauts. Accent sensitivity can be turned off by specifying AI (Accent Insensitive).

These are not the only character settings that can be set. Character data can be set to be stored with sensitivity to width with the designation of WS (Width Sensitive) or WI (Width Insensitive). Width sensitivity applies to Unicode character data and differentiates between UTF-8 (8-Bit Unicode Text Format) and

UTF-16 (16-Bit Unicode Text Format). There is also a setting for Kana sensitivity: KS (Kana Sensitive) and KI (Kana Insensitive). *Kana sensitivity* essentially controls the sorting and searching of Asian Unicode characters (Japanese, Chinese, etc.) that can represent the same words using different script. For example, when Japanese kana characters Hiragana and Katakana are treated differently, it is called *Kana sensitive*; when they are treated the same, it is *Kana insensitive*.

Character data can also be sorted by their binary value. Binary sorting and searching is actually faster than dictionary sorting and searching, but is not as user-friendly. For example, the following script creates a table with two columns. The first column is assigned a character data type with case-sensitive dictionary collation. The second column is assigned a character data type with binary collation:

```
USE TempDB
CREATE TABLE MySortTable
(DictionarySort varchar(10) COLLATE Latin1_General_CS_AS NULL,
 BinarySort varchar(10) COLLATE Latin1_General_BIN)
GO
```

Once the tables are created, you can populate both of them with the same six rows: Alpha, Bravo, Charlie and alpha, bravo, charlie by executing the following command:

```
USE TempDB
INSERT MySortTable
 VALUES ('Alpha','Alpha')
INSERT MySortTable
 VALUES ('Bravo','Bravo')
INSERT MySortTable
 VALUES ('Charlie','Charlie')
INSERT MySortTable
 VALUES ('alpha','alpha')
INSERT MySortTable
 VALUES ('bravo','bravo')
INSERT MySortTable
 VALUES ('charlie','charlie')
GO
```

Now that the tables are created and populated, you can query them. Notice the different order of results using an identical query:

```
SELECT DictionarySort
FROM MySortTable
ORDER BY DictionarySort ASC

DictionarySort
--------------
alpha
Alpha
bravo
Bravo
charlie
Charlie

(6 row(s) affected)


SELECT BinarySort
```

```
FROM MySortTable
ORDER BY BinarySort ASC

BinarySort
----------
Alpha
Bravo
Charlie
alpha
bravo
charlie

(6 row(s) affected)
```

As you can see, server collation can have a profound effect on how your data is stored and retrieved, so careful planning is essential when deciding on a server collation. Fortunately, collation can also be set at the database and column level, so multiple collations are supportable.

> **As a word of caution, though, be careful when implementing incompatible collations on a single server. Issues may arise when the server collation is set to a collation that is not compatible with a database collation. This is because the** `tempdb` **database is set to the default server collation. When temporary objects are created in** `tempdb` **from a user database that uses an incompatible collation, errors can occur.**

Database Engine Configuration

After you have configured the server options, the next stage in the installation process requires you to set additional configuration properties on the Database Engine. It begins with the Account Provisioning screen, which allows you to set the Authentication mode and define administrative users. Authentication and security are covered in great detail in Chapter 6. However, a brief explanation is appropriate at this point.

If the default "Windows Only" configuration is chosen, only connections that have been authenticated by the local Windows security subsystem (or by the domain security subsystem) are allowed to be made to SQL Server. In this scenario, SQL Server validates that the login exists and has been authenticated, but no password verification takes place because SQL Server "trusts" that the login has been validated. A frequent connection error that occurs on servers configured for "Windows Authentication mode" is one that says simply that the login failed (see Figure 2-9).

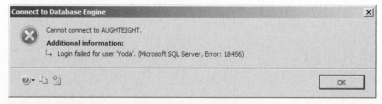

Figure 2-9: Bad login or password error message.

This is admittedly a vague response to a login request and is not the most intuitive message in the world. "Login Failed because it is not a valid Windows account and the server is configured for Windows authentication mode" or something a bit more informative would have been more useful. The message can be even more cryptic, given that the respective SQL login may, in fact, exist. Being in "Windows Authentication mode" does not prevent the database administrator from creating SQL Server login accounts. However, any attempt to connect with a valid SQL Server login when the server is in "Windows Authentication mode" will result in the vague "trusted SQL Server connection" error.

With "Mixed Mode," SQL Server can authenticate Windows logins as well as logins that have been created locally on the SQL Server. Local SQL Server logins are validated by username and password verification. The username and an encrypted version of the password are stored in the master database. When a SQL login connection is requested, the SQL Server security subsystem encrypts the provided password, compares it to the stored password, and allows or refuses the connection based on the credentials provided.

If you choose the "Mixed Mode" option, you will need to specify a password for the sa account. Not setting one, or setting a weak one, would expose your SQL Server to any number of potentially disastrous results.

Invalid credentials (either bad login name or bad password) result in the same "Login failed" message (see Figure 2-9) when SQL Server is configured for "Mixed Mode" security.

Also on this screen you will need to provide at least one Administrator account. Often, you will want to choose the "Add Current User" option (to give yourself rights to the SQL Server), but you may need to include additional users or groups as well. Most common production environments will require you to add a group that identifies all the SQL Server administrators, which can be added through this tool.

The Data Directories tab allows you to change the default locations for data files (which will also change the default location for the system databases, user databases, the tempdb database, and the backup directory).

The last tab in the Database Engine Configuration screen allows you to enable FILESTREAM options. FILESTREAM is turned off by default, and if you don't enable it from here, you can enable and configure it using SQL Server Configuration Manager and SQL Server Management Studio. More information about using FILESTREAM is in Chapter 5.

Analysis Services Configuration

As with the Database Engine, the Analysis Services Engine will require you to specify which users or groups will have administrative control over the Analysis Services instance, as well as the data directories for data, log, temp, and backup files. Note that Analysis Services does not use SQL-based logins. All authentications are done through the Windows Authentication provider.

Reporting Services Configuration

If you are using SQL Server Reporting Services, you may want to specify how reports will be published. As mentioned in Chapter 1, SQL Server Reporting Services no longer uses Internet Information Services (IIS) for hosting access to the Reporting Services Web Service and the Reports virtual directory (both of which are covered in more detail in Chapter 18). In your production environment, you should have already decided whether reports will be published natively from SQL Server, or if they are going to be published on a SharePoint Server. You have the option during installation to configure Reporting Services to use the default "Native Mode" configuration or to use "SharePoint Integrated Mode." There is also a third option that allows you to install the files needed for the SSRS, but configuration will be done using the Reporting Services Configuration tool after the installation has completed.

Error and Usage Reporting

Microsoft also provides an opt-in screen to allow you to send Windows and SQL error reports, as well as feature usage data, to Microsoft. Personally, I see some value in this, as it helps Microsoft identify problems or bugs. That being said, I enable this only on my test and development systems and never in my production systems, unless there is a corporate policy that dictates otherwise. Microsoft Enterprise licensing customers can send error reports to a Corporate Error Reporting server that allows your administrators to selectively choose which events get sent to Microsoft.

Installation Rules

Prior to finally installing the files for SQL Server, one last set of rules is checked. These rules validate your setup configuration options to identify potential problems that would cause undesired behavior or prevent SQL Server from installing. The following table lists the components that are checked before installation begins:

Component	Description
Same architecture installation	Checks whether the installing feature(s) are the same CPU architecture as the specified instance.
Cross language installation	Checks whether the setup language is the same as the language of existing SQL Server features.
Existing clustered or cluster-prepared instance	Checks if the selected instance name is already used by an existing cluster-prepared or clustered instance on any cluster node.
Reporting Services Catalog Database File Existence	Checks whether the Reporting Services catalog database file exists.
Reporting Services Catalog Temporary Database File Existence	Checks whether the Reporting Services catalog temporary database file exists.
SQL Server 2005 Express tools	Checks whether SQL Server 2005 Express Tools are installed.
Operating System supported for edition	Checks whether the SQL Server edition is supported on this operating system.
FAT32 File System	Checks whether the specified drive is FAT32 file system volume. Installing on a FAT32 file system is supported but not recommended as it is less secure than the NTFS file system.
SQL Server 2000 Analysis Services (64-bit) install action	Checks whether a default instance of SQL Server 2000 (64-bit) Analysis Services is installed.
Instance name	Checks whether the specified instance name is already used by an existing SQL Server instance.
Previous releases of Microsoft Visual Studio 2008	Checks for previous releases of Microsoft Visual Studio 2008

Final Steps

After the Install Rules have been validated, a final summary screen appears that provides you with a list of the services and features that will be installed. Clicking "Install" launches the SQL Server installation, and an Installation Progress screen appears (see Figure 2-10). The Installation Progress screen gives summary information about all the different features required by SQL Server and shows when each individual feature is finished installing.

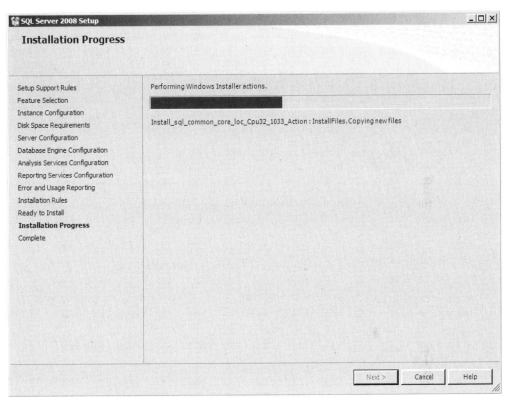

Figure 2-10: Installation Progress screen.

Installing to a Windows Cluster

The most difficult part about installing SQL Server to a cluster is configuring the Windows cluster, which is beyond the scope of this book. It is important to note that planning and configuration of the cluster must be done prior to running SQL Server Setup. There are several dependencies that must be in place, such as clustering the Microsoft Distributed Transaction Coordinator (MS DTC). Once the Windows cluster is installed and configured, the installation of SQL Server to the cluster has some very significant differences from installing to a single server. One of the first things you will most likely notice is that when the pre-installation rule validation process runs, it detects all nodes in the cluster and ensures that they meet the requirements for a SQL Server install (see Figure 2-11).

Because you are installing a SQL Server failover cluster, the installation will be slightly different from that previously described for a single server installation. After choosing to install the failover cluster, the

Instance Configuration screen appears. SQL Server 2008 supports multiple instances in a cluster, as well as in stand-alone scenarios.

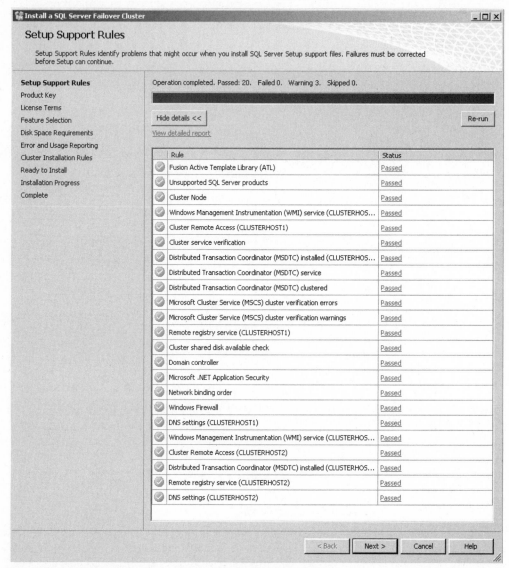

Figure 2-11: Ensuring that the requirements are met for the install.

Configuring the Virtual Server Name

The least-intuitive part of installing a SQL Server failover cluster is the naming configuration. When the Windows cluster was originally installed, a virtual name was designated for the cluster. However, a virtual name must also be specified for the SQL Server installation, and it cannot be the same as the virtual name used for the cluster. For my test cluster, I installed Windows Server 2008 Enterprise Edition on two Virtual PC images and configured the two servers as nodes in a Windows failover cluster. During the SQL Server installation, the setup utility will prompt for the instance configuration information, at which time you can supply both the SQL Server Network Name, which is the name of the SQL Server cluster, and the instance name (Figure 2-12).

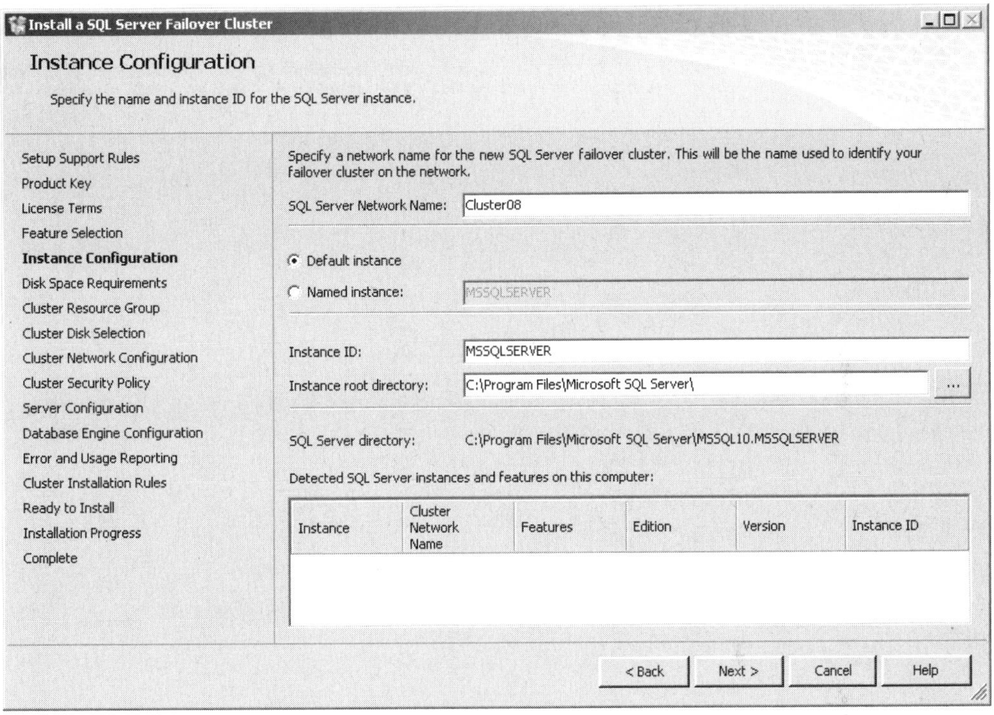

Figure 2-12: Instance Configuration screen.

If you choose a default instance, the name of the SQL Server will be whatever you provide for the SQL Server Network Name. If you choose a named instance, the instance name will be NetworkName\InstanceName.

After specifying the Network Name, a cluster resource group must be created. The resource group is where SQL Server places all failover cluster resources. You will also need to specify the shared disk (or disks) that will be used to store shared SQL Server data (Figure 2-13). Additionally, you will need to designate an IP address that will be used as a listener for the SQL Server cluster.

The last cluster-specific option applies a cluster security policy for services that are installed as part of the cluster. Windows Server 2003 and Windows XP only support the use of domain groups for clustered services. This meant that the service accounts for each SQL Service installed as part of this cluster would be added to the identified domain groups. Windows Vista and Windows Server 2008 include a new feature that uses a Service SID rather than a group (Figure 2-14). This improves security by not requiring the service account to run with unnecessary elevated privileges.

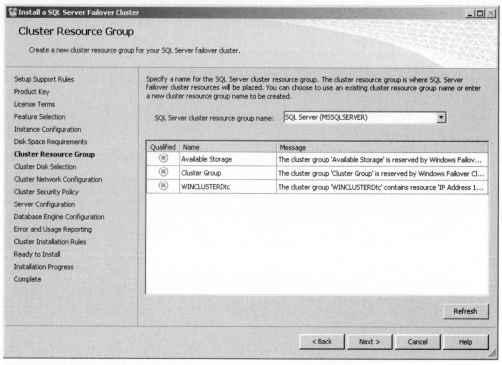

Figure 2-13: Cluster Resource Group screen.

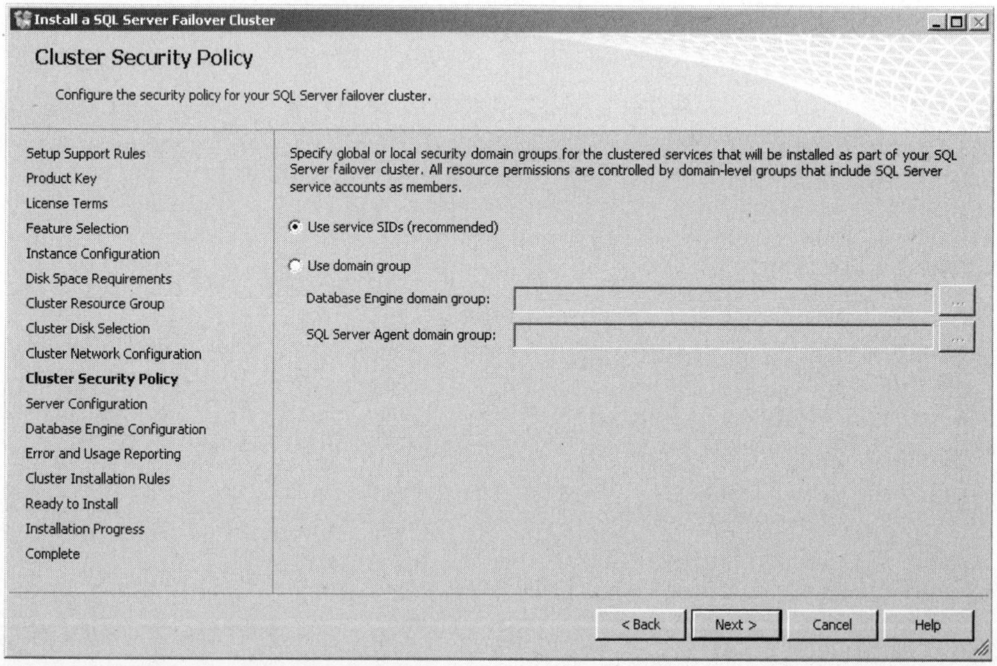

Figure 2-14: Cluster Security Policy screen.

The Cluster Security Policy configuration screen is the last dialog that is different from a stand-alone installation. The summary screen (Figure 2-15) is presented after the services screen, and then the installation begins.

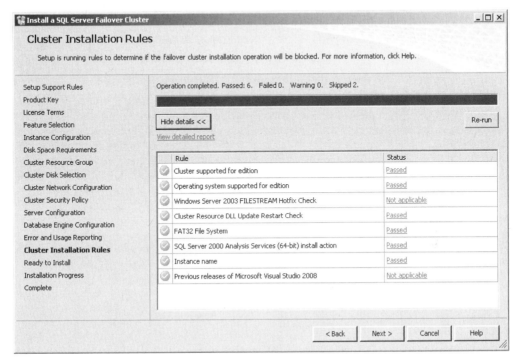

Figure 2-15: Cluster Installation Rules.

Once SQL Server is successfully installed, it can be controlled just like any other SQL Server instance. The only difference is the ability of SQL Server to fail over to the second node automatically in the case of fault tolerance, or manually for scheduled maintenance events.

Sample Databases

Because SQL Server no longer ships with sample databases, in order to follow along with many of the examples in the book, you will need to download and manually install the sample databases from Mirosoft's CodePlex site. There are three databases available that can be found at www.codeplex.com/MSFTDBProdSamples. These include the AdventureWorks2008, AdventureWorksLT2008, and AdventureWorksDW2008 databases. It is important to note that these are not the same databases that shipped with SQL Server 2005. Although they may look similar on the surface, they have a different schema, and they have been optimized for SQL Server 2008. Each of these comes in a platform-specific version (x86, x64, ia64) and gives you several options for download types (.zip and .msi). I prefer the MSI installer myself, as it makes it easy to download and deploy. There is also an installer for some sample scripts that are used in conjunction with the databases.

In most cases, you'll be using the AdventureWorks 2008 OLTP database, but the Analysis Services chapter uses the AdventureWorks DW database.

Installation Review

Not every installation goes flawlessly, and not everything may behave as expected. After installing SQL Server, it is important to review the installation to "inspect," or ensure that what you expected to happen, actually happened. Did the services get installed with the proper credentials? Are they configured to auto-start? Are the program files and database files where they were expected to be? This may seem to be a little overkill, but "An ounce of prevention is better than a pound of cure."

Summary

Careful planning prior to the installation process prevents the need to uninstall and start over. It also prevents a continuous struggle with an installation that is "not quite right." In later chapters, the optimization process, disk and memory access, as well as disaster recovery are discussed in great detail, and the connection to a well-designed infrastructure for installation will become increasingly evident. One of the most important aspects of installing SQL Server is having an understanding of the effects of the options you select. Too many times I've seen production environments where a junior administrator who was given the install media and no direction installed every feature under the sun. This was wasteful and unnecessary.

This chapter described physical storage options, which are a big part of any database configuration. By placing SQL data files and log files on separate physical disks, you decrease the chances of a major disaster and increase the speed of recovery. By placing SQL Server's assets on separate controllers and arrays, you also increase the performance of SQL Server by reducing resource conflicts and maximizing database throughput. It's always a balancing act to try to get the most out of your system performance while staying within a reasonable budget.

When it comes to availability, understand that Microsoft worked very hard to make SQL Server "cluster-friendly." It is fairly easy to configure a failover cluster, but remember that a full discussion of the Windows cluster was not provided. Many resources are available in the Windows Help files, online resources such as TechNet, and in print that cover the topic of clustering in great detail. It is strongly recommended that you research them thoroughly prior to any SQL Server cluster installation.

Chapter 3 will introduce you to the tools used to administer, manage, monitor, and maintain SQL Server 2008. You will learn about a number of improvements that have been made to facilitate the administration of SQL Server 2008.

SQL Server 2008 Tools

Several years ago, when I was beta testing SQL Server 2005, I was surprised to see familiar tools like the Enterprise Manager, a Microsoft Management Console (MMC)-based interface, and the SQL Query Analyzer done away with. In fact, with the exception of the SQL Server Profiler, pretty much everything had been replaced with a new set of applications that were … well, different.

It's been my experience that most database administrators (DBAs) typically fall into one of two distinct groups. The first group is made up of database administrators whose background is system and network administration. The second group is made up of application and database developers who have become responsible for the administration of a SQL Server infrastructure, be it a production system or a test-bed environment. DBAs that fell into the first category, myself included, often responded with trepidation about the new SQL Server management tools, and with good reason. Most of the new tools available were based on the Visual Studio interface. In fact, one of them was indeed Visual Studio (although rebranded to sound less intimidating). What was Microsoft trying to do — make us developers?

Yes. A database administrator must be about half system administrator and half developer in order to be completely successful. Several years ago, when Microsoft announced its Microsoft Certified Database Administrator (MCDBA) certification, it was no real surprise that the required exams were both from the administrative side of database administration and the programming side. Microsoft's intent was clear. To be a database administrator worth his or her salt, it would be absolutely imperative to understand database design and database application development. This was where Microsoft wanted DBAs to go, and they made sure we had the tools to get there. Ironically, the current generation of certifications, the Microsoft Certified Information Technology Professional (MCITP), includes two distinct specializations for Database Administrators and for Database Developers.

There is no doubt that Microsoft considers database administrators to be, at least marginally, developers. However, this does not mean that the tools are not intuitive and easy to use. In fact, after having spent more than three years working with them, I can't ever see myself going back to what some of us jokingly referred to as *Enterprise Mangler*. The tools that you will use today to manage SQL Server 2008 (and supported previous versions) are *more* intuitive and *easier* to use. DBAs will also be able to take advantage of functionality that developers have become used to, such as source control, solution files that manage multiple related files, and a fully functional Integrated Development Environment (IDE).

If you've never worked with SQL before or haven't managed SQL since SQL Server 2000, the new tools may seem daunting. In reality, they are more streamlined, more efficient, and yet more powerful than anything we've had before.

SQL Server Management Studio

SQL Server Management Studio completely replaces Enterprise Manager and Query Analyzer from SQL Server 2000 and earlier. It also replaces some of the functionality formerly found in other applications, such as SQL Analysis Manager. The bulk of work that I often do is performed through SQL Server Management Studio, or SSMS.

On first glance, the SQL Server Management Studio interface looks a lot like the Visual Studio IDE. It should, since it is, in actuality, a Visual Studio shell. The Visual Studio shell brings many very useful tools and features to the creation and organization of database objects, as well as the full feature set of the old tools.

When the SQL Server Management Studio is first launched, the default view is a great deal like the old Enterprise Manager with a slight Query Analyzer influence (see Figure 3-1).

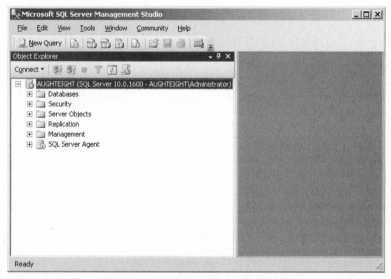

Figure 3-1: SQL Server Management Studio.

Because there are many different windows that can be viewed in the Management Studio, the management of screen real estate becomes critical. Most of the windows have the capability to either be pinned open or configured to fly out when the mouse pointer is placed over the menu bar, or auto-hide when the mouse cursor is placed elsewhere. If you are familiar with the Visual Studio Integrated Development Environment (IDE), this will all be very familiar; if not, it may take a little while to get used to.

If you are unfamiliar with the Visual Studio interface, here's a tip: Any window that supports the pinned or unpinned option will have a pin at the top right of the window. When the window is pinned, the pin will appear vertically oriented. When the window is unpinned, it will be horizontal (see Figure 3-2), and the toolbar will auto-hide or fly out, depending on the mouse cursor location.

Figure 3-2: Object Explorer with a pinned and unpinned window.

As mentioned before, the Visual Studio interface has a bit of a learning curve, but once you get used to it, it's hard to imagine any interface that works as well. The biggest advantage of the interface is that it's heavily customizable. Everything from window placement to colors can be altered to suit your personal management style. I used to drive my old manager (and cowriter), Dan, crazy by setting my Query window to a black background with bright green text (yes, it was hideous). Being able to hide and unhide windows with little effort offers a huge benefit. This conserves a great deal of screen real estate without having to click several menus to expose the features you want. The expanding popularity of Netbook computers with smaller screen sizes and limited resolution makes this a more and more attractive feature for those of us who tend to administer from the road.

Tool Windows

SQL Server Management Studio offers many different tool windows that facilitate the development and modification of database objects, as well as the effective management of SQL Server. The various views are accessible from the View menu as well as the Standard Toolbar. Each window can be configured as Dockable, which is the default, but can also be configured as a Tabbed Document or a Floating window. You can change the state of the window by clicking on the down arrow next to the pushpin in the window's title bar, or if the window is floating, by right-clicking on the title bar (Figure 3-3).

Figure 3-3: Window placement options.

A *dockable window* means that the window can be dragged and docked at almost any location in the environment. If you don't like the Object Explorer window on the left of the Studio, just drag it to the right, top, or bottom, and dock it there. When dragging a tool window, a guide diamond will appear in the center of the screen representing the dockable areas. Dragging the window over one of the area representations (see Figure 3-4) will cause a shadow to appear in that area, indicating that the window can be docked there by releasing the mouse button.

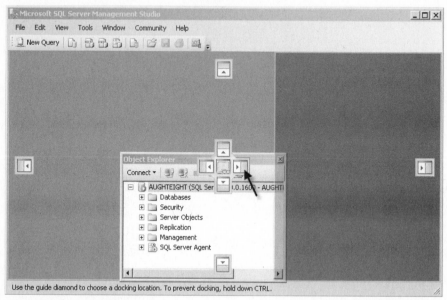

Figure 3-4: Dockable window.

Changing a windows property to Tabbed Document mode changes the window into a tab on the main window. The Floating window option specifies that the tool window is not anchored anywhere and can be moved around the main interface.

Object Explorer

The Object Explorer (see Figure 3-2) is more than just a way to explore the database objects on a server. The Object Explorer is also the tool that will be used to initiate most database management tasks. It is arranged in a standard tree view with different groups of objects nested in folders.

The Object Explorer's functionality is exposed through the context menu. Right-clicking on any object or folder within the Object Explorer exposes a list of context-sensitive options, from creating tables and users to configuring replication and Database Snapshots. The context menu also presents the ability to create scripts that manipulate. For example, right-clicking on a table exposes a context menu that allows the user to either view or modify the table structure through the graphical interface, or create scripts to perform actions against the table or its data (perhaps to be saved and executed later). This functionality exists for virtually every object that is visible in the Object Explorer.

Another great feature of SQL Server Management Studio that is exposed through the Object Explorer and other areas of the Studio interface is the ability to create scripts based on actions performed in the graphical designers. For example, right-clicking on the table folder and choosing to create a new folder launches a graphical interface where the table structure can be defined. Once the table design is complete, you can either save the table (which creates it) or click the "Generate Change Script" button on the Table Designer toolbar (which will write the appropriate T-SQL to complete the task). Using the "Generate Change Script" option can be beneficial when creating objects in a test or development environment that will also need to be created in a production environment.

Likewise, when working with other objects in Management Studio, a Script button will appear at the top of the respective designer, which will cause the actions performed in the designer to be scripted to a new Editor window. This feature is particularly useful when several different objects of the same type are to be created. The first one can be designed in the designer, the script generated for it, and that script modified to create the remaining objects. It can also be a good learning tool, by allowing inexperience database administrators to learn the T-SQL equivalent of a task that is performed through the Graphical User Interface (GUI).

Try It Out — Creating a Script

In the following example, you use the Object Explorer to create a script for a new database called `DVDCollection`:

1. In Object Explorer, right-click Databases. In the context menu that appears, click "New Database."

2. The New Database dialog appears (see Figure 3-5).

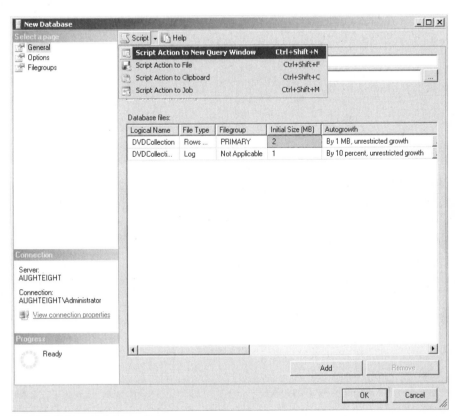

Figure 3-5: New Database dialog.

3.   Enter **DVDCollection** for the name of the database.

4.   Click on the Script button at the top of the New Database dialog.

5.   The Script button causes the appropriate T-SQL code to be written to a new Query window.

Clicking the down arrow to the right of the Script button (Figure 3-5) gives you the option of sending the script to a variety of locations.

6.   In the New Database dialog box, click Cancel. (Clicking OK will cause the database to be created.)

The script remains, but the database is not created unless the script is executed.

Code Editor

The Code Editor in SQL Server Management Studio provides the ability to open, edit, or create new queries. The types of queries supported by the Editor are:

❑   **Database Engine Queries** — These are written in Transact-SQL (T-SQL) against a SQL Server OLTP database.

❑   **Analysis Services MDX Queries** — These use the *MultiDimensional eXpression* (MDX) language. MDX queries are used to retrieve information from multidimensional objects created in Analysis Services.

❑   **Analysis Services DMX Queries** — These are created by using extensions to the Structured Query Language (SQL) called *Data Mining eXtensions* (DMX). DMX queries are written to return information from data-mining models created in SQL Server Analysis Services databases.

❑   **Analysis Services XMLA Queries**

❑   **SQL Server Compact** — As the name implies, these can perform Transact-SQL queries using a SQL Server Compact Edition database file as a data source.

The Code Editor is essentially a word processor. It provides color coding of syntax, multiple query windows, and partial code execution when you highlight the desired code and click on the Execute button or press [F5]. The SQL Server 2008 Books Online documentation will often refer to the Code Editor as the *Query Editor* (its most common moniker), *Text Editor*, or simply the *Editor*, depending on what aspect of SQL Server you are reading about.

The basic functionality that the Code Editor brings is the same for all the possible types of queries it supports. However, more complete functionality is provided for specific languages. For example, when creating MDX, DMX, or XMLA queries, the Code Editor provides basic IntelliSense functions such as those found in Visual Studio. SQL Server 2008 also introduces, for the first time, IntelliSense for Transact-SQL, which includes code completion (for object names) and error handling. For example, while typing the following script, as soon as you type the **H** in *HumanResources*, a dropdown list appears with the HumanResources schema selected. Pressing the period (.) key results in a list of objects that exist within the HumanResources schema, from which you can use the arrow keys to highlight and select the Employee table.

```
USE AdventureWorks2008

Select * from HumanResources.Employee
Where Gender = 'M';
GO
```

Additionally, if you mouse-over the column name, *Gender*, the Query Editor provides you with metadata about the gender column, as shown in Figure 3-6.

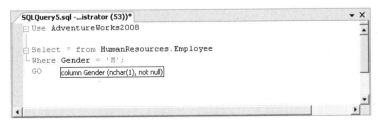

Figure 3-6: IntelliSense displaying column information.

Right-clicking on the Code Editor window, when that window is associated with a Database Engine query, results in a context menu that includes the "Design Query in Editor" option (see Figure 3-7). The Query Designer is also available from the SQL Editor toolbar described later. The Query Designer can be very helpful when writing queries against databases that are not familiar to the query writer.

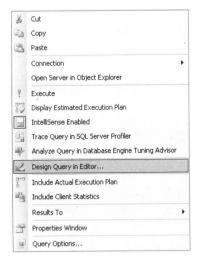

Figure 3-7: Query window context menu.

Solution Explorer

In the past, DBAs and database developers who had to keep track of saved queries that were used together as part of a batch process, or required source control and versioning, often had to manage multiple independent files manually. I don't know how many times I've browsed a common file system and found scattered .sql files stored here and there. SQL Server Management Studio takes full advantage of Visual Studio's solution system by providing the means of grouping various connection objects and scripts into a single solution called a *SQL Server Management Studio Solution*. Each solution can have one or more projects associated with it. For example, if you are developing several objects for a new application that includes both Database Engine and Analysis Engine objects, you can create a new solution that links them all together by creating a new SQL Server Management *Solution* with one or more associated *Projects* (see Figure 3-8).

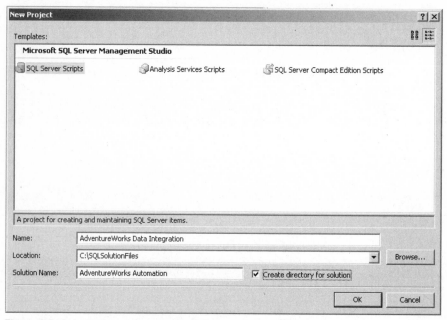

Figure 3-8: Associating projects and solutions.

If no solution is currently open, the Management Studio will create a new one. As you can see in Figure 3-8, there are three types of projects to choose from:

- ❑ **SQL Server Script** — These projects contain T-SQL Database Engine queries.
- ❑ **Analysis Services Script** — These projects contain MDX, DMX, and XMLA analysis queries.
- ❑ **SQL Server Compact Edition Script** — These projects contain SQL Server Compact queries, as you might expect.

The solution is managed through a SQL Server Management Studio Solution file with an .ssmssln extension. The example shown in Figure 3-8 created a new solution folder called *AdventureWorks Automation* that contains a project folder called *AdventureWorks Data Integration*. By default, the solution folder and the first project folder will have the same name, so it is generally a good idea to change the name of the solution. The "Create directory for solution" option can also be cleared and a solution folder specified. In this way, only a project folder will be created in the specified directory. If a solution is already opened, creating a new project can add the project to the solution, or be configured to create a whole new solution and close the open one. Solutions can contain many projects. For example, a project called *AdventureWorks Data Preparation* can be added to organize the files for the sales piece of the solution (see Figure 3-9).

Figure 3-9: Multiple projects.

Projects contain three folders:

❑ **Connection Folders** — These folders store objects that contain connection parameters for the queries in the solution. For example, if you look at the AdventureWorks Data Preparation project shown in Figure 3-9, you will note that there are two connection objects, one for the AughtEight\Administrator account and another for a SQL account named *ChrisL*.

❑ **Queries Folders** — Each of the queries in the *Queries folders* of the project will use one of those configured connection objects. The query will run in the context of the associated connection object.

❑ **Miscellaneous Folder** — This folder can be used to store just about any other file that is pertinent to the project. This may be project documentation, XML files, or even the .NET assemblies used to create managed-code procedures.

The solution folder contains two files:

❑ **Solution File** — One file is the *solution file*, which, in this case, is called *AdventureWorks Automation.ssmssln*. This contains a list of all the projects in the solution and their locations.

❑ **SQL Solution Options File** — The second file is the *SQL Solution Options* file, *AdventureWorks Automation.sqlsuo*. The solution options file contains information about the options that customize the development environment. This file is hidden by default.

The solution folder will contain a project folder for every project added to the solution. The project folder contains all the project files, including the project definition file. The project definition file, or SQL Server Management Studio SQL Project file, is an XML file with the .ssmssqlproj extension. In the previous AdventureWorks Data Integration project example, this file is called *AdventureWorks Data Integration.ssmssqlproj*. The project definition file contains the connection information, as well as metadata about the remaining files in the project.

Properties Window

The Properties window is linked to the Solution Explorer and simply displays the properties for the currently selected item in the Solution Explorer window. Editable properties will be bolded.

Registered Servers

Multiple servers can be registered and managed with the Management Studio. Right-clicking on any blank area in the Registered Servers window or on any server group name (see Figure 3-10) will expose a context menu that allows for the addition of new server registrations. It also allows for the creation of server groups. The Registered Servers window is not visible by default. To open it, use the View menu, and select Registered Servers or press *[Ctrl]+[Alt]+G*.

Figure 3-10: Registered Servers window.

If you have multiple servers in your organization, server groups can be very useful. For example, server registrations can be segregated so that all the test and development servers are in one group and the production servers are in another, or servers could be grouped based on function or department. Instances of the Database Engine, Analysis Services, Reporting Services, Integration Services, and SQL Server Compact can be registered in the Registered Servers window (Figure 3-10). Once registered, the Registered Servers window provides the ability to manage the associated services or launch other SQL Server tools associated with the respective instance.

A new feature of SQL Server 2008 includes the ability to use policy-based management, enforceable on multiple servers simultaneously through the use of Central Management servers. Central Management servers can be registered in the Registered Servers window and can also have Server Groups created to group together services with similar configuration requirements. Policy-based administration can be used to apply policies to the Central Management server, the Server Group, or the individual registered SQL Server. More information about Policy-Based administration is presented in Chapter 8.

Bookmark Window

When working with very large scripts in the Code Editor, it is very useful to be able to mark a location in the script. Bookmarks enable this functionality. The Bookmark window is made visible from the View menu and is enabled when working with any SQL Server script type. Any number of bookmarks can

```
SQLQuery4.sql -...inistrator (53))                                    ▼ ×
          SELECT e.[BusinessEntityID], e.[OrganizationNode], p.[Firs
          FROM [HumanResources].[Employee] e
              INNER JOIN [Person].[Person] as p
              ON p.[BusinessEntityID] = e.[BusinessEntityID]
          WHERE e.[BusinessEntityID] = @BusinessEntityID
          UNION ALL
          SELECT e.[BusinessEntityID], e.[OrganizationNode], p.[Firs
          FROM [HumanResources].[Employee] e
              INNER JOIN [EMP_cte]
              ON e.[OrganizationNode] = [EMP_cte].[OrganizationNode]
              INNER JOIN [Person].[Person] p
              ON p.[BusinessEntityID] = e.[BusinessEntityID]
          )
      -- Join back to Employee to return the manager name
      SELECT [EMP_cte].[RecursionLevel], [EMP_cte].[BusinessEntityID
          [EMP_cte].[OrganizationNode].ToString() AS [OrganizationNo
      FROM [EMP_cte]
          INNER JOIN [HumanResources].[Employee] e
          ON [EMP_cte].[OrganizationNode].GetAncestor(1) = e.[Organi
          INNER JOIN [Person].[Person] p
 Conn...  AUGHTEIGHT (10.0 RTM)  AUGHTEIGHT\Administrat...  AdventureWorks2008  00:00:00  0 rows
```

Figure 3-11: Bookmark window.

be created and then renamed with an intuitive name that identifies the bookmark (see Figure 3-11). If the script is part of a solution, the bookmarks are saved with the solution in the Solution Options file. Bookmarks can be added to a line by pressing *[Ctrl]+K* twice. Navigating bookmarks is easy. In addition to selecting the bookmarks in the Bookmark window, you can use the key combinations of *[Ctrl]+K*, *[Ctrl]+P* and *[Ctrl]+K, [Ctrl]+N* to move to the previous and next bookmarks, respectively. You can also organize your bookmarks into multiple folders for each project, which can make it easier to navigate through bookmarks by function.

Toolbox

The Toolbox window (see Figure 3-12) consists of maintenance plan tasks that can be dragged and dropped into maintenance plan subtasks using the Maintenance Plan Designer, which is described in more detail in Chapter 8.

Figure 3-12: Toolbox
window.

Error List

The Error List can be handy when trying to troubleshoot a query, even simple ones like the example in Figure 3-13, by providing descriptive information about the error, as well as line and position number in the query text. As you can see, the three lines of code have generated four errors. You can now resolve these errors before you execute your query.

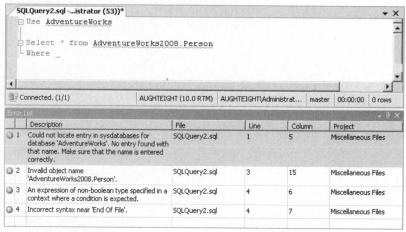

Figure 3-13: Error List window.

Object Explorer Details

The Object Explorer Details window replaces the Summary View from SQL Server 2005. It is a great deal like the List or Detail view in Windows Explorer; however, it also provides a very useful reporting feature. This feature allows the rendering of various server and database reports. The report feature is enabled when right-clicking on an object in the Object Explorer or in the Object Explorer Details window that has reports associated with it, and selecting the Reports option from the context menu. The following table contains a list of all the supported reports and where they can be found:

Report Object	Reports
Server	Server Dashboard
	Configuration Changes History
	Schema Changes History
	Scheduler Health
	Memory Consumption
	Activity — All Blocking Transactions
	Activity — All Cursors
	Activity — Top Cursors

Report Object	Reports
	Activity — All Sessions
	Activity — Top Sessions
	Activity — Dormant Sessions
	Activity — Top Connections
	Top Transactions by Age
	Top Transactions by Blocked Transactions Count
	Top Transactions by Locks Count
	Performance — Batch Execution Statistics
	Performance — Object Execution Statistics
	Performance — Top Queries by Average CPU Time
	Performance — Top Queries by Average I/O
	Performance — Top Queries by Total CPU Time
	Performance — Top Queries by Total I/O
	Service Broker Statistics
	Transaction Log Shipping Status
Server.Database	Disk Usage
	Disk Usage by Top Tables
	Disk Usage by Table
	Disk Usage by Partition
	Backup and Restore Events
	All Transactions
	All Blocking Transactions
	Top Transactions by Age
	Top Transactions by Blocked Transactions Count
	Top Transactions by Locks Count
	Resource Locking Statistics by Objects
	Object Execution Statistics
	Database Consistency History
	Index Usage Statistics
	Index Physical Statistics

Continued

Report Object	Reports
	Schema Changes History
	User Statistics
Server.Database.Service Broker	Service Broker Statistics
Server.Database.Storage.Full Text Catalogs	Active Full Text Catalogs
Server.Security	Login Statistics
	Login Failures
	Resource Locking Statistics by Logins
Server.Management	Tasks
	Number of Errors
Server.Management.Data Collection	Server Activity History
	Disk Usage Summary
	Query Statistics History
SQL Server Agent	Job Steps Execution History
	Top Jobs

Web Browser

SQL Server Management Studio also includes the ability to launch a Web Browser window within the context of the management studio. The browser uses the Internet Explorer renderer, if desired, to minimize the number of open applications and to allow direct access to Internet content from within the Management Studio application. The Web Browser window is made visible from the View menu (or by pressing *[Ctrl]+[Alt]+R*). You can use the address bar at the top of the window to enter a URL, or you can use the Web Browser Search button to take you to the MSDN home page.

Although using a browser within Management Studio might seem unnecessary, it does offer some benefits. For example, it allows tabbed browsing of content or newsgroups that may be pertinent to the current solution. You can search or ask questions without having to switch back and forth between Management Studio and Internet Explorer. Keep in mind that the Web Browser window is just an instance of Internet Explorer embedded in Management Studio. The behavior of the Web Browser window is the same as Internet Explorer, and the security configuration of Internet Explorer is in full effect in the Web Browser window. However, because a separate executable is not launched, it may actually be more efficient from a resource perspective to launch the Web Browser within the context of Management Studio. For example, on my test system, when I opened up a new instance of IE and browsed to www.msdn.com, the process consumes about 13 MB of memory. Launching the Web Browser window in SSMS and clicking on the Web Search button in the toolbar increased the memory utilization for the SSMS process by only 3 MB.

Template Explorer

The Template Explorer (see Figure 3-14) contains hundreds of SQL Server, Analysis Server, and SQL Compact scripts. Each script is grouped into folders based on their function. The template scripts can be opened by being dragged onto an open Query window. If no Query window is open, the templates can be opened by double-clicking with a mouse, using the Edit menu, or right-clicking on a context menu, all of which cause a new Query window to open.

Figure 3-14: Template Explorer.

When using a template, you can modify the text directly in the Query Editor, or you can use the ''Specify Values for Template Parameters'' option to replace the placeholders in the template (see Figure 3-15). This dialog can be launched from the SQL Editor toolbar or through the Query menu.

Toolbars

SQL Server Management Studio includes 14 preconfigured toolbars that contain features from various menus. Each toolbar can be displayed or hidden by using the View ➤ Toolbars menu (see Figure 3-16). The existing toolbars can be customized to display only the buttons that are most often used, or you can create a new toolbar that has only the commands you typically use.

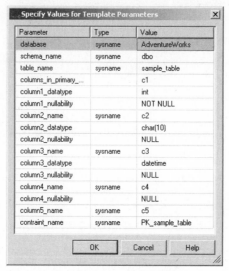

Figure 3-15: Parameter replacement.

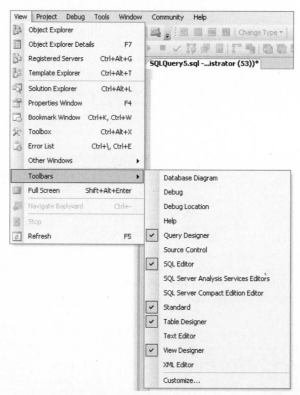

Figure 3-16: Toolbars menu.

Try It Out   **Creating a Custom Toolbar**

Create a new custom toolbar by completing the following steps:

1.   Select the Customize command on the View ≻ Toolbars menu. This will launch the Customize window.

2.   On the Customize window, click on the New button (see Figure 3-17), give your toolbar a new name (for this example, I just created one called *My Toolbar*), and click OK. Your new toolbar will show up in the Toolbars list, as well as a floating toolbar on your screen.

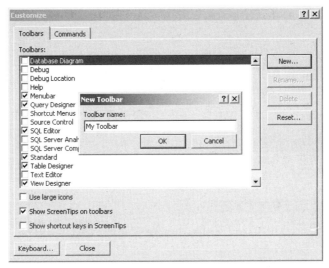

Figure 3-17: Custom toolbar window.

3.   With your new toolbar highlighted, select the Commands tab on the Customize window. Two panes are visible on the Commands tab: Categories and Commands. Each category contains commands specific to that category. For example, the File category contains commands such as Open File, Save Project, and so on.

4.   Select the Edit Category, and drag several commands to the new custom toolbar created in Step 2 (see Figure 3-18). You can also right-click on a button on the toolbar to change some of the options of that toolbar — for example, changing the name or button image used for that command. Once you have all the commands that you want on the new toolbar, you can drag it and dock it in a desired location.

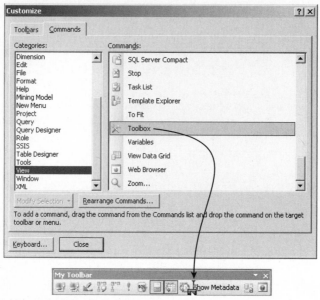

Figure 3-18: Custom edit toolbar.

Creating new toolbars or customizing existing ones can help you manage your screen real estate by allowing you to create more useful and efficient toolbars.

Database Diagram Toolbar

The Database Diagram toolbar (see Figure 3-19) exposes a great deal of functionality for use on database diagrams.

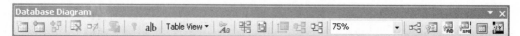

Figure 3-19: Database Diagram toolbar.

The toolbar is not used just for diagramming the database, but also for modifying or creating database objects from within the diagram interface. The Database Diagram toolbar features are described in the following table:

Feature	Purpose
New Table	Enables the creation of new tables from within the database diagram.
Add Table	Adds an existing table from the database to the diagram.
Add Related Tables	If a table in the database diagram is related to one or more additional tables by a declarative Foreign Key constraint, clicking on the Add Related Tables button will add those related tables to the diagram.

Feature	Purpose
Delete Tables from Database	Not only removes the table from the diagram, but deletes the table and its contents as well. Use with caution.
Remove from Diagram	Removes the selected table from the diagram, but not the database.
Generate Change Script	Any changes made to database objects in the diagram (such as the creation, deletion, or modification of attributes) can be sent to a script. If changes are made to underlying objects and the diagram is saved, a prompt is shown asking to confirm changes to the underlying objects.
Set/Remove Primary Key	Sets or removes the primary key assignment to the selected column.
New Text Annotation	Adds a textbox for annotation to the database diagram.
Table View	Enables the changing of table presentation in the diagram, including a customized view to configure exactly which aspects of the table are displayed. The default is Column Names.
Show Relationship Labels	Displays or hides the name of the foreign key constraints.
View Page Breaks	Displays or hides page break lines to enable the organization of diagrams for printing.
Recalculate Page Breaks	Re-centers table objects onto as few pages as possible after being manually arranged on the diagram.
Autosize Selected Tables	Re-sizes the selected table so that all rows and columns are visible.
Arrange Selection	Arranges selected tables so they do not overlap and are viewable in the diagram.
Arrange Tables	Arranges all tables so they do not overlap and are viewable in the diagram.
Zoom	Increases or decreases the zoom factor on the displayed diagram.
Relationships	Launches a dialog that displays existing foreign keys defined on a selected table and enables the defining of additional foreign keys.
Manage Indexes and Keys	Launches a dialog that displays existing primary and unique keys defined on a selected table and enables the defining of additional keys.
Manage Fulltext Indexes	Launches a dialog that displays existing full-text indexes on a selected table and enables the defining of additional full-text indexes on full-text index-enabled databases.
Manage XML Indexes	Launches a dialog that displays existing XML indexes on a selected table and enables the defining of additional XML indexes.
Manage Check Constraints	Launches a dialog that displays existing Check Constraints on a selected table and enables the defining of additional Check Constraints.
Manage Spatial Indexes	Launches a dialog that displays existing Spatial indexes on a selected table and enables the defining of additional indexes on Spatial data types.

Debug Toolbar

The Debug toolbar, as shown in Figure 3-20, includes several tools useful when debugging projects in SQL Server Management Studio that let you step through long queries to help identify potential problem areas.

Figure 3-20: Debug toolbar.

The Debug toolbar's commands are described in the following table:

Command	Purpose
Start Debugging	Begins debug mode and runs the code in the Query Editor against the debugger until a breakpoint is encountered.
Break All	Sets the debugger to break all processes to which it is attached.
Stop Debugging	Exits Debug mode.
Show Next Statement	Moves the cursor to the next statement.
Step Into	Runs the next statement.
Step Over	Skips the statement immediately after the current one and executes the statement after next.
Step Out	Steps out to the next highest calling level in the query structure.
Breakpoints	In Standard mode, this opens the Breakpoints window, which allows you to view and manage Breakpoints in the current query. In Debug mode, this provides a breakpoint menu that includes the ability to open the Locals, Call Stack and Threads window.

Debug Location Toolbar

The Debug Location toolbar (Figure 3-21) displays thread and stack frame information about the current command being executed in the Debug window.

Figure 3-21: Debug Location toolbar.

Help Toolbar

The Help toolbar (see Figure 3-22) provides a very easy and convenient mechanism for consulting online help articles while using the Management Studio.

Figure 3-22: Help toolbar.

The Help toolbar's commands are described in the following table:

Command	Purpose
Web Browser Back/Web Browser Forward	If the Web Browser window is opened in Management Studio, the Web Browser Back and Forward commands can be used to move from a viewed Web page to the previously viewed Web page, and vice versa.
Web Browser Stop	Stops the loading of a Web page in a Web Browser window.
Web Browser Refresh	Refreshes the current Web Browser window.
Web Browser Search	Launches the MSDN web site in a new Web Browser window.
Text Size	Changes of the size of text in the Web Browser window. Clicking this repeatedly will cycle the font size from Smallest, Smaller, Medium, Larger, and Largest.
How Do I	The "How Do I" command launches SQL Server Books Online and loads up the How Do I section, which allows the user to navigate through articles that explain how to perform a myriad of actions with SQL Server 2008.
Search	Launches the search feature of SQL Server Books Online.
Index	Launches the SQL Server Books Online Index.
Contents	Launches the SQL Server Books Online Table of Contents.
Help Favorites	Launches SQL Server Books Online and opens the Help Favorites window for navigating any saved favorites.
Add to Help Favorites	Adds the currently viewed help page to the Help Favorites.
Save Search	Saves the current search in the SQL Server Books Online search page to the Help Favorites.
Sync with Table of Contents	If the SQL Server Books Online Table of Contents is visible, this button will navigate to the location in the Table of Contents that the current article window is opened to.
Ask a Question	Opens the Search Community Forums home page at the MSDN web site. Here you can create a profile and ask questions of other SQL Server professionals or answer other people's questions.
Check Question Status	Once you have an MSDN Community Forum account, your questions are associated with your account, so you can easily check back to see if anyone has replied to your question.
Send Feedback	The Send Feedback command allows you to provide feedback to the SQL Server product team about SQL Server 2008.

Query Designer Toolbar

The Query Designer toolbar (see Figure 3-23) is enabled when a table is opened for editing with Object Explorer.

Figure 3-23: Query Designer toolbar.

To open a table for editing, follow these steps:

1. Right-click on the table you want to open in Object Explorer.

2. Click "Edit Top 200 Rows."

If the Query Designer was not visible, it will be when the table is opened. If it was visible, it will now be enabled. Although opening a table in a test and development environment might be acceptable, opening a table in this manner in a production environment is never recommended. Opening a table with the Object Explorer dumps the data from the table in to an updatable scrollable cursor. What this means is that while the table data is exposed in the results window, any change to the displayed data is also made to the underlying data in the table. There is no confirmation message or warning. The data is just modified. This can be very dangerous. Displaying the entire contents of the table can also consume a great deal of server resources if the table is large. The default behavior of SQL Server Management Studio only exposes the first 200 rows of a table for editing, but this can be changed through the Tools ➤ Options menu. As a general rule, if the entire contents of a table need to be exposed for quick viewing, the best way is to write a query with no filters, such as the following:

```
USE AdventureWorks2008
GO
SELECT * FROM Person.Person
```

This exposes the same information as opening the table, but does not populate an updatable cursor, so the results are Read Only. If the data in that table needs to be updated, an update command is more appropriate than modifying the data in an open table results window.

The Query Designer toolbar features are described in the following table:

Feature	Purpose
Show Diagram Pane	Displays or hides the Diagram Pane, which can be used to add or remove tables from the query, add derived tables, and configure table join criteria.
Show Criteria Pane	Displays or hides the Criteria Pane, which can be used to alias column names, establish sort orders, and configure filter criteria.
Show SQL Pane	Displays or hides the SQL Pane, which displays the resultant SQL syntax from the Diagram Pane. The SQL syntax can also be manipulated in the SQL Pane, resulting in changes to the Criteria and Diagram Panes.
Show Results Pane	Displays or hides the results of the query if it has been executed.
Change Type	Allows changing the type of query from SELECT to INSERT, DELETE, or UPDATE.

Feature	Purpose
Execute SQL	Executes the query against the database.
Verify SQL Syntax	Validates the syntax of the query, but does not execute it.
Add/Remove Group By	Adds a GROUP BY expression and formats the query so that non-aggregated columns in the SELECT list are present in the GROUP BY list.
Add Table	Adds an existing table to the Diagram Pane and SQL Pane.
Add New Derived Table	Adds an empty table to the Diagram Pane and the shell syntax for creating a derived table subquery to the SQL Pane.

Source Control Toolbar

The Source Control toolbar (see Figure 3-24) is enabled when working with scripts and a Source Control plug-in has been configured such as Visual Source Safe 2005. The addition of source-control functionality to SQL Server projects is a great step forward in recognizing the need for a structured solution environment in the development of database solutions.

Figure 3-24: Source Control toolbar.

The following example uses Visual Source Safe 2005 as the source-control tool, but there are other source-control applications available that will interact with SQL Server Management Studio. A full description of Visual Source Safe 2005 configuration and use is beyond the scope of this book, so it will be limited to just the interaction with SQL Server Management Studio.

To configure Management Studio to use source control:

1. Click File, and click Launch Microsoft Visual Source Safe. The Add Visual SourceSafe Database Wizard will launch.

2. Click Next on the Welcome screen. The Database Selection screen will appear, asking for the location of an existing Source Safe database. If you or your organization has already configured a source-control database, select the "Connect to an existing database" option. If this is a new installation, check the "Create a new database" option (see Figure 3-25).

3. The next step is either to choose an existing source control share location or to create one. After choosing to either use an existing share or to create a new one, the summary screen for the Wizard will appear.

4. Clicking Finish on the Wizard will launch the Visual SourceSafe Explorer. The Visual SourceSafe Explorer can be used to create and manage project folders for both SQL Server Management Studio and Visual Studio solutions.

In a previous example, I created a Management Studio solution called *AdventureWorks Automation*. Now that Visual SourceSafe is configured for use with Management Studio, I can add the solution to the source-control database to control the modification of the included files and to provide structured version control.

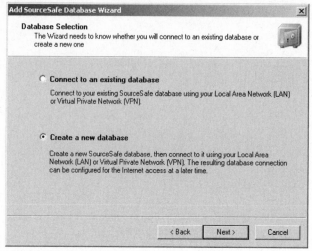

Figure 3-25: Source-control database selection.

Much of the functionality of the Source Control toolbar is only enabled if the current project has already been added to the source-control database.

To add a solution to source control, right-click on the solution in Solution Explorer and select "Add Solution to Source Control." After logging in to source control, choose a location for the solution (see Figure 3-26) and click OK.

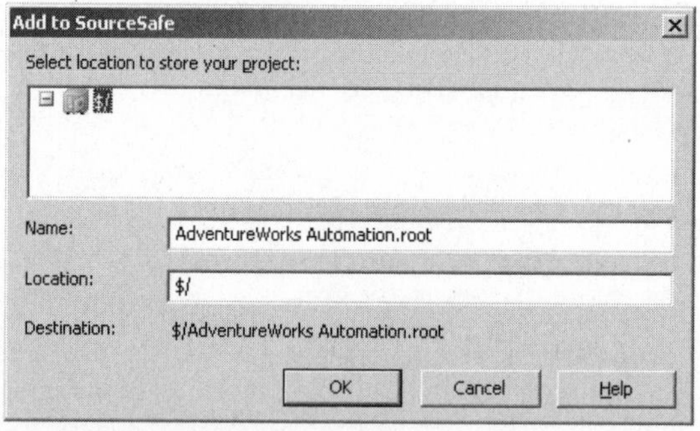

Figure 3-26: Add solution to source control.

Now that the solution has been added to source control, the Source Control toolbar is fully enabled for managing the solution.

The features available on the Source Control toolbar are described in the following table:

Feature	Purpose
Change Source Control	Displays a dialog that enables the linking of new and existing items in the Solution Explorer to a source-control database folder.
Get Latest Version	Opens the latest version of the item or items selected in the Solution Explorer.
Get	Returns a list of all versions of the selected item and allows the selection of a particular version.
Check Out for Edit	Opens the selected item for editing and marks its status in the source-control database as "Open for Edit," preventing other users from editing it at the same time.
Check In	Saves changes and marks the selected item in the source-control database as "Checked In" and allows editing by other users.
Undo Checkout	Discards any changes and marks the selected item in the source-control database as "Checked In" and allows editing by other users.
View History	Displays the history of a project, which includes a list of everything done to the project from creation to deletion.
Refresh Status	Queries the source-control database for the most recent status of all project items.
Share	Allows for a single item to be shared in multiple projects. Changes made to shared items are reflected in all the projects that use the item.
Compare	Compares an item to a previous version to expose the changes made.
Properties	Displays detailed status information on the selected item.
Source Control Manager	Launches the associated source control application as identified in the Management Studio options settings.

SQL Editor Toolbar

The SQL Editor toolbar (see Figure 3-27) becomes visible (or is enabled if already visible) when a new SQL Query window is opened. It provides the most common features used by SQL programmers and DBAs.

Figure 3-27: SQL Editor toolbar.

The supported features available on the SQL Editor toolbar are described in the following table: }

Feature	Purpose
Connect	Queries can be written without being connected to a database, so when it comes time to execute the query or validate its syntax against a database, the Connect button displays a server connection dialog that enables the selection of the applicable server and database.
Change Connection	Enables changing the connected server. A script can be created and tested on a test and development server and then the connection changed to the production server for execution.
Available Databases	Dropdown list box for selecting the database context for the query
Execute	Executes the SQL in the current window (or the highlighted portion of code) against the selected database.
Debug	Opens the current query in the debugger.
Cancel Executing Query	Terminates the active query.
Parse	Checks the SQL in the current window for valid structure and syntax. It does *not* check to ensure that referenced objects actually exist.
Display Estimated Execution Plan	Displays a graphical execution plan for the current window. It does not actually execute the query, but simply checks the metadata of the referenced object and builds a query plan based on current information.
Query Options	Opens a dialog box that allows you to specify query-specific options, such as maximum rows returned, deadlock priority, and ANSI settings. You can also configure the output settings of the query from this dialog.
IntelliSense Enabled	Toggling this button allows you to enable or disable IntelliSense for this query.
Include Actual Execution Plan	A graphical query plan used during execution is returned along with the results of the query.
Include Client Statistics	Client statistics including statistics about the query, network packets, and the elapsed time of the query are returned, along with the query results.
Results to Text	Formats the results of any query executed in the Query Editor as text.
Results to Grid	Query results are returned in a grid. By default, grid results cannot exceed 65,535 characters.
Results to File	When a query is executed a Save Results window will appear, prompting for a filename and location.
Comment Out Selected Lines	Adds inline comment marks to comment out the selected lines.
Uncomment Selected Lines	Removes inline comment marks.
Decrease Indent	Decreases the indent of selected text.
Increase Indent	Increases the indent of selected text.
Specify Values for Template Parameters	Displays a dialog that enables the replacement of template parameters with defined values.

SQL Server Analysis Services Editors Toolbar

The Analysis Services Editors toolbar (see Figure 3-28) also becomes visible (or is active if already visible) when a new Analysis Services query is opened or created. The tools on this toolbar are a subset of the SQL Editor tools, but contain only those tools applicable to Analysis Services queries (DMX, MDX, XMLA).

Figure 3-28: Analysis Services Editors toolbar.

SQL Server Compact Edition Editor Toolbar

The SQL Server Compact Edition Editor toolbar (see Figure 3-29) becomes visible (or enabled) when a new SQL Compact Edition Query window is opened. The tools on the SQL Server Compact Edition toolbar are a subset of the SQL Editor tools that are applicable for SQL Compact queries.

Figure 3-29: Compact Edition Editor toolbar.

Standard Toolbar

The Standard toolbar (see Figure 3-30) provides buttons to execute the most common actions such as opening and saving files. It also provides buttons that will launch new queries and expose additional tool windows.

Figure 3-30: Standard toolbar.

The commands available on the Standard toolbar are described in the following table:

Feature	Purpose
New Query	The New Query command launches a new Database Engine Query window by default.
Database Engine Query	Opens a new Database Engine Query window.
Analysis Services MDX Query	Opens a new MDX Query window.
Analysis Services DMX Query	Opens a new DMX Query window.
Analysis Services XMLA Query	Opens a new XMLA Query window.

Continued

Feature	Purpose
SQL Server Compact Query	Opens a new SQL Server Compact query.
Open File	Opens a file.
Save	Saves the currently selected window, or in the case of a Designer tool, saves the current object.
Print	Sends the selected window or pane to the printer.
Activity Monitor	Opens the SQL Server Activity Monitor.

Table Designer Toolbar

The Table Designer toolbar (see Figure 3-31) becomes visible (or enabled) when a new table is created using Table Designer or an existing table is modified using Table Designer. Table Designer is launched by right-clicking on the Table node in Object Explorer and choosing New Table from the context menu, or by right-clicking on an existing table in the Table node of Object Explorer and choosing Design.

Figure 3-31: Table Designer toolbar.

The following table describes the toolbar:

Feature	Purpose
Generate Change Script	Table creation or modification done with the Designer can be sent to a Query window for later execution.
Set/Remove Primary Key	Sets the selected column of the table as the primary key column or removes the key if it has already been set.
Relationships	Enables the creation of foreign key constraints.
Manage Indexes and Keys	Enables the creation of unique keys and indexes.
Manage Fulltext Index	Launches a dialog that enables the creation of full-text catalogs and full-text indexes.
Manage XML Indexes	Launches a dialog that enables the creation and management of Primary and Secondary indexes.
Manage Check Constraints	Launches a dialog that enables the creation and management of check constraints.
Manage Spatial Indexes	Launches a dialog that enables the creation of Spatial Indexes for the new Geometry and Geography data types.

Text Editor Toolbar

The Text Editor toolbar (see Figure 3-32) offers additional shortcuts to those provided in the other language-specific editors.

Figure 3-32: Text Editor toolbar.

The features are described in the following table:

Feature	Purpose
Display an Object Member List	When editing T-SQL, DMX, MDX, or XMLA scripts, invokes an IntelliSense window that displays a list of possible script members.
Display Parameter Info	Displays the parameter list for System Stored Procedures and functions used with Analysis Services.
Display Quick Info	Displays declaration information for XML objects created or referenced in an XMLA script.
Display Word Completion	Displays possible words to complete a variable, command, or function call. If only one possible option exists, it is implemented.
Decrease Indent	Decreases the indent of selected text.
Increase Indent	Increases the indent of selected text.
Comment Out Selected Lines	Adds inline comment marks to comment out the selected lines.
Uncomment Selected Lines	Removes inline comment marks.
Toggle a Bookmark on the Current Line	Adds or removes a bookmark to the current script at the position of the cursor.
Move the Caret to the Previous Bookmark	Moves the cursor to the previous set bookmark in the current script project.
Move the Caret to the Next Bookmark	Moves the cursor to the next set bookmark in the current script project.
Move the Caret to the Previous Bookmark in the Current Folder	Moves the cursor to the previous set bookmark in the currently selected bookmark folder of the Bookmark window.
Move the Caret to the Next Bookmark in the Current Folder	Moves the cursor to the next set bookmark in the currently selected bookmark folder of the Bookmark window.

Continued

Feature	Purpose
Move the Caret to the Previous Bookmark in the Current Document	Moves the cursor to the previous set bookmark in the current script window.
Move the Caret to the Next Bookmark in the Current Document	Moves the cursor to the next set bookmark in the current script window.
Clear All Bookmarks in All Files	Removes all configured bookmarks from the current project.

View Designer Toolbar

The View Designer toolbar (see Figure 3-33) is almost exactly like the Query Designer toolbar, with the exception of being limited to writing SELECT queries. In addition, queries written with the View Designer are saved as views and not just query scripts. For information about the function of the buttons on the View Designer toolbar, consult the table in the earlier section, "Query Designer Toolbar."

Figure 3-33: View Designer toolbar.

XML Editor Toolbar

The XML Editor toolbar (see Figure 3-34) contains several shortcuts that are specific to managing XML files. This is often used with XMLA scripts.

Figure 3-34: Text Editor toolbar.

The features of the Text Editor toolbar are described in the following table:

Feature	Purpose
Create Schema	Generates a schema file based on the structure of the current XML file.
Reformat Selection	Applies formatting rules to selected text to ensure that the hierarchy is properly displayed.
Format the Whole Document	Applies formatting rules to the entire XML document to ensure that the hierarchy is properly displayed.
Show XSLT Output	Allows you to associate an XSLT style sheet with your XML document to format the output.

Feature	Purpose
Debug XSLT	Starts debugging for the XML and XSLT style sheet.
Cancel XSLT Output	Cancels the output, which can be helpful if the process is taking too long to finish.
Display an Object Member List	When editing T-SQL, DMX, MDX, or XMLA scripts, invokes an IntelliSense window that displays a list of possible script members.
Display Parameter Info	Displays the parameter list for System Stored Procedures and functions used with Analysis Services.
Display Quick Info	Displays declaration information for XML objects created or referenced in an XMLA script.
Display Word Completion	Displays possible words to complete a variable, command, or function call. If only one possible option exists, it is implemented.
Decrease Indent	Decreases the indent of selected text.
Increase Indent	Increases the indent of selected text.
Comment Out Selected Lines	Adds inline comment marks to comment out the selected lines.
Uncomment Selected Lines	Removes inline comment marks.
Toggle a Bookmark on the Current Line	Adds or removes a bookmark to the current script at the position of the cursor.
Move the Caret to the Previous Bookmark	Moves the cursor to the previous set bookmark in the current script project.
Move the Caret to the Next Bookmark	Moves the cursor to the next set bookmark in the current script project.
Move the Caret to the Previous Bookmark in the Current Folder	Moves the cursor to the previous set bookmark in the currently selected bookmark folder of the Bookmark window.
Move the Caret to the Next Bookmark in the Current Folder	Moves the cursor to the next set bookmark in the currently selected bookmark folder of the Bookmark window.
Move the Caret to the Previous Bookmark in the Current Document	Moves the cursor to the previous set bookmark in the current script window.
Move the Caret to the Next Bookmark in the Current Document	Moves the cursor to the next set bookmark in the current script window.
Clear All Bookmarks in All Files	Removes all configured bookmarks from the current project.

SQL Server Management Studio Configuration

Management Studio's look and feel can be customized through the Tools ➤ Options menu (see Figure 3-35), which is accessed by selecting Tools on the main menu and clicking Options.

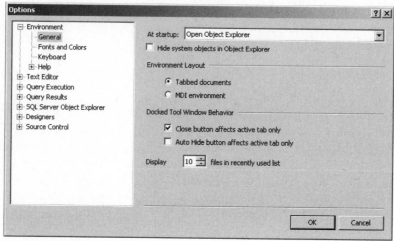

Figure 3-35: Options menu.

The Options dialog enables the customization of the Management Studio IDE. The configuration options are divided into the following seven areas.

Environment

The Environment configuration section is broken down into four subareas:

❑   **General** — Start-up options and environment layout (such as tabbed windows versus MDI windows) and how the windows behave. Recent file history is also configured on this screen.

❑   **Fonts and Colors** — The fonts and colors used in the Text Editor are completely customizable in this area. The colors and fonts used for items such as reserved words, stored procedures, comments, and background colors are just a small portion of what can be changed.

❑   **Keyboard** — For those database administrators who are used to Query Analyzer's keyboard shortcuts, this configuration area enables the setting of the keyboard shortcuts to the same ones used in Query Analyzer. The keyboard configuration area also allows for the addition of custom keyboard shortcuts.

❑   **Help** — The Help area enables the integration of Help into a Management Studio window or launching Help externally. It also allows for customizing local and online help resources.

Text Editor

The Text Editor section enables the customization of the various Text Editors and is divided into the following six subareas:

❑ **File Extension** — File extensions for all the possible script and configuration files can be configured in the File Extension area. Known file extensions such as .sql, .mdx, .dmx, and .xml are not listed, but are automatically associated with their respective editors. They can be reassigned with a "with encoding" option so that Management Studio will prompt for specific language encoding every time an associated file type is opened. Custom file extensions can also be added.

❑ **All Languages** — The All Languages area is divided into two parts, General and Tabs, and provides configuration settings for IntelliSense features, word-wrap, line numbers, and indentation for all script languages.

❑ **Plain Text** — Configuration settings for plain-text documents not associated with a particular scripting language.

❑ **Transact-SQL** — Configuration settings specific to T-SQL. There is also a separate tab here for enabling and configuring IntelliSense for Transact-SQL queries.

❑ **XML** — Configuration settings for XML documents. These settings consist of the same settings from the All Languages area, as well as XML-specific settings such as automatic formatting and schema download settings.

❑ **Editor Tab and Status Bar** — Configuration settings for the status bar, which is displayed at the bottom of the Query Editor window. You can choose the colors of the status bar, as well as what information is included in the display.

Query Execution

The Query Execution section provides configuration options for how queries are executed, as well as connection properties and time-out settings. The Query Execution section is divided into two primary areas:

❑ **SQL Server** — The SQL Server area has configuration options that control the maximum row count and the maximum amount of text or Unicode text that is returned to the Management Studio results window. This area also has options to specify a batch delimiter other than GO and to specify Query Execution time-out settings. There are also Advanced and ANSI areas that provide for the configuration of specific connection level options described in the following table:

Option	Description
SET NOCOUNT	Suppresses the X number rows message from being returned on the connection.
SET NOEXEC	Configures the Query Processor to only parse and compile SQL batches, but not to execute them.
SET PARSEONLY	Configures the Query Processor to only check the validity of SQL batches, but not to compile or execute them.
SET CONCAT_NULLS_YIELDS_NULL	Configures the Query Processor to return a NULL for any string concatenated with a NULL. This setting is selected by default.

Continued

Option	Description
SET ARITHABORT	Configures the Query Processor to terminate the query if an arithmetic error, overflow, divide-by-zero, or a domain error is encountered. This setting is enabled by default.
SET SHOWPLAN_TEXT	Configures the Query Processor to only return the query plan in text format, but not to actually execute the query.
SET STATISTICS TIME	Configures the Query Processor to return the amount of time spent in the parsing, compiling, and execution of a script.
SET STATISTICS IO	Configures the Query Processor to return the amount of scans, physical reads, logical reads, and read-ahead reads required to execute a script.
SET TRANSACTION ISOLATION LEVEL	Provides the option of configuring the isolation level of SQL scripts. The default is READ COMMITTED.
SET DEADLOCK_PRIORITY	Configures the deadlock priority of SQL scripts to either Normal or Low. The default is Normal.
SET LOCK TIMEOUT	Configures the time a connection will wait until terminating a query that is being blocked by a lock. The default setting is -1, which means forever.
SET QUERY_GOVERNOR_COST_LIMIT	Configures the Query Processor to prevent any query from executing that is calculated to take longer than the configured limit. The default value is 0, which disables the time limit.
Suppress provider message headers	Configures the Query Processor to suppress messages returned by data providers such as OLEDB or SQLClient. This setting is enabled by default.
Disconnect after the query executes	Disconnects the active Query window from the database after execution.
SET ANSI_DEFAULTS	Sets all ANSI connection settings to On.
SET QUOTED IDENTIFIER	Configures the Query Processor to allow double quotes as legitimate object delimiters. This setting is enabled by default.
SET ANSI_NULL_DFLT_ON	Specifies that columns created in a CREATE TABLE or ALTER TABLE statement default to allowing NULLS if NOT NULL is not defined in the script. This setting is enabled by default.
SET IMPLICIT_TRANSACTIONS	Configures the Query Processor to begin, but not commit a transaction any time an UPDATE, INSERT, or DELETE statement is executed outside an explicit transaction.

Option	Description
SET CURSOR_CLOSE_ON_COMMIT	When set to ON, causes any open cursor to be closed on a COMMIT TRANSACTION statement or ROLLBACK TRANSACTION statement not associated with a save point.
SET ANSI_PADDING	When set to ON, causes trailing spaces to be added to any fixed-length character string, or trailing zeros to be added to fixed-length binary strings. Trailing spaces or trailing zeros explicitly added to variable-length strings are not trimmed. This setting is enabled by default.
SET ANSI_WARNINGS	When set to ON, causes a warning to be returned if any aggregate function encounters a NULL or an arithmetic function fails. This setting is enabled by default.
SET ANSI_NULLS	When set to ON, equality or inequality operations executed against a NULL value will return an empty set. This setting is enabled by default.

❑ **Analysis Services** — Configuration setting to control the execution time-out setting for Analysis Server queries.

Query Results

The Query Results section provides configuration options for how query results are formatted. As with the Query Execution options, this is also divided into two sections for the SQL Server Database Engine and the Analysis Services Engine.

❑ **SQL Server** — The SQL Server section has configuration options to specify the default location for query results: to a grid, as text, or to a file, as well as the default location for results sent to a file. You can also enable the Windows default beep sound to play whenever a query batch completes. The "Results to Grid" settings are described in the following table:

Option	Description
Include the query in the result text	The query executed is returned as part of the result. This setting is off by default.
Include column headers when copying or saving results.	Results copied to the clipboard or saved to a file include the column header names. This setting is off by default.
Quote strings containing list separators when saving .csv results	When exporting to a .csv file format, quotes will be placed around any column that contains a list separator, such as a comma. This setting is off by default.
Discard results after execution	Queries are executed, but results are immediately cleared from the results window. This setting is off by default.

Continued

85

Option	Description
Display results in a separate tab	Results are sent to a separate tab instead of a results window beneath the query window. This setting is off by default. Note that the new tab will not automatically have focus.
Switch to results tab after the query executes	If the above option is enabled, the Query Results tab will automatically have focus once the results are displayed.
Maximum Characters Retrieved	Grid results are limited to a specified number of characters. By default, this limit is 65,535 characters for non-XML data and 2 MB for XML data.

The "Results to Text" settings are described in the following table:

Option	Description
Output format	The default text output format is column-aligned. Comma, tab, space, and custom delimiters are available.
Include column headers in the result set	Column headers are returned in the text results by default.
Include the query in the result text	The query executed is returned as part of the result. This setting is off by default.
Scroll as results are received	The results window scrolls to expose the last set of rows returned that will fit in the results window. This setting is on by default.
Right align numeric values	This option is only available when column-aligned is selected as the Output format. This setting is disabled by default.
Discard results after query executes	Queries are executed, but results are immediately cleared from the results window. This setting is off by default.
Display results in a separate tab	Results are sent to a separate tab instead of a results window beneath the query window. This setting is off by default.
Switch to results tab after the query executes	If the above option is enabled, the results tab can be given focus by enabling this option. This is off by default.
Maximum characters displayed in each column	Configures the maximum length of any column returned in text format. The default is 256 characters.

Multi-server Result settings include enabling or disabling adding the login name or server name to the results, as well as merging the results from multiple servers into a single output.

❑ **Analysis Services** — Configuration settings for Analysis Services query results include showing grids in separate tabs and playing the default Windows beep when the query completes. Both settings are disabled by default.

SQL Server Object Explorer

The SQL Server Object Explorer options list contains two tabs, one for managing command settings and another for handling scripting behavior. The command settings allow you to specify the number of rows returned used by the menu items for the number of rows returned for the `Select Top <n> Audit records`, `Edit Top <n> Rows`, and `Select Top <n> Rows` commands.

The configurable scripting options are identified in the following table:

Option	Description
Delimit Individual Statements	Separate individual T-SQL statements by using the batch separator. This is on by default.
Include descriptive headers	Adds descriptive comments at the beginning of a script. This is on by default.
Include VarDecimal	Enables the scripting of VarDecimal storage formats. This is off by default.
Script change tracking	Enables including Change Tracking information. This is off by default.
Script for server version	Specifies the version of SQL Server for which the script will be generated. The default is SQL Server 2008, but SQL Server 2005 and SQL Server 2000 are supported.
Script full-text catalogs	Includes scripts for full-text catalogs. This is off by default.
Script USE <database>	Includes the database context in the scripts. This is on by default.
Generate script for dependent objects	Dependent objects will be scripted when this setting is enabled. This is off by default.
Include IF NOT EXISTS clause	This clause checks to see if an object with the same name already exists. This is off by default.
Schema qualify object names	Uses the two-part schema.object convention when including object names in the script. This is on by default.
Script Data Compression Options	This option includes data compression settings in the target script if they exist in the source object. This is off by default.
Script extended properties	Extended properties of an object will also be scripted when this option is enabled. This is on by default.
Script permissions	Permissions will be scripted when this option is turned on. It is off by default.

Continued

Option	Description
Convert user-defined data types to base types	This will force user-defined data types to be converted to their respective base types. This is off by default.
Generate SET ANSI PADDING commands	This will enclose CREATE TABLE statements in SET ANSI PADDING commands. This is on by default.
Include collation	Enables the inclusion of collation settings in column definitions for tables or views. This is off by default.
Include IDENTITY property	This option will include IDENTITY seed and IDENTITY increment definitions. This is on by default.
Schema qualify foreign key references	This enables references to include schema qualifiers for foreign key constraints. This is on by default.
Script bound defaults and rules	This option will include sp_bindefault and sp_bindrule binding stored procedure calls. This is off by default.
Script CHECK constraints	Include CHECK constraints. This is on by default.
Script defaults	Includes default values for columns. This is on by default.
Script file groups	Specifies the ON <filegroup> clause for table definitions. This is on by default.
Script foreign keys	Include FOREIGN KEY constraints. This is on by default.
Script full-text indexes	Includes script for full-text indexes. This is off by default.
Script indexes	Includes script for clustered, non-clustered, and XML indexes. This is off by default.
Script partition schemes	Table partitioning schemes are scripted when this option is enabled. This is off by default.
Script primary keys	Includes script for PRIMARY KEY constraints. This is on by default.
Script statistics	Includes script for user-defined statistics. This is off by default.
Script triggers	This will include scripts for triggers. This is off by default.
Script unique keys	This will include UNIQUE constraints in generated scripts. This is on by default.
Script view columns	This option will declare view columns in view headers. This is on by default.
ScriptDriIncludeSystemNames	When enabled, this option will include system-generated constraint names to enforce declarative referential integrity (DRI). This is off by default.

Designers

The Designers section provides configuration options for the graphical designers used in Management Studio. The Designers section is divided into three subareas:

❑ **Table and Database Designers** — The Table and Database Designers area allows for the configuration of specific designer behavior. The following table describes the Table options:

Option	Description
Override connection string time-out value for table designer updates	Changes the default connection string time-out. When modifying the structure of large tables, more time is often required than the default of 30 seconds. Enabling this option also enables a textbox for entering the new time-out value.
Auto generate change scripts	When this option is enabled, Management Studio will automatically generate a change script and prompt for a location to save the file any time designer modifications are saved. The applicable modifications are executed, as well as a script being generated.
Warn on null primary keys	A primary key placed on a column that allows NULLS will cause an error when the option is enabled. If this option is not enabled, the designer will automatically clear the Allow Nulls attribute from the column designated as a primary key without raising an error.
Warn about difference detection	When selected, Management Studio will raise a warning dialog if the changes made conflict with changes made by any other user.
Warn about tables affected	Management Studio will raise a warning and confirmation dialog if changes to a table affect any other table in the database.
Prevent saving changes that require table re-creation	This will prevent a user from making a change that will require re-creation of a table. This includes actions such as adding a new column to the middle of a table, dropping a column, and changing the data type of a column.

The following table describes the Diagram options:

Option	Description
Default table view	Used to select the default way tables are represented in the database diagram tool. Possible views are: **Standard** — Shows the table header, all column names, data types, and the Allow Nulls setting. **Column Names** — Shows the table header and column names.

Continued

Option	Description
	Key — Shows the table header and the primary key columns.
	Name Only — Shows only the table header with its name.
	Custom — Allows you to choose which columns to view.
`Launch add table dialog on new diagram`	When the Database Diagram Designer is opened, Management Studio automatically prompts for the selection of existing tables to be added to the diagram when this option is selected.

❑   **Maintenance Plans** — The Maintenance Plan Designer options determine the way new shapes are added to the maintenance plan design area, including the precedence constraint and positioning of the new shape relative to an existing shape.

❑   **Analysis Designers** — The Analysis Designers options page provides options to set the connection and query time-out values for the Analysis Designers and the colors for the Data Mining viewers.

Source Control

The Source Control configuration section allows for the integration of a source-control plug-in such as Visual Source Safe 2005. The Source Control section is broken down into three different areas:

❑   **Plug-In Selection** — Here, the specific plug-in can be chosen (such as Visual Source Safe 2005, or Visual Studio Team System).

❑   **Environment** — The Environment section allows for the configuration of the Source Control Environment settings supported by the configured source-control plug-in. For Visual Source Safe 2005, there are three preconfigured settings: Visual Source Safe, Independent Developer, and Custom. These settings determine the automatic Check-In and Check-Out behavior of source-control projects.

❑   **Plug-in Settings** — The Plug-in Settings section provides the ability to customize the source-control actions (such as what to do with unchanged files that have been checked out and how to manage file comparisons and timestamps).

The features available in the Source Control section are dependent on the source control application used. Consult the documentation of the applicable program for more information.

Log File Viewer

The Log File Viewer (see Figure 3-36) is launched from within SQL Server Management Studio. To open it, follow these steps:

1.   Expand the Management node in Object Explorer.

2.   Expand SQL Server Logs.

3.   Right-click on a log, and select "View SQL Server Log."

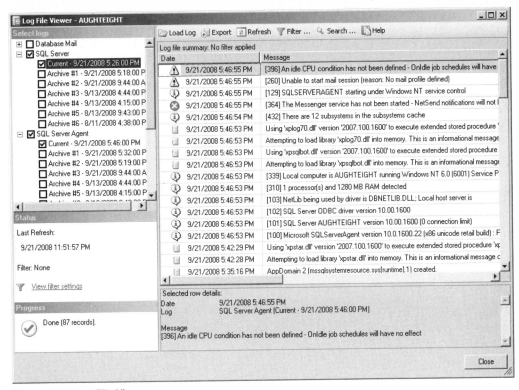

Figure 3-36: Log File Viewer.

One of the benefits of the Log File Viewer is that it allows consolidation of practically all the logs the DBAs are most interested in. SQL Server logs, SQL Agent logs, and Operating System logs can be opened in the same window for easy correlation of system and SQL Server events.

When viewing multiple logs in the Log Viewer, filters can become useful in ensuring that only the information of interest is shown. For example, the filter settings allow the specification of a start date and an end date. Filter settings can also be set to display only those events from a certain subsystem. Applying the appropriate filters helps mitigate the problem of "Information Overload" when trying to sift through thousands of log entries.

SQL Server Business Intelligence Development Studio

When SQL Server 2000 Reporting Services was released, Visual Studio was the only way for users to be able to create and manage reports. However, many non-developers were scared off by an interface that was unfamiliar to them. When SQL Server 2005 was released, Microsoft knew they had to respond to user concerns and provide them with a new interface for not only managing reports, but one that could be used for Analysis Services and Integration Services tasks, as well.

Thus, the SQL Server Business Intelligence Development Studio (BIDS) was born. Users could now feel more confident that they had a tool made especially for their Business Intelligence (BI) needs.

In all actuality, BIDS is, in fact, Visual Studio, and SQL Server 2008 includes Visual Studio 2008. Granted, it's not the full Visual Studio 2008, which includes the templates and compilers for Visual Basic, C#, and ASP.NET, but many DBAs were surprised to find Visual Studio installed on their workstation after installing the SQL Server tools. Regardless of whether you launch the Business Intelligence Development Studio shortcut from the SQL Server 2008 folder or the Visual Studio 2008 shortcut from the Visual Studio folder in your Start menu, they launch the exact same application. If the full Visual Studio suite has not been installed, the only available project templates will be Business Intelligence projects. However, if the full suite is installed, all the installed features and templates will be available.

A complete discussion of the Visual Studio IDE is beyond the scope of this book, but a very brief description is definitely in order.

Microsoft has divided Business Intelligence into three distinct pieces: ETL (Extract-Transform-Load), Analysis, and Reporting. These three parts of the Business Intelligence package are implemented through SQL Server Integration Services, SQL Server Analysis Services, and SQL Server Reporting Services. Correspondingly, BIDS provides Business Intelligence project templates that focus on these three areas. The templates are available when creating a new project from BIDS (see Figure 3-37) by selecting File ➤ New Project from the main BIDS menu.

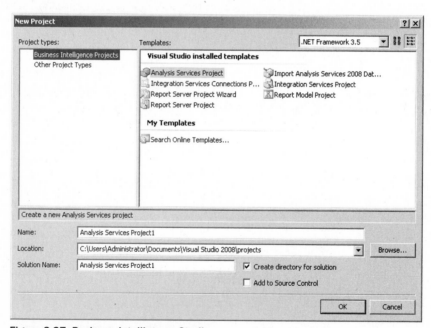

Figure 3-37: Business Intelligence Studio.

Once a template is selected, the template loads with the appropriate tools for the project. The available templates are briefly described in the following table:

Template	Description
Analysis Services Project	Analysis Services projects are used to create SQL Server 2008 Analysis Services databases that expose the objects and features of Analysis Cubes used for complex data analysis.
Import Analysis Services 2008 Database	The import project enables the creation of an Analysis Services project from an existing SQL Server 2008 Analysis Services database. It essentially reverse-engineers the project using an existing database.
Integration Services Connection Project	Integration Services projects are used to create robust Extract-Transform-Load (ETL) solutions to enable the moving and transforming of data. This project type uses a Wizard to generate an ETL package.
Integration Services Project	This project type uses the Integration Services Designer for creating and managing ETL packages.
Report Server Project Wizard	The Report Server Project Wizard offers the same functionality as the Report Server Project, but starts the development of the project in a step-by-step process that guides the user through the various tasks required to create a report. Like many wizards, this one leaves the project in a skeleton phase, which will require more detailed finalization.
Report Model Project	Report Model projects are used to create and deploy SQL Server Reporting Services 2008 report models, which can, in turn, be used by end-users to create reports using Report Builder.
Report Server Project	Report Server projects are used to create and deploy enterprise reports for both traditional (paper) and interactive reports.

SQL Server Profiler

The SQL Server Profiler is an absolutely essential tool for both DBAs and developers alike. Profiler provides the ability to monitor and record virtually every facet of SQL Server activity. It is actually a graphical interface for SQL Trace, which is a collection of stored procedures and functions that are used to monitor and record server activity. SQL Server Profiler can be launched from the Tools menu of SQL Server Management Studio, or from the All Programs ➤ Microsoft SQL Server 2008 ➤ Performance Tools menu.

SQL Server Trace

The Profiler can be used to create and view SQL Server Traces. When creating a new trace, the Profiler will prompt you for the server on which you will be running the trace. Remember that the Profiler is just a graphical interface for SQL Trace, and what is occurring in the background is the execution of stored procedures and functions on the server you connect to. If the server is very busy and is operating at the edge of its capabilities, the additional load of running SQL Trace on it may well put it over the edge. Profiler and SQL Trace procedures are discussed in greater detail in Chapter 10.

Trace Properties

When creating a new trace, the Trace Properties dialog is shown (see Figure 3-38). The Trace Properties dialog includes two tabs: the General tab and the Events Selection tab. A third tab, Events Extraction Settings, will be enabled if any XML SHOWPLAN event is selected in the Events Selection tab.

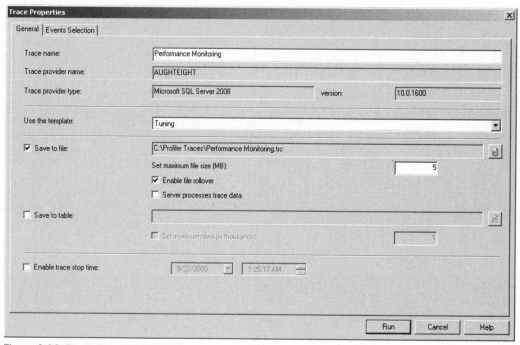

Figure 3-38: Trace Properties dialog.

General Tab

The General tab provides the ability to set the basic structure of the trace (such as the trace name, trace template, saving options, and trace stop time). It also displays the provider name and type, because SQL Server Profiler is not limited to the Data Engine. It can also be used to trace SQL Server Analysis Services.

❑ **Use the Template** — This dropdown list contains several pre-built trace templates. Each template is a pre-defined set of events and filters that provide for the monitoring of SQL Server for particular purposes. These templates can be a good place to start when creating traces to monitor SQL Server. It is also possible to create your own templates, and it is strongly recommended that you do so. The provided templates are fine, but you will undoubtedly want to collect different information from that which the templates provide. To avoid having to create the same custom trace over and over again, create and save a template to capture the information you are interested in.

❑ **Save to File** — Selecting this checkbox will display a dialog prompting for a file location to save the trace data to. The filename defaults to the name assigned to the trace with the .trc extension. However, the name can be changed if desired. The default maximum file size for a trace file is 5 MB, but it can be set to virtually any size. When the "Save to file" option is selected, two additional options are enabled: the "Enable file rollover" option and the "Server processes trace data" option.

  ❑ **Enable File Rollover** — This option causes a new file to be created every time the maximum file size is reached. Each file created is named the same as the original file with a sequential number added to the end of the name. Each sequential file is linked to the preceding file, so that each file can be opened in sequence, or they can all be opened in a single trace window.

  ❑ **Server Processes Trace Data** — This option causes the server that the traces are running on to also process the trace information. By default, the Profiler application processes the trace information. During high-stress operations, if the Profiler processes the data, it may drop some events and even become unresponsive. If the server processes the trace data, no events will be dropped. However, having the server process the trace data and run the trace puts an additional load on the server, which can have a negative impact on server performance.

❑ **Save to Table** — Trace data can also be saved to a table instead of a file by selecting the "Save to table" option. This is very useful if the trace data is going to be analyzed by an external application that requires access to the data stored in a relational format. The down side is that large traces will generate huge amounts of data that will be inserted into the storage table. This can also cause server performance issues, but you can mitigate this by saving trace information to a different server from your production system. If saving trace data to a table, the maximum amount of rows to be stored can also be assigned.

❑ **Enable Trace Stop Time** — Traces can be started and configured to automatically stop at a pre-defined time by enabling the "Enable trace stop time" option and assigning a stop time.

Events Selection Tab

The Events Selection tab provides the ability to choose what SQL Server events are to be traced (see Figure 3-39). Events are grouped in 21 SQL Server event groups with a total of 170 distinct SQL Server events, plus 10 user-definable events. There are also 11 Analysis Services Groups with 38 distinct events. SQL Server Books Online has an excellent reference that describes each group and event. Search for the titles of "SQL Server Event Class Reference" for SQL Server events and "Analysis Services Event Classes" for Analysis Services Events.

❑ **Column Filters** — Also in the Events Selection tab is the option to filter the events that are traced (see Figure 3-40). The ability to filter the data is incredibly useful. For example, if you are troubleshooting a particular application, you can filter on just the events generated by the application of interest and avoid having to sift through all the events generated by SQL Server and other applications.

❑ **Organize Columns** — The Organize Columns button enables you to place the trace columns you are most interested in so that they are easily seen when viewing the trace. Because a great deal of data can be returned, it may very well be that the column you are most interested in is off the screen to the left. The Organize Columns button helps prevent this.

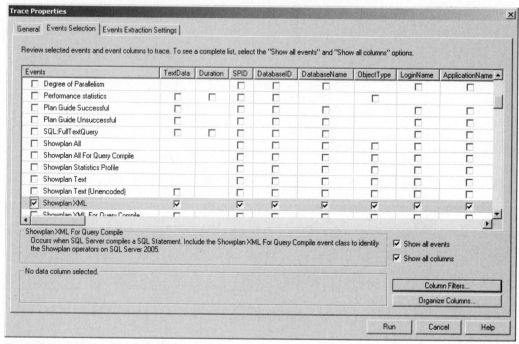

Figure 3-39: Events to be traced.

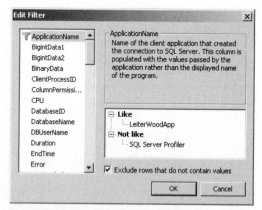

Figure 3-40: Filtering traced events.

Events Extraction Settings Tab

The Events Extraction Settings tab (see Figure 3-41) is enabled when one of the SHOWPLAN XML events is chosen from the Performance event group. This tab is divided into two group boxes. The first provides the ability to save SHOWPLAN information. All SHOWPLAN information can be saved to a single file or multiple XML files that can be opened in SQL Server Management Studio. When opened, they are displayed as graphical execution plans (which are described in detail in Chapter 10). The second group is used for saving graphical deadlock information. Because deadlocks are automatically detected and killed by SQL Server, they are often hard to troubleshoot. SQL Server Profiler provides the ability to trace deadlocks and graphically represent the sequence of events that led to the deadlock.

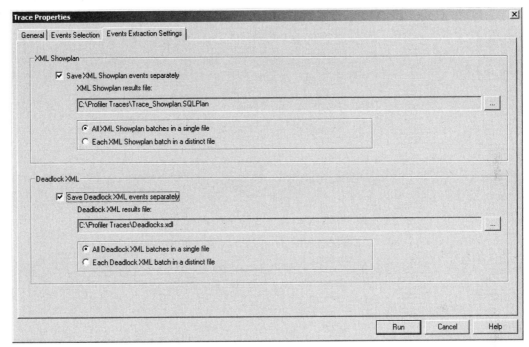

Figure 3-41: Events Extraction Settings.

Chapter 10 describes how to use the SQL Server Profiler to gather pertinent SQL Server data and how to use the profile traces to troubleshoot and optimize SQL Server performance.

Database Engine Tuning Advisor

The Database Engine Tuning Advisor (DTA) can analyze SQL Server scripts or SQL Server Profiler traces to evaluate the effective use of indexes. It can also be used to get recommendations for building new indexes or indexed views, or for creating physical table partitions.

Chapter 11 describes how to use the DTA to help optimize SQL Server databases, so this section is limited to describing the tool and its features. When the DTA is started, it prompts for a server to connect to and then automatically creates a new session. The session is displayed in two tabs: a General tab and a Tuning Options tab.

General Tab

The General tab (see Figure 3-42) is used to define the session name, the workload for analysis, and the database(s) to tune.

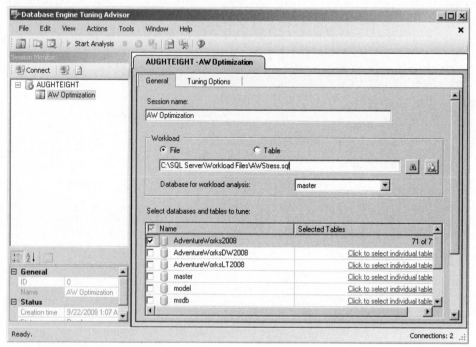

Figure 3-42: DTA General tab.

Following are some options found under this tab:

❑ **Session name** — By default, the *session name* is the name of the logged-on user combined with the current date and time, but it can (and should) be changed to a more descriptive name.

❑ **Workload** — The Workload section provides the ability to retrieve trace information from either a file or a table. The table designated must have been previously created by a SQL Server Profiler trace, and the table must be located on the same server the DTA is running on. The file can be a SQL script, a Profiler trace (.trc) file, or a Profiler trace saved as XML.

❑ **Database for workload analysis** — This option sets the initial connection information for the DTA.

❑ **Select databases and tables to tune** — In this section, you can designate the database or databases to be tuned. Keep in mind that the more objects chosen to monitor, the bigger the performance impact on the server being monitored. The DTA doesn't actually re-run all the activity from the trace, but it does retrieve a great deal of metadata about the objects contained in the workload, along with any available statistics. This activity alone generates a lot of server activity. Both SQL Server Profiler and DTA activity should be as specific as possible for performance reasons because the more specific the monitoring is, the better the results will be.

Another reason for being specific about choosing the right tables to tune is that if the DTA sees no activity for a table that was selected for monitoring, it will recommend dropping any indexes on that table not associated with a constraint.

Tuning Options Tab

The Tuning Options tab (see Figure 3-43) contains the controls used to configure how the DTA analyzes the workload and what kind of recommendations it will return. At the bottom of the tab is a description box that both describes the individual options and provides feedback for incompatible settings.

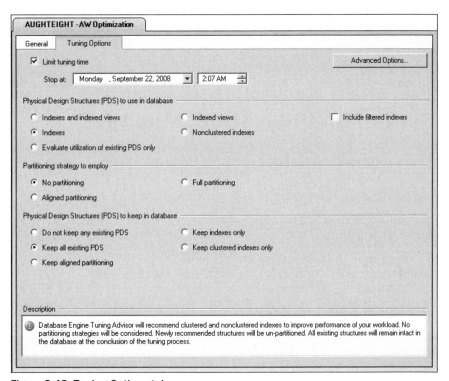

Figure 3-43: Tuning Options tab.

- ❑ **Limit tuning time** — Large workloads can take a very long time to fully analyze and can be very expensive in CPU and Database Engine resources. Limiting the amount of time the DTA spends analyzing the workload will cause it to return any recommendations generated with the amount of workload it was able to analyze in the time allocated. For the best results, the DTA should be allowed to run until it has completed; however, that may not always be possible on production systems. Once analysis has started, it can be stopped by clicking the Stop Analysis button on the DTA toolbar.

- ❑ **Physical Design Structures (PDS) to use in database** — This option group allows the configuration of the type of PDS recommendations the DTA will return. Options include returning recommendations for the creation of all indexes and indexed views, indexes only, non-clustered indexes only, and indexed views only. There is also an option for the DTA to only evaluate the effectiveness of current PDS structures, but not recommend the creation of additional structures. Filtered indexes can also be included.

❑ **Partitioning strategy to employ** — This option group is used to configure the type of physical table partitioning to employ: no partitioning, full partitioning, and aligned partitioning. Physical partitioning is described in Chapter 4.

❑ **Physical Design Structures (PDS) to keep in database** — When the DTA analyzes workloads, if it determines the PDS structure is not beneficial, it may recommend dropping the structure from the database. This option group is used to configure what PDS structures the DTA will *not* recommend dropping. The DTA can be configured to recommend dropping any non-beneficial PDS structure, to keep indexes only, to not recommend dropping any PDS, to keep clustered indexes only, and to keep any aligned partitioning structure.

❑ **Advanced Options** — The Advanced Options dialog is used to configure the maximum amount of disk space to use for recommendations, the maximum number of table columns to include per individual index, and online indexing recommendations.

SQL Server Configuration Manager

The SQL Server Configuration Manager is a Microsoft Management Console (MMC) snap-in and is used to manage all the services and protocols employed by an instance of SQL Server. It combines all the functionality that had been in three separate applications — SQL Server 2000's Service Manager, Client Network Utility, and Server Network Utility. The Configuration Manager is divided into three nodes:

❑ **SQL Server Services** — The Services node offers the similar functionality as the Services applet in the Administrative toolset. However, because it only shows SQL Server services, it is much easier to both control and monitor the status of SQL Server services.

❑ **SQL Server Network Configuration** — The Network Configuration node displays and enables the configuration of all the available server protocols. The protocols available for use with SQL Server 2008 are Shared Memory, Named Pipes, TCP/IP, and Virtual Interface Adapter (VIA). Protocols that are not in use should be disabled (or left disabled) to minimize the attack surface of the SQL Server.

❑ **SQL Native Client 10.0 Configuration** — The SQL Native Client Configuration node displays and enables the configuration of the client protocols used to connect to an instance of SQL Server 2008. The configurations only affect the computer that the Configuration Manager is running on. In addition to protocol configuration, the Native Client Configuration node enables the configuration of server aliases.

Reporting Services Configuration Manager

SQL Server 2008 includes an updated Reporting Services Configuration Manager that is more streamlined and easier to use than configuration tools from prior versions. Depending on which options you chose during the installation of SQL Server Reporting Services ("Native Mode," "SharePoint Integrated mode," or "I Will Configure Later" mode), SQL Server may already be configured and ready to deliver reports.

More information about Reporting Services can be found in Chapter 18. For a thorough discussion of SQL Server 2008 Reporting Services, check out the book Professional Microsoft SQL Server 2008 Reporting Services *by Paul Turley, Thiago Silva, Bryan C. Smith, and Ken Withee (Wiley, 2008).*

Each has its own configuration areas, including the following:

- ❑ **Report Server Status** — Selecting the Server name will display the Service Status area, which allows you to monitor the status and stop and start the Reporting Services service. Although this area is called *Server Status*, it is really only the status of the Reporting Services service.

- ❑ **Service Account** — This area is used to configure the account under which the Reporting Service runs. Best practices recommend using an Active Directory domain account with the minimum permissions required to run SQL Server Reporting Services. If a domain account is not available, the Network Service account may be used. Local System and Local Service accounts will not work very well, unless SQL Server and Reporting Services are installed on the same computer.

- ❑ **Web Service URL** — The Report Server Virtual Directory configuration area enables the viewing or changing of the virtual directory on the SQL Server that hosts the Reporting Services Web Service. Unlike prior versions of Reporting Services, the Web Service does not use IIS. The default virtual directory name is *ReportServer*.

- ❑ **Database** — The Database area is used to create or configure SQL Server 2008 Report Server databases. The Report Server databases provide storage of report definitions, report connections, and intermediately rendered reports. The database can be configured in either Native or SharePoint Integrated mode. If you wish to switch database modes, you will have to create a new database with the correct target mode. You can also configure the credentials that are used by the Report Server to connect to the Report Server database. By default, the Service Account for the Reporting Services engine is used.

- ❑ **Report Manager URL** — This area is where the virtual directory for the administrative interface, Report Manager, is viewed or configured. This is the Virtual Directory that users will access when creating or managing reports.

- ❑ **E-mail Settings** — The SMTP Server settings are very straightforward and simple. However, using the Reporting Services Configuration tool, you can only specify the SMTP server to use and the sender's address. Additional configuration to the e-mail settings must be done manually by editing the Report Server configuration file.

- ❑ **Execution Account** — The Execution Account is used when a report needs resources that are not locally available (such as a graphic stored on a remote server). It can also be used to connect to resources that do not require credentials. Configuration of an Execution Account is optional, but may be necessary when accessing shared resources.

- ❑ **Encryption Keys** — During the installation of Reporting Services, the installation program automatically generates a symmetric key that is used to encrypt security credentials stored in the Report Server database. To preserve access to this encrypted information, it is critical to back up and restore the key during certain Report Server maintenance procedures. For example, if the database is moved to a different server or the service accounts are changed, the key will have to be restored to preserve access to the encrypted information. The Encryption Keys configuration area provides an easy-to-use graphical interface to back up and restore the keys. It also provides the ability to replace the existing encryption key with a newer one, as well as delete all encrypted content, in which case, all the stored security credentials would have to be re-entered. In the past, this functionality was provided only through the RSKEYMGMT command-line utility, which is still available.

❑ **Scale-out Deployment** — SQL Server Reporting Services 2008 provides the ability to scale-out Web Service and report access by allowing multiple Reporting Services instances to share a common Report Server database. Scaling-out provides fault tolerance (for front-end services), as well as being able to handle more concurrent connections and specific report execution loads. SSRS is not "Cluster Aware," but can leverage Network Load Balancing (NLB) for Web Services and clustering of the database through a Fault Tolerant Cluster.

Command-Line Tools

SQL Server 2008 comes with plenty of great graphical tools to accomplish almost everything you could ever need to do, but there also comes a time when a simple command-line tool is the best tool for the job. While there are a few command-line tools out there, this section will look at the more prominent ones, which have historically been SQLCMD (and previously OSQL) and BCP, as well as introduce you to Microsoft's newest, and arguably most powerful, command-line utility, PowerShell.

SQLCMD

The SQLCMD utility replaces OSQL as the utility used to execute Transact-SQL statements, Stored Procedures, and SQL script files from the command prompt. OSQL is still available for backward compatibility, but SQLCMD is a more full-featured tool. SQLCMD uses OLE DB to connect to SQL Server and execute Transact-SQL batches.

The SQLCMD utility includes the ability to use variables, connect to servers dynamically, query server information, and pass error information back to the calling environment. Access to the Dedicated Administrator Connection (DAC) is also provided by the SQLCMD utility. The DAC is a special diagnostic connection that can be used by the DBA to connect to a SQL Server server when all other connection types fail to diagnose and correct server problems.

SQLCMD supports several arguments that change the way it behaves and connects to an instance of SQL Server. An abbreviated list is included in the following table. For a complete list of the argument options, consult SQL Server Books Online under the topic "SQLCMD Utility." Unlike other command-line utilities, SQLCMD command-line arguments are case-sensitive.

Argument	Description
-S	Specifies the SQL Server Instance name for SQLCMD to connect to.
-U	Specifies a username to use when connecting with a SQL Server login.
-P	Specifies the password to use when connecting with a SQL Server login.
-E	Configures SQLCMD to use a trusted connection.
-i	Specifies the Transact-SQL script input file to run.
-o	Specifies the output text file to return the results of a SQLCMD execution.

Argument	Description
-v	Specifies the parameter(s) to pass to a SQLCMD script execution.
-Q	Performs a query passed as a command-line parameter and exits.
-A	Designates the SQLCMD connection as a DAC

The SQLCMD utility is typically used to execute saved Transact-SQL scripts in batch processes. This functionality is further enhanced by the ability of SQLCMD to accept scripting parameters. The following code is an example of a SQLCMD script that accepts a parameter called DBName to back up a designated database to a file named *DatabasenameDB-Month-Day-Year.BAK* to the C:\SQLBackups folder:

```
DECLARE @BackupDest AS varchar(255)
SET @BackupDest = 'C:\SQLBackups\'
+ '$(DBName)'
+ 'DB-'
+ DATENAME(m,GETDATE())
+ '-'
+ DATENAME(dd,GETDATE())
+ '-'
+ DATENAME(yy,GETDATE())
+ '.BAK'
BACKUP DATABASE $(DBName)
TO DISK = @BackupDest
```

If the preceding script is saved to a file called *BackupDBs.SQL* in the C:\SQLBackups folder, it could be executed to back up the Master database on a server called *AughtEight* using Windows authentication with the following command line:

```
SQLCMD -E -S AughtEight -i C:\SQLBackups\BackupDBs.SQL -v DBName="Master"
```

SQL Server Management Studio makes the creation of SQLCMD scripts even easier with its SQLCMD mode. The BackupDBs.SQL script can be written and tested with Management Studio by selecting SQL-CMD mode in the Query menu. However, to fully test it in the Query Editor, the following command must be inserted in the beginning of the script:

```
:SETVAR DBName "Master"
```

The SETVAR command can also be used in the execution of SQLCMD from the command line, but it usually makes more sense to use the -v variable argument.

Multiple variables can be set with the SETVAR command, as well as passed in to a SQLCMD script with the -v argument. The following example shows how to use multiple SETVAR commands:

```
USE AdventureWorks2008
GO
:SETVAR ColumnName "LastName"
:SETVAR TableName "Person.Person"

SELECT $(ColumnName)
FROM $(TableName)
```

If the preceding example is saved to a file called *GetContacts.SQL* with the SETVAR commands omitted, it would look like the following example:

```
USE AdventureWorks2008
GO

SELECT $(ColumnName)
FROM $(TableName)
```

This script could be executed with the SQLCMD utility using the following command line:

```
SQLCMD -E -S AughtEight -i C:\GetContacts.SQL -v ColumnName="LastName"
  TableName = "Person.Person"
```

Dedicated Administrator Connection (DAC)

SQLCMD is particularly useful for creating batch scripting jobs for administrative purposes. However, as an emergency utility to diagnose and hopefully correct server problems, it has no peer. With the -A argument, the SQLCMD utilizes an exclusive connection to SQL Server. If no other connection is possible, the SQLCMD -A command is the last and best hope for diagnosing server problems and preventing data loss. By default, only local DACs are allowed because the DAC components only listen on the loopback connection. However, remote DACs can be enabled using the sp_configure stored procedure by changing the remote admin connections option to true, as the following code illustrates:

```
sp_configure 'remote admin connections', 1
RECONFIGURE
```

Bulk Copy Program (BCP)

The BCP utility is mainly used to import flat-file data into a SQL Server table, export a table out to a flat file, or export the results of a Transact-SQL query to a flat file. In addition, it can be used to create format files that are used in the import and export operations.

The syntax of the BCP utility is as follows:

```
usage: bcp {dbtable | query} {in | out | queryout | format} datafile
[-m maxerrors] [-f formatfile] [-e errfile] [-F firstrow] [-L lastrow]
[-b batchsize] [-n native type] [-c character type] [-w wide character type]
[-N keep non-text native] [-V file format version] [-q quoted identifier]
[-C code page specifier] [-t field terminator] [-r row terminator] [-i inputfile]
[-o outfile] [-a packetsize] [-S server name] [-U username] [-P password]
[-T trusted connection] [-v version] [-R regional enable] [-k keep null values]
[-E keep identity values] [-h "load hints"] [-x generate xml format file]
```

BCP format files can be created in two separate formats: XML and non-XML. These files can then be referenced in the import and export of data. The BCP is well-documented in Books Online, but the following examples show the most common usage of BCP.

Non-XML Format File Example

This example shows how to begin an interactive BCP session to create a non-XML format file based on an existing table. The BCP utility will prompt for a column data type, a prefix length, and a field delimiter.

It is usually best to accept the defaults provided for the data type and the prefix length because these values are determined by the table being referenced in the BCP command. The delimiter value can be any character, but defaults to "None."

The following command uses BCP to create a format file based on the CreditCard table in the AdventureWorks2008 database and Sales schema of the local default instance of SQL Server:

```
BCP AdventureWorks2008.Sales.CreditCard format nul -T -f C:\BCP\CreditCard.fmt
```

It is often better to provide the -S switch and specify the server name. The format argument tells BCP that the desired output is a format file. The absence of an -x switch specifies that the output file is not XML. The nul argument sends a NULL as the username, because the -T switch was used indicating that BCP should use a Windows trusted connection. If -T is not used, the -U username switch is required followed by the -P password switch. If nul is not used, BCP will fail with the error that a username was not provided.

The result of the preceding command, accepting the defaults for the field data type and prefix length, but entering a comma as the field delimiter, is as follows:

```
10.0
6
1    SQLINT       0    4     ","   1   CreditCardID   ""
2    SQLNCHAR     2    100   ","   2   CardType       SQL_Latin1_General_CP1_CI_AS
3    SQLNCHAR     2    50    ","   3   CardNumber     SQL_Latin1_General_CP1_CI_AS
4    SQLTINYINT   0    1     ","   4   ExpMonth       ""
5    SQLSMALLINT  0    2     ","   5   ExpYear        ""
6    SQLDATETIME  0    8     ","   6   ModifiedDate   ""
```

The 10.0 at the top of the results designates the version of BCP. "10.0" is SQL Server 2008, and "9.0" would be SQL Server 2005. The number 6 under the 10.0 specifies how many columns are in the file. Following the column number is the SQL Server data type of the column, followed by the number of bytes needed by the prefix length. The prefix length of a column depends on the maximum number of bytes, whether the column supports NULLs, and the storage type.

If the BCP command is supplied a data format argument (-c or -n), it will output a format file with all columns mapped to the supplied format without any interaction.

XML Format File Example

This example shows how to use the BCP command to generate an XML format file:

```
BCP AdventureWorks2008.Sales.CreditCard format nul -x -T -f C:\BCP\CreditCard.xml
```

As you can see, the syntax is identical, except that the -x switch is used to specify an XML output. The result is as follows:

```
<?xml version="1.0"?>
<BCPFORMAT xmlns=http://schemas.microsoft.com/sqlserver/2004/bulkload/format
        xmlns:xsi="http://www.w3.org/2001/XMLSchema-instance">
 <RECORD>
  <FIELD ID="1" xsi:type="NativeFixed" LENGTH="4"/>
  <FIELD ID="2" xsi:type="NCharPrefix" PREFIX_LENGTH="2" MAX_LENGTH="100"
```

```
            COLLATION="SQL_Latin1_General_CP1_CI_AS"/>
    <FIELD ID="3" xsi:type="NCharPrefix" PREFIX_LENGTH="2" MAX_LENGTH="50"
            COLLATION="SQL_Latin1_General_CP1_CI_AS"/>
    <FIELD ID="4" xsi:type="NativeFixed" LENGTH="1"/>
    <FIELD ID="5" xsi:type="NativeFixed" LENGTH="2"/>
    <FIELD ID="6" xsi:type="NativeFixed" LENGTH="8"/>
  </RECORD>
  <ROW>
    <COLUMN SOURCE="1" NAME="CreditCardID" xsi:type="SQLINT"/>
    <COLUMN SOURCE="2" NAME="CardType" xsi:type="SQLNVARCHAR"/>
    <COLUMN SOURCE="3" NAME="CardNumber" xsi:type="SQLNVARCHAR"/>
    <COLUMN SOURCE="4" NAME="ExpMonth" xsi:type="SQLTINYINT"/>
    <COLUMN SOURCE="5" NAME="ExpYear" xsi:type="SQLSMALLINT"/>
    <COLUMN SOURCE="6" NAME="ModifiedDate" xsi:type="SQLDATETIME"/>
  </ROW>
</BCPFORMAT>
```

Export a Table to a Flat-File Example

Once the format file is created, it can be used to control data export and import operations. To export data to a delimited flat file using the XML format file created in the preceding example, execute the following code:

```
BCP AdventureWorks2008.Sales.CreditCard OUT C:\BCP\CreditCard.dat -T
        -f C:\BCP\CreditCard.XML
```

Import Flat-File Example with a Format File

To test a BCP import, first create a copy of the CreditCard table with the following script:

```
USE AdventureWorks2008
GO
SELECT * INTO Sales.CreditCard2
FROM Sales.CreditCard
TRUNCATE TABLE Sales.CreditCard2
```

Once the destination table exists, the flat file and XML format file can be used to import the data to the new CreditCard2 table with the following code:

```
BCP AdventureWorks2008.Sales.CreditCard2 IN C:\BCP\CreditCard.dat -T
        -f C:\BCP\CreditCard.xml
```

PowerShell

PowerShell is a new command-line shell designed for Systems Administrators. PowerShell is both an interactive console and a scripting interface that can be used to automate many common administrative tasks. A complete explanation of PowerShell is beyond the scope of this book, but this section will provide a summary of how PowerShell can be used for SQL Server Administration.

PowerShell is designed around the Microsoft .NET Common Language Runtime (CLR) and the .NET Framework. It exposes .NET objects through a series of *cmdlets*, which are single-feature commands that interact with objects. Cmdlets are formatted using a verb–noun structure, separated by a hyphen, such as

`Get-Process`, which returns a list of the current running processes. Another benefit of PowerShell is that cmdlets can be piped into one another; for example, you might invoke one command to retrieve information and then use a pipe character (|) on the same line to invoke another command that performs an action or controls formatting and output of the results of the first command. You can pipe several commands as a single function. PowerShell can be installed on Windows XP SP2, Windows Vista, Windows Server 2003, and comes installed in Windows Server 2008.

SQL Server 2008 supports PowerShell for SQL Administration, and, in fact, if it's not already installed on the system, the SQL Server installer will install it for you. SQL Server administrators can use PowerShell to administer any SQL Server running SQL Server 2008, SQL Server 2005, and even SQL Server 2000 SP4, although functionality will be limited.

SQL Server 2008 also includes a limited-functionality shell known as *sqlps*. The sqlps utility is designed to expose access to SQL Server objects and cmdlets automatically, but it is configured to run with a *Restricted* execution policy, which prevents PowerShell scripts from running. This can be changed, if necessary.

It may be preferred to access SQL Server objects from a standard PowerShell environment, in which case, you can create a PowerShell console that includes the snap-ins for SQL Server. The following example shows you how to create a new PowerShell console named *MySQLPS.psc1* with the SQL Server snap-ins, to a new folder called *PSConsoles*. In this case, PowerShell is being invoked from the Run command in the Start Menu.

```
Windows PowerShell
Copyright (C) 2006 Microsoft Corporation. All rights reserved.

PS C:\Users\Administrator> md C:\PSConsoles


    Directory: Microsoft.PowerShell.Core\FileSystem::C:\


Mode                LastWriteTime     Length Name
----                -------------     ------ ----
d----         9/23/2008   9:33 AM            PSConsoles


PS C:\Users\Administrator> cd c:\PSConsoles
PS C:\PSConsoles> add-pssnapin SqlServerProviderSnapin100
PS C:\PSConsoles> add-pssnapin SqlServerCmdletSnapin100
PS C:\PSConsoles> Export-Console -Path MySQLPS.psc1
```

Now that you've created the new console, you can double-click on the file in Windows Explorer, or you can manually invoke the console using the following command from the Run command:

```
powershell.exe -psconsolefile C:\PSConsoles\MySQLPS.psc1
```

So what can you do with PowerShell? Quite a bit, actually. The Object Explorer includes the ability to launch PowerShell using the right-click context menu. The PowerShell console invoked is location-aware, meaning that when you right-click the `HumanResources.Employee` table in the `AdventureWorks2008` database and choose Start PowerShell from the menu, it will start `sqlps` using that object as the current path.

```
PS SQLSERVER:\SQL\AUGHTEIGHT\DEFAULT\Databases\AdventureWorks20
08\Tables\HumanResources.Employee>
```

Try It Out   **Output Data using PowerShell**

In this exercise, you will use PowerShell to invoke a SQLCMD function.

1. In Object Explorer, navigate to Server ➤ Databases ➤ AdventureWorks2008.

2. Right-click on the AdventureWorks 2008 database, and select Start PowerShell (Figure 3-44).

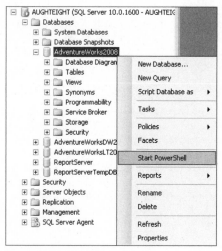

Figure 3-44: Start PowerShell.

3. Type the following commands into the PowerShell shell:

```
md C:\OutFiles
invoke-SQLCMD "Select TOP 10 * from HumanResources.Employee" |
    ConvertTo-html | Out-file C:\OutFiles\Top10Emps.html
```

4. Navigate to C:\OutFiles, and double-click on the Top10Emps.html file. In IE, you should see the HTML-formatted output shown in Figure 3-45.

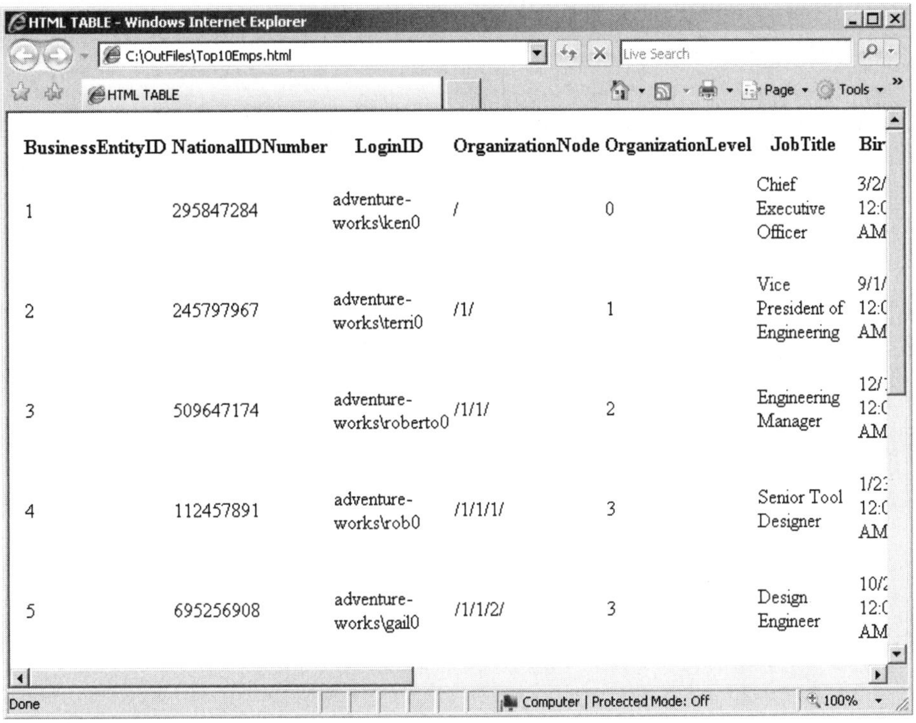

BusinessEntityID	NationalIDNumber	LoginID	OrganizationNode	OrganizationLevel	JobTitle	Bir
1	295847284	adventure-works\ken0	/	0	Chief Executive Officer	3/2/ 12:(AM
2	245797967	adventure-works\terri0	/1/	1	Vice President of Engineering	9/1/ 12:(AM
3	509647174	adventure-works\roberto0	/1/1/	2	Engineering Manager	12/ 12:(AM
4	112457891	adventure-works\rob0	/1/1/1/	3	Senior Tool Designer	1/2 12:(AM
5	695256908	adventure-works\gail0	/1/1/2/	3	Design Engineer	10/ 12:(AM

Figure 3-45 HTML formatted output.

At this point, you've barely scratched the surface of what PowerShell can do, but because the entire set of SQL Management Objects (SMO) is exposed to PowerShell, administration of your SQL Server and its databases can be made much easier by automating and scripting many common processes.

Summary

This Chapter described the primary tools that are used by DBAs. Some of the less-frequently used tools were covered briefly, as they are not often used by the DBA, but instead by an application or Business Intelligence developer. By this point, you should have a good understanding of the tools available to you in your role as a DBA and how to customize those tools to meet your needs.

The most prominent of these tools is, of course, SQL Server Management Studio. SQL Server Management Studio for SQL Server 2008 includes many new and compelling features, such as IntelliSense for T-SQL, PowerShell integration, and expanded toolsets. However, DBAs should also be familiar with Business Intelligence Development Studio (BIDS) and SQL Server Configuration Manager.

Throughout this book, you will be using the tools described in this Chapter to build and manage SQL Server 2008 databases. Having a solid understanding of the tools available will make it easier to perform these tasks.

Chapter 4 describes how SQL Server stores its data physically and logically. It describes the physical architecture of data and log files, as well as how SQL Server manages these files. Since Disk I/O is often the slowest part of any SQL environment, understanding how SQL Server stores and accesses data will be the key to maintaining a solid infrastructure.

SQL Server 2008 Storage Architecture

I had just spent the better part of the day describing the storage architecture to a group of about 30 new database administrators when one of them approached me while the class was on break and asked me pointedly, "Why do I need to know this stuff? I mean, who cares how SQL Server stores data as long as it does it?" They were valid questions. After all, I have no idea how the fuel injection system on my car works, but I drive it anyway. The key difference is that when my car needs service, I take it to a mechanic. If your database doesn't work, who are you going to take it to? Understanding the mechanics of the SQL Server storage will help you make informed decisions on where the data is stored, how the data is indexed, and how to troubleshoot an ailing database.

For years, SQL Server database administrators have grown accustomed to having unrestricted access to system objects. This ability gave the DBA incredible power for both good and for evil. For example, a database administrator could turn on ad hoc updates to the system tables and then modify any value, including password hashes. This ability was certainly useful for correcting some system errors; more damage was just as likely, however.

In the past, Microsoft strongly recommended that system objects not be accessed directly, while sometimes offering solutions to database problems that required directly updating system tables. With the release of SQL Server 2005 and continuing with SQL Server 2008, this apparent contradiction came to an end. Unless Microsoft (or a mysterious third party) releases some hidden secret handshake that unlocks system objects to modification, they are completely inaccessible for updates by the DBA. Even Read Only access to the actual system tables has been restricted and can only be accomplished through the Dedicated Administrator Connection (DAC), and even that allowance is made with the disclaimer "*Access to system base tables by using DAC is designed only for Microsoft personnel, and it is not a supported customer scenario.*"

To Microsoft's credit, they certainly did their homework. They researched the primary reasons that DBAs performed ad hoc updates to system tables and provided mechanisms to perform those actions in a controlled manner without compromising the integrity of the system catalog.

In this chapter, you learn how SQL Server 2008 stores and organizes data. This knowledge will be very helpful in any effort to optimize and tune SQL Server, as well as troubleshoot performance issues.

The Resource Database

A big reason for the locking away of the system objects is because they all have a common source now called the `resource` database. The `resource` database is the physical repository for all system objects and is inaccessible during normal operations of SQL Server. Although the system objects are physically stored in the `resource` database, they are logically presented as the `sys` schema in each database. Microsoft strongly recommends that the `resource` database be left alone, but it can be accessed if SQL Server is started in single-user mode. Even this access, however, is Read Only, as is access to any objects in the `sys` schema. Any attempt to modify a system object will result in an error, even if ad hoc updates to the system catalog are enabled.

Persisting all the system objects in the `resource` database allows for rapid deployment of service packs and upgrades to SQL Server 2008. When installing a service pack, the process is simply one of replacing the `resource` database with a new version and executing whatever modifications are required to the operating system objects. This dramatically reduces the amount of time it takes to update SQL Server.

Even though the `resource` database isn't accessible during normal SQL Server operations, information about the database can be retrieved using system functions and global variables. The following code returns the build number of the `resource` database:

```
SELECT SERVERPROPERTY('ResourceVersion')
```

To return the date and time the `resource` database was last updated, the following code can be executed:

```
SELECT SERVERPROPERTY('ResourceLastUpdateDateTime')
```

The sys *Schema*

As previously mentioned, the system objects stored in the `resource` database logically appear in the `sys` schema of each database. The `sys` schema contains views that can be utilized by the DBA to retrieve information about the objects in a database. Most (but not all) of the information the DBA typically needs access to is available through the use of system functions and stored procedures that return metadata from the system objects. Sometimes, however, it is beneficial to retrieve the metadata directly from the system objects. The views in the `sys` schema are provided for this reason.

If you have ever used SQL Server 2000 system tables, you will find that almost all of the old system table names have been preserved, but now are persisted as views. However, these views are only provided for backward compatibility. They do not expose any SQL Server 2008–specific metadata. Any future operations should be based on the new SQL Server 2008 system views. The views created to replace the functionality of the old system tables are known as *backward compatibility views*, and Microsoft's official word is that these views will be removed in a future release.

A word of caution is needed here. As a general rule, any scripts or applications created to consume system metadata directly from system objects should be built with the knowledge that they may not work in future releases of SQL Server. There is nothing really new about this. Microsoft has cautioned against formalizing processes that directly access system objects for years and has warned that the system objects could be altered by future upgrades and service packs. What this means is that as a rule, dynamic management views and system functions, which are discussed next, along with system stored procedures should be used.

Dynamic Management Views and Functions

In addition to the traditional system objects that can be used to view system metadata, new dynamic views and functions in the sys schema expose some very useful information about SQL Server processes and database activity. The dynamic views and functions are grouped into the following functional categories:

- ❑ Common Language Runtime Related Dynamic Management Views
- ❑ I/O Related Dynamic Management Views and Functions
- ❑ Database Mirroring Related Dynamic Management Views
- ❑ Query Notifications Related Dynamic Management Views
- ❑ Database Related Dynamic Management Views
- ❑ Replication Related Dynamic Management Views
- ❑ Execution Related Dynamic Management Views and Functions
- ❑ Service Broker Related Dynamic Management Views
- ❑ Full-Text Search Related Dynamic Management Views
- ❑ SQL Server Operating System Related Dynamic Management Views
- ❑ Index Related Dynamic Management Views and Functions
- ❑ Transaction Related Dynamic Management Views and Functions
- ❑ Change Data Capture Related Dynamic Management Views
- ❑ Resource Governor Dynamic Management Views
- ❑ SQL Server Extended Events Dynamic Management Views
- ❑ Security Related Dynamic Management Views
- ❑ Object Related Dynamic Management Views and Functions

Many of the dynamic views and functions replace SQL Server 2000 system-stored procedures and Database Consistency Checker (DBCC) commands. Most of the old stored procedures and DBCC commands still exist, but they are provided only for backward compatibility and do not expose new SQL Server 2008 objects and processes. The new views and functions provide much more detailed information and return relational result sets that can be used with ease in custom monitoring applications.

In later chapters, many (but by no means all) of the views and functions are used and explained in the context of describing database maintenance and monitoring tasks. For a complete description of each system view and function, check out SQL Server Books Online under the topic "Dynamic Management Views and Functions."

SQL Server Database Physical Structure

SQL Server stores all of its data in files. These files are divided up into substructures that SQL Server manages to maintain the integrity, structure, and logical organization of the data contained within them. Although this book is meant to be a beginner's guide to SQL Server 2008 database administration, it is still very important for the new DBA to understand such advanced topics as physical database architecture. Knowing how SQL Server stores and maintains data will give you a better understanding of how changes to the data affect performance and will allow you to more effectively diagnose database problems.

Physical Storage Data Types

Before getting started on the physical storage of data, it is important to have a good understanding about the types of data that SQL Server stores. SQL Server 2008 Books Online groups data types into the following seven functional groups:

- ❑ Exact numerics
- ❑ Approximate numerics
- ❑ Date and time
- ❑ Character strings
- ❑ Unicode character strings
- ❑ Binary strings
- ❑ Other data types

Although the functional grouping of data types makes perfect sense when looking at data types from a usability viewpoint, what is relevant to this discussion is how the data is stored. SQL Server data types can essentially be grouped into three storage type groups: fixed-length data types, variable-length data types, and large object data types. In certain circumstances, large object data types can also act like variable-length data types, which are explained later. The data types described in this section are only data types that can be assigned table column data types for the physical storage of the associated data. This precludes the cursor and table data types that are described later in this chapter.

Fixed-Length Data Types

Fixed-length data types are exactly that — *fixed*. The amount of space used to store them in memory or on disk does not change. Following is a list of fixed-length data types:

- ❑ bit — The bit is an integer data type that supports a value of 0 or 1. Contrary to what its name implies, the bit data type actually consumes a byte of space for 8 or less bit data types used.

- ❑ tinyint — The tinyint data type uses 1 byte of storage space to store an unsigned integer value between 0 and 255.

- ❑ smallint — The smallint data type uses 2 bytes of storage space to store a signed integer between –32,768 and 32,767.

- ❑ int — The int data type uses 4 bytes of storage space to store a signed integer between –2,147,483,648 and 2,147,483,647.

- ❑ bigint — The bigint data type uses 8 bytes of storage space to store a signed integer between –9,223,372,036,854,775,808 and 9,223,372,036,854,775,807.

- ❑ decimal and numeric — The decimal and numeric data types are functionally identical. For clarity, you should typically use decimal, because it is more descriptive of the data it is used to store. The decimal data type can be set to consume different fixed amounts of storage space based on how it is used. When using the decimal data type, you have the option of specifying the precision (p) and scale (s) of the data to be stored. This is expressed by decimal(p,s). The precision and scale are specified with positive integer values between 0 and 38. However, the scale value must be less than or equal to the precision value, and can only be specified if a precision value is specified. Storage space is dependent on the value of precision, as described in the following table:

Precision	Storage Bytes
1–9	5
10–19	9
20–28	13
29–38	17

❑ smallmoney — The smallmoney data type stores monetary values between –214,748.3648 and 214,748.3647. The smallmoney data type is accurate to a ten-thousandth of whatever currency unit is being stored and consumes 4 bytes of space.

❑ money — The money data type stores monetary values between –922,337,203,685,477.5808 and 922,337,203,685,477.5807. The money data type is accurate to a ten-thousandth of whatever currency unit is being stored and consumes 8 bytes of space.

❑ real — The real data type is a floating-point number, so its value is approximate. The values supported by real are negative numbers between –3.40E+38 and –1.18E-38, 0, and positive numbers between 1.18E-38 and 3.40E+38. The real data type consumes 4 bytes of space.

❑ float — The float data type is a floating-point number, so its value is also approximate. The range of values supported by float and the resultant storage space required is dependent on the specified precision of the float. The precision is expressed as float(n), where n is the number of bits used to store the mantissa of the number in scientific notation. Allowable precision values are between 1 and 53. Precision values from 1 to 24 require 4 bytes of storage space, and precision values of 25 to 53 require 8 bytes of storage space. With the default precision of 53, the range of values supported by float is negative numbers between –1.79E+308 and –2.23E-308, 0, and positive numbers between 2.23E-308 and 1.79E+308.

❑ smalldatetime — The smalldatetime data type is used to store dates and times between January 1, 1900 and June 6, 2079. It is accurate to the minute and consumes 4 bytes of space. Internally, SQL Server stores smalldatetime data as a pair of 2-byte integers. The first 2 bytes are used to store the number of days since January 1, 1900, and the second 2 bytes are used to store the number of minutes since midnight.

❑ datetime — The datetime data type is used to store dates and times between January 1, 1753 and December 31, 9999. It is accurate to 3.33 milliseconds and consumes 8 bytes of space. Internally SQL Server stores datetime data as a pair of 4-byte integers. The first 4 bytes are used to store the number of days since January 1, 1753, and the second 4 bytes are used to store the number of milliseconds (rounded to 3.33) since midnight.

❑ datetime2 — The datetime2 data type is an extension of the datetime data type with support of a wider range of dates and more accuracy. It can be used to store dates and times between January 1, 0001 and December 31, 9999 and is accurate to up to 100 nanoseconds. Similar to the decimal and numeric data types, it is declared with an optional precision. The precision specifies the storage of fractional seconds with the default precision being seven decimal places, or 100 nanoseconds. It consumes 6 bytes of space for precisions 3 or less, 7 bytes for precisions 4 and 5, and 8 bytes for precisions 6 and 7.

❑ datetimeoffset — The datetimeoffset data type is used to store dates and times between January 1, 0001 and December 31, 9999 along with an offset from UTC (Coordinated Universal Time) ranging from 14 hours before UTC to 14 hours after UTC. Like the datetime2 data type, it is accurate to 100 nanoseconds and uses the optional precision specification.

❑ date — The date data type is used to store date values only between January 1, 0001 and December 31, 9999. It is accurate to 1 day and consumes 3 bytes of space. Internally, SQL Server stores date data as a 3-byte integer that is used to store the number of days since January 1, 0001.

❑ time — The time data type is used to store time values only between 00:00:00.0000000 and 23:59:59.9999999. It is accurate to 100 nanoseconds. Similar to the decimal and numeric data types, it is declared with an optional precision. The precision specifies the storage of fractional seconds with the default precision being seven decimal places, or 100 nanoseconds. It consumes 3 bytes of space for precisions less than 3; 4 bytes for precisions 3 and 4; and 5 bytes for precisions 5, 6, and 7.

❑ char — The char data type is used to store a fixed amount of non-Unicode data between 1 and 8,000 characters, and is expressed as char(n), where n is the number of characters to store. Each character requires 1 byte of storage space.

❑ nchar — The nchar data type is used to store a fixed amount of Unicode data between 1 and 4,000 characters, and is expressed as nchar(n), where n is the number of characters to store. Each character requires 2 bytes of storage space. Unicode types are appropriate if multiple languages must be supported.

❑ binary — The binary data type is used to store a fixed amount of binary data between 1 and 8,000 bytes, and is expressed as binary(n), where n is the number of binary bytes to store.

❑ rowversion or timestamp — rowversion is the data-type synonym for timestamp and consumes 8 bytes of storage space. rowversion should be specified instead of timestamp whenever possible, because it more accurately reflects the true nature of the data type. The timestamp data type has nothing to do with time. It is actually an 8-byte binary string that is used to define a versioning value to a row. When a timestamp or its synonym rowversion is specified as a table column's data type, every insert or update to that table will cause a new value to be generated by SQL Server and placed in the appropriate field.

❑ uniqueidentifier — The uniqueidentifier data type is stored as a 16-byte binary string represented by 32 hexadecimal characters. uniqueidentifiers can be generated by SQL Server with the NEWID() function, or existing uniqueidentifiers can be inserted and stored in a uniqueidentifer column.

Variable-Length and Large Object Data Types

Variable-length data types are used when the exact amount of space required by data cannot be predicted (such as a column that holds a last name of a person). The varchar, nvarchar, and varbinary data types fall into this category.

However, when the (MAX) option is specified for the length of the character or binary string, these variable data types can be treated as Large Object data types. The primary difference is in how the data is stored. Large Object data is stored outside the data row in separate physical structures by default, whereas variable-length data is stored in the data row.

This is explained in the following descriptions:

- ❑ varchar — The varchar data type is used to store a variable amount of non-Unicode data between 1 and 8,000 characters, and is expressed as varchar(n), where n is the maximum number of characters to store. Each character requires 1 byte of storage space. The actual storage space used by a varchar is the value of n plus 2 bytes. The varchar data type also supports an optional (MAX) length specification. When using varchar(MAX), the maximum amount of characters supported is 2,147,483,647, consuming up to 2 GB of storage space. When the (MAX) option is specified, SQL Server will store the varchar data in the data row, unless the amount of data exceeds 8,000 bytes or doing so would exceed the maximum row size of 8,060 bytes. In these cases, SQL Server will move the varchar data out of the row and into a separate Large Object storage space (see the section "Data Pages" later in this chapter).

- ❑ nvarchar — The nvarchar data type is identical to the varchar data type, except that it is used to store Unicode data. Each Unicode character requires 2 bytes of storage, resulting in the maximum number of characters supported being 1,073,741,824.

- ❑ varbinary — The varbinary data type is also very similar to the varchar data type, except that it is used to store binary data and not character data. Other than that, the storage and use of the (MAX) option works the same as the (MAX) option described above.

- ❑ text — The text data type is a Large Object data type and is very similar to the varchar(MAX) data type in that it can also be used to store up to 2 GB of character data. The primary difference is that text data is stored out of the data row by default, and the text data type cannot be passed as a parameter in SQL Server functions, stored procedures, or triggers.

- ❑ ntext — The ntext data type is identical to the text data type, except that it is used to store Unicode data. As a result, the 2 GB of Unicode character data represents only 1,073,741,824 characters.

- ❑ image — The image data type is a Large Object data type and is very similar to the varbinary(MAX) data type. It can also be used to store up to 2 GB of binary data but is always stored outside the data row in separate Large Object data pages.

- ❑ XML — The XML data type is a Large Object type that is used to store XML (Extensible Markup Language) in its native format. Up to 2 GB of XML data can be stored per data row.

- ❑ sql_variant — A sql_variant data type can be used in objects when the actual data type of a value is unknown. The sql_variant data type can be used to store almost any value that consumes less than 8,000 bytes. The type of data that is incompatible with the sql_variant type is text, ntext, image, timestamp, cursor, varchar(MAX), and nvarchar(MAX).

CLR Data Types

SQL Server 2008 includes three different CLR-based data types. The first is hierarchyid, which is used to manage hierarchical data in a table structure. The other two are new spatial data types that are used to represent information about the physical location and shape of geometric objects, such as country boundaries, roads, lakes, and the like. SQL Server 2008's spatial data types conform to the Open Geospatial Consortium (OGC) Simple Features for SQL Specification version 1.1.0.

- ❑ hierarchyid — The hierarchyid data type is used to create tables with a hierarchical structure or to reference the hierarchical structure of data in another location. The amount of storage required depends on the number of records and the number of hierarchies in the rows. To store a hierarchical number for an organization with 100,000 employees divided into seven levels would require 5 bytes. The more rows divided into more hierarchies, the more storage space that is required. The data type is limited to 892 bytes.

❑   geometry — This type represents data in a Euclidean (flat) coordinate system.

❑   geography — The geography data type (geodetic) stores ellipsoidal (round-earth) data, such as GPS latitude and longitude coordinates.

In-Row Data

By utilizing the 'large value types out of row' table option, the DBA can specify that all of the varchar(MAX), nvarchar(MAX), and varbinary(MAX) data is treated as Large Object data and is stored outside the row in separate Large Object data pages. The option can be set to 'ON' or 'OFF', as shown here:

```
sp_tableoption 'tablename', 'large value types out of row', 'ON'

sp_tableoption 'tablename', 'large value types out of row', 'OFF'
```

Likewise, if the DBA wants to keep text or ntext data in the row unless it exceeds a specified size, the table option 'text in row' can be specified. This option allows the DBA to specify a range of data to keep in the row. The supported range is from 24 to 7,000 bytes. Instead of specifying a limit, the word ON can be passed, resulting in a default value of 256 bytes. To turn the option off, the word OFF is passed:

```
sp_tableoption 'tablename', 'text in row', 'number of bytes'

sp_tableoption 'tablename', 'text in row', 'ON'

sp_tableoption 'tablename', 'text in row', 'OFF'
```

FILESTREAM Data

A new enhancement added to SQL Server 2008 is the ability to store unstructured data, such as text documents, images, and videos, outside the database but linked to the row in which the column is defined. FILESTREAM integrates the Database Engine with the NT File System by storing varbinary(MAX) binary large object (BLOB) data as files on the file system instead of on separate Large Object data pages within the data file of the database. Transact-SQL statements can insert, update, query, and back up FILESTREAM data.

In order to use FILESTREAM, the database needs a filegroup that is designated as a FILESTREAM storage area. The following example shows how to add a FILESTREAM filegroup to the AdventureWorks2008 database:

```
USE Master
GO
ALTER DATABASE AdventureWorks2008
ADD FILEGROUP MyFilestreamGroup2
CONTAINS FILESTREAM
GO
ALTER DATABASE AdventureWorks2008
```

```
ADD FILE (NAME = N'FileStreamData'
        ,FILENAME = N'D:\SQLData\FileStreamData')
          TO FILEGROUP MyFilestreamGroup
GO
```

Once the new filegroup is added to the database, tables can be added or modified to store the table's binary Large Object data in the file system as a Database Engine–managed object. The following example shows how to create a table that uses the FILESTREAM storage:

```
USE AdventureWorks2008
GO
CREATE TABLE MyLargeData
(DocumentIdentifier uniqueidentifier ROWGUIDCOL NOT NULL UNIQUE
,DocumentFile VARBINARY(MAX) FILESTREAM NULL)
GO
```

Keep in mind that a table with FILESTREAM-enabled storage must have a non-NULL unique ROWGUID column. To add a FILESTREAM column to an existing column, you must ensure that the table has a ROWGUID column or you must add one.

Other Data Types

As previously noted, SQL Server 2008 has two data types that are not used to store data physically on the disk by being part of a table or index definition. The following data types are used in programming objects to manipulate data:

❑   table — The table data type is used to store a set of rows in memory. It is primarily used with Table-Valued Functions but can be used in any programming object to return an organized result set that has most of the properties of an actual table. A table variable can be declared and instantiated with a set of columns, a specified primary key, check constraints, and a default constraint.

❑   cursor — Transact-SQL performs best with sets of data, but occasionally it is necessary to manipulate data one row at a time. The cursor data type is used for this type of requirement. A cursor holds a complete set of rows from a query and can then be manipulated to return single rows at a time. For a complete discussion of cursors and their uses, check out the book *Beginning T-SQL with Microsoft SQL Server 2005 and 2008* by Paul Turley and Dan Wood (Wiley, 2008).

SQL Server Database Files

SQL Server stores data in data files and transactional records in transaction log files. These files, when grouped together under a logical database name, *are the database*. A SQL Server database can have many data files and multiple transaction log files, although one transaction log file is usually sufficient.

When a database is first created, it will have one primary data file with the default file extension of .mdf. It can also optionally have secondary data files with the default extension of .ndf. These data files can be grouped together in a logical grouping called a *filegroup*, which is explained in Chapter 5. The database will also have, at a minimum, one transaction log file with the default extension of .ldf. The file extensions for SQL Server databases are not enforced, so you can use anything you want, but the default extensions are typically used because they readily identify the file's purpose. The following sections are limited to a description of the physical storage structure of the data and transaction log files. For a complete description of the database creation process and how files are created and used, see Chapter 5.

Data Files

The database master data file (.mdf), or primary data file, and any secondary data files (.ndf) that are part of the database have identical structures. Both files are used to store data, as well as all the metadata that allows SQL Server to efficiently find, read, modify, and add data to the database. All the data from tables and indexes and the metadata that describes that data is organized in storage objects called *extents* and *pages*.

Extents

An *extent* is a SQL Server file storage structure that is 64 KB in size. Extents are comprised of eight contiguous 8-KB pages. There are two types of extents: mixed extents and uniform extents. *Mixed extents* contain pages from more than one object. For example, a mixed extent might contain data pages from Table A, an index page from indexes on Table B, and still more data pages from Table C. Because there are eight pages in an extent, it is possible for eight different objects to share an extent. *Uniform extents* contain eight contiguous pages that belong to the same object. The differences are illustrated in Figure 4-1.

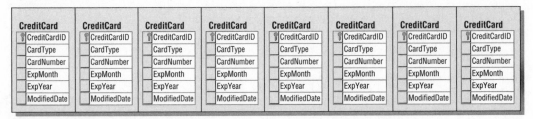

Figure 4-1: Mixed extents and uniform extents.

When data is retrieved or written to disk during database operations, the extent is the basic structure for data retrieval. SQL Server always allocates space in 64-KB increments. This maps very nicely to the way data is organized in memory and on an NT File System (NTFS) formatted partition. As previously noted, however, SQL Server can store pages from different objects in a single extent to maximize the efficiency of the storage process.

Pages

All data and metadata in a SQL Server 2008 database are stored in *pages*. Unlike extents, pages always store data from the same object. This includes rows from tables, rows from indexes, and Large Object data. Pages are 8 KB in size and are organized on 64-KB extents, which are made up of eight contiguous 8-KB pages. Every page has a 96-byte header that contains information about the page, such as the page number, the type of data stored on the page, the amount of free space available on the page, and what object owns the page. SQL Server contains several different types of pages that are used both to store data and to manage data.

Data Pages

Data pages contain data rows from tables. These rows cannot span pages. Because of the page header and row offset information, the maximum row size is limited to 8,060 bytes. Row sizes are determined by the number of columns in the row and the data type defined on each column. To maximize performance, table and index rows should be kept as narrow as possible. For example, if a single table row were 4,100 bytes in width, only one row could be stored on each data page, leaving almost 4,000 bytes of unusable space. Resulting reads from a table with this structure would require 8 KB of data retrieval for only 4,100 bytes of data. This is obviously very inefficient. Physical data page structure is illustrated in Figure 4-2.

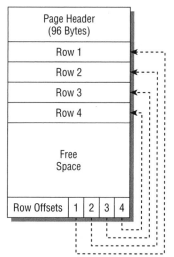

Figure 4-2: Physical storage structure.

Each row-offset block consumes 2 bytes of space for every row stored on a page. Rows from tables are physically arranged differently than their logical definition in order to optimize storage space. When a row is stored on a data page, the row is identified with a 4-byte header, which uniquely identifies the row on the page, followed by the fixed-length data columns, a Null block, a variable block, and then all the variable data columns at the end of the physical row, as shown in Figure 4-3.

The *Null block* contains a 2-byte block that indicates how many columns in the row can contain nulls, followed by a bitmap that indicates whether the nullable column is null. The size of the null bitmap is equal to 1 bit per column, rounded up to the nearest byte. One to eight nullable columns require a 1-byte bitmap. Nine to 16 columns require a 2-byte bitmap, and so on.

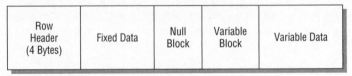

Figure 4-3: Header identifying a row.

The *variable block*, like the Null block, contains 2 bytes that indicate how many variable-length columns are present, followed by a bitmap that indicates what the maximum length of each variable column is. Unlike the Null block, the variable block bitmap contains 2 bytes per column that point to the end of each variable-length column, so that all the variable data can be stored contiguously at the end of the row. If no columns are defined as variable length, the variable block is omitted.

Index Pages

Index pages contain rows from indexes. They have the same structure and limitations as data pages.

Text/Image Pages

When a column is defined with a Large Object data type, SQL Server places a 16-byte pointer in the actual data row and places the Large Object data on separate data pages. This data includes those defined as `text`, `ntext`, `image`, `varchar(MAX)`, `nvarchar(MAX)`, `varbinary(MAX)`, and `XML`.

Global Allocation Map (GAM) and Secondary Global Allocation Map (SGAM) Pages

The *GAM* and *SGAM pages* are allocation pages that manage extents on a file-by-file basis. The second page of every data file is a GAM page, and the third page of every data file is a SGAM page. SQL Server will add additional GAM and SGAM pages as necessary, because each GAM and SGAM page can track only 63,904 extents. The GAM and SGAM pages form a bitmap that indicates whether an extent is a uniform or mixed extent. The GAM and SGAM bitmap also indicates whether the extent is full, empty, or has free data pages.

Page Free Space (PFS) Pages

PFS pages record the status of each page, whether or not a page has been allocated, and the amount of free space on each page.

Index Allocation Map (IAM) Pages

The *IAM page* contains information about the extents that a table or index uses. The IAM page contains the location of the eight initial pages of an object, and a bitmap representing the extents that are in use for that object. Every IAM page can track up to 512,000 data pages. SQL Server uses the IAM and PFS pages to find and allocate new pages for data.

Bulk Changed Map (BCM) Pages

The *Bulk Changed Map pages* contain the location of extents that were modified by bulk operations since the last transaction log backup. Bulk operations include UPDATETEXT, WRITETEXT, SELECT INTO, BULK INSERT, and image operations. BCM pages are used primarily for transaction log backup operations when the database is in BULK-LOGGED recovery mode (see Chapter 9 for a full explanation of the BULK-LOGGED recovery mode).

Differential Changed Map (DCM) Pages

The *Differential Changed Map pages* contain the identifier of any extent that has been modified since the last database backup. The DCM pages are used when performing Differential backups.

Transaction Log

The purpose of the transaction log is to maintain a physical record of all transactions that have occurred on a SQL Server database during a specific interval. The specific interval depends on the database recovery mode.

In the default database configuration, the transaction log keeps a record of all database modifications and is never cleared unless it is backed up or explicitly truncated by a database administrator.

The transaction log is a binary file. It is not simply a traditional log file that can be opened and viewed with a log viewer or Notepad, so its contents are not readily available to the database administrator. There are a couple of third-party products that can be used by the database administrator to open and view the contents of the transaction log. These products can be used to audit database modifications and also can be used to create scripts that will reverse the effects of an unwanted transaction.

The transaction log is maintained on disk as one or more physical files. In most cases, one transaction log file is sufficient, because any additional log files will not be used until the first is completely full and has reached its maximum size. Internally, the physical transaction log file is divided into multiple virtual logs. The number and size of the virtual log files that a physical file or files are divided into are configured dynamically by SQL Server and are not configurable. When SQL Server configures the transaction log internal structure, it tries to keep the number of virtual logs small.

To help SQL Server maintain a smaller number of virtual logs, the initial size of the transaction log should be set to accommodate all expected transactions that may occur between transaction log backups. If the log is configured to auto-grow, the growth increments should be fairly large to avoid small repetitive growths that will cause the creation of multiple small virtual logs.

Transactions

All data modifications occur within a transaction and are recorded in the transaction log. A *transaction* is a single unit of data operations that can be controlled so that either all the modifications in a transaction occur, or none occur. SQL Server has three ways of executing transactions: Implicit Transactions, Explicit Transactions, and Auto-Commit Transactions. Implicit and Auto-Commit Transactions are mutually exclusive.

Auto-Commit

By default SQL Server connections use *Auto-Commit Transactions*. Any INSERT, UPDATE, or DELETE state-ment executed alone or in a batch will automatically be applied to the database. An example of this type of activity is as follows:

```
UPDATE CheckingAccount
SET Balance = Balance + 500
WHERE AccountID = '123456789-CK'

UPDATE SavingsAccount
SET Balance = Balance - 500
WHERE AccountID = '123456789-SV'
```

Both of the updates in this example are transactions. In Auto-Commit mode, they will be applied to the database independently of each other. If the first update succeeds, but the second fails, the bank will have lost $500.00, and there will be no way to roll back the changes. Likewise, if the first update fails and the second succeeds, you will be out $500.00, and the bank will have gained $500.00. To avoid data problems resulting from errors involving dependent data changes, transactions should be used.

Implicit

The ANSI standard for the Structured Query Language specifies that no modifications should be made to data unless explicitly committed. SQL Server supports this specification through a connection property called IMPLICIT_TRANSACTIONS. When IMPLICIT_TRANSACTIONS is set to ON, any data modification will implicitly begin a transaction, but will not close the transaction. The transaction will remain open until it is explicitly committed or rolled back. An example of this is as follows:

```
SET IMPLICIT_TRANSACTIONS ON

BEGIN TRY

  UPDATE CheckingAccount
  SET Balance = Balance + 500
  WHERE AccountID = '123456789-CK'

  UPDATE SavingsAccount
  SET Balance = Balance - 500
  WHERE AccountID = '123456789-SV'

  COMMIT TRANSACTION

END TRY

BEGIN CATCH

  ROLLBACK TRANSACTION
  RAISERROR('Account Transfer Failed', 14,1)

END CATCH
```

In this example, if any error occurs during data modification, the CATCH block will be called to roll back the transaction. If no errors occur, the transaction will be committed. In Auto-Commit mode this same logic would not work, because there was no implicit or explicit transaction to commit or roll back. Turning on IMPLICIT_TRANSACTIONS turns off Auto-Commit.

Explicit

An explicit transaction requires a BEGIN TRANSACTION to begin the transaction and an explicit COMMIT TRANSACTION or ROLLBACK TRANSACTION to close the transaction, as shown in the following example:

```
BEGIN TRY

   BEGIN TRANSACTION

      UPDATE CheckingAccount
      SET Balance = Balance + 500
      WHERE AccountID = '123456789-CK'

      UPDATE SavingsAccount
      SET Balance = Balance - 500
      WHERE AccountID = '123456789-SV'

   COMMIT TRANSACTION

END TRY

BEGIN CATCH

   ROLLBACK TRANSACTION
   RAISERROR('Account Transfer Failed', 14,1)

END CATCH
```

In this example, like the implicit transaction example before it, any error can be used to immediately roll back the transaction, ensuring data integrity.

Much of the documentation available on SQL Server states that a transaction is a "single unit of work that must accomplish entirely, or not at all." However, even if the data modifications are placed in a transaction, this does not guarantee that the transaction will accomplish entirely. Without the TRY and CATCH blocks, an implicit or explicit transaction will work just like the Auto-Commit example. Any successful modifications will be made to the database, and any failed ones will not. Proper error handling is critical to managing transactions.

Recording Transactions

Now that you know what a transaction is, take a look at how SQL Server records them on the disk.

Data modifications are never made directly to the database data file. When a modification is sent by an application, SQL Server finds the data page that contains the data, or, in the case of an insert, a page with enough space in it to accommodate the data in the buffer cache. If the page is not located in the cache, SQL Server will read the page from disk and place it in the buffer cache and then modify it there. At the same time, SQL Server records the data modification on disk in the transaction log. When the page was initially read into the buffer cache, it was a "clean" page. Once the page was modified by the transaction, the page became "dirty."

SQL Server periodically issues an event called a CHECKPOINT. When a CHECKPOINT is issued, all dirty pages in the buffer cache are written to the data file on disk. The purpose of checkpoints is to reduce the amount of dirty data stored in the cache to minimize the amount of time required for SQL Server to recover from a failure. Consider the following sequence of events:

```
BEGIN TRANSACTION 1
UPDATE ...
INSERT ...
UPDATE ...
COMMIT TRANSACTION 1

BEGIN TRANSACTION 2
INSERT ...
UPDATE ...

***CHECKPOINT***

BEGIN TRANSACTION 3
DELETE ...
UPDATE ...
COMMIT TRANSACTION 3

BEGIN TRANSACTION 4
UPDATE ...
***Server Power failure***
```

When SQL Server restarts after the power failure, it will read the transaction log to find the last CHECKPOINT issued. Everything from the last CHECKPOINT to the beginning of the log has been safely written to the disk. However, the only record of data modifications after the CHECKPOINT is in the transaction log. Because Transaction 3 was successfully committed, the calling application was notified of its success and should expect to see all the modifications that were submitted. In light of this, SQL Server will roll the entire Transaction 3 forward and commit the changes to disk. Transaction 2, on the other hand, was never successfully committed, even though the first two modifications were written to disk by the CHECKPOINT. SQL Server will use the information in the transaction log to undo, or roll back, the modifications. Transaction 4 was also never successfully committed, but neither was it written to the disk. Transaction 4 data modifications will essentially be deleted from the transaction log.

Transaction Log Physical Characteristics

The transaction log is implemented as a serialized, sequential, rotary write-back log. As data modifications are written to the log, they are given a Log Sequence Number (LSN). Because the transaction log is used to record more and more transactions, it will eventually fill up. If the transaction log has been set up to auto-grow (see Chapter 5), SQL Server will allocate additional file space to accommodate storage of transaction records. This behavior will continue until the transaction log's maximum size has been reached, or the disk that contains the transaction log fills up. If the transaction log becomes completely full, no data modifications will be allowed on the database.

To keep the transaction log from becoming completely full, it is necessary to periodically remove old transactions from the log. The preferred method of clearing the log is by backing up the transaction log (see Chapter 7). By default, once the transaction log has been successfully backed up, SQL Server will clear the inactive portion of the transaction log. The inactive portion of the transaction log is from the LSN of the oldest open transaction to the earliest LSN in the transaction log. This clearing of the transaction log does not reduce the size of the transaction log, but it does free up space in the log for additional transaction records.

The inactive portion of the transaction log can also be manually cleared, but this is strongly discouraged because doing so deletes all records of data modifications since the last database backup.

As previously noted, the transaction log is a rotary file. Once the end of the physical log is reached, SQL Server will loop back and continue writing the current logical log at the beginning of the physical log, as shown in Figure 4-4.

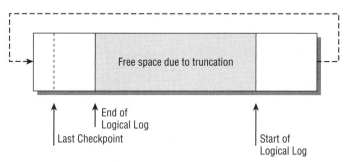

Figure 4-4: Looping back and continuing to write the current logical log.

Summary

This chapter examined how SQL Server physically stores data and transaction records on disk. Although this information may seem a bit esoteric in nature, it will become increasingly valuable as your SQL Server skills advance and you encounter more complex troubleshooting and optimization issues that require a deep understanding of how SQL Server stores and retrieves data. Keep in mind that this chapter just scratched the surface when it comes to the deep inner workings of the Database Engine. For a complete discussion of the Database Engine internals, consult SQL Server 2008 Books Online.

The database is the heart of SQL Server, and Chapter 5 exposes and describes all the parts and pieces that SQL Server uses to manage, modify, and organize the data stored within it. This includes everything from the tables used to store the data to the programming objects used to modify the data, and everything in between.

SQL Server 2008 Databases

The database is the heart of SQL Server 2008, handling everything from storing user information for later retrieval to acting as a temporary storage area for SQL Server operations. Previous chapters discussed the SQL Server installation process and the internal structure of all the files that make up a SQL Server 2008 database. This chapter delves into creating user databases and the various options that can be configured on them.

System Databases

As mentioned in Chapter 1, when SQL Server 2008 is installed, five system databases are created to store system information and support database operations. Four of the system databases (`master`, `model`, `msdb`, and `tempdb`) are visible during normal database operations, but the fifth (the `resource` database, as described in Chapter 4) is not. Distribution databases can also be created if the SQL Server instance is configured as a distributor for SQL Server Replication.

User Databases

User databases are those databases that are created by any server login that possesses the appropriate permissions. In past versions of SQL Server, you had the option to install the `AdventureWorks2008` sample databases that were briefly described in Chapter 1, but this ability has since been removed from the product. You can download the `AdventureWorks2008` sample database and code samples from the "Microsoft SQL Server Community Projects and Samples" located at `www.codeplex.com/sqlserversamples`.

Database Planning

One of the key responsibilities of the database administrator is the management of database creation. All too often, a company will purchase an application from a vendor that requires a SQL Server back-end without fully planning the data tier support. Many times, the vendor will be more than happy to come out, install the SQL Server instance, and create the necessary databases to support the application. In other cases, the application vendor will create setup programs that install and configure the database automatically. I have seen many of these installations, and, with just a few exceptions, the configuration of the supporting databases was either inefficient or flat-out wrong.

This is not to say that the application developers from software vendor companies don't know what they're doing. The problem is much more complex. First, it is almost impossible to accurately predict the hardware platform, database usage, and the amount of data stored for every installation of a database application combination, so default values are almost always wrong. Second, and this comes from a lot of experience, many application developers have no idea how SQL Server really works. They think of it only as a place to stick data. The idea of leveraging the power of the data tier or optimizing the data tier doesn't occur to very many application developers.

Database administrators should worry about how and why a database is performing the way it is. The best time to start managing a database is before it is created. Whether a data application is developed internally or purchased from a software vendor, it is imperative that the database administrator be intimately involved in the planning and creation of the supporting database. With that in mind, here's a closer look at the database creation process and the configuration options available during database creation.

Capacity Planning

One of the first things that must be determined when planning a new database is how much disk space will be required to support the database. The idea is to both ensure that there is sufficient disk space available for data expansion and to reduce the amount of data and log file growths that are performed to accommodate the data expansion to improve database efficiency.

If the database is being built to support an application purchased from a vendor, the capacity planning for the database should be very easy. However, the simplicity depends on the software vendor providing detailed documentation. The documentation must describe the average size of the database after periodic intervals where a defined number of users and transactions were supported. If the documentation is provided, you will have a good idea of what to expect from the database and can configure it accordingly. If the vendor did not provide the information, your job as a database administrator becomes a bit more complicated, and you may just have to guess. However, it must be an educated guess using as much information as you are able to collect. The difficulty is often in the fact that you may not know how the vendor is storing and retrieving data, so the database must be monitored for growth trends to adequately predict the amount of storage space.

If the database is being designed and built internally, there are established techniques for determining how big the data files will need to be. These techniques work because you know how much data is added for every transaction, whereas in a vendor-provided database, that information may not be available.

One such technique that I am sure you will encounter is calculating a database size requirement by calculating table sizes. It looks like this:

1. Add up the total number of bytes used by the fixed-length columns in the table.

2. Average the total number of bytes used by the variable-length columns in the table.

3. Add the number from Step 1 to the number calculated in Step 2.

4. Divide 8,060 (the maximum amount of data bytes in a page) by the number calculated in Step 3, and round down to the nearest whole number. This is the number of rows that will fit on a single page. Remember that rows cannot span pages, which is why you round down.

5. Divide the total number of expected rows by the number of rows per page calculated in Step 4. This is the total number of data pages expected to support the table.

6. Multiply the number calculated in Step 5 by 8,192 (the size of the data page). This is the total number of bytes required for the table.

7. Repeat the process for every table in the database.

Sounds like fun, doesn't it? Here's a tip: *Don't do it*. The results from this algorithm are misleading at best. The calculation doesn't take into account variables that affect storage space, such as whether or not compression is enabled, the number of indexes, the fill-factor used on the indexes, and data fragmentation, just to name a few. So, why did I even bother to explain the process? Because it does give insight into size considerations and because, as I mentioned earlier, you will most likely encounter this technique, and I wanted to make sure you knew its limitations.

There is a more realistic method of determining how big to make a data file. The idea is to take the database prototype (the test or development version of the database) and fill it with an appropriate amount of test data. After the test database has been populated, check the size of the data file on disk, and then multiply it by 1.5. The resulting file size should be sufficient to accommodate the initial data load of the new database with some room to spare. This technique is by no means perfect, but it is a great deal easier than the first technique, and typically much more accurate.

Once the database is put into production, it will become extremely important to monitor the size of the database files in order to analyze growth trends. I prefer to configure alerts that fire off when the database grows to 75 percent full. This will allow you to increase the size of files when necessary, but also to increase them in sufficient percentages so that the increases are seldom executed.

Planning the size of the transaction log file is much more complicated. To accurately plan the log size, you will need to know how big the average transaction is that will be executed on the database, as well as how often the transactions will take place and what the physical structure of the tables being modified is. For example, an insert executed on a table stored in a heap with a row size of 800 bytes and a non-clustered index on an integer column will increase the amount of data in the transaction log by approximately 820 bytes. This is because the new row is recorded in the transaction log along with the new index row. The size of the transaction log is also dependent on the recovery model of the database and how often the database transaction log is backed up. Recovery models are introduced later in this chapter. A complete description of indexes can be found in Chapter 6. Transaction log backups and their effect on the transaction log are described in Chapter 9.

Creating Databases

Databases are usually created either by writing and executing Transact-SQL code or through the graphical user interface. In either case, the only required information during the database creation process is the name of the new database, so the following code will create a database called SampleDB:

```
CREATE DATABASE SampleDB
```

Executing this Transact-SQL will cause SQL Server to create a single data file and one transaction log file in the default location for files specified during the SQL Server 2008 installation process. For a typical installation of a default instance of SQL Server 2008, this code, when executed, will create the following file system objects:

```
C:\Program Files\Microsoft SQL Server\MSSQL10.MSSQLSERVER\
                                        MSSQL\DATA\SampleDB.mdf
C:\Program Files\Microsoft SQL Server\MSSQL10.MSSQLSERVER\
                                        MSSQL\DATA\SampleDB_log.ldf
```

The first file is the database data file, and the second file is the database transaction log file. Although this default behavior is very convenient, it is usually better not to take advantage of it because all databases are not created equal, besides the fact that the system partition is hardly the recommended destination for data and log files. The database creation process allows for the specification of data file(s), transaction log file(s), and database options.

Getting Started

Before creating a database, it is important to understand all the available settings and options that are available. This section explains the process of creating a database with the graphical user interface and examines each configuration setting and option, as well as how it affects the database creation process. Once you have gone through the entire process, I'll show you how to turn all the work into a script that can be run again and again by specifying different values for the database name, filenames, and file locations.

Creating a New Database

Creating a database graphically with SQL Server Management Studio is very easy and intuitive. The first step is to open SQL Server Management Studio from the Start menu and connect to the Database Engine of your SQL Server.

Right-click on the Databases node, and click New Database. The New Database screen appears, as shown in Figure 5-1.

In the "Database name" field, enter the name of the new database. When specifying a database name, keep in mind that it can be a maximum of 128 characters long. SQL Server Books Online also states that a database name must start with a letter or underscore, and then subsequent characters can be a combination of letters, numbers, and some special characters, but this requirement is not enforced. However, data applications may be unable to make the connection to a database if the name does not conform to accepted standards, so it is a very good idea not to deviate from them. As a best practice, database names should be as descriptive as possible, but also kept as short as possible. Embedded spaces in object names are also problematic, because they can cause unexpected problems when the database is accessed programmatically.

The "Owner" field should typically specify SA, which is the built-in SQL Server System Administrator account. When creating a new database in the graphical user interface, this field will default to the value of <default>, which is the login account that is performing the database creation. The owner of the database gains complete control of the database. Database ownership can be modified by using the ALTER AUTHORIZATION T-SQL statement and specifying any valid login as shown in the following example:

```
ALTER AUTHORIZATION ON DATABASE::SampleDB TO SA
GO
```

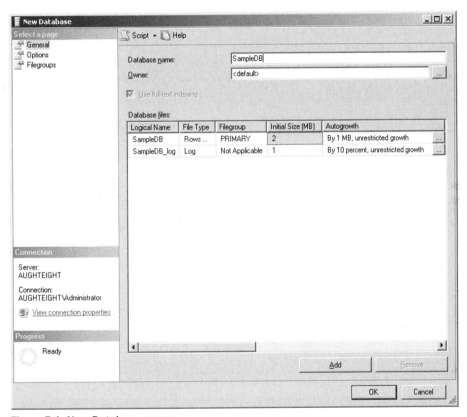

Figure 5-1: New Database screen.

There are two different ways to retrieve information about databases (such as who the owner is). The sp_helpdb stored procedure can be used to retrieve information about all databases or a specific database and is a lot easier to use for a quick look. For all databases, the stored procedure is executed with no parameters. For a specific database, the name of the database is passed to the stored procedure, as demonstrated in the following example:

```
USE Master
GO
EXEC sp_helpdb AdventureWorks2008
```

The results of the stored procedure when executed alone and with a database name are shown in Figures 5-2 and 5-3, respectively.

133

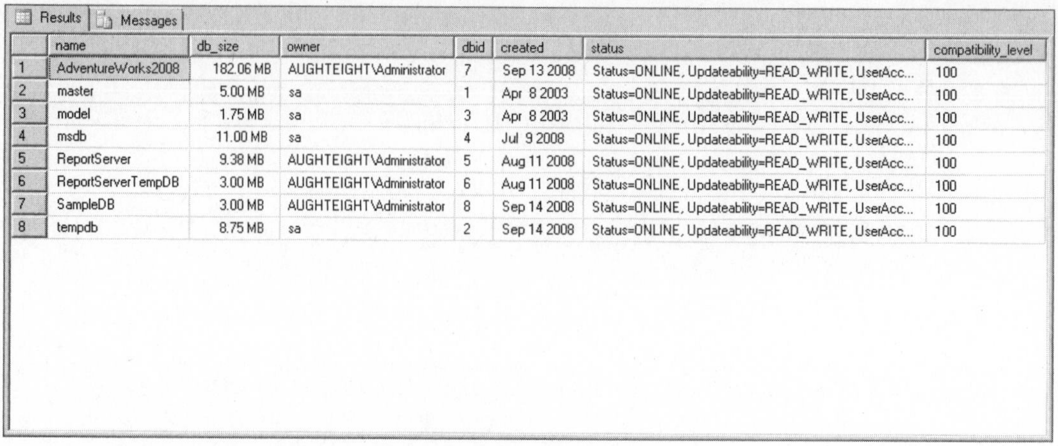

Results | Messages

	name	db_size	owner	dbid	created	status	compatibility_level
1	AdventureWorks2008	182.06 MB	AUGHTEIGHT\Administrator	7	Sep 13 2008	Status=ONLINE, Updateability=READ_WRITE, UserAcc...	100
2	master	5.00 MB	sa	1	Apr 8 2003	Status=ONLINE, Updateability=READ_WRITE, UserAcc...	100
3	model	1.75 MB	sa	3	Apr 8 2003	Status=ONLINE, Updateability=READ_WRITE, UserAcc...	100
4	msdb	11.00 MB	sa	4	Jul 9 2008	Status=ONLINE, Updateability=READ_WRITE, UserAcc...	100
5	ReportServer	9.38 MB	AUGHTEIGHT\Administrator	5	Aug 11 2008	Status=ONLINE, Updateability=READ_WRITE, UserAcc...	100
6	ReportServerTempDB	3.00 MB	AUGHTEIGHT\Administrator	6	Aug 11 2008	Status=ONLINE, Updateability=READ_WRITE, UserAcc...	100
7	SampleDB	3.00 MB	AUGHTEIGHT\Administrator	8	Sep 14 2008	Status=ONLINE, Updateability=READ_WRITE, UserAcc...	100
8	tempdb	8.75 MB	sa	2	Sep 14 2008	Status=ONLINE, Updateability=READ_WRITE, UserAcc...	100

Figure 5-2: `sp_helpdb` **results without a database name.**

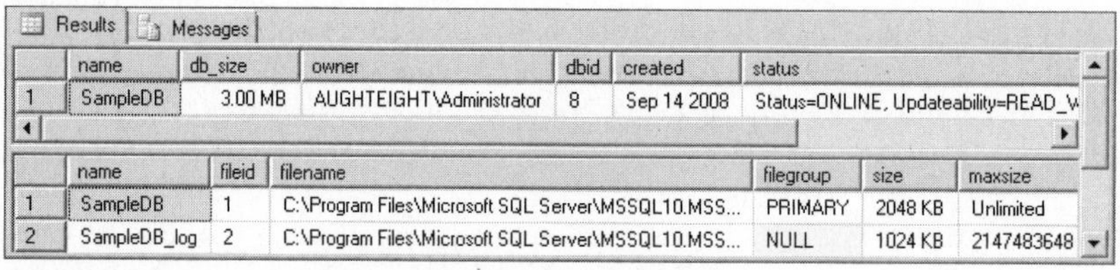

Results | Messages

	name	db_size	owner	dbid	created	status
1	SampleDB	3.00 MB	AUGHTEIGHT\Administrator	8	Sep 14 2008	Status=ONLINE, Updateability=READ_V

	name	fileid	filename	filegroup	size	maxsize
1	SampleDB	1	C:\Program Files\Microsoft SQL Server\MSSQL10.MSS...	PRIMARY	2048 KB	Unlimited
2	SampleDB_log	2	C:\Program Files\Microsoft SQL Server\MSSQL10.MSS...	NULL	1024 KB	2147483648

Figure 5-3: `sp_helpdb` **results with a database name.**

Another way to view database information is by using catalog views, which were introduced in SQL Server 2005. They offer more information than their stored procedure counterparts and allow the use of standard T-SQL commands such as `WHERE` and `GROUP BY`. The following T-SQL statement shows how to take the sys.databases catalog view and join it with the sys.server_principals catalog view to see basic information about all the databases on the server (see Figure 5-4):

```
SELECT db.name AS database_name,

sp.name AS owner,

db.create_date,

db.compatibility_level,

db.recovery_model_desc
FROM sys.databases db INNER JOIN sys.server_principals sp
ON db.owner_sid = sp.sid
```

To avoid any potential issues, the database owner should almost always be SA. See Chapter 6 for more information about the SA account.

Full-text indexing allows for the use of more flexible string-matching queries than Transact-SQL allows. The full-text engine has been moved into the SQL Server 2008 process in this release, allowing better optimization of mixed queries and performance of the index itself.

	database_name	owner	create_date	compatibility_level	recovery_model_desc
1	master	sa	2003-04-08 09:13:36.390	100	SIMPLE
2	tempdb	sa	2008-09-14 08:24:47.977	100	SIMPLE
3	model	sa	2003-04-08 09:13:36.390	100	FULL
4	msdb	sa	2008-07-09 16:46:27.767	100	SIMPLE
5	ReportServer	AUGHTEIGHT\Administrator	2008-08-11 15:14:08.617	100	FULL
6	ReportServerTempDB	AUGHTEIGHT\Administrator	2008-08-11 15:14:10.727	100	SIMPLE
7	AdventureWorks2008	AUGHTEIGHT\Administrator	2008-09-13 09:30:59.623	100	SIMPLE
8	SampleDB	AUGHTEIGHT\Administrator	2008-09-14 10:05:22.007	100	FULL

Figure 5-4: Using catalog views to retrieve database information.

Database Files

In the "Database files" section of the New Database dialog, notice that the Logical Name of the first data file as well as the Logical Name for the first log file have been given names automatically. The first data file is named the same as the database, and the log file is given the name of the database with _log appended to the end. The *logical names* are used to refer to the files programmatically in T-SQL script. Multiple files can be specified during the creation process, and each one could have its own configuration settings (such as initial size and growth behavior).

Click on the Add button at the bottom of the New Database dialog. A new row for an additional file is added to the "Database files" section. The new file defaults to the file type of Rows Data but can be changed to either Log or FILESTREAM Data by selecting it from the dropdown list. Once the database is created, the type of the file cannot be changed.

For this example, leave the file type as Rows Data. Type in a Logical Name for the new data file and then in the Filegroup column, click on the dropdown list, and choose <new filegroup>. The New Filegroup dialog displays, as shown in Figure 5-5.

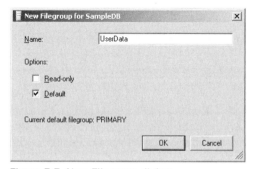

Figure 5-5: New Filegroup dialog.

Filegroups

Databases are created on files that are organized in *filegroups*. *Filegroups* are a logical grouping of data files that hold all data and database objects defined for the database. The data is striped across all files within the filegroup using a proportional fill strategy. This allows all data files to become full at the same time.

The only required filegroup is the one called *Primary*. The *Primary filegroup* is made up of the primary data file and any additional user-defined data files. The purpose of the primary data file is to store all system references for the database including pointers to objects defined in the resource database. The Primary filegroup contains all object definitions for user-defined objects if it is left as the default filegroup as well as all system-created objects. In addition to the Primary filegroup, more user-defined filegroups can be created as needed.

One of the biggest advantages of using user-defined filegroups boils down to one word: *control*. With user-defined filegroups, the database administrator has complete control over what data is stored in what location. Without user-defined filegroups, all data is stored in the Primary filegroup, so the flexibility and scalability of the database are reduced dramatically. Although this may be perfectly acceptable for smaller databases, once the database grows to a large size, it will become increasingly unacceptable to have all the user and system data grouped into the same filegroup.

I wish I could tell you exactly when it becomes necessary to segregate data, but like almost all questions in technology, the answer is, "It depends." It depends on the hardware the SQL Server is running on and how the database is being accessed; there is no hard-and-fast rule. For more information about data segregation and the use of filegroups, check out *Professional Microsoft SQL Server 2008 Administration* by Brian Knight, Ketan Patel, Wayne Snyder, Ross LoForte, and Steven Wort (Wiley, 2008).

Type in a name for the new filegroup, select the Default checkbox, and click OK. This sets the new user-defined filegroup as the default so that all user-created objects will be placed in this filegroup. This essentially segregates system data from user data and allows for more control of the database structure.

One nice feature of using filegroups is the ability to mark all data contained within that filegroup as Read Only. This can be done by selecting the "Read-only" checkbox on the New Filegroup dialog. This can be very advantageous when organizing the different objects in a database. The objects that change can be placed in an updatable filegroup, whereas those that never (or seldom) change can be placed in a Read Only filegroup. This segregation of objects can reduce the amount of data required to be backed up and restored, which is a useful option with very large databases.

Maintenance or Performance?

Should filegroups be implemented to optimize performance or to optimize maintenance tasks? Why not both? Filegroups provide the ability to improve both the performance and the maintainability of a database by separating data across multiple physical files in groups of tables.

The maintenance advantage comes from the ability to back up and restore individual files and filegroups as opposed to backing up entire databases. (File and filegroup backups are described in Chapter 9.) This ability is useful with very large databases separated into multiple filegroups, and even more useful when some of the filegroups are marked as Read Only. This segregation of Read Write data and Ready Only data enables the database administrator to back up only the data that is subject to modification, which can minimize backup and restore time of large databases. This ability, however, does not come without a cost. File and filegroup backup strategies can become quite complex. The complexity of the maintenance plans can quickly outweigh the flexibility that is gained.

Performance advantages that are delivered with filegroups are primarily divided into three areas: The first is parallel Read and Write operations that are made possible by separating the data files across multiple physical devices. However, the same performance gain can be achieved in a single filegroup with many physical files in it. The second is the ability to move non-clustered indexes and Large Object data off the filegroup reserved for the regular data space. Separating non-clustered indexes from the data enables the Database Engine to seek row locations from the index and retrieve the rows from the tables simultaneously using separate threads. Separating infrequently accessed Large Object data from transaction-intensive relational data can improve scan performance in some instances. The third (and most significant) advantage that filegroups enable is the ability to physically partition large tables across multiple filegroups. (Table and index partitioning is described later in this chapter.)

When it comes to performance, filegroups will only offer a small increase in performance to most databases, with the exception of very large databases that can fully exploit physical table partitioning. The best way to improve disk access to data is to implement a robust Redundant Array of Inexpensive Disks (RAID) environment. The primary reasons for using filegroups for most database administrators are the control it offers in the storage of the data and the ability to segregate system and user data, which equates to maintenance concerns.

File Size

In the "Initial Size (MB)" column (see Figure 5-1), a value should be assigned based on how big the file is expected to be within the first few weeks (and maybe even months) of operation. When looking for a house and planning a large family, it would be inadvisable to buy a one-bedroom house and then have to remodel it every time a new child is born. It makes much more sense to buy a large house that would accommodate the family, including future children. The same goes for database files. If a file is expected to hold 1 GB of data within the first few months of its existence, it only makes sense to allocate 1 GB of space to that file. As a best practice, file size modifications should be kept to a minimum. Allocate enough contiguous disk space to accommodate all the expected data plus a percentage of space for growth.

Autogrowth

Click the ellipsis button on the right of the Autogrowth column (see Figure 5-1) for the Primary data file. The Change Autogrowth dialog displays, as shown in Figure 5-6. The Change Autogrowth dialog enables the configuration of the maximum size and file growth setting for each individual file. Ensure that the "Enable Autogrowth" checkbox is checked. Clearing this checkbox sets the `filegrowth` property to zero. For this example, we will use the defaults in the Change Autogrowth dialog box.

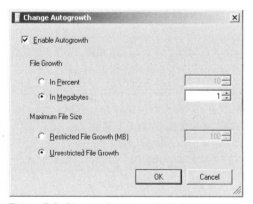

Figure 5-6: Change Autogrowth dialog.

File growth can be set at a fixed allocation size or a percentage of the existing file size. As a best practice, the Autogrowth option should be set to a sufficiently large enough increment to minimize the number of file-growths required to accommodate data growth. Growing files in small increments results in physical fragmentation of the files, which is detrimental to both data and log file performance.

The size of both data and log files can be restricted, allowing one more way to control the sizing of the files. This can be done by selecting the "Restricted File Growth (MB)" option button and specifying a maximum size. This size cannot be exceeded by automatic or manual file-growth operations. It is generally a best practice to set a maximum file size to safeguard against any errant process that may attempt to insert millions of rows (instead of just a few) and also to maintain control of database growth. One thing to keep in mind is that if the database reaches the maximum size, all data modification transactions will fail. If this occurs, the maximum size property can be changed and additional space allocated. The size selected should be the maximum amount of data expected for that file in a determined period of time. This operation should be performed on every file in the database.

Path

To change the path where data and log files are located, either click on the ellipses button on the right of the Path column in the New Database dialog for each data file and select a destination folder for each individual file, or simply type in the correct path in the Path column. When placing files, keep in mind that data files and log files should never be on the same physical disk; doing so puts the data at high risk of loss caused by disk or controller failure. See Chapter 3 for more information on file placement.

Now that all the general settings of your new database are complete, it is time to configure the database options.

Database Options

Click Options in the "Select a page" section in the upper-left of the New Database dialog, as shown in Figure 5-7. The Options window displays, enabling the setting of several database options.

Collation

Click the Collation dropdown list and review the different collation settings that are available, but leave the setting set to <server default>.

As noted in Chapter 2, an instance of SQL Server is assigned a default server collation that determines what characters are supported on the server by default and how those characters are searched and sorted. Collation settings can also be assigned to the database as well. As a result, just because a SQL Server instance has been configured to use the Latin character set doesn't mean that a database built to support Korean characters cannot be created on the same instance. However, also as previously described, collation incompatibilities in the tempdb database may occur if the database collation settings are different from the SQL Server instance collation settings.

Recovery Model

Click the "Recovery model" dropdown list and review the available choices. The available models that can be set are Full, Bulk-Logged, and Simple. If the Model database has not been set otherwise, the default recovery model for new databases is Full. Recovery models are explained in complete detail in Chapter 9, so for now an abbreviated explanation will suffice.

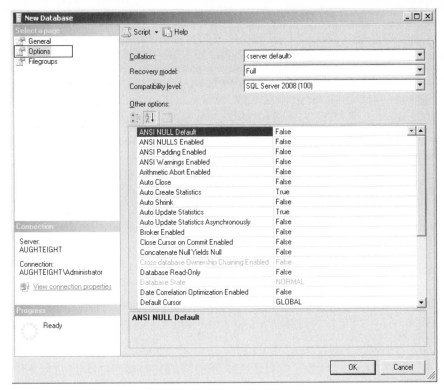

Figure 5-7: Enabling database options.

For all intents and purposes, there are really only two recovery models, Full and Simple. The Bulk-Logged model is meant only as an accessory to the Full recovery model for use during bulk operations. This is because in the Full recovery model, all modifications to the database are fully logged. Although this recovery model offers the greatest level of protection from data loss, it comes at a cost. Because all modifications to a database are fully logged, the transaction log can grow very rapidly to large sizes during certain operations (such as bulk loading of data or table index maintenance operations). The Bulk-Logged recovery model is also known as *minimal logging* and was developed so that the database could be temporarily set to Bulk-Logged during those operations that could cause the transaction log to rapidly swell and then be set back to Full recovery once those operations were complete.

In the Simple recovery model, the transaction log is cleared of all inactive content every time a checkpoint is issued. Checkpoints were described in Chapter 4. The repercussion of the Simple recovery model is that the transaction log cannot be backed up or used for database restore operations. The transaction log is only used for transactional consistency, but no long-term storage of transactional history is maintained.

Compatibility Level

Click the "Compatibility level" dropdown list and review the possible choices. Unless you have specific reasons to change the compatibility level, it should be set to SQL Server 2008 (100). The Compatibility level option changes the behavior of some database operations and is only necessary if an instance of SQL Server 2008 is sharing database responsibilities with a previous release of SQL Server. SQL Server 2008 only allows for the selection of compatibility levels of 80, 90, and 100, which, as the dropdown list indicates, correlates to SQL Server 2000, SQL Server 2005, and SQL Server 2008, respectively. In previous versions, you were able to programmatically change the compatibility level by using the System Stored Procedure `sp_dbcmptlevel`. This System Stored Procedure has been officially deprecated and has been replaced with an addition to the ALTER DATABASE Transact-SQL command. The following code will set the compatibility level of the `AdventureWorks2008` database to SQL 2000:

```
ALTER DATABASE AdventureWorks2008
SET COMPATIBILITY_LEVEL = 80
```

For a complete discussion of all the differences between compatibility levels, there is an excellent description in SQL Server 2008 Books Online under the topic "ALTER DATABASE Compatibility Level (Transact-SQL)." Databases upgraded from SQL Server 2000 or 2005 are configured for a compatibility mode respective to their original version. For example, a SQL Server 2000 database upgraded to SQL Server 2008 will have a compatibility level of 80.

Other Options

By default, the "Other options" section of the New Database screen organizes the options categorically. For purposes of this discussion, we will sort the options alphabetically. For this exercise, leave all the options in their default configurations. Each one is described in the following sections. Some of the database options are also connection options. Where this is the case, the commands to set the database option and the connection-level options are both shown. It's important to know that connection-level options, if specified, will override database-level options. When they are not specified, the database option will be in effect.

Click the alphabetical sort button, which can be identified by an A and a Z with a vertical arrow pointing down. The available options are now listed alphabetically, as shown in Figure 5-7.

ANSI NULL Default

The "ANSI NULL Default" setting specifies whether or not the default for columns added to a table during a CREATE TABLE or ALTER TABLE operation is to allow nulls. When the "ANSI NULL Default" setting is set to `False`, columns added will not allow nulls unless explicitly specified to do so. When connecting to SQL Server with SQL Server Management Studio, the connection setting for new queries defaults to the setting ANSI NULLS ON, which overrides the database setting. To set it at the connection level or database level, the following commands are used:

```
--Connection Settings
SET ANSI_NULL_DFLT_ON OFF --ANSI NULL Default False
SET ANSI_NULL_DFLT_ON ON  --ANSI NULL Default True

--Database Options
ALTER DATABASE AdventureWorks2008 SET ANSI_NULL_DEFAULT OFF
ALTER DATABASE AdventureWorks2008 SET ANSI_NULL_DEFAULT ON
```

ANSI NULLS Enabled

The "ANSI NULLS Enabled" setting controls the behavior of comparisons to NULL values. When set to `True`, any comparison to a NULL value results in an unknown. When set to `False`, comparisons to NULL will return `True` if the values are null. To set it at the connection level or database level, the following commands are used:

```
--Connection Settings
SET ANSI_NULLS OFF
SET ANSI_NULLS ON

--Database Options
ALTER DATABASE AdventureWorks2008 SET ANSI_NULLS OFF
ALTER DATABASE AdventureWorks2008 SET ANSI_NULLS ON
```

The "ANSI NULLS" option is deprecated as of this version of SQL Server. In a future version of SQL Server, the option will be set to ON and will not be allowed to be changed. If an application attempts to set the value to OFF, an error will be thrown. It is recommended that you avoid using it in all new development work and make arrangements to update any applications that currently use it.

ANSI Padding Enabled

When set to `True`, "ANSI Padding Enabled" dictates that trailing spaces for character data and trailing zeros for binary data are appended to the end of character and binary columns that are of fixed length. Character and binary columns that are of variable length are not padded, but trailing spaces or trailing zeros are not trimmed either. When set to `False`, character and binary columns that are of fixed length and set to NOT NULL behave the same as when "ANSI Padding Enabled" is `True`. However, nullable character and binary columns that are of fixed length are not padded, and any trailing spaces or trailing zeros are trimmed. Variable-length columns behave the same as nullable fixed-length columns when "ANSI Padding Enabled" is `False`. To set it at the connection level or database level, the following commands are used:

```
--Connection Settings
SET ANSI_PADDING OFF
SET ANSI_PADDING ON

--Database Options
ALTER DATABASE AdventureWorks2008 SET ANSI_PADDING OFF
ALTER DATABASE AdventureWorks2008 SET ANSI_PADDING ON
```

The "ANSI Padding" option is deprecated as of this version of SQL Server. In a future version of SQL Server, the option will be set to ON and will not be allowed to be changed. If an application attempts to set the value to OFF, an error will be thrown. It is recommended that you avoid using it in all new development work and make arrangements to update any applications that currently use it.

ANSI Warnings Enabled

When "ANSI Warnings Enabled" is set to `True`, warnings will be raised by the Database Engine whenever an aggregate function encounters a null. When set to `False`, no warnings are raised. To set it at the connection level or database level, the following commands are used:

```
--Connection Settings
SET ANSI_WARNINGS OFF
SET ANSI_WARNINGS ON

--Database Options
```

```
ALTER DATABASE AdventureWorks2008 SET ANSI_WARNINGS OFF
ALTER DATABASE AdventureWorks2008 SET ANSI_WARNINGS ON
```

Arithmetic Abort Enabled

Any statement or transaction that encounters an arithmetic overflow or divide-by-zero error will terminate when "Arithmetic Abort Enabled" is set to `True`. When set to `False`, a warning is raised, but the statement or transaction will not be terminated. In order for this option to have the desired effect, the "ANSI Warnings" options must also be set to `False`. To set it at the connection level or database level, the following commands are used:

```
--Connection Settings
SET ARITHABORT OFF
SET ARITHABORT ON

--Database Options
ALTER DATABASE AdventureWorks2008 SET ARITHABORT OFF
ALTER DATABASE AdventureWorks2008 SET ARITHABORT ON
```

Auto Close

When a database is first accessed, SQL Server opens and locks all files that are associated with the database. When "Auto Close" is `True`, the database will be closed, releasing all file locks, when the last user connected to it closes the connection. This setting is OFF by default because the act of opening and closing the database on a server platform is unnecessary and produces unneeded overhead. The exception to this rule is SQL Server Express Edition, because SQL Express is designed to run on a desktop system where resources are more restricted and an open database consumes resources. If no user is connected, those resources can be returned to the system. To set it at the database level, the following commands are used:

```
ALTER DATABASE AdventureWorks2008 SET AUTO_CLOSE OFF
ALTER DATABASE AdventureWorks2008 SET AUTO_CLOSE ON
```

Auto Create Statistics

When "Auto Create Statistics" is set to `True`, the Database Engine will generate statistics for columns without indexes that are missing statistics and when those columns are referenced in a `WHERE` clause, or the `ON` clause of a `JOIN` operation. Statistics are used by the Database Engine to determine the selectivity and distribution of data in a column. If set to `False`, it will be up to the database administrator to create statistics manually wherever needed. To set it at the database level, the following commands are used:

```
ALTER DATABASE AdventureWorks2008 SET AUTO_CREATE_STATISTICS OFF
ALTER DATABASE AdventureWorks2008 SET AUTO_CREATE_STATISTICS ON
```

Auto Shrink

When "Auto Shrink" is set to `True`, the Database Engine will periodically examine the total size of all database files and compare it to the amount of data being stored. If there is more than 25 percent total free space remaining, the Database Engine will perform file-shrink operations on database files to reduce the total free space to 25 percent. This option is set to `False` by default, except for SQL Express Edition, and, apart from the rare instance that a database will increasingly get smaller, it should be left set to False. To set it at the database level, the following commands are used:

```
ALTER DATABASE AdventureWorks2008 SET AUTO_SHRINK OFF
ALTER DATABASE AdventureWorks2008 SET AUTO_SHRINK ON
```

Auto Update Statistics

When "Auto Update Statistics" is set to True, the Database Engine will automatically update statistical information on columns to maintain the most efficient query plans possible. This typically takes place when a query is executed and the Query Processor discovers the out-of-date statistics. If set to False, it will be up to the database administrator to manually keep column statistics up to date. To set it at the database level, the following commands are used:

```
ALTER DATABASE AdventureWorks2008 SET AUTO_UPDATE_STATISTICS OFF
ALTER DATABASE AdventureWorks2008 SET AUTO_UPDATE_STATISTICS ON
```

Auto Update Statistics Asynchronously

When "Auto Update Statistics Asynchronously" is set to True, statistics that are discovered to be out-of-date during queries will be updated, but the query that was being executed when the discovery was made will not wait for the new statistics. Subsequent queries will take advantage of the new statistics. When set to False, query compilation will not occur until after the statistics are updated. To set it at the database level, the following commands are used:

```
ALTER DATABASE AdventureWorks2008 SET AUTO_UPDATE_STATISTICS_ASYNC OFF
ALTER DATABASE AdventureWorks2008 SET AUTO_UPDATE_STATISTICS_ASYNC ON
```

Broker Enabled

When "Broker Enabled" is set to True, the database is configured for participation in a Service Broker messaging system. When this is enabled in a new database, a new Service Broker identifier is created and persisted in the database. If Service Broker is disabled and then re-enabled, the original identifier will be used. For more information on Service Broker, see Chapter 19. To set it at the database level, the following commands are used:

```
ALTER DATABASE AdventureWorks2008 SET DISABLE_BROKER
ALTER DATABASE AdventureWorks2008 SET ENABLE_BROKER
```

Close Cursor on Commit Enabled

When "Close Cursor on Commit Enabled" is set to True, cursors contained in a transaction will be closed after the transaction has been committed or rolled back. When this setting is False, cursors will remain open when the transaction is committed. However, rolling back a transaction will close any cursors except those defined as INSENSITIVE or STATIC when set to False. To set it at the connection level or database level, the following commands are used:

```
--Connection Settings
SET CURSOR_CLOSE_ON_COMMIT OFF
SET CURSOR_CLOSE_ON_COMMIT ON

--Database Options
```

```
ALTER DATABASE AdventureWorks2008 SET CURSOR_CLOSE_ON_COMMIT OFF
ALTER DATABASE AdventureWorks2008 SET CURSOR_CLOSE_ON_COMMIT ON
```

Concatenate Null Yields Null

When a character string is concatenated with a NULL, it will return NULL when the "Concatenate Null Yields Null" setting is True. When set to False, a character string concatenated with a NULL will return the character string. To set it at the connection level or database level, the following commands are used:

```
--Connection Settings
SET CONCAT_NULL_YIELDS_NULL OFF
SET CONCAT_NULL_YIELDS_NULL ON

--Database Options
ALTER DATABASE AdventureWorks2008 SET CONCAT_NULL_YIELDS_NULL OFF
ALTER DATABASE AdventureWorks2008 SET CONCAT_NULL_YIELDS_NULL ON
```

The "Concatenate Null Yields Null" option is deprecated as of this version of SQL Server. In a future version of SQL Server, the option will be set to ON and will not be allowed to be changed. If an application attempts to set the value to OFF, an error will be thrown. It is recommended that you avoid using it in all new development work and make arrangements to update any applications that currently use it.

Cross-database Ownership Chaining Enabled

The "Cross-database Ownership Chaining Enabled" option is not settable in the Options dialog and only indicates what the value is set to. When set to True, it indicates that the database can participate in a cross-database ownership chain. This option is only recognized if the server level option is turned off. To set it at the server level or database level, the following commands are used:

```
--Server Options
sp_configure 'cross db ownership chaining', 0 -- OFF
sp_configure 'cross db ownership chaining', 1 -- ON
RECONFIGURE

--Database Options
ALTER DATABASE AdventureWorks2008 SET DB_CHAINING OFF
ALTER DATABASE AdventureWorks2008 SET DB_CHAINING ON
```

Database Read-Only

The "Database Read-Only" option specifies that no modifications are allowed to the database when set to True. Exclusive access to the database is required to set this option, except for the Master database. To set it at the database level, the following commands are used:

```
ALTER DATABASE AdventureWorks2008 SET READ_ONLY
ALTER DATABASE AdventureWorks2008 SET READ_WRITE
```

Database State

The "Database State" option is not configurable in the graphical interface, and, for the most part, is not directly configurable at all. The exception is the ONLINE, OFFLINE, and EMERGENCY states. The "Database

State" will indicate different values based on what is occurring on the database. The following table describes the various states the database can be in:

State	Description
ONLINE	The database is online and available. This will show up as the NORMAL state.
OFFLINE	The database is unavailable. Databases are set offline by executing the command ALTER DATABASE <DBName> SET OFFLINE. This can be done if the database administrator wants to move a database file from one location to another. In this case, the database would be set OFFLINE, then the ALTER DATABASE <DBName> MODIFY FILE command would be executed, followed by changing the database back to ONLINE.
RESTORING	One or more files are being restored. The database is unavailable.
RECOVERING	The database is being recovered. Except in the case of database mirroring, this is a transient state that occurs during the automatic or manual recovery process. The database is unavailable.
RECOVERY PENDING	A database will be in this state if SQL Server encounters a resource-related error during recovery. The database will be unavailable until the database administrator resolves the resource error and allows the recovery process to be completed.
SUSPECT	One or more database files have been marked as suspect because of a data access or Read error. This may occur if a TORN PAGE has been detected during database Read operations. If a database has been marked as SUSPECT, the database is unavailable until the error has been resolved.
EMERGENCY	The database will be in this state when the database administrator has set the status to EMERGENCY. In this state, the database is in single-user mode and may be repaired or restored. If the database has been marked as SUSPECT, this is the first step in correcting the problem, short of a database restore. Only members of the sysadmin fixed server role can set a database to the EMERGENCY state.

Date Correlation Optimization Enabled

When the "Date Correlation Optimization Enabled" option is set to True, it indicates that the Database Engine will maintain date statistics between two tables with datetime columns joined by a foreign key constraint to optimize queries between those two tables where the datetime field is a filter. To set it at the database level, the following commands are used:

```
ALTER DATABASE AdventureWorks2008 SET DATE_CORRELATION_OPTIMIZATION OFF
ALTER DATABASE AdventureWorks2008 SET DATE_CORRELATION_OPTIMIZATION ON
```

Default Cursor

Unlike local and global variables whose scope is based on connections, cursors are always local to the connection in which they are declared. When the "Default Cursor" option is set to Global, it specifies that a declared cursor can be referenced by any batch, stored procedure, or trigger executing on the same connection. If set to Local, the cursor can only be referenced inside the batch, stored procedure, or trigger in which the cursor was declared. To set it at the database level, the following commands are used:

```
ALTER DATABASE AdventureWorks2008 SET CURSOR_DEFAULT LOCAL
ALTER DATABASE AdventureWorks2008 SET CURSOR_DEFAULT GLOBAL
```

Encryption Enabled

When the "Encryption Enabled" option is set to True, all data and log files will be encrypted. If a database encryption key has not yet been created, trying to set this option will result in an error. See Chapter 6 for more information on "Transparent Data Encryption." To set it at the database level, the following commands are used:

```
ALTER DATABASE AdventureWorks2008 SET ENCRYPTION OFF
ALTER DATABASE AdventureWorks2008 SET ENCRYPTION ON
```

Honor Broker Priority

The "Honor Broker Priority" option is not configurable in SQL Server Management Studio and must be changed through T-SQL script. When this option is turned on, SQL Server will honor priority levels for Service Broker messages. For more information on Service Broker and message priority, see Chapter 19. To set it at the database level, the following commands are used:

```
ALTER DATABASE AdventureWorks2008 SET HONOR_BROKER_PRIORITY OFF
ALTER DATABASE AdventureWorks2008 SET HONOR_BROKER_PRIORITY ON
```

Numeric Round-Abort

When the "Numeric Round-Abort" option is set to True, it means that any numeric rounding that occurs will generate an error. For example, if "Numeric Round-Abort" is set to True, the following code will generate an error:

```
DECLARE @Num1 AS decimal(4,3)
SET @Num1 = 7.00004 / 2.84747
SELECT @Num1 AS Answer

RESULTS:
-----------------------------------------------------------------
Msg 8115, Level 16, State 7, Line 2
Arithmetic overflow error converting numeric to data type numeric.
```

The error is caused because the decimal variable was declared with a scale of 3. Remember that the scale specifies how many digits are supported to the right of the decimal place. To perform this calculation, SQL Server must round the number. If "Numeric Round-Abort" is set to False, this code will succeed:

```
DECLARE @Num1 AS decimal(4,3)
SET @Num1 = 7.00004 / 2.84747
```

```
SELECT @Num1 AS Answer

RESULTS:
-----------------------------------------------------------------
Answer
--------
2.458
```

To set it at the connection level or database level, the following commands are used:

```
--Connection Settings
SET NUMERIC_ROUNDABORT OFF
SET NUMERIC_ROUNDABORT ON

--Database Options
ALTER DATABASE AdventureWorks2008 SET NUMERIC_ROUNDABORT OFF
ALTER DATABASE AdventureWorks2008 SET NUMERIC_ROUNDABORT ON
```

Page Verify

The "Page Verify" option enables the database administrator to set different options for page Write verification. The available options are Checksum, Torn_Page_Detection, and None. As far as performance goes, the best option is None. However, with None set, pages corrupted during disk Write operations (or by some other disk anomaly after the page is written to disk) will not be discovered.

With the Checksum option, SQL Server will calculate a checksum value and store it in the page header. This checksum value is very much like the Cyclic Redundancy Check (CRC) values created when files are written to disk by the operating system. When a data page is read from the disk, SQL Server will re-calculate the checksum and compare it to the one stored in the page header. If the values match, the page is good. If the values do not match, the page is considered corrupted, an error 823 will be raised, and the database status is changed from ONLINE to SUSPECT.

In a typical configuration, only 512 bytes of data are written to the disk with each pass of the disk under a Write head. Therefore, it takes 16 passes to write an 8-KB page. The Torn_Page_Detection option configures SQL Server to write an error bit in the page header at the end of every Write cycle. If the error bit is absent when the page is later read, an error 823 is raised, and the database status is changed from ONLINE to SUSPECT.

When SQL Server raises an 823 error, a record will be added to the suspect_pages table in the msdb database. The record includes the database the error occurred in, the page ID, file ID, and various other pieces of information that will be helpful to restore the page from a backup. This table will be updated when the page is restored, but the records will *not* be removed. It is the database administrator's job to remove any records that are marked as restored or repaired.

Choosing an appropriate Page Verify setting depends on the degree of acceptable risk and CPU utilization. As mentioned earlier, the best option for performance is setting "Page Verify" to None, but this setting exposes your database to the risk of undetected data corruption. The Checksum option offers the best protection from undetected corruption because any modification to the data on disk during or after data Write operations will be detected by the checksum verification. However, the Checksum option costs the most CPU cycles. The Torn_Page_Detection option is a lower-cost method of detecting corrupted pages, but it will only detect page corruption that occurs during the Write operation. The recommended setting is Checksum because of its high degree of data integrity verification. To set it at the database level, the following commands are used:

```
ALTER DATABASE AdventureWorks2008 SET PAGE_VERIFY NONE
ALTER DATABASE AdventureWorks2008 SET PAGE_VERIFY TORN_PAGE_DETECTION
ALTER DATABASE AdventureWorks2008 SET PAGE_VERIFY CHECKSUM
```

Parameterization

"Parameterization" is a very interesting but advanced option that was introduced in SQL Server 2005. By default, the Database Engine auto-parameterizes some queries so the query plans that are created and compiled can be reused even when different values are defined in the WHERE clause. For example, consider this code:

```
USE AdventureWorks2008
GO
SELECT * FROM Person.Person
WHERE LastName = N'Smith'
```

If you type this code in a Query window and then click on the "Display Estimated Execution" button on the SQL Editor toolbar, you will find that the Database Engine compiles the query with the search criteria of LastName = N'Smith' (see Figure 5-8) when the "Parameterization" option is set to Simple. This is because SQL Server decides which queries to parameterize and which ones not to when Simple is set. For this particular query, it determines that it is not worth the extra cost.

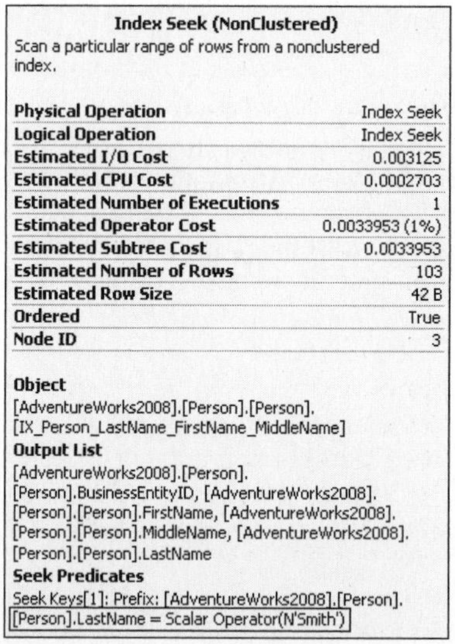

Index Seek (NonClustered)	
Scan a particular range of rows from a nonclustered index.	
Physical Operation	Index Seek
Logical Operation	Index Seek
Estimated I/O Cost	0.003125
Estimated CPU Cost	0.0002703
Estimated Number of Executions	1
Estimated Operator Cost	0.0033953 (1%)
Estimated Subtree Cost	0.0033953
Estimated Number of Rows	103
Estimated Row Size	42 B
Ordered	True
Node ID	3

Object
[AdventureWorks2008].[Person].[Person].
[IX_Person_LastName_FirstName_MiddleName]
Output List
[AdventureWorks2008].[Person].
[Person].BusinessEntityID, [AdventureWorks2008].
[Person].[Person].FirstName, [AdventureWorks2008].
[Person].[Person].MiddleName, [AdventureWorks2008].
[Person].[Person].LastName
Seek Predicates
Seek Keys[1]: Prefix: [AdventureWorks2008].[Person].
[Person].LastName = Scalar Operator(N'Smith')

Figure 5-8: Simple parameterization.

When the option is set to Force, SQL Server will parameterize all queries that can be parameterized, and the same query will result in a parameterized query plan instead (see Figure 5-9). Forcing auto-parameterization can improve performance in some instances, but careful monitoring should be done to ensure that it doesn't have a negative impact on performance.

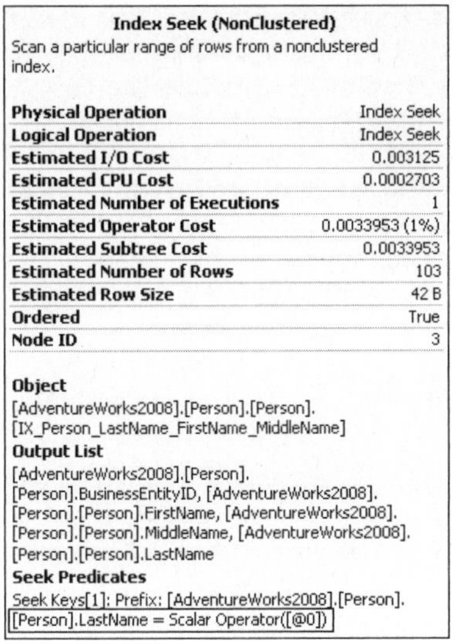

Figure 5-9: Forced parameterization.

To set it at the database level, the following commands are used:

```
ALTER DATABASE AdventureWorks2008 SET PARAMETERIZATION SIMPLE
ALTER DATABASE AdventureWorks2008 SET PARAMETERIZATION FORCED
```

Quoted Identifiers Enabled

By default, SQL Server uses square brackets ("[ ]") to delimit objects. Delimiting objects is only required if the object name contains an embedded space or a reserved word. The ANSI standard delimiter is the double quotation marks. The following examples show how to create and reference an object with an embedded space with both square brackets and double quotation marks.

Following is an example for the ANSI double quote delimiter:

```
USE AdventureWorks2008
GO
CREATE TABLE "Sales.USA Customers"
( AcctNumber int IDENTITY(1,1) NOT NULL
, "Last Name" varchar(75) NOT NULL
, "First Name" varchar(75) NOT NULL)

SELECT AcctNumber, "Last Name", "First Name"
FROM "Sales.USA Customers"
```

Following is an example of the default square bracket delimiter:

```
USE AdventureWorks2008
GO
CREATE TABLE [Sales.USA Customers]
( AcctNumber int IDENTITY(1,1) NOT NULL
, [Last Name] varchar(75) NOT NULL
```

```
, [First Name] varchar(75) NOT NULL)

SELECT AcctNumber, [Last Name], [First Name]
FROM [Sales.USA Customers]
```

When the "Quoted Identifiers" option is True, both square brackets and double quotation marks are accepted. If the "Quoted Identifiers" option is set to False, only square bracket delimiters will be accepted. To set this option at the connection level or database level, the following commands are used:

```
--Connection Settings
SET QUOTED_IDENTIFIER OFF
SET QUOTED_IDENTIFIER ON

--Database Options
ALTER DATABASE AdventureWorks2008 SET QUOTED_IDENTIFIER OFF
ALTER DATABASE AdventureWorks2008 SET QUOTED_IDENTIFIER ON
```

On a completely editorial note, I personally believe that embedded spaces in object names are wrong and should never be used. They typically introduce nothing but problems to your database and application design for the negligible benefit of a natural language name.

Recursive Triggers Enabled

Recursive triggers are considered an advanced programming technique that allows the same trigger to fire more than once, in sequence, in the same transaction. When set to False, this action is not allowed and is the default configuration. Generally it is a good idea to leave this set to False. Recursive logic is difficult at best to debug and can lead to many headaches. Almost all of the time, recursive logic can be rewritten as non-recursive logic. To set it at the database level, the following commands are used:

```
ALTER DATABASE AdventureWorks2008 SET RECURSIVE_TRIGGERS OFF
ALTER DATABASE AdventureWorks2008 SET RECURSIVE_TRIGGERS ON
```

Restrict Access

The "Restrict Access" option enables the database administrator to restrict access to a database to a defined set of logins. The default value of this option is MULTI_USER, which allows multiple non-privileged users to access the database. Two other options exist to restrict access: SINGLE_USER and RESTRICTED_USER.

When the SINGLE_USER "Restrict Access" option is set, only one user account is allowed access to the database at a time.

If the RESTRICTED_USER "Restrict Access" option is set, only members of the db_owner, dbcreator, or sysadmin roles can connect to the database. To set it at the database level, the following commands are used:

```
ALTER DATABASE AdventureWorks2008 SET MULTI_USER
ALTER DATABASE AdventureWorks2008 SET RESTRICTED_USER
ALTER DATABASE AdventureWorks2008 SET SINGLE_USER
```

Service Broker Identifier

The "Service Broker Identifier" option is not configurable in SQL Server Management Studio and cannot be set directly. The Service Broker Identifier is created the first time the database is enabled to use Service

Broker and is used to uniquely identify the database in a messaging infrastructure. See Chapter 19 for more information on Service Broker.

Trustworthy

The "Trustworthy" setting cannot be set through SQL Server Management Studio. The "Trustworthy" option indicates whether or not the instance of SQL Server trusts the database to access external or network resources. If this is set to `False`, database programming components created with managed code, or database components that need to execute within the context of a highly privileged user, are not allowed access to any resource external to the database. When one of those two situations is required, the "Trustworthy" option can be set to `True`. To set it at the database level, the following commands are used:

```
ALTER DATABASE AdventureWorks2008 SET TRUSTWORTHY OFF
ALTER DATABASE AdventureWorks2008 SET TRUSTWORTHY ON
```

VarDecimal Storage Format Enabled

The "VarDecimal Storage Format Enabled" feature was first introduced in Service Pack 2 for SQL Server 2005 and is now deprecated in SQL Server 2008. Row and Page Compression, new features of SQL Server 2008, replace this functionality and are discussed later in the chapter. For SQL Server 2008, it is turned on and cannot be turned off.

Generating Database Creation Scripts

Now that you have gone through all the steps and options of creating a database, let's take a look at how you can script this process so that you don't have to go through it again.

At the top of the New Database dialog is a button called *Script*, as shown in Figure 5-10.

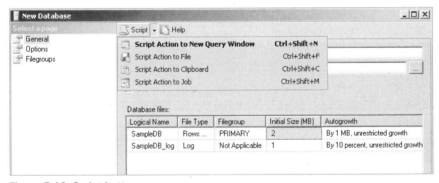

Figure 5-10: Script button.

Click the down arrow to the right of Script, and it will expose the scripting options available. If you have followed along with the last few pages, then clicking any of the Script Action options will generate a script that will duplicate all the settings you specified in the graphical interface. This script can then be used to create new databases with the same options simply by changing the logical and physical names of the database and associated files. The Script Action options are also great for exploring the actual syntax for creating or modifying database objects. Almost every configuration screen for creating or modifying database objects includes the Script Action option.

Another option for reusing scripts is to replace the actual names of objects and files with variables. Then all you have to do is update the variable values and execute the script. The only tricky part in creating Data Definition Language (DDL) scripts is having to use dynamic SQL because variables can't be used directly in a DDL script. The following example demonstrates how to use dynamic SQL to create a new database with a user-defined filegroup marked as the default:

```
DECLARE @DatabaseName AS nvarchar(255)
DECLARE @FileGroupName AS nvarchar(255)

SET @DatabaseName = N'SlateGravel'
SET @FileGroupName = N'UserData'

EXECUTE (
'CREATE DATABASE ' + @DatabaseName +
' ON  PRIMARY
( NAME = ''' + @DatabaseName + '''
, FILENAME = ''S:\SQLDataFiles\' + @DatabaseName + '_data.mdf"
, SIZE = 20MB
, MAXSIZE = 100MB
, FILEGROWTH = 30%)
, FILEGROUP UserData
( NAME = ''' + @FileGroupName + '''
, FILENAME = ''S:\SQLDataFiles\' + @DatabaseName + '_data.ndf''
, SIZE = 2048KB , FILEGROWTH = 20%)
 LOG ON
( NAME = '" + @DatabaseName + '_log''
, FILENAME = ''T:\SQLLogFiles\' + @DatabaseName + '_log.ldf''
, SIZE = 100MB
, FILEGROWTH = 20%);
 ALTER DATABASE ' + @DatabaseName +
' MODIFY FILEGROUP ' + @FileGroupName + ' DEFAULT')
```

This script assumes the presence of an "S" drive, "T" drive, a SQLDataFiles folder, and a SQLLogFiles folder. To run it in your environment, you may have to change the drive letter assignments and folder names.

Schemas

SQL Server 2008 implements the database schema as defined in the ANSI standard. Almost every object in SQL Server 2008 exists within a defined schema. A *schema* is simply a way to organize your database objects and assign permissions to the objects it contains. The schema itself can be owned by any database principal including database roles and application roles while containing many objects owned by various users. Within the schema, objects cannot have duplicate names. However, objects can have the same name if they exist in different schemas. For example, if a table called Inventory is created in the schema Sales on the server AughtEight, its name becomes AughtEight.Sales.Inventory. An additional table called Inventory can still be created in the Marketing schema, and its name would be AughtEight.Marketing.Inventory. Although this is possible, it is not a good idea, in my opinion, as it can lead to confusion for anybody new to the database and may produce unexpected results from queries later on. Where schemas really become powerful is in the ability to form a security scope that can be used by the database administrator to control access to all objects within the schema. This is covered in detail in Chapter 6.

In SQL Server 2008, a database principal is assigned ownership of a schema, and that schema owns the constituent objects such as tables, views, stored procedures, and functions. If a user who owns a schema needs to be deleted, ownership of that schema will have to be assigned to a different user first. The easiest solution is to have the dbo user own all the schemas. The dbo user is a built-in user that is mapped to any member of the fixed server role sysadmin. The dbo user always exists and cannot be dropped, so it is a perfect candidate for schema ownership. For more information about the dbo user, fixed server roles, and SQL Server 2008 security, see Chapter 6.

Schemas and Name Resolution

Because schemas are just containers for objects, it is important to set the context of object references when calling on database objects in SQL Server 2008. Every user is assigned a default schema. When he or she logs in to a SQL Server and calls on database objects, this default schema will play a distinct role in how the objects must be referenced.

For example, assume that a user named *FredF* is created in the AdventureWorks2008 database and assigned the default schema of Sales. If FredF logs in and executes the query SELECT * FROM CreditCard, the CreditCard table will be resolved to AdventureWorks2008.Sales.CreditCard because Fred's default schema is Sales. The Sales.CreditCard table exists, and so the contents of the CreditCard table will be returned.

If FredF executes the query SELECT * FROM Person, the table Person will be resolved to AdventureWorks2008.Sales.Person, a table that does not exist. Because SQL Server is unable to find the Person table in FredF's default schema, it will default to the dbo schema and look for the AdventureWorks2008.dbo.Person table, again with no success. SQL Server will then return the error: "Invalid object name".

Schema Creation

To create a schema, the only required information is the name of the schema. The ownership of the schema defaults to the user who runs the creation script, but any valid database user can be specified as the owner. The simplest approach is to designate dbo as the owner of the schema, but there are situations in which it may be desirable to designate a regular user as the owner. The syntax and an example of the CREATE SCHEMA statement are as follows:

```
CREATE SCHEMA Schema_Name [ AUTHORIZATION owner ]

USE AdventureWorks2008
GO
CREATE SCHEMA Operations AUTHORIZATION dbo
```

Any schema-scoped statements that follow the CREATE SCHEMA statement will fall into the scope of the schema just created, as the following example illustrates:

```
USE AdventureWorks2008
GO
CREATE SCHEMA Operations AUTHORIZATION dbo

  CREATE TABLE DeliveryDriver
```

```
(DriverID int IDENTITY NOT NULL
,LName varchar(75) NOT NULL
,FName varchar(75) NOT NULL)

GRANT SELECT ON DeliveryDriver TO FredF
```

Even though the schema was not specified in the CREATE TABLE statement, this script places the DeliveryDriver table into the Operations schema. Even the GRANT SELECT statement succeeds, although the schema was not designated in the statement it defaulted to the Operations schema, because the CREATE SCHEMA statement set the scope of the schema for all remaining statements in the batch. If the script is changed slightly so that the GRANT SELECT statement is in a different batch, the GRANT SELECT will fail.

```
CREATE SCHEMA Operations AUTHORIZATION dbo

CREATE TABLE DeliveryDriver
(DriverID int IDENTITY NOT NULL
,LName varchar(75) NOT NULL
,FName varchar(75) NOT NULL)

GO

GRANT SELECT ON DeliveryDriver TO FredF
-------------------------------------------------------------------------

Msg 15151, Level 16, State 1, Line 1
Cannot find the object 'DeliveryDriver', because it does not exist or you do
not have permission.
```

The GO keyword placed the GRANT SELECT statement outside the batch that created the schema, and thus the execution context reverted to that of the user executing the script. As a best practice, the schema of an object should always be specified to avoid any unexpected results.

```
CREATE SCHEMA Operations AUTHORIZATION dbo

CREATE TABLE Operations.DeliveryDriver
(DriverID int IDENTITY NOT NULL
,LName varchar(75) NOT NULL
,FName varchar(75) NOT NULL)

GRANT SELECT ON Operations.DeliveryDriver TO FredF
```

Remember that schema scope resolution always starts at the user's default schema and will revert to the dbo schema if a referenced object is not scope-qualified.

Schema Maintenance

As a precaution if you attempt to drop a schema that contains objects, an error will be generated as shown in the following example:

```
DROP SCHEMA Operations                    .

-------------------------------------------------------------------------

Msg 3729, Level 16, State 1, Line 1
```

```
Cannot drop schema 'Operations' because it is being referenced by object
'DeliveryDriver'.
```

If the object in the schema is still required, it can be transferred to a different schema with the ALTER SCHEMA statement:

```
ALTER SCHEMA Production TRANSFER Operations.DeliveryDriver
```

This example alters the schema Production by moving the table DeliveryDriver from the Operations schema to the Production schema. Because that was the last object in the schema, it can now be dropped. Be advised, however, that transferring an object from one schema to another clears any permissions set on the object.

A user who owns a schema cannot be dropped from the database, which is one of the reasons why you may decide to have the dbo user own all schemas. To change the ownership of a schema, the AUTHORIZATION property of the schema is altered. The following example changes the ownership of the Operations schema to FredF:

```
ALTER AUTHORIZATION ON SCHEMA::Operations TO FredF
```

Tables

SQL Server 2008, like all relational database management systems, stores data in objects called *tables*. As mentioned in Chapter 1, it is assumed in this book that you are at least familiar with relational database concepts, so I won't spend much time explaining what a table is or how to create them. What is pertinent to the SQL Server 2008 database administrator is how to maintain and secure tables to optimize the performance and security of the database. Security is discussed in detail in Chapter 6, so for this chapter, the discussion is limited to the maintenance of data tables, but first a little background information is required.

Table Collation

As discussed earlier in this chapter, when creating a database, collation support can be configured that is different from that of the server. This is also true for table columns that contain character data. Each column can be defined with a different collation setting. For example, the AdventureWorks Cycles company wants to enable customers from all over the world to browse and search the product catalog in their own languages. To enable this functionality, a GlobalProductDescription table is built with the following script:

```
USE AdventureWorks2008
GO
CREATE TABLE Production.GlobalProductDescription(
    ProductDescriptionID int IDENTITY(1,1) NOT NULL,
    EnglishDescription nvarchar(400) COLLATE SQL_Latin1_General_CP1_CI_AS NULL,
    FrenchDescription nvarchar(400) COLLATE French_CI_AS NULL,
    ChineseDescription nvarchar(400) COLLATE Chinese_PRC_CI_AI NULL,
    ArabicDescription nvarchar(400) COLLATE Arabic_CI_AS NULL,
    HebrewDescription nvarchar(400) COLLATE Hebrew_CI_AS NULL,
    ThaiDescription nvarchar(400) COLLATE Thai_CI_AS NULL,
    ModifiedDate datetime NOT NULL)
```

Each column is now sorted and searchable using the native language collation settings as defined in the business requirement. Now, don't let me mislead you. SQL Server definitely is not some kind of universal translator. SQL Server just provides the framework for storing multiple languages. You will have to arrange for the proper translation of the descriptions and place them in the appropriate columns, and handle any collation incompatibilities that arise because of `tempdb`'s collation. For more information on collation, see Chapter 2.

Table Architecture

As discussed in Chapter 4, SQL Server uses 8-KB data pages to store information. All data within a table is stored within these data pages, but how the data on the pages is organized will differ depending on how you create the table and what you do with it after creation. By default, all data will be stored in an unorganized manner formally called a *heap*. SQL Server makes no attempt to keep the data organized or sorted in any way and maintains no links between the pages. The following code creates a table that is stored in such a way:

```
CREATE TABLE Employee(
EmployeeId int IDENTITY,
FirstName nvarchar(25) NOT NULL,
MiddleName nvarchar(25) NULL,
LastName nvarchar(25) NOT NULL,
HireDate smalldatetime
)
```

Although this arrangement works great for adding data to a table, it is less than an optimum solution when trying to find a particular row or set of rows in a table. Think of a library. If you managed a library that put all the books on shelves as they came in with no regard to genre, author, or title, it would take very little effort to shelve the books as they came in. However, when it came time to find a particular book, you would be forced to scan through all the shelves looking for the one book you wanted. This is exactly how SQL Server works when it is looking for a record in a heap. Later on in the chapter, we will take a look at indexes and see how they can help with this problem, but first, let's look at how breaking up the table into smaller chunks can help.

Partitioning Tables

SQL Server physically stores all data pages in logical units called *partitions*. Unless specifically separated, tables are stored in a single partition defined on a single filegroup. However, SQL Server provides the ability to separate large tables into smaller manageable units by horizontally partitioning the tables across multiple files managed by filegroup definitions.

The Table Partitioning feature is available only in the Enterprise and Developer editions of SQL Server 2008.

For example, a transaction table with millions of rows can be physically partitioned so that all the transactions for the current year are separated from those for previous years. This way, only a subset of the table will need to be scanned to select, insert, or update current-year transactions.

To illustrate the advantages of physical table partitioning and demonstrate how to implement them, you must first build a table that is a candidate for partitioning. Using the following script, create the dbo.`Transactions` table that will hold your test data. The `Transaction` table has the same basic structure as the `Production.TransactionHistory` and `Production.TransactionHistoryArchive` tables.

```
USE AdventureWorks2008
GO
CREATE TABLE dbo.Transactions(
    TransactionID int NOT NULL,
    ProductID int NOT NULL,
    ReferenceOrderID int NOT NULL,
    ReferenceOrderLineID int NOT NULL,
    TransactionDate datetime NOT NULL,
    TransactionType nchar(1) NOT NULL,
    Quantity int NOT NULL,
    ActualCost money NOT NULL,
    ModifiedDate datetime NOT NULL)
```

To populate the new `Transactions` table, insert all the rows from the `TransactionHistory` and `TransactionHistoryArchive` tables by using a `UNION` operator:

```
USE AdventureWorks2008
GO
INSERT dbo.Transactions
SELECT * FROM Production.TransactionHistory
UNION ALL
SELECT * FROM Production.TransactionHistoryArchive
```

Now that you have a nice-size table to work with, run a query against it to see the performance before partitioning. The table contains a total of 202,696 rows. Of the transaction rows in the table, 12,711 took place in 2001, 38,300 in 2002, 81,086 in 2003, and 70,599 took place in 2004.

```
--Pre Partition Statistics
USE AdventureWorks2008
GO
DBCC DROPCLEANBUFFERS
SET STATISTICS IO ON
DECLARE @BeginDate AS datetime, @EndDate AS datetime
SET @BeginDate = '2002-01-01'
SET @EndDate = '2002-12-31'

SELECT SUM(Quantity) AS TotalQuantity, SUM(ActualCost) AS TotalCost
FROM dbo.Transactions
WHERE TransactionDate BETWEEN @BeginDate AND @EndDate
```

The script uses the `DBCC DROPCLEANBUFFERS` command to clear all pages from the buffer cache. This will allow us to see how many physical Reads are required to bring all needed data into memory. It also turns on statistic reporting with the `SET STATISTICS IO ON` option and then queries the `dbo.Transactions` table to return the total sales amount and total quantity of products sold in 2002.

The results of the query are as follows:

```
TotalQuantity TotalCost
------------- ---------------------
1472494       16427929.3028

(1 row(s) affected)

Table 'Transactions'. Scan count 1, logical reads 1408, physical reads 26, read-
ahead reads 1407, lob logical reads 0, lob physical reads 0, lob read-ahead reads 0.
```

In order to see the results as shown above, you must have the results of the query displayed as text. You can do this by pressing [Ctrl]+T prior to running the query. To switch back to grid view, press [Ctrl]+D and re-run the query.

As you can see, to satisfy the query, SQL Server had to scan the table. To find the 38,300 rows that met the criteria of the WHERE clause, SQL Server had to scan through 202,696 rows. This scan resulted in 1,408 logical reads.

Now, let's see what happens when you physically divide the table into multiple files by partitioning the table so that all the transactions are divided by year.

In a perfect world, you would know that you wanted to physically partition a table before you ever populated it with data, but perfect worlds are rare. In this case, you have decided to physically partition the Transactions table after it has been built. Since the data is stored in a heap, you are forced to create a new partitioned table and move the data to it, and then drop the original table. (I will show you a much easier way to accomplish this later in the chapter.)

The first step in partitioning the table is to create the filegroups that will hold the data files to be used to store the partitions of the table. Remember from the previous discussion on filegroups that tables cannot be assigned to a particular file, only to a filegroup. In this example, each filegroup will contain only one file. This is by no means a requirement. Partitions can be defined to exist on a single file or multiple files.

The following script adds four new filegroups with one file per filegroup to contain the partitioned transaction table. As the names suggest, you will be partitioning the Transactions table by date:

```
USE MASTER
GO
ALTER DATABASE AdventureWorks2008
ADD FILEGROUP FGPre2002
GO
ALTER DATABASE AdventureWorks2008
ADD FILE
  ( NAME = 'AworksPre2002'
  , FILENAME = 'E:\SQLData\AworksPre2002.ndf'
  , SIZE = 20MB
  , FILEGROWTH = 20% )
TO FILEGROUP FGPre2002
GO
ALTER DATABASE AdventureWorks2008
ADD FILEGROUP FG2002
GO
ALTER DATABASE AdventureWorks2008
ADD FILE
  ( NAME = 'Aworks2002'
  , FILENAME = 'E:\SQLData\Aworks2002.ndf'
  , SIZE = 20MB
  , FILEGROWTH = 20% )
TO FILEGROUP FG2002
GO
ALTER DATABASE AdventureWorks2008
```

```
ADD FILEGROUP FG2003
GO
ALTER DATABASE AdventureWorks2008
ADD FILE
  ( NAME = 'Aworks2003'
  , FILENAME = 'E:\SQLData\Aworks2003.ndf'
  , SIZE = 20MB
  , FILEGROWTH = 20% )
TO FILEGROUP FG2003
GO
ALTER DATABASE AdventureWorks2008
ADD FILEGROUP FG2004AndAfter
GO
ALTER DATABASE AdventureWorks2008
ADD FILE
  ( NAME = 'Aworks2004AndAfter'
  , FILENAME = 'E:\SQLData\Aworks2004AndAfter.ndf'
  , SIZE = 20MB
  , FILEGROWTH = 20% )
  TO FILEGROUP FG2004AndAfter
GO
```

This script assumes the presence of an "E" drive and a SQLData folder. To run it in your environment, you may have to change the drive letter assignment.

The next step in partitioning the `Transactions` table is to create a *partition function*. *Partition functions* determine the boundaries for each partition. You must specify what data type the function will work with during creation. All data types are valid with the exception of alias data types, CLR types, or any of the following: `text`, `ntext`, `image`, `xml`, `timestamp`, `varchar(max)`, `nvarchar(max)`, or `varbinary(max)`. For example, the partition function will specify what the ranges of values are (as in 1 through 100,000, 100,001 through 1,000,000, etc.). Keep in mind that when specifying a partitioning function, you can only partition on a single value.

In this example, all data is partitioned by date in order to group together the data in accordance to the most frequent queries run against the table. Run the following script to create a partition function that partitions a table into four groups of dated records. The first group is from NULL to 12/31/2001. The second group is from 1/1/2002 to 12/31/2002. The third group is from 1/1/2003 to 12/31/2003, and the last group is from 1/1/2004 to INFINITY.

```
CREATE PARTITION FUNCTION YearFunction (datetime)
AS RANGE RIGHT FOR VALUES ('1/1/2002','1/1/2003','1/1/2004')
```

When creating a partition function, the option `RANGE RIGHT` or `RANGE LEFT` can be used. This is used to determine which partition the row will be stored in if the value the table is partitioned on is equal to the boundary value. For example, if you use `RANGE LEFT` and the value is equal to the boundary value, then the row would be stored in the partition to the left of the boundary. If you were to use the `RANGE RIGHT` partition function created in the previous script and insert a transaction into your table with a transaction date of 1/1/2003, then the record would be placed into the third group.

Once the function is created to define the boundaries used for partitioning, a *partition scheme* must be created. A *partition scheme* is used to determine where the partitions are physically stored. When defining the partition scheme, you must specify the same number of filegroups as partitions that are defined by the partition function. Run the following script to create a partition scheme that maps the partitions created by the YearFunction to the filegroups that you created earlier:

```
CREATE PARTITION SCHEME YearScheme
AS PARTITION YearFunction
TO (FGPre2002, FG2002, FG2003, FG2004AndAfter)
```

If you wanted to partition the table but store all of the partitions on the same filegroup, you have two choices: You could repeat the filegroup name for each partition or use the ALL TO option with a single filegroup, for example, ALL TO ([PRIMARY]).

You can also specify one additional filegroup following the last one. This filegroup is marked as the "next" filegroup to be used if another partition is created.

All that is left to do now is to create the actual partitioned table and move the data from the original Transactions table into it:

```
USE AdventureWorks2008
GO
CREATE TABLE dbo.PartitionedTransactions(
  TransactionID int NOT NULL,
  ProductID int NOT NULL,
  ReferenceOrderID int NOT NULL,
  ReferenceOrderLineID int NOT NULL,
  TransactionDate datetime NOT NULL,
  TransactionType nchar(1) NOT NULL,
  Quantity int NOT NULL,
  ActualCost money NOT NULL,
  ModifiedDate datetime NOT NULL)
ON YearScheme(TransactionDate)
GO
INSERT INTO dbo.PartitionedTransactions
SELECT * FROM  dbo.Transactions
```

When creating partition functions and partition schemes, remember that they can be used to partition as many tables as needed. The YearFunction and YearScheme can be used to partition any table in the AdventureWorks2008 database that has a datetime column in it.

To see if you have improved the performance of your query, run the same query that you ran before on the Transactions table:

```
--Post Partition Statistics
DBCC DROPCLEANBUFFERS
SET STATISTICS IO ON
SELECT SUM(Quantity) AS TotalQuantity, SUM(ActualCost) AS TotalCost
FROM dbo.PartitionedTransactions
WHERE TransactionDate BETWEEN '1-1-2002' AND '12-31-2002'
The results of the query are as follows:
TotalQuantity TotalCost
```

```
------------- ---------------------
1472494        16427929.3028

(1 row(s) affected)

Table 'PartitionedTransactions'. Scan count 1, logical reads 266, physical reads 5,
read-ahead reads 259, lob logical reads 0, lob physical reads 0, lob read-ahead
reads 0.
```

Now that the table is physically partitioned, the logical Reads required to retrieve the results have gone from 1,408 to 266. The decrease in I/O cost will also cause a decrease in CPU cost, resulting in a much more efficient query. Keep in mind that the savings in performance are on a table with only 202,696 rows. Imagine the savings if the table contained 10 years of data comprising millions of rows and the partitions were defined on each year. The savings when querying a specific year would be much more dramatic.

Although creating partitioned tables was available in SQL Server 2005, the only way to do it was with code. I don't have a problem with writing scripts every once and awhile, but if I can use the GUI to write it for me, I am all over it. SQL Server Management Studio now has the ability to not only create partitioned tables, but also to generate the script for it so that you could run it on any server. Another benefit is that it could perform the operation in place so that you don't have to worry about creating a new table and moving the data into it. Let's walk through the process of partitioning the Production.TransactionHistory table in the AdventureWorks2008 database.

If you were following along with the last section, you will need to drop the table, partition function, and partition scheme in order to do the next section. The following script will accomplish this for you:

```
IF  EXISTS (SELECT * FROM sys.tables WHERE object_id =
    OBJECT_ID('dbo.PartitionedTransactions'))
        DROP TABLE dbo.PartitionedTransactions

IF  EXISTS
    (SELECT * FROM sys.partition_schemes WHERE Name = 'YearScheme')
        DROP PARTITION SCHEME YearScheme

IF  EXISTS
    (SELECT * FROM sys.partition_functions WHERE Name = 'YearFunction')
        DROP PARTITION FUNCTION YearFunction
```

To partition a table from SQL Server Management Studio, right-click on the table you wish to partition, select Storage, and then "Create Partition," as shown in Figure 5-11.

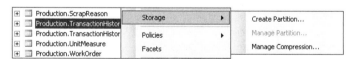

Figure 5-11: Creating a partition using Management Studio.

Use the "Select Partitioning Column" page to identify the column upon which the table will be partitioned (see Figure 5-12). As mentioned earlier, only certain data types are valid for the partitioning column, and the Wizard will only show you columns that are of valid types. In this case, we are going to choose the TransactionDate column.

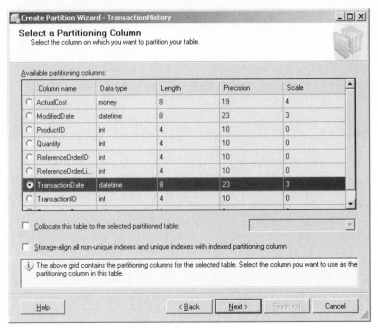

Figure 5-12: Select a Partitioning Column page.

After clicking Next, you will need to choose the partitioning function that you would like to use (see Figure 5-13). If you choose to use an existing function, you will only be able to choose a function that can be used with the column that you selected in the previous page. If there are no partition functions defined in the database for the data type of your selected column, then you will be have to create a new one. Type a name for the new partition function, and click Next.

Now a partitioning scheme needs to be selected for the table (see Figure 5-14). If there is a partition scheme available that has the correct number of filegroups defined for the choosen funtion then it can be reused; otherwise, a new one will need to be created. Click Next to continue.

The Map Partitions page (see Figure 5-15) is used to define the boundaries of the partition function and the mapping between the partitions and filegroups. If the partition column is a date, datetime, smalldatetime, datetime2, or datetimeoffset, then the "Set boundaries" button will be enabled. This allows a very quick way of defining the boundary points for the partition function by specifying the Start Date, End Date, and the Date Range. You can create partitions that are broken up by Day, Month, Quarter, Half-Year, or Year. Once the partitions are defined, they need to be mapped to the desired filegroups. The filegroups must already exist and cannot be created at this point. When defining the mapping, the last one will not map to a boundary point. The filegroup is not marked as the next filegroup but the filegroup that the last partition is placed in. See Figure 5-16 for the completed dialog box.

You now have the option to create a script that will partition the table, do the partitioning immediately, or schedule it for later execution (see Figure 5-17).

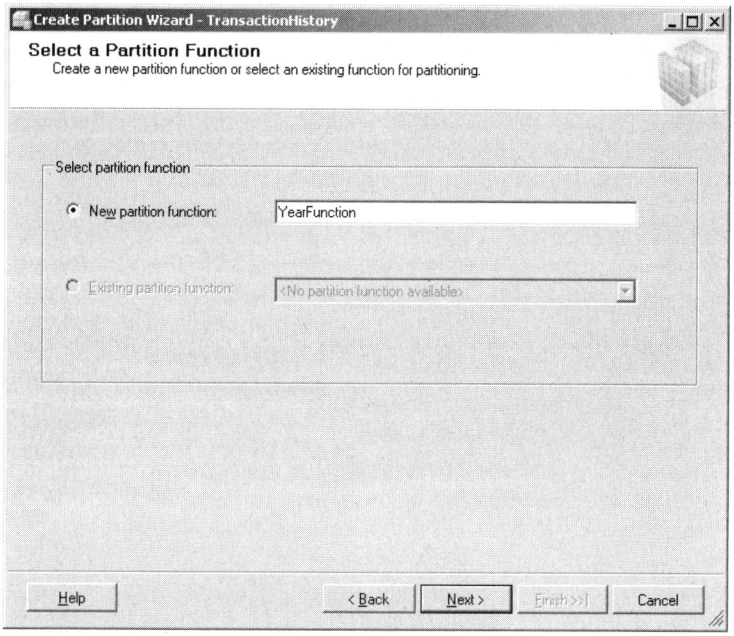

Figure 5-13: Select a Partition Function page.

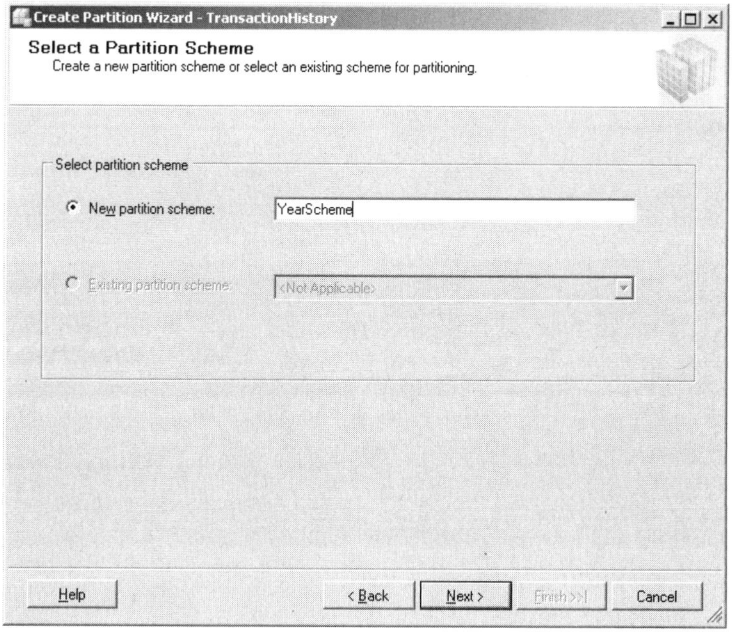

Figure 5-14: Select a Partition Scheme page.

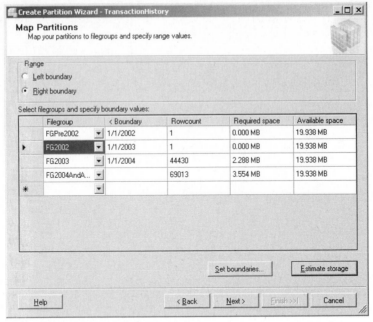

Figure 5-15: Map Partitions page.

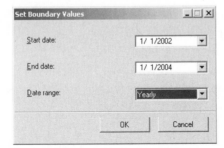

Figure 5-16: Set Boundaries dialog.

Data Compression

SQL Server 2008 introduces the ability to compress data in tables, indexes, or partitions. This can save I/O requests since more data on each page equals fewer pages to read into memory. Additionally, because more data is stored on each data page, more data can be stored in the same amount of memory. The combination of lower I/O and having more data in memory usually translates to increased performance. Data compression is enabled using one of two different modes: row compression or page compression.

Row Compression

Row compression is a descendent of the vardecimal storage format introduced in SQL Server 2005 SP2. Prior to the vardecimal storage format, decimals were stored in a fixed amount of space. The amount of space that the decimal used was based on the scale defined for the column and took anywhere between 5 and 17 bytes. This often contributed to a lot of wasted space depending on the value. For example, if you define a column as a decimal (15, 15), it would take 9 bytes of storage regardless of the value. With vardecimal storage format enabled, only the absolute required space to represent the number is used. This has been extended to all fixed length data types in SQL Server 2008.

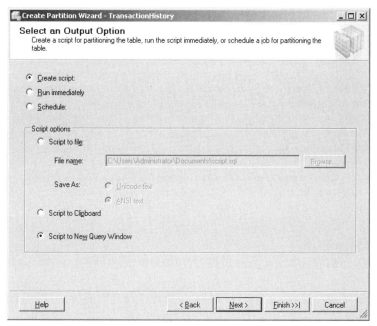

Figure 5-17: Select an Output Option page.

Now that we have seen how SQL Server stores its data in tables and how we could improve performance by partitioning the data, let's look at another way to improve the performance of retrieving data — indexes.

Indexes

As noted previously, SQL Server tables are stored as heaps by default. In order for SQL Server to retrieve any record from a heap, it must perform a full table scan; in other words, it must examine every record to determine if it should be returned. As you are probably already thinking, this is an extremely inefficient way to retrieve data. Heaps work very well for storing data and are very efficient in handling new records, but they are not so great when it comes to finding specific data in a table. This is where indexes come in. SQL Server supports two basic types of indexes: *clustered* and *non-clustered*. Although there is support for other index types such as XML and spatial indexes, which are discussed later in this chapter, they are quite different from the regular relational indexes that will be used to locate the majority of the data in database tables.

The key difference between clustered and non-clustered indexes is in the *leaf level* of the index. In non-clustered indexes, the leaf level contains pointers to the data, whereas in a clustered index, the leaf level of the index contains the actual data.

Clustered Indexes

All data that belongs to a table can be stored in either a heap or a clustered index. Heaps and clustered indexes are thus mutually exclusive. As I mentioned earlier, a *heap* is an unorganized collection of table rows, whereas a *clustered index* is a collection of organized table rows.

The white pages of the phone book are a perfect example of a clustered index. All the rows of the white pages are clustered on the combination of last name and first name. When scanning the white pages looking for a phone number, you are scanning both the index and the data. When the indexed value is found, so is the rest of the pertinent data.

This is also true of SQL Server clustered indexes. Clustered indexes can be created to sort the data by a particular attribute, or column, of the row. Going back to the library example, libraries organize most of the books in a clustered index based on genre and/or topic, and then break that organization down further by author. The clustered key must be unique within the index (this is to support non-clustered indexes, as you will see shortly), but you do not have to mark the column as *unique* in order to create the index. When clustered indexes are created on columns that are not marked as being unique, SQL Server generates a hidden column that holds a 4-byte internal number called a *uniqueifier* to uniquely identify duplicate clustered index keys. The leaf level of a clustered index is the actual data row, not just a pointer to the data.

Non-Clustered Indexes

Non-clustered indexes are more like the indexes in the back of a book. When the indexed value is found, you do not have the actual data row but a pointer that specifies the location of the actual data row. The type of pointer that is included in the leaf level pages will depend on whether the non-clustered index is built on top of a heap or a clustered index.

Non-Clustered Indexes on Heaps

When a non-clustered index is built on a table organized as a heap, the indexed column or columns are sorted along with a pointer to the physical location of the data. The pointer is made up of the file ID, page ID, and slot number that the data is located in. For example, if the data is the 20th record on page 84,593 in the first file, then the SQL would use *1:84593:20* for the value of the pointer. This allows SQL Server to access the data quickly after finding it in the index.

For example, let's go back to the library analogy. If the physical location of every book that came into this unorganized library were recorded in an index as it was placed on the shelf, that index could be referenced to find the location of a book instead of scanning all the shelves. The downside of this technique is that similar records (or, in the library analogy, similar books) could be located in completely different places. For example, searching for books on SQL Server 2008 could return several books, each one located at the opposite end of the library. Retrieving the books may take more effort than would be required if all the SQL Server books were clustered together. In a simple one-column index built on a heap table, the index itself is a great deal like a two-column table. The first column records the indexed value, and the second column records the physical location of the row in which the indexed value can be found.

Non-Clustered Indexes on Clustered Indexes

When a non-clustered index is built on a clustered index, the pointer value in the index is the clustered index key value for that row. Once the indexed value is located, SQL Server uses the clustered key to navigate the clustered index to retrieve all required columns.

For example, in the phone book analogy, you learned that the white pages of the phone book are just like a clustered index in SQL Server. I live in a small town southeast of Seattle, and my phone book contains an interesting additional index just after the white pages. I call them the "slightly off-white pages." These off-white pages contain every published phone number in town listed in sorted order, along with the last name and first name of the phone number's holder. This is a perfect example of a non-clustered index built on a clustered index. The phone number can be used to discover the last name–first name combination, and then the last name–first name combination can be used to find the address, if it is listed.

Whether to create a clustered index or leave the records in a heap is a design decision that is typically driven by how the data is accessed. When data from a table is primarily accessed by a predictable attribute or column, then it may be useful to cluster the rows of the table on that specific column. However, if the column is based on a large data type, creating a clustered index on it will be costly as far as storage and index maintenance.

Included Columns

The functionality of non-clustered indexes can be improved by adding non-key values to the leaf nodes of the index. This allows the index to cover more queries, reducing the number of times the clustered index needs to be traversed in order to retrieve additional values.

For example, imagine we have a table called Contacts that has a clustered index defined on the ContactId column and a non-clustered index defined on the LastName column. The non-clustered index leaf nodes will contain the index value and the clustered key. When a query that requires the ContactId, FirstName, and LastName column is executed using the LastName as a predicate, the non-clustered index on LastName will be used to locate the records but will only contain two of the required columns, LastName and ContactId. SQL Server would then have to make a trip to the clustered index to retrieve the value for the FirstName for each record found. Repeated trips to the clustered index can be eliminated by designing the index as a *covered index*.

Typically, a *covered index* is an index that contains all data needed to satisfy the query. One approach used by DBAs is to create a non-clustered index on both the LastName and FirstName columns. This would place the values to both the LastName and FirstName columns (since these are the index keys) and the ContactId in the leaf nodes. If a query only needing these three columns is executed, a trip to the clustered index would not be necessary. This approach is fine except the index size could grow quickly since all columns that participate in the index are included on all levels of the index. Also, the index needs to be sorted on both columns, which could cause performance problems trying to keep it this way during updates.

Included columns allow us to increase query coverage without incurring the overhead of composite index keys. Columns that are marked as "included" in the index only appear in the leaf nodes of the index and are not considered in the ordering of the rows. To include columns in the leaf nodes, you use the INCLUDE option of the CREATE INDEX command. The following command creates an index on the LastName column and includes the FirstName column of the Person.Person table in AdventureWorks2008:

```
CREATE NONCLUSTERED INDEX IX_Person_LastName
ON Person.Person(LastName)
INCLUDE(FirstName)
```

Filtered Indexes

A *filtered index* is simply an optimized non-clustered index. It allows the creation of an index over a subset of the data keeping the index structure smaller, resulting in a decrease of the amount of time

167

required to build the index and reducing index maintenance costs. Filtered indexes are particularly useful for indexes on columns that contain a high percentage of NULL values or columns that contain ranges of data such as dollar amounts. To create a filtered index, simply include a WHERE clause with the CREATE INDEX statement. The following code creates an index over all products that cost more than $800.00.

```
CREATE NONCLUSTERED INDEX IX_ListPrice_Product
    ON Production.Product(ListPrice)
WHERE ListPrice > 800.00;
```

Hierarchal Indexes

As discussed in Chapter 4, HierarchyId is one of the new data types introduced in SQL Server 2008. To aid in the retrieval of hierarchal data, indexes can be built on columns of this type using two different approaches: breadth-first or depth-first.

Breadth-First Indexes

Breadth-first indexes keep all the records that are within the same level grouped together. This allows SQL Server to very quickly respond to queries where all records have a common parent. For example, all records for employees who report to the IT Manager would be grouped together. The following code creates a breadth-first index on the employee table:

```
-- Breadth-First
IF  EXISTS (SELECT * FROM sys.indexes
        WHERE Name = 'IX_Employee_OrganizationLevel_OrganizationNode')
        DROP INDEX IX_Employee_OrganizationLevel_OrganizationNode
        ON HumanResources.Employee

CREATE NONCLUSTERED INDEX IX_Employee_OrganizationLevel_OrganizationNode
ON HumanResources.Employee
(
OrganizationLevel,
OrganizationNode
)
```

Depth-First Indexes

Depth-first indexes keep all the records for a chain grouped together. This allows SQL Server to quickly answer queries that are looking for a hierarchy. For example, say we need the record for Peter and all the people that Peter reports to, up to the CEO.

To create a depth-first index, all you need to do is create an index on the HierarchyId column.

The following code creates a depth-first index on the employee table:

```
-- Depth-First
IF  EXISTS (SELECT * FROM sys.indexes WHERE Name = 'IX_Employee_OrganizationNode')
        DROP INDEX IX_Employee_OrganizationNode ON HumanResources.Employee

CREATE NONCLUSTERED INDEX IX_Employee_OrganizationNode
ON HumanResources.Employee
```

```
(
OrganizationNode
)
```

Spatial Indexes

SQL Server 2008 includes support for spatial data through two new CLR data types: `geometry` and `geography`. The `geometry` data type is designed for planer (flat earth) space, while the `geography` data type is used for geodetic (round earth) space. For more information on these data types, see Chapter 4.

A common operation on spatial data is to find all records that intersect with a given area. For example, we need to find all stores that are within a 50-mile radius of a specific location and then sort them based on distance. Finding the intersection of regions is an expensive operation especially on complex data regions. If all the regions that have no chance of intersecting with the given region could be eliminated, then the cost of finding the valid records could be substantially reduced. This is where spatial indexes help.

The creation of a spatial index goes through two phases: decomposition and tessellation. During the *decomposition phase*, SQL Server breaks down a finite area into a grid structure (think "Excel worksheet"). Each cell of the grid is then mapped onto another grid structure, forming a more detailed level. This process continues until four levels are created. The grid in each level can be configured to be a 4×4, 8×8, or 16×16 cell grid. As you can see, the number of cells can grow very quickly. For example, if you were to have a 16×16 cell grid in each level, you would end up with approximately 4 billion cells.

During the tessellation phase, each spatial value in the table is mapped onto each of the resulting grid levels. SQL Server evaluates the cells that the value "touches" and records them into the actual spatial index. The spatial index can then be used to locate objects in space relative to other objects that are also stored in the index.

Many spatial indexes can be built on a single spatial data column, each covering an independent area of space. Since a flat plane continues infinitely in all directions, when using the `geometry` (flat earth) data type, a finite space must be specified by using the `BOUNDING_BOX` option. For example, we may only want to index storage-location data for stores within the state of Washington. Conceptually, it is very similar to a filtered index in that we are only indexing a subset of the data, but instead of providing a `WHERE` clause to limit the records indexed, we provide a bounding rectangle.

XML Indexes

Another type of index supported in SQL Server 2008 is the XML index. SQL Server 2005 introduced the ability to store native XML in tables, and with that comes the ability to build indexes on that XML to help locate and retrieve specific data within the XML text. XML data is stored as a Binary Large Object (BLOB) in the SQL Server database. To search for specific elements, attributes, or values in the XML document, SQL Server must first open the BLOB and then shred its contents. The act of shredding is what SQL Server does to create a collection of XML objects that it can then navigate. It essentially extracts the XML data structure and stores it in temporary relational structures.

XML indexes, like their relational counterparts, come with some overhead, but XML index overhead is more significant than regular indexes. For this reason, XML indexes should be reserved for columns in which the XML data is seldom modified.

It is typically much more efficient to have the database applications store and retrieve complete XML documents, rather than inserting and modifying parts and pieces of the document, which results in shredding. However, there are business cases that call for just this type of functionality, so the ability to create XML indexes was included to avoid the necessity of shredding complete documents.

XML indexes are essentially pre-shredded sections of the XML data linked to the primary key of the table. There are four types of XML indexes: The first XML index must be a primary XML index. In addition to the primary index, three secondary indexes can be created that build on the primary. Each additional index type will improve XML query performance for certain types of queries, but will also adversely affect XML data modification.

Primary XML Indexes

The primary XML index really isn't built on the XML column itself but, rather, is a clustered index that is built on an internal table that is created during the index creation process. This internal table is known as the *node table*. The node table is directly linked to the clustered index of the table where the XML index is being created. To create an XML index, the table with the XML column must have a clustered index on its primary key. The node table is used to support the primary XML index but is not directly accessible, although information about it can be exposed using system views. The primary XML index stores a relational representation of the XML field and assists the Query Optimizer in creating efficient query plans to extract data from an XML field. An example of the syntax to create a primary XML index is as follows:

```
USE AdventureWorks2008
GO
CREATE PRIMARY XML INDEX XML_IX_Illustration
ON Production.Illustration (Diagram)
```

Primary XML indexes can also be graphically created in Management Studio. To create a new set of XML indexes, first create a table to use. To create a copy of the `Person.Person` table that contains an XML column, execute the following code, which creates the `MyContact` table and then creates a clustered index on the primary key, which is required to create XML indexes:

```
USE AdventureWorks2008
GO
SELECT * INTO dbo.MyPerson FROM Person.Person
GO
ALTER TABLE dbo.MyPerson
ADD CONSTRAINT PK_MyPerson_BusinessEntityId
PRIMARY KEY CLUSTERED (BusinessEntityId)
```

Now that you have a table to play with, expand the `AdventureWorks2008` database in Object Explorer, expand Tables, and then expand the `dbo.MyPerson` table.

You may have to refresh the Tables node to get the `MyPerson` *table to appear.*

Right-click on the `MyPerson` table and click Design. The table structure will appear to the right of the Object Explorer, and the Table Designer toolbar will appear.

Click on the `AdditionalContactInfo` column, and then click on the "Manage XML Indexes" button on the Table Designer toolbar (see Figure 5-18). If the Table Designer toolbar is not visible, select it on the View ➢ Toolbars menu.

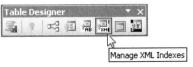

Figure 5-18: "Manage XML Indexes" button.

On the XML Indexes dialog (see Figure 5-19), click Add and then change the name of the new primary XML index to *PXML_MyPerson_AdditionalContactInfo*, and give it a short description such as "Primary XML Index."

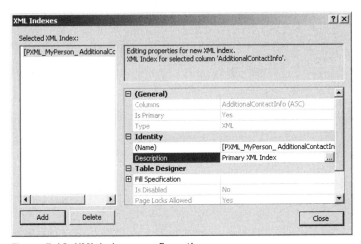

Figure 5-19: XML Indexes configuration.

Notice that the "Is Primary" property is set to Yes and cannot be changed. This is because this is the first XML index, and the first XML index created on an XML column must be a primary XML index.

Primary XML indexes can also be created through the New Index dialog by right-clicking on the Indexes node under the Table node in Object Explorer, clicking "New Index," and then choosing "Primary XML" from the list in the "Index type" dropdown box, as shown in Figure 5-20. However, secondary indexes cannot be created this way.

Secondary XML PATH Indexes

XML PATH indexes can improve the performance of XML queries that specify path expressions against the XML column. For example, if you use queries that check for the existence of an XQuery expression such as /Invoice/LineItem[@ProductID="9834"], then a PATH secondary index may improve performance. PATH secondary indexes (like all other secondary XML indexes) are built on the nodes provided by the primary XML index. An example of the syntax to create a secondary PATH index is as follows:

```
USE AdventureWorks2008
GO
CREATE XML INDEX IXML_MyPerson_AdditionalContactInfo_Path
  ON dbo.MyPerson(AdditionalContactInfo)
```

```
USING XML INDEX PXML_MyPerson_AdditionalContactInfo
FOR PATH
```

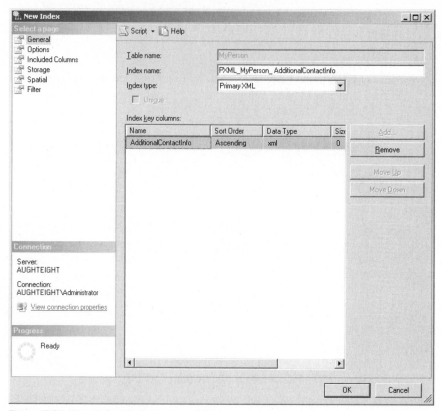

Figure 5-20: New Index dialog.

Creating secondary indexes graphically is the same as creating the primary index, except that the secondary index type can now be chosen from the Secondary Type dropdown list. To create a Secondary XML index, click on the Add button again on the XML Indexes configuration window. Now that a Primary XML index has been added, the next index type defaults to Secondary, the Is Primary property is set to No, and a new Secondary Type dropdown list appears (see Figure 5-21).

To commit the changes to the table and actually create the indexes, the table must be saved after closing the XML Indexes configuration window.

Secondary XML VALUE Indexes

XML VALUE indexes are designed to support XML queries where the path is not fully specified, or where a value is being searched by a wildcard. For example, if you are trying to retrieve all LineItem nodes that are for Product Id 9834 regardless of which invoice it belongs to using the XQuery such as

`//LineItem[@ProductID="9834"]`, then a `VALUE` index may improve performance. An example of the syntax for creating a secondary `VALUE` index is as follows:

```
CREATE XML INDEX IXML_MyPerson_AdditionalContactInfo_Value
   ON dbo.MyPerson(AdditionalContactInfo)
   USING XML INDEX PXML_MyPerson_AdditionalContactInfo
   FOR VALUE
```

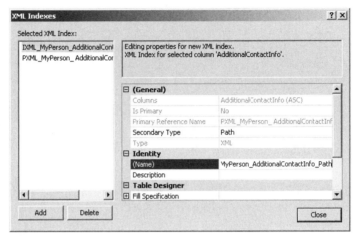

Figure 5-21: Secondary XML Indexes configuration.

Secondary XML PROPERTY Indexes

XML `PROPERTY` indexes are used to optimize queries that retrieve the value of nodes specifying full paths to the nodes. For example, if you are trying to return the Product ID for the first `LineItem` node in the document using an XQuery such as `(/Invoice/LineItem/@ProductID)[1]`, then a `PROPERTY` index may improve performance. An example of the syntax for creating a secondary `PROPERTY` index is as follows:

```
CREATE XML INDEX IXML_MyPerson_AdditionalContactInfo_Property
   ON dbo.MyPerson(AdditionalContactInfo)
   USING XML INDEX PXML_MyPerson_AdditionalContactInfo
   FOR PROPERTY
```

Maintaining Tables

Now that you have a better idea of how the data is organized in tables and explored ways to optimize retrieving the data, we need to look at maintaining this environment. Table maintenance can be classified into two basic categories:

❑   The maintenance of indexes

❑   The creation and maintenance of index statistics

Index Fragmentation

One of the leading causes of poor query performance is poorly maintained indexes. As indexes are updated, they can become fragmented. This occurs because indexes are a collection of contiguous, sorted data. To maintain the sorted order of indexes, SQL Server must split full data pages to make room for more data.

For example, extent 72 (see Figure 5-22) contains a clustered index defined on the LastName column of the fictitious Slate.Employee table. Each data page in the extent is completely full.

The code in the following example is shown for illustration purposes only and is not intended to be executed.

Extent 72

Page 110	Page 111	Page 112	Page 113	Page 114	Page 115	Page 116	Page 117
Desai	Dillon	Eaton	Faeber	Friske	Galos	Gates	Groth
Desalvo	Dixon	Ecoffey	Ferrier	Frum	Galvin	Gee	Gubbels
Dewer	Dobney	Edwards	Fine	Fuentes Espino	Ganio	Gehring	Guo
D'Hers	Dockter	Eldridge	Finley	Fulton	Gao	Geist	Gupta
Diaz	Dodd	Ellerbrock	Flood	Funk	Garcia	German	Gustafson
Dickmann	Dominguez	Elliott	Flores	Gaffney	Garden	Getzinger	Gutierrez
Dickson	Donovan	Elson	Fluegel	Gage	Garza	Giakoumakis	Guzik
Dievendorff	Earls	Emanuel	Focht	Gallagher	Gash	Gibbens	Haemon

Figure 5-22: Full data pages.

The following batch is executed to insert a new row in to the Slate.Employee table:

```
INSERT Slate.Employee
(LastName, FirstName, Title, EmailAddress, Phone, ModifiedDate)
VALUES
('Flintstone','Fred','Mr.','fredf@slategravel.com','123-456-7890',GETDATE())
```

An immediate page split occurs. This is because there is no room on the data page for a new record. To maintain the order of the rows, SQL Server splits Page 113 and moves approximately 50 percent of the rows to a new unallocated data page (see Figure 5-23).

As a result of this page split, when SQL Server reads the data pages to retrieve the contents of the Slate.Employee table, it will have to switch from Extent 72 to Extent 119, and then back to Extent 72 again to continue the scanning of rows. After many more employees are added, additional page splits will occur. These page splits cause index fragmentation. The fragmentation of the indexes will eventually cause SQL Server to perform an excessive number of Reads to retrieve data, resulting in poor query performance.

To check for fragmentation on all the indexes of a table or specific indexes, the dynamic management function sys.dm_db_index_physical_stats is used. This function returns a great deal of information about the indexes on a table, including the amount of data on each data page, the amount of fragmentation at the leaf and non-leaf levels of the indexes, and the average size of records in an index.

When querying this table-value function, I am most interested in the fragmentation level and the average percentage that each page is full. The fragmentation level will let me know which indexes need to be rebuilt, and the average percentage that each page is full tells me how soon I can expect more page splits to occur. To query the sys.dm_db_index_physical_stats dynamic management view, the following syntax can be used:

```
SELECT {* | column list} FROM
sys.dm_db_index_physical_stats
({database_id | NULL}
,{object_id | NULL}
,{index_id | NULL}
,{partition_number | NULL
,{mode | NULL | DEFAULT}
```

Extent 72

Page 110	Page 111	Page 112	Page 113	Page 114	Page 115	Page 116	Page 117
Desai	Dillon	Eaton	Faeber	Friske	Galos	Gates	Groth
Desalvo	Dixon	Ecoffey	Ferrier	Frum	Galvin	Gee	Gubbels
Dewer	Dobney	Edwards	Fine	Fuentes Espino	Ganio	Gehring	Guo
D'Hers	Dockter	Eldridge	Finley	Fulton	Gao	Geist	Gupta
Diaz	Dodd	Ellerbrock		Funk	Garcia	German	Gustafson
Dickmann	Dominguez	Elliott		Gaffney	Garden	Getzinger	Gutierrez
Dickson	Donovan	Elson		Gage	Garza	Giakoumakis	Guzik
Dievendorff	Earls	Emanuel		Gallagher	Gash	Gibbens	Haemon

Extent 73-118

Page ...	Page ...	Page ...	Page ...	Page ...	Page ...	Page ...	Page ...

Extent 119

Page 494	Page 495	Page 496	Page 497	Page 498	Page 499	Page 500	Page 501
Yee	Yukish	Flintstone					
Yonekura	Yvkoff	Flood					
Yong	Zabokritski	Flores					
Young	Zare	Fluegel					
Youtsey	Zeman	Focht					
Yu	Zeng						
Yuan	Zhang						
Yuhasz	Zhao						

Figure 5-23: Splitting Page 113.

As the syntax indicates, the sys.dm_db_index_physical_stats function requires five parameters to be passed to it when retrieving index information. The following table describes the parameters:

Parameter	Description
database_id	The integer ID value assigned by SQL Server to the database. If this is unknown, the output of the DB_ID() function can be passed. For example, the value DB_ID(AdventureWorks2008) can be provided in lieu of the integer. If NULL is passed, the information for all indexes in all databases will be returned. If NULL is specified, you must also specify NULL for object_id, index_id, and partition_number.
object_id	The integer ID value for the table hosting the indexes to be examined. If the object_id value is unknown, the output of the OBJECT_ID() function can be passed. For example, the value OBJECT_ID('Person.Person') can be provided. If NULL is passed, the information for all tables will be returned. If NULL is provided for object_id, you must also specify NULL for the index_id and partition_number.
index_id	The integer value of the index on the table. If NULL is passed, the information for all indexes will be returned. If NULL is provided as the value, you must also specify NULL for partition_number. Finding the value of index_id requires querying the sys.indexes catalog view. For example, finding the name and index_id for all the indexes on the Person.Person table would require the following query: ```USE AdventureWorks2008\nGO\nSELECT name, index_id\nFROM sys.indexes\nWHERE object_id = OBJECT_ID('Person.Person')```
partition_number	If the index is partitioned then this is the integer value for the partition. Indexes that are not partitioned have a partition number of 1. Because partitions can be stored on separate physical files, their fragmentation can be different on each partition. If NULL is provided as the value for partition_number, all partitions will be returned. To discover the partition_numbers for an index, the following query can be used: ```USE AdventureWorks2008\nGO\nSELECT *\nFROM sys.dm_db_partition_stats\nWHERE object_id = OBJECT_ID('Person.Person')```
mode	Mode specifies what level of index analysis is performed and has only three valid options: LIMITED, SAMPLED, or DETAILED, with LIMITED being the default. The LIMITED mode is the fastest, but it only scans the index pages above the leaf level, which makes it the least accurate. The SAMPLED mode samples only 1 percent of the data pages to return the analysis information. If there are fewer than 10,000 pages, SQL Server will use DETAILED instead. The DETAILED mode scans all pages.

To practice examining and maintaining indexes, run the following command to create the MyPersons table that is used in the next few examples:

```
USE AdventureWorks2008
GO
SELECT BusinessEntityId, LastName, FirstName, Title, ModifiedDate
INTO dbo.MyPersons
FROM Person.Person
CREATE CLUSTERED INDEX IX_MyPersons_LastName ON dbo.MyPersons(LastName)
```

To query the sys.dm_db_index_physical_stats view to return all the possible data in relation to the MyPersons table, the following query can be used:

```
DECLARE @dbID smallint, @objectID int
SET @DbID = DB_ID('AdventureWorks2008')
SET @ObjectID = OBJECT_ID('dbo.MyPersons')

SELECT *
FROM sys.dm_db_index_physical_stats(@DbID, @ObjectID, NULL, NULL , 'DETAILED')
```

However, running this query returns more information than is generally needed. Because I am more particularly interested in just the fragmentation of the leaf level of the index and the fill percentage of the data pages, I can limit the amount of data returned. The reason that I am less concerned about the non-leaf level is that the non-leaf level is typically very small. It can, indeed, get very fragmented, but the fragmentation of the non-leaf level of the index does not have anywhere near as much impact on performance as leaf-level fragmentation.

To reduce the information returned by the sys.dm_db_index_physical_stats query, it can be limited to just the columns of interest and the leaf level of the index, as follows:

```
DECLARE @dbID smallint, @objectID int
SET @DbID = DB_ID('AdventureWorks2008')
SET @ObjectID = OBJECT_ID('dbo.MyPersons')

SELECT index_id, avg_fragmentation_in_percent, avg_page_space_used_in_percent
FROM sys.dm_db_index_physical_stats(@DbID, @ObjectID, NULL, NULL , 'DETAILED')
WHERE index_level = 0
Results:

index_id    avg_fragmentation_in_percent
       avg_page_space_used_in_percent
--------    --------------------------    ----------------------------
1           0                             98.9983815171732
```

This query only returns the fragmentation level and page space used for the leaf level of all the indexes, which is where the worst fragmentation (as far as performance is concerned) will occur.

The precise definition of fragmentation as a measurement is the percentage of pages where the next physical page is not the next logical page, as shown in Figure 5-24.

Extent 72

Page 110	Page 111	Page 112	Page 113	Page 114	Page 115	Page 116	Page 117
Desai	Dickmann	Dobney	Earls	Ellerbrock	Ferrier	Fluegel	Fulton
Desalvo	Dickson	Dockter	Eaton	Elliott	Fine	Focht	Funk
Dewer	Dievendorff	Dodd	Ecoffey	Elson	Finley	Friske	Gaffney
D'Hers	Dillon	Dominguez	Edwards	Emanuel	Flood	Frum	Gage
Diaz	Dixon	Donovan	Eldridge	Faeber	Flores	Fuentes	Gallagher

Figure 5-24: Impact of filling the data pages.

The MyPersons table contains 19,972 rows. Now, insert some more records in the MyPersons table. The following script inserts 3,994 additional records, which constitutes a 20 percent increase in rows:

```
INSERT dbo.MyPersons
(BusinessEntityId, LastName, FirstName, Title, ModifiedDate)
SELECT BusinessEntityId, LastName, FirstName, Title, ModifiedDate
FROM Person.Person WHERE BusinessEntityId % 5 = 4
```

Querying the sys.dm_db_index_physical_stats dynamic management view now returns some very interesting data:

```
DECLARE @dbID smallint, @objectID int
SET @DbID = DB_ID('AdventureWorks2008')
SET @ObjectID = OBJECT_ID('dbo.MyPersons')

SELECT index_id, avg_fragmentation_in_percent, avg_page_space_used_in_percent
FROM sys.dm_db_index_physical_stats(@DbID, @ObjectID, NULL, NULL , 'DETAILED')
WHERE index_level = 0

RESULTS:
-------------------------------------------------------------------------
index_id    avg_fragmentation_in_percent
        avg_page_space_used_in_percent
--------    ----------------------------          ------------------------------
1           97.8571428571428                      59.4185322461082
```

Because of the additional rows that have been added to the MyPersons table, almost 97 percent of the time when SQL Server was reading the data pages, the next physical page was not the next logical page. In addition to the fragmentation, the data pages are now only 59 percent full.

The combination of the fragmented indexes and the partially filled data pages causes SQL Server to read 274 logical extents, when only about 40 logical extent Reads should have been required. This information is available through a deprecated Database Console Command (DBCC) command called DBCC SHOWCONTIG. DBCC SHOWCONTIG will be removed in a future release of SQL Server, but for now, see what it tells you about the MyPersons table:

```
USE AdventureWorks2008
GO
```

```
DBCC SHOWCONTIG('dbo.MyPersons')

RESULTS:
--------------------------------------------------------------------------
- Pages Scanned...............................: 280
- Extents Scanned............................: 38
- Extent Switches............................: 274
- Avg. Pages per Extent......................: 7.4
- Scan Density [Best Count:Actual Count].......: 12.73% [35:275]
- Logical Scan Fragmentation .................: 97.86%
- Extent Scan Fragmentation ..................: 13.16%
- Avg. Bytes Free per Page...................: 3284.7
- Avg. Page Density (full)...................: 59.42%
```

Although historically, DBCC has been known to stand for Database Consistency Checker, *many DBCC commands now go beyond just checking database consistency. For this reason, DBCC can also be used to as an acronym for Database Console Command.*

The DBCC SHOWCONTIG command shows you that SQL Server scanned 38 extents to retrieve all the data in the MyPersons table, but to scan those 38 extents, it had to switch between them 274 times!

It has already been established that SQL Server uses indexes to quickly find rows in data pages for reading, updating, or deleting. However, if all you ever did was insert data in tables, you would not need an index. The general rule is that indexes help Read performance and hurt insert performance. Here is an analogy and a confession.

I am a home-improvement organizational slob. I am just incapable of putting things back where they belong. As a result, when I am finished with a particular home project, I invariably grab all the tools I have used and throw them on my workbench. Putting stuff away never takes me very long. However, as I start the next project, I invariably spend a huge amount of time just trying to find my hammer. Out of desperation, I sometimes just go buy another one. The home-improvement stores love me. If I just spent the extra time required to put things back where they belong, I could save time and money.

The same goes for databases. Planning and building indexes take time and effort; so does maintaining the indexes once they are built. However, even the most insert- and update-intensive database can usually be found to perform five Reads for every Write. That means that maintaining indexes at peak performance is going to pay off fivefold. With that firmly in mind, take a look at how to mitigate index fragmentation and correct it once it has occurred.

Mitigating Fragmentation with Fill-Factor

To mitigate fragmentation caused by page splits, the database administrator can design or rebuild the indexes so that data pages are not completely filled. This option is called the *fill-factor*. When building or rebuilding the index, a fill-factor percentage can be specified. If an index page is only filled 90 percent of the way, it will take more inserts to the index to cause page splits and thus longer for fragmentation to occur. With the previous example, take a look at what impact filling the data pages to 90 percent would have (see Figure 5-24).

As you can see, now that the data pages are not completely full, adding additional contacts will not cause the pages to split as quickly. The fill-factor is only effective when the indexes are built or rebuilt. After a few inserts, the indexes will again fill and page splits will occur. However, the page splits will not occur immediately, and the amount of time between index rebuilds can be lengthened.

Only filling the index pages partially does have its drawbacks, as you knew it would. First, because the pages are not completely full, the amount of disk space needed to store the index will increase. Also, since there is less data on each page, the number of reads required to retrieve the data will increase. As a result, there is a definite point of decreasing returns when setting a fill-factor. I personally believe that the fill-factor of indexes should rarely be less than 90 percent. On heavily updated and queried tables, this percentage might go as low as 85 percent, but keep in mind that at an 85 percent fill-factor, SQL Server will have to perform 15 percent more Reads than is strictly required to retrieve the records at a 100 percent fill-factor. As a result, a 10 percent fragmentation level may have about the same effect as a 90 percent fill-factor.

Removing Fragmentation

There are three ways to remove fragmentation: The indexes can be dropped and re-created, rebuilt in place, or reorganized. Each method has its advantages and disadvantages. The drop and re-create option is used with the CREATE INDEX command. The rebuild and reorganize options are used with the ALTER INDEX command. Let's take a look at how to use each of these approaches.

Create Index with Drop Existing

The main advantage of dropping and re-creating an index is that almost everything about the index can be changed. For example, the columns that the index is defined on can be changed, the FILLFACTOR of the index can be modified, or the index can be changed from a non-clustered index to a clustered index as long as a clustered index does not already exist. However, when using the DROP_EXISTING option with the CREATE INDEX command, a specific index must be specified. When using the rebuild or reorganize options of the ALTER INDEX command, all the indexes on a table can be processed at once.

Rebuilding an index with the DROP_EXISTING option removes index fragmentation by rebuilding all the index pages in indexed order. It also compacts the index pages so that empty space created by page splits is filled. Both the leaf level and the non-leaf level of the indexes are rebuilt.

The following is an example of the syntax for dropping and re-creating an index with the CREATE INDEX command:

```
CREATE UNIQUE CLUSTERED INDEX PK_Address_AddressID
    ON Person.Address(AddressID)
    WITH (FILLFACTOR = 90, DROP_EXISTING = ON)
```

Rebuilding Indexes

When an index is rebuilt using the ALTER INDEX command, SQL Server actually drops and re-creates the index much like the CREATE INDEX command. The difference is that the columns of the existing index cannot be changed, nor can the type of index. However, the FILLFACTOR can be modified. It is also possible to execute the command only once and have it rebuild all the indexes on that table.

Another very useful feature is the ONLINE option. If ONLINE is on, SQL Server will not place any long-term locks on the table being indexed, resulting in a much lower impact on user performance. In order to do this, SQL Server leverages the tempdb database for index creation and maintenance. Indexes are created or rebuilt in the tempdb database and then moved to the appropriate database. This decreases the impact on users in the database, but it can cause unanticipated growth of the tempdb database. The ONLINE index option is only available with the Enterprise and Developer editions of SQL Server.

Like the DROP_EXISTING option, the REBUILD option of ALTER INDEX rebuilds both the leaf and non-leaf levels of the index.

The following is an example of rebuilding an individual index and then all the indexes on a table with a FILLFACTOR of 90 percent and the ONLINE option on:

```
USE AdventureWorks2008
GO

ALTER INDEX AK_Product_ProductNumber ON Person.Product
REBUILD WITH (FILLFACTOR=90,ONLINE=ON)

USE AdventureWorks2008
GO

ALTER INDEX ALL ON Person.Product
REBUILD WITH (FILLFACTOR=90,ONLINE=ON)
```

Reorganizing Indexes

Reorganizing indexes consumes the least amount of system resources, but doesn't do as thorough a job as an index rebuild. When SQL Server reorganizes an index, it rearranges and compacts the data pages so that their logical order matches their physical order. Index reorganization only affects the leaf level of the index and is always performed online.

The guideline on when to perform index reorganization versus when to perform a rebuild is the 30 percent fragmentation level. If the level of fragmentation is less than or equal to 30 percent, a reorganization will take less time than an index rebuild and consume much fewer system resources. If the fragmentation is greater than 30 percent, index reorganization will most likely take longer than a rebuild, but it will still consume fewer resources.

In general, if the indexes are rebuilt periodically with an appropriate FILLFACTOR, the need for index reorganization between those periods is reduced. However, intervals of high transaction activity may necessitate an intervening reorganization to prevent fragmentation from exceeding 30 percent and potentially causing performance issues.

Statistics

Statistics are used by SQL Server to find the most efficient means of retrieving data from database tables by storing information about the selectivity of data in a column, as well as the distribution of data in a column. They can be created manually and automatically. Chapter 10 describes statistics in greater detail.

Enforcing Data Integrity

As mentioned in previous chapters, the assumption of this book is that you are at least marginally familiar with database theory, so I will not expound on the purpose of constraints to maintain data integrity. Instead, what is covered in this section is how to create these constraints, as well as other database objects that are used to maintain the integrity and consistency of data.

Primary Key Constraints

A table can have one and only one *primary key constraint*. This value is the one that is used to uniquely identify every row in the table. A primary key constraint can be defined on either a single column or a combination of columns if it takes more than one column to uniquely identify each row. It is critical that you understand how SQL Server enforces uniqueness of the key values specified in a primary key definition. It does so by creating a unique index on the column or columns participating in the key.

It would be very inefficient to try to enforce uniqueness without sorting the data. The problem with SQL Server in this respect is that it defaults to a unique clustered index if a clustered index does not already exist. Decisions on which column or columns participate in a primary key and which ones define the physical structuring of the table's data are completely different. It should not be assumed that the primary key should also be the table's cluster key. Remember that all the table's non-clustered indexes will include the clustered index key as the pointer back to the data row. If the primary key length is large, using a clustered index to support the primary key could prove to be very detrimental to non-clustered index storage and retrieval.

Primary keys can be created by selecting the column or columns in the Table Designer window and then clicking on the "Set Primary Key" button on the Table Designer toolbar, or by using Transact-SQL in a CREATE TABLE or ALTER TABLE command. The following are examples of setting a primary key on tables during and after creation.

When using the CREATE TABLE statement, you can either define the constraint as part of the column definition or at the end of all the column definitions as part of the table definition. The first example shows how to create the primary key as part of the column definition of the CREATE TABLE command:

```
USE AdventureWorks2008
GO
CREATE TABLE dbo.CreditCards(
    CreditCardID int IDENTITY(1,1) NOT NULL
    CONSTRAINT PK_CreditCardID PRIMARY KEY NONCLUSTERED (CreditCardID),
    CardType nvarchar(50) NOT NULL,
    CardNumber nvarchar(25) NOT NULL,
    ExpMonth tinyint NOT NULL,
    ExpYear smallint NOT NULL,
    ModifiedDate datetime NOT NULL)
```

This next example also creates a primary key constraint in the CREATE TABLE command, but does so as part of the table definition at the end of all the column definitions:

```
CREATE TABLE dbo.CreditCards(
    CreditCardID int IDENTITY(1,1) NOT NULL,
    CardType nvarchar(50) NOT NULL,
    CardNumber nvarchar(25) NOT NULL,
    ExpMonth tinyint NOT NULL,
    ExpYear smallint NOT NULL,
    ModifiedDate datetime NOT NULL,
    CONSTRAINT PK_CreditCardID PRIMARY KEY NONCLUSTERED (CreditCardID))
```

In both cases, the CONSTRAINT keyword and name for the constraint are optional. If the name is omitted, SQL Server will assign a system-generated name. I recommend that you provide a name for all constraints since this is what will be displayed within SQL Server Management Studio and in any error message generated by SQL Server, and a friendlier name could prove to be helpful. The name that you choose must be unique within the scheme that contains the table.

The last example shows how to add a primary key constraint to an already existing table by using the ALTER TABLE command:

```
ALTER TABLE dbo.CreditCards
ADD CONSTRAINT PK_CreditCardID PRIMARY KEY NONCLUSTERED (CreditCardID)
```

In addition, remember that if the NONCLUSTERED keyword is omitted, SQL Server will create a clustered index to enforce the key if one is not already defined. Be sure this is what was intended as it is a common mistake.

Unique Constraints

Whereas only one primary key constraint is allowed on a table, many *unique constraints* can be specified. For example, a delivery company that employs drivers may want to record information about its drivers in a table like the following example:

```
CREATE TABLE dbo.Driver(
    DriverID int IDENTITY(1,1) NOT NULL
        CONSTRAINT PK_DriverId PRIMARY KEY CLUSTERED,
    LastName varchar(75) NOT NULL,
    FirstName varchar(75) NOT NULL,
    MiddleInitial varchar(3) NULL,
    SocSecNum char(9) NOT NULL,
    LicenseNum varchar(25) NOT NULL)
```

In this example, the employer would probably want to ensure that both the Social Security number and the driver's license number were unique in addition to the primary key. You may be thinking, "Why don't we just use the Social Security number or driver's license number as the primary key?" There are many reasons why these columns are not good candidates for a primary key.

When it comes to the Social Security number, security can be a big issue. Because most primary keys are used as foreign keys, the Social Security number would be duplicated in several places. Given the sensitivity placed on private information, this would become a management nightmare. Another reason applies to both the Social Security number and the driver's license number. Because both these numbers are not numbers at all, but rather strings of characters, they are not the best values to use to enforce referential integrity, because the join criteria would be large instead of a more efficient integer value.

One other thing to think about is whether the values are unique after all. Social Security numbers can be reused, and you may end up with problems. This usually only occurs if you plan to keep your data for a very long time, but it does happen.

To create a unique constraint, you have two choices: Create a unique index or create a unique constraint on the table. A unique index behaves like a unique constraint, and SQL Server will create a unique index to enforce the unique constraint. It is almost a case of "What comes first: the chicken or the egg?" However, there is a difference — albeit a small one. If you create a unique constraint, the only way to drop the unique index is to remove the constraint. You will not be able to use the DROP INDEX command.

To create unique indexes or constraints graphically, first open the table for modification by right-clicking on the table name and clicking Design.

On the Table Designer toolbar, click on the "Manage Indexes and Keys" button (see Figure 5-25).

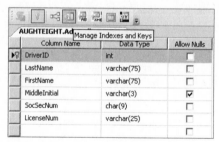

Figure 5-25: "Manage Indexes and Keys" button.

On the Indexes/Keys dialog (see Figure 5-26), click Add and then specify the properties of the new index or key. Notice in the Type property that either Index or Unique Key can be chosen. If the "Is Unique" property is set to True, then either Index or Unique Key will have the same effect.

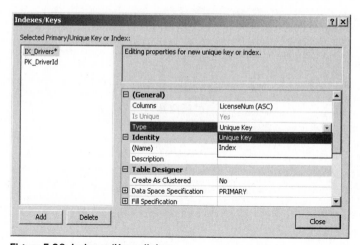

Figure 5-26: Indexes/Keys dialog.

To enforce uniqueness on the LicenseNum column, one of the following commands can be used as they will both have the same outcome:

```
ALTER TABLE dbo.Driver
ADD CONSTRAINT UX_LicenseNum UNIQUE NONCLUSTERED(LicenseNum)

CREATE UNIQUE NONCLUSTERED INDEX UX_LicenseNum
ON dbo.Driver(LicenseNum)
```

Foreign Key Constraints

Foreign key constraints are created to guarantee referential integrity between tables. To create a foreign key constraint on a table, the column or columns defined in the foreign key must map to a column or columns in a primary key table, where the columns are designated as either the primary key or have a unique constraint (both unique constraints and unique indexes qualify).

The following examples are based on the `dbo.Driver` table created earlier and the `dbo.DriverRecord` table, which can be created with the following script:

```
CREATE TABLE dbo.DriverRecord(
   RecordID int IDENTITY (1,1) NOT NULL PRIMARY KEY NONCLUSTERED,
   DriverID int,
   InfractionID int NOT NULL,
   RecordDate datetime NOT NULL)
```

To create a foreign key constraint with the graphical tools, expand the `DriverRecord` table in Object Explorer. Right-click on the Keys node and click "New Foreign Key." The Foreign Key Relationships dialog will display (see Figure 5-27).

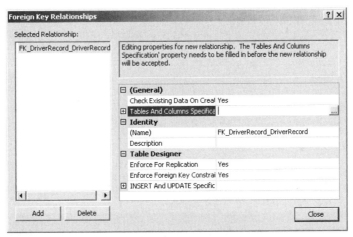

Figure 5-27: Foreign Key Relationships dialog.

Click the ellipses to the right of the "Tables And Columns Specification" property to select the primary key and foreign key columns.

In the resulting Tables and Columns dialog (see Figure 5-28), choose `Driver` as the primary key table and `DriverID` as the column in both the Primary key and Foreign key tables as shown in Figure 5-28. Once you close the Wizard and the Table Designer page, you should be able to see the newly created foreign key under the Keys folder in the tree view. If you don't, right click the `DriverRecord` table and select Refresh.

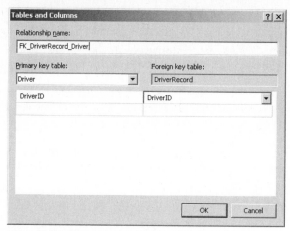

Figure 5-28: Tables and Columns dialog.

Foreign Key Constraint Options

Foreign key constraints have several advanced options that change the way they behave during creation and after creation that are described in the following sections. These options can be set in the General and Table Designer sections of the Foreign Key Relationships dialog, or through Transact-SQL. Examples of the code necessary to create foreign keys and set their options are given with each description.

The following examples all use the same constraint name. To execute the examples in succession, it will be necessary to drop the existing constraint prior to re-creating it. Constraints can be deleted using SQL Server Managements Studio's Object Explorer or by executing the script ALTER TABLE dbo. DriverRecord DROP CONSTRAINT FK_DriverRecord_Driver.

WITH CHECK

WITH CHECK is the default setting when adding a foreign key constraint. This setting specifies that any existing data in the foreign key table should be validated to conform to the constraint:

```
ALTER TABLE dbo.DriverRecord WITH CHECK
ADD CONSTRAINT FK_DriverRecord_Driver FOREIGN KEY (DriverID)
    REFERENCES dbo.Driver (DriverID)
```

WITH NOCHECK

The WITH NOCHECK setting specifies that existing data is not validated to conform to the new constraint. This option can make the creation process more efficient when you know that all existing data already conforms to the constraint, but it is important to keep in mind that any non-conforming records will be ignored during the creation. However, during subsequent updates to the non-conforming row, the constraint will be enforced, resulting in an error.

```
ALTER TABLE dbo.DriverRecord WITH NOCHECK
ADD CONSTRAINT FK_DriverRecord_Driver FOREIGN KEY (DriverID)
    REFERENCES dbo.Driver (DriverID)
```

Cascading Constraints

Foreign keys prevent the updating or deletion of parent values (primary or unique values) by default. However, there are times when this is not desirable. SQL Server provides the option of specifying what action is taken on the child records if a parent record is deleted or updated.

ON DELETE NO ACTION and ON UPDATE NO ACTION are the default settings for foreign keys. These settings specify that any attempt to delete a row or update a key referenced by foreign keys in existing rows in other tables will fail.

In addition to the default NO ACTION setting, the options CASCADE, SET NULL, and SET DEFAULT are possible, which allow for deletions or updates of key values to cascade in a defined manner to the tables defined to have foreign key relationships.

ON DELETE CASCADE

This option specifies that all child records will be deleted when the parent row is deleted. If the child record also has child records, the foreign key options on those tables will be enforced and either cascade or fail.

```
ALTER TABLE dbo.DriverRecord WITH NOCHECK
ADD CONSTRAINT FK_DriverRecord_Driver FOREIGN KEY (DriverID)
    REFERENCES dbo.Driver (DriverID)
    ON DELETE CASCADE
```

ON UPDATE CASCADE

When a parent key is updated, the update will cascade to any child records that reference the parent keys.

```
ALTER TABLE dbo.DriverRecord WITH NOCHECK
ADD CONSTRAINT FK_DriverRecord_Driver FOREIGN KEY (DriverID)
    REFERENCES dbo.Driver (DriverID)
    ON UPDATE CASCADE
```

ON DELETE SET NULL

With this setting, any child record's foreign key will be set to NULL if the parent row is deleted. The foreign key column must allow nulls for this option to work.

```
ALTER TABLE dbo.DriverRecord WITH NOCHECK
ADD CONSTRAINT FK_DriverRecord_Driver FOREIGN KEY (DriverID)
    REFERENCES dbo.Driver (DriverID)
    ON DELETE SET NULL
```

ON UPDATE SET NULL

Any child record's foreign key will be set to NULL if the corresponding parent key is updated. The foreign key column must allow nulls for this option to work.

```
ALTER TABLE dbo.DriverRecord WITH NOCHECK
ADD CONSTRAINT FK_DriverRecord_Driver FOREIGN KEY (DriverID)
    REFERENCES dbo.Driver (DriverID)
    ON UPDATE SET NULL
```

ON DELETE SET DEFAULT

When a parent record is deleted, the corresponding child key value will be set to the value specified by any DEFAULT constraint defined on that column. If no DEFAULT constraint exists, the value will be set to NULL as long as the foreign key column is nullable. The value specified in the DEFAULT constraint must have a corresponding row in the parent table.

```
ALTER TABLE dbo.DriverRecord WITH NOCHECK
ADD CONSTRAINT FK_DriverRecord_Driver FOREIGN KEY (DriverID)
    REFERENCES dbo.Driver (DriverID)
    ON DELETE SET DEFAULT
```

ON UPDATE SET DEFAULT

When a parent key value is updated, any corresponding child records will be updated to the value specified in the DEFAULT constraint defined on the foreign key column. Like the previous option, the default value must exist in the parent table. If there is no DEFAULT defined and the foreign key column is nullable, the child value will be set to NULL.

```
ALTER TABLE dbo.DriverRecord WITH NOCHECK
ADD CONSTRAINT FK_DriverRecord_Driver FOREIGN KEY (DriverID)
    REFERENCES dbo.Driver (DriverID)
    ON UPDATE SET DEFAULT
```

The various cascade settings can be combined and mixed. For example, the cascade option for a DELETE can be set to CASCADE, but NO ACTION for an UPDATE.

Check Constraints

Check constraints are used to ensure that the data in a field conforms to a defined expression. The check constraints can be created graphically by following these steps on the dbo.Driver table that was created earlier:

1. Expand the dbo.Driver table in Object Explorer.

2. Right-click on the Constraints node and click "New Constraint." This will launch the Check Constraints dialog.

3. In the Check Constraints dialog (see Figure 5-29), change the name of the constraint to **CK_DriverSocialSecurityNumber** in the Identity section and change the description to **Enforce numeric values for SSN's**.

4. Edit the expression for the constraint by typing in the following expression:

```
(SocSecNum LIKE '[0-9][0-9][0-9][0-9][0-9][0-9][0-9][0-9][0-9]')
```

This expression ensures that any Social Security numbers added to the table will be nine contiguous integers with no dashes. Validating a Social Security number (SSN) is far more complicated than this makes it out to be. For example, the first three numbers of an SSN range only between 001 and 772, but this would become very messy using a simple LIKE operator.

Notice that as you are working within either the Foreign Key Constraint or Check Constraint dialog boxes (see Figure 5-29), there are no OK or Cancel buttons. If you open the dialog, a constraint is automatically added for you, so if you decided not to add the constraint, you would actually have to delete it before closing the dialog. Here is the Transact-SQL command to create the same constraint:

```
ALTER TABLE dbo.Driver ADD CONSTRAINT
  CK_DriverSocialSecurityNumber
  CHECK (SocSecNum LIKE '[0-9][0-9][0-9][0-9][0-9][0-9][0-9][0-9][0-9]')
GO
```

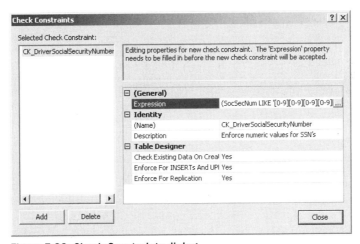

Figure 5-29: Check Constraints dialog.

Default Constraints

Default constraints specify a value to be inserted in a table if no value is specified during an insert. They can be applied to a table when it is created or added afterwards. To create a default constraint with the graphical tools, first select the column you want to apply the default to, and then specify a default value or binding in the Column Properties window of the Table Designer, as shown in Figure 5-30.

Bindings are links to a Database Default or Rule and are discussed later in the chapter.

For this example, specify the string '000000000' as the default value for the SocSecNum column.

The Transact-SQL command for accomplishing this same task is as follows:

```
ALTER TABLE dbo.Driver ADD CONSTRAINT
    DF_Driver_SocSecNum DEFAULT '000000000' FOR SocSecNum
GO
```

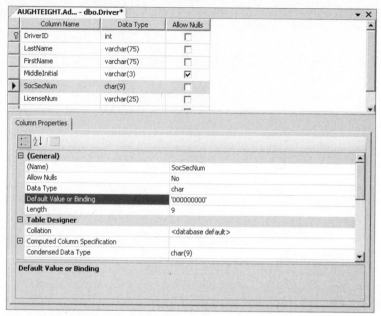

Figure 5-30: Creating a default constraint.

Database Diagrams

Once the database and its objects have been created, it is often convenient to be able to create entity relationship diagrams that are linked to the underlying structures. That way, any changes that must be made (especially the creation of foreign key constraints) can be made and applied to the database in a convenient graphical environment. The *database diagram* feature in SQL Server Management Studio provides this functionality. The database diagram feature, however, is not a replacement for full-fledged database design tools. It is more often used in the test and development phase of database deployment.

The database diagram feature is accessed in Object Explorer of SQL Server Management Studio in the individual database node. Before you can create your first *database diagram*, you will need to install the diagram support objects. This can be done by right-clicking on the Database Diagrams node and selecting "Install Diagram Support." If you don't do this, then the first time you try to create a database diagram, an informational message will display notifying you that "One or more support objects" are missing, and asking whether or not you want to install them. Either installing the support objects or selecting Yes will cause SQL Server to create a system-owned table called dbo.sysdiagrams that will contain the definitions of all diagrams created.

The following steps will guide you through the creation and modification of a database diagram:

1. Expand the Databases node and then the AdventureWorks2008 database node. Right-click on the Database Diagrams node in AdventureWorks2008 and click "New Database Diagram." The Database Diagram pane will appear, as well as an Add Table dialog that alphabetically lists all the user tables in the database.

2. Select the `Address(Person)` table. Click Add to add the `Person.Address` table to the diagram and then click Close on the Add Table dialog. (You can also double-click on the table in the list to add it to the diagram.)

3. Right-click on the `Address(Person)` table and then click "Add Related Tables." This causes all tables that have a defined relationship to the `Person.Address` table to be added to the diagram. This feature comes in handy when you are unfamiliar with the structure of the database.

Notice that all the tables are just piled on top of each other in the diagram. You can manually reorder them, or just right-click on an empty space on the diagram and click "Arrange Tables." SQL Server arranges the tables neatly on the diagram pane so that the tables and their relationships are easily viewed.

Because there is limited space in the diagram, you can create multiple diagrams that divide the database into functional areas, or you can display page breaks on the diagram and divide a large diagram into many pages. To display page breaks, right-click on an empty space on the diagram and click "View Page Breaks."

Right-clicking on any table provides the option of changing the way the table is displayed on the diagram, deleting the table from the database, removing the table from the diagram, as well as several table modification options normally available from the Table Designer toolbar.

Views

SQL Server 2008 *views* are simply saved queries that are named and can be managed independently of the tables they reference. They are very much like the tables they reference, except that they are, by default, logical objects and not physical objects. The one exception to this is when a unique clustered index is created on a view, causing the view to be "materialized." Views are typically created to abstract complex database design, to simplify permissions by granting access to one view instead of multiple tables, and to arrange data for export to other data stores.

The creation of views and other programming objects is unfortunately beyond the scope of this book. For more information on how to create views and why to create views, check out *Beginning T-SQL with Microsoft SQL Server 2005 and 2008* by Paul Turley and Dan Wood (Wiley, 2008). For information about securing views take a look at Chapter 6.

System Views

System views, as noted in Chapter 4, are the database administrator's view of system objects. There are too many system views to describe here, and most are documented in SQL Server 2008 Books Online. System views can be divided into four categories:

❑ **Information Schema Views** — Information Schema views are pre-defined views that belong to a special schema known as `INFORMATION_SCHEMA`. SQL Server 2008 implements the ISO standard definition for the `INFORMATION_SCHEMA` and provides a consistent view of SQL Server metadata that is generally stable from one release to another.

❑ **Catalog Views** — Catalog views are another method for retrieving metadata from SQL Server. Because the catalog views represent the most general interface into metadata about SQL Server, it is recommended that you use these over the Information Schema views. They provide a great deal of useful information that can be used in the troubleshooting and maintenance of SQL Server 2008. If using them in permanent scripts, be sure to specify the columns by name. Microsoft reserves the right to add additional columns to the end of the catalog views, which could break existing code. In fact, this occurred in select catalog views between SQL Server 2005 and SQL Server 2008.

❑ **Dynamic Management Views** — Dynamic Management views return server state information that can be used to monitor SQL Server processes, diagnose problems, and tune performance. They are briefly described in Chapter 4.

❑ **Compatibility Catalog Views** — Because the system tables from SQL Server 2000 are no longer available, SQL Server 2008 provides many views that carry the same name as the previous system tables. These views return only the features of SQL Server 2008 that are compatible with SQL Server 2000 and are provided strictly for use with objects and scripts designed on SQL Server 2000. Future development work should use the new catalog views that return SQL Server 2008 specific information since these will be removed in a future release.

Synonyms

Synonyms are a means to give a name to a SQL Server schema-scoped database object that can be used by database applications instead of its defined two-part, three-part, or four-part names. For example, a database application that references a table on another server would typically need to use a four-part name. Defining a synonym essentially presents an alias that maps directly to the table without having to fully qualify the table. The following code will create a synonym called `Products` in the `AdventureWorks2008` database that references the `dbo.DimProduct` table in the `AdventureWorksDW2008` database:

```
USE AdventureWorks2008
GO

CREATE SYNONYM dbo.Products
FOR AdventureWorksDW2008.dbo.DimProduct
GO
```

Now that you have a new synonym, open a new Query window and type in the following code:

```
USE AdventureWorks2008
GO
SELECT ProductKey, EnglishProductName, StandardCost
FROM dbo.Products
```

Notice that the query returns 606 rows from the `AdventureWorksDW` database without having to qualify the object name, like the following example:

```
USE AdventureWorks2008
GO
SELECT ProductKey, EnglishProductName, StandardCost
FROM AdventureWorksDW2008.dbo.DimProduct
```

Synonyms can reference views, tables, stored procedures, and functions on any database, or a linked server to simplify the application data access.

Programming Objects

As previously noted, the creation and logic behind programming objects are beyond the scope of this book, but the purpose of the objects and their basic use is pertinent. The database administrator needs to understand how programming objects can affect the behavior of the database. The most important aspect is typically security, which is addressed in Chapter 6.

Stored Procedures

A *stored procedure* is a named collection of Transact-SQL or managed code that is stored on the server in a database. SQL Server stored procedures are very similar to procedures from other programming languages in that they are used to encapsulate repetitive tasks. They support user-declared variables, conditional execution, and many other programming features.

Stored procedures can be written in traditional Transact-SQL or in any .NET managed language such as C# or VB.NET. Chapter 14 discusses the advantages of using managed code to create complex stored procedures that would push the limits of Transact-SQL.

The major purpose of stored procedures is to encapsulate business functionality and create reusable application logic. Because the stored procedures are stored on the server, changes to the business logic can be accomplished in a single location.

Stored procedures also provide controlled modification of data in the database. Giving users permission to modify data in database tables is typically a very bad idea. Instead, stored procedures can be created that perform only the modifications that are required by the application. Users can then be given the permission to execute the stored procedure to perform the required data modification.

User-created stored procedures can be more efficient than ad hoc Transact-SQL, and much more secure. They also drastically reduce the number of network packets needed to query and modify databases and are compiled and cached for long periods of time for efficient reuse.

In addition to user-created stored procedures, SQL Server provides literally hundreds of *System Stored Procedures*. These System Stored procedures are used to retrieve system information, as well as make changes to the underlying system objects. They range from simple stored procedures that return a list of all the logged-in users, to complex stored procedures that create database maintenance jobs. Some of these stored procedures are covered in later chapters as they apply to the topic at hand.

Functions

SQL Server 2008 provides support for three types of user-defined functions: scalar functions, table-valued functions, and aggregate functions. SQL Server functions are very similar to functions in other programming languages. They accept parameters, perform some action based on the input parameters, and return a value. Table-value functions always return a `table` data type. Scalar and aggregate functions can return any data type except `text`, `ntext`, and `image`.

User-defined functions can be created with Transact-SQL or managed code with the exception of aggregate functions, which are always created in managed code. User-defined functions offer many of the same benefits as stored procedures as far as efficiency and security are concerned. One area in which they differ is that functions are not allowed to execute any code that modifies the state of the database, whereas stored procedures can.

System functions are separated into categories in Object Explorer of SQL Server Management Studio. Some functions are used to manipulate user data (such as aggregate and string functions), whereas others are used to retrieve system information (such as security and metadata functions).

Triggers

Triggers are stored Transact-SQL or managed-code objects that are executed because of some other action within the system and cannot be executed directly. Two types of triggers exist in SQL Server 2008: DML and DDL triggers.

DML Triggers

Data Manipulation Language (DML) triggers are executed as a result of a DML command (INSERT, UPDATE, DELETE) being executed. There are two types of DML triggers in SQL Server 2008: After triggers and "Instead Of" triggers.

After Triggers

Traditional triggers are known as *After triggers* because they execute "after" the DML statement is executed on the table with the defined trigger. The code in the trigger is implicitly part of the transaction that caused the trigger to execute. Any ROLLBACK command in the body of the trigger will cause the trigger and the associated transaction to be rolled back.

"Instead Of" Triggers

"Instead Of" triggers are so named because the commands in the trigger are executed "instead of" the actual transaction that caused the trigger to be executed. "Instead Of" triggers were created primarily as a method of sending updates to tables referenced in views containing a UNION operator, because these views cannot be directly updated. For information about "Instead Of" triggers and these partitioned views, check out *Beginning T-SQL with Microsoft SQL Server 2005 and 2008* by Paul Turley and Dan Wood (Wiley, 2008).

DDL Triggers

Data Definition Language (DDL) triggers are executed as a result of a DDL command (CREATE, DROP, ALTER) being executed and can be scoped at either the database or server scope. DDL triggers provide the ability to audit or prevent database and server modifications.

The following example demonstrates how to create a database-level DDL trigger to audit modifications made to the database.

First, you create a table to record all the DDL events that occur on the database. Do this by running the following script:

```
USE AdventureWorks2008
GO
CREATE TABLE AuditLog (
   EventID    int IDENTITY(1,1) NOT NULL,
   LoginName  varchar(75) NOT NULL,
   EventTime  datetime NOT NULL,
   DDLEvent   varchar(100) NULL,
```

```
    Eventdata  xml NOT NULL)
GO
```

Next, create a trigger that will execute whenever any DDL level event is executed. This trigger uses a system function called EVENTDATA that returns an XML resultset containing all the information about the DDL event. The trigger uses XQUERY commands to shred the XML data into a relational resultset to be inserted into the audit table.

```
USE AdventureWorks2008
GO

CREATE TRIGGER DatabaseAudit
ON DATABASE
FOR DDL_DATABASE_LEVEL_EVENTS
AS
DECLARE @data XML = EVENTDATA()

INSERT AuditLog(LoginName, EventTime,DDLEvent,EventData)
VALUES
 (SYSTEM_USER
 ,GETDATE()
 ,@data.value('(/EVENT_INSTANCE/TSQLCommand)[1]', 'nvarchar(2000)')
 ,@data)
RETURN
GO
```

Now, test the trigger by creating and dropping a table called TriggerTest and then querying the audit table to see if you captured the information you wanted:

```
USE AdventureWorks2008
GO

CREATE TABLE TriggerTest (
  Column1 int
 ,Column2 int)

DROP TABLE TriggerTest

SELECT * FROM AuditLog
```

You should get two rows that look similar to Figure 5-31 (of course, your LoginName and EventTime will vary).

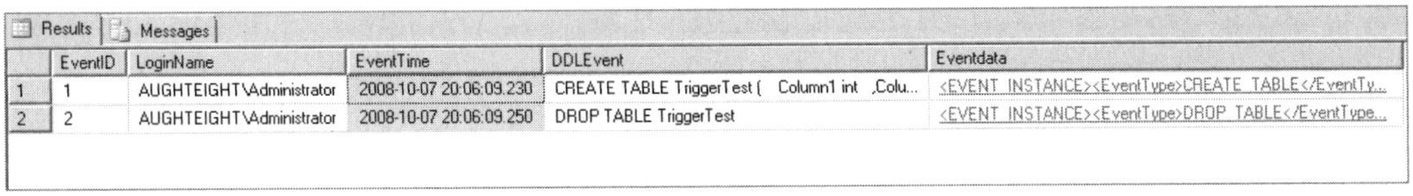

	EventID	LoginName	EventTime	DDLEvent	Eventdata
1	1	AUGHTEIGHT\Administrator	2008-10-07 20:06:09.230	CREATE TABLE TriggerTest (Column1 int ,Colu...	<EVENT_INSTANCE><EventType>CREATE_TABLE</EventTy...
2	2	AUGHTEIGHT\Administrator	2008-10-07 20:06:09.250	DROP TABLE TriggerTest	<EVENT_INSTANCE><EventType>DROP_TABLE</EventType...

Figure 5-31: DDL Trigger Audit results.

To ensure that this trigger does not interfere with other exercises later in the book, you may want to drop it by executing the following command:

```
DROP TRIGGER DatabaseAudit ON DATABASE
```

Assemblies

Assemblies are files that contain database programming objects and are created using Visual Studio. They can include stored procedures, functions, triggers, aggregates, and data types written in any managed language such as C# or Visual Basic.NET. They are directly accessible in the Database Engine through the integration of the Common Language Runtime (CLR). Using managed code offers a significant advantage over traditional Transact-SQL programming in certain situations such as those that require intensive and recursive mathematical operations or complex string manipulation. Chapter 14 describes CLR objects and integration in more detail.

As inferred in Chapter 14, there is a definite tension between database administrators and developers. Often, this tension is exacerbated by the database administrator's lack of programming skills. With the integration of the CLR and the Database Engine, it is more important than ever that the database administrators understand programming and communicate with the developers who interact with their systems.

CLR assemblies can be imported into the database with Visual Studio, Transact-SQL, or with SQL Server Management Studio. This discussion focuses on just Transact-SQL and SQL Server Management Studio. In order for you to follow along with me here, you will need a file to upload. Later in Chapter 14 we will cover the creation of this file, but for now, just use your imagination.

To add a new assembly using SQL Server Management Studio, expand Databases, expand `AdventureWorks2008`, expand Programmability, right-click Assemblies, and click "New Assembly."

In the New Assembly dialog (see Figure 5-32), browse to the assembly, specify an owner for the assembly, and set the permissions for the assembly.

The permission set defines how much access the assembly is given to perform the contained actions. "Safe" limits the assembly to the current database and connection. "External Access" enables the assembly to interact with the operating system, network, and file system. "Unrestricted" allows the assembly all the privileges of External Access, as well as the ability to make calls to unmanaged code. Assembly permission sets are discussed in more detail in Chapters 6 and 14.

Now that the assembly has been added to the database, a stored procedure, function, trigger, type, or aggregate can be added to the database that links to the assembly. (For this exact process, check out Chapter 14.)

Types

Types are a collection of system data types, user-defined data types, user-defined table types, and user-defined types, as well as any XML schema collections used in the database. System data types were covered in Chapter 4, so let's look at the remaining types.

User-Defined Data Types

User-defined data types are aliases for system types. These aliases exist only within the database they are created in. User-defined data types are most often used to provide an intuitive data type name and maintain data type consistency across different tables.

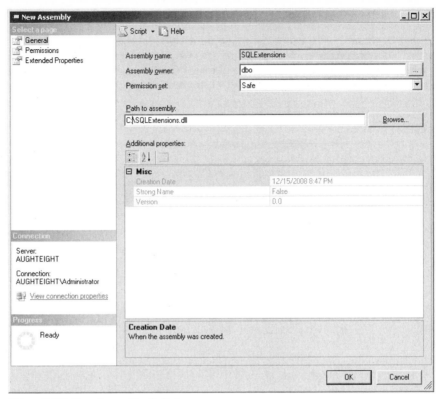

Figure 5-32: New Assembly dialog.

For example, if I were to ask five different database developers to create a table that stores information about an individual, I would most likely get five different solutions. The table will probably contain columns for the individual's last name, first name, address, and phone number, but chances are that the five different database developers would provide at least three differing data types to store any one of the fields specified. For example, one developer may use a varchar(13) to represent a phone number, thinking that phone numbers would be represented as **(111)111-1111**. Another developer may decide to think globally and provide for international codes as well, and specify a phone number of varchar(25). To avoid possible type conflicts later, you can specify that user-defined data types be used.

To create a user-defined data type graphically, expand Databases in Object Explorer, expand AdventureWorks2008, expand Programmability, expand Types, right-click "User-defined data types," and click "New User-defined data type."

Figure 5-33 illustrates the creation of a ZipCode data type in the dbo schema that is based on the system type char(5). User-defined data types can also be bound to database defaults and rules by specifying them in the appropriate textboxes. Defaults and rules are described later in this chapter.

There are a few drawbacks of user-defined data types. For one, they are not transparent to database applications. For example, an application programmer would not be able to instantiate a variable in the application layer that used the `ZipCode` data type. The programmer would have to know that the base type was a `char(5)`. In addition to the application-layer visibility, user-defined data types only exist in the database in which they are created. For example, a `ZipCode` data type in the `AdventureWorks2008` database may not be the same as a `ZipCode` data type in the `AdventureWorksDW2008` database. Also, once created, it cannot be altered. In other words, if later you wanted to change the `ZipCode` data type to be a `char(9)` to hold zip+4, you would have to drop and re-create it. Unfortunately, in order to drop it, it can't be used anywhere.

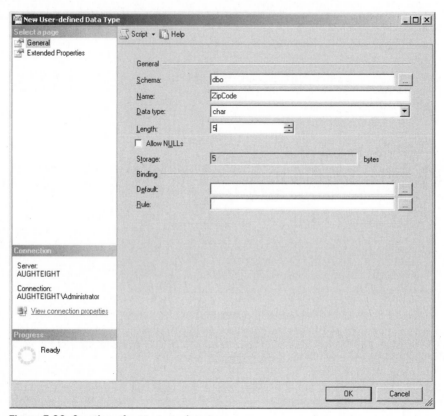

Figure 5-33: Creation of a `ZipCode` data type.

User-Defined Table Types

SQL Server 2008 provides the ability to create user-defined types that represent table definitions. You could use user-defined table types to declare variables or as parameters for stored procedures and functions, making it far easier to work with sets of information. To create a user-defined table type, you use the CREATE TYPE statement providing the definition for the table. The following code creates a table structure that is used to represent a set of customers and then uses it as an input parameter to a stored procedure:

```
CREATE TYPE Customers AS TABLE
( CustomerName varchar (50),
```

```
   CreditLimit decimal,
   Address varchar(50),
   PhoneNumber varchar(10) );
GO

DECLARE @customers Customers
INSERT INTO @customers(CustomerName, CreditLimit, Address, PhoneNumber)
VALUES ('', 2300.00, '', ''),
('', 2300.00, '', ''),
('', 2300.00, '', '')
GO

EXEC usp_AddCustomers @customers
GO
```

The preceding code is for demonstration purposes only and will not function since there is no stored procedure called usp_AddCustomers *in the* AdventureWorks *database.*

User-Defined Types

User-defined types (UDTs) are very similar to user-defined data types, except that they are created using managed code and defined in an assembly that is imported into a SQL Server database. UDTs can be very complex and can define custom data types that have no parallel system type. For example, a UDT could be created to define a true Social Security number data type that really was stored as a number, but didn't truncate leading zeros. Also, we would be able to take advantage of regular expressions in the managed code to validate the Social Security number much more easily and be more accurate.

The other advantage of UDTs is that they are visible from the application layer as well. Because they are defined in an assembly, that assembly can be referenced in a database application so that parameters could be instantiated using the native UDT. But user-defined types are not perfect, and they can be troublesome when it comes to cross-database applications because the UDT is database-specific. However, if the same assembly is referenced in the creation of the UDT in each database, this limitation is reduced. As previously noted, Chapter 14 contains more information about CLR assemblies and the database objects that can be created with them, including UDTs.

Defaults

Instead of creating a default constraint on a column in a table, a stand-alone *default* can be created at the database level and then bound to any table column in the database. Defaults have been marked for deprecation, and it is recommended that you do not use them in any new development work. They are found in the Programmability node of databases in Object Explorer, but must be created with Transact-SQL. The following example demonstrates how to create a default Social Security number and then bind it to the SocSecNum column on the dbo.Driver table:

```
USE AdventureWorks2008
GO
IF EXISTS(SELECT * FROM sys.default_constraints WHERE name = 'DF_Driver_SocSecNum')
        ALTER TABLE dbo.Driver DROP CONSTRAINT DF_Driver_SocSecNum
CREATE DEFAULT dfltSocSecNum AS '000000000'
GO
sp_bindefault 'dfltSocSecNum', 'dbo.Driver.SocSecNum'
```

Rules

Rules, like defaults, have been deprecated. A *rule* is like a check constraint. However, it is created once at the database level and then bound to any column that matches the data type specified. The following example demonstrates how to create a rule that enforces numeric data on a character-based column and then how to bind that rule to the SocSecNum column:

```
USE AdventureWorks2008
GO
CREATE RULE AllNumRule AS
@value LIKE '[0-9][0-9][0-9][0-9][0-9][0-9][0-9][0-9][0-9]'
GO
sp_bindrule 'AllNumRule','dbo.Driver.SocSecNum'
```

Summary

This chapter has covered a great deal of information, and we have barely scratched the surface. An entire book could be written on just the SQL Server database and all the features it includes; however, this is not that book. The purpose of this chapter was to expose you to many of the objects that can be found in a SQL Server database and how to create and manage them. Future chapters dive into various other areas of SQL Server 2008 from the database administrator's perspective.

In Chapter 6, you will look at how to secure a SQL Server 2008 server, database, and all the associated objects that comprise SQL Server. Many new features (such as SQL Server certificates, credentials, and encryption) are described in detail, and it also covers the core security features so that you can ensure your server is as secure as it possibly can be.

SQL Server 2008 Security

Security is often one of the most challenging aspects of designing and managing a database system. As a DBA, you want your servers to be as secure as possible without having to invest an inordinate amount of money or sacrifice user functionality. Unfortunately, many administrators and application developers are often skeptical about the benefits of security, believing that they are somehow immune to the myriad of threats that are out there. In reality, as long as users have access to data, there is a risk of a security breach. So what do you do? Take the SQL Server offline, put it in a locked room that only you have access to, and require that all database requests be processed manually through you?

Security isn't about guaranteeing a completely attack-proof system. It's about mitigating and responding to risk. It's about ensuring that you take the necessary steps to minimize the scope of the attack. Remember that simply giving users access to the database through the network will introduce an element of risk. This chapter takes a look at SQL Security from the outside in. You will learn about the different types of accounts and principals that are available. You will see how to control access to database objects, and how to encrypt and protect your data. This chapter also includes some guidelines for providing a secure solution for deploying and managing your SQL Server.

Because SQL Server 2008 is designed to work with Windows Server 2008, some of the examples in this chapter may behave a little differently in other operating systems, such as Windows Vista, Windows XP, or Windows Server 2003. All examples in this chapter use Windows Server 2008 as the baseline. Also, many of the examples used in this chapter refer to the server AughtEight, which I configured in Chapter 2. Remember to replace *AughtEight* with your own server name.

SQL Server Authentication Modes

Microsoft SQL Server 2008 offers two options for authenticating users. The default mode is *Windows Authentication mode*, which offers a high level of security by using the operating system's authentication mechanism to authenticate credentials that will need access to the server. The other, *SQL Server and Windows Authentication mode*, offers the ability to allow both Windows-based and SQL-based authentications. For this reason, it is also sometimes referred to as *Mixed mode*. Although Windows Authentication mode typically provides better security than SQL Server and Windows Authentication mode, the design of your application may require SQL-based logins.

Windows Authentication mode allows you to use existing accounts stored in the local computer's Security Accounts Manager (SAM) database, or, if the server is a member of an Active Directory domain, accounts in the Microsoft Windows Active Directory database. The benefits of using the Windows Authentication mode include reducing the administrative overhead for your SQL or database administrators by allowing them to use accounts that already exist and the ability to use stronger authentication protocols, such as Kerberos or Windows NT LAN Manager (NTLM).

In Windows Authentication mode, SQL does not store or need to access password information for authentication. The Windows Authentication Provider will be responsible for validating the authenticity of the user.

Mixed mode authentication allows you to create logins that are unique to the SQL Server and do not have a corresponding Windows or Active Directory account. This can be helpful for applications that require users who are not part of your enterprise to be able to authenticate and gain access to securable objects in your database. When SQL logins are used, the SQL Server stores username and password information in the `master` database, and the SQL Server is responsible for authenticating these credentials.

When deciding on the authentication method, it is important to identify how users will be connecting to the database. If the SQL Server and your database users are all members of the same Active Directory forest, or even different forests that share a trust, using Windows Authentication can simplify the process of creating and managing logins. However, if your SQL Server is not in an Active Directory domain or your database users are not internal to your organization, consider the use of SQL-based logins to create a clear distinction between security contexts.

In Chapter 2, you learned how to install Microsoft SQL Server 2008, and you selected which authentication mode to use. If you wish to change the authentication mode after the installation, be aware that this will require you to restart the SQL Server service.

Changing the Authentication Mode from Management Studio

To change the authentication mode from Management Studio, follow these steps:

1. Launch SQL Server Management Studio.
2. In Object Explorer, select your server.
3. Right-click on your server and select Properties.
4. Under the "Select a page" pane, select Security.
5. Under the heading "Server authentication," select or review the appropriate authentication mode (Figure 6-1).

Using the `xp_instance_regwrite` Extended Stored Procedure

You can also change the authentication mode using the `xp_instance_regwrite` extended stored procedure, as long as you have administrative permissions on the local server. The following example shows you how to change the authentication mode to SQL Server and Windows Authentication mode:

```
USE master
EXEC xp_instance_regwrite N'HKEY_LOCAL_MACHINE',
N'Software\Microsoft\MSSQLServer\MSSQLServer', N'LoginMode', REG_DWORD, 2
```

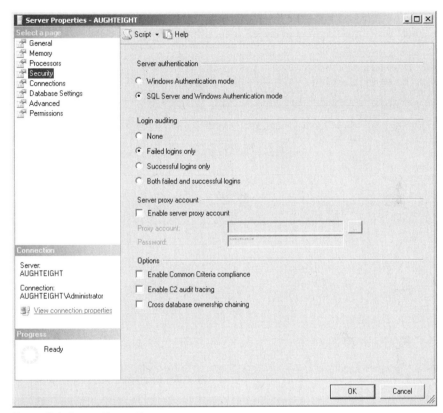

Figure 6-1: Server Properties screen.

You can also change the authentication mode to Windows Authentication mode by changing the DWORD value to 1, as shown in this example:

```
USE master
EXEC xp_instance_regwrite N'HKEY_LOCAL_MACHINE',
N'Software\Microsoft\MSSQLServer\MSSQLServer', N'LoginMode', REG_DWORD, 1
```

During the installation of SQL Server, the sa account is disabled by default. If you are changing the authentication mode from Windows Authentication mode to SQL Server and Windows Authentication mode, the account remains disabled with the password you specified during the Installation Wizard. I recommend against using the sa account in a production environment, especially when multiple people have administrative access to the SQL Server because of the lack of accountability. When multiple people can log in as the sa account, you lose the ability to associate an auditable action with a specific person.

Principals

The term *principal* is used to describe individuals, groups, and processes that will interact with the SQL Server. The resources available to a principal are dependent on where the principal resides. Microsoft SQL Server supports several different types of principals defined at three different levels: the Windows level, the SQL Server level, and the database level. Each type of principal is identified here, and the way they are used. To prepare for some of the exercises in this chapter, you will want to create some local Windows accounts as follows:

  1. From the Start Menu, right-click My Computer and select Manage.

  2. In the Server Manager window, expand Configuration, then "Local Users and Groups" (see Figure 6-2).

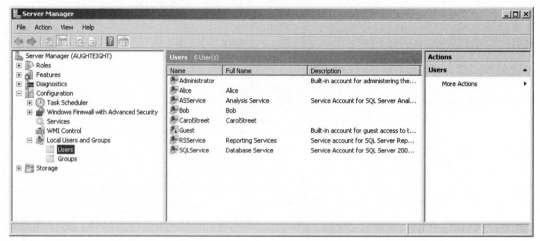

Figure 6-2: Server Management screen.

  3. Right-click on the Users folder and select "New User."

  4. In the User Name box, enter **Bob**.

  5. In the Password and Confirm Password boxes, enter **P@ssw0rd**.

  6. Clear the check next to the "User must change password and next login" box.

  7. Click Create.

  8. In the User Name box, enter **CarolStreet**.

  9. In the Password and Confirm Password boxes, enter **P@ssw0rd**.

  10. Clear the check next to the "User must change password and next login" box.

  11. Click Create.

  12. In the User Name box, enter **Alice**.

  13. In the Password and Confirm Password boxes, enter **P@ssw0rd**.

  14. Clear the check next to the "User must change password and next login" box.

  15. Click Create.

  16. Click Close.

17. Right-click on the Groups folder and select "New Group."

18. In the Group Name Box, enter **G NorthWest Sales**.

19. Click Create.

20. Click Close.

21. Close the Server Manager window.

Logins

Microsoft SQL Server 2008 offers two kinds of logins for authentication. *Windows logins* are associated with user or group accounts stored in the Active Directory or the local Security Accounts Manager (SAM) database. *SQL logins* are used to represent an individual or entity that does not have a Windows account and, therefore, must rely on the SQL Server for storage and management of account information.

Windows logins, whether they represent an individual or a group, are bound by the password policy of either the domain or the SAM in which the account exists. When a login is created for a Windows user or group, no password information is stored in the SQL Server. The password for a Windows login is stored as NULL, but even if this field is populated with a value, the value is ignored. Windows logins are also authenticated prior to connecting to the SQL Server. This means that Active Directory or the operating system will have already verified the principal's identity.

When a Windows login is created for a group, all members of that group have the ability to authenticate against the SQL Server without having to create separate logins for each user.

SQL Server logins, however, must authenticate against the SQL Server. This makes the SQL Server responsible for verifying the user's identity. SQL stores the login and a hash of the login's password information in the master database. It is important that passwords for SQL logins adhere to security best practices, such as enabling complexity requirements, prohibiting non-expiring passwords, and requiring that passwords be changed regularly. In fact, options in Microsoft SQL Server 2008 allow you to enforce requirements for password complexity and expiration for SQL logins based on your Windows or Active Directory policies. Complex passwords are typically defined as having a combination of at least three of the following four criteria:

❑ Uppercase alpha characters

❑ Lowercase alpha characters

❑ Non-negative integers (0–9)

❑ Special characters ($, %, *, &)

> *If the SQL Server is a member of an Active Directory domain, the password policy is usually defined in a Group Policy object linked to the domain. For SQL logins, or logins based on a local Windows account, this may be superseded by a Group Policy object linked to an Organizational Unit. If the SQL Server is not a member of an Active Directory domain, the password policy is defined in the Local Group Policy object or the Local Security Policy (which is a subset of the local GPO).*

Unlike previous versions of SQL, SQL Server 2008 does not automatically create logins for the [BUILTIN\Administrators] group, which would allow anyone with local administrative rights on the server to log in to the SQL Server. Instead, administrators must be added during the user-provisioning step in the Installation Wizard (see Chapter 2), or added to the sysadmin role (discussed later in the chapter) after installation. A SQL login, sa, is also created. The sa account has full administrative access to all SQL functions. During installation, you are prompted to specify a password for the sa account. Regardless of whether you install SQL Server using Windows Authentication mode or Mixed mode, the sa account is disabled and remains disabled until you choose to enable the account.

Another new feature in SQL Server 2008 is the ability to create a SQL Server login that is mapped to a certificate or asymmetric key through the GUI. SQL Server 2005 had allowed this mapping to be created only through T-SQL. This mapping must be specified during login creation, and the certificate or asymmetric key must be created before the login can be mapped to it. Creation and management of certificates and symmetric keys are covered later in this chapter.

Creating Logins in Management Studio

To create logins from Management Studio, follow these steps:

1. From Object Explorer, expand your server.
2. Expand the Security folder.
3. Right-click Logins and select "New Login."
4. In the Login–New dialog box (see Figure 6-3), either type the Login name you want to add or click the Search button to browse for a Windows account.

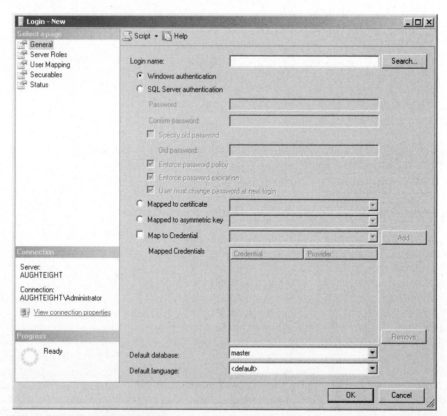

Figure 6-3: New login dialog box.

5.   If you are creating a SQL Login, select the "SQL Server authentication" radio button.

6.   Also, when you select "SQL Server authentication," you can choose not to enforce the password policies.

7.   You may also want to change the user's default database and language.

Try It Out   **Creating a New Login for Alice**

To create a new login for Alice, follow these steps:

1.   From Object Explorer, expand your server.

2.   Expand the Security folder.

3.   Right-click Logins and select "New Login."

4.   In the New Login dialog box, click Search.

5.   In the "Select User or Group" dialog box, type **Alice** and click OK.

6.   Select `AdventureWorks2008` as the default database.

7.   Click OK.

Creating Logins Using T-SQL

Alternatively, you can use the CREATE LOGIN statement. CREATE LOGIN allows you to create either Windows or SQL logins. This statement is designed to replace two stored procedures that were used in previous versions of SQL, `sp_grantlogin` and `sp_addlogin`. Both of these stored procedures are still available in SQL Server 2008, primarily for backward compatibility, but they have been deprecated and may be removed in a future version of SQL. Use the following format for the CREATE LOGIN statement:

```
CREATE LOGIN [name] {WITH <options> | FROM <source>}
```

The following tables show the options available with this statement:

Option	Description
`PASSWORD = 'password'`	Creates a new password for SQL logins. If this value is already hashed, use the HASHED option. Passwords are case-sensitive. See the "Best Practices" section in this chapter for more information on password guidelines.
`HASHED`	When a password is created for a SQL login, the password is stored in the database using a one-way hashing algorithm. This provides several benefits. Because the password is not stored in plain text, it cannot be read by simply querying a system view. Because the hashing process is one-way, the password cannot be extrapolated from the hash value. This also secures the password in transmission, because the SQL Authentication process will send the hashed value of the password, not the actual plain-text password.

Continued

Option	Description
MUST_CHANGE	Requires the user to change his or her password at the next login. This is valid for SQL logins only. CHECK_POLICY and CHECK_EXPIRATION must be set to ON for this to work.
CREDENTIAL = credential_name	Maps an existing credential to a login. Credentials are discussed later in this chapter.
SID = sid	Allows you to manually specify a SID (Security Identifier) for a new user. If this value is left blank, the SID will be automatically generated.
DEFAULT_DATABASE = database	Assigns the default database for the login. If not specified, the master database will be assumed. This should be configured to a user database for most business users.
DEFAULT_LANGUAGE = language	Assigns the default language for the login. If not specified, the default language of the server at the time the login was created will be used. This will not change if the server's default language is changed.
CHECK_POLICY = { ON | OFF }	This statement allows you to enforce your Windows-based password policies to SQL logins. This is ON by default.
CHECK_EXPIRATION = { ON | OFF }	A complement to the CHECK_POLICY option, this allows your Windows-based password expiration policy to also apply to SQL logins. If CHECK_POLICY is ON, then this will default to ON. Otherwise, the default value is OFF.

Sources	Description
WINDOWS	Identifies that a login will be created based on an existing Windows user or group.
CERTIFICATE certname	Associates a pre-existing certificate with a login. Certificates are discussed later in this chapter.
ASYMMETRIC KEY asym_key_name	Associates a pre-existing asymmetric key with a login. Symmetric and Asymmetric keys are discussed later in this chapter.

SQL Server will automatically hash a password before storing it in the database. Be careful about using the HASHED option unless you are sure that the password you are supplying has already been hashed by SQL Server. For example, if you type the following statement:

```
CREATE LOGIN Bill WITH PASSWORD = 'P@ssw0rd' HASHED
```

SQL will assume that P@ssw0rd is a hash of another value. So, when Alice tries to log in with P@ssw0rd, the authentication will fail. You can use the loginproperty function to obtain the hashed value of an existing user's password, as shown in the following example:

```
SELECT LOGINPROPERTY('bill', 'passwordhash')
```

Managing Logins

SQL Server Management Studio includes several property sheets to configure logins, which are addressed later in this chapter. In addition to the General property sheet, you should also be familiar with the Status page, which allows you to enable or disable the login, unlock the login, and specifically grant or deny access to connect to this SQL Server.

From the General property sheet, you can change the following attributes:

❏ Password

❏ Password Policy

❏ Password Expiration

❏ Force the user to change the password at the next login

❏ Default Database

❏ Default Language

Logins can also be managed using the ALTER LOGIN statement. In addition to many of the options listed previously for the CREATE LOGIN statement, the ALTER LOGIN statement uses the following format:

```
ALTER LOGIN name {<status> | WITH <options>}
```

The following table shows the additional options available with this statement:

Option	Description
Status {Enable | Disable}	Enables or disables the login as needed.
OLD_PASSWORD = 'oldpassword'	Specifies the current password when changing the password for the login. The HASHED keyword cannot be used when specifying an old password.
NAME = login_name	Allows you to rename a login. If renaming a Windows-based login, the SID of the Windows object must match the SID for the login in SQL Server. SQL Server–based logins must not contain a backslash (\) character.
NO CREDENTIAL	Removes the mapping between the login and a server credential.
UNLOCK	A SQL Server login may become locked out after too many invalid password attempts. If that occurs, this option can remove the lock.
ADD CREDENTIAL	Associates an Extensible Key Management (EKM) provider credential to the login. EKM is covered later in this chapter.
DROP CREDENTIAL	Removes an associated Extensible Key Management (EKM) provider credential from the login. EKM is covered later in this chapter.

Using CREATE LOGIN

To create a new login in Transact-SQL, use the CREATE LOGIN statement. The following example creates a new login for a user account named *Bob* on the AughtEight server:

```
CREATE LOGIN [AughtEight\Bob] from Windows;
GO
```

To create a new login for a Windows group, use the following example:

```
CREATE LOGIN [AughtEight\G NorthWest Sales] from Windows;
GO
```

To create a new SQL Server login for Carol, use the following syntax:

```
CREATE LOGIN Carol
WITH PASSWORD = 'Th1sI$|\/|yP@ssw0rd';
GO
```

To change Carol's password to use the all-lowercase *newpassword*, use the following command:

```
ALTER LOGIN Carol WITH PASSWORD = 'newpassword',
CHECK_POLICY=OFF;
GO
```

To remove an existing login, use the DROP LOGIN statement. For example, if you want to remove Bob's login (remember, Bob has a Windows-based login), use the following:

```
DROP LOGIN [AughtEight\Bob];
GO
```

For More Information

For backward compatibility, Microsoft SQL Server 2008 supports the stored procedures for managing logins listed in the following table. Because these stored procedures have been deprecated, you should use the CREATE LOGIN and ALTER LOGIN statements.

Stored Procedure	Description
sp_grantlogin:	Creates a new Windows-based login.
sp_revokelogin:	Removes a Windows-based login.
sp_addlogin:	Creates a new SQL Server login.
sp_droplogin:	Removes a SQL Server–based login.

Credentials

Microsoft SQL Server 2008 also includes a feature for mapping SQL Server logins to external Windows accounts. This can be extremely useful if you need to allow SQL Server logins to interact with the resources outside the scope of the SQL Server itself (such as a linked server or a local file system). They can also be used with assemblies that are configured for EXTERNAL_ACCESS permissions.

Credentials can be configured as a one-to-one mapping or a many-to-one mapping, allowing multiple SQL Server logins to use one shared Windows account for external access. In SQL Server 2008, logins can now be associated with multiple credentials, whereas SQL Server 2005 only allows a login to be mapped to a single credential. Credentials can also be configured to use an EKM provider

Creating a New Credential

When creating a new credential, follow these steps:

1. In Object Explorer, expand your server.

2. Expand the Security folder.

3. Right-click Credentials and select "New Credential" (see Figure 6-4).

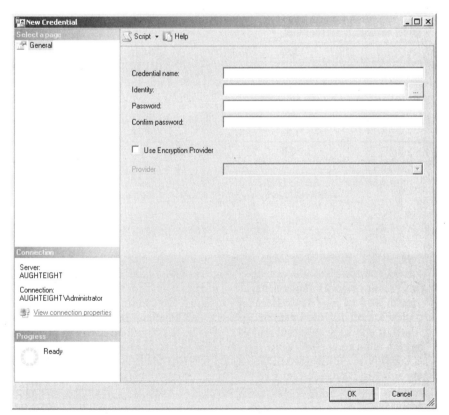

Figure 6-4: New Credential properties screen.

4. Type a name for the credential.

5. In the Identity section, either type the name of a Windows account or click the " ... " button to browse for an account.

6. Enter the password for the account.

7. Re-enter the password to confirm.

8. Enable Use Encryption Provider (if desired).

9. Select a valid External Key Management provider (if the above option is selected).

10. Click OK.

Using Transact-SQL

You can use the CREATE CREDENTIAL statement as an alternative means to create a new SQL credential object. The syntax is as follows:

```
CREATE CREDENTIAL name WITH IDENTITY = 'identity_name' [, SECRET = 'secret']
  [FOR CRYPTOGRAPHIC_PROVIDER provider_name]
```

Likewise, the ALTER CREDENTIAL statement can be used to alter the name of the credential, the identity it's associated with, and the password. Once the credential is no longer needed, it can be removed with the DROP CREDENTIAL command, as follows:

```
DROP CREDENTIAL name
```

Try It Out   Create a New Credential for a Windows Account

Earlier in the chapter, you created a Windows account named CarolStreet with a password of P@ssw0rd. You will now create a new credential named StreetCred for that user. When running the following script, replace *AughtEight* with your own server name:

```
USE master
CREATE CREDENTIAL StreetCred
WITH IDENTITY = 'AughtEight\CarolStreet',
SECRET = 'P@ssw0rd';
GO
```

You can then associate Carol's SQL Server login with the StreetCred credential:

```
ALTER LOGIN Carol WITH CREDENTIAL = StreetCred;
GO
```

Server Roles

Microsoft SQL Server 2008 defines eight server-level roles that are available to simplify management (and the delegation of management) for SQL logins. These are often referred to as *fixed server roles* because membership is the only thing you can change about these roles. The fixed server roles are designed to allow you to automatically assign a common set of permissions to a login, based on the purpose of the role.

Additionally, SQL Server 2008 also includes a public server role. In addition to customizing the member list of the public server role, you can also define protocol-specific permissions for Tabular Data Stream

(TDS) endpoints. These endpoints are covered in more detail in Chapter 7. By default, all logins are members of the `public` server role.

Using Fixed Server Roles

The following table shows the fixed server roles in the order they appear on the server:

Role	Description
sysadmin	Members have full administrative access to the SQL Server and can perform any action. Users and groups added through the User Provisioning function of SQL Server setup are added to this group.
serveradmin	Members of this role can change server-wide configurations and shut down the server.
securityadmin	Members can manage SQL logins, including changing and resetting passwords as needed, as well as managing GRANT, REVOKE, and DENY permissions at the server and database levels.
dbcreator	Members can create, drop, alter, and restore any database for the server.
diskadmin	Members can manage disk files for the server and all databases.
processadmin	Members can manage and terminate processes on the SQL Server.
setupadmin	Members can add and remove linked servers.
bulkadmin	Members of this role can execute the BULK INSERT statement for any database on the server.

To add a login to a fixed server role, use the `sp_addsrvrolemember` stored procedure. The stored procedure uses the following format:

```
sp_addsrvrolemember [ @loginame= ] 'login' , [ @rolename = ] 'role'
```

Simply provide the login name and the role name. To add Ted to the `securityadmin` role, use the following command:

```
USE master
CREATE LOGIN Ted WITH PASSWORD = 'P@ssw0rd';
GO
EXEC sp_addsrvrolemember 'Ted', 'securityadmin';
GO
```

Use `sp_dropsrvrolemember` to remove a login from a fixed server role. The syntax is similar to the `sp_addsrvrolemember` stored procedure, as shown in the following example:

```
USE master
EXEC sp_dropsrvrolemember 'Ted', 'securityadmin';
GO
```

For More Information

You can query the Security Catalog Views to find out more information about principals at the server scope. The following table shows views that identify server-level principals:

View	Description
sys.server_principals	Returns information about all server-level principals.
sys.sql_logins	Returns information about SQL Server logins.
sys.server_role_members	Returns the role ID and member ID for each member of a server role.
sys.credentials	Returns a list of all credentials configured on the SQL Server.
sys.server_principal_ credentials	Returns a list containing the principal_id and credential_id for each principal mapped to a credential.

Database Users

Database users are another component of the security model employed by Microsoft SQL Server 2008. Users are granted access to securable database objects, either directly or through membership in one or more database roles. Users are also associated with ownership of objects such as tables, views, and stored procedures.

When a login is created, unless it is a member of a fixed server role with administrative privileges to all databases, that login has no explicit permissions within the various databases attached to the server. When this happens, the login is associated with the guest database user and inherits the permissions of that user account.

When managing database users in SQL Server Management Studio, you have several options from which to select. On the General property sheet (see Figure 6-5), you will be able to specify a name for the user and associate the user with an existing login. Note that the username does not have to match the login name. For ease of administration, it is best practice to try to use a consistent naming convention, but it is not required. Also, note that there are radio buttons that show whether the user is mapped to a login, a certificate, a key, or without any association. Through the Graphical User Interface (GUI), you can only create a user mapped to a login. In the next section, you see how to create users with other mappings.

Other options you can configure from the General page include specifying the user's default schema, schemas owned by this user (if any), and to which database roles the user belongs. In the Securables page, you can list all the securable objects the user has permissions to and what permissions they have. Finally, you have the Extended Properties page, which allows you to designate or view additional metadata information about this user.

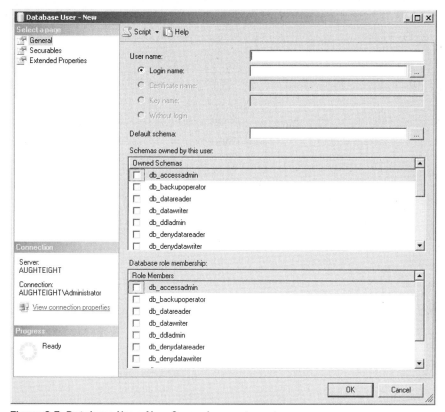

Figure 6-5: Database User–New General property page.

Try It Out   Create a New User and Default Schema

For this example, you will create a new database user in the `AdventureWorks2008` database for Carol and set her default schema to the `Sales` schema.

1. In Object Explorer, expand Databases.

2. Expand `AdventureWorks2008` (see Figure 6-6).

3. Expand Security.

4. Right-click Users and select "New User."

5. Type **Carol** in the User Name box.

6. Type **Carol** in the "Login name" box, or select her login using the "..." button.

7. Type **Sales** in the "Default schema" box.

8. Click OK.

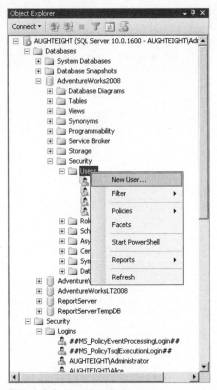

Figure 6-6: New database user.

Now that Carol has a database user account in the `AdventureWorks2008` database, she has inherited the permissions granted to the public database role. Database roles and permissions are covered later in this chapter.

CREATE USER

The `CREATE USER` statement can also be used for creating new database users. `CREATE USER` offers more options over how the user is created than the GUI allows. For example, you can create a user based on an existing certificate or key, or even create a user who is not associated with a login. Although reasons for implementing these types of users will be limited, they can have access to database objects without being associated with a specific login. They can be used to access resources that have specific security requirements. For example, a stored procedure might contain the `EXECUTE AS` clause, in which case, the stored procedure runs as the user associated with a particular certificate, or asymmetric key. The caveat, though, is that these users are valid only in the database in which they were created. If they attempt to access resources in another database, they will access the other database as `guest`. If the `guest` user is disabled in the other database, then they will be denied access.

Each database has two users created by default. The `dbo` user (also known as the *database owner*) has all rights and privileges to perform any operation in the database. Members of the fixed server role, `sysadmin`, as well as the `sa` account, are mapped to `dbo`. Any object created by a `sysadmin` is automatically owned by `dbo`. The `dbo` user is also the owner of the default schema, also called `dbo`. The `dbo` user cannot be deleted.

The `guest` account is also present in every database, but is disabled by default. The `guest` account is commonly used when a person has login access to the SQL Server, but no explicit user access to a database. If the database has a `guest` account and it is enabled, then the login will connect to that database with guest access. `guest` is a member of the `public` role and has all of the permissions assigned to that role, but can be granted explicit permissions to securables as well.

You may also notice two other "users," `sys` and `INFORMATION_SCHEMA`. Although they are not users in the conventional sense, they do own objects in the database, primarily for storing and retrieving metadata. These users are not mapped to any login and are disabled by default.

The following is the syntax and options for the `CREATE USER` statement:

```
CREATE USER name [{{FOR | FROM} source | WITHOUT LOGIN]
    [WITH DEFAULT_SCHEMA = schema_name]
```

The following tables explain the options that are available:

Source Options	Description
Login login_name	This option specifies the login name to associate with this user. If this value is not present, SQL Server assumes that the user you are trying to create is using the same name as an existing login. If there is not a login with the same name as the user, the operation will fail.
CERTIFICATE cert_name	This option allows you to create a user associated with a certificate, rather than with a login. The certificate must already exist in this database for the operation to succeed. Certificates are discussed later in this chapter.
ASYMMETRIC KEY key_name	This option allows you to create a user associated with an asymmetric key, rather than with a login. The asymmetric key must already exist in the database. Keys are discussed later in this chapter.

Other Options	Description
WITHOUT LOGIN	This option allows you to designate that the user is created without any association to a login, or other objects such as asymmetric keys or certificates.
WITH DEFAULT_SCHEMA = schema	This option lets you specify the schema in which the user will operate. The benefit to users is that whenever they create or access an object within their default schema, they can use the object name by itself. The users may still be able to access objects in other schemas, permission allowing, by using the `schema.object` naming convention.

Try It Out   Create a New User

Take a look at the CREATE USER statement in action. In an earlier example, you created a new SQL Server login called Carol and an associated user in the AdventureWorks2008 database. If you wanted to create a user for Carol in the tempdb database, you could execute the following statement:

```
USE tempdb;
CREATE USER Carol;
GO
```

That's all there is to creating a new user.

Look at another example. If you executed the DROP LOGIN [AughtEight\Bob] statement earlier, you'll need to re-create his login. In this example, you'll create a database user named BillyBob who will be mapped to Bob's login, and set BillyBob's default schema to the Sales schema:

```
USE master;
CREATE LOGIN [AughtEight\Bob] FROM WINDOWS;
USE AdventureWorks2008;
CREATE USER BillyBob FOR LOGIN [AughtEight\Bob]
WITH DEFAULT_SCHEMA = sales;
```

The last example shows creating a new user from an existing certificate. Certificates are covered later in this chapter, but for this example, create the certificate first, and then create the user:

```
USE AdventureWorks2008;
CREATE CERTIFICATE SalesCert
    ENCRYPTION BY PASSWORD = 'P@ssw0rd'
    WITH SUBJECT = 'Sales Schema Certificate',
    EXPIRY_DATE = '12/31/2010';
GO
CREATE USER SalesSecurity FOR CERTIFICATE SalesCert;
GO
```

You can also use the ALTER USER statement to make changes to a user account. This is another example where Transact-SQL gives you greater flexibility than Management Studio. ALTER SCHEMA lets you modify both the name property and the DEFAULT_SCHEMA property. If you wish to change the Windows or SQL login that the account is associated with, you can use the LOGIN = option, as well. Be aware that the LOGIN option can only be used to associate a user to a login that is the same type as the one it was originally created as. This will not work for users created as certificate or keys. These options are illustrated in the following examples:

```
USE AdventureWorks2008
ALTER USER SalesSecurity
WITH NAME = SalesSchemaSecurity;
GO

USE AdventureWorks2008
ALTER USER BillyBob
WITH DEFAULT_SCHEMA = Production;
GO

--Create a new login
```

```
USE master
CREATE LOGIN TempCarol WITH PASSWORD = 'MyPassword',
CHECK_POLICY = OFF;
GO
USE tempdb
ALTER USER Carol WITH Login = TempCarol;
GO
```

Finally, once a user has outlived its usefulness, use the DROP USER statement to remove it from the database. The DROP USER statement is straightforward, as seen in the following example:

```
USE AdventureWorks2008
DROP USER BillyBob;
GO
```

Older versions of SQL explicitly tied an object owner into the naming context of the object. For example, if a user named BillyBob created a table called Orders, the table would be called BillyBob.Orders. SQL Server 2008 allows you to separate an object's schema from its owner. This helps to minimize orphaned objects when a user is dropped by keeping those objects part of a schema that may be owned by a role or a Windows group. Although it was easier to manage objects that were all owned by dbo, as seen in previous versions, using schemas helps provide a more logical, hierarchical security design.

Fixed Database Roles

Every SQL database has a list of fixed database roles that allow you to delegate permissions to users as necessary. As with the fixed server roles, membership is the only thing you can change about these roles. It is important to know how and when to use these roles.

The following table shows the fixed database roles:

Role	Description
db_accessadmin	This role can add or remove access for Windows logins, Windows groups, and SQL Server logins.
db_backupoperator	This role has the right to back up the database.
db_datareader	Members of this role can read data from all user tables.
db_datawriter	Members of this role can write data to all user tables.
db_ddladmin	This role can execute data definition language (DDL) statements for any object in the database.
db_denydatareader	This role is explicitly excluded from being able to read from any user table with the database.
db_denydatawriter	This role is explicitly excluded from being able to write to any table in the database.

Continued

Role	Description
db_owner	Members of this role can perform any activity within the database. This role can also drop the database from the server. The dbo user is automatically a member of this role.
db_securityadmin	This role can manage permissions and role membership within the database.
public	Membership in the public role is automatic. Permissions that apply to the public role apply to everyone who accesses the database.

Note that the fixed database roles include db_denydatareader and db_denydatawriter. These roles explicitly deny Read or Write access to user tables in the database and should be used sparingly. Deny permissions are authoritative and cannot be overridden.

User-defined database roles offer greater control over managing permissions and access to resources within a database. Frequently, when using a role-based security model, you may find that built-in principals (such as groups in Windows or roles in SQL) offer either too much access or not enough. In this case, you can create user-defined roles that allow you to control access to securable objects for an entire collection of users at once. Database roles are very similar in concept to Windows groups. You can create a database role to identify a group of users, all of whom need access to a common set of resources, or you can use roles to identify the permissions being granted to a securable in the database. Regardless of the purpose of your role, its function should be clearly identified by the name of the role.

Creating a New User-Defined Database Role in Management Studio

In the New Role dialog box, you are prompted to provide a name for the role, as well as identify an owner for the role. The owner of the role can modify it at any time. You can also select existing schemas that will be owned by this role and add users as members to this role. In addition to the General property sheet, you also have the Securables page and the Extended Properties page, which you can use to assign permissions or set additional attributes, respectively.

In this example, you can create a new database role called ProductionRole and then add Carol as a member:

1. In Object Explorer, expand Databases.

2. Expand AdventureWorks2008 and then expand Security.

3. Expand Roles and then expand Database Roles.

4. Right-click "Database Roles" and select "New Database Role."

5. In the "Role name" box, type **ProductionRole** (see Figure 6-7).

6. Under the list of members of this role (which should be empty), click Add.

7. Enter **Carol** in the window and click "Check Names." This should resolve her name. Click OK.

8. In the Database Role–New window, click OK.

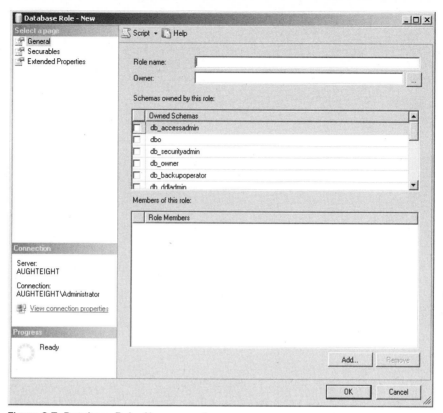

Figure 6-7: Database Role–New properties screen.

CREATE ROLE

CREATE ROLE is the Transact-SQL equivalent for creating a new user-defined database role. When using the CREATE ROLE statement as shown here, you can also specify the owner of the role. Note that if you are assigning a user as the owner of a role, you must have the IMPERSONATE permission, and if you're assigning another role as the owner, you must either be a member of that role or have ALTER permission on the role. The following statement creates a role called SalesStaff, designating Carol as the owner:

```
USE AdventureWorks2008
CREATE ROLE SalesStaff
AUTHORIZATION Carol;
GO
```

The ALTER ROLE statement is fairly limited, allowing you to change only the name of the role:

```
USE AdventureWorks2008
ALTER ROLE SalesStaff
WITH NAME = SalesStaffRole;
GO
```

`DROP ROLE rolename` will let you remove a role from the database once it is no longer needed:

```
USE AdventureWorks2008
DROP ROLE SalesStaffRole;
GO
```

As with fixed server roles, database roles (both fixed and user-defined) can have users added to them either through SQL Server Management Studio or through a stored procedure. The stored procedure for database roles is `sp_addrolemember`. Unlike the stored procedures for adding and dropping members from server roles, `sp_addrolemember` and `sp_droprolemember` identify the role as the first variable and the user as the second.

The following example adds the database user `Carol` to the `db_datareader` role:

```
USE AdventureWorks2008
EXEC sp_addrolemember 'db_datareader', 'Carol';
GO
```

To remove Carol from the `db_datareader` role, use the following stored procedure:

```
USE AdventureWorks2008
EXEC sp_droprolemember 'db_datareader', 'Carol';
GO
```

Application Roles

Another type of role that can be used to help secure the database environment is the *application role*. Application roles are quite different from standard role types. They do not have members, and they can (and should) be configured to authenticate with a password. Application roles are typically used when database access must be the same for all users who run a particular application. Rather than depending on the individual user to have the appropriate access for the application to work properly, the application can instantiate the application role without prompting the user to provide a username and password.

You can create a new application role from the Application Roles folder within SQL Server Management Studio. The dialog box for creating a new application role is very similar to the standard database role dialog, with the exception of the password field and the lack of a members list.

Try It Out   Create an Application Role

In this example, you create a new application role named `PurchasingOrderEntry`, with a password of `POEpass1`:

1. In Object Explorer, expand Databases.
2. Expand `AdventureWorks2008` and then expand Security.
3. Expand Roles and then expand Application Roles.
4. Right-click "Application Roles" and select "New Application Role."
5. Type **PurchasingOrderEntry** for the Role name (see Figure 6-8).

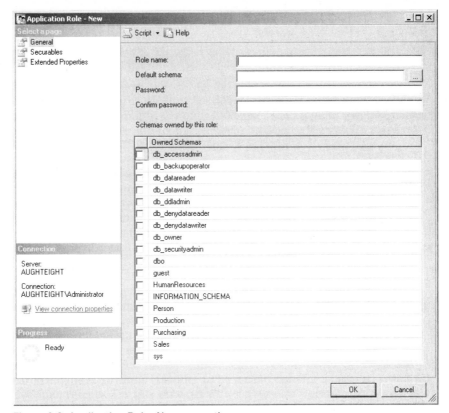

Figure 6-8: Application Role–New properties screen.

6.   Set the Default schema to "Purchasing."

7.   Enter **POEpass1** in the Password and "Confirm password" boxes.

8.   Click OK.

In the next section, you see how to instantiate that role.

Using CREATE APPLICATION ROLE

The CREATE APPLICATION ROLE does what the name suggests. When using this statement, specify the name of the application role, a password for the application role, and, optionally, a default schema for the application role. The following example creates an application role named SalesApp:

```
USE AdventureWorks2008
CREATE APPLICATION ROLE SalesApp
WITH PASSWORD = 'P@ssw0rd',
DEFAULT_SCHEMA = Sales;
GO
```

To use an application role, you can execute the `sp_setapprole` stored procedure. This can be called from an application, or you can test it from your Query window. The stored procedure includes options to activate the application role by providing an encrypted password, creating a cookie, and setting information in the cookie. The following command activates the `SalesApp` application role and then returns the username:

```
USE AdventureWorks2008
GO
DECLARE @cookie varbinary(8000);
EXEC sp_setapprole 'SalesApp', 'P@ssw0rd'
    , @fCreateCookie = true, @cookie = @cookie OUTPUT;
GO
SELECT USER_NAME();
```

Once you've executed the preceding script, all activity performed from that connection operates under the application role. When the connection is closed, the application role session ends.

With the `ALTER APPLICATION ROLE` statement, you can change the name of the application role, the password, and the default schema. The following example changes the `SalesApp` role name to `OrderEntry` and sets a new password:

```
USE AdventureWorks2008
ALTER APPLICATION ROLE SalesApp
WITH NAME = OrderEntry,
PASSWORD = 'newP@ssw0rd';
GO
```

If you intend to run the `ALTER APPLICATION ROLE` script listed previously, ensure that you don't do it while connected as that application role. Opening a new Query window under your own credentials will prevent errors.

`DROP APPLICATION ROLE rolename` will remove an application role from the database. Ensure that you do not have any applications still using the application role; otherwise, the application will be unable to connect to the database. For example:

```
USE AdventureWorks2008
DROP APPLICATION ROLE OrderEntry;
GO
```

For More Information

The following Security Catalog Views can be used to identify which principals exist in your database, and their role membership:

View	Description
sys.database_principals	Returns information about all database-level principals.
sys.database_role_members	Returns the ID of each database role and its members.

For backward compatibility, Microsoft SQL Server 2008 supports the following stored procedures. Keep in mind that these stored procedures are considered "legacy" tools and may disappear in a future update or release of SQL Server.

Stored Procedure	Description
sp_adduser	Creates a new database user.
sp_grantdbaccess	Creates a new database user.
sp_dropuser	Removes a database user.
sp_revokedbaccess	Removes a database user.
sp_addrole	Creates a new user-defined database role.
sp_droprole	Removes a user-defined database role.
sp_addapprole	Creates a new application role.
sp_approlepassword	Changes the password for an application role.
sp_dropapprole	Removes an application role from the database.

Permissions

A well-implemented security solution answers three questions about security access. Who are you? What can you do? And what have you done? The Kerberos security protocol, which was developed at MIT, is designed to answer these questions through the processes of Authentication (who are you?), Authorization (what can you do?), and Auditing (what have you done?). In an Active Directory forest, SQL Server uses Microsoft's implementation of the Kerberos protocol (named after the three-headed dog who guarded the entrance to Hades), for the Authentication of logins that are associated with Active Directory accounts. Permissions, or Authorizations, are managed from within SQL Server itself and may be configured on server or database objects.

A typical statement to define the permissions on an object or resource will be structured to define a permission state, an action, the object to which the permission and action will apply, and the security principal to whom the permission and action will apply on the defined object. Put simply, it will look like the following:

```
PermissionState Action ON Object TO Principal
```

or

```
GRANT SELECT ON Person.EmailAddress TO Carol
```

To begin with, you should understand there are essentially three permission states that exist: GRANT, GRANT_W_GRANT, and DENY. In addition, when a principal does not have an explicit permission defined, the permission is considered "revoked." The following table shows the different permission states:

Permission	Description
GRANT	This state means that you have been given the right to perform this action or interact with this resource based on what the actual permission is.
GRANT_W_GRANT	Not only can you perform this action, but you also have the right to give others the ability to perform this action.
DENY	You cannot perform this action. This is also known as an "explicit deny" because nothing will allow you to perform this action.
REVOKE	This is not really a permission state as much as it is the absence of a permission state. Revoked permissions will not show up in a sysprotects table or sys.sysprotects view, and are considered an "implicit deny." The idea is that if you haven't been granted this permission, either directly or indirectly, such as through membership in a role with that permission, it is safe to assume that you shouldn't be doing that. Therefore, you will not be doing that.

To control permission states, you can use Object Explorer or Transact-SQL. The three commands that you can use to control permission states are GRANT, REVOKE, and DENY, which are described in the following table:

Command	Description
GRANT	This command allows you to grant the right to perform an action or interact with an object in a specific way. The GRANT statement includes the WITH GRANT OPTION statement, which also allows the grantee the ability to become a grantor of this permission. Note that WITH GRANT OPTION follows the TO *Principal* portion of the command.
REVOKE	This command removes any explicit permission granted to the grantee, either grant or deny. Revoked permissions will remove the ability to perform that task. Remember that if the user is a member of another role, he or she may still have the ability to perform the action, unless an explicit deny is specified.
DENY	This command creates an entry that will prevent the user from performing the action. Denied permissions cannot be overridden by grant permissions. For example, if a user specifically had deny insert permission on a table, but belonged to a role that was given grant insert permission on that same table, the user's deny permission would win.

The following table shows a general list of the actions you can grant, deny, or revoke, and the types of objects on which you can grant them. A short description is provided for each:

Action	Description	Securable
SELECT	Controls the ability to retrieve data.	❑ Synonyms ❑ Table-valued functions ❑ Tables and columns ❑ Views and columns
INSERT	Controls the ability to add a new row to a table or view.	❑ Synonyms ❑ Tables and columns ❑ Views and columns
UPDATE	Controls the ability to change data rows in a table or view.	❑ Synonyms ❑ Tables and columns ❑ Views and columns
DELETE	Controls the ability to remove data rows from a table or view.	❑ Synonyms ❑ Tables and columns ❑ Views and columns
EXECUTE	Controls the ability to launch programmability objects.	❑ Procedures ❑ Scalar and aggregate functions ❑ Synonyms
ALTER	Controls the ability to change all the properties of an object except ownership. ALTER ANY can also be used when assigning permissions to all objects of a specific type at the server scope.	❑ Procedures ❑ Scalar and aggregate functions ❑ Service Broker queues ❑ Tables ❑ Table-valued functions ❑ Views
REFERENCES	Allows a user to write to an object (using an INSERT or UPDATE statement) that contains a foreign key reference without having SELECT permissions on the underlying object.	❑ Scalar and aggregate functions ❑ Service Broker queues ❑ Tables and columns ❑ Table-valued functions ❑ Views and columns

Continued

227

Action	Description	Securable
VIEW DEFINITION	Controls the ability to return metadata information about objects.	☐ Procedures ☐ Service Broker queues ☐ Scalar and aggregate functions ☐ Synonyms ☐ Tables ☐ Table-valued functions ☐ Views
VIEW CHANGE TRACKING	Allows the user to view Change Tracking information for objects on which it is enabled.	☐ Tables ☐ Schemas
TAKE OWNERSHIP	Controls the ability to take ownership of an object. Object owners can change permissions of the object.	☐ Procedures ☐ Scalar and aggregate functions ☐ Synonyms ☐ Tables ☐ Table-valued functions ☐ Views
CONTROL	Controls the ability to have full control of an object. This is similar to the ALTER permission but includes TAKE OWNERSHIP.	☐ Procedures ☐ Scalar and aggregate functions ☐ Service Broker queues ☐ Tables ☐ Table-valued functions ☐ Views
RECEIVE	Controls the ability to retrieve one or more messages from a queue.	Service Broker queues

Now that you understand the permissions and permission states, take a look at the specific permissions available. SQL Server 2008 uses a hierarchical security model that allows you to specify permissions that can be granted at the server, database, schema, or object levels. You can also assign permissions within tables and views for selected columns.

The next section identifies the scopes in which the different securable objects reside and how you can use them to control access to your data. Best practices recommend using a role-based administrative model to simplify the process of creating a secure environment, not only for your databases and database servers, but also for all of your operations.

There are two key strategies you should use when securing your database servers:

❑ The first strategy you should use when granting permissions is known as the *principle of least privilege*. This strategy mandates that you give your users appropriate permissions to do their jobs, and nothing more. By keeping such tight constraints on your database environment, you can offer a solution that minimizes the attack surface of your servers while maintaining operational functionality.

❑ The second key strategy is *defense in depth*. A good security implementation will provide security at all layers of a database application. This might include using IPSec or SSL for communications between clients and servers, strong password encryption on your authentication servers, and configuring column-level permissions within a table or view.

When evaluating the different securable objects within SQL Server, you should have a good understanding of where and how permissions apply and how you can use some of the native features of the hierarchical model to your advantage. Permission applied to a specific class of objects at a higher level in the hierarchy allows for permission inheritance. For example, if you want Ted to be able to update any row on every table within the Sales schema, you could simply use the following command:

```
USE AdventureWorks2008
--First, create the user
CREATE USER Ted WITH DEFAULT_SCHEMA = Sales;
-- Next, Grant Ted update permissions on the Sales Schema
GRANT UPDATE ON SCHEMA :: Sales to Ted;
GO
```

Alternatively, if you wanted Ted to have the ability to update any object in the database, you could use the following:

```
Use AdventureWorks2008
GRANT UPDATE TO Ted;
GO
```

Take a quick look at the different levels in your security hierarchy. Figure 6-9 outlines the different levels of security you need to manage. In the Windows scope, you create and manage Windows and Active Directory security principals (like users and groups) and manage the files and services needed by the SQL Server and the behavior of the server itself. In the server scope, you manage logins, endpoints, and databases. In the database scope, you work with users, keys, certificates, roles, assemblies, and other database objects. Also in this scope are schemas, which aren't really objects as much as they are object containers. Finally, within the schema scope, you have data types, XML schema collections, and objects. These objects include your tables, views, stored procedures, and more.

Server Permissions

Server control permissions can be managed by simply specifying the permission and the login the permission will be assigned to. For example, to grant permissions to create databases to the login Ted, you could use the following statement:

```
USE master
GRANT CREATE ANY DATABASE TO Ted;
GO
```

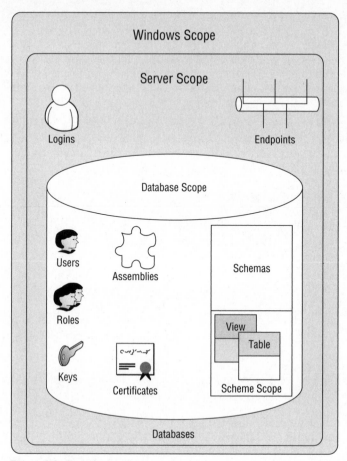

Figure 6-9: Security levels.

If you also wanted Ted to be able to have the permissions to alter logins and to allow others to alter logins, you could use the following statement:

```
USE Master
GRANT ALTER ANY LOGIN TO Ted
WITH GRANT OPTION;
GO
```

To remove Ted's ability to alter logins, you could use the following statement:

```
USE master
REVOKE ALTER ANY LOGIN TO Ted CASCADE;
GO
```

The CASCADE keyword is required because you gave Ted the GRANT_W_GRANT permission. This ensures that not only will Ted lose his ability to alter any login, but so will anyone that Ted granted the ALTER ANY LOGIN permission. If you had not used GRANT OPTION, the CASCADE keyword would have been optional.

Note that the preceding example revokes a permission that had been previously granted to Ted. If Ted were a member of the securityadmin fixed server role, he would still have the ability to alter logins for that server.

Now, if you want to prohibit Ted from being able to create a new database, you could use the DENY statement as follows:

```
USE master
DENY CREATE ANY DATABASE TO Ted;
GO
```

Contrary to what I said earlier, the DENY permission state isn't always the end-all be-all answer to whether or not a login or user will be able to perform a certain action. If a login is a member of the sysadmin fixed server role, that login has complete control over the SQL Server and its resources, and it wouldn't make a lot of sense to prevent that login from being able to access any object on the server. Even if the DENY permission statement were successfully executed on an object, the sysadmin role can always change the permissions on that object.

Also, if the GRANT OPTION was specified in the GRANT statement, as with the REVOKE keyword, you will need to ensure that you use the CASCADE option.

The following table identifies the permissions that can be used to control the server, as well as granting blanket permissions to any resource of a particular type on the server. You can control access by using the following statement:

```
{GRANT | REVOKE | DENY} action on object to principal WITH {options}
```

Action	Securable
ADMINISTER BULK OPERATIONS	
ALTER	❑ ANY CONNECTION
	❑ ANY CREDENTIAL
	❑ ANY DATABASE
	❑ ANY ENDPOINT
	❑ ANY EVENT NOTIFICATION
	❑ ANY LINKED SERVER
	❑ ANY LOGIN
	❑ RESOURCES
	❑ SERVER STATE
	❑ SETTINGS
	❑ TRACE
AUTHENTICATE SERVER	

Continued

231

Action	Securable
CONNECT SQL	
CONTROL SERVER	
CREATE	❑ ANY DATABASE ❑ ANY DDL EVENT NOTIFICATION ❑ ENDPOINT ❑ TRACE EVENT NOTIFICATION
EXTERNAL ACCESS ASSEMBLY	
SHUTDOWN	
UNSAFE ASSEMBLY	
VIEW	❑ ANY DATABASE ❑ ANY DEFINITION ❑ SERVER STATE

Endpoints are server-level objects that use a slightly different syntax from server permissions when granting, revoking, or denying. The following example creates an endpoint named ServiceBroker that will be used for a Service Broker application (endpoints are covered in Chapter 7, and Service Broker is introduced in Chapter 19), and then grants the ALTER permission for that endpoint to Ted:

```
CREATE ENDPOINT ServiceBroker
STATE = STARTED
AS TCP( LISTENER_PORT = 5162 )
FOR SERVICE_BROKER (AUTHENTICATION=WINDOWS);
GO

USE master
GRANT ALTER ON ENDPOINT :: ServiceBroker TO Ted;
GO
```

The following table lists the permissions you can grant for endpoints:

Action	Description
ALTER	Modify all properties of an endpoint, except ownership.
CONNECT	Connect to an endpoint.
CONTROL	Modify all properties of an endpoint, including ownership.
TAKE OWNERSHIP	Take ownership of an endpoint.
VIEW DEFINITION	View metadata about an endpoint.

The next server-level object you can set permissions for is logins. The syntax for setting permissions on logins is similar to the syntax for setting permissions on endpoints. For example, to give Carol the ability to alter Ted's login, you would use the following statement:

```
USE master
GRANT ALTER ON LOGIN :: Ted TO Carol
WITH GRANT OPTION;
GO
```

The following table shows how you can control these permissions for logins:

Action	Description
ALTER	Change any property of an existing login except ownership.
CONTROL	Change all properties of an existing login including ownership.
IMPERSONATE	Perform an action as that login.
VIEW DEFINITION	View metadata information about that login.

Finally, the last object type at the server level is the database object. Unlike logins and endpoints, database permissions are specified for database users. This keeps the security of the database within the database itself. Additional options may be available based on whether you are granting, denying, or revoking. The following table lists permissions that can be granted on the database object.

Action	Securable
ALTER	❑ ANY APPLICATION ROLE
	❑ ANY ASSEMBLY
	❑ ANY ASYMMETRIC KEY
	❑ ANY CERTIFICATE
	❑ ANY CONTRACT
	❑ ANY DATABASE DDL TRIGGER
	❑ ANY DATABASE EVENT NOTIFICATION
	❑ ANY DATASPACE
	❑ ANY FULLTEXT CATALOG
	❑ ANY MESSGE TYPE
	❑ ANY REMOTE SERVICE BINDING
	❑ ANY ROLE
	❑ ANY ROUTE
	❑ ANY SCHEMA

Continued

Action	Securable
	❑ ANY SERVICE
	❑ ANY SYMMETRIC KEY
	❑ ANY USER
AUTHENTICATE	
BACKUP	❑ DATABASE
	❑ LOG
CHECKPOINT	
CONNECT	
CONNECT REPLICATION	
CONTROL	
CREATE	❑ AGGREGATE
	❑ ASSEMBLY
	❑ ASYMMETRIC KEY
	❑ CERTIFICATE
	❑ CONTRACT
	❑ DATABASE
	❑ DATABASE DDL EVENT NOTIFICATION
	❑ DEFAULT
	❑ FULLTEXT CATALOG
	❑ FUNCTION
	❑ MESSAGE TYPE
	❑ PROCEDURE
	❑ QUEUE
	❑ REMOTE SERVICE BINDING
	❑ ROLE
	❑ ROUTE
	❑ RULE
	❑ SCHEMA
	❑ SERVICE
	❑ SYMMETRIC KEY

Action	Securable
	❏ SYNONYM
	❏ TABLE
	❏ TYPE
	❏ VIEW
	❏ XML SCHEMA COLLECTION
DELETE	
EXECUTE	
INSERT	
REFERENCES	
SELECT	
SHOWPLAN	
SUBSCRIBE QUERY NOTIFICATIONS	
TAKE OWNERSHIP	
UPDATE	
VIEW	❏ DATABASE STATE
	❏ DEFINITION

Database Scope Permissions

In the database scope, there are additional permissions you can assign based on the different types of securable objects you have. Permissions assigned to an object class allow you to perform the defined action on all members of that class. However, an object can be explicitly identified by declaring the class and then the object name. The syntax for assigning permissions to database securables is as follows:

```
{GRANT | REVOKE | DENY} action ON class :: object TO principal
```

In the following example, you can grant the CONTROL permission for the Sales schema to the user Alice:

```
USE AdventureWorks2008
CREATE USER Alice FOR LOGIN [AughtEight\Alice]
WITH DEFAULT_SCHEMA = SALES;
GO

GRANT CONTROL ON SCHEMA :: Sales TO Alice;
GO
```

The following table lists the various permissions and the database objects and classes to which you can assign them:

Action	Securable
ALTER	❑ APPLICATION ROLE ❑ ASSEMBLY ❑ ASYMMETRIC KEY ❑ CERTIFICATE ❑ CONTRACT ❑ FULLTEXT CATALOG ❑ MESSAGE TYPE ❑ REMOTE SERVICE BINDING ❑ ROLE ❑ ROUTE ❑ SCHEMA ❑ SERVICE ❑ SYMMETRIC KEY ❑ USER
CONTROL	❑ APPLICATION ROLE ❑ ASSEMBLY ❑ ASYMMETRIC KEY ❑ CERTIFICATE ❑ CONTRACT ❑ FULLTEXT CATALOG ❑ MESSAGE TYPE ❑ REMOTE SERVICE BINDING ❑ ROLE ❑ ROUTE ❑ SCHEMA ❑ SERVICE ❑ SYMMETRIC KEY ❑ USER

Action	Securable
DELETE	SCHEMA
EXECUTE	❑ ASSEMBLY
	❑ SCHEMA
IMPERSONATE	USER
INSERT	SCHEMA
REFERENCES	❑ ASSEMBLY
	❑ ASYMMETRIC KEY
	❑ CERTIFICATE
	❑ CONTRACT
	❑ FULLTEXT CATALOG
	❑ MESSASGE TYPE
	❑ SCHEMA
	❑ SYMMETRIC KEY
SELECT	SCHEMA
SEND	SERVICE
TAKE OWNERSHIP	❑ ASSEMBLY
	❑ ASYMMETRIC KEY
	❑ CERTIFICATE
	❑ CONTRACT
	❑ FULLTEXT CATALOG
	❑ MESSAGE TYPE
	❑ REMOTE SERVICE BINDING
	❑ ROLE
	❑ ROUTE
	❑ SCHEMA
	❑ SERVICE
	❑ SYMMETRIC KEY
UPDATE	SCHEMA
VIEW CHANGE TRACKING	SCHEMA

Continued

Action	Securable
VIEW DEFINITION	❏ APPLICATION ROLE
	❏ ASSEMBLY
	❏ ASYMMETRIC KEY
	❏ CERTIFICATE
	❏ CONTRACT
	❏ FULLTEXT CATALOG
	❏ MESSAGE TYPE
	❏ REMOTE SERVICE BINDING
	❏ ROLE
	❏ ROUTE
	❏ SCHEMA
	❏ SERVICE
	❏ SYMMETRIC KEY
	❏ USER

Schema Scope Permissions

Finally, within the scope of a schema, there are additional permissions you can assign to objects, data types, and XML schema collections. When granting permissions to schema-level objects, the syntax is similar to what you saw earlier:

```
{GRANT | REVOKE | DENY} action ON class :: securable TO principal
```

When the class is an OBJECT, you can omit OBJECT : : as long as the schema name is included with the object name, as in the following example:

```
Use AdventureWorks2008
GRANT SELECT, UPDATE ON Person.Person to Alice;
GO
```

Schema objects include the following:

❏ Aggregates

❏ Constraints

❏ Functions

❏ Procedures

- ❑ Queues
- ❑ Statistics
- ❑ Synonyms
- ❑ Tables
- ❑ Views

The following table lists the schema classes and the permissions that can be set for each of them. Remember that not all permissions are valid for every object type. You can't expect to grant EXECUTE on a table, or SELECT on a stored procedure.

Class	Permissions
OBJECT	❑ ALTER ❑ CONTROL ❑ DELETE ❑ EXECUTE ❑ INSERT ❑ RECEIVE ❑ REFERNCES ❑ SELECT ❑ TAKE OWNERSHIP ❑ UPDATE ❑ VIEW CHANGE TRACKING ❑ VIEW DEFINITION
TYPE	❑ CONTROL ❑ EXECUTE ❑ REFERNCES ❑ TAKE OWNERSHIP ❑ VIEW DEFINITION
XML SCHEMA COLLECTION	❑ ALTER ❑ CONTROL ❑ EXECUTE ❑ REFERNCES ❑ TAKE OWNERSHIP ❑ VIEW DEFINITION

Using SQL Server Management Studio for Managing Permissions

You can also use Object Explorer in SQL Server Management Studio to set or view permissions on objects. In this section, you will learn how to use the GUI to control access to SQL resources.

The first thing to look at is auditing permissions on the objects themselves.

For the next example, create a new login, a new database user for the AdventureWorks2008 database, and then grant control permissions to the Sales schema for this new user. Use the following code:

```
USE master
CREATE LOGIN Chris WITH PASSWORD = 'P@ssw0rd',
DEFAULT_DATABASE = AdventureWorks2008;
GO

USE AdventureWorks2008
CREATE USER Chris WITH DEFAULT_SCHEMA = Sales;
GO

GRANT CONTROL ON SCHEMA :: SALES TO Chris;
GO
```

Now, use Object Explorer to see what permissions have been granted to Chris. First, look at the database itself:

1. Expand your server.
2. Expand Databases.
3. Right-click AdventureWorks2008 and select Properties.
4. Select Permissions.
5. In the Users or Roles pane, select "Chris."

Under "Explicit permissions for Chris," scroll down until you find "Connect." Note that the user who granted the permission, in this case the dbo, is also listed in the Grantor column.

Next to the list of explicit permissions for this user, there is an "Effective Permissions" tab. Clicking on this tab will give you a list of the permissions the user has for this resource, including those that were granted through membership in a role or group. This new feature can really help simplify the process of auditing your security settings, or troubleshooting why a user is having problems accessing a resource.

Because you granted control of the Sales schema to Chris, take a look at what permissions have actually been assigned to that schema and the objects within it. To do this, open the property sheet for Chris's user account in the AdventureWorks2008 database (see Figure 6-10):

1. Close the Database Properties — AdventureWorks2008 window by clicking OK or Cancel.
2. In Object Explorer, expand AdventureWorks2008.

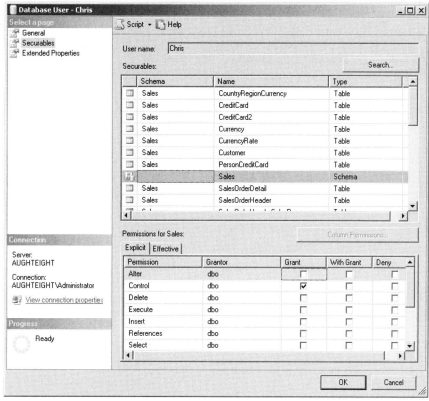

Figure 6-10: Property sheet for Chris.

3. Expand Security.

4. Expand Users.

5. Right-click "Chris" and select "Properties."

6. Select the Securables page and click Search.

7. Select "All objects belonging to the schema."

8. From the "Schema name" dropdown list, select "Sales."

9. Click OK.

If you look at the list of explicit permissions on the Sales schema, notice that Chris only has CONTROL permissions. Clicking the "Effective Permissions" tab will show you that the user has full access to any object in the schema.

Now, take a look at specific objects in the Sales schema. Select CreditCard in the list of Securables, and select the "Effective Permissions" tab.

Look at the list of explicit permissions for `Sales.CreditCard` (see Figure 6-11), and notice that Chris has no explicit permissions on this table. Clicking the "Effective Permissions" tab will show you that the user has full access to the table and its contents.

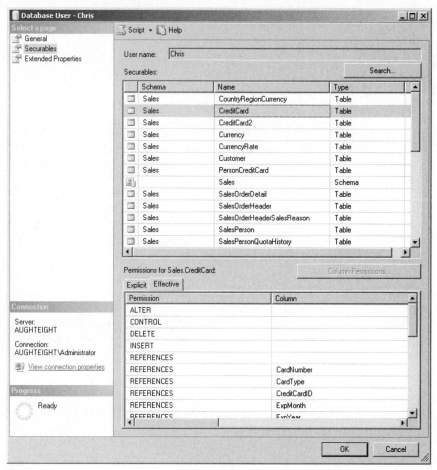

Figure 6-11: `Sales.CreditCard` **permissions.**

You now have a user with full access to the Sales schema, but no access to resources outside of it. Any attempt to query a view in another schema will result in the following error:

```
SELECT * FROM HumanResources.vEmployee
----------------------------------------------------------------------------

Msg 229, Level 14, State 5, Line 1
SELECT permission denied on object 'vEmployee', database 'AdventureWorks2008',
 schema 'HumanResources'.
```

Also note that you can add permissions for database objects in the User Properties dialog box. You can use the Management Studio to assign permissions by editing the properties of the securable, or by editing the properties of a principal.

SQL Server Encryption

Protecting data, both in storage and during transmission, is important for the integrity of your applications and services. Microsoft SQL Server 2008 offers several options for both. In this section, you will see some of the tools available for protecting your data.

First of all, whether you're using symmetric keys, asymmetric keys, or certificates, there are two main components to encrypting data: the *encryption algorithm* and the *key value*. The encryption algorithms available include Data Encryption Standard (DES), Triple Data Encryption Standard (3DES), RC4, and Advanced Encryption Standard (AES_256), as well as others. An encryption algorithm is simply a mathematical formula that dictates how to turn the data from plain text into cipher text. The key is a value that is used within that formula to determine the actual output based on the input. It's not unlike basic algebra, where you take a statement like $x + y = z$. In this case, x is the plain-text value, y is the encryption key, and z is the cipher text. Fortunately, the encryption algorithms are significantly more complex than that, but you get the idea.

Keys come in two flavors: symmetric and asymmetric. *Symmetric keys* use the same data key value to both encrypt and decrypt data. This is actually very good for encrypting large amounts of data, but has a relatively low level of security. *Asymmetric keys* use one key value for encrypting data and a different value for decrypting data. This provides a higher level of security than symmetric keys, but is a costly operation and not good for large amounts of data. A well-designed encryption method encrypts data using symmetric keys, and encrypts the symmetric keys using asymmetric keys. Certificates use asymmetric keys, but have additional functionality that can be used for authentication and non-repudiation.

Now, take a look at how SQL provides encryption services. Figure 6-12 shows a high-level overview of the encryption hierarchy used by SQL Server 2008. At the top level is the Windows layer, which includes the Windows Data Protection API (DPAPI). The DPAPI is responsible for encrypting the server's service master key using the server's local machine key. The *service master key* is the top of the encryption food chain within the SQL environment. The service master key is automatically generated the first time a lower-level key is created.

Beneath the service master key is the *database master key*. The database master key can protect the private keys of all certificates and asymmetric keys within a database. It is a symmetric key that is encrypted using the 3DES algorithm and a password. Copies of the key are encrypted using the service master key and are stored in both the master database and the database for which it was created. If the database is moved to another server, the database master key can be decrypted by using the OPEN MASTER KEY statement and providing the password used to encrypt it.

Also in the database scope are symmetric and asymmetric keys you can create for encrypting data, as well as certificates that can also be used for digital signing and non-repudiation. Creating and managing the different key types are discussed in the next section.

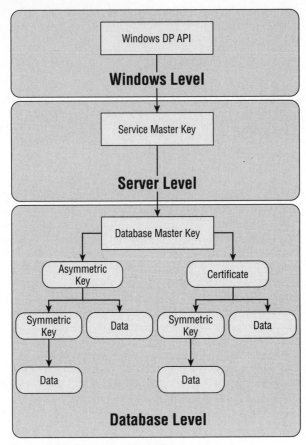

Figure 6-12: Encryption hierarchy.

One of the first steps you should take is creating the database master key. Remember that the database master key is a symmetric key that encrypts all private key data within the database. This is helpful if you are using asymmetric keys or certificates, in that they can be created without having to supply a password or other mechanism to protect the private keys associated with both. To create a new master key for the AdventureWorks2008 database, you can execute the following command:

```
USE AdventureWorks2008
CREATE MASTER KEY
ENCRYPTION BY PASSWORD = 'P@ssw0rd';
GO
```

Creation of a master key requires CONTROL permission on the database. Also, if you already have a master key created, you must drop the existing one if you need to create a new master key. An existing master key cannot be dropped if it is being used to encrypt a private key in the database.

Once you've created your master key, you can query the sys.databases catalog view to see if the database master key has been encrypted using the service master key by looking at the value of the `is_master_key_encrypted_by_server` column. This column uses a Boolean value to indicate whether the database master key is encrypted with the service master key. The value may be 0 if the database master key was created on another server.

```
SELECT NAME, [is_master_key_encrypted_by_server] FROM sys.databases
GO
```

Before continuing on to the subject of working with other keys to encrypt database information, let's look at the topic of backing up your service master key and database master keys. This can be extremely valuable in case you have to perform a disaster-recovery operation and need to recover data that had been protected or encrypted with one of these keys. The syntax for both keys is similar, but an additional step is required to back up an encrypted database master key.

Let's start with the service master key first. Quite simply, use the BACKUP SERVICE MASTER KEY statement with a file path, which can be a local or UNC path, and a password that meets your password-complexity requirements. Using a password on the backup file prevents someone from being able to restore your master key on another server and then being able to decrypt your database master keys. The following example will save a backup of the service master key to a folder called *C:\KeyBackups* (this folder must already exist):

```
BACKUP SERVICE MASTER KEY TO FILE = 'C:\KeyBackups\ServiceMasterKey'
ENCRYPTION BY PASSWORD = 'c@MplexP@ssw0rd';
GO
```

If you need to restore the service master key, you can issue the following statement:

```
RESTORE SERVICE MASTER KEY FROM FILE = 'C:\KeyBackups\ServiceMasterKey'
DECRYPTION BY PASSWORD = 'c@MplexP@ssw0rd';
GO
```

To back up and restore a database master key, use the following examples:

```
--Backup the database master key
USE AdventureWorks2008;
OPEN MASTER KEY
 DECRYPTION BY PASSWORD = 'P@ssw0rd'
BACKUP MASTER KEY TO FILE = 'C:\KeyBackups\AWorksMasterKey'
ENCRYPTION BY PASSWORD = 'dn9e8h93ndwjKJD';
GO
--Restore the database master key
USE AdventureWorks2008;
RESTORE MASTER KEY FROM FILE = 'c:\KeyBackups\AWorksMasterKey'
DECRYPTION BY PASSWORD = 'dn9e8h93ndwjKJD'
ENCRYPTION BY PASSWORD = 'P@ssw0rd'
GO
```

There are a couple of things to note about the previous example. First, in order to back up the database master key, you must decrypt it by using the password that was originally used to encrypt it. Also note that when you use the RESTORE MASTER KEY statement, you need to provide a password for encrypting the database master key. The command will fail without this step.

Extensible Key Management (EKM)

One of the most important new features of SQL Server 2008 is Extensible Key Management, or EKM for short. EKM works with the Microsoft Cryptographic API (MSCAPI) to allow encryption keys that are used for data encryption, as well as encryption of other keys, to be generated and stored outside of the SQL Server 2008 environment. This provides a more robust and flexible mechanism for key management, given that you can now separate the keys from the data they protect.

This is often accomplished through the use of Hardware Security Models (HSM). HSM vendors can create a provider that will interface with the MSCAPI, exposing at least some of the features of the HSM to SQL Server 2008 and other applications that leverage the MSCAPI. Unfortunately, because MSCAPI acts as a middle tier between the HSM and the SQL Server, not all of the features of the HSM may be exposed to the SQL Server.

In order to use EKM, you must first enable it on the server. It is turned off by default, but can be turned on with the sp_configure command. Because enabling EKM is considered an advanced feature, the show advanced configuration must also be specified. The following example shows you how to turn on EKM for your server:

```
sp_configure 'show advanced', 1;
GO
RECONFIGURE
GO
sp_configure 'EKM provider enabled', 1;
GO
RECONFIGURE
GO
```

With EKM enabled, you can now store your encryption keys on HSM modules, smart cards, or USB devices. Whenever data is encrypted using a key stored on one of these devices, that same device must be present in order to decrypt the data. This can protect against an unauthorized user copying and attaching the database files to a rogue SQL Server and being able to access all your confidential data.

EKM can also be leveraged to provide the following benefits:

❑ Additional authorization checks

❑ Easier key recovery

❑ Encryption key retrieval

❑ External key generation and storage

❑ External key retention and rotation

❑ Higher performance when using hardware-based encryption and decryption

❑ Manageable key distribution

❑ Secure key disposal

Encryption Tools

Now that you understand some of the basics of encryption, take a look at creating and managing encryption tools. Each of the objects in this section serves a specific purpose. After you learn how to create symmetric keys, asymmetric keys, and certificates, you will learn how to use them.

Symmetric Keys

As mentioned earlier, symmetric keys offer an efficient model for being able to encrypt large amounts of data. The resource overhead is minimized by using the same keys for both encryption and decryption. Here's the syntax for generating symmetric keys:

```
CREATE SYMMETRIC KEY name [AUTHORIZATION owner] [FROM PROVIDER] providername
 WITH options
ENCRYPTION BY mechanism
```

The following table shows the arguments that can be used:

Argument	Description
AUTHORIZATION owner	Identifies who the owner of the key is.
FROM PROVIDER	Specifies that an EKM provider will be used and the name of the provider.
KEY_SOURCE pass phrase	Identifies a pass phrase used to derive the key.
ALGORITHM	Choose one of the following: DES, TRIPLE_DES, TRIPLE_DES_3KEY, RC2, RC4, RC4_128, DESX, AES_128, AES_192, AES_256.
IDENTITY_VALUE pass phrase	Used to generate a GUID for identifying data that has been encrypted with this key.
CREATION_DISPOSITION	When using an EKM device, you can specify to create a new key on the device or map the symmetric key to an existing one by using the following options: ❑ CREATE_NEW ❑ OPEN_EXISTING
ENCRYPTION BY mechanism	One or more of the following methods for encrypting the symmetric key: ❑ CERTIFICATE certificate_name ❑ PASSWORD = 'password' ❑ SYMMETRIC KEY symmetric_key_name ❑ ASYMMETRIC KEY asym_key_name

Try It Out   Create a Symmetric Key

The following example creates a new symmetric key named SalesKey1, which uses the 192-bit Triple DES 3-Key algorithm:

```
USE AdventureWorks2008
GO
--Create Symmetric Key
```

```
CREATE SYMMETRIC KEY SalesKey1
    WITH ALGORITHM = TRIPLE_DES_3KEY,
    KEY_SOURCE = 'The quick brown fox jumped over the lazy dog',
    IDENTITY_VALUE = 'FoxAndHound'
    ENCRYPTION BY PASSWORD = '9348hsxasnA@B';
GO
```

You can add or remove methods for encrypting the key with the ALTER SYMMETRIC KEY statement, and you can remove a symmetric key by using the DROP SYMMETRIC KEY statement.

In this example, use the SalesCert certificate created in the earlier section, "Database Users," to encrypt the symmetric key and remove the password encryption from the previous example:

```
--Open the symmetric key
OPEN SYMMETRIC KEY SalesKey1
 DECRYPTION BY PASSWORD = '9348hsxasnA@B'
--Add encryption using the certificate created earlier
ALTER SYMMETRIC KEY SalesKey1
 ADD ENCRYPTION BY CERTIFICATE SalesCert
--Remove the password encryption
ALTER SYMMETRIC KEY SalesKey1
 DROP ENCRYPTION BY PASSWORD = '9348hsxasnA@B'
--Close the symmetric key
CLOSE SYMMETRIC KEY SalesKey1
```

Asymmetric Keys

Asymmetric keys use a pair of keys rather than a single one. These keys are often referred to as the *public key* and the *private key*. One key is used for encryption, and the other is used for decryption. It doesn't really matter which key is used for encryption, but the data cannot be decrypted without the corresponding key. The process for creating an asymmetric key pair is similar to creating a symmetric key. Here's the syntax for generating symmetric keys:

```
CREATE ASYMMETRIC KEY name [AUTHORIZATION owner] [FROM key_source]
    WITH ALGORITHM = algorithm [ENCRYPTION BY PASSWORD = 'password']
```

The following table shows the arguments that can be used:

Argument	Description
AUTHORIZATION owner	Identifies who the owner of the key is. The owner cannot be a role or a group.
FROM key source	Specifies the key source that will be used.
FILE = 'path to filename'	Specifies a strong-name file that can be used as a source for the key pair.
EXECUTABLE FILE	Specifies an executable file that can be used to load the key pair.

Argument	Description
ASSEMBLY	Specifies an assembly file that can be used to load the key pair.
ENCRYPTION BY PASSWORD = 'password'	Specifies the password used to encrypt the private key. The password is limited to 128 characters.
ALGORITHM	Choose one of the following: RSA_512, RSA_1024, or RSA_2048.
KEY_NAME key	When using EKM, this allows you to specify the key name from the external provider.
CREATION_DISPOSITION	When using an EKM device, you can specify to create a new key on the device or map the symmetric key to an existing one by using the following options: ❑ CREATE_NEW ❑ OPEN_EXISTING

When creating an asymmetric key pair, you can specify the owner of the key pair and the key source (which is either a strong-name file, an assembly, or an executable assembly file). Alternatively, you can use an algorithm that determines the number of bits used by the private key, selecting a key length using 512, 1,024, or 2,048 bits. You can also use the ENCRYPTION BY PASSWORD option to encrypt the private key. If you do not specify a password, the database master key will encrypt the private key.

```
USE AdventureWorks2008
CREATE ASYMMETRIC KEY HumanResources
    WITH ALGORITHM = RSA_2048;
GO
```

You can use the ALTER ASYMMETRIC KEY statement to change the properties of a key pair. You can use the REMOVE PRIVATE KEY option to take the private key out of the database (make sure you have a backup of the private key first!), or you can change the way the private key is protected. For example, you can change the password used to encrypt the private key and then change the protection from password to database master key, or vice versa.

In the following example, use the following code to encrypt the private key from the HumanResources key pair created in the earlier example using a password:

```
USE AdventureWorks2008
ALTER ASYMMETRIC KEY HumanResources
    WITH PRIVATE KEY (
    ENCRYPTION BY PASSWORD = 'P@ssw0rd');
GO
```

In the next example, you can change the password used to encrypt the private key by first decrypting it, and then re-encrypting it with a new password:

```
USE AdventureWorks2008
ALTER ASYMMETRIC KEY HumanResources
```

```
WITH PRIVATE KEY (
DECRYPTION BY PASSWORD = 'P@ssw0rd',
ENCRYPTION BY PASSWORD = '48ufdsjEHF@*hda');
GO
```

Certificates

Certificates (also known as *public key certificates*) are objects that associate an asymmetric key pair with a credential. Certificates are objects that can be used not only for encryption, but also for authentication and non-repudiation. This means that not only can you obfuscate data that would normally be in plain text, but you can also provide a means of guaranteeing the source, the trustworthiness of that source, or that the data has not changed since it was signed.

The details of a certificate identify when the certificate was created, the validity period of the certificate, who created the certificate, and what the certificate can be used for. It also identifies the public key associated with the certificate and the algorithm that can be used for digitally signing messages.

The ability to create and use certificates is a feature that was first introduced in SQL Server 2005, and one that even experienced DBAs may have trouble grasping at first. Certificates are part of the bigger scope of application security and identity, and the functionality extended to SQL Server 2008 is no different from how you would use certificates with other applications and services. This topic is almost like opening a Pandora's Box, but once you understand the basics of how certificates work and how they can be used to protect your services and data, you will appreciate their flexibility.

Certificates also have a feature that lets you trace the genealogy of the certificate, its "family tree," if you will (see Figure 6-13). This certificate hierarchy identifies not only what *Certification Authority* (CA) issued the certificate, but what CA generated the certificate used by the CA to generate the certificate you have. This is known as the *certificate chain*. The certificate chain can be used to identify either a common Root CA (the highest authority in a chain) that can be trusted for authentication or another Root CA that is considered a trustworthy source. Many applications and operating systems include a list of commercial CAs that are automatically trusted. When the certificate from a Root CA is trusted, it is assumed that any certificate that can trace its genealogy back to that root is also trusted. If the certificate is not from a trusted certificate chain, the user may be warned that the certificate is not trusted, and they should proceed with caution. Commercial CAs are often used to obtain Server Authentication and SSL certificates, simply because many Web browsers already trust the most popular Root CAs.

Many organizations have developed their own *Public Key Infrastructure* (PKI). These companies have found it necessary to deploy and use certificates for a variety of reasons. Some might use certificates with smart cards for logging in to their computers. Some may use certificates for encrypting data on the NTFS file system, using Encrypting File System (EFS). Some organizations may use certificates for digitally signing applications and macros, so that their users can verify where the application came from or that it hasn't been modified. These organizations often have their own CA hierarchy. They may have a Root CA they manage themselves, or they may have the ability to generate their own certificates that are part of a third-party certificate chain.

Microsoft SQL Server 2008 has the ability to create its own self-signed certificates. In a way, SQL can be its own CA, but don't expect these certificates to be automatically trusted outside of the SQL instance. The certificates generated by SQL Server conform to the X.509 standard and can be used outside of the SQL Server if necessary, but they are not part of a trusted hierarchy. A more common approach is to use a certificate generated by another CA and import that into SQL Server. Certificates can be just as widely used in SQL Server as they can outside SQL. You can use them for server authentication, encryption, and digital signing.

Figure 6-13: Certificate information.

On the subject of encryption, public key certificates operate in the same way as asymmetric keys. The key pair, however, is bound to this certificate. The public key is included in the certificate details, and the private key must be securely archived. Private keys associated with certificates must be secured using a password, the database master key, or another encryption key. When encrypting data, the best practice is to encrypt the data with a symmetric key and then encrypt the symmetric key with a public key.

When creating a certificate that will be self-signed, you can use the CREATE CERTIFICATE statement. You can choose to encrypt the private key using a strong password or by using the database master key. You can also use the CREATE CERTIFICATE statement to import a certificate and private key from a file. Alternatively, you can create a certificate based on a signed assembly.

Once the certificate has been created, you can modify the certificate with the ALTER CERTIFICATE statement. Some of the changes you can make include changing the way the private key is protected or removing the private key from the SQL Server. Removing the private key should be done only if the certificate is used to validate a digital signature. If the public key had been used to encrypt data or a symmetric key, the private key should be available for decryption.

It is a good idea when creating certificates to make a backup of the certificate and the associated private key with the BACKUP CERTIFICATE statement. You can make a backup of the certificate without archiving the private key, and use the public key for verification or encrypting messages that can only be decrypted with the private key.

Once a certificate is no longer needed, you can get rid of it with the DROP CERTIFICATE statement. Be aware that the certificate can't be dropped if it is still associated with other objects.

Try It Out   Create a New Certificate

In the following example, create a new certificate named `PersonnelDataCert`, which you will use later to encrypt data. After creating this certificate, back up the certificate to the file system (you can either change the path in the example or create a new folder on your C: drive called *certs*). Once that is done, the last step is to import the certificate into the `tempdb` database.

```
-- Create the Personnel Data Certificate
USE AdventureWorks2008;
CREATE CERTIFICATE PersonnelDataCert
    ENCRYPTION BY PASSWORD = 'HRcertific@te'
    WITH SUBJECT = 'Personnel Data Encryption Certificate',
    EXPIRY_DATE = '12/31/2011';
GO

--Backup the certificate and private key to the file system
Use AdventureWorks2008
BACKUP CERTIFICATE PersonnelDataCert TO FILE = 'c:\certs\Personnel.cer'
    WITH PRIVATE KEY (DECRYPTION BY PASSWORD = 'HRcertific@te',
    FILE = 'c:\certs\Personnelkey.pvk' ,
    ENCRYPTION BY PASSWORD = '@notherPassword' );
GO

--Import the certificate and private key into the TempDB database
USE tempdb
CREATE CERTIFICATE PersonnelDataCert
    FROM FILE = 'c:\certs\Personnel.cer'
     WITH PRIVATE KEY (FILE = 'c:\certs\Personnelkey.pvk',
    DECRYPTION BY PASSWORD = '@notherPassword',
     ENCRYPTION BY PASSWORD = 'TempDBKey1');
GO
```

In the next example, change the password used to encrypt the private key using the ALTER CERTIFICATE statement:

```
Use tempdb
ALTER CERTIFICATE PersonnelDataCert
    WITH PRIVATE KEY (ENCRYPTION BY PASSWORD = 'P@ssw0rd789',
    DECRYPTION BY PASSWORD = 'TempDBKey1');
GO
```

Now you can remove the private key from the `AdventureWorks2008` database. Because the certificate and the private key are backed up, you can perform this action safely.

```
Use AdventureWorks2008
ALTER CERTIFICATE PersonnelDataCert
    REMOVE PRIVATE KEY
GO
```

Finally, clean up the `tempdb` database:

```
USE tempdb
DROP CERTIFICATE PersonnelDataCert;
GO
```

Encrypting Data

Now that you've seen the different objects that can be used for encryption or non-repudiation, take a look at how you can actually use them. First of all, not everything needs to be encrypted. Because the process of encrypting and decrypting data can be resource-intensive, you should be mindful of what data you need to encrypt. Data that should be kept confidential (such as credit card or Social Security numbers) might fall into this category. An employee's middle name, no matter how embarrassing it might be, would not. Also note that not every data type can be encrypted with the encryptbykey function. The valid data types are nvarchar, char, wchar, varchar, and nchar.

It is also a good idea to know *when* to encrypt the data, and when not to. Frequently queried columns in tables or views should *not* be encrypted, because the process of decrypting large amounts of data that is queried over and over again can often become counterproductive. In this case, a better strategy might be to store the sensitive information in a separate table that has much tighter security on it. Remember that you can give insert or update permissions on a row in a foreign table without having to grant select permissions on that related table. HSMs may offset some of the overhead involved with the decryption process, but that may require significant testing to verify how well it will perform in production.

Prior to encrypting data, you must open the key that will perform the encryption process. Again, data is commonly protected with a symmetric key, which is, in turn, protected with an asymmetric key pair. If the symmetric key is protected with a password, then any user with ALTER permissions on the symmetric key and the password can open and close the symmetric key. If the symmetric key is protected by an asymmetric key or certificate, the user also needs CONTROL permissions on the asymmetric key or the certificate.

Try It Out   **Create an Encrypted Column**

Use the following sample code to create an encrypted column in the Sales.CreditCard table. In this example, use the symmetric key SalesKey1 and the certificate SalesCert, both created earlier in this chapter:

```
ALTER TABLE Sales.CreditCard
    ADD EncryptedCardNumber varbinary(128);
GO

OPEN SYMMETRIC KEY SalesKey1 DECRYPTION BY
 CERTIFICATE SalesCert WITH PASSWORD = 'P@ssw0rd'

UPDATE Sales.CreditCard
SET EncryptedCardNumber
    = EncryptByKey(Key_GUID('SalesKey1'), CardNumber);
GO

CLOSE SYMMETRIC KEY SalesKey1;
GO
```

Because the symmetric key was used to encrypt the data, it will also be used for decryption. Using the preceding example as a template, you could use the following commands to create another new column that stores the decrypted data. A SELECT statement is included that allows you to view the original data, the encrypted data, and the decrypted data columns:

```
ALTER TABLE Sales.CreditCard
    ADD DecryptedCardNumber NVARCHAR(25);
```

```
GO

OPEN SYMMETRIC KEY SalesKey1 DECRYPTION BY
 CERTIFICATE SalesCert WITH PASSWORD = 'P@ssw0rd';
GO

UPDATE Sales.CreditCard
SET DecryptedCardNumber
    = DecryptByKey(EncryptedCardNumber);
GO

CLOSE SYMMETRIC KEY SalesKey1;
GO

Select TOP (10) CreditCardID, CardNumber AS Original, EncryptedCardNumber AS
 Encrypted, DecryptedCardNumber AS Decrypted
FROM Sales.CreditCard;
GO
```

You don't have to create a whole new column to view the decrypted data, though. The DECRYPTBYKEY function can be executed in a SELECT statement to view the unencrypted data. The following example shows you how:

```
OPEN SYMMETRIC KEY SalesKey1 DECRYPTION BY
 CERTIFICATE SalesCert WITH PASSWORD = 'P@ssw0rd';
GO

SELECT CreditCardID, CardNumber,EncryptedCardNumber
    AS 'Encrypted Card Number',
    CONVERT(nvarchar, DecryptByKey(EncryptedCardNumber))
    AS 'Decrypted Card Number'
    FROM Sales.CreditCard;
GO

CLOSE SYMMETRIC KEY SalesKey1;
GO
```

Transparent Data Encryption

Another new feature of SQL Server 2008 is Transparent Data Encryption (TDE). TDE is designed to perform real-time I/O encryption, using a Database Encryption Key (DEK), of the database and transaction log files for databases that have TDE enabled. The benefit of TDE is that it protects all data "at rest." This means that anything not currently being read into memory is protected using the DEK. However, when a query is run, the data that is retrieved from that query is decrypted as it is being read into memory. Unlike the use of symmetric and asymmetric keys for decrypting data in a single table or column, it is not necessary to invoke a decryption function when reading from or writing to a table in a database protected by TDE (hence the use of the word *Transparent*).

Setting up TDE is slightly more complex than other encryption methods, in that there are certain dependencies that must be in place before you can enable it.

1. First of all, a Database Master Key must exist in the `master` database.

2. Secondly, you must either create a certificate or install a certificate in the `master` database that can be used to encrypt the DEK; or you may use an asymmetric key from an EKM provider.

3. Then you will need to create the DEK in the database that you will be encrypting. Finally, enable encryption on that database. The following script provides an example of these steps:

```
USE master
CREATE MASTER KEY ENCRYPTION BY PASSWORD = 'MyStrongP@ssw0rd';
GO
CREATE CERTIFICATE AughtEightTDE WITH SUBJECT =
 'TDE Certificate for the AUGHTEIGHT Server';
GO
USE AdventureWorks2008
CREATE DATABASE ENCRYPTION KEY
WITH ALGORITHM = TRIPLE_DES_3KEY
ENCRYPTION BY SERVER CERTIFICATE AughtEightTDE;
GO
ALTER DATABASE AdventureWorks2008
SET ENCRYPTION ON;
GO
```

You can also use SQL Server Management Studio to manage the Transparent Encryption Properties of a database. Do this by performing the following steps:

1. In Object Explorer, expand Databases.

2. Right-click on the `AdventureWorks2008` database, and select Tasks, then "Manage Database Encryption."

As you can see in Figure 6-14, you have several options you can perform from this window, including "Re-Encrypt Database Encryption Key" using a server certificate or server asymmetric key (stored in the master database), as well as regenerating the key using an AES 128, AES 192, AES 256, or Triple DES encryption algorithm. You can also enable or disable TDE for this database by checking (or unchecking) the box next to "Set Database Encryption On."

Digital Signatures

Digital signatures provide authentication and non-repudiation. Often, with public key pairs, the private key is used to digitally sign a message (or, in the case of a code-signing certificate, an application or assembly). Take a look at how digital signing works with e-mail messages as an example.

Bob sends Alice a message, and his e-mail client is configured to automatically add his digital signature to all outgoing messages. In this case, while the message is being prepared for delivery, a key is generated and passed to a hashing algorithm for a one-way transformation of the data into a hash value. The hash value is attached to the message, and the key that was used to generate the hash is encrypted with Bob's private key.

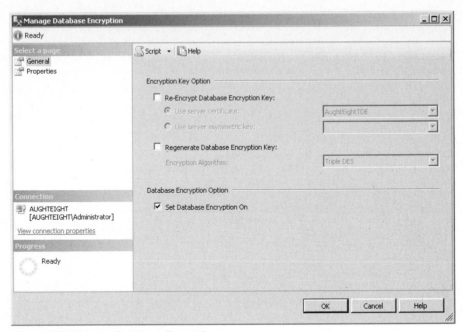

Figure 6-14: Manage Database Encryption.

The message is delivered to Alice, who receives the message in plain text, as well as receiving the hashed version of the message. Alice, who has access to Bob's public key, uses it to decrypt the key that was used to generate the hash. The key is then passed through the hashing algorithm, and a new hash is generated. If the new hash matches the hash that was sent with the message, Alice can feel confident that the message hasn't been changed during delivery. If the hash values do not match, then the message may have been altered since it was transmitted and should not be trusted.

In a similar vein, you can use digital signatures to sign SQL Server components (such as stored procedures) to associate the stored procedure with a hash value. If the stored procedure changes by a single bit, then the hash values will differ; and you'll know that someone must have used an ALTER PROCEDURE statement on it!

You can use both asymmetric keys and digital certificates to sign stored procedures, functions, or DML triggers in SQL Server. The following code creates a simple stored procedure called Sales.DisplaySomeVendors. You can then add a signature to that stored procedure using the SalesCert certificate from earlier. The private key will need to be decrypted to digitally sign the stored procedure.

```
CREATE PROCEDURE Sales.DisplaySomeVendors AS
    SELECT TOP (20) * FROM Purchasing.Vendor;
GO

USE AdventureWorks2008;
ADD SIGNATURE TO  Sales.DisplaySomeVendors
    BY CERTIFICATE SalesCert WITH PASSWORD = 'P@ssw0rd';
GO
```

If you look at the properties of the stored procedure, you can now see that the stored procedure has been digitally signed, and it was signed by the SalesCert certificate (see Figure 6-15). You can also query the sys.crypt_properties catalog view. This view will show any objects that have been digitally signed. In the next example, you will query the sys.crypt_properties view to see the digital signature assigned to the Sales.DisplaySomeVendors stored procedure. Then you can alter the procedure, query the view again, and note that the procedure is no longer digitally signed.

```
SELECT * FROM sys.crypt_properties
GO
ALTER PROCEDURE Sales.DisplaySomeVendors AS
 SELECT TOP (10) * FROM Purchasing.Vendor
GO
SELECT * FROM sys.crypt_properties
```

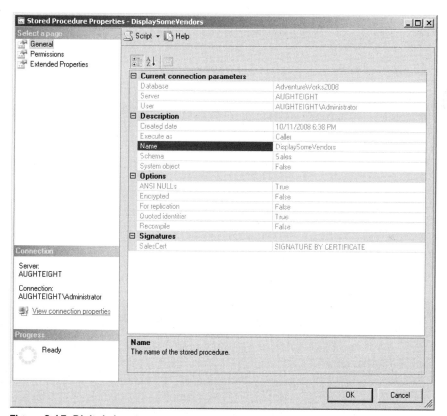

Figure 6-15: Digital signature.

Best Practices

Like any other application or server product, there are a few guidelines you should follow to help increase the level of security in place. Remember that you will never be able to plan for and protect against every possible threat, but you can make it more difficult for malicious users to gain access to your data.

❑ **Use Strong Passwords** — As mentioned earlier in this chapter, you should take advantage of the password policies and require users to create complex passwords that get changed regularly. You should educate your users about the importance of strong passwords. While password policy enforcement for SQL Logins is managed at the server, you should provide an application or tool that allows users a way to change their passwords and be notified when their passwords are about to expire.

❑ **No One Should Log on as sa** — The sa account should rarely (if ever) log in. To provide more accurate auditing information, users should be forced to use their own logins (or log in through the membership in a group) in order to track what users are performing which actions. If everyone has the sa password and everyone is able to log in as that account, nothing would stop them from being able to steal or destroy your data. You wouldn't be able to hold that person accountable, because you may not know who that person is!

❑ **Use Least-Privilege Accounts for SQL Services** — Apply the principle of least privilege, and use accounts that have exactly the rights and permissions needed by the services, and nothing else. While it might be tempting to make the SQL Server account or the SQL Server Agent account a member of an administrative group, it is not necessary. Identify what resources outside of the SQL Server each of these accounts will be interacting with, and assign only the required permissions.

❑ **Audit Principals Regularly** — A diligent administrator will know what accounts have been created and who is responsible for these accounts, and identify what steps must be taken to disable or remove superfluous accounts.

❑ **Disable or Remove Any Unused Network Protocols** — In the SQL Configuration Manager, you have the ability to enable or disable protocols used by the SQL Server. Additionally, consider disabling the NetBIOS protocol for your network adapter if NetBIOS will not be used by your server or applications.

❑ **Use On-the-Wire Encryption to Protect Your Data in Transit** — It's not enough for you to protect the data while it sits idly on the server. As a database administrator, you should use technologies like Secure Sockets Layer (SSL) encryption and Internet Protocol Security (IPSec) to protect the data while it's moving from client to server, server to client, or server to server.

❑ **Do Not Place the SQL Server in a Location with Poor Physical Security** — There is a well-known article published by the Microsoft Security Response Center known as the "10 Immutable Laws of Security." The first law dictates that if a malicious user has physical access to your computer, it's no longer your computer. Unless you can provide the means to control access to the hardware, your data can easily be stolen, compromised, damaged, or destroyed. Hardware locks, secure server rooms, and security personnel can all be instrumental in helping to protect your data.

❑ **Minimize the Visibility of the Server** — SQL Servers should never be publicly available. The Slammer worm should never have been a problem, had application architects and database administrators taken the necessary precautions to protect against that type of attack. Slammer was able to propagate so much, so fast, because few organizations recognized the harm in publishing SQL connectivity through their firewalls. A well-designed database application will use a robust and secure front-end, minimizing the exposure to the Database Engine.

❑ **Remove or Disable Unnecessary Services and Applications** — You should minimize the attack surface of your SQL Server as much as possible by turning off services and features that will not be used. Typically, it's a good idea to avoid running other services such as IIS, Active Directory, and Exchange on the same machine as SQL. Each one of these services can be a potential entry point for a malicious user to exploit, thereby granting the user access to your data. Because SQL Server Reporting Services no longer requires IIS, this can help reduce the attack surface of your system.

❑ **Use Windows Authentication Whenever Possible** — Windows and Kerberos authentication are inherently more secure than SQL Authentication, but this is a design decision that you, your application developers, and security team must address.

❑ **Do Not Use Column Encryption on Frequently Searched Columns** — Encrypting frequently accessed or searched columns may cause more problems than it solves. If encrypting a column is the best, or only, way to protect the data, make sure that the performance impact is tested before implementing encryption in production.

❑ **Use TDE to Protect Data at Rest** — Encrypting the database and transaction log files can reduce the likelihood that someone can copy your data files and walk away with sensitive business data.

❑ **Always Back up Data Encryption Keys** — This is probably pretty self-explanatory, but make sure that any of the keys you use to back up your data, or other encryption keys, are safely and securely backed up. Test your backup and recovery strategy, as well.

❑ **Understand Your Role in the Company's Security Policy** — Most organizations have a documented security policy that defines acceptable use for the network and expectations for server or service behavior. As a database administrator, your responsibilities to configure and secure your servers may be documented as part of the overall security policy. What is expected of you and of your servers must be unambiguous. Your liabilities should also be clearly stated.

Summary

In this chapter, you learned about many of the security features available to you in SQL Server 2008. You should have a good understanding of the way security is applied to SQL Server from the top down, including:

❑ How to configure the different authentication modes

❑ How to create and manage server and database principals

❑ How to assign and control permissions

❑ How to protect your data on the server

You should also be able to apply some of the best practices discussed in this chapter to your own environments. Remember that you will never have a server that is 100 percent secure, and you should never be overconfident of your security design, because complacency leads to sloppiness, which leads to *ginormous* holes in your security design. But having read this chapter, you should feel confident in implementing the security mechanisms covered.

In Chapter 7, you will learn about creating and managing SQL endpoints and how you can enable access to database resources using a variety of connectivity methods.

Configuring SQL Server Network Communication

SQL Server 2008 is a client-server application designed to efficiently exchange data and instructions over multiple network connections. Understanding the network connections and how they can be configured is a big part of a DBA's job. Microsoft has made your job easier by minimizing the number of network protocols that SQL Server 2008 supports to the most commonly implemented protocols, but at the same time, the job of the DBA is made more complex by the ability to configure multiple connection types with each protocol with the endpoint server object. This chapter discusses the different endpoints that can be configured, as well as the protocol configurations that the endpoints rely on. The chapter also takes a brief look at the client configurations that can be configured with SQL Server 2008.

SQL Server 2008 Network Protocols

SQL Server 2008 provides support for four protocols:

❏   Shared Memory

❏   TCP/IP

❏   Named Pipes

❏   Virtual Interface Adapter (VIA)

By default, the only network protocols enabled for most editions of SQL Server are TCP/IP and Shared Memory. The Developer and Enterprise Evaluation editions are configured with all protocols except Shared Memory disabled during installation, but the remaining protocols can be enabled if required. If a protocol is not enabled, SQL Server will not listen on an endpoint that is configured to use that protocol. This helps reduce the attack surface of SQL Server.

SQL Server Configuration Manager is used to configure server protocols. With this tool, each supported protocol can be enabled, disabled, and configured as required. The configuration options of the network protocols may not be intuitive, so they justify a little explanation.

Opening SQL Server Configuration Manager displays a node for configuring SQL Server services, SQL Server network protocols, and SQL Native Client protocols. To configure the Server protocols, expand the SQL Server 2008 Network Configuration node and select the instance to be configured. The right-hand pane shows all four of the supported protocols and their status. To display the configurable properties of any of the protocols, double-click on the protocol or right-click on the protocol and select Properties to launch the corresponding Properties window.

Shared Memory

The Shared Memory protocol can only be used by local connections, because it is a shared memory and process space used for inter-server communication. It has only one configurable property: `Enabled`. The `Enabled` property can be set to `Yes` or `No`, resulting in a status of `Enabled` or `Disabled`. Applications or tasks that are designed to run locally on a SQL Server can take advantage of the Shared Memory protocol.

Named Pipes

Named Pipes uses Interprocess Communication (IPC) channels for efficient inter-server communication, as well as local area network (LAN) communication. The Named Pipes protocol has some enhancements in SQL Server 2008 including support for encrypted traffic, but because of the excessive overhead of Named Pipes when connecting across networks or firewalls and the additional port that Named Pipes requires to be opened (445), it is generally a good idea to leave the Named Pipes protocol disabled. However, there are many applications, particularly older applications, that require the Named Pipes protocol because they were designed around NetBIOS or other LAN-based protocols. Named Pipes provides easy access to Remote Procedure Calls (RPC) within a single security domain and thus is advantageous to these applications. If you need to support one of these applications and the SQL Server is not exposed to external traffic, the risk of enabling the Named Pipes protocol and corresponding endpoint is minimal.

Named Pipes has two configurable properties: `Enabled` and `Pipe Name`. The `Enabled` property works the same as the Shared Memory protocol. The `Pipe Name` specifies the inter-process pipe that SQL Server will listen on. The default pipe is `\\.\pipe\MSSQL$<instance_name>\sql\query`.

TCP/IP

The TCP/IP protocol is the primary and preferred protocol for most SQL Server installations. It is configured on two separate tabs on the TCP/IP Properties window: the Protocol tab and the IP Addresses tab, as shown in Figure 7-1.

The Protocol tab has the following three configurable properties:

❑   `Enabled` — This works the same as the other protocols.

❑   `Keep Alive` — This specifies how many milliseconds SQL Server waits to verify that an idle connection is still valid by sending a `KEEPALIVE` packet. The default is 30,000 milliseconds.

❑   `Listen All` — This specifies whether SQL Server will listen on all IP addresses configured on the server.

As you can see in Figure 7-1, the "IP Addresses" tab contains configuration settings for each configured IP address on the server and one section for the configuring of all IP addresses. In addition to IPv4, SQL Server 2008 now includes support for IPv6 addresses.

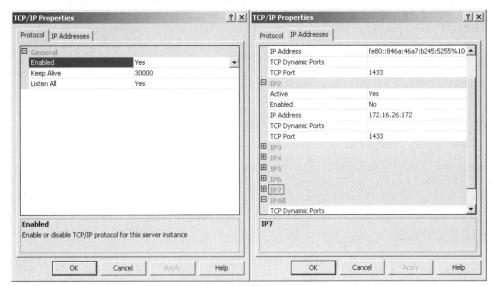

Figure 7-1: Tabs for configuring the TCP/IP protocol.

A detailed explanation of the pros and cons of IPv6 is outside the scope of this book, but you should be aware that it is not uncommon for a single physical adapter to have multiple IPv6 addresses associated with it. Unlike IPv4 addresses, which allow variable-length network masks, IPv6 addresses use fixed-length fields for the network portion and the host portion of the address (each portion uses 64 bits, or half, of the available address). A single host may belong to one or more networks, as defined by the IPv6 protocol. For example, a single host computer will have one IPv6 address to identify it on a non-routed network segment, a second IPv6 address to identify it on a LAN that may include multiple routes, and a third IP address to uniquely identify it on the Internet. What is interesting about IPv6 is that in all cases, the host portion of the address (the second half) stays the same (and is usually a variant of the hardware, or MAC address of the adapter), and the network portion of the address (the first 64 bits) will be different, to identify the networks to which the host machine is connected.

SQL Server will have more than one IPv4 address as well, if only to include the loopback (127.0.0.1) address. All IP addresses, whether version 4 or version 6, are managed from the "IP Addresses" tab of the TCP/IP Properties window.

IP address settings are described in the following table:

Setting	Description
Active	Specifies whether the individual address is active and available on the server. This setting is not available for the IPALL configuration (shown in the bottom of the right-hand pane in Figure 7-1).
Enabled	If the Listen All property on the Protocol tab is set to No, this property indicates whether SQL Server is listening on the IP address. If the Listen All property on the Protocol tab is set to Yes, the Enabled property is ignored. This setting is not available for the IPALL configuration.

Continued

263

Setting	Description
IP Address	Specifies the IP address for individual configuration, not available for the IPALL configuration.
TCP Dynamic Ports	Specifies whether the TCP port will be dynamically generated at start-up. If left blank, dynamic assignment is disabled. A setting of 0 (zero) specifies that dynamic assignment is enabled.
TCP Ports	Specifies the TCP port to be used for all addresses in the IPALL section or the port for a specific address in an individual IP address section. If dynamic port assignment is enabled, this property will display the value of the dynamically configured port.

Virtual Interface Adapter (VIA)

SQL Server 2008, like its predecessors, also supports the Virtual Interface Adapter protocol, which is used with supported hardware and network configurations. The Virtual Interface Architecture was jointly developed by Compaq (now HP), Intel, and Microsoft, and was designed as a high-performance protocol that could reduce much of the overhead of traditional networking protocols by operating in a user-mode context instead of in a kernel-mode context. VIA network clients connect to a System Area Network (not to be confused with a Storage Area Network, despite the fact that they share an acronym).

SQL Native Client Configuration

The same four server-side protocols are supported for the SQL Native Client, and, again, SQL Server Configuration Manager is used to enable, disable, or configure these protocols. In addition to the configuration of the client protocols, the binding order of the protocols can also be set. You can do this by expanding the SQL Native Client Configuration node and selecting Client Protocols. In the right-hand pane, right-click on a protocol and select Order to set the order of all enabled protocols, as shown in Figure 7-2.

As Figure 7-2 shows, if the Shared Memory protocol is enabled, it is always first in the binding order. It is not available for manual ordering.

Aliases can be created using the SQL Native Client Configuration. Aliases are very useful in enabling clients to connect to a server even though the name of the server does not match that in the client's connection string. For example, a standby server may be brought up to take the place of a failed server that serves an application with a hard-coded connection string. Without an alias, either the application's connection string would need to be changed, or the server name would have to be changed. By specifying an alias, client requests can be directed to the server without changing the server name. Aliases can also be used to replace a complicated named-instance name.

Figure 7-3 shows the alias YODAHOME being configured for the named instance AUGHTEIGHT\DAGOBAH. To launch the New Alias dialog, right-click on the Aliases node and select "New Alias." Once the alias has been created, new connections can be created by referencing the alias name in lieu of the instance name.

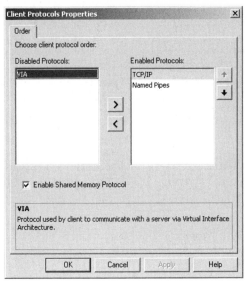

Figure 7-2: Setting the order of enabled protocols.

Figure 7-3: Configuring the alias YODAHOME.

SQL Server Endpoints

When SQL Server 2005 came out, there was a lot of confusion and trepidation about SQL Server Endpoints. More to the point, I think a lot of people I worked with were unsure about what they were and why they would use them. The term *endpoint* simply refers to a point of termination on a network, or to be perfectly precise, an *endpoint* is the name for the entity on one end of a transport layer connection. In previous releases of SQL Server, the default network endpoints were UDP port 1434 for the SQL Server Resolution Service and TCP port 1433 for the default instance of SQL Server. Additional TCP ports could be configured for the default and/or any additional named instances. Most database administrators didn't really think of the server listener as an endpoint, but that's what it is, and that's what it will remain. SQL Server 2008 leverages connection objects as endpoints, allowing SQL Server 2008 to listen on different ports, using different transport protocols for different services.

SQL Server provides four different types of endpoints:

❑   TSQL (both default and TCP)
❑   Database Mirroring
❑   SOAP
❑   Service Broker

Each endpoint provides separate functionality and can be uniquely configured to control access to the Database Engine and associated services.

Default TSQL Endpoints

TSQL endpoints are essentially the same as the standard endpoints that existed in earlier versions of Microsoft SQL Server. During installation, five TSQL endpoints are created:

❑   TSQL Default TCP
❑   TSQL Default VIA
❑   TSQL Named Pipes
❑   TSQL Local Machine
❑   Dedicated Administrator Connection (DAC)

The TSQL endpoints are created to provide connection services for the four supported protocols (TCP, VIA, Named Pipes, and Shared Memory). These protocols correspond to the Default TCP, Default VIA, Named Pipes, and Local Machine endpoints. The fifth endpoint created to support the DAC listens on a dedicated TCP port that is configured at start-up to support an administrative connection. The configured port is logged in the current SQL Server log file. (SQL Server log files are described in Chapter 10.)

Regardless of the condition of the network protocol, TSQL endpoints have two states: *started* and *stopped*. If the network protocol is enabled and the endpoint is started, SQL Server will listen and accept connections on that endpoint. A stopped endpoint still listens, but actively refuses new connections. If the corresponding protocol is disabled, the TSQL endpoint will not listen and will not respond to client requests.

TSQL endpoints are also known as *Tabular Data Stream* (TDS) endpoints. TDS has been around since Sybase created it in 1984 to support its fledgling relational Database Engine. Microsoft inherited the protocol during its joint venture with Sybase and has since made many changes to the protocol to make it more efficient and secure. It remains the primary protocol for transmitting data from SQL Server to clients via the TCP, Named Pipes, VIA, and Shared Memory protocols.

TSQL Default TCP

The TSQL Default TCP endpoint is created during the installation of a SQL Server instance and is automatically configured to listen on port 1433 for default instances. Named-instance TSQL Default TCP endpoints are randomly assigned a TCP port every time the named instance starts up. However, the port number for named instances can be statically configured with SQL Server Configuration Manager. Configuring a static port can simplify client access and reduce the dependency on the SQL Server Browser Service that enumerates named instances.

To statically configure the port that a named instance of SQL Server will listen on, open SQL Server Configuration Manager, expand the SQL Server 2008 Network Configuration node, and select the instance to configure. Double-click on the TCP/IP protocol in the right-hand pane, or right-click on it and click Properties to launch the TCP/IP Properties window. By default, SQL Server is configured to listen on all available IP addresses, and so the only place that the static port needs to be set is in the IPALL section of the IP Addresses tab on the TCP/IP Properties window (see Figure 7-4). This behavior can be changed by setting the `Listen All` property to `No` on the Protocol tab and individually configuring each IP address.

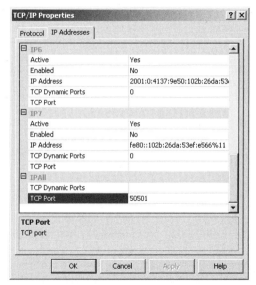

Figure 7-4: The IPALL section of the IP Addresses tab.

Figure 7-4 shows the TCP port for the named instance DAGOBAH being statically set to port 50101. When configuring ports for named instances, it is best practice to choose a port above 50,000, because many ports below 50,000 are associated with other applications. To retrieve a list of reserved and well-known ports, visit the Internet Assigned Numbers Authority (IANA) web site at www.iana.org/assignments/port-numbers.

Keep in mind that the supported protocols are separate from endpoints, and multiple endpoints can be configured for each protocol. In fact, it might be necessary to create multiple TCP endpoints, either for security reasons, such as publishing a SQL Server through a firewall using the non-default port; or for enabling connections that execute against specific processors with Non-Uniform Memory Access (NUMA).

By default, all users have access to the Default TCP endpoint. However, access to the endpoint, as well as any user-created endpoints, can be more tightly controlled with the GRANT CONNECT | DENY CONNECT | REVOKE CONNECT commands.

The state of any endpoint can also be changed with the ALTER ENDPOINT command, as shown in the following example:

```
USE Master;
GO
ALTER ENDPOINT [TSQL Default TCP]
STATE=STOPPED;

USE Master;
GO
ALTER ENDPOINT [TSQL Default TCP]
STATE=STARTED;
```

TSQL Default VIA

The VIA protocol is used to support VIA hardware devices such as VIA System Area Networks (SAN). The VIA protocol is dependent on vendor implementations, so a discussion of the VIA endpoint is somewhat difficult without seemingly endorsing one hardware vendor over another. The VIA configurations are usually very straightforward and only require a port assignment. If you are using a VIA hardware implementation for your SAN configuration, make sure you get all the technical documentation you can from your supplier.

TSQL Named Pipes

The Named Pipes endpoint is created to support Named Pipes protocol connections. The Named Pipes protocol was described earlier in this chapter.

TSQL Local Machine

The TSQL Local Machine endpoint allows connections to occur using the Shared Memory protocol. Shared Memory is only accessible on the local machine, hence the TSQL Local Machine designation for this endpoint. Installations of the Enterprise Evaluation and Developer editions of SQL Server 2008 use this endpoint exclusively, unless additional protocols are enabled.

Dedicated Administrator Connection (DAC)

The Dedicated Administrator Connection (DAC) endpoint is used to support limited administrative actions when other connections are unavailable or unresponsive. It uses its own memory area, dedicated TCP port, and CPU scheduler. By default, the DAC endpoint only listens for local connections. Remote DAC connections can be enabled by executing the following code:

```
USE Master;
GO
sp_configure 'remote admin connections', 1;
GO
RECONFIGURE;
GO
```

DAC connections are facilitated through the SQLCMD command-line tool.

TSQL TCP Endpoints

In addition to the default TCP endpoints created automatically, additional TSQL TCP endpoints can be created. These TSQL TCP endpoints can be created to support special security or application requirements. However, an important fact to keep in mind is that when a new TSQL TCP endpoint is created, SQL Server automatically revokes all connect permissions to the default endpoint. If connection support is still required for the default endpoint, explicit GRANT CONNECT permissions will be necessary to use the default endpoint. SQL Server helps you remember this important fact by always returning a message informing you of the impact of creating a new TCP endpoint, as shown in the next example.

If an additional TSQL TCP endpoint is needed, it can be created using T-SQL. The following example creates an additional TSQL TCP endpoint that is configured to listen on port 50102 and all IP addresses and shows the resulting message warning about permissions:

```
USE Master;
GO
CREATE ENDPOINT DagobahEP
STATE = STARTED
AS TCP
    (LISTENER_PORT = 50102, LISTENER_IP = ALL)
FOR TSQL();
GO

RESULTS:
-------------------------------------------------------------------------
Creation of a TSQL endpoint will result in the revocation of any 'Public' connect
  permissions on the 'TSQL Default TCP' endpoint.  If 'Public' access is desired on
  this endpoint, reapply this permission using 'GRANT CONNECT ON ENDPOINT::[TSQL
  Default TCP] to [public]'.
```

If a single IP address is needed, the LISTENER_IP argument can be set to a specific value inside parentheses, as the following example illustrates:

```
USE Master;
GO
CREATE ENDPOINT DagobahEP
STATE = STARTED
AS TCP
    (LISTENER_PORT = 50102, LISTENER_IP = (192.168.1.101))
FOR TSQL();
GO
```

As mentioned earlier, IPv6 is also supported by SQL Server 2008. The address can be configured by passing in the hexadecimal IPv6 address as a binary string in single quotes enclosed in parentheses, as the following example illustrates:

```
USE Master;
GO
CREATE ENDPOINT DagobahEPv6
STATE = STARTED
AS TCP
```

```
    (LISTENER_PORT = 50102
    , LISTENER_IP = ('fe80::846a:46a7:b245:5255'))
FOR TSQL();
GO
```

In a previous example, the TCP/IP protocol was configured for the named instance DAGOBAH to listen on port 50101. With the additional endpoint and associated port, it will be necessary to add the port to the TCP/IP protocol with SQL Server Configuration Manager. This is done by simply adding another port to the port assignment delimited by a comma, as shown in Figure 7-5.

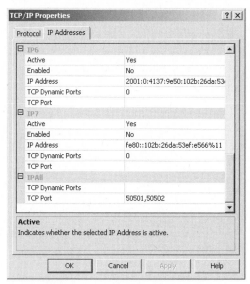

Figure 7-5: Adding another port to the port assignment.

Database Mirroring Endpoints

SQL Server 2008 uses a mirroring endpoint for exclusive use of the server that is configured to participate in a database mirroring configuration. In mirroring, which is described in Chapter 12, each instance of SQL Server is required to have its own dedicated database mirroring endpoint. All mirroring communication uses this database mirroring endpoint, but client connections to a database configured with a mirror use the standard TDS endpoint.

The configuration of an exclusive mirroring endpoint ensures that database mirror process communication is handled in a separate process from all other database activities. The easiest way to configure mirroring endpoints is to run the Mirroring Wizard as explained in Chapter 12. To create and configure a mirroring endpoint manually and enforce secure encrypted communication over the endpoint, the following code can be used:

```
CREATE ENDPOINT AughtEightDagobahMirror
  AUTHORIZATION sa
  STATE=STARTED
```

```
AS TCP (LISTENER_PORT = 5022, LISTENER_IP = ALL)
FOR DATA_MIRRORING
(ROLE = PARTNER, AUTHENTICATION = WINDOWS NEGOTIATE
,ENCRYPTION = REQUIRED ALGORITHM RC4);
```

This example can be used to create the mirroring endpoint on either the principal or mirror server. It assumes that the same domain account is used for the SQL Server service on both the principal and the mirror. For the witness server, the ROLE argument would need to be changed to WITNESS.

If different accounts are used for each MSSQLSERVER service on the servers, logins that are mapped to the service accounts from each server will need to be granted the CONNECT permission to the other servers participating in the mirroring configuration. The following script can be run to ensure encrypted authenticated communication between the three servers configured to take part in a mirroring relationship. AughtEight is the principal server, Dagobah is the mirror server, and Tatooine is the witness server. In this example, all three instances are running on the same physical server, which is why each endpoint is configured with a different port number. In the case of separate physical servers, the port numbers could be configured consistently.

```
--Run on AughtEight

USE Master;
GO
CREATE ENDPOINT AughtEightDagobahPrincipal
 AS TCP (LISTENER_PORT = 5022)
 FOR DATA_MIRRORING (ROLE = PARTNER, ENCRYPTION = REQUIRED ALGORITHM RC4);
GO
CREATE LOGIN [AughtEight\DagobahSQL] FROM WINDOWS;
CREATE LOGIN [AughtEight\TatooineSQL] FROM WINDOWS;
GO
GRANT CONNECT ON ENDPOINT::AughtEightDagobahPrincipal
 TO [AughtEight\TatooineSQL];
GRANT CONNECT ON ENDPOINT::AughtEightDagobahPrincipal
 TO [AughtEight\DagobahSQL];

--Run on Dagobah
USE Master;
GO
CREATE ENDPOINT AughtEightDagobahMirror
  AS TCP (LISTENER_PORT = 5023)
   FOR DATA_MIRRORING (ROLE = PARTNER, ENCRYPTION = REQUIRED ALGORITHM RC4);
GO
CREATE LOGIN [AughtEight\AughtEightSQL] FROM WINDOWS;
CREATE LOGIN [AughtEight\TatooineSQL] FROM WINDOWS;
GO
GRANT CONNECT ON ENDPOINT::AughtEightDagobahMirror
TO [AughtEight\AughtEightSQL];
GRANT CONNECT ON ENDPOINT::AughtEightDagobahMirror
TO [AughtEight\TatooineSQL];

--Run on Tatooine
USE Master;
GO
CREATE ENDPOINT AughtEightDagobahWitness
  AS TCP (LISTENER_PORT = 5024)
```

```
        FOR DATA_MIRRORING (ROLE = WITNESS, ENCRYPTION = REQUIRED ALGORITHM RC4);
    GO
    CREATE LOGIN [AughtEight\AughtEightSQL] FROM WINDOWS;
    CREATE LOGIN [AughtEight\DagobahSQL] FROM WINDOWS;
    GO
    GRANT CONNECT ON ENDPOINT::AughtEightDagobahWitness
    TO [AughtEight\AughtEightSQL];
    GRANT CONNECT ON ENDPOINT::AughtEightDagobahWitness
    TO [AughtEight\DagobahSQL];
```

The preceding commands set up the communication framework for mirroring, but do not actually initialize mirroring. See Chapter 12 for more information on how to configure and monitor mirroring.

SOAP Endpoints

Simple Object Access Protocol (SOAP) is a platform-independent protocol that defines how to use XML and HTTP to access services, objects, and servers. SOAP endpoints are created to publish SQL Server programming objects over data-tier Web Services without the use of IIS as a Web server.

Data-tier Web Services provide a very powerful alternative to XML Web Services and provide the means of exposing stored procedures and functions over HTTP the same as conventional Web Service architecture. In addition to stored procedures and functions, SOAP endpoints can be configured to allow ad hoc queries, but as a general rule, ad hoc access should be avoided.

Although SOAP endpoints were introduced in SQL Server 2005, they have been considered deprecated in SQL Server 2008. Microsoft intends to remove SOAP endpoints in a future version of SQL Server. Microsoft recommends that existing applications that use SOAP endpoints should instead switch to using either ASP.NET or Windows Communications Foundation (WCF). The information provided in this section regarding the configuration of SOAP endpoints should be treated as reference only, and development of applications that use SOAP endpoints in SQL Server should be discouraged.

SOAP endpoints return SOAP messages consisting of an XML document with a header and a body. SOAP messages are essentially one-way transmissions from a sender to a receiver. SOAP does not define any application semantics such as a programming model or implementation-specific details. Web Services, on the other hand, require a request/response model. The solution is to send SOAP messages within the body of an HTTP request and response. This solution provides the required model for Web Services, and SOAP endpoints provide the structure to accomplish the communication.

In order to be able to create SOAP endpoints successfully, the URL must already be registered with the HTTP.sys kernel-mode driver. This will ensure that requests for the SOAP endpoint URL are passed to the SQL Server, and not handled by other applications, such as IIS. If the SQL Server service account has full administrative permissions on the local machine, this can be performed by using the `sp_reserve_http_namespace` stored procedure. However, since it is generally not recommended to run SQL Server services under an administrative account, you may have to register the URL manually using the `netsh` Windows configuration tool (for Windows Server 2003 environments, use the `httpcfg` Windows system tool) before executing the `sp_reserve_http_namespace` stored procedure.

The following syntax is used for creating a SOAP endpoint:

```
CREATE ENDPOINT endPointName [ AUTHORIZATION login ]
STATE = { STARTED | STOPPED | DISABLED }
AS HTTP (
PATH = 'url'
  , AUTHENTICATION =( { BASIC | DIGEST | INTEGRATED | NTLM | KERBEROS }
    [ ,...n ] )
  , PORTS = ( { CLEAR | SSL} [ ,... n ] )
  )

FOR SOAP (
  [ { WEBMETHOD ['namespace'.] 'method_alias'
  (    NAME = 'database.schema.name'
  )
  } [ ,...n ] ]
  [ , DATABASE = { 'database_name' | DEFAULT }
  [ , HEADER_LIMIT = int ])
```

Because syntax specifications can be a bit arcane, the following example is provided to demonstrate the creation of a SOAP endpoint. The example creates a SOAP endpoint called *AWSales* that uses Windows integrated security to control access to a Web Service that is published at the location `http://AughtEight/AdventureWorks2008/Sales`. The endpoint exposes the stored procedure `AdventureWorks2008.dbo.uspGetBillOfMaterials` as the Web method `GetBillOfMaterials`. The SOAP document that is created by this Web Service can be viewed by opening Internet Explorer and navigating to the Web Service URL and appending a Web Service Description Language (WSDL) query to the end of the URL:

```
http://AughtEight/AdventureWorks2008/Sales?wsdl
```

Keep in mind that you will most likely have to change the server name in your environment.

```
USE master;
--Turn on Advanced Options for the sp_configure utility
EXEC sp_configure 'show advanced option', '1';
RECONFIGURE
GO
-- enable xp_cmdshell
EXEC sp_configure 'xp_cmdshell', '1';
RECONFIGURE
GO
--Allow SQL to create the reservation (Windows Server 2008/Vista only)
EXEC xp_cmdshell 'netsh http add urlacl url=
http://AughtEight:80/AdventureWorks2008 user=AughtEight\SQLService delegate=yes';
GO

--Reserve the URL
EXEC sp_reserve_http_namespace N'http://AughtEight:80/AdventureWorks2008';
GO
```

```
-- Create the SOAP endpoint
USE Master;
GO
CREATE ENDPOINT AWSales
STATE = STARTED
AS HTTP(
        PATH = '/AdventureWorks2008/Sales'
        ,AUTHENTICATION = (INTEGRATED)
        ,PORTS = ( CLEAR )
        ,SITE = 'AughtEight')
FOR SOAP(
WEBMETHOD 'GetBillOfMaterials'
        (NAME='AdventureWorks2008.dbo.uspGetBillOfMaterials'
        ,FORMAT=ROWSETS_ONLY)
        ,WSDL = DEFAULT
        ,DATABASE = 'AdventureWorks2008'
        ,NAMESPACE = 'http://AughtEight/'
     );
GO
```

In the preceding example, the xp_cmdshell extended stored procedure was used to execute the necessary netsh command to allow SQL to register the URL, although this can be just as easily done from a command line. Because xp_cmdshell is disabled by default, the sp_configure stored procedure had to be run to enable its use.

Although Internet Explorer can be used to view the SOAP document, the real use for data-tier Web Services is for applications that are created to connect to and consume XML Web Services. Later in this chapter, you will see how to do this.

The HTTP arguments available for configuration in a CREATE ENDPOINT statement are described in the following table:

Argument	Description
PATH	Specifies the path of the Web Service. An analogous setting would be the virtual directory name in IIS. Thus, the PATH setting specifies what comes after the http://Servername, as specified in the SITE argument.
AUTHENTICATION	The AUTHENTICATION argument is used to specify what type or types of authentication are allowed for the endpoint. One or more of the following settings can be configured: BASIC, DIGEST, NTLM, KERBEROS, or INTEGRATED. Multiple settings can be specified by comma-delimiting the settings.
PORTS	Specifies whether HTTP or HTTPS is used with the endpoint. When CLEAR is specified, HTTP is used. SSL specifies that requests must use HTTPS. Both CLEAR and SSL can be configured concurrently, enabling communication with either HTTP or HTTPS.

Argument	Description
SITE	The SITE argument specifies the host name used along with the PATH configuration. Possible choices are '*', '+', or 'webSite'. ❑ The asterisk ('*') specifies that the endpoint will listen to all available hostnames that are not reserved. ❑ The plus sign ('+') specifies that the endpoint will listen to all configured hostnames. ❑ webSite is used for a specific server name (e.g., _AughtEight_).
CLEAR_PORT	Specifies the clear port to use. The default is 80.
SSL_PORT	Specifies the SSL port to use. The default is 443.
AUTH_REALM	AUTH_REALM defaults to NONE, but when the AUTHENTICATION argument is DIGEST, AUTH_REALM can be used to return the digest realm hint to the client.
DEFAULT_LOGON_DOMAIN	When AUTHENTICATION is set to BASIC, this setting specifies the default login domain. The default is NONE.
COMPRESSION	When set to ENABLED, SQL Server will process requests where gzip encoding is accepted and return compressed responses. The default setting is DISABLED.

The configurable SOAP arguments are described in the following table:

Argument	Description
WEBMETHOD	The published method that will be exposed through an HTTP SOAP request to an endpoint. More than one WEBMETHOD clause can be defined to publish multiple SQL Server functions and stored procedures. In the preceding example, the WEBMETHOD was GetBillOfMaterials.
(WEBMETHOD) NAME	The physical name of the function or procedure published as the Web method, as in AdventureWorks2008.dbo.uspGetBillOfMaterials.

Continued

Argument	Description
(WEBMETHOD) SCHEMA	Determines whether an inline XSD schema will be returned for the Web method in SOAP responses. The possible choices are NONE, STANDARD, and DEFAULT. ❏ NONE omits the Web method from the schema if a schema is returned. ❏ STANDARD specifies that an XSD schema is returned. ❏ DEFAULT specifies that the endpoint SCHEMA option setting is to be used.
(WEBMETHOD) FORMAT	Specifies the format of data returned by the endpoint. The possible choices are ALL_RESULTS, ROWSETS_ONLY, and NONE. The default is ALL_RESULTS. ❏ ALL_RESULTS specifies that a result set or row count, including any error message or warnings, is returned. ❏ ROWSETS_ONLY specifies that just the result set is returned without errors, warnings, or row count information. ❏ NONE configures the endpoint not to return any SOAP-specific formatting with the result. If this option is used, the stored procedure or function is responsible for proper formatting of the result set as well-formed XML.
BATCHES	The BATCHES argument specifies whether ad-hoc batches can be sent to the endpoint. It can be set to ENABLED or DISABLED. The default setting is DISABLED.
WSDL	*WSDL* stands for "Web Services Description Language." The WSDL setting is used to determine how a SOAP endpoint responds to a WSDL request. The possible configuration settings are NONE, DEFAULT, or the name of a stored procedure that returns the desired WSDL information. ❏ NONE specifies that the endpoint will not return any information to a WSDL request. ❏ DEFAULT specifies that basic metadata about the published Web method will be returned to a WSDL request. This information includes any possible parameters and the type of data returned. ❏ Proc_Name is a procedure created to return a custom WSDL document to a WSDL request.

Argument	Description
SESSIONS	When set to ENABLED, allows multiple SOAP request/response message pairs in a single SOAP session. The default is DISABLED.
LOGIN_TYPE	Specifies which type of Login authentication is supported by the endpoint. The choices are WINDOWS and MIXED. The choices correspond to the Server Authentication Mode. If WINDOWS is specified, only Windows logins will be allowed. If MIXED is specified, both Windows and SQL Server logins are allowed.
SESSION_TIMEOUT	Specifies how long a session will stay open without activity. The value is an integer and specifies the number of seconds to wait before closing a session. Subsequent requests that use an expired session ID will return an exception.
DATABASE	Specifies the database context that the Web method will be executed in.
NAMESPACE	Specifies an XML namespace to be used with the endpoint. If no namespace is specified, or if the DEFAULT option is used, the namespace will be configured as http://tempuri.org.
SCHEMA	Like the WEBMETHOD SCHEMA argument, this option specifies whether inline XML Schema Definition (XSD) data is returned. The possible choices are NONE and STANDARD. ❑ NONE configures the endpoint not to return inline XSD data with the SOAP response. ❑ STANDARD specifies that inline XSD data is returned with the SOAP response. If the SCHEMA setting is omitted in the WEBMETHOD section, the Web method will use the setting specified here.
CHARACTER_SET	Specifies what to do with result data that is not valid in an XML document. The two choices are XML and SQL. ❑ XML specifies that all characters are returned as XML or delimited XML, and is the default setting. ❑ SQL specifies that non-XML characters are encoded as character references, and are returned with the XML data.
HEADER_LIMIT	Configures the maximum size of the header section in the SOAP envelope. The default size is 8 K. If the SOAP headers are larger than the configured size, a parsing exception will be thrown.

Service Broker Endpoints

As described in Chapter 19, Service Broker is a powerful feature of SQL Server 2008 that enables database applications to communicate asynchronously with other database applications in a Service-Oriented Architecture (SOA). Service Broker endpoints are only required if the two instances of the broker service are located on separate instances of SQL Server. They are created in much the same way as SOAP endpoints. The basic CREATE ENDPOINT command is used, but instead of the FOR SOAP clause that defines the endpoint as a SOAP endpoint, the FOR SERVICE_BROKER clause is used. The syntax for creating a Service Broker endpoint is as follows:

```
CREATE ENDPOINT endPointName [ AUTHORIZATION login ]
STATE = { STARTED | STOPPED | DISABLED }
AS TCP (
  LISTENER_PORT = listenerPort
  [ [ , ] LISTENER_IP = ALL | ( 4-part-ip ) | ( "ip_address_v6" ) ]
)
FOR SERVICE_BROKER (
  [ AUTHENTICATION = { WINDOWS [ { NTLM | KERBEROS | NEGOTIATE } ]
  | CERTIFICATE certificate_name
  | WINDOWS [ { NTLM | KERBEROS | NEGOTIATE } ] CERTIFICATE certificate_name
  | CERTIFICATE certificate_name WINDOWS [ { NTLM | KERBEROS | NEGOTIATE } ]
} ]
  [ [ , ] ENCRYPTION = { DISABLED | { { SUPPORTED | REQUIRED }
    [ ALGORITHM { RC4 | AES | AES RC4 | RC4 AES } ] }
  ]
  [ [ , ] MESSAGE_FORWARD_SIZE = forward_size ]
)
```

An example of this syntax put in use to create a Service Broker endpoint is as follows:

```
CREATE ENDPOINT MyEndpoint
STATE = STARTED
AS TCP ( LISTENER_PORT = 50001 )
FOR SERVICE_BROKER ( AUTHENTICATION = WINDOWS );
```

In all likelihood, when creating Service Broker or mirroring endpoints, certificates will be used to ensure authenticated and encrypted traffic between endpoints, especially if the endpoints are located on different physical servers. For more information on the workings of Service Broker, take a look at Chapter 19. For information about creating and using certificates, see Chapter 6.

Securing Endpoints

A critically important aspect of all endpoints is securing them so that only connections that are authorized can enumerate and call the Web methods or other services that the endpoint provides. The key permission for endpoints is the CONNECT permission. Only those logins that have been explicitly granted the CONNECT permission will be able to expose the functionality behind the endpoint. In addition, the login will need permissions to the underlying objects that the endpoint provides access for.

Data-Tier Web Services

To re-create this exercise requires that you have Visual Studio 2008 installed, as well as SQL Server 2008. As described in Chapter 2, the SQL Server 2008 installation installs a piece of Visual Studio, but it does not install everything you need to create database applications. The following examples and descriptions assume that you have installed either C# or VB.NET (or both). If you haven't, the information is still very useful, but you will not be able to practice or re-create it. The examples using Visual Studio may seem to be a bit out of context in this book. However, it is difficult to describe the use of SOAP endpoints without using a Visual Studio application to demonstrate the purpose of data tier Web Services.

Create the Endpoint

The first step is to create the endpoint that will publish the two stored procedures you want to make available via a data-tier Web Service where they can be used by any SOAP-compliant application. Execute the following code to create the SOAP endpoint HRWebService that publishes the uspGetEmployeeManagers and uspGetManagerEmployees stored procedures as the GetEmployeeManagers and GetManagerEmployees Web methods:

```
USE Master;
GO
CREATE ENDPOINT HRWebService
STATE = STARTED
AS HTTP(
        PATH = '/AdventureWorks2008/HR'
        ,AUTHENTICATION = (INTEGRATED)
        ,PORTS = ( CLEAR )
        ,SITE = 'AughtEight')
FOR SOAP(
        WEBMETHOD 'GetEmployeeManagers'
          (NAME='AdventureWorks2008.dbo.uspGetEmployeeManagers'
          ,FORMAT=ROWSETS_ONLY)
        ,WEBMETHOD 'GetManagerEmployees'
          (NAME='AdventureWorks2008.dbo.uspGetManagerEmployees'
          ,FORMAT=ROWSETS_ONLY)
        ,WSDL = DEFAULT
        ,DATABASE = 'AdventureWorks2008'
        ,NAMESPACE = 'http://AughtEight/'
    );
GO
```

Once the endpoint has been created to make the procedures visible through the Web Service, a SOAP-compliant application will be able to enumerate and reference the Web methods specified in the endpoint.

1.   Start Visual Studio 2008 and create a new VB.NET or C# Windows Application Project by clicking on the File menu, selecting New, and then Project.

2.   In the New Project window, select either Visual Basic or Visual C# from the Project Types pane, and then choose Windows Forms Application from the Templates pane, as shown in Figure 7-6. Ensure that .NET Framework 2.0 is selected (this will not work with later versions of .NET).

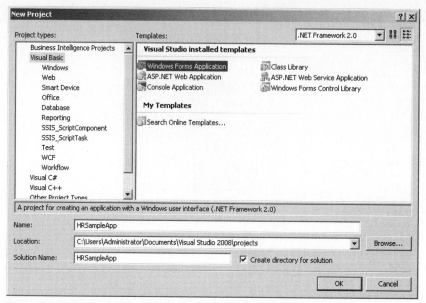

Figure 7-6: Selecting "Windows Forms Application" from the Templates pane.

3. Give the project a name such as *HRSampleApp*. Choose a folder for the solution to be created in, and click OK. A design window showing a blank Windows form will appear.

4. From the toolbox (to the left of the form designer by default), select and drag a button control to the upper-left-hand side of the form. Then drag a textbox and place it to the right of the button. Lastly, drag a datagridview control onto the form, and place it under the button and textbox controls, as shown in Figure 7-7. If the toolbox is not visible, it can be launched by pressing [Ctrl]+[Alt]+X or by selecting it from the View menu.

5. You may want to adjust the size of the form and the datagridview control to accommodate multiple columns and rows. After creating the form, right-click on the project name in the Solution Explorer window, and select "Add Web Reference," as shown in Figure 7-8.

The Add Web Reference window will display where the data-tier Web Service can be added as a Web reference to the project.

6. In the URL dropdown textbox, type in the appropriate address for your server followed by a WSDL query command. In my case, the URL and query take the form of `http://AughtEight/Adventureworks2008/hr?wsdl`.

7. Click the GO button to query the SQL Server for information regarding any Web methods published at that location. You should see results similar to those shown in Figure 7-9.

8. In the "Web reference name" field, type in the name **HRWebService**, and click OK.

Now that all the foundation work has been completed, it is time to write the code that will call on the Web methods made available with the SOAP endpoint.

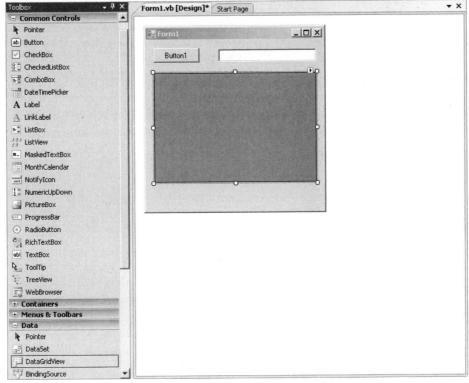

Figure 7-7: Placing a datagridview control.

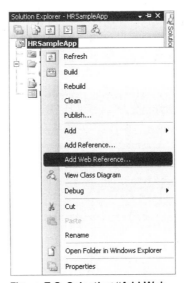

Figure 7-8: Selecting "Add Web Reference."

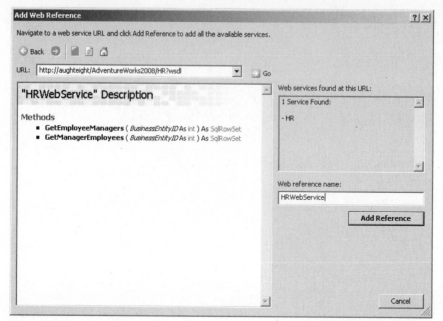

Figure 7-9: Viewing the results of a query for information regarding Web methods.

9. Double-click on the Button1 button on the Form Designer. This will launch the Code Editor window and create the basic code to handle the button `click` event. In the button `click` event handler, type in the code shown in the next example. There is one set of code for a VB.NET application, and another for Visual C# application.

Following is the Visual C# code:

```
private void button1_Click(object sender, EventArgs e)
{
  DataSet dsEmployees;
          HRWebService.HRWebService proxy =
              new HRSampleApp.HRWebService.HRWebService();
          proxy.Credentials = System.Net.CredentialCache.DefaultCredentials;

          try
          {
              Int32 intMgrID;
              intMgrID = Convert.ToInt32(textBox1.Text);
              dsEmployees = proxy.GetManagerEmployees(intMgrID);
              dataGridView1.DataSource = dsEmployees;
              dataGridView1.DataMember = dsEmployees.Tables[0].TableName;
          }
          catch (Exception ex)
          {
              MessageBox.Show(ex.Message);
          }
    }
}
```

Following is the Visual Basic.NET code:

```
Private Sub button1_Click(ByVal sender As System.Object, _
ByVal e As System.EventArgs) Handles btnGetEmployees.Click

    Dim Proxy As New HRWebService.HRWebService
    Proxy.Credentials = System.Net.CredentialCache.DefaultCredentials

    Try

        Dim dsEmployees As DataSet = Proxy.GetManagerEmployees(textBox1.Text)
        dataGridView1.DataSource = dsEmployees
        dataGridView1.DataMember = dsEmployees.Tables(0).TableName

    Catch
        MsgBox(Err.Description)
    End Try

End Sub
```

Notice that the amount of code required to consume the Web Service is actually very small. Not counting error-handling code, there are only five lines of code for VB.NET and eight lines for Visual C#. This is one of the features that make consuming Web Services so attractive; most of the work has been done at the Web Service side.

10. Once the code has been entered into the button `click` event, press [F5] or click the green triangle on the menu to start the application debugging process. If everything goes well, what you should see is the Windows form created earlier.

11. Enter the number **1** in the textbox, and click Button1. Your results should look like those in Figure 7-10.

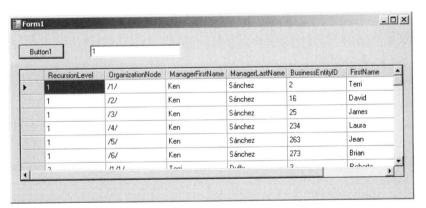

Figure 7-10: Results of entering 1.

SOAP endpoints can be created to not only return data, but also to manipulate data in the database. The amount of code required does not change dramatically.

283

As a database administrator, this may all seem a bit over the top, but it is very important to understand why developers may want to use SOAP endpoints and exactly what they do. Keep in mind, however, that SOAP endpoints are no longer supported in SQL Server 2008. Instead, encourage your developers to use Windows Communications Foundation in the newer versions of .NET Framework.

Summary

SQL Configuration Manager offers the database administrator a one-stop shop for troubleshooting and configuring SQL Server connection objects and networking devices. The tools you will use to manage these objects are simple, if not intuitive. Diagnosing networking problems has never been easier. Using the information in this chapter, you should be able to configure and secure the network protocols and endpoints that make it possible to make the most of SQL Server 2008 services and features. With the introduction of Service Broker and mirroring, the database administrator's responsibility for network and transport security has never been greater. Be sure to carefully evaluate all the security and configuration options available for each networking object to ensure the highest level of security and functionality.

In Chapter 8, you will learn about automating SQL Server 2008 administrative and maintenance processes. You'll learn to configure jobs and alerts that will keep you informed of SQL Server performance, and keep it performing at peak efficiency.

Automating Administrative Tasks

"Set it and forget it!" Wouldn't it be nice if SQL Administration were that easy? Unfortunately, that's not a realistic goal for many of us. SQL Server is a product that needs regular maintenance and monitoring to ensure the health and stability of your servers. Fortunately, there are several tools available out-of-the-box to help DBAs manage and maintain their systems. Even better are the tools you can use to automate some of these processes that can also make your job easier.

Managing the SQL Servers in your organization can be a full-time job. In fact, it might be yours! Realistically, the complexities of our database systems and applications (both supported and supporting) might be overwhelming at first, but there are many ways that you can keep your system in shape. This chapter will introduce you to some of the more common tools and features that Database Administrators can leverage to take control of their servers.

- ❑   Policy-Based Management
- ❑   Database Mail
- ❑   Event Notifications
- ❑   SQL Server Agent
- ❑   SQL Server Maintenance Plans

As you begin this chapter, understand that some of what you will learn will serve as an introduction to topics that are covered in later chapters. Backups, replication, performance monitoring, and the Service Broker are just a few of the topics that can be managed or automated through many of the tools and examples that you will see in this chapter.

> *The examples in this chapter use the local server configured as both a Simple Mail Transfer Protocol (SMTP) server and a Post Office Protocol (POP3) server. Both features are available out-of-the-box with Windows Server 2003. However, the POP3 server has been removed from Windows Server 2008. Configuration of SMTP and POP3 is beyond the scope of this book; however, there are some free POP3 servers available.*

Policy-Based Management

One of the most compelling additions to SQL Server 2008 for Database Administrators is the new Policy-Based Management feature. To simplify, Policy-Based Management allows you to define criteria that can control object creation and behavior, as well as gather information about objects that are out of compliance. It is both an automated management tool as well as a management auditing tool.

If you are familiar with how group policy objects work in the Active Directory, it's somewhat similar, in that you have a wide variety of settings that can be configured, locked, or reported on. All Policy-Based Management is configured from the Management folder of the server in SQL Server Management Studio. As you can see in Figure 8-1, there are three subfolders for the different types of management objects: Policies, Conditions, and Facets.

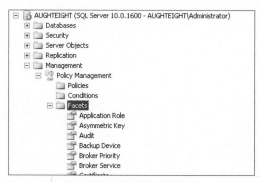

Figure 8-1: Policy Management folder.

By default, no policies are installed; however, there are several policy templates that are included when SQL Server is installed. You can import these policies from the SQL Server installation directory, which, if you used the default settings, is C:\Program Files\Microsoft SQL Server\100\Tools\Policies\DatabaseEngine\1033. These policies are disabled when they're imported, but you can enable them after you've had a chance to review and configure them.

Before creating and using policies, you should understand some of the basic components of Policy Management. These components include:

❑ Targets

❑ Facets

❑ Conditions

❑ Policies

❑ Policy categories

❑ Effective policies

Each of these topics is introduced in greater detail in the following sections.

Targets

A *target* is simply a specific entity or object that is managed by one or more policies. A target might be a single index or table, or it might be every database attached to the local server. The Database Engine itself might be the target of a policy.

Targets can also be grouped in sets, such as defining all tables that belong to a particular schema. For example, you might have a policy that specifies every table in the `Person` schema in the `AventureWorks2008` database as a target set.

Facets

Facets are collections of properties that represent all or some portion of a target object that are grouped together based on behavior or characteristics. There are 74 facets that are available from the default installation of SQL Server 2008. These include facets for databases, schemas, logins, tables, and full text catalogs, to name a few. In some cases, a facet might be just a subset of properties from another facet. For example, the Login facet includes properties such as `Name`, `LoginType`, `IsPasswordExpired`, `CreateDate`, and `DateLastModified`; whereas the Login Options facet only includes a subset of these properties, excluding `DateLastModified` and `IsPasswordExpired`, among others. Facets are used when defining a *condition*, described in the next section.

Conditions

Conditions are one or more Boolean expressions that are associated with the properties of a specific facet. When more than one expression is defined, you can decide whether to use the `AND` operator or the `OR` operator when evaluating these expressions. For example, I can create a condition called *Login Errors*, which uses the Login facet and checks to see if the `@IsDisabled`, `@IsLocked`, or `@IsPasswordExpired` properties are true. See Figure 8-2 for reference.

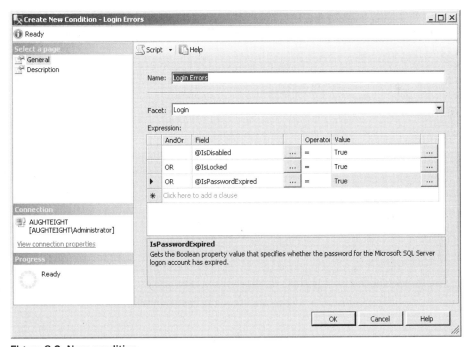

Figure 8-2: New condition.

If you import the pre-defined polices from the SQL Server installation folder, several conditions on which those policies are based will also be added to your SQL Server instance.

Policies

Policies are what you can use to evaluate, configure, or restrict your server and the objects that reside on it. Each policy consists of five main elements that must be defined. The first, obviously, is a unique name for the policy. Then, a condition that will be evaluated must be selected for the policy. The third element defines the targets against which the condition will be evaluated and to which the policy will be applied. Next, you must choose the Evaluation mode that the policy will execute against. Depending on the type of policy you are creating, you can select one of four available evaluation modes:

- ❑ **On Demand** — The policy must be run manually.

- ❑ **On Change: Prevent** — Uses DDL triggers to prevent a non-compliant event from occurring. This might be useful if, for example, you want to standardize the naming conventions on certain object types. This option will specifically prevent objects that do not comply with the naming rules from being created.

- ❑ **On Change: Log Only** — Uses DDL triggers to log non-compliant events, but will not prevent them from executing.

- ❑ **On Schedule** — Creates a SQL Server Agent job (described later in this chapter) to automatically evaluate policies.

Finally, you can also define a *Server restriction property*. This might be useful if you want to prevent the policy from applying to a specific version of SQL Server or a particular platform. Figure 8-3 shows a sample policy that uses a Login Errors condition (shown in Figure 8-2) and evaluates it manually against SQL Server 2005 and later platforms.

Note that the Enabled checkbox is grayed out. This is because the On Demand evaluation mode has been selected. If I change the evaluation mode of the policy, you can enable it as part of a scheduled operation.

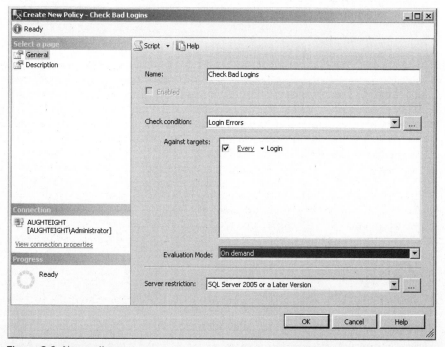

Figure 8-3: New policy.

Policy Categories

On the description page of the policy, I can set additional properties that allow me to better manage multiple policies on my server. With the default policies imported, I can see a list of available "Microsoft Best Practice" categories, or I can create my own, as shown in Figure 8-4.

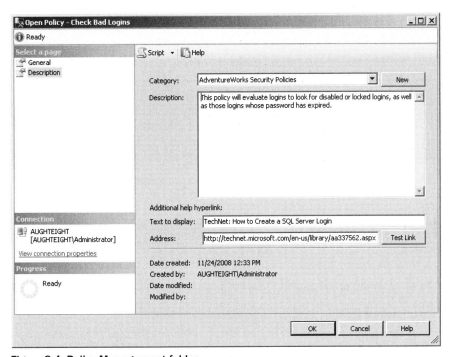

Figure 8-4: Policy Management folder.

Databases can be *subscribed* to a category, meaning that all policies within that category will automatically be evaluated against the database. Although a policy can only belong to one category, a single database can subscribe to more than one policy. This is done by right-clicking the database, choosing Policies from the context menu, and selecting Categories. From there, you will see a dialog box that lists all the available policy categories you want this database to subscribe to. By default, policy categories are enforced at the server level, automatically applying to all databases. This can be managed by right-clicking the Policy Management node in Object explorer and choosing Manage Categories. Deselecting the "Mandate Database" option for a category will allow you to subscribe individual databases to that category.

Also note in Figure 8-4 that I provided descriptive text as well as information in the additional Help hyperlink section. This allows me to provide a reference to a URL that might contain more information about that specific policy. For example, if I am creating a policy that requires a specific naming convention for certain object types, I might include a URL for the document that defines that policy.

Effective Policies

Effective policies are all policies that are being applied to an object by meeting three criteria:

❑ The policy must be enabled. This rules out policies that are configured to run "On Demand."

❑ The target identified, such as a table, must belong to the target set of the policy. A login policy has no effect on that table.

❑   The target, or a parent object in the target hierarchy, must subscribe to the policy category that contains the effective policies. This means that a policy may be applied to a table if its schema, database, or server subscribes to that policy.

Try It Out   Creating a Naming Policy

In this example, you will be creating a new policy that specifies a naming convention for tables that belong to the `Sales` schema of the `AdventureWorks2008` database. You will use this to prevent the creation of new tables that don't meet this policy condition, as well as get an accounting of tables that already exist that are not compliant with this naming policy.

1.   Begin by creating a new Policy Condition called `AWSalesTableNames`. Navigate to the Conditions folder, right-click, and select "New Condition."

2.   Enter the **AWSalesTableNames** for the Name, and select "Multipart Name" for the Facet.

3.   For the first row of the expression line, select `@Name` for the field.

4.   Select `LIKE` as the operator.

5.   Enter **AW_Sls_%** in the Value field.

6.   Add a new row, using the `OR` operator.

7.   Select `@Schema` for the Field value.

8.   Set the Operator to `!=`.

9.   Enter **Sales** for the Value field. Click OK to create the new condition.

10.   Right-click on the Policies folder in Object Explorer, and click "New Policy."

11.   Enter **AW Sales Name** for the Policy Name.

12.   In the Check condition list, scroll down until you find the `AWSalesTableNames` condition (it will be under the "Multipart Name" header).

13.   Select the check next to the `"Every Table in Every Database"` line, and click the dropdown arrow next to "Database."

14.   Select "New Condition."

15.   Enter **AdventureWorks2008 DB** for the name of the new condition.

16.   Select the Database Facet.

17.   Set the Condition Expression to `@Name = 'AdventureWorks2008'`, and click OK.

18.   Change the Evaluation Mode to "On change: prevent."

19.   Leave the server restriction as None.

20.   Check the Enable checkbox underneath the Name property.

Your settings should resemble Figure 8-5.

Now let's test the new policy:

1.   First, ensure that you can create a table in any schema other than `Sales` that doesn't require this naming convention.

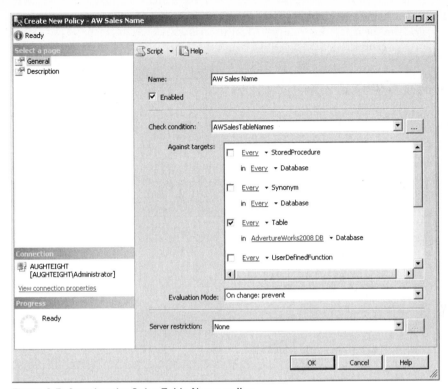

Figure 8-5: Creating the Sales Table Name policy.

2. Enter the following code to create a new table in the `Person` schema:

```
Use AdventureWorks2008;
Create Table Person.Foo (
Col1 Int,
Col2 nvarchar(25)
);
```

The command should succeed as expected.

3. Next, try to create a table called *Foo* in the `Sales` schema using the following code:

```
Use AdventureWorks2008
Create Table Sales.Foo (
Col1 Int,
Col2 nvarchar(25)
);
```

4. At this point, the operation should fail, indicating that the expected name isn't provided. So now you should create a new table that *does* follow the expected naming convention. Enter the following code to create the new table:

```
Use AdventureWorks2008
Create Table Sales.AW_Sls_Foo (
Col1 Int,
```

```
Col2 nvarchar(25)
);
```

This should complete successfully.

You have now created a policy that enforces a specific naming convention on a particular schema in the `AdventureWorks2008` database. As you explore the different facet and condition options, it is easy to see how powerful the Policy-Based Management system can be.

Because several objects already existing in the `Sales` schema don't meet our required naming convention, we can get an audit of those tables that are in violation of the policy. Keep in mind that the policy will only apply the DDL trigger to new objects. Existing objects will still function. To get a list of non-compliant objects, navigate to the AW Sales Name policy, right-click on it, and select Evaluate. Your results should look similar to Figure 8-6.

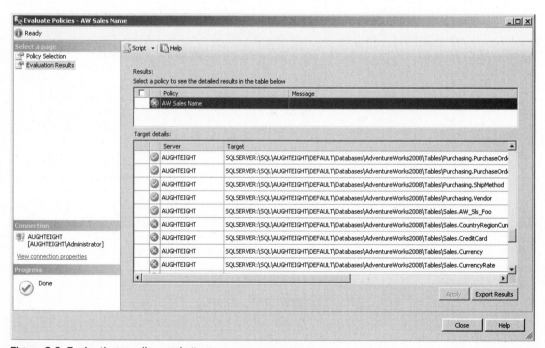

Figure 8-6: Evaluating a policy against `AdventureWorks2008`.

Central Management Servers

One of the most important concerns for a DBA is how to find the best way to manage multiple servers at once. The examples in the previous section regarding Policy-Based Management were designed around a single instance; however, if you browse through some of the options for Policy-Based Management (or PBM, for short), you will notice that there are options that allow you to specify to which platform and version of SQL Server these policies will apply.

"How can that be," you might ask, "if PBM doesn't exist in prior versions of SQL?" The answer is through the use of Central Management Servers (CMS). More than simply an extension of PBM, the concept of Central Management Servers is to allow not only policies, but also queries to be executed against several servers simultaneously. This can be extremely useful if, for example, you have a database that is distributed among multiple SQL Servers and you're not sure on which server a particular row exists. You could write a query that includes a select statement against all servers, specifying the full object name in a separate line, or you could add these servers to a Central Management group and execute the query in a single operation.

There are, however, two key factors to keep in mind when considering a Central Management Server:

❑ First of all, the Central Management Server and all registered target servers *must* use Windows-based logins for authentication and management. SQL Login creation and management will not be replicated among servers that are members of a management group.

❑ The other important item to note is that a Central Management Server cannot have itself as a target. This means that policies that are applied at the CMS are applied to the registered servers, but not the CMS itself.

To define a new CMS, you need to display the Registered Servers window. You can access this from SQL Server Management Studio by selecting View ➤ Registered Servers. The Registered Servers window will display two categories:

❑ The first is the Local Server Groups category. This is where you can add a list of servers you regularly manage for easy access, without having to connect Object Explorer to them every time. You can create folders known as *Server Groups* to logically arrange and collect the servers you typically manage.

❑ The second category is where you will define (if any) the Central Management Servers. After you have defined a server as a Central Management Server, you will need to create a new server group and register servers you want to centrally manage in that new server group

In Figure 8-7, you can see that I have created a new Local Server Group called *MyServers*, of which AughtEight is a member. I have also defined AughtEight as a Central Management Server, with a new server group called *Bespin*. This server group contains the AughtEight\Dagobah and AughtEight\Hoth instances.

Figure 8-7: Registered Servers.

By right-clicking on my CMS, I can choose the "Evaluate Policies" option, which allows me to evaluate one or more policies against the managed servers. I will need to specify the policy from the file system, or I could use a policy that exists on a server (including the CMS). If you look at Figure 8-8, you will see the results of evaluating the Check Bad Logins policy I created.

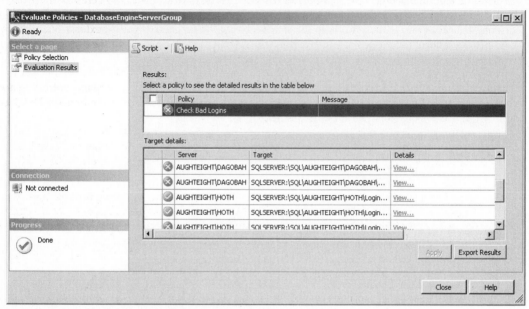

Figure 8-8: Evaluating policies against multiple servers.

Database Mail

Microsoft SQL Server 2008 includes a simple method for message delivery to and from the SQL Server. This feature, known as *Database Mail*, allows SQL Server to send and receive messages through SMTP delivery. One of the many benefits of SQL Server's Database Mail service is that it will work with any SMTP service, regardless of whether or not it requires authentication (which it should, but that's a security discussion that is beyond the scope of this chapter).

The Database Mail feature in SQL Server 2008 is a tool that allows you to generate and send e-mail messages from your server, which can be relayed through a corporate mail system. This can provide several advantages, including using an alternate method of returning information to your users, notifying the appropriate personnel that certain events or conditions have been met, or providing status information about jobs and SSIS packages. Database Mail was designed with security, scalability, and reliability in mind.

> *Be aware that the Database Mail feature is not included with the Express Edition of SQL Server 2008.*

How It Works

Database Mail uses SMTP for message delivery. Messages can be generated from within SQL and can include attachments from outside the SQL environment. One of the primary benefits of the Database Mail feature is its ability to use any SMTP server to relay messages. This is a significant improvement over prior versions of SQL Server that use SQL Mail, which requires a MAPI-compliant mail server (such as Microsoft Exchange) and a MAPI client (such as Microsoft Outlook). SQL Mail still exists in SQL Server 2008 but is considered a legacy feature and should not be used.

Another benefit of Database Mail is that it allows you to configure authentication credentials if required by your SMTP server to forward messages, as well as allowing you to configure different servers for delivery, in case your preferred server is not available. SQL Server also uses an external executable, DatabaseMail.exe, to handle message delivery to an SMTP server. This allows the SQL Server to isolate itself from the process that relays the messages to the SMTP server.

The msdb database is used for storing configuration information about Database Mail, controlling access to the feature, and queuing messages until they are ready for delivery. Prior to configuring Database Mail, there are a few things you should consider:

❑ First, you should know which SMTP servers are available for use and what credentials are needed. As you'll see in the next section, you can configure multiple servers, with multiple accounts, if necessary.

❑ Another consideration is which messages will be retained, and how long they need to be retained. By default, all Sent messages and their attachments are stored in the msdb database. Be aware of your company's security and retention policies for e-mail messages. You may also be under a legal obligation to keep messages for a specific amount of time.

The Database Mail feature uses *accounts* to configure access to SMTP servers and *profiles* to configure access to mail accounts. However, profiles and accounts can be mutually exclusive. You can create accounts without an association to a profile, and you can use the same account with multiple profiles, if necessary.

How to Configure Database Mail

The easiest way to configure SQL Server to use Database Mail is through the Database Mail Configuration Wizard in SQL Server Management Studio. This section steps you through the different pages in the Wizard and explains what each page configures:

1. To launch the Wizard, navigate to the Management section of your server in Object Explorer (see Figure 8-9).

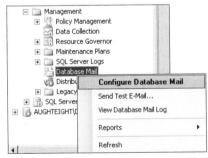

Figure 8-9: Launching the Database Mail Wizard.

295

2. Expand Management, right-click "Database Mail," and select "Configure Database Mail."

3. The first page you will see is simply a start page that explains each of the following steps in the Wizard. If you don't want to see this page again, select the checkbox at the bottom of the page indicating that you wish to skip this page in the future.

4. On the next screen, you'll be asked to identify which configuration task you're using the Wizard to perform. You can use this to initialize Database Mail for use on the server; or, if it's already configured, you can manage existing mail profiles and configured accounts. You can also change system settings. For this run, select the first option to set up Database Mail (see Figure 8-10).

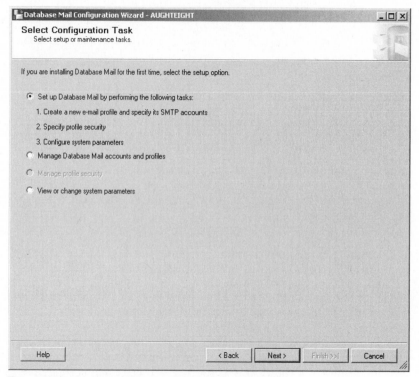

Figure 8-10: Choosing a Database Mail configuration task.

5. Database Mail is disabled by default. If this is the first time you've run this Wizard and you have not manually enabled Database Mail, you will be prompted to enable it. Once you've enabled Database Mail, the next screen will ask you to provide information for a new Database Mail profile. Enter a name for the profile and, optionally, a description to help identify the profile and how it will be used. For this example, enter **AdventureWorksSalesProfile** as the profile name.

    Once that information has been entered, you must configure at least one account that this profile will use. The ability to configure multiple accounts under a single profile helps guarantee the availability of the Database Mail feature to users who need to receive information, and the path of delivery isn't relevant. The order in which the accounts are listed will determine the order of precedence when sending messages. Accounts listed at the top of the list will be preferred over those listed below them.

6. To create a new account, click on the Add button. In the New Database Mail Account screen (see Figure 8-11), enter an account name and description, and then information about the account, including the e-mail address that the messages will originate from, the display name for that address, the reply-to address, and the name or IP address of the SMTP server. There is also a box where you can enter the port number used by the SMTP server. Unless you know that your server uses a different port, you should use the standard SMTP port, 25. If your server uses Secure Sockets Layer (SSL) to protect the data in transit, select the appropriate checkbox.

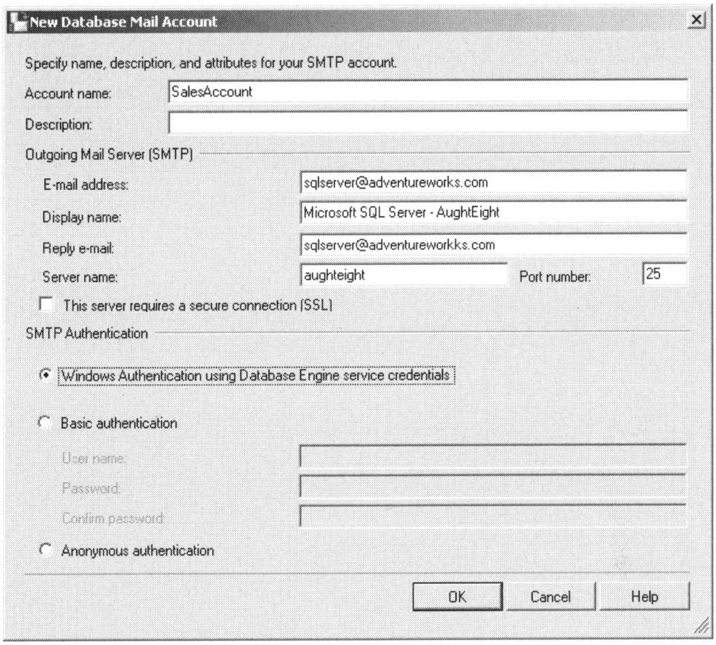

Figure 8-11: New Database Mail Account screen.

7. Also on the new Database Mail Account screen, you will select the method of authentication that the SMTP server requires. By default, Anonymous authentication is selected, but this is not the preferred method for most SMTP servers. If your SMTP server is Windows-based (such as in the case of Microsoft Exchange or IIS) and is a member of the same domain or a different domain that shares a trust relationship, you may be able to use Windows Authentication with Database Engine service credentials. Otherwise, you can use Basic authentication, providing a username and password manually. Be aware that if SSL is not used between the SQL Server and the SMTP server, the authentication information may be sent in clear text and may be vulnerable to interception.

In this example, I am using an SMTP service installed on the local machine through IIS. You can use the information in Figure 8-11 to configure your mail account appropriately for your mail server.

8. Once you've entered in the information about the account, click OK to close the New Database Mail Account window. You can enter in more accounts to be used by the same profile, or you can continue on to the next screen by clicking Next.

9. On the Manage Profile Security screen, you can use the Public Profiles tab (see Figure 8-12) to elect to make the profile public. When a profile is *public*, it means that the profile will be available to all users who are members of the DatabaseMailUserRole role in the msdb database. You can also define which public profile is the default public profile. The default profile is the one that is used when a profile is not specified during the Send mail operation. For private profiles, you can specify (on a per-user basis) which profiles are available to that user (see Figure 8-13). Each user can also have a default profile available to them. The user must already exist in the msdb database. For this example, mark the profile as *public*, and make it the default. Once you've configured the Profile Security options, click Next.

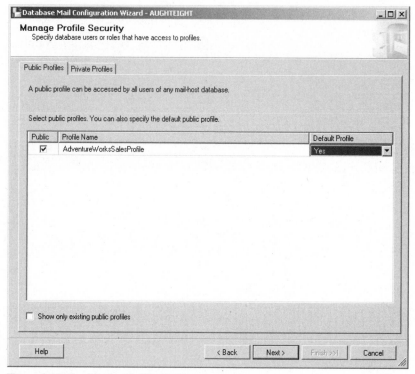

Figure 8-12: Configuring Public Profiles.

10. On the final input page of the Wizard, you can change the system configuration values for mail messages sent from the SQL Server. You can identify the information shown in the following table:

Option	Description
Account Retry Attempts	The number of retry attempts that SQL Server will make for a mail account within a profile before it moves on to the next account
Account Retry Delay	The amount of time (in seconds) that the SQL Server will wait between retries

Option	Description
Maximum File Size	Maximum size (in bytes) of file attachments
Prohibited Attachment File Extensions	List of file extensions that the SQL Server will not send
Database Mail Executable Minimum Lifetime	The time-out value for the external executable if there are no more messages in queue
Logging Level	Choose one of the following: ❑ **Normal** — Logs only errors. ❑ **Extended** — Errors, Warnings, and Informational messages. This is the default setting. ❑ **Verbose** — Extended logging, plus success messages and internal messages

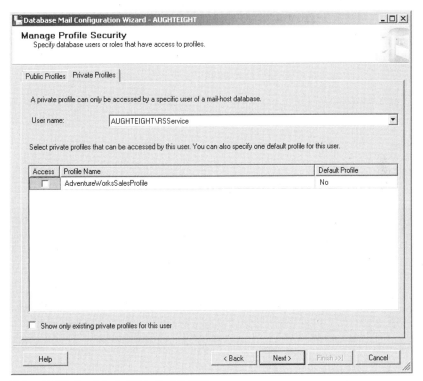

Figure 8-13: Configuring Private Profiles.

11. Click Next on the Configure System Parameters page to move to the last page in the Wizard. Once you've provided the appropriate values to the Wizard, it gives you a summary page with the options you've selected. Clicking Finish will commit your changes and give you a quick report on the success or failure of each step.

Configuring Database Mail Options

Alternatively, you can enable Database Mail using the `sp_configure` stored procedure. Once Database Mail has been enabled, you can use the `sysmail_configure_sp` stored procedure to configure Database Mail settings. The syntax of the `sysmail_configure_sp` stored procedure is as follows:

```
sysmail_configure_sp [ @parameter_name = ] 'name' , [ @parameter_value = ]
    'value' , [ @description = ] 'description'
```

Similar to the options listed here, you can use the values in the following table for the parameters:

Parameter	Description
AccountRetryAttempts	The number of retry attempts SQL Server will make for a mail account within a profile before it moves on to the next account
AccountRetryDelay	The amount of time (in seconds) that the SQL Server will wait between retries
DatabaseMailExeMinimumLifeTime	The time-out value for the external executable if there are no more messages in queue
DefaultAttachmentEncoding	The default encoding for e-mail attachments
MaxFileSize	Maximum size (in bytes) of file attachments
ProhibitedExtensions	List of file extensions that the SQL Server will not send
LoggingLevel	Choose one of the following numeric values: 1. Normal 2. Extended 3. Verbose

The `sysmail_configure_sp` stored procedure (as do many of the Database Mail stored procedures) lives in the `msdb` database. When executing these stored procedures, you'll have to qualify them from within your application or T-SQL statements. Use the following example to set the maximum file size for all attachments sent by Database Mail to 4 MB:

```
EXECUTE msdb.dbo.sysmail_configure_sp
    'MaxFileSize', '4194303', 'Max Size 4 MB'
```

Note that the description parameter is optional. Although it may not be required, it is always a good idea to use it to define or explain why a particular configuration value is used.

Managing Profiles and Accounts

Profiles are commonly used as a unit of management for SMTP accounts. However, as mentioned earlier, there is no one-to-one relationship between the two. You can use the Database Mail Configuration Wizard, or you can use a series of stored procedures to create and delete profiles and accounts as needed.

Because you've already been exposed to the different elements of the Wizard, you should easily be able to fumble through the different pages to find what you need to configure the accounts and profiles you want. In this section, you learn about the stored procedures used to create and manage Database Mail accounts and profiles.

sysmail_add_profile_sp

The first stored procedure you should know is `sysmail_add_profile_sp`. This stored procedure allows you to create a new profile to be used by the Database Mail service and uses the following syntax:

```
sysmail_add_profile_sp [ @profile_name = ] 'name' , [ @description = ] 'desc',
[ @profile_id = ] profile_id OUTPUT
```

The following table shows the available options.

Option	Description
profile_name	The name of the profile
description	An optional description that provides information about the profile
profile_id	An optional parameter that displays the unique value generated by SQL to identify the profile
OUTPUT	Keyword used to output the profile_id value

Try It Out   Create a New Profile

The following example creates a new mail profile and returns the integer value generated for the profile ID. Begin by declaring the variable for the `profile_id`:

```
DECLARE @profileID INT;

EXECUTE msdb.dbo.sysmail_add_profile_sp
        @profile_name = 'HumanResourcesMail',
        @description = 'Mail Profile for the Human Resources team.',
        @profile_id = @profileID OUTPUT ;

SELECT @profileID ;
```

Note the ID returned from the SELECT statement. You'll use this in the next example.

The `sysmail_help_profile_sp` stored procedure will return information about the profiles created on the SQL Server. It will return the profile ID, the profile name, and the description, if any. You can also use the @profile_id or @profile_name variables to limit the results to just the specific profile you're interested in.

```
EXEC msdb.dbo.sysmail_help_profile_sp @profile_id=2
```

You can also query the sysmail_profile table in the msdb database to return information about the profiles that have been created. In addition to the information returned from the sysmail_help_profile_sp stored procedure, you can identify who last modified the account and when.

```
SELECT * FROM msdb.dbo.sysmail_profile
```

sysmail_add_account_sp

To create a new account, use the sysmail_add_account_sp stored procedure. This stored procedure will create an account that is not associated with a profile. A different stored procedure can be used to add accounts to a profile, which is discussed later in this chapter.

Creating accounts, as you've seen from the Database Mail Configuration Wizard, is a little more complex than creating profiles, because the accounts may vary from server to server. The following table lists the options you can use with the sysmail_add_account_sp procedure:

Parameter	Description
@account_name = name	The name of the new account
@email_address = address	The e-mail address associated with the account
@display_name = display	How messages sent from this account display the sender's name
@replyto_address = address	The address that will be used for replies when the client is responding to a message sent to this account
@description = desc	An optional description for this account
@mailserver_name = server	Name or IP address of the SMTP server this account will use
@mailserver_type = servertype	Made available for future technology, SMTP is currently the only value supported, and is the default.
@port = serverport	TCP port used by the SMTP server. The default is 25.
@username = username	Used if your SMTP server requires authentication.
@password = password	The password to be provided for authentication to the SMTP server
@use_default_credentials = [0|1]	A value of 1 indicates that the SQL Server service account will be used for SQL authentication.
@enable_ssl = [0|1]	A value of 1 indicates that SSL will be used between the SQL Server and the SMTP server.
@account_id = accountID OUTPUT	Returns the account ID generated when the account is created.

Try It Out **Create a New Account**

So, take a look at this in action. Use the following example to create a new account:

```
DECLARE @accountID INT;

EXECUTE msdb.dbo.sysmail_add_account_sp
    @account_name = 'Mail Sender',
    @description = 'Generic Account for sending mail',
    @email_address = 'mailsender@adventureworks.com',
    @display_name = 'SQL Database Mail Account',
    @mailserver_name = 'mail.adventureworks.com',
    @username = 'MailSender',
    @password = 'P@ssw0rd',
    @account_id = @accountID OUTPUT ;

SELECT @accountID;
```

Note the account ID returned. You can use this in the next example.

To find out more about the accounts that have been created, use the `sysmail_help_account_sp` stored procedure. This will give you information about the account, such as the ID, the name, and the server options for this account. Use the `@account_id` or `@account_name` variables to limit the results to a specific account.

```
EXECUTE msdb.dbo.sysmail_help_account_sp
```

To limit the output to just the account you're interested in, use the following:

```
EXECUTE msdb.dbo.sysmail_help_account_sp @account_id=2
```

You can also return a simple list of configured accounts by querying the `sysmail_account` table, which includes the `datetime` information of when the account was last modified and who last modified it:

```
SELECT * FROM msdb.dbo.sysmail_account
```

sysmail_add_profileaccount_sp

So, you've created a new profile and a new account. Now you can associate that account with that profile. Remember that accounts can be associated with more than one profile, and each profile can be configured to use more than one account.

To create the mapping, you can use the `sysmail_add_profileaccount_sp` stored procedure. This allows you to map an account to a profile using the profile name or profile ID and the account name or account ID. Another option you can specify is the sequence number of the account ID. This is used to determine the order of preference for the account within that profile.

Because this is a fairly simple stored procedure, you will see a couple of examples that use the profiles and accounts created previously.

In this first example, you will use the account created during the Database Mail Configuration Wizard and add it to the profile you created from the `sysmail_add_profile_sp` stored procedure example. This example has you use the `profile_id` of the `HumanResourcesProfile` and the name of the `SalesAccount` account. You can easily mix and match, as long as you declare the correct parameter.

```
EXECUTE msdb.dbo.sysmail_add_profileaccount_sp
    @profile_id = 2,
    @account_name = 'SalesAccount',
    @sequence_number = 1;
```

In the next example, add the account created from the `sysmail_add_account_sp` stored procedure to the `HumanResourcesProfile` profile, only this time, you will refer to the profile by name, and the account by ID number.

```
EXECUTE msdb.dbo.sysmail_add_profileaccount_sp
    @profile_name = 'HumanResourcesMail',
    @account_id = 2,
    @sequence_number = 2;
```

To find out what mappings exist between the accounts and profiles, you can use the `sysmail_help_profileaccount_sp` stored procedure. You can limit your results using `@account_id`, `@account_name`, `@profile_id`, or `@profile_name`. Each row returned identifies the profile ID, the profile name, the account ID, the account name, and the sequence number for the account.

```
EXECUTE msdb.dbo.sysmail_help_profileaccount_sp
```

Querying the `sysmail_profileaccount` table in the `msdb` database returns the IDs of profiles and associated accounts, but not the names. It also returns the sequence number for those accounts and the last modified information.

```
SELECT * FROM msdb.dbo.sysmail_profileaccount
```

sysmail_update_profile_sp

Quite simply, you can use this stored procedure to change the name or description of an existing profile. If you're changing the description of the profile, you can refer to it using `@profile_id` or `@profile_name`. If you want to change the name of the profile, you will use `@profile_id`.

Use the following example to change both the name and the description of the `HumanResourcesMail` profile created earlier. Assuming that you did not create any new accounts or profiles other than those used in the examples, the `profile_id` of `HumanResourcesMail` should be 2.

```
EXECUTE msdb.dbo.sysmail_update_profile_sp
    @profile_id = 2,
    @profile_name = 'HRMail',
    @description = 'Human Resources Mail Profile';

EXECUTE msdb.dbo.sysmail_help_profile_sp;
```

This will produce the following output:

```
profile_id  name                      description
----------- ------------------------- -------------------------------------
```

```
1              AdventureWorksSalesProfile  NULL
2              HRMail                      Human Resources Mail Profile
```

sysmail_update_account_sp

This stored procedure can be used to update the properties of a mail account after it has been created. Unlike profiles, accounts have a lot more parameters that can be modified or adjusted as needed. The same parameters from the `sysmail_add_account_sp` procedure can be used, and not unlike the `sysmail_update_profile_sp` procedure, you can identify the account by `account_name` or `account_id`.

In this example, you reconfigure the name, `replyto_address`, and the description of the `SalesMail` profile. Unfortunately, with this stored procedure, you cannot cherry-pick which values you want to update. You will have to specify the values for all parameters, as shown here:

```
EXECUTE msdb.dbo.sysmail_update_account_sp
    @account_id = 1,
    @account_name = 'SalesMail',
    @display_name = 'Microsoft SQL Server - AughtEight',
    @replyto_address = 'administrator@adventureworks.com',
    @description = 'Sales Mail Account',
    @mailserver_name = 'AughtEight',
    @mailserver_type = 'SMTP',
    @port = 25,
    @username = NULL,
    @password = NULL,
    @use_default_credentials = 1,
    @enable_ssl = 0;

EXECUTE msdb.dbo.sysmail_help_account_sp
```

sysmail_update_profileaccount_sp

If you want to change the sequence in which the accounts will be used within a profile, you can use the `sysmail_update_profileaccount_sp` stored procedure. Specify the profile and the account by either name or ID, and then enter the preferred sequence number. Be aware that more than one account within a profile can have the same sequence number. If this is the case, SQL will arbitrarily decide which one to use. Use the following example to change the sequence numbers of the accounts in the `HRMail` profile:

```
-- Assigns the Mail Sender account a sequence of 1

EXECUTE msdb.dbo.sysmail_update_profileaccount_sp
    @profile_id = 2,
    @account_id = 2,
    @sequence_number = 1;

-- Assigns the SalesMail account a sequence number of 2

EXECUTE msdb.dbo.sysmail_update_profileaccount_sp
    @profile_name = 'HRMail',
    @account_name = 'SalesMail',
    @sequence_number = 2;

EXECUTE msdb.dbo.sysmail_help_profileaccount_sp
```

sysmail_add_principalprofile_sp

This stored procedure is used to control access to a mail profile. In order for the profile to be accessible, the profile will be made available to specific database principals within the msdb database. The following table outlines the parameters for the sysmail_add_principalprofile_sp stored procedure:

Option	Description
@principal_id	The ID of the user or role in the msdb database. Use the value 0 to specify the public role. The principal must be specified by either the ID or name.
@principal_name	The name of the user or role in the msdb database. Use the public role if the profile is a public profile.
@profile_id	The ID of the profile. Use either the ID or name to specify the profile.
@profile_name	The name of the profile. Use to identify the profile.
@is_default	Indicates that this profile is the default profile for the specified principal.

Take a look at this stored procedure in action. In this first example, create a new profile with a new account. Then, ensure that the profile is public.

```
-- Create the profile
EXECUTE msdb.dbo.sysmail_add_profile_sp
       @profile_name = 'Purchasing',
       @description = 'Purchasing Mail Profile';

-- Create the account
EXECUTE msdb.dbo.sysmail_add_account_sp
     @account_name = 'PurchasingMail',
     @description = 'Purchasing Mail Account',
     @email_address = 'purchasing@adventureworks.com',
     @display_name = 'AdventureWorks Purchasing Application',
     @mailserver_name = 'localhost',
     @use_default_credentials = 1;

-- Associate the profile and the account
EXECUTE msdb.dbo.sysmail_add_profileaccount_sp
      @profile_name = 'Purchasing',
      @account_name = 'PurchasingMail',
      @sequence_number = 1;

-- Make the profile public
EXECUTE msdb.dbo.sysmail_add_principalprofile_sp
     @principal_name = 'public',
     @profile_name = 'Purchasing',
     @is_default = 0;
```

To view the security configuration, use the sysmail_help_principalprofile_sp stored procedure. You can specify the principal_id, principal_name, profile_id, and/or profile_name. Note that you should only provide either the ID or the name for each, not both. For example, if you wanted to see which profiles are available to the public role, use the following example:

```
EXECUTE msdb.dbo.sysmail_help_principalprofile_sp
    @principal_name = 'public';
```

If you've been following all the steps in this chapter so far, you should expect to see the following output:

```
principal_id   principal_name   profile_id   profile_name                 is_default
-----------    --------------   ----------   -------------------------    ----------
0              public           1            AdventureWorksSalesProfile   1
0              public           3            Purchasing                   0
```

Interestingly enough, if you execute the sysmail_help_principalprofile_sp stored procedure without any parameters (such as the principal_name as in the previous example), it returns results for the guest account, not the public role. This is not surprising, though, because the guest account, when available, is used when the requestor does not have a user mapping in the msdb database.

In the next example, you learn how to create a new profile, account, and database user named *AWOrderProcessing*. You'll then see how to configure the new profile as the default for that user.

```
-- Create the user
-- In the real world, you would map this to an existing server credential.
USE msdb
CREATE USER AWOrderProcessing
    WITHOUT LOGIN;
GO

-- Create the profile
EXECUTE msdb.dbo.sysmail_add_profile_sp
        @profile_name = 'OrderEntry',
        @description = 'OrderEntry Mail Profile';

-- Create the account
EXECUTE msdb.dbo.sysmail_add_account_sp
    @account_name = 'Orders',
    @description = 'Order Entry Primary Mail Account',
    @email_address = 'orders@adventureworks.com',
    @display_name = 'AdventureWorks Purchasing Application',
     @replyto_address = 'administrator@adventureworks.com',
    @mailserver_name = 'localhost',
    @use_default_credentials = 1;

-- Associate the profile and the account
EXECUTE msdb.dbo.sysmail_add_profileaccount_sp
        @profile_name = 'OrderEntry',
        @account_name = 'Orders',
        @sequence_number = 1;

--Configure the purchasing account as a backup account
EXECUTE msdb.dbo.sysmail_add_profileaccount_sp
        @profile_name = 'OrderEntry',
```

```
        @account_name = 'PurchasingMail',
        @sequence_number = 2;

    -- Make the profile available to the AWOrderProcessing user
    EXECUTE msdb.dbo.sysmail_add_principalprofile_sp
        @principal_name = AWOrderProcessing,
        @profile_name = 'OrderEntry',
        @is_default = 1;

    -- Show which profiles the AWOrderProcessing user has access to.
    EXECUTE msdb.dbo.sysmail_help_principalprofile_sp
        @principal_name = 'AWOrderProcessing';
```

One thing you should note when you return the list of profiles available to the AWOrderProcessing user is that both of the profiles available to the public role are also available to this user. Also note that the public role and the AWOrderProcessing user each has a default profile. When a database user or a role that is not public has a default profile defined, that profile will be the one used if a profile isn't identified. If the user or role does not have a default profile specified, the default profile of the public role will be used.

sysmail_update_principalprofile_sp

Each principal can only have one default profile defined. If you need to change which of the available profiles is the default, use the sysmail_update_principalprofile_sp stored procedure. As with the sysmail_add_principalprofile_sp, you can identify the principal and the profile either by name or ID. The only value you can alter with this stored procedure, though, is the @is_default parameter. Using the last example, if you changed the @is_default option for AWOrderProcessing, then the user would need to manually specify the appropriate profile. Otherwise, in this case, the default profile would come from the public role.

```
    -- Remove the default profile for AWOrderProcessing
    EXECUTE msdb.dbo.sysmail_update_principalprofile_sp
        @principal_name = AWOrderProcessing,
        @profile_id = 4,
        @is_default = 0;

    -- Show which profiles the AWOrderProcessing user has access to.
    EXECUTE msdb.dbo.sysmail_help_principalprofile_sp
        @principal_name = 'AWOrderProcessing';
```

sysmail_delete_principalprofile_sp

If you need to remove the association between a principal and a profile, use the sysmail_delete_principalprofile_sp stored procedure. Note that this does not delete the principal or the profile from the database but, rather, removes the explicit mapping between the two. You might want to use this if you have to remove the public role's access to the specified profile, for example. The syntax is very straightforward, requiring you to identify both the principal and the profile; but again, you can use the name or ID value for either. Use the following example to remove the Purchasing profile from the public role:

```
    EXECUTE msdb.dbo.sysmail_delete_principalprofile_sp
        @principal_name = 'public',
        @profile_name = 'Purchasing';

    EXECUTE msdb.dbo.sysmail_help_principalprofile_sp
        @principal_name = 'public';
```

sysmail_delete_profileaccount_sp

If you want to remove an account from a profile, simply use the sysmail_delete_profileaccount_sp stored procedure. You need to specify both the profile and the account either by name or ID. The following example removes the Orders account from the OrderEntry profile:

```
EXECUTE msdb.dbo.sysmail_delete_profileaccount_sp
    @profile_name = 'OrderEntry',
    @account_name = 'Orders';

EXECUTE msdb.dbo.sysmail_help_profileaccount_sp;
```

sysmail_delete_account_sp

Next, to remove an account from the msdb database entirely, use the sysmail_delete_account_sp stored procedure. This will not only remove the account, but all references to the account in all profiles where it was configured, as in the following example. If the account to be deleted is the only account in the profile, the profile will remain, but will be empty.

```
EXECUTE msdb.dbo.sysmail_delete_account_sp
    @account_name = 'Orders';

EXECUTE msdb.dbo.sysmail_help_account_sp;
```

sysmail_delete_profile_sp

Finally, to remove a profile from the msdb database, use the sysmail_delete_profile_sp stored procedure. This removes the profile but will not delete the accounts in the profile. This is because the accounts may be used in other profiles.

```
EXECUTE msdb.dbo.sysmail_delete_profile_sp
    @profile_name = 'OrderEntry';

EXECUTE msdb.dbo.sysmail_help_profileaccount_sp;
```

Guidelines for Deleting Mail Objects

As a general rule, be careful about deleting accounts or profiles. If you are going to delete an account, profile, or account mapping, use the following guidelines:

- ❏ Deleting a profile/account mapping is non-destructive. It simply removes the relationship between the profile and account. If necessary, this can be easily re-created. If another account is properly configured within the profile, this should not disrupt operations.

- ❏ Deleting an account removes its availability in all profiles. If the profiles already have another valid account configured, then you (or your users) shouldn't notice any problems. If you are deleting an account that is the only account in one or more profiles, those profiles will not be able to send mail.

- ❏ Deleting a profile removes a list of configured accounts, not the accounts themselves. If, however, your application is configured to use a mail profile you've recently deleted, once again, your SQL Server will be unable to send messages.

Sending Mail

This chapter has spent a lot of time looking at the elements and configuration of Database Mail, so now let's see where your efforts have gotten you. Sending mail is an easy process. This section introduces the parameters of the `sp_send_dbmail` stored procedure, as well as a couple of useful examples of how to prepare data for sending.

sp_send_dbmail

As mentioned earlier, the stored procedure for sending mail using the Database Mail feature is `sp_send_dbmail`. As with the other Database Mail stored procedures covered earlier in this chapter, this one lives in the `msdb` database; and if you're going to be instantiating it from outside of that database, you'll need to qualify it, as you have been doing throughout the chapter.

Keep in mind that although a mail profile may be made public and is available to the members of the public role, the `sp_send_dbmail` can only be executed by members of the DatabaseMailUserRole. Ensure that all logins that need access to the `sp_send_dbmail` stored procedure are mapped to a user in the `msdb` database and are members of the DatabaseMailUserRole.

The following table identifies the different parameters available to `sp_send_dbmail` and their descriptions:

Parameter	Description
@profile_name	Name of the profile the stored procedure will use. If a default profile is specified for the user or one has been defined for the `public` role, this value is optional.
@recipients	List of e-mail addresses that will receive your message. Use semicolons between values. Although this value is technically optional, you must specify at least one recipient through @recipients (To:), @copy_recipients (CC:), or @blind_copy_recipients (BCC:).
@copy_recipients	The same as using the CC: (also called Carbon Copy) field in a standard e-mail client. As with the recipients list, you can use semicolons between multiple values.
@blind_copy_ recipients	The same as using the BCC: (also known as Blind Carbon Copy) field in a standard e-mail client. This value will indicate a list of recipients for your messages, but the addresses are obfuscated by e-mail clients. Use semicolons between multiple values.
@subject	Subject of the mail message. Defaults to `SQL Server Message` with no value specified.
@body	Text of the message. The default is `NULL`.
@body_format	Message delivery format. Choose between `TEXT` and `HTML`. The default is `TEXT`.
@importance	Allows you to specify a value indicating how the client should treat the message. Choose between `Low`, `Normal`, and `High`. The default is `Normal`.

Parameter	Description
@sensitivity	Allows you to define a sensitivity level for the message, interpreted by the client. Choose from `Normal`, `Personal`, `Private`, and `Confidential`. The default is `Normal`.
@file_attachments	Allows you to provide a list of external files that can be attached to the e-mail message. The user executing the stored procedure must specify (and have access to) the absolute file path where the files reside. Use a semicolon between file paths to specify multiple files.
@query	Identifies a query whose results will be sent as part of the message. The query results can be added to the body of the message or attached as a file.
@execute_query_database	Identifies the database context in which the aforementioned query will run. This defaults to the current database, and is only used if the `@query` option is used.
@attach_query_result_as_file	Specifies if the query result is returned as part of the message body or an attached file. It uses a bit value of `0` to append to the body, and a value of `1` to attach a file with the results. Defaults to `0`.
@query_attachment_filename	Allows you to define the filename that will be attached if `@attach_query_result_as_file` is set to `1`. If a filename is not provided, SQL will make one up for you.
@query_result_header	Bit value that specifies if column headers are included with the results. Not surprisingly, `0` equals no, and `1` equals yes. Defaults to `1`.
@query_result_width	Allows you to specify the line width by maximum number of characters. This is an `int` value with a range between 10 and 32,767. The default is 256.
@query_result_separator	Allows you to define a single character delimiter between columns in a query output. The default is a single space (`' '`).
@exclude_query_output	This option allows you to define (when using a query in a mail message) whether to output the query results to the console. This defaults to `0`, which will display the results.
@append_query_error	If an error is returned from a query, setting this value to `1` will include the error in the e-mail message. The default of `0` does not include error information.
@query_no_truncate	Setting the value of this option to `1` will override the default behavior, which is to truncate variable-length columns greater than 256. If you override the default, be aware that columns that store a large amount of data may take longer to process and send.
@mailitem_id id OUTPUT	This option allows you to return the `mailitem_id` after the message has been generated. You can use this to review or clean up sent messages.

Take a look at some examples of how to send mail messages from within SQL Server.

In this first example, you can create a simple mail message that doesn't rely on any additional data source. This can be executed as a `SendMail` task upon completion of a job, or through an event notification. This one will send a simple message, indicating that an import task has been successfully completed.

```
EXECUTE msdb.dbo.sp_send_dbmail
    @profile_name = 'HRMail',
    @recipients = 'Gregory.House@adventureworks.com',
    @copy_recipients = 'Administrator@adventureworks.com',
    @body = 'Your data has been successfully imported!',
    @subject = 'Import Notification Message - Success';
```

In order for the message to actually be delivered, you must be running SMTP and POP3 services for the `adventureworks.com` domain, and you must also have Gregory.House and the Administrator accounts configured as POP3 recipients. If you have a different SMTP server configured, you can change the `@recipients` and `@copy_recipients` parameters to valid mail accounts. The Query window will simply return "Mail Queued." The resulting e-mail should look something like Figure 8-14.

Figure 8-14: Simple mail message.

Another example uses a query within the `sp_send_dbmail` stored procedure to send the results to the intended recipient list. In this example, you're going to use a query that returns the first names, last names, and hire dates of all employees hired in the year 2002:

```
EXECUTE msdb.dbo.sp_send_dbmail
    @profile_name = 'HRMail',
    @recipients = 'Lisa.Cuddy@adventureworks.com',
    @blind_copy_recipients = 'Gregory.House@adventureworks.com;
Administrator@adventureworks.com',
    @body = 'Per your request, here are the employees hired in 2002.',
    @query = 'SELECT Person.Person.FirstName AS First,
        Person.Person.LastName AS Last,
```

```
HumanResources.Employee.HireDate AS [Date of Hire]
        FROM Person.Person INNER JOIN HumanResources.Employee
        ON Person.Person.BusinessEntityID =
HumanResources.Employee.BusinessEntityID
        WHERE HireDate > ''2002-01-01" AND HIREDATE < ''2003-01-01''
        ORDER BY HireDate',
    @execute_query_database = 'AdventureWorks2008',
    @subject = 'Employees Hired in 2002',
    @attach_query_result_as_file = 1;
```

The resulting attachment should look something like Figure 8-15.

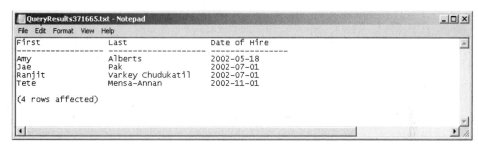

Figure 8-15: Raw output of 2002 new hires.

One more example shows you how to take the information in a query and prepare it as an HTML document. You can then e-mail the HTML document as the body of the mail message, and as long as the recipient's mail reader can render HTML, the recipient will have a nice-looking display.

```
USE AdventureWorks2008
DECLARE @tableHTML NVARCHAR(MAX) ;

SET @tableHTML =
    N'<H1>Employees Hired in 2002</H1>' +
    N'<table border="1">' +
    N'<tr><th>First Name</th><th>Last Name</th>' +
    N'<th>Hire Date</th>' +
  CAST ((SELECT td = Person.Person.FirstName,       '',
            td = Person.Person.LastName, '',
            td = HumanResources.Employee.HireDate, ''
            FROM Person.Person INNER JOIN HumanResources.Employee
            ON Person.Person.BusinessEntityID =
HumanResources.Employee.BusinessEntityID
            WHERE HireDate > '2002-01-01' AND HIREDATE < '2003-01-01'
            Order by HireDate
        FOR XML PATH('tr'), TYPE
        ) AS NVARCHAR(MAX) ) +
    N'</table>';

EXEC msdb.dbo.sp_send_dbmail @recipients='administrator@adventureworks.com',
  @subject = '2002 New Hires',
  @body = @tableHTML,
    @body_format = 'HTML';
```

This will return the output shown in Figure 8-16 to the mail client.

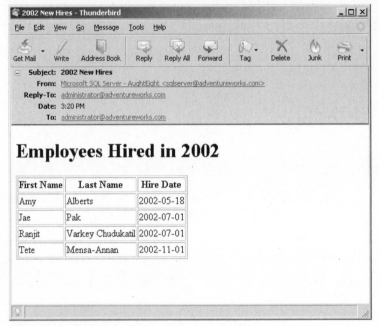

Figure 8-16: HTML document as body of e-mail message.

Managing Messages

As mentioned earlier, Database Mail messages are retained on the server. If you want to view which messages have been retained, you can query the sysmail_mailitems table in the msdb database. This returns detailed information about each message, such as who the recipients were, what the body of the message contained, and which profile sent the message.

```
SELECT * FROM msdb.dbo.sysmail_mailitems
```

You can also delete messages from the server by using the sysmail_delete_mailitems_sp stored procedure. This will allow you to delete messages that have either failed or succeeded, or delete just messages older than a specific date. Service Pack 1 requires that you provide either the @sent_before or @sent_status option.

To delete messages from before January 31, 2009, use the following example:

```
EXECUTE msdb.dbo.sysmail_delete_mailitems_sp
    @sent_before = 'January 31, 2009' ;
```

To delete messages that show a specific status value, use the following examples:

```
EXECUTE msdb.dbo.sysmail_delete_mailitems_sp
    @sent_status = 'failed';

EXECUTE msdb.dbo.sysmail_delete_mailitems_sp
```

```
        @sent_status = 'retrying';

EXECUTE msdb.dbo.sysmail_delete_mailitems_sp
        @sent_status = 'unsent';

EXECUTE msdb.dbo.sysmail_delete_mailitems_sp
        @sent_status = 'sent';
```

Event Notifications

Event Notifications are database objects that send information about server and database events to a Service Broker. They execute in response to data definition language (DDL) statements and SQL Trace events by sending information about these events to a Service Broker service. You can use Event Notifications either to log activity within a database or to execute an action asynchronous to an event. They are designed to be an alternative to creating DDL triggers or using SQL Trace functions.

Because Event Notifications run outside the scope of a transaction, they can be used inside a database application to respond to events without using any resources defined by the immediate transaction. Event Notifications operate independently of whether or not the transaction commits. They can also be used to perform an action inside an instance of SQL Server in response to a SQL Trace event.

Every Event Notification has its own exclusive Service Broker conversation between an instance of SQL Server and the target service you specify. The conversations usually remain open as long as the Event Notification still exists on the server. Ending a conversation prevents the target service from receiving more messages, and the conversation will not reopen when the Event Notification fires again.

Event information is an XML data type that provides information about when the event occurs, the object it affects, the batch statement involved, and more. This data can be used by applications that help SQL Server track progress and make decisions.

When designing an Event Notification, you must define both the scope of the notification and the statement or batch that raises the notification. For example, the Event Notification can occur as a response to a statement made on all objects in the AdventureWorks2008 database. You can also define the scope as being server-wide, such as triggering Event Notifications when new databases or logins are created.

More information about the architecture used to create services and queues is covered in Chapter 19. However, you should be aware that some of the mechanisms discussed in this section are also applicable to the next topic, the SQL Server Agent Service. For this reason, you should ensure that the msdb database is configured to manage Service Broker objects and process Event Notifications. Two important elements of this are ensuring that the SQL Server can trust the database and the object within it, and that the database is configured for Service Broker message delivery. To do this for the msdb database, use the following ALTER DATABASE statement:

```
ALTER DATABASE msdb
SET TRUSTWORTHY ON,
ENABLE_BROKER;
GO
```

Because the SQL Server Agent Service may have an active connection to the msdb database, it may be necessary to stop the service prior to running this statement and then restart it once the command has completed successfully.

There is also a feature in SQL Server 2008 known as *SQL Server Extended Events*. A full description of Extended Events is beyond the scope of this book; however, you should be aware that they can be used for more advanced troubleshooting and diagnostics. One of the key benefits of using Extended Events is the ability to associate SQL events with operating system or database application events, through the use of Event Tracing for Windows (ETW). More information on Extended Events can be found under the topic "Introducing SQL Server Extended Events" in Books Online.

SQL Server Agent

This section explains how to automate SQL Server tasks using the Microsoft SQL Server Agent Service. The SQL Server Agent Service runs as a Windows service that is dependent on the SQL Server service. Each instance of SQL Server will have its own SQL Server Agent Service to manage jobs, schedules, operators, and alerts. You learn about the essential components of the SQL Server Agent Service for single and multiple server management configurations.

The primary purpose of the SQL Server Agent is to make your job easier. In a perfect world, you could configure your servers, let them run, and never worry about losing data or the database going offline. But this isn't a perfect world. Things happen. And because you can't realistically monitor every server every minute of every day, you can use the SQL Server Agent to leverage against what you can't do.

The SQL Server Agent Service is not available in SQL Server 2008 Express Edition.

Configuring the SQL Server Agent Service

In Chapter 2, you learned about installing SQL Server and defining which accounts are used by the SQL Server service and the SQL Server Agent Service. A common configuration is to use the same account for both services, but this is not required. In fact, because of certain job or administrative requirements, you may need to use completely different credentials for each. Regardless of whether or not you use the same account, the account used by the SQL Server Agent must be a member of the sysadmin fixed server role and must have the following rights in the Windows operating system where the server is installed:

❑ Adjust memory quotas for a process.

❑ Act as part of the operating system.

❑ Bypass traverse checking.

❑ Log on as a batch job.

❑ Log on as a service.

❑ Replace a process-level token.

These rights can be granted by an administrator editing the Local Security Policy. If the SQL Server Agent will be interacting with services and features outside the local system, an Active Directory domain account should be used. This allows the SQL Server Agent to use an authenticated account to connect to a remote file system, Web Service, or another SQL Server.

An out-of-the-box installation of SQL Server with no changes to the default configuration does not start the SQL Server Agent Service but, instead, requires manual control over the start and stop behavior of the service. *Don't do this.* If you are going to use the SQL Server Agent for automation or alerting features, it needs to be running. If the SQL Server Agent is stopped, no scheduled jobs can run, and no operator will receive notification indicating that a job did or did not run successfully. When installing SQL Server, it is a good practice to configure the SQL Server Agent to run automatically when Windows starts.

If, however, you did not configure the SQL Server Agent to start automatically, you'll need to know how to start it manually. There are actually four different ways you can start and stop the SQL Server Agent Service.

One way is to use the NET START command from a Windows command prompt:

```
NET START SQLSERVERAGENT
```

To stop the service, use the NET STOP command:

```
NET STOP SQLSERVERAGENT
```

You can also use the Services snap-in from the Administrative Tools menu or the Computer Management console. From this tool, you can also configure the account that the service runs under, change the start-up behavior, choose service recovery options, and view the dependencies of the service. In Chapter 3, you learned how to use SQL Server Configuration Manager. You can use that similarly to configure the account used by the SQL Server Agent Service and the start-up behavior, as well as error reporting options. Finally, you can use SQL Server Management Studio to configure the behavior and properties of the SQL Server Agent Service.

This section will spend more time going into depth about configuring the various properties of the service, so you have a good understanding of each of the configurable elements from within a familiar tool. In Object Explorer, you can right-click "SQL Server Agent" and either stop or start the service as needed. To configure the service, select Properties from the context menu.

General Properties

From the General Properties sheet (see Figure 8-17), you can see the current state of the service, and you can configure both the SQL Server and SQL Server Agent to automatically restart if they stop unexpectedly. You can also change the location of the error log and elect to include execution trace messages in the logs for advanced troubleshooting. There is also an option to use an original equipment manufacturer (OEM) file. This allows the log information to store data in a non-Unicode format, which can take up less space on the system. However, if the error logs contain any Unicode data, it may be more difficult to read or interpret. Finally, the NET SEND RECIPIENT indicates an operator that can be notified of messages that SQL Server writes to the log file.

> *The messenger service is disabled by default in Windows Server 2003 and Windows Server 2008. The ability to use* NET SEND *may not be available.*

Advanced Properties

In the Advanced Properties sheet (see Figure 8-18), you can enable event forwarding, which will re-direct SQL Server events to a different server. To configure this, enable the checkbox next to "Forward events to a different server," and then select an available server or instance from the dropdown list. Once this is configured, you can also determine what type of events will get forwarded. "Unhandled events" are those that do not have alerts defined by the SQL Server Agent system, or you can select "All events." You can also decide to forward events with a minimum severity level. Severity-level values are discussed in detail later in this chapter.

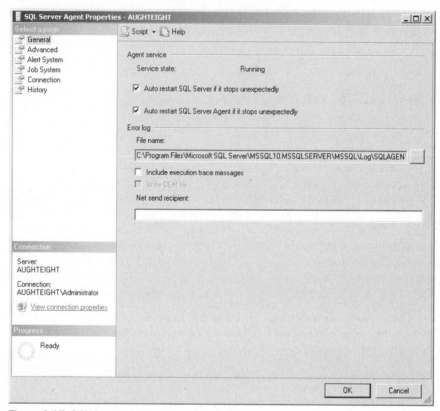

Figure 8-17: SQL Server Agent General Properties.

From this window, you can also define the CPU idle threshold. This can be useful if you have any job schedules that define the job and should be run when the CPU is idle, such as backing up the transaction log. In this case, the default values indicate that CPU usage must fall below 10 percent for 10 minutes. You can adjust this as necessary to meet your performance needs.

Alert System Properties

You can configure the Alert System properties from this page (see Figure 8-19) by first defining if the SQL Server Agent Mail service is enabled. If you want your operators to receive alert notifications by e-mail, you should enable this feature. You can also decide if you are going to use the Database Mail feature or the SQL Mail feature. Remember that SQL Mail is provided for backward compatibility only and should not be used with new applications because it will be phased out. If you are upgrading from a previous version of SQL, you should try to convert your applications to use Database Mail as soon as possible.

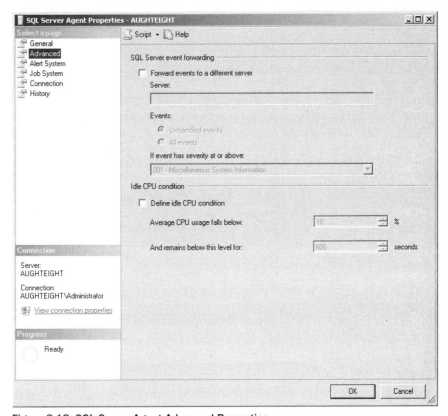

Figure 8-18: SQL Server Agent Advanced Properties.

Once you've selected your mail system (Database Mail, preferably), you can then select an appropriate profile to use. If you are using SQL Mail, you can test the MAPI connectivity and allow Sent messages to be saved in the Sent Items folder of the Microsoft Outlook profile.

If you will be paging operators, you can configure options for formatting addresses in the To, CC, and Subject lines of the message. You can also elect to include the body of the e-mail message in the page. Additionally, you can define a fail-safe operator and methods for notifying that person. The role of the fail-safe operator is discussed in more detail later in this chapter.

Finally, there is the option to replace tokens for all job responses to alerts. Tokens are a feature (similar to variables) of job steps that are discussed later in this chapter. For now, though, you should understand that this enables token replacement, replacing the variable with an actual value, for any job executed by the alert systems.

Job System Properties

You can specify the time-out value for jobs in the Job System Properties window (see Figure 8-20). This option configures how long the SQL Server Agent will wait for a job to complete before forcefully terminating the job. The default is 15 seconds, but be aware of how long certain jobs may need to take (because of their complexity) or the type of operations being performed.

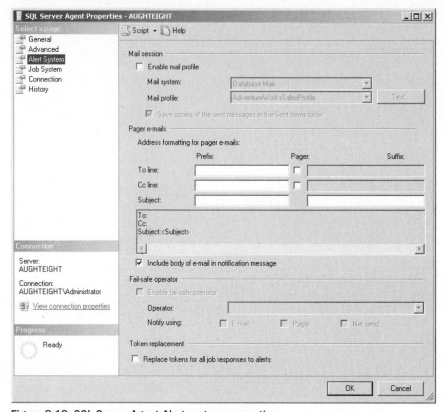

Figure 8-19: SQL Server Agent Alert system properties.

There is also an option to configure a non-administrative account as a proxy account for job steps. This is only applicable if you are using SQL Server Management Studio to manage an older version of SQL Server and its corresponding Agent service. You can specify the authentication information for the account by providing a username, password, and domain name. Configuring a proxy account for SQL Server 2008 job steps is covered in the section, "Creating Jobs," later in this chapter.

Agent Connection Properties

If you need to connect to an instance of SQL Server that uses a non-standard connection property, you can enter an alias used by the SQL Server to allow the SQL Server Agent Service to establish and maintain a connection (see Figure 8-21). You can also specify whether you require the SQL Server Agent Service to use Windows authentication or SQL Server authentication. If you select SQL Server authentication, you must provide a valid login and password for an account that is a member of the sysadmin fixed server role.

Job History Properties

Finally, the History page allows you to configure retention settings for job logs in the msdb database. By default, a maximum of 1,000 rows are stored in the sysjobhistory table, and each job can use no more than 100 rows in that table. You can use this window to remove or change the limit to the size of the job history table (see Figure 8-22).

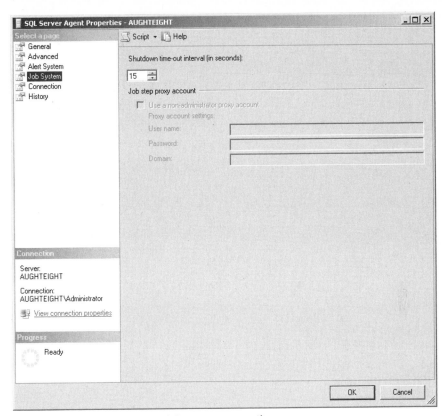

Figure 8-20: SQL Server Agent Job system properties.

You can also have the SQL Server Agent service automatically purge old job history rows from the `sysjobhistory` table. This feature is disabled by default. However, if enabled, it allows you to specify how many days, weeks, or months old a job history record must be before it can be purged from the database. If you need to maintain the job history indefinitely or need to have greater control over what gets purged, consider creating a custom job that will meet your needs.

SQL Server Agent Security

When planning to use the SQL Server Agent Service, or allowing other users to access it, you need to ensure that appropriate access is granted. By default, only members of the sysadmin fixed server role have complete access to the SQL Server Agent Service. In the `msdb` database, additional roles are created with varying levels of rights and permissions, but these roles are empty until a user is explicitly added to one or more of these roles. This section identifies each of these roles and the permissions assigned to them.

SQLAgentUserRole

The SQLAgentUserRole is the most limited of the three SQL Server Agent roles. Users who are members of this role have the ability to create new jobs and schedules and can manage only those jobs and schedules they create. However, they cannot view the properties of other jobs on the system, nor can they define operators or proxies. If they need to assign an operator or proxy to a job step, it must have already been defined. Members of this role also cannot delete job history information, even for jobs they own, unless they are granted EXECUTE permission on the sp_purge_jobhistory stored procedure. Another important limitation on this role is the inability to create or manage multi-server jobs. This means that any job created by members of this role is limited to the server on which it was created.

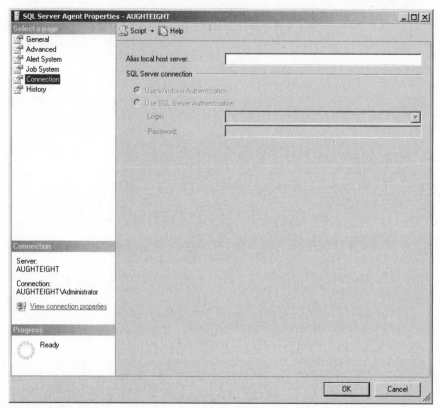

Figure 8-21: SQL Server Agent Connection properties.

SQLAgentReaderRole

The SQLAgentReaderRole role can enable users to create local jobs and schedules and manage only those that they create. In addition to these permissions, they can also view the properties of other local jobs, as well as multi-server jobs. This gives them the ability to audit the configuration of other jobs on the server, without having any rights to change those settings. This role is also prevented from creating multi-server jobs, but the job histories of all local and remote jobs are available for review. Members of this role, too, are prohibited from deleting the history of jobs they own, unless granted EXECUTE permission on sp_purge_jobhistory.

SQLAgentOperatorRole

Members of this role can create local jobs, as well as manage and modify jobs they own. They can also view and delete the job history information for all local jobs. To a limited extent, they can also enable or disable jobs and schedules owned by other users. However, they are still prohibited from creating and managing operators and proxies. They are also limited to Read Only access for multi-server jobs, as well. Outside of the sysadmin fixed server role, this role is granted the most rights and privileges to the job system in the SQL Server Agent Service.

Creating Jobs

Jobs are really at the core of the SQL Server Agent service. *Jobs* are operations that perform through a sequence of steps that run Transact-SQL scripts and launch command-prompt applications, ActiveX script tasks, replication tasks, and a variety of other tasks. Each task is defined as a separate job step. Part of the design of the job system is to build each task so that you can build dependencies and workflows between the job steps. A very simple example of this would be a backup job that ran nightly and then e-mailed an administrator to inform him or her that the job was complete. The simplicity and complexity of a job depend on what you need it to do. In some cases, you'll want to create multiple jobs, rather than a single, overly complex one, because of the time-out settings mentioned earlier.

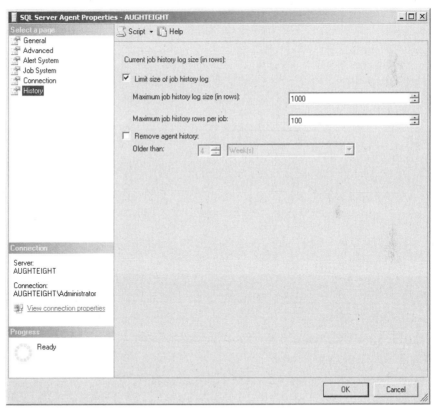

Figure 8-22: SQL Server Agent History properties.

Try It Out   Creating a New Job

Begin by creating a new job in SQL Server Management Studio. For this example, you're going to populate only the most basic information about the job from the General Properties page. Feel free to browse through the other property pages in this exercise, but be aware that the configurable elements in those pages are covered later in this chapter.

1. In Object Explorer, expand SQL Server Agent.

2. Right-click Jobs and select "New Job."

3. In the New Job dialog box (see Figure 8-23), enter **Simple Backup** as the job name.

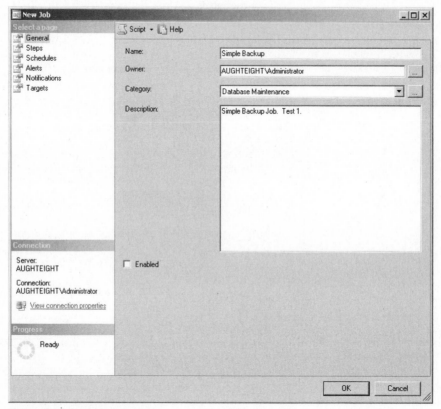

Figure 8-23: New Job properties.

4. Leave the Owner as the default.

5. Select Database Maintenance in the Category dropdown list.

6. In the description, enter **Simple Backup Job. Test 1**.

7. Remove the check next to Enabled.

8. Click OK.

This creates a new job and prevents the job from running once you close the New Job window. Because the job has no steps, there would have been little harm in letting it run, but it's a habit you will want to get into, until you've tested your jobs to ensure that they work as expected.

Now look at how to create a new job using Transact-SQL. The `sp_add_job` stored procedure allows you to create a new job and set configurable options on the job. The following table lists all the options for `sp_add_job`:

Option	Description
@job_name	The name of the job
@enabled	The default value of 1 indicates the job is enabled, and a value of 0 means the job is disabled. Disabled jobs can still be manually executed.
@description	An optional description of the job. If no value is specified, the field is populated with `No description available`.
@start_step_id	In more complex jobs, where you have multiple steps built around dependencies and error handling, you can actually have the job start at a step other than the first one. Use the integer-based job ID value for the initial job step.
@category_name	Allows you to type a category name to assign the job. Categories make it easier to group and manage jobs that have similar functions. Be aware that if you misspell an existing job category (as in "Databizase Maintenance"), it will return an error. You must use an existing category name.
@category_id	Allows you to use the `category_id` value rather than category name. Category names and IDs are stored in msdb.dbo .syscategories.
@owner_login_name	Allows a system administrator to set a different login as the owner of the job.
@notify_level_eventlog	Indicates what information should be added to the Windows Application Log. This is an `int` data type with the following values: 0 — Never 1 — On success 2 — On Failure (Default) 3 — Always
@notify_level_email	Indicates when to send e-mail messages regarding this job, using the levels described in @notify_level_eventlog. The default is 0.
@notify_level_netsend	This value indicates when a NET SEND message should be sent. The Messenger service must be started on both the sender and the recipient machines for this to work. With a default value of 0, the levels for @notify_level_eventlog can be used to change its behavior.

Continued

Option	Description
@notify_level_page	Indicates when to send messages to an SMTP-enabled pager, using the same values as @notify_level_eventlog. The default is 0.
@notify_email_operator_name	The name of an operator that will receive e-mail messages if e-mail notification is enabled. Do not use the e-mail address but, rather, the sysname value of the operator.
@notify_netsend_operator_name	The name of an operator that will receive NET SEND messages
@notify_page_operator_name	The name of the operator that will receive SMTP pages
@delete_level	Indicates when to delete the job, using the values defined in @notify_level_eventlog. If the level is set to 3, the job is deleted upon completion, and no further instances of this job will run. The default is 0.
@job_id job_id OUTPUT	Returns the value of the job_id. The job_id is of the uniqueidentifier data type.

Take a look at using the sp_add_job stored procedure to create a new job with only the basic elements. After creating other elements such as schedules, operators, and alerts, you will add those into the jobs you create in this section. For this example, you will create a new job that will be used for data retrieval tasks:

```
DECLARE @job_id uniqueidentifier;

EXECUTE msdb.dbo.sp_add_job
 @job_name = 'Poor Performers Report',
 @description = 'Monthly task to indicate which sales team members have less
                 than remarkable sales figures over previous year',
 @job_id = @job_id OUTPUT;

SELECT @job_id
```

One thing you should notice about the job_id parameter is that it uses the uniqueidentifier data type. This is also referred to as a Globally Unique Identifier (GUID). GUIDs are used for both jobs and schedules if either will be used for multi-server jobs. Multi-server jobs are covered later in this chapter.

If you're adding a job using the sp_add_job stored procedure, you will also need to ensure that the job can run on the server by using the sp_add_jobserver stored procedure. If the job is going to run on the local server, all you need to define is the job either by job_id or job_name, as in the following example:

```
EXECUTE msdb.dbo.sp_add_jobserver
    @job_name='Poor Performers Report';
```

So, now you have two new jobs available to your SQL Server Agent Service. Neither job has any steps defined, so running them won't accomplish anything, other than receiving a failure message. (But hey, if that's what you're after, go for it.) Before adding steps to your jobs, take a look at how to manage job categories.

Categories

The easiest and preferred method for managing job categories is through SQL Server Management Studio. Although you could directly edit the `syscategories` table, it's not recommended. You can add new categories and delete user-created categories. Be aware that you cannot delete built-in categories. In this example, you will add a new category called *AW–Performance Tasks*.

Try It Out   Creating a New Category

1. From Object Explorer, expand your server, and then expand SQL Server Agent.

2. Next, right-click Jobs, and select "Manage Job Categories."

3. In the Manage Job Categories window (see Figure 8-24), click Add.

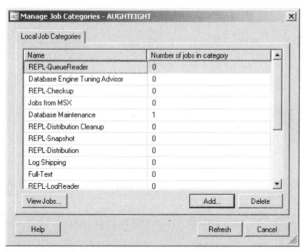

Figure 8-24: Manage Job Categories screen.

4. For the category name, enter **AW–Performance Tasks**.

5. Check the box next to "Show all jobs."

6. Check the box in the row for the Poor Performers Report job.

7. Click OK.

8. Click Cancel to close the Manage Job Categories window.

You have now successfully created the AW–Performance Tasks category and added the Poor Performers Report job to it. This category will now be available for any new jobs you want to create.

Creating Job Steps

Now that you have a couple of jobs you can work with, add some simple steps to these jobs. Before doing this, though, take a look at the different types of job steps you can define, as shown in the following table:

Step Type	Description
Windows Executable (CmdExec)	This will run Windows executable code, including files with the following extensions: .exe, .bat, .cmd, .com. For fully automated tasks, the executable may contain command-line parameters that can be passed to control execution.
Transact-SQL	Any T-SQL script that will execute in the context of the job owner if not otherwise specified. The Transact-SQL script can contain multiple batches and can include executing stored procedures.
ActiveX Script	Can use any language supported by the Windows Scripting Host. Common examples use VBScript and JavaScript. The script itself is written into the job task.
Replication	Used to initiate replication agents for the different replication types. Chapter 16 introduces replication and the function of these agents.
Analysis Services	Can be either command steps or queries.
Integration Services	Can execute a SQL Server Integration Services (SSIS) package. For more information about SSIS, see Chapter 13.

For each job step type, you can identify one or more proxy accounts that can be used to execute that step type, in case the owner of the job, or the login under which the job is run, does not have permissions to execute that type of task. It allows you to let users run jobs that contain steps that they would not be able to run under their own credentials. You learn about creating and managing proxies later in this chapter.

This first example uses SQL Server Management Studio again to edit the properties of the Simple Backup job. You're going to add a Transact-SQL step that will perform a full backup of the AdventureWorks2008 database onto the local disk. Before beginning, you should create a folder called dbBackups on your C: drive.

1. From Object Explorer, expand your server, and then expand SQL Server Agent.

2. Expand Jobs.

3. Right-click "Simple Backup," and select Properties.

4. Under the "Select a Page" list, select Steps.

5. Click on the New button.

6. In the "Step Name" box, enter **AdventureWorks2008 Backup**.

7. In the Type dropdown list, ensure that Transact-SQL is listed.

8. Leave "Run as" empty.

9. Ensure that master is the selected database.

10. Enter the following code in the command window:

```
BACKUP DATABASE AdventureWorks2008 TO DISK = 'C:\dbBackups\AWFull.bkf';
```

11. Click OK to close the New Job Step window.

12. Click OK to close the Job Properties window.

13. In the SQL Server Management Studio Note, it informs you that the last step will be changed from "Go to Next Step" to "Quit with Success." Click Yes.

You have now created a simple job step. Feel free to enable the job by right-clicking on the job and selecting Enable from the context menu. You can also manually run the job at any time, even if it's disabled, by right-clicking and selecting "Start Job." The job should execute with success.

If you go back into the job step properties and look at the Advanced Properties page, you will notice options to configure how the job responds when this step completes. If the job is successful, you can have it perform one of the following tasks:

❑ Go on to the next step.

❑ Quit the job reporting success.

❑ Quit the job reporting failure.

❑ Go to Step: (number).

The option to go to a numbered step is only available if you have more than one step in the job. Be careful about creating cyclical jobs where the first step will go to the next step, and the second step will go to the first step.

On this page, you can also identify the number of retry attempts and how long (in minutes) the server should wait between retries. If the job step cannot be completed successfully, you can also define how the job should behave. You have the same options for defining what to do when the step fails as when it succeeds.

Also, depending on the type of step being executed, you can define additional options or parameters. For example, with Transact-SQL steps, you can specify an output file, log the output to a table, and include output information with the job history. You can also identify who the step should run as.

sp_add_jobstep

You can use the `sp_add_jobstep` stored procedure to add steps to an existing job. Using this procedure allows you to append a step to an existing job or insert a new step between two existing steps. The following table provides a breakdown of the parameters for `sp_add_jobstep`:

Parameter	Description
@job_id	The `uniqueidentifier` value of the job. You can use this or `job_name` to refer to the job to which you are adding the step.
@job_name	The display name of the job. Use either this or the `job_id`, but not both.
@step_name	A display name for the step
@step_id	A unique number indicating where this step should be added into the job step order. If no value is specified, the `step_id` will auto-increment by 1. If the value specified already exists, this will insert this step and increment the step that previously held this value (and all steps that follow it) by 1.
@subsystem	This parameter allows you to identify which subsystem will be used to interpret the step. The available values are: `ACTIVESCRIPTING` — ActiveX script `CMDEXEC` — Windows command or executable `DISTRIBUTION` — Replication Distribution job `SNAPSHOT` — Replication Snapshot job `LOGREADER` — Replication Log Reader Agent job `MERGE` — Replication Merge Agent job `QueueReader` — Replication Queue Reader Agent job `ANALYSISQUERY` — MDX or DMX Analysis Services query `ANALYSISCOMMAND` — XMLA Analysis Services command `Dts` — Integration Services Package `PowerShell` — Invokes a PowerShell script. `TSQL` — Transact-SQL script. This is the default.
@command	The command that will be executed as the job step. The syntax will vary depending on the subsystem used to process the command.
@additional_parameters	This is not implemented but may be used in a future version.
@cmdexec_success_code	Value returned by the CmdExec subsystem. Uses `int` data type, and the default is `0`.

Parameter	Description
@on_success_action	Allows you to specify what to do if the step is successful. Use one of the following values: 1 — Quit with success (default). 2 — Quit with failure. 3 — Go to the next step. 4 — Go to step `on_success_step_id`.
@on_success_step_id	The ID of the step to go to if option 4 is selected above
@on_fail_action	The same values as `on_success_action` except `on_success_step_id` is replaced by `on_fail_step_id`
@on_fail_step_id	The ID of the step to go to if option 4 is selected for `on_fail_action`
@database_name	The database in which a Transact-SQL step will execute. If no value is specified, the Master database is used. If the step is an ActiveX script, this can be used to identify the scripting language.
@database_user_name	The user account under which the Transact-SQL step will execute
@retry_attempts	The number of attempts a step will make before it fails. The default is 0.
@retry_interval	The number of minutes before `retry_attempts`. The default is 0.
@os_run_priority	This is not available in this version of SQL Server, but may be implemented in the future.
@output_file_name	An external file in which step output is saved. Valid for Transact-SQL and CmdExec steps.
@flags	Options that control output behavior. Uses the following values: 0 — Overwrite output file (default). 2 — Append to output file. 4 — Write T-SQL step output to step history. 8 — Write log to table, overwriting existing history. 16 — Write log to table, appending to existing history.
@proxy_id	The ID of a proxy account that will be used for this job step, if needed
@proxy_name	The name of a proxy account that will be used for this job step, if needed

*There are additional parameters listed in SQL Server Books Online that are identified as "reserved."
Because they are not configured, they are not included in this list.*

Now take a look at creating a couple of job steps for the Poor Performers Report job. The first step will
generate an e-mail message that identifies sales employees who have not exceeded their previous year
sales by $200,000 (slackers!). The second step will e-mail an administrator indicating that the job has been
successful:

```
-- Create the First Step
EXECUTE msdb.dbo.sp_add_jobstep
 @job_name = 'Poor Performers Report',
 @step_id = 1,
 @step_name = 'Send Report',
 @subsystem = 'TSQL',
 @command = 'DECLARE @tableHTML NVARCHAR(MAX) ;
        SET @tableHTML =
            N''<H1>Lowest Sales Increase</H1>" +
            N''<table border=1>" +
            N''<tr><th>First Name</th><th>Last Name</th>" +
            N''<th>Current Year Sales</th>" +
            N''<th>Previous Year Sales</th>" +
         CAST ((SELECT td = pC.FirstName, '''',
                    td = pC.LastName, '''',
                    td = sP.SalesYTD, '''',
                 td = sP.SalesLastYear, ''''
               FROM AdventureWorks2008.Sales.SalesPerson AS sP INNER JOIN
               AdventureWorks2008.HumanResources.Employee AS hrE ON
             sP.BusinessEntityID = hrE.BusinessEntityID INNER JOIN
               AdventureWorks2008.Person.Person AS pC
 ON hrE.BusinessEntityID = pC.BusinessEntityID AND
            hrE.BusinessEntityID = pC.BusinessEntityID
             WHERE (sP.SalesYTD - sP.SalesLastYear) < 200000
          FOR XML PATH(''tr''), TYPE
          ) AS NVARCHAR(MAX) ) +
            N''</table>'';

      EXECUTE msdb.dbo.sp_send_dbmail
            @recipients = ''Gregory.House@adventureworks.com'',
            @subject = ''First to go...'',
            @body = @tableHTML,
            @body_format = ''HTML'';';




-- Create Step 2
EXECUTE msdb.dbo.sp_add_jobstep
 @job_name = 'Poor Performers Report',
 @step_id = 2,
 @step_name = 'Notify Administrator',
 @subsystem = 'TSQL',
 @command = 'EXEC msdb.dbo.sp_send_dbmail
            @recipients = ''administrator@adventureworks.com'',
            @subject = ''Message Sent'',
```

```
@body = ''The Monthly Sales Report has been sent'',
@body_format = ''HTML'';';
```

Now, you must tell the step that you created earlier to go to the next step once the first step has been completed. For this, use the `sp_update_jobstep` stored procedure, as follows:

```
EXECUTE msdb.dbo.sp_update_jobstep
  @job_name = 'Poor Performers Report',
  @step_id = 1,
  @on_success_action = 3;
```

Remember that when `on_success_action` is set to 3, the step will go to the next step.

Token Replacement

SQL Server 2008 uses tokens in job steps as parameter placeholders. These tokens allow the SQL Server Agent Service to replace the token with an actual value at run time (this token will *not* be replaced when executed as a query in SQL Server Management Studio). This is similar to using a variable within a script or an application. When writing jobs, consider using some of these tokens to provide accurate reporting of job status. These tokens can also allow your jobs to be more flexible. The following table provides a list of tokens supported by the SQL Server Agent Service:

Token	Description
$(A-DBN)	Database name, used in jobs launched by alerts
$(A-SVR)	Server name, used in jobs launched by alerts
$(A-ERR)	Error number, used in jobs launched by alerts
$(A-SEV)	Error severity, used in jobs launched by alerts
$(A-MSG)	Message text, used in jobs launched by alerts
$(DATE)	Current date (YYYYMMDD)
$(INST)	Instance name. The default instance returns an empty value.
$(JOBID)	Job ID
$(MACH)	Computer name
$(MSSA)	Master SQL Server Agent Service name
$(OSCMD)	Prefix for the program used to run CmdExec steps
$(SQLDIR)	The SQL Server installation directory
$(STEPCT)	The number of times this step has executed, excluding retries. Can be used to force a multi-step loop to terminate.
$(STEPID)	Step ID
$(SRVR)	Name of the computer running SQL Server, including the instance name, if any

Continued

333

Token	Description
$(TIME)	Current time (HHMMSS)
$(STRTTM)	The time (HHMMSS) the job began executing
$(STRTDT)	The date (YYYYMMDD) the job began executing
$(WMI(property))	The value of the property specified by property, when the job is launched by a Windows Management Instrumentation (WMI) alert

Using Tokens in Job Steps

When SQL Server 2005 Service Pack 1 was released, it significantly changed the way tokens are used in job steps. Prior to that release, you could simply use a token like a variable, as seen in the following example:

```
PRINT 'The database backup of $(A-DBN) is now complete.'
```

If your job backed up the AdventureWorks2008 database, the job step would have returned the output:

```
'The database backup of AdventureWorks2008 is now complete.'
```

Job steps in SQL Server 2008 require the use of an escape macro to successfully replace the token. The escape macros are used to prevent parsing errors that may exist because of invalid characters in the data that replaces the token. For example, if you installed SQL Server to a folder called *C:\Finance Department's Database* and tried to use the $(SQLDIR) token, your job step might fail, believing that the value ended at the word *Department*. There are four possible escape macros. The following table lists the escape macros and their uses:

Escape Macro	Usage
$(ESCAPE_SQUOTE(token))	This allows any single quotation mark in the replacement token string to be replaced by two single quotation marks.
$(ESCAPE_DQUOTE(token))	This escape macro replaces a double quotation mark with two double quotation marks.
$(ESCAPE_RBRACKET(token))	Use this escape macro to replace a right bracket character with two right bracket characters.
$(ESCAPE_NONE(token))	This allows the token to be replaced without escaping any characters. This is designed for backward compatibility.

So, the correct way to use a token is to use the appropriate escape macro when calling the token. For example, the following will prevent a database name that contains a single quote (which is possible) from causing the command to end prematurely:

```
PRINT 'The database backup of $(ESCAPE_SQUOTE(A-DBN)) is now complete.'
```

In SQL Server 2008, because users that have Write permissions on the Windows Event Log can access job steps that are activated by SQL Server Agent alerts or WMI alerts, use of any token that launched by an alert is disabled by default. To enable these tokens, you can enable the "Replace tokens for all job responses to alerts" option in the Alert System page of the SQL Server Agent properties.

Creating Schedules

To automate many of the tasks you need to perform to maintain your SQL Server, you must define schedules for when your jobs run. Schedules, not unlike categories, can be created and managed independently of the creation and management of jobs. This allows you to use the same schedule for multiple jobs.

Each job can also use multiple schedules. For example, you may create a job that performs a Transaction Log backup. If your operation is not a 24/7 business, you might want to create a schedule so that the transaction log is backed up more frequently during business hours. Let's use every 2 hours as an example. Then, you may want to continue to back up the transaction log after normal business hours, but because there is less activity after hours, and therefore fewer changes to your database, you could back up the transaction log every 4 hours. On the weekends, you may want to back up the transaction logs every 8 hours. Not that you would expect a lot of activity, but if someone comes in to work over the weekend, you will want to have a backup of any changes.

You can also enable or disable individual schedules as needed. When a schedule is disabled, any job that uses that schedule will not run under that schedule. However, if a job is configured to use other schedules, the job will run under those schedules. If the job itself is disabled, it will not run under any schedule.

Take a look at the tools used to manage schedules. In this first example, you're going to create a new schedule for your Simple Backup job that will run the job every weekday at noon:

1. From Object Explorer, expand your server, and then expand SQL Server Agent.
2. Right-click Jobs and select "Manage Schedules."
3. In the Manage Schedules window, click New.
4. In the New Job Schedule window (see Figure 8-25), enter **Weekdays–Noon** for the schedule name.
5. Ensure that the schedule type is Recurring, and ensure that the schedule is Enabled.
6. In the Frequency section, make sure that the schedule is set to occur weekly.
7. Select the checkboxes for Monday, Tuesday, Wednesday, Thursday, and Friday.
8. If selected, remove the check in the box next to Sunday.
9. In "Daily frequency," select the radio button marked "Occurs once at:" and set the time to **12:01:00 PM**.
10. Leave the "Start date" as the current date, and ensure that "No end date" is selected.
11. Click OK.

At this point, you can either add the job to the schedule, or you can add the schedule to the job in the properties. Let's look at both methods.

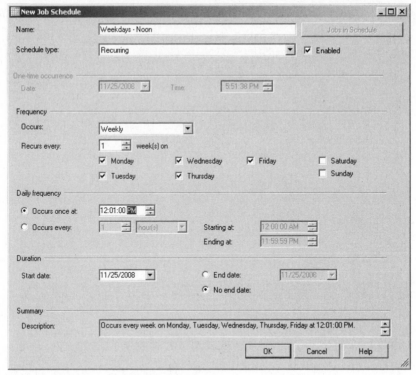

Figure 8-25: New Job Schedule screen.

First, in the Manage Schedules window (which should be open, unless you closed it), you should notice that the "Jobs in schedule" column for the Weekdays–Noon schedule contains the value 0, which is also a hyperlink.

1. Click on the number 0 (note that it is a hyperlink) in the "Jobs in schedule" column for the Weekdays–Noon schedule (see Figure 8-26).

2. In the "Jobs Referencing a Schedule" dialog box, click the checkbox in the Selected column for the Simple Backup schedule (see Figure 8-27).

3. Click OK. Note that the number of jobs in this schedule has incremented.

4. Click OK to close the Manage Schedules window.

If you want to add the schedule to the job through the Job Properties dialog box, follow these instructions:

1. In Object Explorer, expand the Jobs folder.

2. Right-click on the Poor Performers Report job, and select Properties.

3. Under the "Select a page" section, click Schedules.

4. Under the Schedule list, click Pick (see Figure 8-28).

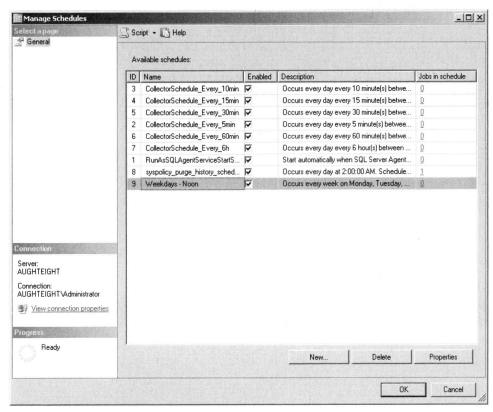

Figure 8-26: Manage Schedules window.

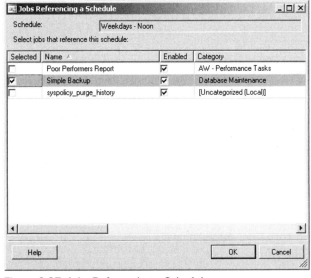

Figure 8-27: Jobs Referencing a Schedule.

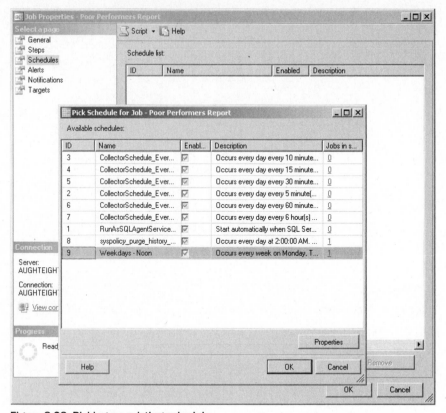

Figure 8-28: Picking an existing schedule.

5. A list of available schedules will appear. Select the "Weekdays–Noon" schedule, and click OK.

6. Click OK to close the Job Properties window.

Note that you can also create a new schedule from this window, as well. One of the benefits of SQL Server 2008, and especially of SQL Server Management Studio, is that you usually have more than one option for performing a task. Use whichever tool or method best suits your administrative needs.

sp_add_schedule

You can also create new schedules with the sp_add_schedule stored procedure. When you create the new schedule, you can specify the parameters shown in the following table:

Option	Description
@schedule_name	Friendly name of the schedule
@enabled	The default value of 1 means that the schedule is enabled. A value of 0 will disable the schedule.

Option	Description
@freq_type	Integer value indicating the frequency type of the schedule, using the following values: 1 — Once 4 — Daily 8 — Weekly 16 — Monthly 32 — Monthly relative to freq_interval 64 — Run when the SQL Server Agent starts. 128 — Run when CPU is idle.
@freq_interval	The days the job is executed. See the next table for options. This option is not used with all freq_type values.
@freq_subday_type	Identifies the units for freq_subday_interval, with the following values: 1 — At the specified time 2 — Seconds 4 — Minutes 8 — Hours
@freq_subday_interval	The number of freq_subday_type periods between executions
@freq_relative_interval	This value is the occurrence of freq_interval in each month if the value of freq_interval is 32. Can use the following values: 1 — First 2 — Second 4 — Third 8 — Fourth 16 — Last
@freq_recurrence_factor	Number of weeks or months between executions. Used only if freq_type is 8, 16, or 32. The default is 0.
@active_start_date	Date the job can start. This uses the YYYYMMDD format, and the date must be greater than 19900101. The default is NULL.
@active_end_date	Last date the job will run on this schedule. This also uses the YYYYMMDD format, but has a default of 99991231.

Continued

Option	Description
@active_start_time	Time of day on any day between the active_start_date and active_end_date to start a job. The default is 000000 using a 24-hour HHMMSS format.
@active_end_time	Time of day on any day between the active_start_date and active_end_date to end a job. The default is 235959 using a 24-hour HHMMSS format.
@owner_login_name	The name of the login that owns the schedule. By default, the creator of the schedule becomes the owner.
@schedule_uid uid OUTPUT	A uniqueidentifier for the schedule
@schedule_id id OUTPUT	The ID for the schedule using an int data type

The following table shows the values of freq_type and options for freq_interval:

Value of freq_type	Options for freq_interval
1	No recurrence
4	Every freq_interval days
8	Use one or more of the following values. Add the values together to allow multiple days to be selected. For example, to specify the schedule for Tuesday, Wednesday, and Thursday add the values 4 + 8 + 16 for a total value of 24. 1 — Sunday 2 — Monday 4 — Tuesday 8 — Wednesday 16 — Thursday 32 — Friday 64 — Saturday
16	On the freq_interval day of the month
32	Uses one of the following values for monthly relative: 1 — Sunday 2 — Monday 3 — Tuesday

Value of `freq_type`	Options for `freq_interval`
	4 — Wednesday
	5 — Thursday
	6 — Friday
	7 — Saturday
	8 — Day
	9 — Weekday
	10 — Weekend day

You've probably been able to figure out why SQL Server Management Studio is the preferred method for managing jobs and schedules. But look at an example for creating a new schedule. In this example, you're going to create a new schedule that will run the associated job(s) every 8 hours on the weekend. Some comments have been added to help make sense out of some of the values.

```
DECLARE @schguid UNIQUEIDENTIFIER
DECLARE @schid INT

EXECUTE msdb.dbo.sp_add_schedule
  @schedule_name = 'Weekend Schedule',
  @freq_type = 8,  -- Weekly
  @freq_interval = 65,  -- Combination of Saturday(64) and Sunday(1)
  @freq_subday_type = 8,  -- Hours
  @freq_subday_interval = 8,  -- specifies that the job runs every 8 hours
  @freq_recurrence_factor = 1,
  @active_end_date = 20101031,
  @active_end_time = 235959,
  @schedule_uid = @schguid OUTPUT,
  @schedule_id = @schid OUTPUT

SELECT @schguid as GUID,@schid as ID
```

sp_attach_schedule

Creating the schedule will not associate the schedule with any of the jobs you have created, so either you can go back and use SQL Server Management Studio or you can use the sp_attach_schedule stored procedure. When you created the schedule from the previous example, it should have returned both the GUID and the ID of the schedule.

When creating the mapping between a schedule and a job, you can use either the ID or the name of either element. Note that the schedule_id is an int value for the local ID, and not the uniqueidentifier GUID.

```
EXECUTE msdb.dbo.sp_attach_schedule
  @schedule_name = 'Weekend Schedule',
  @job_name = 'Simple Backup';
```

Creating Operators

Operators are objects that represent a unit of notification for SQL Server Agent jobs and alerts. They can represent an individual person, or a group. Operators are not associated with database or server principals, but are exclusive to the SQL Server Agent Service. Earlier in this chapter, you learned how to configure the SQL Server Agent Service to use either Database Mail or SQL Mail for the alert system. Whichever one you configured, the SQL Server Agent Service will use that to notify the appropriate operators.

When you create a new operator, you assign a name to the operator and then define the methods for notifying the operator. Your options for notifying an operator include e-mail, NET SEND using the Windows Messenger service, and SMTP-enabled pager.

In this example, you create a new operator for the administrator account. This operator will be available for paging only on the weekend.

1. From Object Explorer, expand your server, and then expand SQL Server Agent.

2. Right-click on the Operators folder, and select "New Operator."

3. In the New Operator window (see Figure 8-29), enter **Server Administrator** in the Name field.

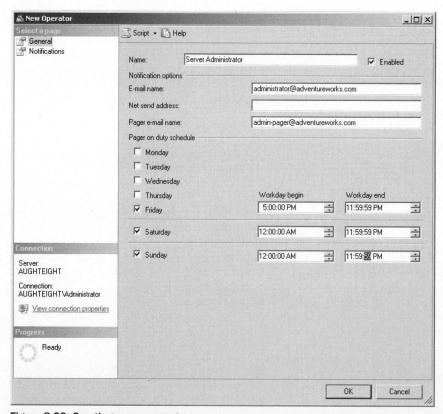

Figure 8-29: Creating a new operator.

4. Ensure that the Enabled box is checked.

5. In the "E-mail name" field, enter **administrator@adventureworks.com**.

6. Leave the "Net send address" field empty.

7. In the "Pager e-mail name" field, enter **admin-pager@adventureworks.com**.

8. In the "Pager on duty schedule," set the following values:

    a. "Friday": **5:00:00 PM** and **11:59:59 PM**

    b. "Saturday": **12:00:00 AM** and **11:59:59 PM**

    c. "Sunday": **12:00:00 AM** and **11:59:59 PM**

9. Click OK to close the New Operator properties window.

If you open the properties of the operator you just created, you will notice there are two additional pages. The Notifications page displays a list of jobs and alerts that have sent notifications to this operator. The History page reports the time of the last notification attempt for each notification type.

sp_add_operator

Use the `sp_add_operator` to create a new operator. You can use the values shown in the following table:

Parameter	Description
@name	Name of the operator
@enabled	The default value is 1. A value of 0 will disable the operator.
@email_address	The e-mail address used to notify the operator
@pager_address	The SMTP address of the pager
@weekday_pager_start_time	This value marks the time during the week when the SQL Server Agent will page the operator if necessary. Time is in the 24-hour HHMMSS format.
@weekday_pager_end_time	This value marks the time during the week when the SQL Server Agent will no longer page the operator. Time is in the 24-hour HHMMSS format.
@saturday_pager_start_time	This value marks the time on Saturday when the SQL Server Agent will page the operator if necessary. Time is in the 24-hour HHMMSS format.
@saturday_pager_end_time	This value marks the time on Saturday when the SQL Server Agent will no longer page the operator. Time is in the 24-hour HHMMSS format.

Continued

343

Parameter	Description
`@sunday_pager_start_time`	This value marks the time on Sunday when the SQL Server Agent will page the operator if necessary. Time is in the 24-hour HHMMSS format.
`@sunday_pager_end_time`	This value marks the time on Sunday when the SQL Server Agent will no longer page the operator. Time is in the 24-hour HHMMSS format.
`@pager_days`	Allows you to indicate the days the operator will be available for paging. To enable multiple days, simply add the following values: 1 — Sunday 2 — Monday 4 — Tuesday 8 — Wednesday 16 — Thursday 32 — Friday 64 — Saturday
`@netsend_address`	The network address of the operator the SQL Server Agent will send a message to
`@category_name`	The name of the category for this operator

In this example, you create a new operator that represents the Sales Managers group and enable paging for the group between 8:00 a.m. and 5:30 p.m.:

```
EXECUTE msdb.dbo.sp_add_operator
  @name = 'Sales Managers',
  @email_address = 'Sales.Managers@adventureworks.com',
  @pager_address = 'Sales.Managers.Pagers@adventureworks.com',
  @weekday_pager_start_time = 080000,
  @weekday_pager_end_time = 173000,
  @pager_days = 62;
```

To add the operator to an existing job, you can use the `sp_update_job` stored procedure. You can use this to specify that the operator should be notified using any of the defined methods for that operator. The following example notifies the Sales Managers by e-mail when the Poor Performers Report succeeds, and pages them if the job fails:

```
EXECUTE msdb.dbo.sp_update_job
  @job_name = 'Poor Performers Report',
  @notify_email_operator_name = 'Sales Managers',
  @notify_page_operator_name = 'Sales Managers',
  @notify_level_email = 1, -- on success
  @notify_level_page = 2; -- on failure
```

You can also edit the properties of an existing job to notify an operator when a job fails or succeeds, or both by using the "When the job completes" option. Also on this page, you can configure the job to write an event to the application log and have the job automatically deleted if one of the completion conditions is met.

The Fail-Safe Operator

After you have created at least one operator, you can designate an operator as the *fail-safe operator*. The *fail-safe operator* is an operator whose contact information is cached in memory while the SQL Server is running. This ensures that the operator can still be contacted in case the msdb database becomes unavailable. The fail-safe operator can also be notified if the primary operators for a job or alert cannot be notified. It is defined in the SQL Server Agent properties window. In the Alert System page, there is a dropdown list allowing you to select an existing operator as the fail-safe operator, and you can use the checkboxes to determine the methods of notification for this operator.

Creating Alerts

"Danger, Will Robinson, Danger!" The term *alerts* tends to carry such negative connotation. You may think of loud klaxons going off, the emergency lights turning on, and people shoring up the doors to keep the zombies out. You know, stuff like that. But alerts in SQL Server 2008 don't necessarily mean the end of the world. Alerts can be simply informational, such as letting a manager know that someone on the sales staff is deleting rows from the Customers table.

Creating alerts consists of three steps:

1. Name the alert. You should use a name that will be descriptive, which may also include information about the severity of the event that triggered the alert.

2. Define the event or performance condition that will trigger the alert.

3. Identify what this alert will actually do. Will it notify an operator, or will it run a job?

Alerts typically fall into one of three categories:

❑ **Event-Based Alerts** — These are generated on database- or system-level events. These can be system-defined, or you can write your own events.

❑ **Alerts on Performance Conditions** — These use SQL Server Performance counters to indicate that a threshold value has been met.

❑ **WMI Events** — You can also create alerts based on WMI events.

SQL Server Event-Based Alerts

SQL Server event-based alerts can be used to execute a task or notify an operator based on a pre-defined SQL Server event. These events exist as both *system-created*, usually referring to system-wide activity, or they can be *user-created*, allowing you to define conditions within a specific database. Before you create an alert, you should learn how to create an event.

SQL Server events are defined as an instance of an action being performed or a condition being met. Although that may sound like a very broad definition, events themselves can be very broad in scope. SQL Server 2008 has several events already defined for you. In fact, the number of events defined is almost 8,900 just for the English language! These events can be generated when a query contains too many referenced tables, or when an index is corrupted. There is also a mechanism for you to create your own events that may be system-wide or database-specific, as needed.

Each event is defined with a unique numerical ID, a severity level, the text of the message, and a language ID number. Severity levels are values between 0 and 25 and are used to categorize the event.

Error messages configured with a severity level of 9 or less will not actually raise a system-level exception. This comes in handy when you want to create an alert on a SQL Server event, but you don't want to throw an exception to the calling application. The following table lists the different severity levels and what they represent:

Severity Level(s)	Description
0–9	Messages with a severity level between 0 and 9 indicate informational messages that do not raise a system error. SQL Server will treat a severity level of 10 as a 0.
11	The object or entity does not exist.
12	Indicates that the query does not use locking because of special query hints. Read operations may result in inconsistent data.
13	Deadlock errors
14	Security errors
15	Syntax errors
16	General errors
17	The SQL Server has run out of resources or has reached an administrator-defined limit.
18	There is a problem in the database engine, but the statement has been executed, and the connection has been maintained.
19	A non-configurable limit has been reached, and the current batch has stopped. Events with a severity level of 19 or higher are automatically logged.
20	A problem has occurred in the current statement.
21	A problem that affects the entire database has occurred, but the database may not have been damaged.
22	A table or index has been damaged by a hardware or software problem.
23	The database has been damaged by a hardware or software problem.
24	General media failure
25	User-defined

Querying the sysmessages catalog view returns a list of all events defined on the server. To create your own messages that can be used by events, you can use the sp_addmessage stored procedure. When using sp_addmessage, you can use the values shown in the following table. All values default to NULL unless otherwise stated. The only required values are @msgnum, @severity, and @msgtext.

Option	Description
@msgnum	This is the ID number of the message. You must use a value greater than 50,000 for all user-defined messages.
@severity	Use an appropriate severity level for this event.
@msgtext	This is an nvarchar(255) field that contains the message text. You can use parameter placeholders such as %d for decimal values and %s for string values. When the event is raised, these placeholders are replaced with the actual values.
@lang	The language for the message. Each message can be stored for multiple languages, allowing you to localize the message.
@with_log	Use TRUE to have the event logged in the Windows Application log. FALSE is the default.
@replace	Use the value replace if you are overwriting an existing message.

Take a look at an example of the sp_addmessage stored procedure. In this exercise, you create a simple error message that contains notification information whenever a user adds a row to the Sales.CreditCard table. In the next step, you'll create a stored procedure that will insert a row into the Sales.CreditCard table, and then you'll execute that stored procedure.

```
-- Create the message
EXECUTE sp_addmessage
@msgnum = 60001,
@severity = 10,
@msgtext = 'Credit Card ID #%d has been added by %s as %s',
@with_log = 'True';
GO

-- Create a stored procedure for inserting credit card data that will raise
-- the error
USE AdventureWorks2008;
GO

CREATE PROCEDURE AddNewCreditCard
@CardType nvarchar(50),
@CardNumber nvarchar(25),
@ExpMonth tinyint,
@ExpYear smallint
AS
DECLARE @username varchar(60)
DECLARE @loginame varchar(60)
DECLARE @CreditCardInfo Table(CreditCardID INT)
DECLARE @CreditCardID INT
```

```
SET @loginame = suser_sname()
SET @username = user_name()

BEGIN TRANSACTION
INSERT Sales.CreditCard(CardType,CardNumber,ExpMonth,ExpYear)
 OUTPUT INSERTED.CreditCardID
  INTO @CreditCardInfo
 VALUES (@CardType,@CardNumber,@ExpMonth,@ExpYear);

SET @CreditCardID = (Select CreditCardID FROM @CreditCardInfo)

RAISERROR (60001, 10, 1, @CreditCardID, @loginame, @username)
COMMIT TRANSACTION;
GO

-- Run the stored procedure and return the message
EXECUTE AddNewCreditCard
@CardType='Veesa',
@CardNumber='111187620190227',
@ExpMonth='2',
@ExpYear='2011'
```

This should result in the following output:

```
(1 row(s) affected)
Credit Card ID #19238 has been added by AUGHTEIGHT\Administrator as dbo
```

Now that you have an event, you should create an alert on that event. In this next exercise, you create an alert that will use the error message created in the previous example and have a notification sent to the Sales Managers operator:

1. In Object Explorer, expand SQL Server Agent.

2. Right-click Alerts and select "New Alert."

3. For the name, enter **NewCCAlert** (see Figure 8-30).

4. Ensure that "Type" is "SQL Server event alert."

5. Select AdventureWorks2008 as the database.

6. Under "Alerts will be raised based on," select "Error number."

7. Type **60001** for the error number.

8. Switch to the Response page.

9. Select "Notify Operators."

10. Select "E-mail for Sales Managers."

11. Switch to the Options page.

12. Select "E-mail" under "Include error alert text in."

13. Click OK.

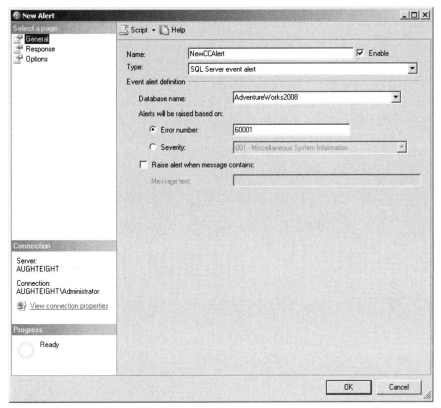

Figure 8-30: Creating a new alert.

The following example shows you how to use the sp_add_alert stored procedure to create a new alert, and the sp_add_notification stored procedure to associate the alert with operators that will be notified. Because you cannot have two alerts defined for the same event in the same database, you will need to delete the "NewCCAlert" you created in the previous step first.

```
EXECUTE msdb.dbo.sp_delete_alert
@name = 'NewCCAlert';

EXECUTE msdb.dbo.sp_add_alert
 @name = 'New Credit Card Alert',
 @message_id = 60001,
 @include_event_description_in = 1,
 @database_name = 'AdventureWorks2008';

EXECUTE msdb.dbo.sp_add_notification
 @alert_name = 'New Credit Card Alert',
 @operator_name = 'Sales Managers',
 @notification_method = 1;
```

The `sp_add_alert` stored procedure includes a number of options for creating and adding alerts. The following table identifies all the parameters available, but be aware that, depending on the type of alert you are creating, not all options will be used, and, in fact, some cannot be used together.

Option	Description
`@name`	The name of the alert
`@message_id`	The error number of the alert. Only messages written to the application log can cause an alert to be sent.
`@severity`	The severity level for messages that will generate the alert. If you specify this option, all messages with this severity level will issue this alert.
`@enabled`	The default value of 1 enables the alert.
`@delay_between_responses`	The wait period between alert responses in seconds. Raising this value decreases the likelihood of multiple alerts being generated within a short time.
`@notification_message`	Optional additional message
`@include_event_description_in`	The notification type, if any, the message text will be included in. The values here are also used with the `sp_add_notification` stored procedure. Adding the values indicates multiple notification types: 0 — None 1 — E-mail 2 — Pager 4 — Net Send
`@database_name`	Identifies the database for which this alert is active. If you do not specify a database name, the alert will be active for all databases.
`@event_description_keyword`	This option uses a pattern match to generate the alert only if certain keywords or phrases are present in the error message.
`@job_id`	ID number of a job that will run as a response to the alert
`@job_name`	Name of a job that will run as a response to the alert. Use either `job_id` or `job_name`, not both.
`@raise_snmp_trap`	The default is 1. Changing the value to 0 will not raise an SNMP trap message.

Option	Description
@performance_condition	Allows you to define a performance condition alert in the format of ItemComparatorValue: Item — Performance object or counter Comparator — Using greater than (>), less than, (<), or equal to (=) Value — Numeric value for the counter
@category_name	Name of the alert category
@wmi_namespace	Namespace used for WMI queries when using WMI Event alerts
@wmi_query	A WQL query for WMI providers that report on health or state information

Performance Condition Alerts

Performance condition alerts use SQL Server performance objects and counters to allow alerts to be defined on server or database activity. For example, you can use this to trigger an alert when the number of transactions per second for the AdventureWorks2008 database rises above a specific value. In this example, you create an alert that will notify you when the transaction log of AdventureWorks2008 is above 85 percent full:

1. In Object Explorer, expand SQL Server Agent.
2. Right-click Alerts and select "New Alert."
3. For the name, enter **AWXtactLogSpace** (see Figure 8-31).
4. Select "SQL Server performance condition alert" as the Type.
5. From the Object dropdown list, select SQLServer:Databases.
6. From the Counter dropdown list, select "Percent Log Used."
7. From the Instance dropdown list, select AdventureWorks2008.
8. From the "Alert if counter" dropdown list, select "rises above."
9. Enter **85** for the value.
10. Switch to the Response page.
11. Select "Notify Operators."
12. Select "E-mail and Pager for the Server Administrator."
13. Click OK.

You've now created a new performance alert that will notify an administrator whenever the transaction log for AdventureWorks2008 grows above 85 percent. Alternatively, you could create a job that would back up and truncate the transaction log. For more information about performance objects and counters, see Chapter 10.

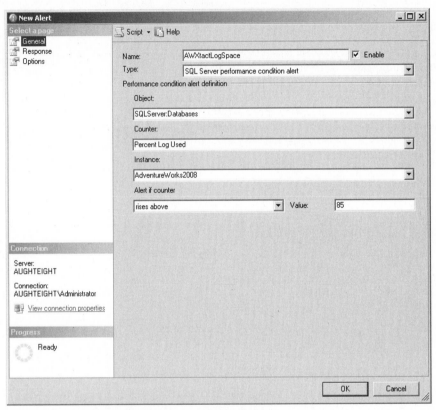

Figure 8-31: Creating a performance condition alert.

WMI Event Alerts

SQL Server 2008 can use WMI to collect events for alerting operators. SQL Server uses the WMI Provider for Server Events to make the SQL Server an object manageable by WMI. Any event that can generate Event Notification can be managed by WMI. SQL Server alerts use WMI Query Language (WQL) to retrieve an event type for a specific database or database object. WQL is similar to SQL, but with extensions specific to WMI. When an alert is created for a WMI Event, the WMI Provider for Server Events translates a WMI query into an Event Notification. The WMI provider will dynamically create a service and queue in the msdb database. The provider reads the data from the queue and returns it to the application in a managed object format.

To be able to successfully create a WMI Event alert, you must ensure that the WMI Performance Adapter service is running. The service is set to be started manually, but if you plan to make WMI Event alerts part of your administrative solution, you may want to configure the service to start automatically. Also, ensure that Service Broker service is enabled in the msdb database, as well as any databases that you will be managing through WMI.

WMI is a very powerful and complex tool, and with it, there are several different Data Definition Language (DDL) and trace events that you can watch for with WMI alerts. I recommend reading the topic entitled "WMI Provider for Server Events Classes and Properties" in Books Online for a list of available events.

Creating Proxies

SQL Server Agent properties allow you to execute specific job steps with a different security account. This allows you greater flexibility over your application and maintenance designs. It also allows you to create job steps that can be executed by users whose security context would normally prohibit them from running a task. The benefit of this is that the user who creates the job need only have access to the proxy account. The user does not need to create credentials or users or be given elevated permissions to execute a job step. You can create proxies for the following types of job steps:

❑ ActiveX Script

❑ Operating System (CmdExec)

❑ Replication Distributor

❑ Replication Merge

❑ Replication Queue Reader

❑ Replication Snapshot

❑ Replication Transaction-Log Reader

❑ Analysis Services Command

❑ Analysis Services Query

❑ SSIS Package Execution

❑ PowerShell

There is also a folder for creating and managing unassigned proxies. Note that a single proxy can be used for multiple task types, if needed.

Try It Out   **Creating a New Proxy**

Take a look at the process for creating a new proxy. First of all, proxies use credentials to execute. In Chapter 6, you learned how to create a new credential, but in case you've deleted it or you're not reading this book from cover to cover, you can create a new credential now. Begin by first creating a new Windows user:

1. Navigate to the Local Users and Groups folder on your system. This may vary depending on which Operating System you are using.

2. Expand Local Users and Groups, and select the Users folder.

3. Right-click on the Users folder and select "New User."

4. In the User name box, enter **ScriptRunner**.

5. Enter **P@ssw0rd** as the password, and remove the check next to "User must change password at next logon."

6. Click Create.

7. Click Close.

8. Close Server Manager (or Computer Manager, depending on your OS).

So, now that you have a new user, create a credential for this user:

1. Go back to SQL Server Management Studio.

2. In Object Explorer, expand your server, and expand Security.

3. Right-click Credentials and select "New Credential" (see Figure 8-32).

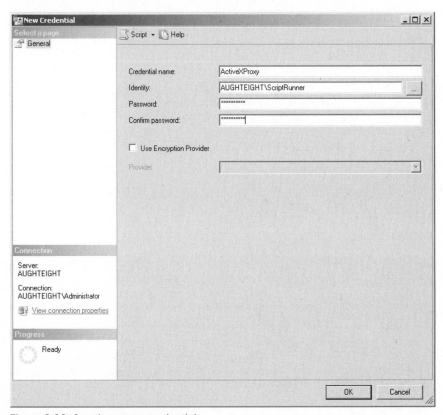

Figure 8-32: Creating a new credential.

4. For the name, enter **ActiveXProxy**.

5. In the identity box, enter **AughtEight\ScriptRunner** (or use your server and domain name in place of *AughtEight*).

6. Enter **P@ssw0rd** for the Password and "Confirm password" fields.

7. Click OK.

You now have a new Windows user with an associated credential on your server. Now you can use that credential to create one or more proxies:

1. In Object Explorer, expand SQL Server Agent.

2. Expand Proxies and select "ActiveX Script."

3. Right-click "ActiveX Script" and select "New Proxy."

4. Enter **ScriptRunner** as the "Proxy name" (see Figure 8-33).

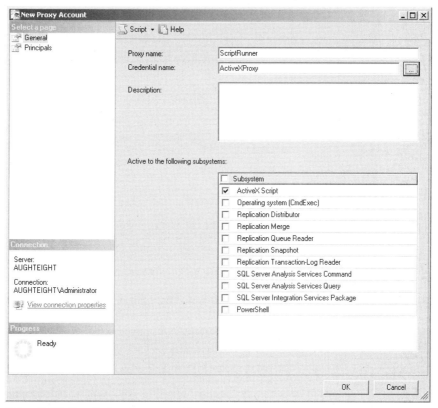

Figure 8-33: Creating a proxy account.

5. Enter **ActiveXProxy** as the "Credential name."

6. Ensure that "ActiveX Script" is selected under "Active to the following subsystems."

7. Alternatively, add additional subsystems or use the Principals page to identify SQL Server logins, server roles, or msdb database roles that can reference this proxy in job creation.

8. Click OK.

Now that you've created a new proxy, let's see how it can be used in a job step. In this next example, you add a new step to your Poor Performers Report job that will contain an ActiveX script. It'll be a fairly useless script, but "Hello World" always makes for great proof of concept!

```
EXECUTE msdb.dbo.sp_add_jobstep
  @job_name = 'Poor Performers Report',
  @step_id = 2,
  @step_name = 'Hello World',
  @subsystem = 'ACTIVESCRIPTING',
  @database_name = 'VBScript',
  @command = 'Sub main()
              Print ("Hello World.")
            End Sub',
  @on_success_action = 3,
  @proxy_name = 'ScriptRunner';
```

Now that this has been added, you can execute the job and review the job history to see the successful execution of the script as the ScriptRunner.

Multi-Server Jobs

SQL Server also supports the ability to create and manage jobs on one server that can be run on multiple SQL Servers. This functionality grants you the ability to administer and control multiple servers at once. This can be beneficial when performing system-level tasks, such as backing up the system databases, or controlling database-level tasks like replication.

Multi-server jobs are configured by first defining a *master server*. This master server acts as the source for all jobs that will be run on multiple *target servers* (see Figure 8-34). When defining a multi-server configuration, be aware that although you can enlist multiple target servers on which remote jobs will run, not every multi-server-enabled job will run on all target servers. In fact, you can specify which target servers a multi-server job will run. The downside to this is that each target server can only have one master server. Plan your multi-server job configuration carefully.

There are a few things you need to know about setting up multi-server jobs:

❑ Jobs running on multiple servers that have steps running under a proxy account use the proxy account on the target server. Ensure that you have a proxy server on both the master and target servers that has the same access and permissions.

❑ Each target server can have only one server for all jobs.

❑ If you are going to change the name of a target server, you must remove it from the master server, through a process known as *defecting*, and then re-enlist it after the name change.

❑ When removing a multi-server configuration, first defect all target servers before decommissioning the master.

To create multi-server jobs, you must first define the master servers and the target server. You can begin by running the Master Server Wizard in SQL Server Management Studio:

1. In Object Explorer, right-click "SQL Server Agent," and select "Multi Server Administration," then "Make this a Master." The Wizard begins with an introductory page that informs you of the steps that will be taken in this Wizard.

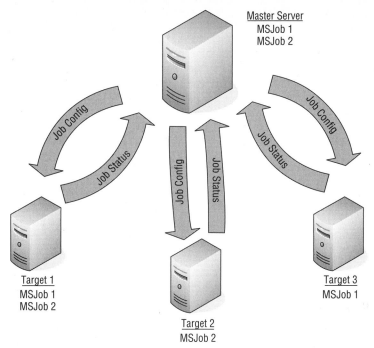

Figure 8-34: Multi-server configuration.

2. The next step creates an MSXOperator account. This operator is used to send information about multi-server jobs. You can provide an e-mail address, pager address, and NET SEND address for message delivery.

3. Then, you will specify at least one server that will be identified as a target server. SQL Server 2008 includes a compatibility check to ensure that the target server will work with the master server.

4. The final step identifies the credentials that will be used to establish authentication and authorization between the two servers. As a best practice, you should use Windows Active Directory domain accounts for the SQL Server Agent service on your master server and all target servers, so that the accounts use the benefit of Active Directory security without having to create duplicate accounts on the servers. If the login for MSXOperator does not exist on the target server, the Wizard will ask you if you want to create it.

Once this has completed, the Wizard will perform the following tasks:

❑ Create the MSXOperator.

❑ Ensure that the SQL Server Agent Service is running on the master server.

❑ Ensure that the SQL Server Agent Service account on the target server has rights to log in as a target server.

❑ Enlist the target server into the master server.

Once the Wizard has completed successfully and the server is configured as a master server, you can create new jobs that will run on the local server, remote servers, or both. You will also be able to go back into an existing job, and specify that job will run as a multi-server job. You can then select on which servers the job will run. This is managed in the Targets property sheet.

Maintenance Plans

SQL Server Management Studio includes a very robust platform for creating and managing maintenance plans. Plans can be created with a wizard or manually with the Maintenance Plan Designer. Maintenance plans are actually created as Integration Services packages. To create and use Maintenance Plans, Integration Services must be installed.

Maintenance Plan Wizard

Microsoft SQL Server 2008 includes a wizard for checking database integrity, as well as running tasks that help reorganize the data and re-index the data. As you step through the Wizard, you are asked to choose which tasks to perform, and then you will provide the configuration options for each task, including which databases to perform the tasks on. The available tasks include the following:

❑   Checking database integrity

❑   Shrink the database

❑   Reorganize indexes

❑   Rebuild indexes

❑   Update statistics

❑   Clean up history

❑   Executing a SQL Server Agent job

❑   Backing up databases using full, differential, or transaction log backups

Once you've specified which options to include and configured them in your maintenance plan, you can schedule the job to run on a recurring basis. This creates a job that will execute an Integration Service package, which contains each of the steps defined in the maintenance plan. You can execute the maintenance plan from the Maintenance Plan folder under the Management node in Object Explorer, or simply execute the job that was created. You can also modify the maintenance plan at any time, and add or remove tasks as needed.

Maintenance Plan Designer

Although the Wizard is an easy way to create a new maintenance plan, it lacks the flexibility that creating a plan with the Designer provides. To create a new maintenance plan, right-click on the Maintenance Plans folder in SQL Server Management Studio, and click "New Maintenance Plan."

In the resulting New Maintenance Plan dialog, enter a name in the Name field and click OK. This will launch the Maintenance Plan Designer, which is based on Integration Services (see Figure 8-35).

To create a maintenance plan, drag the desired tasks from the Toolbox onto the design surface. Once the task is on the surface, you can either double-click on the task or right-click on the task and then select Edit from the context menu to configure the task's properties. Additional tasks can be added to the Designer and joined by precedence constraints. Each task added is configured with a Success constraint by default. However, right-clicking on the constraint (see Figure 8-36) displays a context menu where the constraint can be configured for Success, Failure, or Completion.

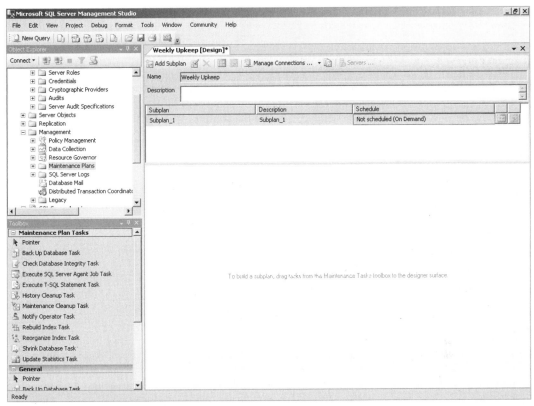

Figure 8-35: Maintenance Plan Designer.

Figure 8-36 shows a Rebuild Index Task configured to rebuild the indexes on the Person.Person table. This task will execute a Notify Operator task called "Notify Failure" in the event that it fails and a Backup Database task if it succeeds. The Backup Database task that performs a Full backup of AdventureWorks2008 will also execute the Notify Operator task if it fails, but it executes the Maintenance Cleanup Task if it succeeds. The Maintenance Cleanup Task is configured to delete any backup files more than 4 weeks old, and then to notify an operator that the plan has succeeded if it succeeds, or notify of failure if it fails.

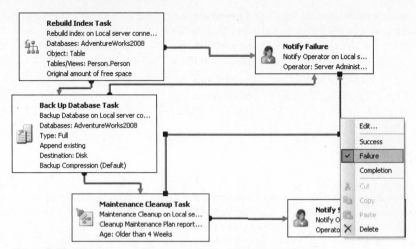

Figure 8-36: Maintenance Plan precedent constraints and tasks.

Maintenance plans are configured to run on-demand by default, but they can be configured with a recurring schedule by clicking the ellipses to the right of the Schedule field and setting the properties of the schedule in the resulting schedule screen.

Best Practices

Here are some guidelines that can help you automate administration of your servers:

❑ **Use Database Mail instead of SQLMail** — SQLMail is included for backward compatibility only, and its dependence on an extended MAPI client and server configuration can make it more cumbersome than it's worth.

❑ **Configure Database Mail to Use Multiple Accounts and Multiple SMTP Servers for Each Profile** — This will help increase the ability to deliver messages to the appropriate operators and personnel.

❑ **Configure the SET TRUSTWORTHY ON and ENABLE_BROKER Options for the msdb Database** — This will help ensure that your Event Notification messages and alerts can be delivered to the appropriate personnel.

❑ **Configure the SQL Server Agent to Start Automatically When Windows Starts, and Configure Automatic Restart if the Service Fails** — This helps ensure that scheduled jobs are able to run in case the system is accidentally shut down or restarted.

❑ **Configure the SQL Server Agent to Use a Domain User Account** — This allows you to use several features, including the ability to run and control multi-server jobs using a single account, as well as having better auditing capabilities of how that account is used.

❑ **Configure Proxy Accounts with Only the Level of Access Needed to Perform the Tasks They Were Designed for and Nothing Else** — Use the principle of least privilege in all layers of your administrative model.

❑ **Designate Groups Rather than Individuals as Operators** — You can specify the e-mail address of a group or distribution list rather than an individual user. This gives you the flexibility of modifying the group membership and, thereby, changing the target delivery without having to change the job, operator, or notification method.

❑ **Use Maintenance Plans to Define a Comprehensive Set of Steps That Will Check the Integrity of Your Database and Help Resolve Performance Issues** — Schedule the maintenance plan to run regularly, but at a time when it least impacts your users.

Summary

In this chapter, you learned about the different tools that can be used to help automate the management of SQL Server 2008. Beginning with an introduction to the new Policy-Based Management tools, you also learned about Central Management Servers. Database Mail is one of the more essential features to help you administer your server, in that you can use it for notification of both critical and non-critical server events. Its flexibility in its ability to use any standard SMTP server allows you to provide a robust solution without incurring some of the costs of a large-scale enterprise mail solution. You were also introduced to the topic of Event Notifications, which can provide you with an alternative method of receiving notifications of system or database events.

Finally, you got an exhaustive look at the elements of the SQL Server Agent, including administrative tools for managing jobs, schedules, operators, alerts, and proxy accounts. In the next few chapters, you are going to learn about different tools and resources to manage the SQL Server environment. This chapter should serve as a building block for the materials from the next chapters, in that you should be able to take the concepts you've learned here and apply them to backing up your databases, covered in Chapter 9, and performance monitoring and optimization, which are covered in Chapters 10 and 11.

Disaster Prevention and Recovery

"There are two things that every database administrator can't live without. The first is an effective backup and restore plan. The second is an up-to-date résumé. If you have the first, you may never *need* the second, but if you don't have the first, sooner or later the résumé will be critical to your future employment." I give that speech to every group of database administrators that I address, and I address a lot of them. It is a fact that disks fail and data gets corrupted. We have all probably suffered from some form of data loss that could have been prevented if the data had been properly backed up. As the individual responsible for the stability and integrity of the organization's data, the database administrator must be diligent and meticulous about planning a database backup strategy so that in the event of equipment failure, user error, or intentional data corruption, the database can be returned to service in as short as time as possible with minimal loss of data.

This chapter is about the mechanics of database backup and recovery, with a little bit of strategy thrown in for good measure. I will try not to give specific recommendations since no cookie-cutter recommendation will work for each situation. It is up to you as the database administrator to examine all possible backup and restore operations and come up with a plan that will prevent data loss and minimize downtime. There are people counting on you, and the very organization that you work for may succeed or fail because of your efforts. It is a pretty heavy responsibility to bear, but as more and more line-of-business applications are built on top of SQL Server, it is a very real responsibility. So take a deep breath, and learn all that you can about disaster prevention and recovery to ensure that you are always the hero and never the person to blame for lost data.

Chapter Preparation

The AdventureWorks2008 database is a fairly large sample database. To reduce the amount of time and disk space required to practice the examples in this chapter, we're first going to create a smaller version of AdventureWorks2008. The following script creates a database called SmallWorks made up of a Primary filegroup and two additional filegroups with one data file each. It then creates a table in each filegroup and populates it with data from the AdventureWorks2008 database. The last action of the script is to set the Read Only attribute on the second user-defined filegroup. The script assumes the existence of the C:\SQLData path.

```
CREATE DATABASE SmallWorks ON   PRIMARY
( NAME = 'SmallWorksPrimary'
, FILENAME = 'C:\SQLData\SmallWorks.mdf'
, SIZE = 10MB
, FILEGROWTH = 20%
, MAXSIZE = 50MB)
, FILEGROUP SWUserData1
( NAME = 'SmallWorksData1'
, FILENAME = 'C:\SQLData\SmallWorksData1.ndf'
, SIZE = 10MB
, FILEGROWTH = 20%
, MAXSIZE = 50MB)
, FILEGROUP SWUserData2
( NAME = 'SmallWorksData2'
, FILENAME = 'C:\SQLData\SmallWorksData2.ndf'
, SIZE = 10MB
, FILEGROWTH = 20%
, MAXSIZE = 50MB)
 LOG ON
( NAME = 'SmallWorks_log'
, FILENAME = 'C:\SQLData\SmallWorks_log.ldf'
, SIZE = 10MB
, FILEGROWTH = 10%
, MAXSIZE = 20MB)
GO
USE SmallWorks
GO
ALTER DATABASE SmallWorks
MODIFY FILEGROUP SWUserData1 DEFAULT
GO

CREATE TABLE dbo.Person(
  PersonID int NOT NULL
, FirstName varchar(50) NOT NULL
, MiddleName  varchar(50) NULL
, LastName varchar(50) NOT NULL
, EmailAddress nvarchar(50) NULL
) ON SWUserData1

CREATE TABLE dbo.Product(
  ProductID int NOT NULL
, ProductName varchar(75) NOT NULL
, ProductNumber nvarchar(25) NOT NULL
, StandardCost money NOT NULL
, ListPrice money NOT NULL
) ON SWUserData2

INSERT dbo.Person
(PersonID, FirstName, MiddleName, LastName, EmailAddress)
SELECT DISTINCT TOP 5000
    P.BusinessEntityID
```

```
    , P.FirstName
    , P.MiddleName
    , P.LastName
    , LOWER(P.FirstName + '.' + P.LastName + '@adventureworks.com')
FROM AdventureWorks2008.Person.Person P
INNER JOIN AdventureWorks2008.Person.EmailAddress E
ON P.BusinessEntityID = P.BusinessEntityID
WHERE P.FirstName NOT LIKE '%.%'
ORDER BY P.BusinessEntityID

INSERT dbo.Product
(ProductID, ProductName, ProductNumber, StandardCost, ListPrice)
SELECT ProductID
    , Name
    , ProductNumber
    , StandardCost
    , ListPrice
FROM AdventureWorks2008.Production.Product

ALTER DATABASE SmallWorks MODIFY FILEGROUP SWUserData2 READONLY
```

Database Recovery Models

SQL Server has three possible recovery models; however, only two are meant for regular use — the *Simple* and *Full* recovery models. The third recovery model, *Bulk-Logged*, is designed to be an adjunct to the Full recovery model. Each recovery model has its advantages and disadvantages. It is absolutely critical that you have a complete understanding of each model so that you can make an informed and appropriate decision as to what recovery model to operate each database in. Recovery models change the behavior of the transaction log, what backups can be performed, and how data is recovered.

Full Recovery Model

In the *Full recovery model*, all activity that affects the database is logged in the transaction log in some way or another. Some events are minimally logged, like the TRUNCATE TABLE command, which completely clears the contents of a table. When the TRUNCATE TABLE command is executed, SQL Server logs only the de-allocation of the data pages affected by the truncation. However, all regular database activity is fully logged, including the rebuilding of indexes, bulk copy, SELECT INTO, BULK INSERT, and BLOB (Binary Large Object) updates. The advantage of this full logging is that every transaction can be recovered in the event of a failure. You never have to worry about a lost transaction due to loss of a data file. With the loss of the actual transaction log, all transactions since the last CHECKPOINT would be lost.

The disadvantage of the Full recovery model is the same as the advantage: Almost everything that affects the database is fully logged. As a result, the transaction log can fill up very quickly. If it is set to auto-grow, it can also get very large, very quickly. When the database is set to Full recovery model, it is imperative that an effective plan for backing up the transaction log on a regular basis be developed and implemented. Backing up the transaction log clears it of all old transactions and makes room for new ones.

In the Full recovery model, the transaction log contains a record of all the modifications made to the database since the last BACKUP LOG event. It can be used to recover those transactions, as described later in this chapter.

Bulk-Logged Recovery Model

The *Bulk-Logged recovery model*, as previously noted, is an adjunct model to the Full recovery model. There are times when the full logging behavior of the Full recovery model can be detrimental to performance and cause unacceptable log file-growth. In these situations, the database can be configured to minimally log bulk operations by changing the recovery model to Bulk-Logged. In the Bulk-Logged recovery model, the following database operations are minimally logged:

- ❑ Index Creation
- ❑ Index Rebuild
- ❑ Bulk Copy operations
- ❑ BULK INSERT
- ❑ SELECT INTO
- ❑ BLOB operations

Minimal logging means that the operations listed are logged as having occurred, but the individual rows affected are not logged. In addition to the record of the operation being logged, a record of the physical extents allocated or affected by the operation is recorded in the transaction log. During the next BACKUP LOG event, the affected physical extents are copied to the log backup. Bulk-Logged recovery keeps the log smaller by minimally logging data-intensive operations, but the log backups can actually be larger. Because the log backups rely on the physical data being intact during the log backup, if the disks are damaged or unavailable, the log backup will fail.

In Bulk-Logged recovery, the transaction log contains a record of all the fully logged modifications made to the database and the identification of changed extents modified by minimally logged operations since the last BACKUP LOG event. Like the transaction log in the Full recovery model, the transaction log in Bulk-Logged recovery is available to restore transactions in the event of a database failure.

Simple Recovery Model

In the *Simple recovery model*, the inactive portion of the log is truncated every time SQL Server issues a checkpoint. As explained in Chapter 4, Checkpoints are issued periodically by SQL Server to keep the amount of time necessary to recovery a database to a minimum. The inactive portion of the log is essentially the portion of the log from the oldest open transaction to the end of the log.

The Simple recovery model has the advantage of decreasing the administrative overhead of transaction log management. Because the inactive portion of the log is basically cleared after every Checkpoint, the log, if planned appropriately, should never grow and should never need to be managed. However, the transaction log cannot be backed up and used for data recovery since it does not have a complete record of all the transactions that have modified the database.

SQL Server 2008 Database Backup

For years I stated that the best part of native SQL Server backups is the price of the backup software, which is free. Other than the price, however, native SQL Server backups offered little in the area of performance and flexibility that most enterprise database administrators needed. As a result of this shortcoming, several third-party software vendors created excellent backup software that would back up SQL Server databases up to 10 times faster than the native utility while compressing and encrypting the backup at the same time. With the release of SQL Server 2008, Microsoft has significantly improved the native backup system so that it now adds some exciting new features to database backup routines. The first is that SQL Server 2008 backups are faster than those of previous editions. The speed is made even more impressive by the fact that SQL Server 2008 also provides the ability to compress the backups and that compressed backups are even faster than non-compressed backups. On my copy of SQL Server 2008, a backup of the AdventureWorks2008 database takes 6 seconds when using compression and 9 seconds without. SQL Server 2008 provides the ability to encrypt backups as well.

SQL Server 2008 backups can be performed during normal database activity. There is no need to disconnect users or shut down any services. Backups can be sent to disk or tape. To send backups to tape, the tape device must be locally attached to the Database Server. This limitation can be overcome by using third-party products or mounting the tape device on a SAN that presents the drive as a logical disk device.

Disk destinations are identified by a physical or Universal Naming Convention (UNC) location as the following examples illustrate:

```
--Full database backup of SmallWorks to a drive location
BACKUP DATABASE SmallWorks
TO DISK = 'D:\SQLBackups\FullSmallWorks.BAK'
WITH DESCRIPTION = 'SmallWorks DB Full Backup'

--Full database backup of SmallWorks to a UNC location
BACKUP DATABASE SmallWorks
TO DISK = '\\AUGHTEIGHT\SQLBackups\FullSmallWorks.BAK'
WITH DESCRIPTION = 'SmallWorks DB Full Backup'
```

Backup Devices

Tape or disk locations can be mapped to a backup device. A backup device is an alias to the disk or tape location. The only real advantage of backup devices is that they make the syntax of the backup command simpler. However, since the backup devices are usually created once to hold many backups, the device name will typically be less descriptive than is usually desired.

The following example shows how to create a backup device and then back up the Master database to it:

```
--Create a device for backups of the Master database
sp_addumpdevice 'Disk'
                , 'MasterDBBackups'
                , 'D:\SQLBackups\masterDB.Backups.BAK'

--Backup the Master database to the new device
```

```
BACKUP DATABASE Master TO MasterDBBackups
WITH DESCRIPTION = 'Master DB Full Backup'
```

Backup devices can also be created graphically by expanding the Server Objects node in Object Explorer of SQL Server Management Studio, right-clicking on "Backup Devices," and clicking on "New Backup Device."

Try It Out   SQL Server Database Backups

Regardless of the type of database backup executed, SQL Server performs the following actions:

- ❑ Logs the BACKUP statement in the transaction log.
- ❑ Issues a Checkpoint causing all outstanding dirty buffer pages to be written to the disk.
- ❑ Writes all data pages specified by the FULL, DIFFERENTIAL, FILE, or FILEGROUP backup options to the backup media.
- ❑ Writes all data modifications recorded in the transaction log that occurred during the backup to the backup media.
- ❑ Logs the completion of the backup in the transaction log.

Back up the Master database by executing the following command in SQL Server Management Studio:

```
--Full database backup of the Master database
BACKUP DATABASE Master
TO DISK = 'D:\SQLBackups\FullMaster.BAK'
WITH DESCRIPTION = 'MASTER DB FULL Backup'
```

The script performs a Full database backup of the Master database. It assumes that you have a "D" volume and a folder named *SQLBackups*. The backup command will create designated files, but it will not create folders.

Databases can also be backed up using the graphical tools provided with Management Studio. To accomplish the same results as the previous script, follow these steps:

1. Expand the Databases and then the System Databases nodes in Object Explorer of Management Studio.

2. Right-click on the Master database, then click Tasks ➤ Back Up to launch the Back Up Database dialog (Figure 9-1).

3. Click on the Remove button to remove the default backup location.

4. Click on the Add button to specify a new destination for the database backup.

5. In the Select Backup Destination dialog, type in a new destination for the backup such as **D:\SQLBackups\Master.BAK**.

6. Click OK to start the backup.

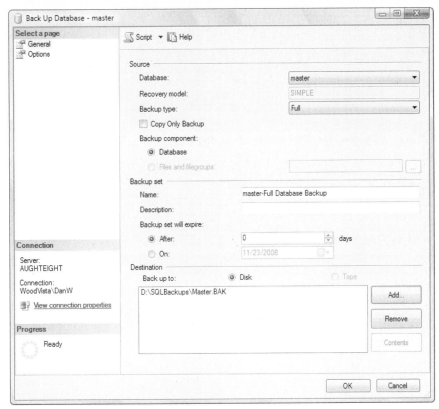

Figure 9-1: The Backup Database dialog.

SQL Server 2008 Backup Types

SQL Server 2008 supports several backup types that can be combined or used independently to create backup strategies. In this section, we'll explore the different types, and then in the next section, we'll examine the backup options and how to combine the backup types into an effective backup strategy. Most of the backups are performed the same way using the graphical tools, and the interface is very intuitive. With that in mind, in the following examples, each backup type will only be accompanied by the appropriate Transact-SQL to use to perform the backup.

Full Backup

Probably the most common and easy way to implement backups is the Full backup. The *Full backup* simply backs up all the data in the database and records all database file locations. SQL Server logs the beginning of a Full database backup in the transaction log and then records all modifications made to the database for the duration of the backup in the transaction log. When all the data pages from the database data files have been transferred to the backup media, SQL Server logs the completion of the backup and transfers the portion of the transaction log that occurred during the backup to the backup media. Full backups can be used in any recovery model.

The advantage of the Full backup is that it is exceptionally simple. However, Full backups take longer than other backup methods and typically result in the same unchanged data being backed up over and over again along with the new and updated data.

```
--Full database backup of SmallWorks
BACKUP DATABASE SmallWorks
TO DISK = 'D:\SQLBackups\SmallWorksFull.BAK'
WITH DESCRIPTION = 'SmallWorks FULL Backup'
```

Differential Backup

Differential backups are used to back up only the data that has changed since the last Full backup. Like the Full backup, the Differential backup also consists of the portion of the transaction log that contains database modifications that occurred during the backup. Because Differential backups only contain the extents of data files that have changed since the last Full backup, they take less time to execute than Full backups. However, each consecutive Differential backup will in most cases become progressively larger. If just 1 byte of a 64-KB extent is modified, the Differential backup will back up the entire extent. The Differential backup is available regardless of the database recovery model and requires a base Full database backup.

```
--Differential database backup of SmallWorks
BACKUP DATABASE SmallWorks
TO DISK = 'D:\SQLBackups\SmallWorksDiff.BAK'
WITH DIFFERENTIAL, DESCRIPTION = 'SmallWorks Differential Backup'
```

File/Filegroup Backup

When a database is divided across many files and filegroups, these files and filegroups can be backed up individually. This type of backup is particularly useful for very large databases. File and Filegroup backups work similarly as Full and Differential backups in that the data pages of the file and then all transactions made against the file or filegroup are added to the backup media.

```
--Backup of the "SWUserData1" User-Defined Filegroup
BACKUP DATABASE SmallWorks
FILEGROUP = 'SWUserData1'
TO DISK = 'D:\SQLBackups\SmallWorksUserData1FG.BAK'
WITH DESCRIPTION = 'SmallWorks SWUserData1 Filegroup Backup'
--Backup of the SmallWorks data file "SmallWorksData1"
--The logical name of the file **NOT the physical file name**
BACKUP DATABASE SmallWorks
FILE = 'SmallWorksData1'
TO DISK = 'D:\SQLBackups\SmallWorksData1File.BAK'
WITH DESCRIPTION = 'SmallWorks UserData1 File Backup'
```

File/Filegroup with Differential

An additional option available when backing up files or filegroups is the ability to perform a *Differential File or Filegroup backup*. This option works exactly like the typical Differential backup; only the changes to the file or filegroup since the last full File or Filegroup backup are captured as well as any changes to the files during the backup.

```
--Differential Filegroup Backup of the "SWUserData1" User-Defined Filegroup
BACKUP DATABASE SmallWorks
FILEGROUP = 'SWUserData1'
TO DISK = 'D:\SQLBackups\SmallWorksUserData1FGDIFF.BAK'
WITH DIFFERENTIAL, DESCRIPTION = 'SmallWorks Filegroup Differential Backup'
```

File and Filegroup backups are only available if the database is in Full or Bulk-Logged recovery model, with one exception. If a filegroup is marked as Read Only and the database is configured in the Simple recovery model, then that filegroup can be backed up.

Transaction Log Backup

In Full or Bulk-Logged recovery models, it is imperative that periodic Transaction Log backups are completed to both maintain the size of the transaction log within reasonable limits and to allow for the recovery of data with the least amount of data loss.

Transaction Log backups come in three forms: Pure Log backups, Bulk Log backups, and Tail Log backups.

❑ **Pure Log Backup** — A Pure Log backup contains only transactions and is completed when the database is in Full recovery model or Bulk-Logged recovery model, but no bulk operations have been executed.

```
--Pure or Bulk Log Backup of SmallWorks
BACKUP LOG SmallWorks
TO DISK = 'D:\SQLBackups\SmallWorksLog.TRN'
WITH DESCRIPTION = 'SmallWorks Log Backup'
```

❑ **Bulk Log Backup** — Bulk Log backups contain both transactional data and any physical extents modified by bulk operations while the database was in Bulk-Logged recovery.

❑ **Tail Log Backup** — Tail Log backups are completed when the database is in Full or Bulk-Logged recovery prior to a database restoration to capture all transaction log records that have not yet been backed up. It is possible in some instances to execute a Tail Log backup even if the database is damaged.

```
--Tail Log Backup of SmallWorks
BACKUP LOG SmallWorks
TO DISK = 'D:\SQLBackups\SmallWorksTailLog.TRN'
WITH NO_TRUNCATE, DESCRIPTION = 'SmallWorks Tail Log Backup'
```

Partial Backup

A *Partial database backup* consists of the Primary filegroup, Read Write filegroups, and any Read Only filegroup specified. The idea behind the Partial backup is that the Primary filegroup, which contains all the information necessary to bring the database online, and all the filegroups subject to modifications can be backed up together, leaving the filegroups that do not change to be backed up separately and not as often, saving both time and backup media space.

```
BACKUP DATABASE SmallWorks READ_WRITE_FILEGROUPS
TO DISK = 'D:\SQLBackups\SmallWorksPartial.BAK'
WITH DESCRIPTION = 'Partial Backup of all Read/Write filegroups'
```

Copy Only Backup

Copy Only backups can be performed on database files and transaction logs to create a backup without affecting the chain of backups required to restore a database. They are essentially non-logged backups that can be used outside the maintenance environment. For instance, if a copy of the database is needed for test and development, a Copy Only backup can be performed so as not to break the backup chain. Backup chains are discussed in the "Restoring Databases" section later in this chapter.

```
BACKUP DATABASE SmallWorks
TO DISK = 'D:\SQLData\SmallWorksCopyOnly.BAK'
WITH COPY_ONLY, DESCRIPTION = 'Copy only backup'
```

Backup Options

As previously described, backups can be sent to either a disk or tape destination. When sent to these destinations, the choice can be made to compress the database backup. Another possibility for backup destinations is to send the backups to multiple destinations at the same time. The multiple destinations can be configured as a stripe of the backup or a mirror.

Backup Stripe

Striping a backup across multiple devices may save time in the backup process since multiple physical devices are being written to simultaneously. To create a backup stripe, simply add multiple destinations to the backup command as shown in the following code:

```
BACKUP DATABASE SmallWorks
TO DISK='D:\StripedBackupsA\SmallWorksStripe1.bak'
 , DISK='E:\StripedBackupsB\SmallWorksStripe2.bak'
 , DISK='F:\StripedBackupsC\SmallWorksStripe3.bak'
WITH DESCRIPTION = 'Striped Backup'
```

Once a stripe set has been created, each file will only accept backups that also include all the members of the stripe. The three files are now a set made up of three family members. In order to send a backup to just one of the members, the FORMAT option must be specified. Although the striped backup can improve performance of the backup, a loss or corruption of any file in the stripe will result in a total loss of the backup.

Mirrored Backup

I received a call late one night from a colleague who had taken over my position after I had moved on to another job. He was desperate. He explained to me that their main database server had suffered a catastrophic failure. They had rebuilt the server and were in the process of restoring from tape when the tape drive inexplicably decided to devour the tape and the redundant drive I had set up was out of commission. I listened intently to his story, but in the end I could only respond with "If you have another copy of the tape, simply get a different tape drive and restore from the copy. If you don't have another copy, restore from the most recent copy you do have and update your résumé."

I tell every SQL Server Administration class I teach this story. I do so to highlight the importance of having redundant backups. It is too easy to feel safe and secure in the knowledge that you are regularly backing up your data. However, your backups are just as vulnerable as the data that they are ostensibly protecting. I have encountered many organizations who wouldn't dream of storing their data on anything but redundant arrays, yet they back up their critical data to a single device and don't make copies of it.

In the past, creating redundant backups meant backing the database up and then backing up the backups or using a hardware solution that mirrored the backups while they were being created. SQL Server 2008 provides the built-in ability to mirror database backups.

Mirrored backups are not supported through the visual tools. The following code demonstrates how to back up a database to one destination and mirror the entire backup to another destination simultaneously. The `WITH FORMAT` option is required to create a new mirrored backup set.

```
BACKUP DATABASE SmallWorks
      TO DISK='D:\MirroredBackupsA\SmallWorksMirror1.bak'
MIRROR TO DISK='E:\MirroredBackupsB\SmallWorksMirror2.bak'
WITH FORMAT, DESCRIPTION = 'Mirrored Backup'
```

Compressed Backup

As I mentioned previously, compressed backups actually are faster than non-compressed backups. They also restore faster. However, this speed does not come without a cost. Compressed backups consume significantly more CPU resources than non-compressed backups. If your database server is already overworked in the area of CPU usage, you may want to avoid compressed backups or schedule them for low-CPU-usage time periods. The following code demonstrates how to create a compressed backup:

```
BACKUP DATABASE SmallWorks
      TO DISK='D:\SQLBackups\SmallWorksCompressed.bak'
WITH COMPRESSION, DESCRIPTION = 'Compressed Backup'
```

`WITH` Options

The following table lists and briefly describes each option that can be included in the `WITH` clause of a database backup command:

Option	Description
`BLOCKSIZE = integer`	Specify a specific block size. If not specified, SQL Server will attempt to choose a block size that is optimum for the tape or disk destination.
`CHECKSUM	NO_CHECKSUM`	The `CHECKSUM` option specifies that SQL Server will validate any page checksum or torn page information when reading the page. SQL Server will also generate page checksums that can be used to validate backups with the `RESTORE` command. The `CHECKSUM` option will decrease the speed and `performance` of the backup. The `NO_CHECKSUM` setting is the default setting and configures SQL Server to not generate or validate page checksum data during the backup.

Continued

Option	Description
STOP_ON_ERROR | CONTINUE_AFTER_ERROR	The default setting of STOP_ON_ERROR aborts the backup if a bad page checksum or torn page is detected during the backup. The CONTINUE_AFTER_ERROR setting overrides this behavior, allowing the database to be backed up even if there are errors in the database.
DESCRIPTION = string	A description of the database backup is often useful to identify the backup media. The description property supports a description length of 255 characters.
DIFFERENTIAL	Specifies that a Differential backup is to be performed on the associated database or data file/filegroup.
EXPIREDATE = datetime	A date specification used to identify when the backup is no longer required and may be overwritten
RETAINDAYS = integer	Specifies the number of days the backup is required. This option or the EXPIREDATE option is used to control this behavior.
PASSWORD = string	A password can be assigned to a backup so that the password is required to use the backup during a restore operation. The password protection is very weak and should *not* be relied on to guarantee the security of a backup. The PASSWORD option is deprecated and will be removed in a future release.
FORMAT | NOFORMAT	The FORMAT option is used to create a new backup media set. It will overwrite any existing media set at the destination. NOFORMAT is the default setting that would prevent an inadvertent overwriting of a backup file that was participating in a backup stripe set.
INIT | NOINIT	The default setting of NOINIT specifies that any backups sent to the destination will be appended to the backup file. INIT specifies that subsequent backups will overwrite the existing backup file contents.
NOSKIP | SKIP	The NOSKIP default setting configures SQL Server to check the backup media's expiration date to prevent inadvertent overwriting of previous backups. The SKIP setting ignores the expiration date information
MEDIADESCRIPTION = string	A maximum length string of 255 characters used to describe the backup media
MEDIANAME = string	The backup media's logical name with a maximum of 128 characters

Option	Description
MEDIAPASSWORD = *string*	Like the PASSWORD option that defines a password for an individual backup, the MEDIAPASSWORD sets a password on the backup media set. The MEDIAPASSWORD is also very weak and should not be relied on for media set security. This option is deprecated.
NAME = *string*	A maximum length of 128 characters to identify the name of the backup set
NOREWIND | REWIND	This option is only used when the backup destination is specified as TAPE. The default REWIND option configures SQL Server to rewind the tape when the backup is completed or the end of the tape is reached during a backup.
NOUNLOAD | UNLOAD	This option is only used with tape backups. The default setting is UNLOAD, which configures SQL Server to rewind and eject the tape when the backup is complete. NOUNLOAD overrides this default behavior and leaves the tape open and mounted.
RESTART	This option does absolutely nothing. It does not generate an error when used and is included to prevent old scripts from previous releases from failing.
STATS = *percentage as integer*	Configures SQL Server to return progress information every time the specified percentage is reached. The default is 10.
COPY_ONLY	COPY_ONLY backups do not affect the transaction log sequence. These backups cannot be used for a Differential or Transaction Log backup base.
COMPRESSION	COMPRESSION backups average about 80 percent smaller in size than uncompressed backups. The compression will vary depending on the type of data stored in the database
NORECOVERY	The NORECOVERY option backs up the database and then places it in the non-accessible "Restoring" mode. This is useful for a last backup of a database before taking it offline or moving it to a new location

Backup Strategies

As previously mentioned, the various backup types provided by SQL Server 2008 can be used in different combinations to create a variety of backup strategies. In this section, we will cover just a few of the more commonly used backup strategies.

Full Backup Only

The Full backup strategy (Figure 9-2) uses periodic Full database backups with no Log or Differential backups. It is a very useful and simple strategy but is generally limited to small databases configured in the Simple recovery model and for system databases. This strategy exposes the database to the risk of losing one period of data modifications. For example, if the database is backed up every day at 1:00 a.m. and there is a database failure anytime before 1:00 a.m., the most recent restore point will be 1:00 a.m. of the previous day. For small databases with very few daily updates, this may be acceptable.

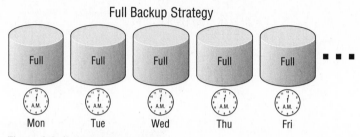

Figure 9-2: Full backup strategy.

Full Backup with Differential

Like the Full backup strategy, the Full backup with Differential (Figure 9-3) is generally limited to databases configured in Simple recovery model because it does not provide for any management of the transaction log. However, the addition of a periodic Differential backup makes this backup strategy more appropriate for slightly larger changing databases where the management of a transaction log is not desired. Because only data modified since the last Full backup is copied to the backup media, the periodic Differential backups will be smaller when compared to the Full backups and will take less time to execute.

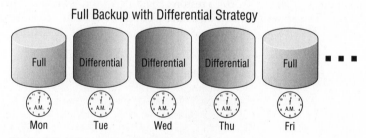

Figure 9-3: Full backup with Differential strategy.

Full Backup with Transaction Log

The disadvantages of the Full and Full with Differential plans are that they expose the database to the risk of data loss equal to the periodicity of the backup. By introducing Transaction Log backups into the backup plan (Figure 9-4), this risk is reduced dramatically. However the management of transaction logs introduces more complexity to the administration of database files. As previously discussed, when the database is not in Simple recovery model, the transaction log must be periodically backed up to prevent it from growing too large and filling up. The alternative method of maintaining the log is to periodically clear it, but this is strongly discouraged as described later.

In the event of a database failure, the database can be restored up to the moment of failure by performing periodic Transaction Log backups between Full backups. The number of log backups and the periodicity of the backups depend on how busy the database is and what the acceptable degree of data loss is. In a worst case scenario, both the database and the transaction log could be lost. If that is the case, then like the Full and Differential backup plans, the database can only be restored to the end of the previous Transaction Log backup. However, if only the data files are damaged, the database backup, log backups, and online log can be used to restore the database to the moment of failure.

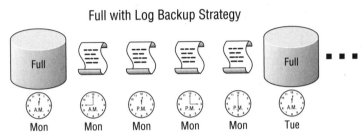

Figure 9-4: Full with Log backup strategy.

Because Transaction Log backups are typically smaller and faster, they can be scheduled to occur as often as necessary. It is not uncommon to see Transaction Log backups scheduled for every 10 minutes on databases that are subject to very frequent modifications.

Full and Differential Backup with Transaction Log

The disadvantage of performing several Transaction Log backups between Full backups is that in order to restore a database, the Full backup and all the logs must be sequentially restored. This can be burdensome if there are a large number of log backups to restore. To minimize this issue, a Differential backup (Figure 9-5) can be performed to capture all the changes to the database since the last Full backup. To restore the database, the log backups between the Full and the Differential can be ignored.

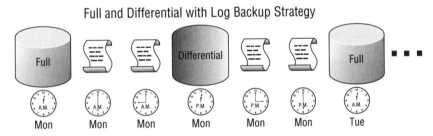

Figure 9-5: Full and Differential with Log backup strategy.

File and Filegroup Backup

With very large databases, it is sometimes more efficient to back up the database in slices. This offers a great deal of flexibility in the backup plan, but it also introduces a proportionate increase in the complexity of the backup plan. Database data files and filegroups can be backed up and restored individually, enabling the administrator to avoid a time-consuming and unnecessary restore of a large database in its entirety. This method is especially useful if some of the filegroups contain Read Only data. These filegroups can be backed up once and then recovered later in the event of a failure with no loss of interim data. For example, a production database is comprised of four 25-GB filegroups. One of the filegroups contains tables that are updated about once every three months. The other three contain transactional data that is updated on a regular basis. The first filegroup can be configured as Read Only and backed up. The remaining three can be backed up on a rotating basis interspersed with Transaction Log backups, as Figure 9-6 illustrates.

Figure 9-6: File/Filegroups backup strategy.

Filegroup with Differential

If the Filegroup strategy still backs up too much data that does not change, a File or Filegroup backup can be combined with a File or Filegroup Differential backup. This way only the changes to the respective file or filegroup will be backed up. However, since the straightforward File/Filegroup backup increases complexity, adding a Differential backup to the mix will complicate things even more, and this strategy will require a great deal of planning and maintenance.

Partial Backup

As previously described, the Partial backup (Figure 9-7) backs up the Primary filegroup and all READ_WRITE configured filegroups by default. In addition, any READONLY configured filegroups can be added to the backup set by specifying them in the BACKUP statement. The purpose behind this strategy is to back up the Read Only filegroups once and then to periodically backup only the filegroups subject to modification.

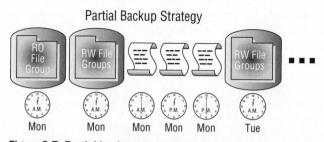

Figure 9-7: Partial backup strategy.

Backup Summary

As you can see, there are quite a few different ways to combine backup types to develop an appropriate backup strategy. Each backup type has its advantages and disadvantages. I wish I could give a prescriptive guide to backing up your databases, but I can't. Each environment is unique, from the size of the database and number of transactions per hour to the disk subsystem supporting the database. It is critically important to develop a backup strategy that mitigates the risk of data loss while at the same time allowing for a realistic and effective data recovery strategy.

Restoring Databases

I have met with many database administrators who were shocked to discover that their database backup plan did not lend itself to a problem-free recovery. If having an effective backup plan is critical, then having an effective restoration plan is even more critical. SQL Server is very lenient in allowing different backup types at different times, but it is a bit pickier about how those backups are restored. The critical issue in most restoration plans is the sequence of backups. This section will describe the restore process, how to prepare a database for restoration, and how to restore databases backed up using the strategies outlined previously.

Restore Process

The restore process is made up of three phases: the *Data Copy phase* in which data pages are copied from the backup media to the data file(s); the *Redo phase* in which the record of committed transactions is restored from a log backup or the log portion of a database backup; and finally, the *Undo phase* in which uncommitted transactions are rolled back from a log backup or the log portion of a database backup.

The Data Copy and Redo phases can span multiple backups. For example, a database is backed up with a Full backup, followed by a Differential backup and then a Transaction Log backup. To restore the database to its most recent state would require restoring the Full backup and then the Differential backup as part of the Data Copy phase. The log portion of the Differential backup would begin the Redo phase, followed by the committed transactions in the Transaction Log backup. After all committed transactions are reapplied to the database, the Undo phase begins in which all uncommitted transactions are rolled back and the database is brought online.

Each phase is linked to the next. If any backup is missing from the sequence, the process stops at the end of the backup preceding the missing sequence. Figure 9-8 illustrates a lost or corrupted log backup. Even though there are an additional two good log backups, they cannot be used because the effects of the transactions recorded in the 12:01 p.m. Transaction Log backup are unknown. The database can only be restored to the end of the 9:00 a.m. Transaction Log backup.

Missing Backup

Figure 9-8: Missing backup.

Delaying Recovery

When restoring a sequence of backups such as a Full backup and a series of Transaction Log backups, the Undo phase and database recovery will have to be delayed so that each additional backup can be restored. Once a database has been recovered, no additional backups can be applied. To delay recovery, the option NO RECOVERY must be specified along with the RESTORE DATABASE command.

RESTORE Command

Although databases can be restored effectively with the graphical tools provided in Management Studio, there are many advanced restore options that are only available by utilizing Transact-SQL. The simplified RESTORE command syntax is as follows:

```
RESTORE DATABASE | LOG database_name
[File | FileGroup]
[FROM <backup_media> [ ,...n ] ]
[WITH
    [CHECKSUM | NO_CHECKSUM]
    [[,] FILE = file_number]
    [[,] MOVE 'logical_file_name' TO 'operating_system_file_name'] [,...n]
    [[,] RECOVERY | NORECOVERY | STANDBY = standby_file_name]
    [[,] REPLACE]
    [[,] STOPAT = date_time
]
```

For simplicity, let's break down the RESTORE command into its constituent pieces. The first is the actual RESTORE command, which is typically followed by the argument DATABASE or LOG and then the target database name. However, the RESTORE command can also be used to expose backup media metadata and to verify the integrity of a backup set. The following table gives the various RESTORE commands that expose information about the backup without actually restoring the database. The table is followed by descriptions of the actual restore process.

Command	Description
RESTORE HEADERONLY	Exposes information from the backup media such as the name, description, and type of backup, as well as information about the backed-up database.
RESTORE FILELISTONLY	Exposes the name of the files contained in the backup set.
RESTORE LABELONLY	Retrieves media information such as the media name and description.
RESTORE VERIFYONLY	Checks the integrity of the backup media. If the backup set was created using the CHECKSUM option, the VERIFYONLY command will read the page checksums as well as check to make sure that the backup set is readable.

RESTORE DATABASE *database_name*

Specifies that the restore process is for a database and specifies the name of the target database to restore to. The database name specified does not need to exist or be the same name as the backed-up database.

FILE

The RESTORE DATABASE *database_name* statement can be followed by the logical name of a database data file so that only that file is restored from the backup media. A file can be specified for Full, File, and Filegroup backups.

```
RESTORE DATABASE SmallWorks
FILE = 'SmallWorksData2'
FROM DISK = 'D:\SQLBackups\SmallWorksFull.BAK'
```

FILEGROUP

The RESTORE DATABASE *database_name* statement can also be followed by the name of a database filegroup so that only that filegroup is restored from the backup media. A filegroup can be specified for Full and Filegroup backups.

```
RESTORE DATABASE SmallWorks
FILEGROUP = 'SWUserData2'
FROM DISK = 'D:\SQLBackups\SmallWorksFull.BAK'
```

READ_WRITE_FILEGROUPS

The READ_WRITE_FILEGROUPS option only restores those filegroups in the database not marked as Read Only. This option can be used with Full and Partial backups.

```
RESTORE DATABASE SmallWorks
READ_WRITE_FILEGROUPS
FROM DISK = 'D:\SQLBackups\SmallWorksFull.BAK'
```

PAGE

To recover from Torn Page or checksum errors that identify one or more corrupted data pages, the RESTORE DATABASE *database_name* statement can specify the 8-K data page to be restored. The page restore option requires the file ID and page ID to be passed, as the following example illustrates:

```
RESTORE DATABASE SmallWorks PAGE = '1:14'
FROM DISK = 'D:\SQLBackups\SmallWorksFull.BAK'
```

RESTORE LOG *database_name*

The RESTORE LOG statement specifies that the restore process is for a database transaction log. The backup must be from a BACKUP LOG process. The restoration of the transaction log must be applied to an existing database. The first Log Sequence Number (LSN) of the log backup being restored must be the next consecutive LSN after the last LSN of the previous Log or database backup.

```
RESTORE LOG SmallWorks
FROM DISK = 'D:\SQLBackups\SmallWorksLog.BAK'
```

FROM *Options*

When restoring a database from either a database backup or a log backup, the RESTORE command expects a backup media location to be specified in the FROM clause of the RESTORE statement. If no backup media location is specified, then the recovery operation is executed. During the recovery operation, SQL Server rolls forward all complete transactions from the existing transaction log and rolls back all incomplete transactions, as this example shows:

```
RESTORE DATABASE SmallWorks
```

With this syntax, the database is recovered in place. This may be necessary if the database is left in a RECOVERING state but there are no additional backups to be applied.

Other than the recover in place option, the following arguments are valid.

FROM DISK

The FROM DISK = *file_location* specifies that the backup media resides on one or more physical disks identified by a drive letter and location or a network location identified by a UNC, as the following code illustrates:

```
RESTORE DATABASE SmallWorks
FROM DISK = 'E:\SQLBackUps\SmallWorksFull.BAK'

RESTORE DATABASE SmallWorks
FROM DISK = '\\AughtEight\SQLBackUps\SmallWorksFull.BAK'
```

FROM TAPE

The FROM TAPE = *tape_device* specifies that the backup media resides on one or more tapes identified by a tape UNC, as shown in the following code:

```
RESTORE DATABASE SmallWorks
FROM TAPE = '\\.\tape1'
```

FROM DATABASE_SNAPSHOT

The DATABASE_SNAPSHOT option specifies that the online database will be restored back to the state it was in when the specific Database Snapshot was created. Database Snapshots will be discussed at the end of this chapter.

WITH *Clause*

After the FROM clause and its arguments comes the WITH clause. The WITH clause of the RESTORE command has several options. The most commonly used are described in the following sections.

RECOVERY | NORECOVERY

When restoring a database from a sequence of backups, all but the last backup must be restored with the NORECOVERY option. This allows for additional backups to be applied to the database. The RECOVERY option completes the Redo/Undo phase of restoration as previously described, making the database available to client connections and preventing further restore operations. WITH RECOVERY is the default setting, so it is important to override it until the final backup is being applied. There is no "UnRecover" command that will allow you to restart the restoration process. Once the database is recovered, the entire restore process must be restarted to apply additional backups. However, if all the available backups have been applied but the database was not recovered, the RESTORE DATABASE command can be specified without designating a source for the restore to invoke the recovery process with the current transaction log.

```
RESTORE DATABASE SmallWorks
FROM DISK = 'E:\SQLBackups\SmallWorksFull.BAK'
WITH NORECOVERY

RESTORE LOG SmallWorks
FROM DISK = 'E:\SQLBackups\SmallWorksTailLog.BAK'
WITH RECOVERY
```

STANDBY

The NORECOVERY option leaves the database in a state of recovering and prevents access to the database. The STANDBY option functions much the same way except it allows for Read Only access to the database. It does this through the use of a standby file that stores all the Undo information that would normally be used to recover the database. The STANDBY option allows for a copy of the database to be maintained on a separate server and periodically updated with additional transaction log restores. This functionality is at the heart of Log Shipping, which is described in Chapter 12.

```
RESTORE DATABASE SmallWorks
FROM  DISK = 'E:\SQLBackups\SmallWorksFull.BAK'
WITH STANDBY = 'E:\SQLBackups\SmallWorksUndoRollback.DAT'
```

CHECKSUM | NO_CHECKSUM

The CHECKSUM option specifies that page checksum information is verified before the data is rewritten to the database during a restore operation. If the backup was not created using the checksum option, the RESTORE ... WITH CHECKSUM command will fail. It will also throw an error if any checksum errors are encountered during the restore process.

```
BACKUP DATABASE SmallWorks
TO DISK = 'E:\SQLBackups\SmallWorksCheckSumFull.BAK'
WITH CHECKSUM

--Capture the tail of the log prior to restore operation
BACKUP LOG SmallWorks
TO DISK = 'E:\SQLBackups\SmallWorksTailLog.BAK'
WITH NO_TRUNCATE

RESTORE DATABASE SmallWorks
FROM DISK = 'E:\SQLBackups\SmallWorksCheckSumFull.BAK'
WITH CHECKSUM
```

CONTINUE_AFTER_ERROR | STOP_ON_ERROR

The CONTINUE_AFTER_ERROR option specifies that the restore operation will continue regardless of errors found in the backup media. The default setting of STOP_ON_ERROR will cause the restore operation to fail if any error is encountered.

FILE

One of the more confusing aspects of the RESTORE command is that there is a FILE = option in the RESTORE clause that specifies a logical filename and another FILE = option in the WITH clause, where an integer value that represents the backup location in the file is specified. Since multiple backups can be stored in a single location identified with a name, it is important to be able to differentiate them. When sending multiple backups to the same file location, it is essentially like storing files within files. To differentiate between the different backups stored in a single file, the FILE = *backup_number* option is specified. The following example shows multiple backups being sent to the same destination. The first is a Full backup, the second is a Differential backup, and the last is a Tail Log backup. The example goes on to show restoration of the backups from the same file.

```
--Initialize the backup file and backup the SmallWorks database to the file
BACKUP DATABASE SmallWorks
TO DISK = 'E:\SQLBackups\SmallWorksBackups.BAK'
WITH INIT, DESCRIPTION = 'Full Backup of SmallWorks'

--Send an Additional backup to the file
BACKUP DATABASE SmallWorks
TO DISK = 'E:\SQLBackups\SmallWorksBackups.BAK'
WITH DIFFERENTIAL, DESCRIPTION = 'Differential Backup of SmallWorks'

--Capture the tail of the log prior to restore operation
BACKUP LOG SmallWorks
TO DISK = 'E:\SQLBackups\SmallWorksBackups.BAK'
WITH NO_TRUNCATE, DESCRIPTION = 'Tail Log Backup of SmallWorks'

--Restore the Full Backup with NORECOVERY
RESTORE DATABASE SmallWorks
FROM DISK = 'E:\SQLBackups\SmallWorksBackups.BAK'
WITH FILE = 1, NORECOVERY

--Restore the Differential Backup with NORECOVERY
RESTORE DATABASE SmallWorks
FROM DISK = 'E:\SQLBackups\SmallWorksBackups.BAK'
WITH FILE = 2, NORECOVERY

--Restore the Tail Log Backup with RECOVERY
RESTORE LOG SmallWorks
FROM DISK = 'E:\SQLBackups\SmallWorksBackups.BAK'
WITH File = 3, RECOVERY
```

MOVE ... TO ...

When restoring databases it is sometimes necessary to change the physical name or location of the database file. The MOVE *logical_filename* TO *operating_system_filename* accomplishes this. For instance, a new database server has been installed, and you need to move a database from the old server to the new server. The new server's file system is not organized the same as the old server so new locations must be specified. The following example shows how to move the SmallWorks database from its original location to the new drives identified for data files and log files.

```
RESTORE DATABASE SmallWorks
FROM  DISK = 'E:\SQLBackups\SmallWorksFull.BAK'
WITH MOVE 'SmallWorksPrimary' TO 'S:\SQLData\SmallWorks.mdf'
```

```
, MOVE 'SmallWorks_log' TO 'T:\SQLLogs\SmallWorks_log.ldf'
, MOVE 'SmallWorksData1' TO 'S:\SQLData\SmallWorksData1.ndf'
, MOVE 'SmallWorksData2' TO 'S:\SQLData\SmallWorksData2.ndf'
, REPLACE
```

PARTIAL

The PARTIAL option specifies that the Primary filegroup and any designated user-defined filegroups will be restored. Partial restores are described later in this Chapter.

REPLACE

The REPLACE option overrides the normal database restoration safety checks and specifies that the backup files referenced should replace the existing files. This is sometimes necessary if the transaction log is not available for a Tail Log backup, but the restore operation fails with errors because of no Tail Log backup existing. The REPLACE option also enables the backup of one database to be restored over an existing database even if the files and names are different.

Database Restore Preparation

There are a few different reasons to restore a database, and only one of them involves a failure of the database. It may very well be that the only time you will be required to restore a database is to move a database from one server to another or to restore a test and development database, in which case there is still some pre-planning to do.

Generally the preparation tasks are as follows:

1. Isolate the database by placing it in SINGLE_USER mode (if it is accessible).

2. Back up the tail of the transaction log if in Full or Bulk-Logged recovery model. This captures all the recent activity.

3. Gather information about all the backups that are required to restore the database to the most recent consistent state.

Isolate the Database

Isolating the database is typically required because when restoring a database that is still online, SQL Server essentially drops and then recreates the database from the backup media. As we learned earlier, a database cannot be dropped if someone is connected to it. Some documentation specifies that the database should be set to RESTRICTED_USER instead of SINGLE_USER. However, when a database is set to RESTRICTED_USER access, it will still allow multiple connections. SQL Server just limits those connections to privileged users such as the DBO or SA. If there are multiple DBO users in your organization, RESTRICTED_USER will not prevent them from connecting to the database. RESTRICTED_USER will also not prevent you from opening multiple windows and multiple connections to the database you are trying to restore, thus preventing the restore from occurring. Each Query Window and Object Explorer in Management Studio uses its own connection. To ensure that the restore operation will succeed, it is much easier to just place the database in SINGLE USER access. Ironically, to change the database from MULTI_USER to SINGLE_USER or RESTRICTED_USER access, you must have exclusive access to the database, which equates to SINGLE_USER.

Capture Recent Activity

Backing up the tail of the log ensures that the most recent transactions (since the last backup) are recorded and recoverable. Often, this is not an optional step, and restore operations will not be permitted until the Tail Log backup has been completed.

Gather Backup Information

This last step can be made easier if the entire database server has not suffered a failure. SQL Server records all database backup and restore history in the msdb database. To see what backups SQL Server Management Studio thinks need to be restored, in Object Explorer right-click Databases, click "Restore Database," and then choose the database to restore from the "Source for Restore" database dropdown list. Management Studio will automatically choose the backups to restore, as shown in Figure 9-9. Keep in mind that this is for a complete restore. If you are restoring a file or filegroup, Management Studio is not as helpful. It will list all the File and Filegroup backups performed, but it will not select any for recovery. You will have to do that manually. Likewise, if the choices made by Management Studio are not what you want, you are able to override the selected backups. If the backup history is not available, the "From device" option can be used to select a file or backup device, and the appropriate backups can be chosen.

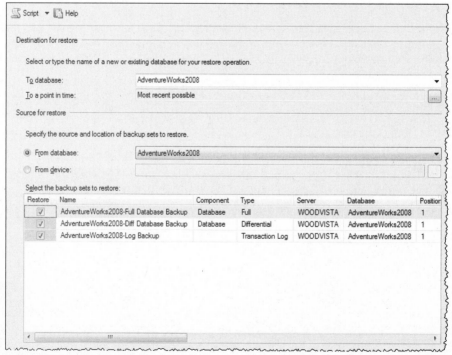

Figure 9-9: Multiple file restore.

As previously described, backup media information can also be retrieved through the use of three RESTORE command arguments: RESTORE HEADERONLY, RESTORE FILELISTONLY, and RESTORE LABELONLY.

Restoring User Databases

The backup strategies outlined earlier in this chapter apply mostly to user databases. Although system databases do need to be backed up, the strategy for backing them up is very straightforward and is typically confined to Full database backups only. This is because system databases do not change as often and are typically quite small. This section, therefore, describes the process of restoring user databases from the backup strategies defined earlier.

Full Restore

The periodic Full backup of a database is the simplest of all backup strategies and is also a very simple restore strategy. If the database needs to be restored, simply find the most recent Full backup, and use it to restore the database. Figure 9-10 illustrates a database that is damaged at 9:00 a.m. The most recent backup was completed at 12:02 a.m. In this case, the 12:02 a.m. backup would be restored with recovery.

```
RESTORE DATABASE SmallWorks
FROM DISK = 'E:\SQLBackups\SmallWorksWed0002.BAK'
WITH RECOVERY
```

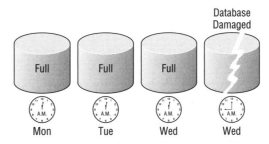

Figure 9-10: Full restore scenario.

Full with Differential Restore

Differential backups require a Full backup to be applied prior to the restoration of the Differential. Figure 9-11 illustrates a failure of the SmallWorks database at 9:00 a.m. on Wednesday. Since a Differential backup was completed at 12:02 a.m. on Wednesday, the Differential backup on Tuesday can be ignored. The recovery process is the Monday Full backup followed by the Wednesday Differential backup.

```
RESTORE DATABASE SmallWorks
FROM DISK = 'E:\SQLBackups\SmallWorksFullMon0002.BAK'
WITH NORECOVERY

RESTORE DATABASE SmallWorks
FROM DISK = 'E:\SQLBackups\SmallWorksDiffWed0002.BAK'
WITH RECOVERY
```

Full with Transaction Log Restore

Like the Differential backup and restore process, the Transaction Log backup also requires a baseline restore before it can be applied. Figure 9-12 illustrates a SmallWorks database damaged at 3:00 p.m. Since the database is in Simple or Bulk-Logged recovery model, the tail of the transaction log may be able to be backed up to capture all the most recent changes to the database. In this way, very little to no data may be lost. The Tail Log backup is completed at 3:10 p.m. After the Tail Log backup is complete, the restoration process can be executed, starting at the Monday Full backup and then proceeding through the remaining Transaction Log backups.

```
BACKUP LOG SmallWorks
TO DISK = 'E:\SQLBackups\SmallWorksTailLogMon1510.BAK'
WITH NO_TRUNCATE

RESTORE DATABASE SmallWorks
FROM DISK = 'E:\SQLBackups\SmallWorksFullMon0002.BAK'
WITH NORECOVERY

RESTORE LOG SmallWorks
FROM DISK = 'E:\SQLBackups\SmallWorksLogMon0900.BAK'
WITH NORECOVERY

RESTORE LOG SmallWorks
FROM DISK = 'E:\SQLBackups\SmallWorksLogMon1202.BAK'
WITH NORECOVERY

RESTORE LOG SmallWorks
FROM DISK = 'E:\SQLBackups\SmallWorksTailLogMon1510.BAK'
WITH RECOVERY
```

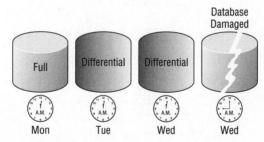

Figure 9-11: Differential restore scenario.

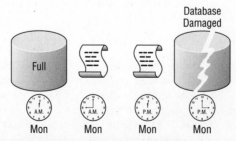

Figure 9-12: Transaction Log restore scenario.

Full and Differential with Transaction Log Restore

When using both Differential and Transaction Log backups to capture changes to the database, the important thing to remember is *sequence*. Each Differential backup contains the changes made to the database that were recorded in transaction logs during the interval between the Full backup and any Differential backup completed. Figure 9-13 illustrates this behavior. Since the database is damaged at 6:00 p.m., a Tail Log backup is completed to capture all activity between 3:00 p.m. and 6:00 p.m. The database is then restored using the Full, Differential regular Transaction Log and Tail Log backups.

```
BACKUP LOG SmallWorks
TO DISK = 'E:\SQLBackups\SmallWorksTailLogMon1810.BAK'
WITH NO_TRUNCATE, NORECOVERY

RESTORE DATABASE SmallWorks
FROM DISK = 'E:\SQLBackups\SmallWorksFullMon0002.BAK'
WITH NORECOVERY

RESTORE DATABASE SmallWorks
FROM DISK = 'E:\SQLBackups\SmallWorksDiffMon1202.BAK'
WITH NORECOVERY

RESTORE LOG SmallWorks
FROM DISK = 'E:\SQLBackups\SmallWorksLogMon1500.BAK'
WITH NORECOVERY

RESTORE LOG SmallWorks
FROM DISK = 'E:\SQLBackups\SmallWorksTailLogMon1810.BAK'
WITH RECOVERY
```

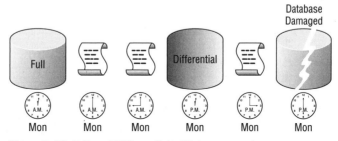

Figure 9-13: Full and Differential with Log scenario.

File and Filegroup Restore

File and Filegroup restore processes vary depending on the recovery model the database is configured for and whether the file or filegroup is marked as Read Only. If the database is in Simple recovery model, the only files or filegroups that can be restored independently of the complete database are those that are marked as Read Only. Since the database is in Simple recovery model, no Tail Log backups are allowed, and any restoration of a Read Only file or filegroup will result in that file or filegroup being immediately available for queries. The syntax and process for individual file or individual filegroup restores are identical.

Try It Out   File Restore Example 1

This first example shows the process of restoring a single damaged file in the SmallWorks database when it is configured in Full Recovery.

1.   Back up the tail of the active transaction log.

```
--Capture the tail of the transaction log
BACKUP LOG SmallWorks
TO DISK = 'E:\SQLBackups\SmallWorksTailLog.BAK'
WITH INIT, NO_TRUNCATE, NORECOVERY
```

2.   Restore the damaged data file.

```
--Restore the damaged or corrupted file
RESTORE DATABASE SmallWorks FILE = 'SmallWorksData1'
FROM  DISK = 'E:\SQLBackups\SmallWorksFull.BAK'
```

At this point the SmallWorksData1 file is offline, and any queries that reference the dbo.Person table, which resides in the SmallWorksData1 file, will fail.

3.   Restore the tail of the log, which returns the SmallWorksData1 file to an online status.

```
--Restore the tail of the log to bring the SmallWorksData1 file online
RESTORE LOG SmallWorks
FROM DISK = 'E:\SQLBackups\SmallWorksTailLog.BAK'
WITH RECOVERY
```

Try It Out   File Restore Example 2

This second example shows the process of restoring a single damaged data file that resides in a Read Only filegroup. In this example, the capture of the tail of the log and the restoration of the tail to bring the file online are unnecessary. This is because the file resides on a Read Only filegroup. There are no changes to capture.

```
--Restore the damaged or corrupted file
RESTORE DATABASE SmallWorks FILE = 'SmallWorksData2'
FROM  DISK = 'E:\SQLBackups\SmallWorksFull.BAK'
```

Once the restoration of the SmallWorksData2 file is complete, the database is completely online and accessible.

Partial Restore

The Partial restore process is very similar to the File/Filegroup restoration process. The significant difference is that Partial restores always include the Primary filegroup.

Try It Out   Partial Restore Example 1

The following example shows the SmallWorks database being backed up with a Partial backup and then the restore process to bring the database back online after suffering a failure of both the SWUserData1 READWRITE filegroup and the Primary filegroup.

1.   Perform the Partial backup:

```
BACKUP DATABASE SmallWorks READ_WRITE_FILEGROUPS
TO DISK = 'E:\SQLBackups\SmallWorksFull.BAK'
WITH INIT
```

2.   Sometime later the READ_WRITE configured filegroups including the Primary filegroup experience a failure. The first step after the failure is to capture all the recent activity and place the database in a state to recover from the failure.

```
BACKUP LOG SmallWorks
TO DISK = 'E:\SQLBackups\SmallWorksTailLog.BAK'
WITH INIT, NORECOVERY, NO_TRUNCATE
```

3.   Restore the READ_WRITE configured filegroups. In the case of the SmallWorks database, that is the Primary and SWUserData1 filegroups.

```
RESTORE DATABASE SmallWorks
FROM  DISK = 'E:\SQLBackups\SmallWorksFull.BAK'
WITH PARTIAL, NORECOVERY
```

4.   Restore the tail of the log and bring the database online

```
RESTORE LOG SmallWorks
FROM DISK = 'E:\SQLBackups\SmallWorksTailLog.BAK'
WITH RECOVERY
```

5.   Even though the database is online, the user-defined filegroups are still inaccessible because of restoring the Primary filegroup. To bring the user-defined filegroups online, we use the RESTORE DATABASE command but do not specify a source for the restore. This completes the recovery process for the filegroups and is near instantaneous since no data is actually being restored.

```
RESTORE DATABASE SmallWorks FILEGROUP = 'SWUserData1'
WITH RECOVERY

RESTORE DATABASE SmallWorks FILEGROUP = 'SWUserData2'
WITH RECOVERY
```

The SmallWorks database is now completely online.

Try It Out   **Partial Restore Example 2**

In this example, only the SWUserData1 READWRITE filegroup is damaged so it is unnecessary to restore the Primary database.

1. Start off again with a Partial backup of the SmallWorks database.

    ```
    BACKUP DATABASE SmallWorks READ_WRITE_FILEGROUPS
    TO DISK = 'E:\SQLBackups\SmallWorksFull.BAK'
    WITH INIT
    ```

2. Sometime later the file in the SWUserData1 filegroup is damaged. When it is discovered, the tail of the transaction log is captured and the database is put into a state to support recovery.

    ```
    BACKUP LOG SmallWorks
    TO DISK = 'E:\SQLBackups\SmallWorksTailLog.BAK'
    WITH INIT, NORECOVERY, NO_TRUNCATE
    ```

3. Restore just the SWUserData1 filegroup and then the tail of the log to bring the database completely online.

    ```
    RESTORE DATABASE SmallWorks FILEGROUP = 'SWUserData1'
    FROM  DISK = 'E:\SQLBackups\SmallWorksFull.BAK'
    WITH NORECOVERY

    RESTORE LOG SmallWorks
    FROM DISK = 'E:\SQLBackups\SmallWorksTailLog.BAK'
    WITH RECOVERY
    ```

Point-in-Time Restore

SQL Server 2008 supports the recovery of both databases and transaction logs to a specific point in time, but only if the database is configured in the Full or Bulk-Logged recovery models. As previously discussed, the Bulk-Logged recovery model should only be used as an adjunct to the Full recovery model. This is especially true because of the impact of the Bulk-Logged recovery on point-in-time restores. If the database is configured for Bulk-Logged recovery and the transaction log contains bulk operations, point-in-time recovery is not possible; the transaction log must be restored in its entirety.

Point-in-time database restore operations are useful to restore a database to a point just prior to data corruption because of a malicious or accidental modification of data. For example, an accidental update to the SmallWorks database occurs at 3:00 p.m. but is not detected until 6:15 p.m. A scheduled database backup was completed at 4:00 p.m., and a scheduled Transaction Log backup occurred at 5:00 p.m. To restore the database to just before the accidental update, a point-in-time restore is used. The sequence of events to restore the database is as follows:

```
RESTORE DATABASE SmallWorks
  FROM  DISK = 'E:\SQLBackups\SmallWorksFull1600.BAK'
  WITH STOPAT = '12/05/2008 14:59:00'
```

```
,NORECOVERY

RESTORE LOG SmallWorks
 FROM  DISK = 'E:\SQLBackups\SmallWorksLog1700.BAK'
 WITH STOPAT = '12/05/2008 14:59:00'
,RECOVERY
```

Recovering System Databases

System databases are just as vulnerable to failure as User databases, and it is very important to ensure that they are adequately protected. Essentially you have two choices when it comes to recovering System databases. You can restore them from backup, or you can rebuild them from scratch. I highly recommend the backup and restore approach, since rebuilding them from scratch means a ton more work.

Because system databases are usually small, they don't require a great deal of time to back up, and they don't take up much space when backed up. How often the structure of your system databases change will determine how often you will need to back them up to minimize the post-restore tasks.

Recovering the Master Database

There are two scenarios for recovering the Master database. In the first scenario, the server is accessible. And in the second, SQL Server is not accessible.

If you can connect to SQL Server, the server instance must be started in single-user mode in order to restore and recover the Master database:

1. To start an instance of SQL Server in single-user mode, type the following command at the command prompt:

```
sqlservr.exe -m
```

2. If the server supports multiple instances of SQL Server, be sure to start the right one. The default instance of SQL Server is located in the folder \Program Files\ Microsoft SQL Server\MSSQL.1\MSSQL\Binn. Each additional instance will have its own *MSSQL.X* folder, but depending on the installation sequence, they may not be in numerical order.

3. Once the server is started in single-user mode, the Master database can be restored. To accomplish this, start another command prompt window and log in to the SQL Server instance with SQLCMD. The following example shows a login command to an instance of SQL Server called *AughtEight* (-S) using Windows Security (-E).

```
C:\>SQLCMD -S AughtEight -E
```

> *For a complete description of the SQLCMD syntax, consult SQL Server 2008 Books Online under the topic "Using the sqlcmd Utility."*

4. After successfully logging in to the server, the restoration of the Master database can be completed through the normal RESTORE syntax.

```
1>RESTORE DATABASE MASTER FROM DISK = 'E:\SQLBackups\MasterFull.BAK'
2>GO
Processed 360 pages for database 'Master', file 'master' on file 1.
Processed 2 pages for database 'Master', file 'mastlog' on file 1.
The master database has been successfully restored. Shutting down SQL
Server.
SQL Server is terminating this process.
```

As shown in the preceding example, once the Master database has been restored, SQL Server will automatically shut down the instance so that it can be restarted with the newly restored Master database.

The only database that can be restored in single-user mode is the Master database. Once Master is restored, restart SQL Server to continue restoring any other system or user databases.

If the instance of SQL Server is not accessible because of a corrupted Master database or total server failure, then the Master database will have to be rebuilt. In previous versions of SQL Server this could be done through a command prompt utility. However, Microsoft discontinued support of that utility. In order to rebuild the Master database, you must re-install SQL Server. Once SQL Server has been re-installed, the most recent backup of the Master database can be used to restore the server using the same procedure outlined previously.

Once the Master database has been restored and the instance of SQL Server restarted, the remaining system databases and user databases should be remounted automatically. If the backup of the Master database is not up-to-date or does not exist at all, the remaining system and user databases may not automatically remount and will have to either be restored or attached. Assuming that the remaining database files are still intact in the file system, it is much faster and easier to attach the databases. The simplest way to attach the existing databases is to use the graphical tools in SQL Server Management Studio:

1. To attach a database, right-click Databases and click Attach; the Attach Databases window will appear.

2. Click on the Add button to browse to the location of the database's MDF file and select it.

   Each database's MDF file contains the metadata that identifies the location of all the database's constituent files. As long as none of the files are identified with a "Not Found" message, the database should attach with no difficulty.

3. If a data file is missing, the database will not be able to be attached. However, if only the transaction log file is missing, the database can still be successfully attached by selecting the missing log file and clicking Remove. Once the log file is removed from the list, click OK to attach the database. SQL Server will re-create a log file using the metadata of the original.

Orphaned Users

After the Master database and all the other databases have been restored or attached, it may be necessary to check the user databases for orphaned users. Orphaned users occur when a SQL Server login has been added to the Master database and granted access to a database, but the backup of the Master database was performed before the login was created. When the user database was attached or restored, the user database contained the database user, but the login in the Master database did not exist.

To find and fix orphaned users, two methods are available. The first is the ALTER USER command. If the user FredF is orphaned, the following code can be used to re-associate the database user to the server login:

```
USE SmallWorks
GO
ALTER USER FredF
WITH LOGIN = FredF
```

The second method is to use a deprecated stored procedure called sp_change_users_login. The sp_change_users_login procedure has three modes defined by the input parameter @Action. The three supported actions are defined in the following table:

Action	Description
Report	Returns a list of all database users not associated with a valid SQL Server login.
Auto_Fix	Links the database user to a SQL Server login with the same name. For example: ❏ USE SmallWorks ❏ GO ❏ sp_change_users_login 'Auto_Fix', 'FredF' This example links the SmallWorks database user FredF to a Server login with the same name if one exists.
Update_One	Links a specific database user to a specific SQL Server Login. ❏ USE SmallWorks ❏ GO ❏ sp_change_users_login 'Update_One', 'FredF', 'SQLFredFLogin' This example links the SmallWorks database user FredF to a SQL Server login called *SQLFredFLogin*.

Database Restore Summary

Like the backup strategy, it is exceptionally important to have a restore plan. A good restore plan will cover any combination of possible failures and list the steps required to restore the database in the shortest time possible and with the least amount of data loss. There is no way I could cover every possible combination in the few pages devoted to this topic. It is up to you to analyze your infrastructure and choose the backup and restore plan that best fits your environment.

Database Snapshots

Database Snapshots can't really be used for disaster recovery in the case of a complete database loss. However, they can be very useful in reversing the effects of database modifications. They are also useful in re-directing queries away from a busy transactional database.

What is a Database Snapshot? A *snapshot* is a point-in-time, static, Read Only view of a database. The creation of a snapshot is instantaneous because the database that is the source of the snapshot is not actually copied to create the snapshot. Instead, data files are created that will only hold the data pages from the source database that have changed since the snapshot was created. This functionality is called *Copy On Write*. When the Database Snapshot is initially created, near-identical data files are created to hold the contents of the snapshot. The difference in the data files is that they have separate physical locations from the source database, and they initially consume very little disk space.

The easiest way to understand Database Snapshots is to create and use one. The following script creates a snapshot of the SmallWorks database.

```
CREATE DATABASE SmallWorksSnapShot ON
  (NAME = 'SmallWorksPrimary'
, FILENAME = 'D:\SQLSnapShotData\SmallWorksPrimary.mdf')
,(NAME = 'SmallWorksdata1'
, FILENAME = 'D:\SQLSnapShotData\SmallWorksData1.ndf')
,(NAME = 'SmallWorksdata2'
, FILENAME = 'D:\SQLSnapShotData\SmallWorksData2.ndf')
AS SNAPSHOT OF SmallWorks
```

A look in the file system reveals that the SmallWorks snapshot data files are all 10 MB, as they were when you created the database (your size may vary based on any modifications you made to the SmallWorks database), but the files are only consuming 128 KB for the primary file and 64 KB for each secondary data file for a total of 256 KB. SQL Server reserves the same amount of disk space that the database is presently using, but it only allocates enough to store the metadata of the database structure.

Now let's take a look at the data in the SmallWorks and SmallWorksSnapshot databases and see what happens to the snapshot database and the data when changes are made to the source database.

1. First write a query to return some data from the first three rows of the dbo.Person table in the SmallWorks database and the SmallWorksSnapshot database, as shown in the following example:

    ```
    USE SmallWorks
    GO
    SELECT FirstName, LastName, EmailAddress
    FROM dbo.Person
    WHERE PersonID < 4

    FirstName    LastName     EmailAddress
    ---------    --------     --------------------------------
    Ken          Sánchez      ken.sánchez@adventureworks.com
    Terri        Duffy        terri.duffy@adventureworks.com
    ```

```
Roberto        Tamburello      roberto.tamburello@adventureworks.com

(3 row(s) affected)

USE SmallWorksSnapShot
GO
SELECT FirstName, LastName, EmailAddress
FROM dbo.Person
WHERE PersonID < 4

FirstName    LastName    EmailAddress
---------    --------    -------------------------------
Ken          Sánchez     ken.sánchez@adventureworks.com
Terri        Duffy       terri.duffy@adventureworks.com
Roberto      Tamburello  roberto.tamburello@adventureworks.com

(3 row(s) affected)
```

Notice that both of the databases return the same results. In actuality, the query to the snapshot database was re-directed to the source database since the data pages containing the contact information had not been changed since the snapshot was created.

2. Now, let's update the data in the source database by changing the last name of all the people in the database. We'll update all of them so we can more easily examine the changes to the physical data files hosting the snapshot database.

```
USE SmallWorks
GO
UPDATE dbo.Person
SET LastName = 'Flintstone'

(5000 row(s) affected)
```

The SmallWorksSnapShot data files now consume about 1.2 MB of space (your results may vary). Updating the 5,000 rows in the SmallWorks database caused the original data pages containing those rows to be copied to the snapshot, resulting in an increase in the size of the snapshot.

3. Now let's query the two databases again to see what the results are. The source database is, indeed, changed, reflecting the update of the LastName column.

```
USE SmallWorks
GO
SELECT FirstName, LastName, EmailAddress
FROM dbo.Person
WHERE PersonID < 4

FirstName    LastName    EmailAddress
---------    --------    -------------------------------
Ken          Flintstone  ken.sánchez@adventureworks.com
Terri        Flintstone  terri.duffy@adventureworks.com
```

```
    Roberto        Flintstone        roberto.tamburello@adventureworks.com

(3 row(s) affected)
```

However, the snapshot database still reflects the data as it appeared when the snapshot was created. This is what is meant by a "static, Read Only copy" of the database.

```
USE SmallWorksSnapShot
GO
SELECT FirstName, LastName, EmailAddress
FROM dbo.Person
WHERE PersonID < 4

FirstName      LastName        EmailAddress
---------      --------        --------------------------------
Ken            Sánchez         ken.sánchez@adventureworks.com
Terri          Duffy           terri.duffy@adventureworks.com
Roberto        Tamburello      roberto.tamburello@adventureworks.com

(3 row(s) affected)
```

You can create as many snapshots as you want of a database, but keep in mind that each additional snapshot is going to add additional overhead to your source database. The overhead is created because every command that updates or deletes data or objects will cause a Write to the snapshot database to record the previous version of the database.

Database Snapshot Limitations

There are some limitations of Database Snapshots and limitations on the source database created with the snapshot:

❑   Database Snapshots cannot be backed up. Since the snapshot is a combination of data retrieved from the source database and data stored internally, it is impossible to actually back up the snapshot.

❑   Database Snapshots cannot be modified.

❑   Source databases cannot be dropped while a snapshot exists.

❑   Source databases cannot be restored to a point in time prior to the creation of the snapshot while the snapshot exists.

Disaster Recovery and Database Snapshots

How exactly do Database Snapshots fit in to the realm of disaster recovery? That is an excellent question! Snapshots can be used to undo updates to a source database because they have the original copy of the data as it looked prior to the modification.

Undoing Updates

In the previous example, we updated all 5,000 rows of the Person table with the last name of *Flintstone*. To reverse the effects of this frivolous update, the following script can be used:

```
USE SmallWorks
GO
```

```
UPDATE dbo.Person
SET LastName = S.LastName
FROM dbo.Person P
JOIN SmallWorksSnapShot.dbo.Person S
ON S.PersonID = P.PersonID
```

A query of the source database will now reveal that all the last names have been put back to their original values.

Undoing Deletes

Consider the following command that deletes 50 of the rows from the dbo.Person table:

```
DELETE dbo.Person
WHERE PersonID < 51
```

If this was a malicious or accidental update, the normal pattern for restoring the data would be to restore the database to a test server and then copy the data from the test server back to the production database. With a Database Snapshot there is no need to involve the database backups.

To restore the data, simply insert the data back into the source database table by selecting from the snapshot.

```
USE SmallWorks
GO
INSERT dbo.Person
(PersonID, FirstName, LastName, EmailAddress)
SELECT PersonID, FirstName, LastName, EmailAddress
FROM SmallWorksSnapShot.dbo.Person
WHERE PersonID < 51
```

Undoing Drops

If a database object is dropped from the source database, it can be scripted and re-created from the snapshot database. If it was a table, the table can then be repopulated using the previous method for undoing deletes.

```
--Inadvertant deletion of the Person table
USE SmallWorks
GO
DROP TABLE dbo.Person

--Recreate the Person Table
USE SmallWorks
GO
CREATE TABLE dbo.Person(
PersonID int NOT NULL,
FirstName varchar(50) NOT NULL,
MiddleName varchar(50) NULL,
LastName varchar(50) NOT NULL,
EmailAddress nvarchar(50) NULL
) ON SWUserData1
--Repopulate the table
INSERT dbo.Person
(PersonID, FirstName, LastName, EmailAddress)
```

```
SELECT PersonID, FirstName, LastName, EmailAddress
FROM SmallWorksSnapShot.dbo.Person
```

Restoring from Snapshots

If several undesired changes have been made to the source database, it can be restored to the point in time when the snapshot was created by specifying the snapshot as the source of the restore operation. Remember that if multiple snapshots exist, the database cannot be restored to a point in time before a snapshot was created. Those snapshots will have to be dropped first. The following command demonstrates how to restore the SmallWorks database from a database snapshot:

```
USE MASTER
GO
RESTORE DATABASE SmallWorks
FROM DATABASE_SNAPSHOT = 'SmallWorksSnapShot'
```

Summary

In this chapter, we examined the different ways to back up and restore databases. We also took a look at the different aspects of disaster recovery, which is most important to minimizing data loss and preserving our jobs. Hopefully, you have arrived at the planned conclusion to this chapter. That conclusion is that it is all about planning. As database administrators we are ultimately responsible for maintaining the integrity and security of the data entrusted to us. In order to accomplish this important goal, it is imperative that we plan for disaster and, even more importantly, plan how to recover from any disaster with the absolute minimum amount of data loss and downtime.

Monitoring SQL Server

One of the primary responsibilities of the database administrator is the ongoing monitoring of SQL Server. Monitoring is done for a variety of reasons, including performance, storage, security, and standards compliance. Much of this monitoring can be automated, but for the most part, the monitoring results must be interpreted and acted on in a systematic approach by the DBA. The monitoring job never ends, and it can become quite complex. Knowing what to monitor, when to monitor, and what constitutes acceptable and unacceptable behavior can become a full-time job. Making things even more challenging is the fact that each SQL Server installation is different, making a global recommendation about what indicators identify unacceptable and acceptable performance very difficult.

This chapter explains the various tools used to monitor SQL Server and provides guidelines on how to use these tools to identify potential security problems and areas for optimization. Monitoring SQL Server can be a challenging process. SQL Server interacts heavily with every operating system subsystem. Some applications rely heavily on RAM, whereas others are CPU- or disk-intensive. SQL Server can be all three at the same time. SQL Server can also be very network-intensive, especially with distributed applications, replication, or database mirroring. Many database administrators find the whole process of monitoring and optimizing arcane and nebulous. However, it doesn't have to be all that mysterious. A good understanding of the tools, as well as a familiarity with the different objects requiring monitoring, will go a long way toward making your monitoring tasks less intimidating.

Whole books have been written on the subject of monitoring, along with several web sites dedicated to the subject. I won't attempt to tell you everything you need to know about monitoring SQL Server in this book, but I will describe the fundamentals, which, as in all things, is the best place to start.

Performance Monitoring

SQL Server 2008 performance monitoring can essentially be divided into five basic areas:

- ❑ System resources
- ❑ SQL Server itself
- ❑ The database
- ❑ The database application
- ❑ The network

Before getting into the specifics of performance monitoring, it is very important to understand the methodology. Monitoring for the sake of monitoring is useless. You monitor your hardware and SQL Server implementations to anticipate and prevent performance problems. To do this, you must have some kind of plan — a strategy that will enable you to invest the right amount of time and the right amount of resources to maintain and improve the performance of your SQL Server.

Performance Monitoring Strategy

The strategy for monitoring and optimizing SQL Server is fairly straightforward and is made up of the following steps:

1. **Create a Performance Baseline** — Without a baseline of your database server, it is very unlikely that you will be able to make changes to the server platform with complete confidence that the changes will accomplish the improvements you are looking for. A baseline contains measurements from all the systems previously mentioned (system resources, SQL Server, the database, the database application, and the network). Specific counters and measurements are discussed later in this chapter. When evaluating the baseline, you may identify areas that warrant immediate optimization. If changes are made, a new baseline must be created.

2. **Complete Periodic Performance Audits** — After the baseline is completed, periodic performance audits are performed to ensure that performance has not degraded from when the baseline was created. This step is often supplemented or replaced by reactive audits that are performed in response to complaints of poor server performance. I prefer to be proactive and schedule the audits, but there will invariably be times when a reactive audit will be required because unexpected performance problems arise.

3. **Make Changes and Evaluate Their Impact** — After performing audits, you may find areas that require modification. When making these changes, it is important to be meticulous. As a rule, you should not make multiple changes at once. Instead, make one or two changes, and then evaluate the measurements that prompted the changes to be made. This makes it much easier to identify what changes have the greatest impact on performance. Chapter 11 goes into more detail on what specific changes you can make to optimize SQL Server when your performance audit identifies a problem area.

4. **Reset the Baseline** — After completing all the modifications, create another baseline to measure future performance trends.

The Mad Clicker

I work with a colleague that we affectionately call the "Mad Clicker." When something goes wrong in the server room, he invariably gets involved and starts clicking away, making sweeping changes to configuration settings in an attempt to correct the problem. Often, he is successful, but it is next to impossible to duplicate his actions in the future because even he doesn't know everything he changed. Don't be a "Mad Clicker." Complete a modification, and then measure and document the results. This makes it easy to duplicate and easy to roll back if the modifications resulted in a degradation of performance instead of an improvement.

Creating a Performance Baseline

It is very important when creating a baseline that typical activity is monitored. Monitoring performance during a monthly import may give you some interesting data, but it will not help you evaluate and improve overall system performance. There are different ways of creating baselines. Most database administrators have their own preferences on how to gather and compare performance data. They also have their own favorite counters and system views that they feel give them insight into how the database is performing. SQL Server performance monitoring and optimization is more of an art than a science.

I have seen many different recommendations on what System Monitor counters to collect and what SQL Server–specific activity to monitor. All of them were different. Some database administrators recommended monitoring everything, whereas others recommended monitoring a small selection of processes. I support the small selection philosophy for two different reasons. The first is that there is definitely such a thing as "too much information." Collecting every conceivable bit of performance data will most likely result in a case of not seeing the forest because of the trees. There is just too much data to sift through. The second reason (and maybe even more importantly) is the performance factor.

Gathering performance information is not free. The more information you gather, the more it costs in terms of performance. This creates an interesting paradox. To adequately monitor performance, you must introduce performance-degrading actions to the database. The quandary that creates is one in which you can never be completely positive that your monitoring actions are not at least marginally responsible for unacceptable performance.

Limiting the data retrieved will reduce this uncertainty, but it is also important to keep in mind that you should not look at any particular counter in isolation. For example, heavy disk activity might be caused by memory limitations, and unsatisfactory CPU performance can be caused by poorly written queries and missing indexes. No one subsystem exists in a vacuum.

So, what should you have in your baseline? Over the years, I have condensed the list of objects and processes that I monitor for baselines and performance audits. Those counters are described in the following pages.

The main tool for creating a performance baseline is Performance Monitor. However, Dynamic Management Views (DMVs) are used as well to give more context to the baseline. After explaining the counters used for a baseline and performance audits, this chapter digs deeper into the SQL Server–specific tools and explores how to identify misbehaving processes.

Performance Counters

The following are some of the most useful counters to use when auditing performance. This discussion is not meant to be all-inclusive. It is made up of the counters I and a few of my colleagues have come to rely on for a "big picture" view of SQL Server performance. There are many more counters that can be used to diagnose performance issues and to dig deeper into the nuts and bolts of SQL Server activity. But these few will most likely provide the information you need to quickly evaluate the health of your server.

Processor Counters

Processor counters are used in conjunction with other counters to monitor and evaluate CPU performance and identify CPU bottlenecks.

❑ **Processor: % Processor Time** — The Processor: % Processor Time counter displays the total percentage of time spent processing non-idle threads. On a multiple-processor machine, each individual processor can be monitored independently. If the CPU affinity settings have been customized, you may want to monitor a specific CPU. Other than that, I normally use the _total instance identifier to see the combined processor utilization. CPU activity is a good indicator of SQL Server CPU activity and is a key way to identify potential CPU bottlenecks. Recommendations on what this counter should look like vary. As a general rule, if total % Processor Time is consistently greater than 70 percent, you probably have a CPU bottleneck, and you should look at either optimizing current application processes, upgrading the CPU, or both. Use this counter along with the Processor Queue Length counter to positively identify CPU bottlenecks.

❑ **Process: % Processor Time (sqlservr)** — The Process: % Processor Time counter (when set to monitor information from the SQL Server process) can be used to determine how much of the total processing time can be attributed to SQL Server.

❑ **System: Processor Queue Length** — The Processor Queue Length counter displays the number of threads waiting to be processed by a CPU. If the average queue length is consistently greater than two times the number of processors, then you may have a CPU bottleneck, because the processors can't keep up with the number of requests.

Use the Processor Queue Length and the % Processor Time counters together to determine if you have a CPU bottleneck. If both counters are out of acceptable ranges, there is most assuredly a CPU bottleneck.

If the Processor Queue Length is not within acceptable limits, but the % Processor Time is, you may not have a CPU bottleneck, but a configuration problem instead. Ensure that the max worker threads server setting has not been set to a value that is too high for your system. The default setting for max worker threads is 0, which configures SQL Server to automatically set max worker threads in accordance to the values shown in the following table. However, in addition to 0, it is possible to configure any value between 128 and 32,767. SQL Server Books Online gives the acceptable range as 32 through 32,767, which is incorrect. The graphical interface *will* accept any value between 0 and 32,767, but any value between 1 and 127 results in a setting of 128.

CPUs	32-bit	64-bit
1	256	512
2	256	512
4	256	512
8	288	576
16	352	704
32	480	960

Disk Counters

Several disk counters return disk Read and Write performance information, as well as data transfer information, for each physical disk or all disks. Physical disk statistics, when combined with memory statistics, give a very accurate view of total I/O performance on the server.

❑ **PhysicalDisk: Avg. Disk Queue Length** — As the last mechanical component in modern computer systems, the disk is inherently the slowest, even with the built-in memory cache that virtually all disk controllers are configured with. The Avg. Disk Queue Length counter returns the average number of Read and Write operations that were queued for an individual disk or all disks. The requests are queued because the disk or disks are too busy, and the controller's onboard memory cache has no space to temporarily store the Read or Write request. This counter should remain below the number of physical disks multiplied by two. For example, if your database is located on a 10-disk array, the counter should remain below 20.

❑ If this counter is consistently greater than the desired value, the most likely cause is an inadequacy in the disk subsystem, or an inadequate amount of memory on the server. A lack of memory can cause the disk subsystem to be overworked by SQL Server's inability to cache data in memory for long periods of time, resulting in more physical disk Reads. Spreading the database across multiple disks and multiple controllers may increase performance. Adding memory, if possible, to the disk controller may also alleviate the disk bottleneck.

❑ **PhysicalDisk: % Disk Time** — This counter measures how busy a physical disk or hardware disk array is. The % Disk Time counter shouldn't consistently run at more than 60 percent. If it does, check out the % Disk Read and % Disk Write counters to determine what type of activity the disk is primarily performing. If more than one array is used for the database, this counter can be used to determine if the disk workload is equally divided among all the arrays.

Memory Counters

As previously noted, memory counters (along with disk counters) are used by the DBA to get an overall picture of database I/O. A lack of memory will have a direct impact on disk activity. When optimizing a server, adding memory should always be considered. SQL Server loves memory and effectively allocates it to minimize the amount of disk access required for database operations. If you are looking for a SQL Server performance panacea, adding memory is as close as you're going to get.

❑ **Memory: Pages/Sec** — The Pages/Sec counter measures the number of pages per second that are paged out of memory to disk or paged into memory from disk. The official recommendation for this counter is that it should never be consistently greater than zero. In all likelihood, it will regularly spike higher than zero, then return to near zero, and then spike high again, as Figure 10-1 shows. This is perfectly normal, but if the counter is consistently above zero, it indicates a possible memory bottleneck. The solution, of course, is to add memory. However, it may also be that the maximum server memory setting is set too low if there is plenty of memory on the server. The memory counter Available Bytes will show how much memory is available on the system.

Another possible cause of steady memory paging is an application other than SQL Server running on the same server. Ideally, SQL Server should be the only application supported by the server. Sometimes this is not possible, but it is still the ideal configuration.

❑ **Memory: Available Bytes** — The Available Bytes counter indicates how much memory is available to processes. The official recommendation is that there should always be at least 5 MB of available memory, but this is a particularly low number, and it should probably be at least 10 times as much.

❑ **Process: Working Set (sqlservr)** — The SQL Server instance of the Working Set counter shows how much memory is in use by SQL Server. If this number is always lower than the minimum server memory setting or significantly lower than the maximum server memory setting, SQL

Server is most likely configured to use too much memory. This is not necessarily a bad thing, as long as it is not interfering with other server processes.

❑ **SQL Server: Buffer Manager: Buffer Cache Hit Ratio** — The Buffer Cache Hit Ratio counter measures the percentage of time that data was found in the buffer without having to be read from disk. This counter should be very high, optimally 90 percent or better. When it is less than 90 percent, disk I/O will be too high, putting an added burden on the disk subsystem.

❑ **SQL Server: Buffer Manager: Page Life Expectancy** — The Page Life Expectancy counter returns the number of seconds a data page will stay in the buffer without being referenced by a data operation. The minimum value for this counter is approximately 300 seconds. This counter, along with the Buffer Cache Hit Ratio counter, is probably the best indicator of SQL Server memory health. A higher number for both counters is better.

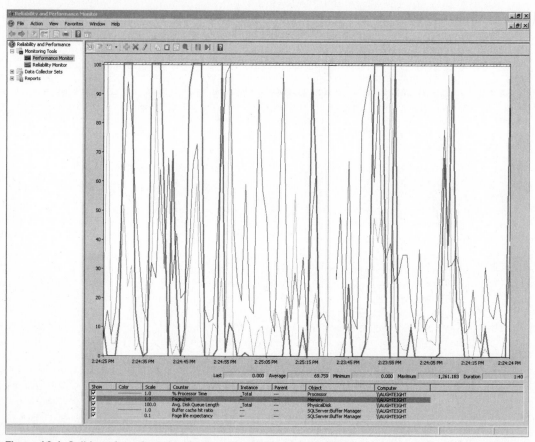

Figure 10-1: Spiking of number of pages in and out of memory to disk.

Network Counters

For most network counters, there is no hard-and-fast recommendation for what you should see. The only guidance that can possibly be given is to ensure that the network traffic being generated on the server is well within the capacity of the network connection. Network counters, however, are a good way to measure the network traffic over a period of time to evaluate trends to determine if some type of scaling or load balancing may be in order.

❑ **Network Interface: Bytes Total/Sec** — The Bytes Total/Sec counter measures the total number of bytes that are being sent back and forth between the server and the network. If the server is configured exclusively for SQL Server, almost all of the traffic should belong to SQL Server. As mentioned, this counter is very useful in analyzing network traffic trends. This information is very useful for planning scale-out and upgrade requirements.

SQL Server Counters

After installing SQL Server, a plethora of SQL Server performance objects and counters are configured to assist in the performance monitoring and optimization of SQL Server. If you are like 99 percent of all database administrators, you will most likely never look at a majority of these counters. However, there will be a special few that you will come to completely rely on. The following SQL Server–specific counters are extraordinarily useful in the establishment of a baseline, and comparing activity against the baseline to establish SQL Server performance health:

❑ **SQL Server: General Statistics: User Connections** — The User Connections counter displays the number of user connections that are currently connected to SQL Server. This counter is especially useful in monitoring and tracking connection trends to ensure that the server is configured to adequately handle all connections. Keep in mind that this counter displays the number of user connections, not users. Some applications will create more than one connection per user, whereas others may create only one connection but support multiple users.

❑ **SQL Server: Locks: Average Wait Time** — The Average Wait Time counter is an excellent counter to monitor and track the average amount of time that user requests for data resources have to wait because of concurrent blocks to the data. With the baseline and subsequent audits, this counter will be a leading indicator of database application performance. However, it is just an indicator. Resolving long-term locking requires running traces to record lock information. Traces are discussed later in this chapter.

❑ **SQL Server: Locks: Deadlocks/Sec** — Deadlocks occur when two or more transactions hold a lock on different resources and the transactions require access to the resources held by the opposing transaction. If this sounds very confusing, see the sidebar "Sample Events Resulting in a Deadlock" for a simple example illustrating the sequence of events that results in a deadlock.

❑ **SQL Server Access Methods: Page Splits/Sec** — As described in Chapter 5, *page splits* occur when SQL Server attempts to insert a row in a clustered or non-clustered index page, but there is not sufficient space available to accommodate the new row. To maintain the contiguousness of the index page, SQL Server splits about half of the data out of the original page and moves it to a free page. This splitting of data is necessary to maintain the indexes, but it causes excessive I/O because logically contiguous data is no longer physically contiguous. As more and more rows are inserted, the fragmentation of data will become worse.

The Page Splits/Sec counter enables the monitoring of page split activity to determine how fast table indexes are becoming fragmented. Although a certain amount of page splitting is normal, excessive page splits will cause a steady deterioration of database performance. Chapter 5 explains how to detect, correct, and mitigate this fragmentation.

When monitoring page split activity, create a baseline shortly after rebuilding the indexes. As subsequent performance audits are completed, compare the page split activity. When the counter begins to spike, it is probably time for the indexes to be rebuilt again with an appropriate fill-factor.

Sample Events Resulting in a Deadlock

Two stored procedures are executed at the same time on separate connections. The first stored procedure, `Proc1`, updates one or more rows in `TableA`. The second stored procedure, `Proc2`, updates one or more rows in `TableB`. At this time, `Proc1` has an exclusive lock on the updated rows in `TableA`, and `Proc2` has an exclusive lock on the rows in `TableB`.

Next, `Proc1` attempts to update the same rows in `TableB` that `Proc2` has updated. It will not be able to, because `Proc2` already has an exclusive lock. At this point, `Proc1` is blocked by `Proc2`. `Proc2` then attempts to update the rows that `Proc1` has updated and is also blocked. This mutual blocking is a *deadlock*.

SQL Server does not allow deadlocks to continue. The Database Engine monitors for deadlocks, and, if one is detected, it will select a victim process and kill that process. The error raised by a terminated deadlock looks like the following message:

```
Msg 1205, Level 13, State 51, Line 6
Transaction (Process ID 53) was deadlocked on lock
resources with another process and has been chosen as the
deadlock victim. Rerun the transaction.
```

The selection process is based on cost. Whichever process would cost the least to roll back is terminated, and the remaining process or processes are allowed to continue. The most significant cause of deadlocks is the updating of tables in an inconsistent process. When database developers are creating procedures for data modification, they should update multiple objects in the same order whenever possible. For example, if `Proc1` and `Proc2` both update `TableA` first, and then `TableB`, a short-term blocking lock may have occurred, but a deadlock would not have.

Deadlocks may occur occasionally, but they should not be a regular occurrence. Because they are automatically detected and killed, they are sometimes difficult to troubleshoot. The Profiler tool can be used to identify the offending processes involved in a deadlock, as discussed later in this chapter.

Dynamic Management Views

SQL Server 2008 provides many Dynamic Management Views (DMVs) that can be used in the gathering of baseline information and for diagnosing performance problems. Some of these views offer the same information as performance counters, but in a relational and instantaneous format. Other views provide more specific database performance information. I won't try to cover all the views in this section, but the following views can prove very helpful in the creation and comparison of performance baselines:

❏   `sys.dm_os_performance_counters` — A very interesting Dynamic Management View as far as operating system information is concerned is `sys.dm_os_performance_counters`. This view provides much the same information as Performance Monitor, except that the information is returned in a relational format and the values returned are instantaneous. Because the data is instantaneous, per-second counters will have to be queried at least twice to determine their true value. The columns that are returned by this view are described in the following table:

Column Name	Description	
object_name	Counter category, such as SQLServer:Wait Statistics or SQLServer:Buffer Manager	
counter_name	Name of the counter	
Instance_name	Name of the counter instance, such as database name or instance description. Server-level counters will not have an instance value.	
cntr_value	Instantaneous value of the counter	
cntr_type	Counter types fall into the following type categories:	
	65792	Numeric (integer) counter
	1073874176	Average value counter
	1073939712	Base value counter
	272696576	Per second counter
	537003264	Ratio value counter

❑ sys.dm_db_index_physical_stats — As described in Chapter 5, this view returns information about the indexes on a table, including the amount of data on each data page, the amount of fragmentation at the leaf and non-leaf level of the indexes, and the average size of records in an index.

❑ sys.dm_db_index_usage_stats — The sys.dm_db_index_usage_stats view collects cumulative index usage data. This view can be used to identify which indexes are seldom referenced and, thus, may be increasing overhead without improving Read performance. The following code example demonstrates one possible use of this view by joining it with the sys.indexes system view to return the index name, table name, and index usage information:

```
USE AdventureWorks2008;
GO
SELECT object_name(S.object_id) AS TableName
,I.name AS IndexName, S.user_seeks AS Seeks
,S.user_scans AS Scans, S.user_updates AS Updates
,S.last_user_seek AS LastSeek, S.last_user_scan AS LastScan
FROM sys.dm_db_index_usage_stats S
JOIN sys.indexes I ON S.object_id = I.object_id
AND S.index_id = I.index_id
WHERE S.object_id > 100000 --Return only user owned index data
ORDER BY Seeks, Scans;
```

Tools and Techniques for Monitoring

Chapter 3 described many of the tools available from a feature point of view. This chapter examines the tools from an implementation point of view and discusses how to use them to actually perform some key database-monitoring tasks. The discussion also examines a few more tools that were not described in Chapter 3, because they are intricately tied in to SQL Server Management Studio.

Log File Viewer

The Log File Viewer is an excellent tool for the viewing of SQL Server and operating system logs in a one-time correlated view. For example, memory subsystem errors from the system log can be correlated with SQL Server errors, indicating out-of-memory conditions and allowing you to isolate the problem away from SQL Server. To open the Log File Viewer, expand the Management folder in SQL Server Management Studio, expand SQL Server Logs, right-click on the log you want to view, and select "View SQL Server Log." Once the Log File Viewer is open, you can choose to open additional SQL Server logs and/or operating system logs by expanding and selecting the logs you want to review (see Figure 10-2). Notice that you can also open up log files for the SQL Server Agent and Database Mail.

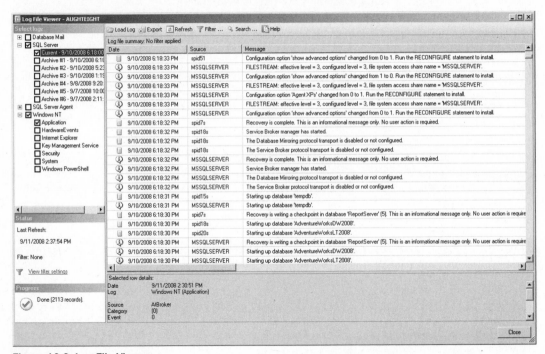

Figure 10-2: Log File Viewer.

SQL Server and SQL Server Agent log files are closed and a new log is opened every time the respective service is restarted. In a production system this may not occur very often, resulting in a large log file. To avoid unacceptably large log files, the contents of the log files should be exported and the files cycled. To cycle the SQL Server Log, execute the sp_cycle_errorlog stored procedure. To cycle the Agent Log, the sp_cycle_agent_errorlog stored procedure is used. These procedures clear the contents of the logs without requiring a service restart.

The number of logs that SQL Server keeps can be configured by right-clicking on the SQL Server Logs folder and selecting Configure (see Figure 10-3). The minimum and default number of logs is 6, but it can be increased to as many as 99. The number cannot be less than 6.

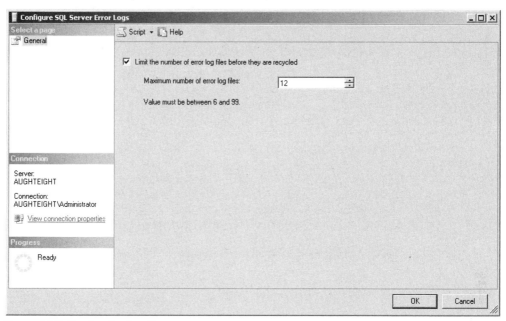

Figure 10-3: Configuring log files.

Activity Monitor

Microsoft bundled a surprise with the final release candidate of SQL Server 2008 when they included a completely overhauled Activity Monitor. This was a surprise to the community because Activity Monitor was moved from its traditional location, leading a number of concerned DBAs to flood the support forums with postings. Apparently this was also a surprise to the Microsoft Books Online team, whom as of this writing were still referencing the documentation for the old Activity Monitor!

Activity Monitor in SQL Server 2008 is now a feature-rich, near-real-time, graphical performance dashboard. The new Activity Monitor has a similar look and feel to the system Reliability and Performance Monitor included in Vista and Server 2008. The first thing that experienced DBAs will notice is that Activity Monitor is no longer located in the Management node of SQL Server Management Studio. Now you will find Activity Monitor on the context menu of a SQL Server instance.

Activity Monitor is a great tool for gaining a deeper understanding of the overall health and performance of your server. Compared to prior versions, it is no longer limited to displaying simple process and lock information. Activity Monitor now shows intuitive graphs, detailed process and lock information, file I/O statistics, and information about long-running queries. In addition, all of the grid views can now be sorted and filtered. Activity Monitor cannot replace a good set of Data Management Views in the hands of an experienced DBA, but it is very useful in answering the basic question "Why is my server running slowly?"

In order to run Activity Monitor, you will need the view server state permission. To kill any processes, you will also need to be a member of either the sysadmin or processadmin server roles. The new Activity Monitor will work on SQL Server 2005, but not on prior versions.

Activity Monitor is comprised of five major sections, titled Overview, Processes, Resource Waits, Data File I/O, and Recent Expensive Queries:

❑ **Overview** — The Overview section displays four near-real-time graphs that represent key performance metrics. Right-clicking on a graph will allow you to adjust the refresh rate or pause data collection.

❑ **Processes** — The Processes section lists a row for every connection to SQL Server, along with several columns describing the process (such as the user associated with the connection, the database context, and the command presently running, as well as any wait status and blocking information). Right-clicking on a process and selecting Details will bring up the last command executed on that connection and provide the capability to kill the process, if necessary. Right-clicking on a process will display a context menu with the option to trace the process in SQL Server Profiler. Figure 10-4 illustrates this behavior. Also notice in Figure 10-4 that Process 59 is suspended, because it is waiting on the resource that is locked by Process 57, which, in turn, is waiting on the resource that is locked by Process 60.

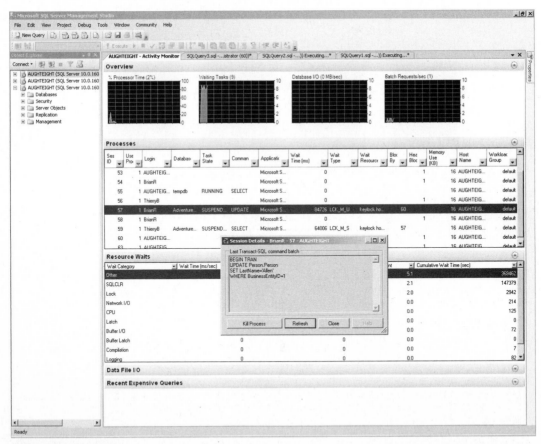

Figure 10-4: Processes.

❑ **Resource Waits** — The Resource Waits section displays a complete list of all resource waits (CPU, Latch, Memory, Buffer I/O, etc.). This list does not provide any drill-in capability, but you can filter and sort the results.

❑ **Data File I/O** — The Data File I/O section displays file activity totals by database file. The list can be filtered and sorted.

❑ **Recent Expensive Queries** — This is a welcome addition to the Activity Monitor! The Recent Expensive Queries section shows all recent, costly queries and allows you to open the complete query statement or the detailed execution plan in a new Query window. Figure 10-5 displays this section and shows the context menu options for an expensive query.

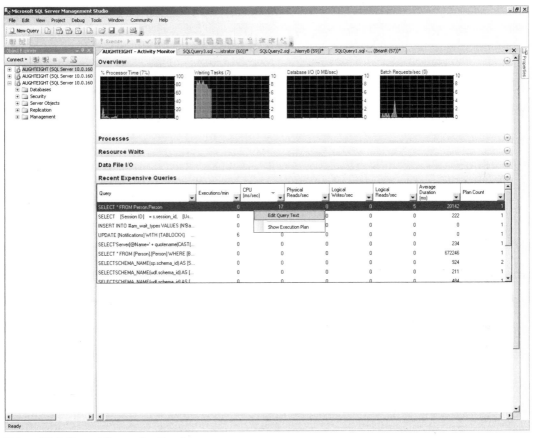

Figure 10-5: Recent Expensive Queries.

By default, Activity Monitor will refresh the display every 10 seconds. To configure Activity Monitor for a different refresh rate, right-click on any of the graphs, and select the desired Refresh Interval or select Pause to disable refreshing. Keep in mind that frequent refreshing of process information can cause degradation of SQL Server's performance.

System Stored Procedures

Although Activity Monitor is a great graphical tool to view processes and the resources they are using, often the simpler output of System Stored Procedures is more appropriate for identifying current processes and identifying any contention.

413

sp_who and sp_who2

The sp_who2 stored procedure is an undocumented system procedure that offers a distinct advantage over its documented sibling procedure, sp_who. They both return information about current SQL Server processes, but the sp_who2 procedure's information is more comprehensive.

These stored procedures are essentially equivalent to Activity Monitor's Processes page. The output of sp_who or sp_who2 can be restricted by specifying a process ID as an input parameter. The syntax of the sp_who and sp_who2 procedures is as follows:

```
sp_who [process_ID] | login_name | [ACTIVE]
```

```
sp_who2 [process_ID] | [ACTIVE]
```

The sp_who stored procedure returns nine columns described in the following table:

Column Name	Description
spid	Server Process ID. The spid represents the session ID of the connection. Every connection has one spid.
ecid	Execution Context ID. The ecid value indicates what thread the process was executed on. An ecid of 0 indicates that the process was executed on the main thread.
status	The status of the session. Possible status values are as follows: Running — The session is performing some work. Runnable — The session has performed some work, but it currently has no work to perform. Sleeping — The session is waiting to perform work. Background — Background processes (typically those owned by the system) that periodically activate to perform an action Suspended — The session has work to do but has been stopped because it is waiting for a process (such as I/O) to complete. Dormant — The session is being re-set by SQL Server. Rollback — The session is currently rolling back a transaction. Pending — The session is waiting on an available thread. Spinloop — The session is waiting on a spinlock to become free. Spinlocks are used for fast protection of critical memory regions on multi-CPU machines.
loginame	The login associated with the session
hostname	Host name associated with the session
blk	The spid of the session that is blocking the session if one exists. If not, a 0 is returned.

Column Name	Description
dbname	The name of the database connected to by the session
cmd	The type of command executing on the session
request_id	The integer identifier of the request running in the session

The sp_who2 stored procedure returns 13 columns, although it returns one column, spid, twice — once on the left side of the result set and once on the right to make the result set easier to read. The columns are described in the following table:

Column Name	Description
SPID	Server Process ID. The spid represents the session ID of the connection. Every connection has one spid.
Status	The status information is the same as for the sp_who command.
Login	The login associated with the session
HostName	Host name associated with the session
BlkBy	The spid of the session that is blocking the session if one exists
DBName	The name of the database connected to by the session
Command	The type of command executing on the session
CPUTime	The cumulative CPU usage for this process
DiskIO	The cumulative Disk I/O for this process
LastBatch	The last time the client process executed a remote stored procedure call or an EXECUTE statement. If the process is a system process, the time is the time that SQL Server was last started.
ProgramName	The name of the application (if reported) associated with the session (e.g., *Microsoft SQL Server Management Studio*)
SPID	Duplicate of the spid recorded in the first column of the results
REQUESTID	The integer identifier of the request running in the session

When the "Active" option is added to sp_who or sp_who2, SQL Server does not return any session that has the Command of "Awaiting Command," which specifies that the session is waiting on input from a user process.

sp_lock

The sp_lock stored procedure returns the number and types of locks held by active database processes. The object locked or requested to be locked is returned with the lock status and any identifying information (such as the object's integer identifier), along with the index ID, if any.

SQL Server Locking

To interpret the information returned by sp_lock, it is important to understand the lockable resource types and the modes these locks can take. The possible resource types are described in the following table:

Resource Type	Description
RID	A RID lock is a row lock on a heap. The identifier is in the format FileID:PageNumber:RID, where FileID is the data file containing the row, PageNumber is the integer identifier of the 8K data page, and RID identifies the specific row on the data page.
KEY	A KEY lock is a row-level lock when a clustered index exists. The KEY is a hexadecimal number that the Database Engine uses internally to track individual clustered index keys.
PAG	PAG indicates that the lock is requested or held on an 8-K data page. The value of PAG is the combination of the data file FileID and the integer identifier of the data page.
EXT	An EXT lock is a lock of an entire 64-K extent. The value of EXT is the data file FileID and the identifier of the first page on the extent.
TAB	TAB locks are table locks. No resource information is returned for TAB locks because the ObjID column already contains the Object_ID of the table.
DB	DB indicates a database lock. No resource information is returned for DB locks because the dbid column already contains the identifier for the database locked.
APP	APP indicates a lock request held on an application resource. Application locks are issued explicitly through the use of the sp_getapplock stored procedure and are fairly rare.
FIL	A FIL lock is a lock held on a data file. The resource information contains the integer value of the file identifier.
MD	MD locks are metadata locks. MD locks are typically on XML collection data.
HBT	A lock on a Heap or B-Tree index
AU	A lock on an Allocation Unit

Locks on resource types are requested and granted by mode. The sp_lock stored procedure returns information that identifies the mode of the lock (e.g., whether the lock is a shared or exclusive lock). The following table describes the most common modes:

Lock Mode	Description
Sch-S	**Shared Schema Lock** — Prevents processes from altering the schema of a resource while it is in use. The Sch-S lock mode is compatible with other shared locks.
Sch-M	**Schema Modification Lock** — Required to modify the schema of a resource. This lock mode is not compatible with any other lock mode.
S	**Shared Lock** — A Shared lock is compatible with all other locks except Exclusive locks.
U	**Update Lock** — An Update lock is used to prevent deadlocks by specifying that a resource is locked for eventual updating.
X	**Exclusive Lock** — For any resource that is being modified, created, or dropped, a process will have an Exclusive lock during the modification.
IS	**Intent Shared Lock** — Intent locks are used on resources higher in the resource hierarchy to prevent more exclusive locks from being issued. For example, an Intent Shared lock can be placed on a data page if an individual row is being read. This prevents an Exclusive lock from being placed on the page and trapping the shared process. Intent Shared locks are compatible with all locks except Exclusive.
IU	**Intent Update Lock** — These locks function in the same way as Intent Shared locks to prevent more exclusive locks from being granted higher in the resource hierarchy. Intent Update locks are compatible with all locks except Update and Exclusive.
IX	**Intent Exclusive Lock** — These locks work the same as the other two Intent locks. Intent Exclusive locks are only compatible with other Intent Exclusive locks.
SIU	**Shared Intent Update** — The SIU lock mode is a combination of the Shared and Intent Update locks. It is compatible with all other locks except Exclusive, Intent Exclusive, Shared with Intent Exclusive, and Update with Intent Exclusive.
SIX	**Shared with Intent Exclusive** — The SIX lock mode is less restrictive than the IX lock mode and allows for compatible shared locks higher in the resource hierarchy.
UIX	**Update with Intent Exclusive** — The UIX lock mode is a combination of the Update and Intent Exclusive locks. It is only compatible with Intent Shared locks.
BU	**Bulk Update** — Bulk Update locks are issued to bulk load table operation processes when the TABLOCK hint is used or when the Table Lock On Bulk Load table option is set. Bulk Update locks are incompatible with all locks except other Bulk Update locks.

KILL

Although not a stored procedure, the KILL command enables the database administrator to kill an offending process just like the "Kill Process" button on the Process Property dialog shown in Figure 10-4. The syntax for the KILL command is as follows:

```
KILL spid
```

The KILL command is very useful, but it should be used with great caution. Although it is sometimes necessary to kill a stalled process, it is very important to gather as much information as possible about that process before killing it. For example, killing a transaction that has updated a thousand rows will result in a thousand row rollbacks, resulting in some undesired consequences such as a full transaction log or lost data.

Try It Out   System Stored Procedures

Take a look at what information is returned by the System Stored Procedures and how you can use them to isolate troublesome processes.

1.   Open a Query window. Type and execute the following code:

```
USE AdventureWorks2008;
GO
BEGIN TRAN
UPDATE Person.Person
SET LastName = 'Gates'
WHERE BusinessEntityID = 1;
```

2.   Open a second Query window. Type and execute the following code:

```
USE AdventureWorks2008;
GO
SELECT * FROM Person.Person
WHERE BusinessEntityID = 1;
```

You will not see any results returned when executing this statement. It will not complete until the first query releases its locks.

3.   Open a third Query window and run the sp_who System Stored Procedure by executing the following command:

```
EXEC sp_who;
```

Notice that one of the processes shows that it is being blocked by another session. In the case shown in Figure 10-6, SPID 59 is being blocked by SPID 60.

4.   Execute the sp_who2 stored procedure, but restrict the result set to the Server Process ID (SPID) that is responsible for the block in progress. In my case, the spid is 60.

```
EXEC sp_who2 60;
```

	spid	ecid	status	loginame	hostname	blk	dbname	cmd	request_id
22	22	0	background	sa		0	NULL	UNKNOWN TOKEN	0
23	23	0	background	sa		0	master	BRKR TASK	0
24	24	0	sleeping	sa		0	master	TASK MANAGER	0
25	25	0	sleeping	sa		0	master	TASK MANAGER	0
26	27	0	sleeping	sa		0	master	TASK MANAGER	0
27	28	0	sleeping	sa		0	master	TASK MANAGER	0
28	29	0	background	sa		0	master	FT GATHERER	0
29	30	0	sleeping	sa		0	master	TASK MANAGER	0
30	31	0	background	sa		0	master	FT GATHERER	0
31	51	0	sleeping	AUGHTEIGHT\SQLService	AUGHTEIGHT	0	msdb	AWAITING COMMAND	0
32	52	0	sleeping	AUGHTEIGHT\Administrator	AUGHTEIGHT	0	master	AWAITING COMMAND	0
33	53	0	sleeping	AUGHTEIGHT\Administrator	AUGHTEIGHT	0	master	AWAITING COMMAND	0
34	54	0	sleeping	BrianR	AUGHTEIGHT	0	master	AWAITING COMMAND	0
35	55	0	sleeping	AUGHTEIGHT\Administrator	AUGHTEIGHT	0	tempdb	AWAITING COMMAND	0
36	56	0	sleeping	ThierryB	AUGHTEIGHT	0	master	AWAITING COMMAND	0
37	57	0	sleeping	BrianR	AUGHTEIGHT	0	AdventureWorks2008	AWAITING COMMAND	0
38	58	0	sleeping	AUGHTEIGHT\RSService	AUGHTEIGHT	0	ReportServer	AWAITING COMMAND	0
39	59	0	suspended	ThierryB	AUGHTEIGHT	60	AdventureWorks2008	SELECT	0
40	60	0	sleeping	AUGHTEIGHT\Administrator	AUGHTEIGHT	0	AdventureWorks2008	AWAITING COMMAND	0
41	62	0	runnable	AUGHTEIGHT\Administrator	AUGHTEIGHT	0	AdventureWorks2008	SELECT	0
42	63	0	sleeping	AUGHTEIGHT\SQLService	AUGHTEIGHT	0	msdb	AWAITING COMMAND	0

Figure 10-6: Result of running `sp_who` System Stored Procedure.

The more comprehensive results of the `sp_who2` stored procedure execution return very useful information (such as the program and user responsible, as well as when the session executed the command responsible for the lock contention).

5. Identify what object is being contested by the two processes. Execute the `sp_lock` stored procedure. The results of this procedure, like the `sp_who` and `sp_who2` stored procedures, can be restricted by passing in the appropriate process ID.

6. Type and execute the following command to display the information about the SPID being blocked. This is the SPID that returned a value in the BlkBy column of the `sp_who2` results. For me, it was 59, but remember that your SPID will most likely be different:

```
EXEC sp_lock 59;
```

The results are shown in Figure 10-7.

	spid	dbid	ObjId	IndId	Type	Resource	Mode	Status
1	59	7	0	0	DB		S	GRANT
2	59	7	1509580416	0	TAB		IS	GRANT
3	59	7	0	0	MD	14(10000:0:0)	Sch-S	GRANT
4	59	7	1509580416	1	PAG	1:4320	IS	GRANT
5	59	7	0	0	MD	14(10001:0:0)	Sch-S	GRANT
6	59	7	1509580416	1	KEY	(010086470766)	S	WAIT

Figure 10-7: `sp_lock` results.

In Figure 10-7, notice that several locks have been requested and granted, but the shared lock on the clustered index key 010086470766 (which represents the contact in the Person.Person table with the

BusinessEntityID of 1) is in a WAIT status. This is because spid 60 is currently modifying that particular row and has an exclusive lock on that key.

To terminate the blocking process, execute the KILL command specifying the appropriate SPID, which, for me, is 60:

```
KILL 60;
```

Use caution when killing a process. SPID 60 is the process on my computer. Your results may vary!

Using Profiler

Chapter 3 described the basic features of Profiler. This section shows you how to gather performance information to isolate and correct database application problems. The guidelines for the traces provided can be combined into a comprehensive trace or run individually.

Another important consideration for using Profiler is overhead. Running Profiler interactively can create a great deal of server overhead and create a large uncertainty factor. Profiler is just a graphical interface for viewing the results of a SQL trace. It is an excellent tool, but for large databases with a heavy transaction load, you will probably want to use the sp_trace_setevent, sp_trace_setfilter, sp_trace_setstatus, and sp_trace_create stored procedures to create, configure, and run traces with the trace data collected in files. The data can then be viewed using Profiler straight from the collected files, or you can import the data into a database for analysis.

Try It Out   Analyzing Deadlocks with Profiler

As mentioned earlier, detecting deadlocks is easy using Performance Monitor. Finding out why deadlocks are happening is more difficult and requires the running of traces and examining the data collected with Profiler.

1. Open SQL Server Management Studio, and connect to a server that hosts the AdventureWorks2008 database. After connecting, launch SQL Server Profiler from the Tools menu, and create a new trace based on the Blank template, as shown in Figure 10-8.

2. On the Events Selection tab, select the Lock events Deadlock graph and Lock:Deadlock Chain, as shown in Figure 10-9. Notice that when Deadlock graph is selected, the Events Extraction Settings tab appears.

3. To limit the data returned to Profiler, click on the "Column Filters" button, and then select Database Name. In the "Not Like" box, enter **MSDB** to prevent SQL Agent and scheduled monitoring activity from being traced. Click OK.

Figure 10-10 shows the desired configuration. Be careful when filtering databases. It may seem like the best filter would be one that specifies only a particular database by creating the filter where the database ID or database name is like a specific value. However, there are many Profiler events that do not have a specific database context, and these will not display if you set the filter this way. Instead, you must tell Profiler what databases you don't want to monitor. The deadlock graph is one such event.

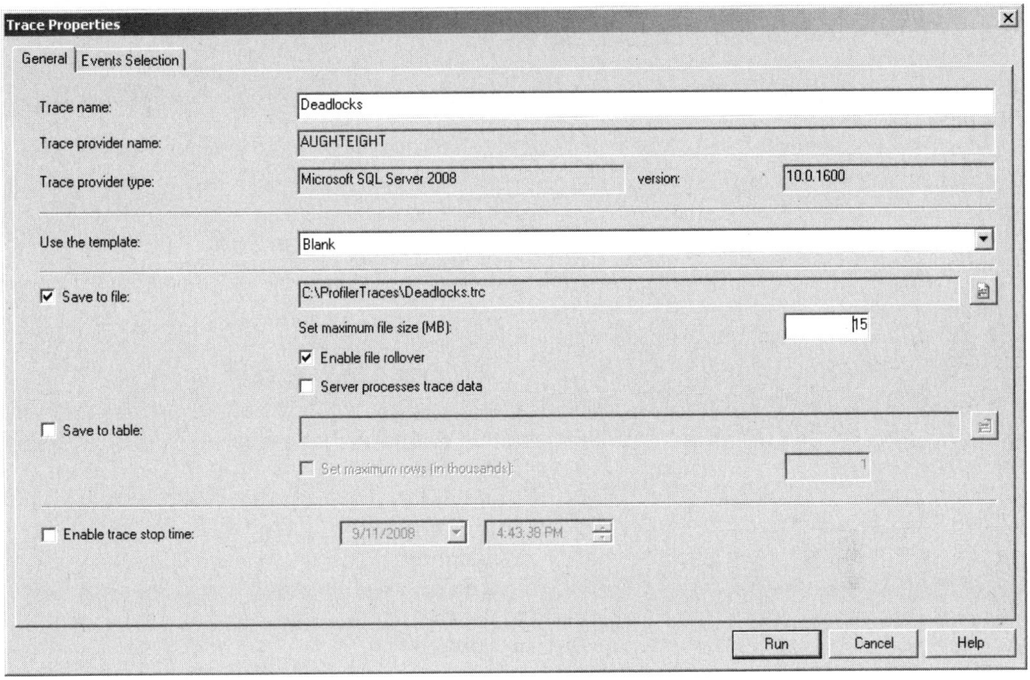

Figure 10-8: Creating a new trace based on the Blank template.

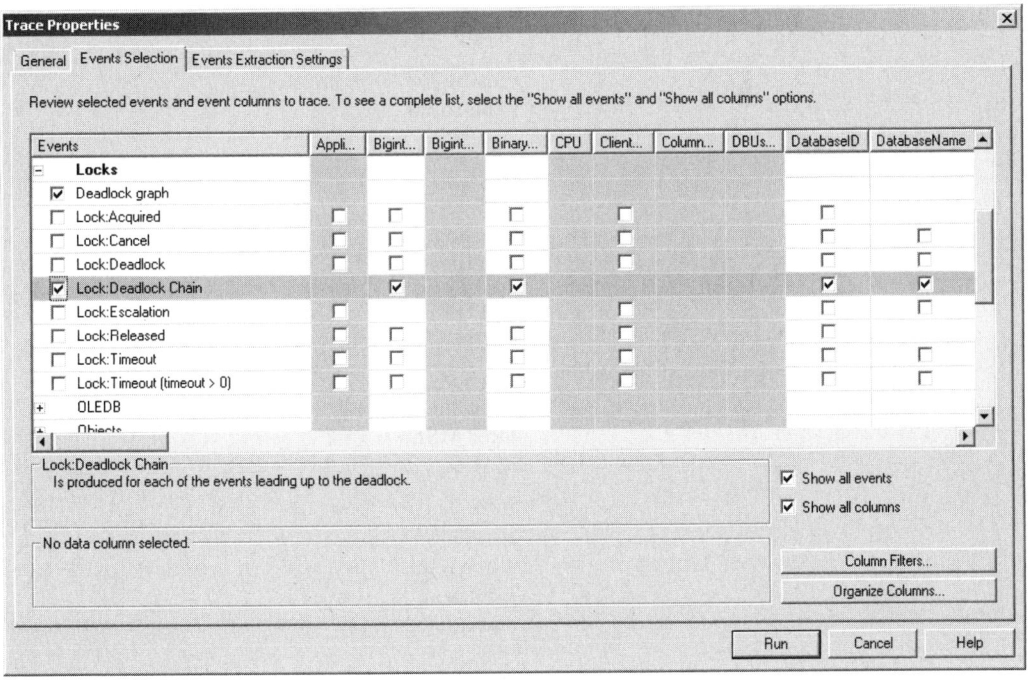

Figure 10-9: Selecting Deadlock graph **and** Lock:Deadlock Chain.

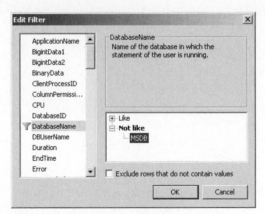

Figure 10-10: Desired configuration.

4. In the Event Extraction Settings tab, check the "Save Deadlock XML events separately" check-box, and enter a destination to save the files (see Figure 10-11). Select the option to save "Each Deadlock XML batch in a distinct file," and click Run.

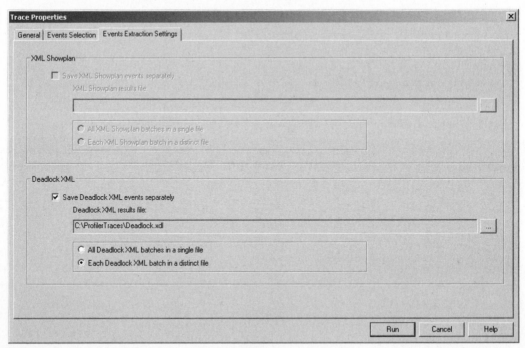

Figure 10-11: Entering a destination to save the files.

5. In SQL Server Management Studio, open two new Query windows.

6. In the first Query window (which is probably called *SQLQuery1.sql*), type the following code and execute it:

```
--Connection 1
USE AdventureWorks2008;
GO

BEGIN TRAN

UPDATE Person.Address
SET City = 'Redmond'
WHERE AddressID = 1;
```

7. In the second Query window, type the following code and execute it:

```
--Connection 2
USE AdventureWorks2008;
GO
BEGIN TRAN
UPDATE Person.Person
SET LastName = 'Gates'
WHERE BusinessEntityID = 1;

UPDATE Person.Address
SET AddressLine1 = '1 Microsoft Way'
WHERE AddressID = 1;
```

This update will not complete because the transaction in Connection 1 has an exclusive lock on the row being updated in the Person.Person table. What is occurring at this point is a blocking lock. The transaction in Connection 2 wants to update the row that is being locked by Connection 1. Blocking locks are allowed and will continue indefinitely unless a lock time-out has been set, the blocking transaction completes, or an administrator terminates the blocking transaction.

8. On the first connection, write and execute the following code to update the Person.Person table:

```
--Connection 1
UPDATE Person.Person
SET FirstName = 'Bill'
WHERE BusinessEntityID = 1;
```

This update causes a deadlock to occur because both connections hold exclusive locks on resources that the opposing transaction requires to complete. The deadlock is detected and one of the deadlocked processes is killed (the deadlock victim). The remaining process will then succeed.

9. Return to Profiler, stop the trace, and select the Deadlock graph event class row. The deadlock graph shows the server process IDs and locked resources that were deadlocked. Hovering the mouse over one of the processes will expose the process that participated in the deadlock, as shown in Figure 10-12.

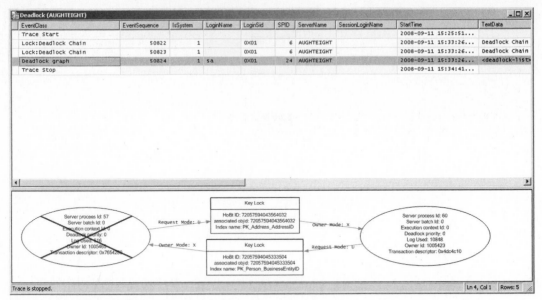

Figure 10-12: Exposing the process that participated in the deadlock.

To restore the Person.Person table to its original state, be sure to execute a ROLLBACK state-ment on the transaction not killed by the deadlock.

10. To capture the script that was used to run this trace, click on the File menu within SQL Profiler, and select the Export ➤ Script Trace Definition ➤ For SQL Server 2005–2008 (see Figure 10-13). A "Save as" dialog will be displayed. Save the script as *DeadLockTrace.SQL*.

11. Open the DeadLockTrace.SQL file that you just saved with SQL Server Management Studio. This is the script that SQL Server ran to create the trace you just practiced. By saving this script, it can be run at any time without having to launch and run Profiler. For more information about each of the stored procedures, consult SQL Server Books Online, which contains a very thorough description of each procedure.

Once the trace file is captured, it can either be opened with SQL Profiler or, in the case of larger traces, it can be inserted into a table for analysis with conventional T-SQL queries. To move the data into a table, the fn_trace_gettable table-valued function can be used. This table-valued function requires two values: the name of the trace file to be imported and the maximum number of rollover files to collect. The default for the number of files is the maximum number of files set with the trace. The following example shows how the trace collected earlier can be added to a table called DeadLockTraceTable in the AdventureWorks2008 database:

```
USE AdventureWorks2008;
GO
SELECT * INTO DeadLockTraceTable
FROM fn_trace_gettable(C:\ProfilerTraces\DeadLocks.trc', NULL);
```

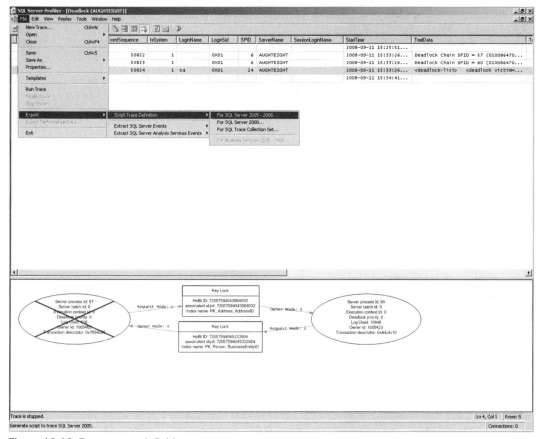

Figure 10-13: Export trace definition.

Detect and Analyze Long-Running Queries with Profiler

Profiler is a great tool for analyzing locks, as well as debugging stored procedures and database applications. It is also very useful in the identification and analysis of long-running queries that interfere with the performance of SQL Server. Profiler can return query execution information that can be examined by the database administrator to isolate the cause of the lengthy query. Is it poorly written? Are there no indexes to support the query, or is it just a monster query?

Try It Out **Analyzing Queries**

To analyze queries, follow these steps:

1. Start Profiler and create a new trace called `QueryTuning` using the Blank template. Select the following events on the Events Selection tab:

   ❑ Performance: `Showplan XML`

❑   Stored Procedures: `SP:Completed`

❑   TSQL: `SQL:BatchCompleted`

2.   Click on the "Column Filters" button, create a filter in which the database name is like `AdventureWorks2008`, and click OK to apply the filter.

3.   Click on the "Organize Columns" button. Find the Duration column and move it up to the top of the column list to make it easy to read duration data.

4.   On the Events Extraction Settings tab, select the "Save XML Showplan events separately" check-box. Choose a destination to save the ShowPlan information, title the file **QueryTuning**, and then choose the option to save each XML ShowPlan in a separate file. *SQLPlan* is the file extension given to ShowPlan data. The ShowPlan data is stored as XML and can be viewed with Management Studio, as you will see later. When saving query plans in separate files, each file is given the name of the file defined in the destination, along with a numerical identifier appended to the end of the name.

5.   Click Run to start the trace.

6.   Next, open a new Query window in SQL Server Management Studio. Type and execute the following code:

```
USE AdventureWorks2008;
GO
SELECT P.ProductID, P.name AS Product, TH.TransactionDate,
       SUM(TH.Quantity), SUM(TH.ActualCost), SUM(P.StandardCost)
FROM Production.Product P
INNER JOIN Production.TransactionHistory TH
ON P.ProductID = TH.ProductID
GROUP BY P.ProductID, P.Name, TH.TransactionDate;
GO
EXEC dbo.uspGetManagerEmployees 109;
GO
EXEC dbo.uspGetEmployeeManagers 1;
GO
SELECT P.name AS Product, SUM(SOD.OrderQty) AS SumQty
    , SUM(SOD.UnitPrice) AS SumPrice, SUM(SOD.LineTotal) AS SumTotal
    , CONVERT(char(10), SOH.OrderDate,101) AS orderDate
    , CONVERT(char(10), SOH.ShipDate,101) AS ShipDate
    , CONVERT(char(10), SOH.DueDate,101) AS DueDate
FROM Sales.SalesOrderDetail SOD
INNER JOIN Sales.SalesOrderHeader SOH
ON SOH.SalesOrderID = SOD.SalesOrderID
INNER JOIN Production.Product P
ON P.ProductID = SOD.ProductID
GROUP BY P.Name, SOH.OrderDate, SOH.ShipDate, SOH.DueDate;
```

After the query completes, stop the trace and examine the results. Notice that the longest-running process is the last one that references the `Sales.SalesOrderHeader`, `Sales.SalesOrderdetail`, and `Production.Product` tables.

7.   Navigate to the ShowPlan destination folder and examine the contents. You should see four files named *QueryTuning_1.SQLPlan* through *QueryTuning_4.SQLPlan*.

8. Double-click on the QueryTuning_4.SQLPlan file. It will open with SQL Server Management Studio as a graphical execution plan, as shown in Figure 10-14.

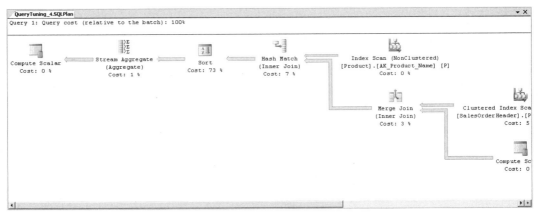

Figure 10-14: SQL Server Management Studio as a graphical execution plan.

The ShowPlan files are very useful in evaluating the actual process that the Database Engine uses to optimize queries and in identifying areas for improvement. The ShowPlans are read from right to left. Hovering the mouse over an icon will display additional information about the process depicted, often providing insight into how the process can be optimized. For example, if a process shows an unnecessary implied conversion, the data types can be more strictly passed to avoid the implied conversion.

> *The information represented in Figure 10-14 is actually saved as XML. This is of particular interest to organizations that want to consume the ShowPlan data with analysis applications such as the Database Tuning Advisor that are built to analyze query plans and identify areas for improvement. Change the name of the QueryTuning_4.SQLPlan to QueryTuning_4.XML. Right-click on the QueryTuning_4.XML file and choose "Open with ... Internet Explorer." The ShowPlan file displayed is rendered with Internet Explorer's built-in XML parser and is readily identified as an XML file.*

Monitoring Files

One of the more mundane (but imminently important) monitoring tasks for every database administrator is that of monitoring and managing file sizes. The default setting for both data files and log files is to grow automatically with no maximum size. This is probably not the most ideal configuration. Generally, during the database design and planning phase, a determination of database size is made. This determination should identify the starting size of the database files and the anticipated rate of growth of each file type. However, unexpected growth, especially with the log file, is very typical. This makes the monitoring of file sizes especially important. If a data file fills to capacity, no data modifications will be allowed. The same goes for the log files.

Disk Usage Report

There are several ways to monitor database file sizes. The Disk Usage report in SQL Server Management Studio (see Figure 10-15) is one. This report is very informative and can be used to find the tables that are consuming the most space, as well as index structures and files. The disadvantage of the Disk Usage report is that you have to run the report to get it.

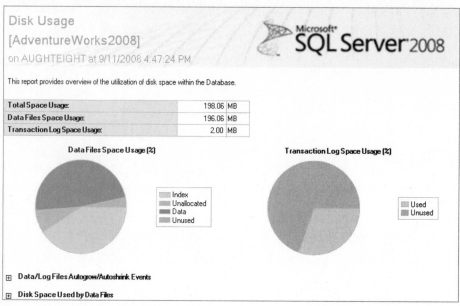

Figure 10-15: Disk Usage report.

sp_spaceused

The sp_spaceused stored procedure can also be used to return some of the same information as the Disk Usage report, but the sp_spaceused stored procedure will only return space information for the entire database if no object name parameter is passed with it or a single object. The following example shows how to run sp_spaceused to retrieve information from the AdventureWorks2008 database and a table in the AdventureWorks2008 database:

```
SET NOCOUNT ON;
USE AdventureWorks2008;
GO
SELECT 'AdventureWorks2008 Space Used Data'
EXEC sp_spaceused; --Return total database size and available disk space

SELECT 'Person.Person Space Used Data'
EXEC sp_spaceused 'Person.Person'; --Return allocation data for Person.Person
```

The results of this script are as follows (your results will look a little different, because I formatted the results to fit on the page):

```
-------------------------------
AdventureWorks2008 Space Used Data

database_name          database_size         unallocated space
-----------------      --------------        ------------------
```

```
AdventureWorks2008      198.06 MB          15.40 MB

reserved              data                index_size          unused
------------------    ------------------  ------------------  ------------------
185000 KB             96312 KB            82112 KB            6576 KB
```

```
------------------------------
Person.Person Space Used Data
```

name	rows	reserved	data	index_size	unused
Person	19972	83752 KB	30488 KB	52560 KB	704 KB

sys.sysfiles

The system view sys.sysfiles is another great way to retrieve information about files in the database, but the default data returned is not the most intuitive. For example, the size attribute is not a file size, but the number of 8-K data pages, and the maxsize attribute returns –1 if no maximum size is specified. To make the results more concise and readable, you can create a script like the one that follows:

```
SELECT Name, FileName
, CAST((Size * 8192 / 1048576) AS varchar(10)) + 'MB' AS FileSize
, MaxSize =
    CASE MaxSize
        WHEN -1 THEN 'Unlimited'
        ELSE CAST((Maxsize / 128) AS varchar(10)) + 'MB'
    END FROM sys.sysfiles;
```

The results of this query are simple and easy to understand (see Figure 10-16). They can also be consumed by an application and programmatic decisions made based on the results.

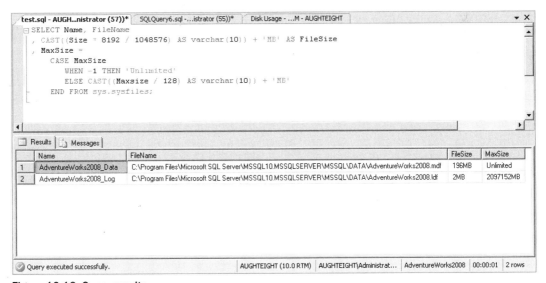

Figure 10-16: Query results.

Monitoring Files with Performance Monitor

Probably the most efficient way of keeping abreast of the amount of free space in data and log files is to use performance counters. The SQL Server:Databases performance object has several counters that can be used to monitor disk and log file sizes. You can use these counters to create alerts as described in Chapter 8. This way, SQL Server does the monitoring for you and sends you notifications when a data file has exceeded a preconfigured size or the transaction log has filled to a percentage greater than a certain value.

Auditing

At its root, *auditing* is simply the process of monitoring and tracking changes to a system. Increasingly, DBAs are required to implement auditing to satisfy application security and business requirements. Monitoring access to and changes to database data, in many cases, may be employed to satisfy industry mandatory compliance in terms of HIPAA, SOX, and other regulatory measures.

Auditing is one of those topics that is very simple conceptually, but traditionally has been very difficult in practice, often requiring custom solutions and extensive commitments of time and resources, with varying degrees of success. SQL Server 2008 aims to change that by making auditing a more integrated, standardized, and automated task, while at the same time increasing audit reliability and reducing the overall system overhead.

At the core of the new auditing capabilities, SQL Server 2008 introduces the SQL Server Extended Events engine. The Extended Events engine potentially allows any process to define and raise events, and consumers to receive events. Events are handled in a completely decoupled fashion, allowing a single event to be efficiently dispatched to multiple consumers while ensuring that events are never lost.

With the wide variety of auditing tools available in SQL Server, a database administrator is able to easily craft a comprehensive, customized auditing strategy to meet the needs of his particular organization. In this section, I will introduce the various auditing tools and processes and attempt to give you some insight on how you can use them effectively in your environment.

SQL Server Audit

SQL Server 2008 Enterprise Edition introduces a new automatic auditing option known as *SQL Server Audit*. An SQL Server Audit is made up of a number of different elements working together to track and log events that occur on the system. The elements are known as the *SQL Server Audit Package*, the *Server Audit Specification*, the *Database Audit Specification*, and the *Audit Destination* (also known as the *target*).

To understand the elements that make up an SQL Server Audit and how they interact, it is useful to compare it to a more well-known construct — a report. A *report* is the output generated by combining a report definition with a data source. Similarly, an *audit* is the output generated by combining an audit object with an audit specification.

> The term *audit* can be a bit confusing because the same word is used in many different contexts. SQL Server uses the term *audit* to describe the audit package, the auditing process itself, and the output of the auditing process! It is no wonder that the terminology can cause some confusion.

The basic process for creating a SQL Server Audit is as follows:

1. Create a SQL Server Audit Package and define a destination for the output.

2. Create a Server Audit Specification and/or one or more Database Audit Specifications that define the audit event criteria.

3. Enable the Audit Specification(s).

4. Enable the Audit.

5. View and analyze the captured audit events. Depending on the audit destination, results can be viewed using the Windows Event Viewer, the Log File Viewer in the SQL Server Management Console, or by using the `fn_get_audit_file` function.

Before actually creating an audit, I will go over each element in a little more detail. Then I will present an example that ties it all together.

Audit Package

An *Audit Package* defines an audit, acts as the event consumer for captured audit events, and directs the captured events to a target destination. Audit Packages can be managed from the Security ➤ Audits folder of a server instance.

In addition to the target, there are only two other settings that you can change:

❑ **Queue Delay** — This setting indicates the number of milliseconds to buffer events before forcing them to be processed. The default value is 1,000 (1 second). Setting this value to zero will force events to be processed immediately. Buffering helps to minimize the performance impact of the audit on the server, so in most cases I recommend leaving it at the default value.

❑ **Shut Down Server on Audit Log Failure** — When this flag is set, SQL Server will shut down if it is unable to write events to the target. Most commonly, this occurs when the disk volume where the logs are being written runs out of space. It is important to mention that if this flag is set and you run out of log space, you will not be able to restart the server until you free up additional space or start SQL Server using the *-f* flag to disable auditing.

An Audit Package can contain at most one server audit specification and one database audit specification for each database. If necessary, you can create multiple audits that each map to a different specification.

Audit Packages are always created in the disabled state. Enabling the Audit Package will allow it to send captured events to the target.

Server Audit Specification

A Server Audit Specification determines which server-level events should be included in the audit. Server Audit Specifications are defined at the SQL Server instance level, so there can only be one per audit. Server Audit Specifications are located in the Security ➤ Server Audit Specifications folder of each server instance.

The Server Audit Specification can include multiple server-level action groups, where each group is a pre-defined collection of related events. The specified events are included in the audit and saved to the destination. Most of the action groups have an equivalent security audit event category, as described later in this chapter.

The following table shows the available server-level-only action groups and briefly describes the events that are included:

Group	Description
SUCCESSFUL_LOGIN_GROUP	A principal (user or role) successfully logs in.
LOGOUT_GROUP	A principal logged out.
FAILED_LOGIN_GROUP	A principal failed to successfully log in.
LOGIN_CHANGE_PASSWORD_GROUP	The password is changed for any server login.
SERVER_ROLE_MEMBER_CHANGE_ GROUP	A login is added or removed from a fixed server role.
BACKUP_RESTORE_GROUP	A backup or restore command is issued.
SERVER_OPERATION_GROUP	Any security audit operations are performed, such as altering settings or resources.
SERVER_STATE_CHANGE_GROUP	The server service state is changed.
SERVER_OBJECT_CHANGE_GROUP	A CREATE, ALTER, or DROP command is used on a server object.
SERVER_PRINCIPAL_CHANGE_GROUP	A server principal is created, altered, or dropped.
SERVER_PRINCIPAL_IMPERSONATION_ GROUP	Impersonation is used in a server context, such as with Execute As <login>.
SERVER_PERMISSION_ CHANGE_GROUP	A GRANT, REVOKE, or DENY is issued for permissions at the server scope, such as creating a login.
SERVER_OBJECT_PERMISSION_ CHANGE_GROUP	A GRANT, REVOKE, or DENY is issued for server object permissions, such as when changing ownership.
BROKER_CONVERSATION_GROUP	An audit broker conversation is created.
BROKER_LOGON_GROUP	Audit messages related to Service Broker transport security are reported.
DATABASE_MIRRORING_ACTION_ GROUP	Audit messages related to database mirroring transport security are reported.
TRACE_CHANGE_GROUP	A trace is created, configured, or filtered.

In addition to the server-level-only action groups, you can also use any of the database action groups in a Server Audit Specification. When you use a database action group at the server level, it applies to all databases on the server. The database action groups are described in the next section.

Database Audit Specification

A Database Audit Specification works in the same way as a Server Audit Specification, but at the database level. An audit can include one Database Audit Specification for each database on the server. Database Audit Specifications can be managed from the Security ➤ Database Audit Specifications node of each database. A Database Audit Specification can include multiple database-level action groups or single audit events.

The following table shows the action groups that are available at the database level and briefly describes which events they represent:

Group	Description
APPLICATION_ROLE_CHANGE_PASSWORD_GROUP	An application role password is changed.
AUDIT_CHANGE_GROUP	An audit is created, modified, or deleted.
DATABASE_ROLE_MEMBER_CHANGE_GROUP	A login is added or removed from a database role.
DATABASE_OPERATION_GROUP	Specific database operations occur, such as checkpoint or subscribe query notification.
DATABASE_CHANGE_GROUP	A database is created, altered, or dropped.
DATABASE_OBJECT_CHANGE_GROUP	A CREATE, ALTER, or DROP statement is used on any object in the database, including schemas.
DATABASE_PRINCIPAL_CHANGE_GROUP	A user or role is created, modified, or dropped. Password changes are included in this group.
DBCC_GROUP	Any DBCC command is issued.
SCHEMA_OBJECT_CHANGE_GROUP	A schema is created, altered, or dropped.
DATABASE_PRINCIPAL_IMPERSONATION_GROUP	An impersonation event occurs in the database, such as Execute As <Principal> or SETPRINCIPAL.
DATABASE_OWNERSHIP_CHANGE_GROUP	The owner of a database is changed.
DATABASE_OBJECT_OWNERSHIP_CHANGE_GROUP	The owner is changed for any object in a database.
SCHEMA_OBJECT_OWNERSHIP_CHANGE_GROUP	When permission to change the owner of any object is checked.
DATABASE_PERMISSION_CHANGE_GROUP	Any database permission is changed, such as granting access to a database.
DATABASE_OBJECT_PERMISSION_CHANGE_GROUP	Permissions are changed for any object in a database, including schemas.

Continued

Group	Description
SCHEMA_OBJECT_PERMISSION_CHANGE_GROUP	When permission to change the permissions of any object is checked
DATABASE_OBJECT_ACCESS_GROUP	Any access to any database or database object, such as certificates or symmetric keys
SCHEMA_OBJECT_ACCESS_GROUP	Whenever an object permission is used in a schema

A powerful feature of the Database Audit Specification allows auditing of specific actions on specific objects, performed by a specific principal (user or role). The actions that can be audited are DELETE, EXECUTE, INSERT, RECEIVE, REFERENCES, SELECT, and UPDATE.

If you select a specific action in a Database Audit Specification, then you must also specify an object name *and* a principal name. You can use the "public" principal to include all users and roles, since everyone is automatically a member of "public." You will not be able to save a specification that includes an incomplete row.

Audit Destination

The audit destination (also known as the target of the audit) determines where the captured events will be written. The destination of the audit can be one of the following:

❑ **File** — Saves the audit to a file. In addition to the file path, you can specify the maximum number of rollover files, the maximum size of each file, and whether or not to reserve the necessary space. The security of this selection will depend on the file system permissions that are assigned to the file.

❑ **Security Log** — Writes the audited events to the Windows Security log. This is probably the best choice for a high-security environment, but before selecting this destination, you will likely need to modify a couple of system policies. Refer to the section below on targeting the security log for more information.

❑ **Application Log** — Sets the audit destination to the Windows Application log. Remember when choosing this destination that by default, the application log is readable by ordinary users. Some audit information might be sensitive in nature and not fit for general consumption. This choice may not be appropriate for a high-security environment.

Targeting the Security Log

In order to write events to the Security log, the SQL Server service account will need to be added to the "Generate Security Audits" policy, and the "Audit Object Access" security policy will need to be enabled for both success and failure. This can be accomplished either from the security policy snap-in (secpol.msc) or, in Windows Vista or Server 2008, by using the command-line audit policy program (auditpol.exe).

To enable targeting the security log using the security policy snap-in:

1. Open the security policy snap-in by entering **secpol.msc** in Start ➤ Run.

2. Expand "Local Policies," and then click on "User Rights Assignment."

3. Open the "Generate Security Audits" policy, and add the SQL Server service account to the local security setting.

4. Next, select "Audit Policy" from the left-hand pane.

5. Open the "Audit Object Access" policy, and check both success and failure on the Local Security setting tab.

6. Close the security policy snap-in.

By default, the Local System, Local Service, and Network Service are part of the Generate Security Audits policy. If you are running SQL Server under one of these accounts, then you will only need to configure the "Audit Object Access" policy.

Try It Out   Auditing Security Events

To audit security events, follow these steps:

1. Open SQL Server Management Studio, and connect to the server that hosts the AdventureWorks2008 database. Expand the Security node in Object Explorer, then right-click on the Audits folder and select New Audit. Create the new audit as shown in Figure 10-17.

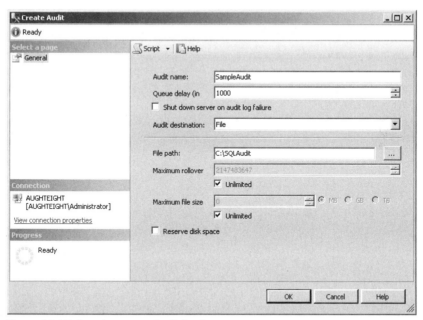

Figure 10-17: Creating a new Audit Package.

> If the file path does not exist, you will receive an error when you click OK on the Create Audit dialog. If necessary, you can leave the dialog open, use Explorer to create the desired folder, and then complete the dialog.

2.   Right-click on the Server Audit Specifications folder, and select New Server Audit Specification. In the Audit box, select the audit that you created above, and then add the following action groups:

❑   SERVER_PRINCIPAL_CHANGE_GROUP

❑   SERVER_PRINCIPAL_IMPERSONATION_GROUP

❑   LOGIN_CHANGE_PASSWORD_GROUP

3.   Save the Audit Specification, and then right-click on it and select "Enable Server Audit Specification." The icon on the Audit Specification should change to show that it is enabled.

4.   Expand the AdventureWorks2008 database, and create a new Database Audit Specification from the Security ➤ Database Audit Specifications folder. Map this specification to the Audit Package created above, and then add the following action groups as shown in Figure 10-18:

❑   SELECT: Object Class "Schema", Object Name "Person", Principal Name "public"

❑   DATABASE_OBJECT_PERMISSION_CHANGE_GROUP

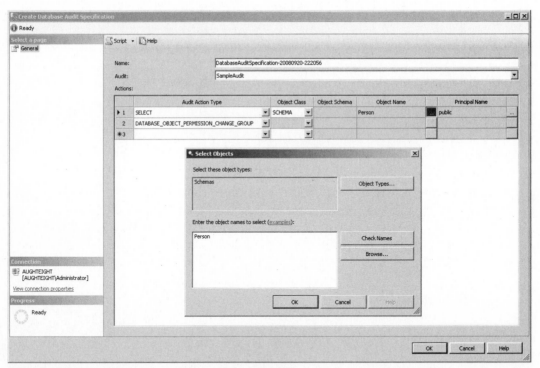

Figure 10-18: Creating a new Database Audit Specification.

5.   Save and enable the Audit Specification. The icon for the Database Audit Specification should change to show that it is enabled.

6. Now enable the audit itself to begin receiving the included events. Once the audit is enabled, type the following into a new Query window and execute it:

```
-- Create a new server login
EXEC sp_addlogin 'Paul', 'Microsoft123', 'AdventureWorks2008';
GO

-- Exclude this login from OS policy constraints
ALTER LOGIN Paul WITH CHECK_POLICY = OFF
GO

-- change password
EXEC sp_password @old = 'Microsoft123', @new = 'Microsoft456', @loginame =
'Paul'
GO

-- Allow this user to access AdventureWorks2008
USE AdventureWorks2008
GO
CREATE USER Paul FOR LOGIN Paul
GO

-- Try to select as Paul, no permissions yet!
EXECUTE AS LOGIN='Paul'
SELECT * FROM Person.Person WHERE BusinessEntityID=1;
REVERT
GO

-- Assign permissions
GRANT SELECT ON Person.Person TO Paul;
GO

-- Now the select should succeed
EXECUTE AS LOGIN='Paul'
SELECT * FROM Person.Person WHERE BusinessEntityID=1;
REVERT
GO

-- Clean up
DROP USER Paul
GO
EXEC sp_droplogin 'Paul';
GO
```

Notice when you run the script that both a result set and an exception are displayed. This is expected and is intended to highlight the ability of an audit to detect both successful and failed access attempts. The exception was generated when user Paul attempted to read data from the Person.Person table before permission was granted.

7. Finally, disable the audit and then right-click on the audit and select "View Audit Logs" to display the results in the Log File Viewer. Your results should look similar to Figure 10-19.

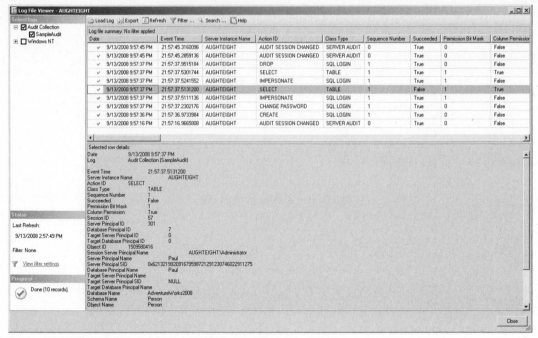

Figure 10-19: Viewing audit results using Log File Viewer.

Notice in the audit result that all the targeted events were captured; including the failed SELECT attempt.

You can also view audit results as a table by using the new `fn_get_audit_file` function. If you would like to try this, execute the following code in a new Query window:

```
SELECT * FROM
fn_get_audit_file('C:\SQLAudit\*',default,default)
```

Login Auditing

The most fundamental auditing to manage and implement is Login Auditing. Login Auditing simply records successful login attempts, failed login attempts, or both. Support for auditing logins is built into SQL Server and can be enabled with the SQL Server Management Console from the security page of the Server Properties dialog, as shown in Figure 10-20. After changing the login auditing level, you must restart the server instance before the new setting will take effect.

Login success and failure events are written to the Windows Application Log as well as to the SQL Server Log. Exactly the same information is written to both logs with one key exception. The SQL Server Log receives an extra entry for a failed login that includes a special *State* code that describes in more detail what caused the login failure. The most common state code values are listed in the following table:

Error State	Error Description
2 or 5	Invalid user ID
6	Attempt to use a Windows login name with SQL authentication
7	Login disabled and password mismatch
8	Password mismatch
9	Invalid password
11 or 12	Login is valid, but user does not have any access to the server.
13	SQL Server service paused.
16	Login failed while trying to connect to the specified target database.
18	Password change is required.
23	Server is in the process of shutting down.
27	Unable to determine the initial database

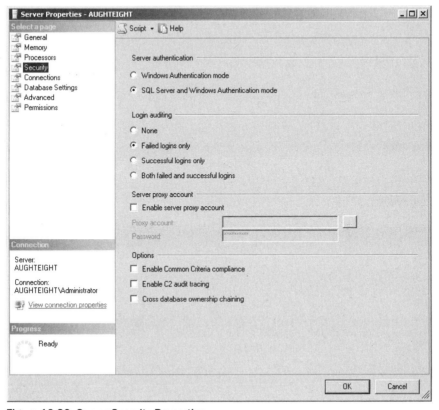

Figure 10-20: Server Security Properties.

C2 Audit Mode

C2 Audit Mode is a set of ratings originally established by the U.S. Department of Defense that applies to levels of security in a computer system, based on their auditing and access control capabilities. SQL Server has been C2-compliant since version 2000. This mode of operation may be required for government agencies and contractors.

C2 auditing goes beyond simple server events, such as login and logout, extending to include successful and failed attempts to access all statements and objects. This can be of benefit when you are attempting to identify possible security violations, but as you can imagine, it can also consume a massive amount of storage as well as negatively affect performance. In a high-volume environment, the C2 logs will probably be much larger than the database itself!

If you are using C2 Audit Mode and your server runs out of physical storage space for the log files, then SQL Server will shut itself down to preserve the integrity of the audit. If this happens, you will not be able to restart SQL Server until you either free up additional space or you disable auditing by using the *-f* flag when starting the server instance.

To enable C2 Audit Mode, right-click on a server instance in SSMS Object Explorer, select Properties, select the Security page, and check the "Enable C2 audit tracing" setting. To disable C2 Audit Mode, clear the "Enable C2 audit tracing" checkbox. After changing this setting, you must restart your server instance before it will take effect.

You can also enable or disable C2 Audit tracing using transact-SQL as follows:

```
-- Enable c2 audit mode
sp_configure 'show advanced options', 1
GO
RECONFIGURE
GO
sp_configure 'c2 audit mode', 1
GO
RECONFIGURE
GO

-- Disable c2 audit mode
sp_configure 'show advanced options', 1
GO
RECONFIGURE
GO
sp_configure 'c2 audit mode', 0
GO
RECONFIGURE
GO
```

As with the SMSS method, after changing the C2 Audit Mode setting, you must restart your server instance before the change will take effect.

The C2 Audit log trace files are always stored in the server instance data directory. You can read these files either by using SQL Server Profiler or with the sys.fn_trace_gettable system function.

Security Audit Event Category

If you like SQL Profiler as much as I do, you will be pleased to discover that you can use this ubiquitous tool to monitor a wide variety of security audit events, such as successful and failed login attempts, new users, and password changes. These events can all be found in the Security Audit section when selecting the events to include in your trace.

The Security Audit Events allow you to selectively monitor much of the same information as a full C2 Audit, but when using SQL Profiler, you get to pick and choose exactly what you want to monitor and only incur the overhead of monitoring when it is needed.

Try It Out   Auditing Security Events with SQL Server Profiler

To audit security events with SQL Server Profiler, follow these steps:

1. Start SQL Server Profiler, and create a new trace called `SecurityAudit` using the Blank template. Select the following events in the Security Audit section of the Events Selection tab:

  ❏ Audit Add DB User Event.

  ❏ Audit Add Member to DB Role Event.

  ❏ Audit Login Change Password Event.

  ❏ Audit Server Principal Management Event.

2. Click the "Organize Columns" button. Find the `EventSubClass`, `TargetLoginName`, `TargetUserName`, `RoleName`, and `ObjectName` columns, and move them to the top of the column list just after the `EventClass` column to make it easier to read the results.

3. Click Run to start the trace.

4. Open a new Query window in SQL Server Management Studio. Type and execute the following code:

```
-- Create a new server login
EXEC sp_addlogin 'Paul', 'Microsoft123', 'AdventureWorks2008';
GO

-- Exclude this login from OS policy constraints
ALTER LOGIN Paul WITH CHECK_POLICY = OFF
GO

-- change password
EXEC sp_password @old = 'Microsoft123', @new = 'Microsoft456', @loginame = 'Paul'
GO

-- Allow this user to access AdventureWorks2008
USE AdventureWorks2008
GO
CREATE USER Paul FOR LOGIN Paul
GO
EXEC sp_addrolemember N'db_owner', 'Paul'
```

```
GO

-- Clean up
DROP USER Paul
GO
EXEC sp_droplogin 'Paul';
GO
```

After the query completes, stop the trace and examine the results. Notice that each selected security related event is recorded. Your output should look something like Figure 10-21.

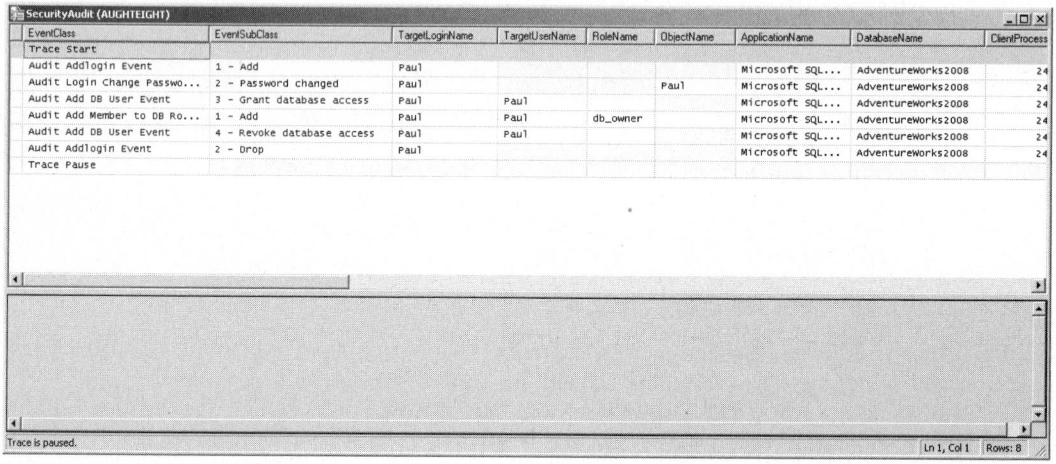

Figure 10-21: Security Audit Trace.

As always, if you save the trace files, you can consume the trace data in a table in SQL Server by using the `sys.fn_trace_gettable` system function.

SQL Trace

SQL Trace provides an alternative to using SQL Server Profiler to capture events. With SQL Trace, you use System Stored Procedures to define traces in T-SQL. This is especially useful for organizations that want to develop their own customized audit solutions.

The basic process for setting up a SQL Trace is as follows:

1. Create a trace with `sp_trace_create`.
2. Add the events that you want to include using `sp_trace_setevent`. When adding events, you must execute the stored procedure once for every event and column combination that you want included in your trace. A complete list of events and column ID numbers is available from SQL Server Books Online.
3. If desired, use `sp_trace_setfilter` to define a filter for captured events.

Once a trace has been created, you can use the `sp_trace_setstatus` stored procedure to start, stop, and close the trace.

The following code will create and start a trace that is equivalent to the SQL Server Profiler example included in the "Security Audit Event Category" section. The trace will continue to run until it is stopped with the `sp_trace_setstatus` stored procedure or until the server instance is restarted.

```
-- Create a new trace
Declare @id int
exec sp_trace_create @id output, 0, N'C:\ProfilerTraces\SecurityAudit'
select @id 'traceid'  -- Display the trace id

-- Add some events
Declare @On bit
SET @On=1
-- Event 109 = Audit Add DB User Event
exec sp_trace_setevent @id, 109, 21, @On  -- EventSubClass
exec sp_trace_setevent @id, 109, 42, @On  -- TargetLoginName
exec sp_trace_setevent @id, 109, 39, @On  -- TargetUserName
exec sp_trace_setevent @id, 109, 38, @On  -- RoleName
exec sp_trace_setevent @id, 109, 34, @On  -- ObjectName
-- Event 104 = Audit Add Login Event
exec sp_trace_setevent @id, 104, 21, @On  -- EventSubClass
exec sp_trace_setevent @id, 104, 42, @On  -- TargetLoginName
exec sp_trace_setevent @id, 104, 39, @On  -- TargetUserName
exec sp_trace_setevent @id, 104, 38, @On  -- RoleName
exec sp_trace_setevent @id, 104, 34, @On  -- ObjectName
-- Event 110 = Audit Add Member to DB Role Event
exec sp_trace_setevent @id, 110, 21, @On  -- EventSubClass
exec sp_trace_setevent @id, 110, 42, @On  -- TargetLoginName
exec sp_trace_setevent @id, 110, 39, @On  -- TargetUserName
exec sp_trace_setevent @id, 110, 38, @On  -- RoleName
exec sp_trace_setevent @id, 110, 34, @On  -- ObjectName
-- Event 107 = Audit Login Change Password Event
exec sp_trace_setevent @id, 107, 21, @On  -- EventSubClass
exec sp_trace_setevent @id, 107, 42, @On  -- TargetLoginName
exec sp_trace_setevent @id, 107, 39, @On  -- TargetUserName
exec sp_trace_setevent @id, 107, 38, @On  -- RoleName
exec sp_trace_setevent @id, 107, 34, @On  -- ObjectName

-- Start the trace
exec sp_trace_setstatus @traceid=@id, @status=1  -- Starts the trace
GO
```

The following code will stop and close the trace. Make sure to substitute the trace ID that was returned when you started the trace.

```
-- Stop and close the trace
Declare @id int
SET @id=3   -- enter the value recorded above

exec sp_trace_setstatus @traceid=@id, @status=0  -- Stops the trace
exec sp_trace_setstatus @traceid=@id, @status=2  -- Closes the trace
GO
```

Tracking Changes

Tracking changes to table data has long been a challenge for database administrators. This task has typically required a complex combination of triggers, custom tables, timestamps, and stored procedures; even then, success was still difficult.

SQL Server 2008 introduces not one, but two, different methods of tracking changes! The first method is Change Data Capture, which is a full-featured, highly customizable change and data tracking solution. The second method is its lightweight cousin, Change Tracking, which leaves out the ability to track the data. Both methods of tracking changes are able to track DML changes (such as inserts, updates, and deletes) and DDL changes (such as new columns) at the column level.

One of the key difficulties with custom Change Tracking solutions is how to determine what has changed after a given point in time. This is more complex than it first appears. Timestamps can partially solve the problem, but they are "stamped" at the beginning of a transaction, not when it is committed. In addition, timestamps only apply to a single table, whereas what is really required is a database-global metric that can be used.

Change Data Capture and Change Tracking both solve this problem by using log sequence numbers (LSNs). LSNs are assigned when a change is committed, and they are globally ordered so they can be used as a single-value baseline for an entire database. With Change Tracking, this process is abstracted by another level, and you are presented with an integer value that represents the database change level.

In my opinion, these are some of the best new features of SQL Server 2008.

Change Data Capture

Another of the many new features of SQL Server 2008 is Change Data Capture (or CDC). CDC is an innovative new approach to an old problem, specifically, "How can you efficiently record all changes to data in a table?" Prior to CDC, the most common answer was "Use triggers in a custom developed solution," which is not really the answer that most DBAs want to hear. Now this process has been standardized, and while it is still not without some issues and limitations, CDC goes a long way in the right direction.

Change Data Capture works by processing the SQL Transaction Log at scheduled intervals looking for all INSERT, UPDATE, DELETE, and Data Definition Language (DDL) changes that occur on tables for which CDC has been enabled. Figure 10-22 gives you the 10,000-foot view of CDC.

Information about what changed and when the change occurred is saved in change tables that are created when CDC is enabled. The data in these tables is designed to be easily consumed by other applications.

A classic example of where this would be useful is in maintaining a data warehouse. The old approach usually involved either periodically rebuilding the entire warehouse, or trying to develop a custom solution using timestamps to discover recent changes. Of course, timestamps won't do any good if the record has been deleted, so a method of saving "tombstones" (deleted records) would have to be devised as well. Ouch! With CDC all the legwork is done for you, and you can focus on processing the changed information rather than wasting time just trying to find out what changed.

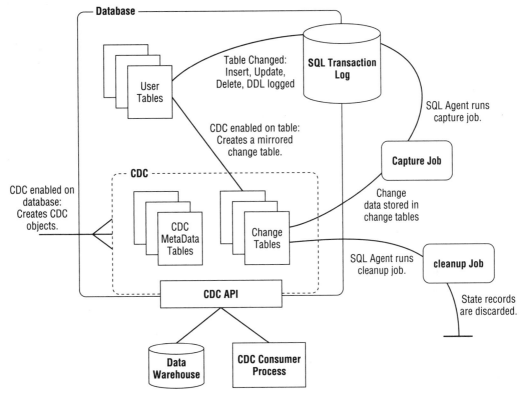

Figure 10-22: Visualizing Change Data Capture.

As mentioned previously, CDC uses log sequence numbers (LSNs) to determine the sequence in which changes occurred to a table. Functionally this is superior to using timestamps; however, humans are generally more comfortable working with time than with sequence numbers, so to support the humans, CDC keeps a cross-reference between LSN values and the associated time value. To make it a bit easier, functions are provided that will translate between the two values as needed.

At present, there is no built-in user interface to configure this powerful feature; however, some third-party configuration utilities are already starting to appear. In this section, I will show you how to use the CDC stored procedures and functions to configure, query, and administer Change Data Capture, and I will discuss some of the limitations of the current implementation.

Configuration

Before you can use Change Data Capture, it must be configured. The configuration process is very straightforward:

1. Enable Change Data Capture on the database using the `sys.sp_cdc_enable_db` stored procedure.

2. Enable Change Data Capture for one or more tables in the database using the `sys.sp_cdc_enable_table` stored procedure.

Enabling Change Data Capture on a database creates all of the necessary metadata tables and supporting stored procedures, functions, and data management views. You must be a member of the sysadmin fixed server role in order to enable CDC on a database. The CDC process will exclusively use a schema named *cdc* and a database user named *cdc*. If a schema or a user already exists in the database with this name, then you will not be able to enable CDC until you rename or remove the conflicting object. The following example will enable Changed Data Capture for the AdventureWorks2008 database:

```
Use AdventureWorks2008
GO

-- Enable Change Data Capture
EXEC sys.sp_cdc_enable_db
GO
```

Once the database is CDC-enabled, you can enable CDC on specific tables using the sys.sp_cdc_enable_table stored procedure. In its basic form, you specify the source schema and source table name as shown in the example below:

```
Use AdventureWorks2008
GO

-- Enable Person.Person table for Change Data Capture
EXEC sys.sp_cdc_enable_table 'Person','Person', @role_name=NULL,
    @supports_net_changes = 1
GO
```

The role_name parameter is used to control access to the Change Table, while the supports_net_changes parameter creates an additional function that returns a consolidated list that combines all of the individual changes for a given key into a single result row. To support net changes, the table must have a primary or unique key. When you enable a table for Change Data Capture, CDC will create a corresponding Change Table that mirrors the source table schema with some extra metadata columns. In addition, two jobs are created — a Capture Job to process the SQL transaction log and a Cleanup Job to purge rows from the Change Tables that are older than the specified retention period. You need to make sure that SQL Server Agent Service is running to process these jobs. By default, all columns will be tracked that exist at the time the table was CDC-enabled, but if necessary, you can limit tracking to specific columns by using the advanced @captured_column_list parameter.

If you would like to get a list of databases and/or tables that are enabled for CDC, you can do so by using the is_cdc_enabled column in sys.databases, or the is_tracked_by_cdc column in sys.tables. The following sample code demonstrates how to query the system views for CDC-enabled objects:

```
-- Display the name of every database enabled for cdc
SELECT name FROM sys.databases WHERE is_cdc_enabled=1

-- Display the name of every table enabled for cdc in AdventureWorks2008
Use AdventureWorks2008
GO
SELECT name FROM sys.tables WHERE is_tracked_by_cdc=1
GO
```

To disable CDC on a table, use the `sys.sp_cdc_disable_table` stored procedure. When a table is disabled, the corresponding Change Table will be removed from the database. The following example shows how to disable Change Tracking on the `Person.Person` table:

```
USE AdventureWorks2008
GO
EXEC sys.sp_cdc_disable_table 'Person','Person','All'
GO
```

The final parameter in the example above represents the specific capture instance to disable. Use `'All'` *to disable all capture instances for the indicated schema and name.*

Finally, you can disable Change Tracking for an entire database using the `sys.sp_cdc_disable_db` stored procedure. When you disable CDC, all of the associated metadata tables, Change Tables, and management objects will be dropped from the database:

```
Use AdventureWorks2008
GO

-- Disable Change Data Capture
EXEC sys.sp_cdc_disable_db
GO
```

Using Change Data Capture

Once Change Data Capture is configured, then at some point you will probably want to query the Change Tables to learn if anything changed and, if so, what. There are two Table-Valued Functions (TVFs) for each Change Table that are used for this purpose:

❑   `cdc.fn_get_all_changes_<schema_table>` — Returns a complete list of changes for the specified Change Table. To use this function, you must specify a valid beginning and ending log sequence number. For updates, you can also optionally include the prior values.

❑   `cdc.fn_get_net_changes_<schema_table>` — This function returns a consolidated list of changes, with one output row representing the final version of each row that changed. As with the previous function, you must specify a valid LSN range. This is a great time-saver if all you need to do is synchronize a data warehouse with the latest values!

In order to properly use the Change Table TVFs, you will need some help to determine the appropriate log sequence numbers and column positions. As you might expect, there are several "helper" functions that you can use for this purpose (see the following table):

helper Function	Description
`sys.fn_cdc_is_bit_set`	Determines if changes occurred to data in a specific column. This function is typically used in conjunction with the `sys.fn_cdc_get_column_ordinal` function.
`sys.fn_cdc_get_column_ordinal`	Looks up the column ordinal associated with the specified column. This value is typically used to determine the "position" of the column for the `sys.fn_cdc_is_bit_set` function.

Continued

helper Function	Description
sys.fn_cdc_get_min_lsn	Returns the earliest valid log sequence number for a given capture table.
sys.fn_cdc_get_max_lsn	Returns the maximum valid log sequence number for any capture table.
sys.fn_increment_lsn	Returns the next valid log sequence number after a specified LSN.
sys.fn_decrement_lsn	Finds the prior log sequence number before a specified LSN.
sys.fn_cdc_map_time_to_lsn	Finds the nearest valid log sequence number for the specified tracking time. This function is very useful to translate time values into log sequence numbers for use with the Table-Valued Functions.
sys.fn_cdc_map_lsn_to_time	Returns the date and time associated with a specified log sequence number.

The following example will display all changes that have been captured for the Person.Person table, as well as indicate whether the change occurred to the LastName column:

```
USE AdventureWorks2008
GO
Declare @from_lsn binary(10)
Declare @to_lsn binary(10)
Declare @lastname_ordinal int

-- Get the available log sequence range
SET @from_lsn=sys.fn_cdc_get_min_lsn('Person_Person')
SET @to_lsn=sys.fn_cdc_get_max_lsn()

-- Get the ordinal value for the LastName column
SET @lastname_ordinal=sys.fn_cdc_get_column_ordinal('Person_Person','LastName')

-- Return the list of changes and whether or not the change
-- affected in the LastName column
SELECT sys.fn_cdc_is_bit_set(@lastname_ordinal, __$update_mask) 'LastNameChanged',
  * FROM cdc.fn_cdc_get_all_changes_Person_Person(@from_lsn, @to_lsn, 'all')
GO
```

For this example to function, you must first enable the Person.Person table for Change Data Tracking as described in the Configuration section.

> One word of caution: It is very important to set the parameters properly for the
> Change Table TVFs. If anything goes wrong, a very misleading error will be
> returned:
>
> ```
> Msg 313, Level 16, State 3, Line X
> An insufficient number of arguments were supplied for the procedure
>     or function ...
> ```
>
> If you receive this error, you probably did supply the right number of arguments,
> but one or more of the arguments were invalid or out of range. The reason that a
> seemingly incorrect error is returned is because at present it is not possible to raise
> an explicit error from within a TVF. Microsoft decided that rather than failing
> silently when the parameters were invalid, they would raise an error, even if it was
> misleading.

Job Control

As mentioned earlier, Change Data Capture uses a Capture Job and a Cleanup Job to keep the Change
Tables up to date and of a manageable size. These jobs are automatically created when the first table in
a database is enabled for Change Data Capture. You have no control over the default configuration of
these jobs; however, you can modify them after they are created by using the sys.sp_cdc_change_job
stored procedure.

*If you have enabled transactional replication on the database, then the Capture Job will be disabled, and
the Change Tables will be updated by the transactional replication process.*

You can use sys.sp_cdc_help_jobs to view the current job configurations. By default, the Capture Job is
enabled immediately and will scan the SQL transaction logs once every 5 minutes, processing a maximum
of 1,000 transactions per cycle. The Cleanup Job is automatically configured to run once per day at 2 a.m.
It will remove change records that are more than three days old, with a limit of 5,000 deletions per delete
statement.

Changes to job configurations will not take effect until the job is stopped and restarted. The
sys.sp_cdc_stop_job and sys.sp_cdc_start_job stored procedures provide a convenient way to
accomplish this.

The following example shows how to change the Cleanup Job to retain change data for 5 days:

```
USE AdventureWorks2008
GO

-- Change the Cleanup Job retention to 6000 minutes
-- 5 days * 24 hours/day * 60 minutes/hour = 6000 minutes
EXEC sys.sp_cdc_change_job @job_type='cleanup', @retention=6000
GO

-- Stop and restart the job
```

```
-- Note: The stop_job command will generate an error if the job is not
-- actually running.  This is fine and the error can be ignored.
EXEC sys.sp_cdc_stop_job 'cleanup'
GO
EXEC sys.sp_cdc_start_job 'cleanup'
GO

-- View the configuration to confirm that the change was made
EXEC sys.sp_cdc_help_jobs
GO
```

Related Dynamic Management Views

Several dynamic management views are provided to help administrators monitor the status of the Change Data Capture processes. These are described in the following list:

❑ sys.dm_cdc_log_scan_sessions — Displays details about each log scan session that has run since the server was last restarted.

❑ sys.dm_repl_traninfo — Displays information about each replicated transaction. This will only be relevant with regard to Change Data Capture if you are using CDC and replication together.

❑ sys.dm_cdc_errors — This view returns information about any errors that occurred in any of the last 32 sessions.

Limitations

Change Data Capture is a powerful and reasonably easy-to-use generalized solution to tracking content changes; however, its current incarnation does have some limitations and side-effects that you should be aware of.

❑ **Supported Editions** — First the bad news: CDC is only available in SQL Server 2008 Enterprise, Development, and Evaluation editions. Many of us would like to see this feature extended to other editions, but for now this is it.

❑ **Supported Data Types** — As of this writing, CDC does not support any of the new data types introduced with SQL Server 2008. You can still track changes on tables that contain these types of columns, but you will have to exclude them from the column list when enabling the table.

❑ **DDL Changes** — This is a mixed bag; some DDL changes will be reflected in the Change Tables, and some will not. The tracked column list is set when the table is enabled for CDC. Any columns added after the table was enabled will *not* be included in the Change Table, and any columns that are deleted from the source table will remain in the Change Table. On the other hand, changes to the data types of source columns will be mirrored in the Change Table. The data type change will fail if the new data type is not compatible with existing data in the associated Change Table. In this situation, you can either disable Change Tracking for the table, or you can manually update the Change Table to make sure that existing data can be successfully converted. Finally, you must be a member of the sysadmin, db_owner, or db_ddladmin security roles in order to make changes to the structure of any source tables that are enabled for CDC. This is true even if explicit rights are granted to a specific user on a table.

❑ **Mirroring** — Mirroring is fully supported in conjunction with Change Data Capture; however, you will need to manually create and enable the Capture and Cleanup Jobs in the mirror database after a failover.

❑ **Restoring the Database** — If a CDC-enabled database is restored to the same server, then Change Data Capture will remain enabled. If, on the other hand, the database is restored to a different server, then CDC will be disabled and all related objects will be removed from the database. You can override this behavior by using the KEEP_CDC option when restoring the database. Attaching the database will always keep CDC enabled, but will fail if you attempt to attach a CDC-enabled database to a server running an edition of SQL Server that does not support CDC.

❑ **Sparse Columns** — Change data will be captured for a source table that uses sparse columns, but only when column sets are not used.

❑ **XML** — Changes to data in XML columns will be captured, but not for individual elements.

Tables

When Change Data Capture is first enabled for a database, several new tables will be created to help manage the CDC processes. Microsoft recommends that you don't try to query these tables directly, but if you are like me, then that is just an irresistible invitation to peruse! Nothing will suddenly break if you decide to take a look, but I do recommend that you avoid making any changes. When you are ready to play by the rules, each table has an associated stored procedure or function that should be used instead (see the following table):

Table	Description
cdc.<schema_table>_CT	These are the tables where changes to the source tables are actually recorded. One Change Table will be created for every source table for which you enable Change Data Capture. The structure of these tables will vary depending on which source columns are being tracked. In general, you should avoid querying these tables directly and use the cdc.fn_get_all_changes_<schema_table> and cdc.fn_cdc_get_net_changes_<schema_table> functions instead.
cdc.captured_columns	This table contains a list of all tracked columns. You can limit which columns are included by specifying a column list when you enable CDC for a table. Use the sys.sp_cdc_get_source_columns stored procedure to display the captured columns.
cdc.change_tables	Contains a list of all source tables that have been enabled for CDC. The preferred method to view this information is by using the sys.sp_cdc_help_change_data_capture stored procedure.
cdc.ddl_history	This table returns one row for each data definition language (DDL) change made to a CDC-enabled source table. The associated stored procedure is sys.sp_cdc_get_ddl_history.
cdc.lsn_time_mapping	Maps log sequence number (LSN) commit values to the time the transaction committed. This table is used when you execute the sys.fn_cdc_map_lsn_to_time and sys.fn_cdc_map_time_to_lsn helper functions.

Continued

Table	Description
cdc.index_columns	Contains information about the unique identifier for rows in the source table. This can be either the primary key or a unique index as specified when CDC is enabled on a source table. Use the sys.sp_cdc_help_change_data_capture stored procedure to return index column information.
dbo.cdc_jobs	This table holds the configuration parameters for Capture and Cleanup Jobs. You won't find it with the other tables; it is stored in **MSDB** instead. The sys.sp_cdc_help_jobs stored procedure will display the list of jobs.

Change Tracking

Change Tracking is essentially Change Data Capture without the "data." Change Tracking can determine if any changes have been made to a row in a table, but it will not provide details about the actual data that was changed. This makes Change Tracking a lighter-weight alternative to Change Data Capture, provided that all you need is the current values for changed rows.

In addition to just recording the fact that a row has changed, Change Tracking can also optionally identify the specific column(s) that were updated. It also captures data definition language (DDL) changes. Cleanup is done automatically behind the scenes.

This adds up to an ideal tool for use when developing synchronization solutions for custom disconnected applications. In fact, Change Tracking was designed with this in mind, supporting both single and bidirectional synchronization scenarios.

To begin using Change Tracking, you must first alter the database and set the CHANGE_TRACKING flag. The example below shows how to enable Change Tracking in the AdventureWorks2008 database:

```
ALTER DATABASE AdventureWorks2008
  SET CHANGE_TRACKING = ON
  (CHANGE_RETENTION = 2 DAYS, AUTO_CLEANUP = ON)
GO
```

Once Change Tracking is enabled in the database, individual tables can be tracked by altering them to enable Change Tracking. The following example shows how to enable Change Tracking in the Person.Person table:

```
USE AdventureWorks2008
GO

ALTER TABLE Person.Person
  ENABLE CHANGE_TRACKING
  WITH (TRACK_COLUMNS_UPDATED = ON)
GO
```

That's it! With SQL Server 2008, it really is that easy to set up a low-overhead, full-featured, and reliable Change Tracking system.

Functions and Views

The functions and views in the following table are created when Change Tracking is enabled on a database:

Function or View	Description
CHANGETABLE	Returns the list of changes to tracked tables that have occurred after the specified version. If you enter null for the version, all available changes will be returned.
CHANGE_TRACKING_MIN_VALID_VERSION	Returns the minimum valid version number. This is typically used to validate that synchronization is possible.
CHANGE_TRACKING_CURRENT_VERSION	Returns the current version number. This value would typically be saved by an external application for use later with the CHANGETABLE function to return the net changes.
CHANGE_TRACKING_IS_COLUMN_IN_MASK	This helper function will interpret the column data to determine if a particular column has been changed.
WITH CHANGE_TRACKING_CONTEXT	Allows the originator of change to be recorded, so that system changes can be differentiated from user changes.
sys.change_tracking_databases	Returns a list of all databases that are enabled for Change Tracking.
sys.change_tracking_tables	Returns a list of all tables in the current database that are enabled for Change Tracking.

Try It Out   Synchronizing with an External Application

Assume for a moment that you have an external application that needs to synchronize with Person.Person. The most difficult task involved in this is trying to determine what has changed since your last update. This is where Change Tracking really shines. I think that you will be surprised at how easily this can be accomplished.

> *Before beginning, make sure that Change Tracking is enabled on the* AdventureWorks2008 *database and then on the* Person.Person *table, as shown earlier in this section.*

Change Tracking sequences all of changes using an internal database-global versioning system. You will need to know what version to start from in order to get the net changes since the last synchronization. If this were the initial load, then the current version number would be recorded, and the source data would be copied in full to establish the initial baseline. To get the starting point for our simulated synchronization, follow these steps:

1.   Enter the following into a Query window and execute it:

```
SELECT CHANGE_TRACKING_CURRENT_VERSION()'current_version'
```

2.   Write down the result. You will need it later on.

3. At this point imagine that the external application has disconnected. Changes that occur after this point will need to be synchronized when the external application reconnects. Type the following into a Query window and execute it to make some changes to the Person.Person table:

```
USE AdventureWorks2008
GO

-- Change some data in the Person table
UPDATE Person.Person
SET FirstName='Paul', LastName='Allen'
WHERE BusinessEntityID=1
GO

-- Change the same record again
UPDATE Person.Person
SET FirstName='Bill', LastName='Gates'
WHERE BusinessEntityID=1
GO

-- Insert a new row
INSERT Person.Person (BusinessEntityID,PersonType,FirstName,LastName)
VALUES (310,'SC','Joan','Ballmer')
GO

-- Update the new row
UPDATE Person.Person
SET FirstName='Steve'
WHERE BusinessEntityID=310
GO
```

4. Next, the external application reconnects and wants to synchronize. To do so, it needs to know what has changed since its last synchronization. Change Tracking can provide this information using the initial version number that you recorded previously. Enter the following into a command window and execute it, making sure to substitute the version value that you recorded earlier:

```
USE AdventureWorks2008
GO

Declare @sync_version bigint
SET @sync_version = [INSERT YOUR VALUE HERE!]


SELECT CHANGE_TRACKING_CURRENT_VERSION()'current_version';


-- Identify the changes made after an earlier version
SELECT CT.BusinessEntityID,p.FirstName, p.LastName,CT.SYS_CHANGE_OPERATION,
CT.SYS_CHANGE_COLUMNS, CT.SYS_CHANGE_CONTEXT
FROM CHANGETABLE(CHANGES Person.Person,@sync_version) CT
left join Person.Person p on CT.BusinessEntityID=p.BusinessEntityID
GO
```

This should return a result set that looks something like Figure 10-23.

	current_version					
1	42					

	BusinessEntityID	FirstName	LastName	SYS_CHANGE_OPERATION	SYS_CHANGE_COLUMNS	SYS_CHANGE_CONTEXT
1	1	Bill	Gates	U	0x0000000005000000007000000	NULL
2	310	Steve	Ballmer	I	NULL	NULL

Figure 10-23: Synchronization change summary.

Notice a few interesting things about this result set:

❑ It displays the "end result" for each primary key, consolidating all of the changes.

❑ Only the primary key for the table is saved in the Change Table. The current values are being retrieved by looking them up in the source table.

❑ For updates, there is a value in the "SYS_CHANGE_COLUMNS" column that we could use to determine if a change occurred to any given column. Insert and Delete operations simply report NULL for this value because all columns are affected.

The actual synchronization process would delete records with a change operation of "D," update those with a "U," and insert new records for entries with an "I." Finally, the new "current version" value would be saved by the external application in preparation for the next synchronization.

It is possible that the external application might be disconnected for so long that the change records are no longer available. This can be easily determined by using the CHANGE_TRACKING_MIN_VALID_VERSION *function and making sure that the saved baseline version is greater than the minimum version. If not, then the external application would need to get a full copy of the synchronized object(s) and establish a new baseline.*

Data Collection

Data Collection is a new feature in SQL Server 2008 that automatically collects different customizable sets of management data into a data warehouse, where you can analyze and report on the data. This is different from the other monitoring features described in this chapter in that Data Collection repeatedly captures snapshots of the data on a schedule, allowing you to monitor how it is changing over time and look for trends.

Data Collection provides significant benefits beyond simply using the SQL Trace and Performance Monitor, for example:

❑ It provides a central collection point for management data across multiple servers.

❑ It allows you to control exactly which management metrics you want to capture.

❑   It allows reporting using SQL Server Reporting Services.

❑   It is extensible via a richly featured API.

The Management Data Warehouse is not a new concept, but typically it takes more work for an administrator to implement than the benefit (or perceived benefit) that they receive. Data Collection provides a new invitation to administrators to give the Management Data Warehouse another try.

This feature is disabled by default, but configuration is easy, and it only takes a few minutes to start capturing a wide array of performance-related data using pre-defined objects.

Terminology

Before we get too far, it will help to have a common understanding of the terminology that is used in the context of data collection. The table below defines these key terms:

Term	Definition
Target	This term can refer to the database itself or anything in the database that can be managed. Yes, the term *target* is really that wide open. In this context, it is just a fancy pronoun that means "that thing."
Target type	Defines what type of object the target is. To continue the analogy above, the target type would be the answer to the question "What is that thing?"
Data provider	A data provider enables access to a source of data of a specific type. Data providers are used to provide data to a collector type.
Collector type	A logical container encompassing the SQL Server Integration Services (SSIS) package that actually collects the data and uploads it to the Management Data Warehouse
Collection item	An instance of a collector type in a collection set, created with specific input parameters and a defined collection frequency
Collection set	A group of collection items and associated metadata
Collection mode	The method used to collect the data. At this point it is either "cached" or "non-cached."
Management Data Warehouse	A relational database where the collected data is stored

Architecture and Processing

Data Collection is like many of the new subsystems in SQL Server in that it is comprised of several lower-level technologies combined in new, innovative ways. In this case, SQL Server Integration Services (SSIS) and SQL Server Agent have been combined with a new external process called the *Data Collector*.

The following explanation uses a lot of specific terms! If you get lost, review the terminology section or try to line things up using Figure 10-24!

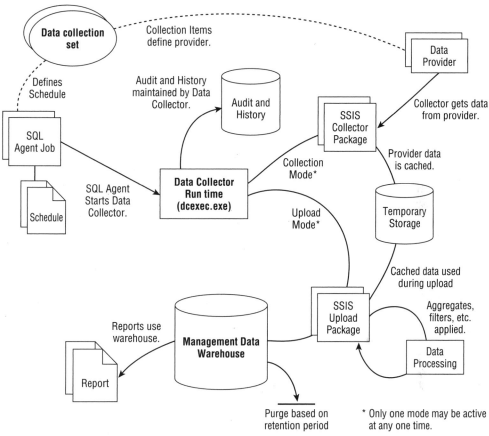

Figure 10-24: Data Collection architecture overview.

The Data Collector is the central object that ties everything together. It relies on Data Collection Sets to define the data providers, schedule, and retention period to use for collected data. SQL Server Agent uses the schedule defined in the collection set to run the Data Collector, which, in turn, executes an SSIS package to collect the requested data from the data provider. Using a separate schedule in the collection set, SQL Server Agent again runs the Data Collector, which this time runs an SSIS package to process and upload the collected data into the Management Data Warehouse. The Data Collector also maintains audit and history information so that administrators can easily identify and resolve problems. Figure 10-24 shows an overview of the Data Collection architecture.

The Data Collector uses MSDB to store most of its control data. This includes configuration, run time, auditing, and collection history information. You will not be able to use Data Collection if the MSDB database is not present on the server.

In order to use the Data Collector, a user must be a member of one of the defined Data Collector security roles (in MSDB). There are only three roles, as listed below:

❑ **dc_admin** — Grants full administrator rights for the Data Collector configuration. Membership in this role also grants membership in SQLAgentUserRole and inherits the permissions granted to dc_operator.

❑ **dc_operator** — Allows Read and update access necessary for running and configuring collection sets. Membership in this role also grants membership in db_dtsltduser so that the operator can list and view collector packages.

❑ **dc_proxy** — Grants Read access to data collection sets and allows users to execute packages that they own.

Now that you know how it works, I will explain how to configure data collection.

Configuring Data Collection

Data collection must be configured before you will able to create or enable any collection sets. Configuration can be accomplished in SSMS, and it is relatively straightforward:

1. If you do not already have a Data Management Warehouse database, then you will need to create one.

2. After creating the database, you will then be able to set up data collection.

> There is a clear advantage in using a single management warehouse database to consolidate data from multiple servers. When configuring data collection in this way, you must make sure that the service account used by SQL Server Agent has the necessary rights on the foreign machine. As an alternative, you can configure the individual data collection sets to use a proxy.

Both of these tasks can be performed from SSMS by using the Configure Management Data Warehouse Wizard, which is located on the context menu of Data Collection within the Management node of a server instance. You may need to run this Wizard twice, first to create a new storage database and then again to set up data collection. You can select which task to perform on the first page of the Wizard, as shown in Figure 10-25.

When creating a new Management Data Warehouse:

1. You must specify where the storage database is located.

2. If you don't have a storage database, you can create a new one from the same dialog by clicking on the New button. Figure 10-26 shows the storage selection page of the Wizard.

3. After selecting a storage database, the next step is to indicate what level of access, if any, should be assigned to specific users or groups. Data Collection uses three pre-defined security roles as described below:

   ❑ **mdw_admin** — Members of this role can perform any task in the data warehouse.

❏ **mdw_writer** — Members of this role can upload data to the data warehouse. Any data collector that stores data in the warehouse must be a member.

❏ **mdw_reader** — This role is designed to support troubleshooting and to view historical data. Members can only read data that is related to these tasks.

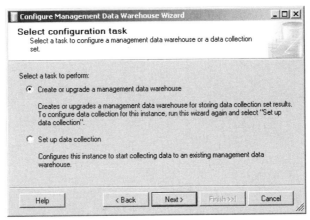

Figure 10-25: Configure Management Data Warehouse Wizard.

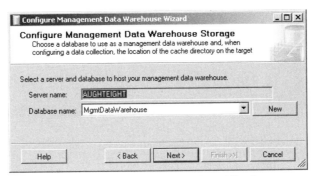

Figure 10-26: Configure Management Data Warehouse Storage.

Figure 10-27 shows the page of the Wizard where you map logins and users to data collection roles.

After creating a Management Data Warehouse, you will need to run the Wizard to set up data collection. For this task, there are only two options that need to be set:

❏ The name of the Management Data Warehouse database to use for storage

❏ The name of the directory to use for cache files

This page of the Wizard is shown in Figure 10-28.

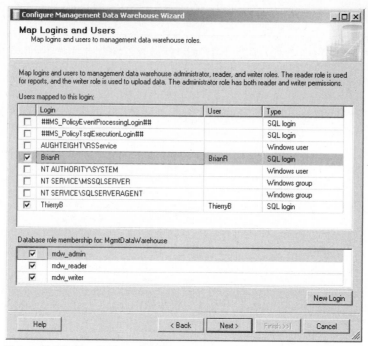

Figure 10-27: Map Logins and Users.

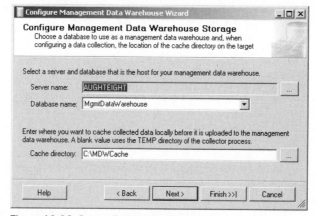

Figure 10-28: Set up Data Collection.

When the "Set up data collection" Wizard is completed and setup is finished, SQL Server 2008 will enable Data Collection and start the system data collection sets. The icon next to the Data Collection node will change, and you will be able to enable/disable data collection and manage individual data collection sets.

Data Collector Types

Before discussing the data collector sets, I will spend a minute and introduce Data Collector types. *Data Collector types* define the data providers that can be used to gather data for a data collection set. At present, Microsoft only provides four different collector types, but there are hints that they will soon be adding more (perhaps a WMI type?). Even so, the current collector types cover a lot of ground and can be used to gather a wide variety of data. Each collector type uses an XML schema to define its input criteria (Microsoft Books Online describes these schemas in detail). The list below covers the currently available types:

❑ **T-SQL Query Collector Type** — This is perhaps the most flexible of the collector types. It will accept any T-SQL select statement. The input criteria include a list of databases that the collector will be applied to.

❑ **SQL Trace Collector Type** — Collects data gathered from a SQL Trace. When collecting data, the SQL Trace will save results to a file, and then during the upload phase, the file will be processed using `fn_trace_gettable`. The input criteria allow filters to be defined.

❑ **Performance Counters Collector Type** — This collector type takes snapshots of Performance Monitor counters. The input criteria permit limited use of wildcards.

❑ **Query Activity Collector Type** — This is a custom collector type that includes internal processing that gathers information about most performance-affecting queries. It correlates query activity, statistics, plans, and the actual query text.

Data Collection Sets

Data collection sets gather data from one or more collection items and upload the data to the data warehouse. Each collection item is based on a Data Collector type that is configured using input parameters (in XML format). A collection set also defines the schedules for data collection and upload, the account under which to run the jobs, and the retention period for uploaded data.

Out-of-the-box, SQL Server 2008 installs three system data collection sets. By default, these are automatically enabled when you first set up data collection. They include a wide variety of performance metrics and can consume between 250 MB and 350 MB of storage per day; however, the bulk of the data is only retained for 2 weeks. The system data collection sets cannot be deleted; however, you can disable or reconfigure them. Each set is described below:

❑ **Disk Usage** — Tracks the size and growth of all database and log files. This collection set uses a T-SQL collector type to gather data from `sys.partitions`, `sys.allocation_units`, `sys.dm_io_virtual_file_stats`, and `DBCC SQLPERF (LOGSPACE)`. By default, data is collected every 60 seconds, uploaded every 6 hours, and is retained for 730 days.

❑ **Server Activity** — Snapshots a wide variety of performance metrics that are useful in determining resource usage, contention, bottlenecks, and blocking problems. Two different collector types are used. First, a T-SQL collector samples data from `sys.dm_os_wait_stats`, `sys.dm_os_latch_stats`, `sys.dm_os_schedulers`, `sys.dm_exec_sessions`, `sys.dm_exec_requests`, `sys.dm_os_waiting_tasks`, `sys.dm_os_process_memory`, and

`sys.dm_os_memory_nodes`. Then, a performance counter collector gathers data from a selection of system and SQL Server performance counters. This collection set gathers a high volume of data, so its default settings are quite different from those of the previous collection set. The default settings collect data every 60 seconds and upload the data every 15 minutes, but only retain the data for
14 days.

❑ **Query Statistics** — Gathers data about query statistics, query plans, and specific queries, including individual query text. This data can be linked to system-level statistics to allow drilldown to an individual query, enabling you to better detect and analyze poorly performing queries. The logic that ties this information together is custom-coded inside the query activity collector type and cannot be changed. By default, this collection set will gather data every 10 seconds, upload it every 15 minutes, and retain the data for 14 days.

Each of the system data collection sets has an associated report, which you can view in SSRS by right-clicking on the Data Collection node and selecting Reports ➢ Management Data Warehouse. The available reports are named *Server Activity History*, *Disk Usage Summary*, and *Query Statistics History*.

You are also free to define your own custom data collection sets using the `sp_syscollector_create_collection_set` System Stored Procedure. At present, you must use T-SQL to create a new data collection set, since there is no GUI available.

Try It Out   Create a Custom Data Collector Set

One of the primary uses for the Data Collector is to collect and monitor performance data; however, the default collector set may actually include too much information. In some cases, it might be more appropriate to monitor just a few targeted counters, as described in the "Performance Monitoring" section earlier in this chapter.

This example will demonstrate how to create a new Data Collector set that includes a few CPU-specific performance counters that are useful in detecting CPU bottlenecks. It should also be a good starting point for you to create your own collector sets later on.

Before beginning, make sure that you have configured Data Collection on your server as described earlier in this section.

1. Create a new custom Data Collector set. Enter the following into the new Query window and execute it:

```
--STEP 1
USE msdb
GO

DECLARE @collection_set_id int
DECLARE @collection_set_uid uniqueidentifier
SET @collection_set_uid = '9170CBA3-2C8D-402f-82F5-CD427F75D221'

exec dbo.sp_syscollector_create_collection_set
@name = 'CPU Bottlenecks',
```

```
@target = '',  -- use this for another server '/Server[@Name=''MSSQLSERVER'']'
@collection_mode = 0,
@days_until_expiration=5, -- Only keep the data for five days
@description = 'Collects selected PerfMon CPU counters',
@logging_level = 0,    -- 0-2 are valid, in increasing verbosity
@schedule_name=N'CollectorSchedule_Every_5min',
@collection_set_id = @collection_set_id OUTPUT,
@collection_set_uid = @collection_set_uid OUTPUT

SELECT @collection_set_id 'collection set id',
       @collection_set_uid 'collection set uid'
GO
```

2. Write down the value returned in the "collection set id" column. You will need it later!

3. Add a new collection item using the Performance Counters Data Collector type. This collection item will reference three CPU counters that are useful in identifying CPU bottlenecks. Enter the following into a new Query window and execute it, making sure to substitute the value you recorded above for the collection set ID:

```
-- STEP 2
USE msdb
GO

DECLARE @collector_type_uid uniqueidentifier, @collection_item_id int,
    @collection_set_id int
SET @collection_set_id=[YOUR VALUE]  -- use the value you recorded above!

-- Get collector type uid
SELECT @collector_type_uid=collector_type_uid
FROM [dbo].[syscollector_collector_types]
WHERE name = N'Performance Counters Collector Type';

-- Add a new collection item
EXEC [dbo].[sp_syscollector_create_collection_item]
  @name='Perfmon CPU counters',
  @parameters='
  <ns:PerformanceCountersCollector xmlns:ns="DataCollectorType">
    <PerformanceCounters Objects="System"
    Counters="Processor Queue Length" Instances="*" />
    <PerformanceCounters Objects="Processor"
     Counters="% Processor Time" Instances="_Total" />
    <PerformanceCounters Objects="Process"
     Counters="% Processor Time" Instances="sqlservr" />
  </ns:PerformanceCountersCollector>',
  @frequency=5,  -- every 5 seconds
  @collection_set_id=@collection_set_id,
  @collector_type_uid=@collector_type_uid,
  @collection_item_id=@collection_item_id OUTPUT

Select @collection_item_id 'collection item id'
GO
```

4. At this point, the new collection set is ready to go. In fact, it will now be visible in the SQL Server Management Console. Using the SSMC, expand the Management ➤ Data Collection node for the server. You should see a new entry named *CPU Bottlenecks*. Right-click on the CPU Bottlenecks data collection set, and select Properties. You should see something similar to Figure 10-29.

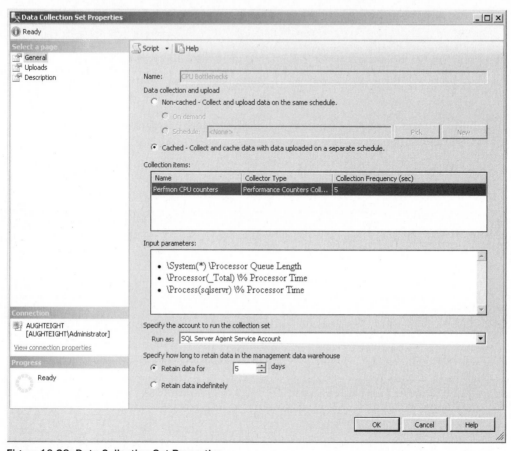

Figure 10-29: Data Collection Set Properties.

5. You need to start the new data collection set so that it can begin storing the performance monitor counters in the data warehouse. Close the Data Collection Set Properties dialog, then right-click on the CPU Bottlenecks data collection set and select "Start Data Collection Set."

At this point, relax for a few minutes and have a cup of coffee or whatever your beverage of choice might be. The data collection set will capture data every 5 seconds, but will only upload the data to the data warehouse every 5 minutes. So before you query the warehouse, you will need to wait at least 5 minutes to make sure some data has actually been uploaded.

After you are done with your beverage, enter the following into a new Query window and execute it:

```
-- STEP 3
-- Report the captured data
```

```
USE MgmtDataWarehouse
GO

DECLARE @collection_set_uid uniqueidentifier, @endtime datetime
SET @collection_set_uid = '9170CBA3-2C8D-402f-82F5-CD427F75D221'

SELECT pci.[object_name], pci.counter_name, pci.instance_name, pc.*
FROM snapshots.performance_counter_values AS pc
   INNER JOIN core.snapshots s ON s.snapshot_id = pc.snapshot_id
   left join snapshots.performance_counter_instances pci on
      pc.performance_counter_instance_id=pci.performance_counter_id
WHERE s.collection_set_uid = @collection_set_uid
ORDER BY pc.performance_counter_instance_id,pc.collection_time
GO
```

The output should look similar to Figure 10-30.

	object_name	counter_name	instance_name	performance_counter_instance_id	snapshot_id	collection_time	formatted_value	raw_value_first	raw_value_second
5	Process	% Processor Time	sqlservr	223	152	2008-09-21 23:11:00.0000000 -07:00	1.20174030582073	8686590704	128665374600137664
6	Process	% Processor Time	sqlservr	223	152	2008-09-21 23:11:05.0000000 -07:00	1.1902769642707	8687191568	128665374650618688
7	Process	% Processor Time	sqlservr	223	152	2008-09-21 23:11:10.0000000 -07:00	0.198814103572015	8687291712	128665374700989360
8	Process	% Processor Time	sqlservr	223	152	2008-09-21 23:11:15.0000000 -07:00	1.2210955523365	8687892576	128665374750196320
9	Process	% Processor Time	sqlservr	223	152	2008-09-21 23:11:20.0000000 -07:00	0.796525524863425	8688293152	128665374800486736
10	Process	% Processor Time	sqlservr	223	152	2008-09-21 23:11:25.0000000 -07:00	3.43039729908965	8689995600	128665374850115040
11	Process	% Processor Time	sqlservr	223	152	2008-09-21 23:11:30.0000000 -07:00	0.400580101940244	8690195888	128665374900114528
12	Process	% Processor Time	sqlservr	223	152	2008-09-21 23:11:35.0000000 -07:00	1.00104854997502	8690696608	128665374950134080
13	Process	% Processor Time	sqlservr	223	152	2008-09-21 23:11:40.0000000 -07:00	0	8690696608	128665375000153632
14	Process	% Processor Time	sqlservr	223	152	2008-09-21 23:11:45.0000000 -07:00	0.5997870703195	8690997040	128665375050243408
15	Process	% Processor Time	sqlservr	223	152	2008-09-21 23:11:50.0000000 -07:00	0	8690997040	128665375100423472
16	Process	% Processor Time	sqlservr	223	152	2008-09-21 23:11:55.0000000 -07:00	0.604386850071698	8691297472	128665375150132032
17	Process	% Processor Time	sqlservr	223	152	2008-09-21 23:12:00.0000000 -07:00	2.19789866981304	8692399056	128665375200251904
18	Process	% Processor Time	sqlservr	223	152	2008-09-21 23:12:05.0000000 -07:00	1.201017380354	8692999920	128665375250281488
19	Process	% Processor Time	sqlservr	223	152	2008-09-21 23:12:10.0000000 -07:00	0.401385449953795	8693200208	128665375300180656
20	Process	% Processor Time	sqlservr	223	152	2008-09-21 23:12:15.0000000 -07:00	0.591962214292402	8693500640	128665375350932544
21	Process	% Processor Time	sqlservr	223	152	2008-09-21 23:12:20.0000000 -07:00	0	8693500640	128665375400289984
22	Process	% Processor Time	sqlservr	223	152	2008-09-21 23:12:25.0000000 -07:00	1.00145025485061	8694001360	128665375450289472
23	Process	% Processor Time	sqlservr	223	152	2008-09-21 23:12:30.0000000 -07:00	4.01789339519053	8696004240	128665375500138480

Figure 10-30: Performance counter data in the Management Data Warehouse.

Notice that the requested counters were captured every 5 seconds. The data in the warehouse could easily be reported or even graphed using SQL Server Reporting Services. Now that the data collection set has been created, it can be started, stopped, and managed using SSMC.

Error Handling

Given the number of components involved in the data collection processes and the fact that the data sources themselves may be located on foreign machines, it is no surprise that errors may occur somewhere along the line. In many cases, errors are caused by connectivity issues, permission issues, or unexpected shutdowns. The error will always be logged by the Data Collector, and depending on the type of error, the Data Collector may try again, or it may elect to disable the collection set.

You can view the log either through SSMS by selecting "View Logs" from the context menu of the Data Collection node or from the context menu of any Data Collection Set.

The following table shows how the Data Collector handles some of the more common errors:

Type of Error	Data Collector Response
Unable to connect to a data provider	The collection set is stopped and disabled.
Data provider connection is dropped	After a short delay, the connection is tried again. If the connection fails a second time, then the collection set is disabled.
Unable to connect to the management data warehouse	The connection is re-attempted up to four times with short delays between attempts. If after four tries the connection is still unavailable, then the collection set is disabled.
The connection to the data management warehouse is dropped during upload	This error is handled in the same way as the previous error. Any uploaded data will be kept except for the transaction that was in process when the connection dropped.
An error is received from a data provider	The collection set is stopped and disabled. This error happens most often during development and testing.
There is an error in the data flow	The number of failures is counted and reported, unless the error is critical, in which case, the collection set is disabled. This error is typically caused by data type conversion errors, expression evaluation errors, or lookup failures.

Reporting

The Data Collector component includes three built-in reports for use with the built-in data collector sets. These can be run from the SSMC by right-clicking on the Data Collection node and selecting a report from Reports ➤ Management Data Warehouse. The three reports are titled *Server Activity History*, *Disk Usage Summary*, and *Query Statistics History*. Microsoft put quite a bit of effort into making some great-looking reports to highlight what is possible when using the Data Collector. A sample of the Server Activity report is shown in Figure 10-31.

Now for the bad news, if you want reports like that for your own custom data collection sets, then you will need to design them yourself. When you are ready to get started with reporting, take a look at Chapter 18.

Management Data Warehouse

The *Management Data Warehouse* is the database where all of the data that is captured by the Data Collector eventually ends up. Data is written to a series of tables in the Management Data Warehouse during the upload phase of the data collection process. You will need to know a little bit about these tables in order to develop your own custom queries and reports.

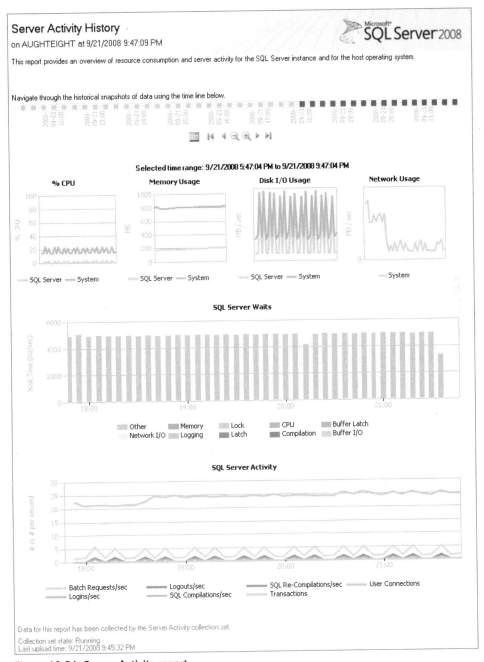

Figure 10-31: Server Activity report.

The `core.snapshots` view is at the top of the food chain. It contains one row for each snapshot that has been uploaded for a collection item in a collection set. Below `core.snapshots`, each different collector type uses a different set of tables to store its uploaded data. I won't attempt to detail all of the custom tables used by the system collector sets, but it would help you to know the standard tables used by each collector type (see the following table for details):

Collector Type	Tables/Views Used
Performance Counters	Data is captured into `snapshots.performance_counter_values`, and a description of the counters themselves is stored in `snapshots.performance_counter_instances`. There is also a view named `snapshots.performance_counters` that combines the data from the two tables for you.
SQL Trace	The `snapshots.trace_info` table contains data that describes each trace, and the `snapshots.trace_data` table contains the captured trace data.
Query Activity	The primary table is `snapshots.query_stats`; however, the internal logic of this collector type generates several support tables that allow drill-in capability for individual queries.
T-SQL	This one works a bit differently. A new table is created in the `snapshots` schema with a name corresponding to the name of the collection item. The table structure will include a few metadata columns and then mirror the provided T-SQL output. The system collection sets make heavy use of this collector type. For example, the Disk Usage collection uses T-SQL collectors for its `disk_usage`, `log_usage`, and `query_stats` collection items.

Remember to assign the proper permissions to any logins or users that require access to the Management Data Warehouse. As discussed earlier in this section, the available security roles are mdw_admin, mdw_writer, and mdw_reader, in decreasing level of access.

I will leave you with a sample query that may help to get you started creating your own. The following query will display the results of the last disk usage snapshot:

```
SELECT c.collection_set_uid,ss.*
FROM snapshots.disk_usage ss
inner join core.snapshots c on ss.snapshot_id=c.snapshot_id
WHERE ss.snapshot_id=(select MAX(snapshot_id) from snapshots.disk_usage)
```

Monitoring Database Modifications

Like many people in the information technology field, I cut my teeth in desktop support, then moved on to network support, and finally settled in with SQL Server. I can't begin to count how many times I began a support conversation with, "Have you changed anything recently?" only to hear the canned response, "No, I haven't done anything. It just stopped working." I bet you can relate. As a database administrator, your audience has changed a bit, but when a database application suddenly quits working, I can almost guarantee that you will hear the same answer from database and application developers — "I didn't do anything, it just stopped working."

A very powerful feature in SQL Server 2008 gives the DBA the ability to debunk that claim with solid audit evidence that, indeed, something was changed to break the database. This feature is the ability to monitor and even prevent database modifications through the use of Data Definition Language (DDL) triggers and event notifications.

Data Definition Language (DDL) Triggers

DDL triggers can be defined at the database and server scope. Like traditional Data Modification Language (DML) triggers, DDL triggers fire *after* the event that the trigger is defined on. If a trigger is defined to prevent the dropping of a database, the database will be dropped first and then put back when the trigger fires with a ROLLBACK statement in it. This can prove to be very costly, but may be less costly than having to restore the database from scratch.

Unlike traditional triggers, DDL triggers are defined on a particular statement or group of statements, regardless of the object that the statement is directed to, and are not assigned to a particular object. As a result, a DROP_DATABASE trigger will fire no matter what database is dropped.

In traditional DML triggers, a great deal of the functionality of the trigger is gained from access to the Deleted and Inserted tables that exist in memory for the duration of the trigger. DDL triggers do not use the Inserted and Deleted tables. Instead, if information from the event needs to be captured, the EVENTDATA function is used.

SQL Server Books Online contains a complete hierarchical listing of server- and database-level events that can be used with DDL triggers. You can find the list under the topic, "Event Groups for Use with DDL Triggers."

EVENTDATA *Function*

The EVENTDATA function returns an XML document that contains pre-defined data about the event that caused the trigger to execute. The type of data largely depends on the event that caused the trigger to execute, but all triggers return the time the trigger was fired, the ID of the process that caused the trigger to execute, and the type of event.

The following example creates a server-scoped DDL trigger that will execute any time a database is created, altered, or dropped:

```
USE Master;
GO
CREATE TRIGGER ServerDBEvent
ON ALL SERVER
FOR CREATE_DATABASE, DROP_DATABASE, ALTER_DATABASE
AS
DECLARE @Data AS xml
DECLARE @EventType AS nvarchar(25)
DECLARE @PostTime AS nvarchar(25)
DECLARE @ServerName AS nvarchar(25)
DECLARE @DBName AS nvarchar(25)
DECLARE @Login AS nvarchar(25)
```

```
DECLARE @TSQLCommand AS nvarchar(MAX)

    SET @Data = EVENTDATA()
    SELECT @EventType =
      @Data.value(' (/EVENT_INSTANCE/EventType)[1] ', 'nvarchar(25) ')
    , @PostTime = @Data.value(' (/EVENT_INSTANCE/PostTime)[1] ', 'nvarchar(25) ')
    , @ServerName =
      @Data.value(' (/EVENT_INSTANCE/ServerName)[1] ', 'nvarchar(25) ')
    , @Login = @Data.value(' (/EVENT_INSTANCE/LoginName)[1] ', 'nvarchar(25) ')
    , @DBName =
      @Data.value(' (/EVENT_INSTANCE/DatabaseName)[1] ', 'nvarchar(25) ')
    , @TSQLCommand =
      @Data.value(' (/EVENT_INSTANCE/TSQLCommand)[1] ', 'nvarchar(max) ')

    PRINT @EventType
    PRINT @PostTime
    PRINT @ServerName
    PRINT @login
    PRINT @DBName
    PRINT @TSQLCommand;
GO
```

To test the trigger, execute the following code and examine the output:

```
USE Master;
GO
CREATE DATABASE SampleDB;
GO
ALTER DATABASE SampleDB SET RECOVERY SIMPLE;
RESULTS:
--------------------------------------------------------
CREATE_DATABASE
2008-09-22T00:48:11.240
AUGHTEIGHT
AUGHTEIGHT\Administrator
SampleDB
CREATE DATABASE SampleDB;

ALTER_DATABASE
2008-09-22T00:48:11.960
AUGHTEIGHT
AUGHTEIGHT\Administrator
SampleDB
ALTER DATABASE SampleDB SET RECOVERY SIMPLE;
```

Try It Out   Database Scoped DDL Trigger

In this exercise, you create a DDL trigger that prevents modifications to the database and records information about who tried to modify the database and how they tried to modify it in an audit table. Follow these steps:

1. Create a table that will contain the auditing information gathered from the DDL trigger. To do that, type and execute the following code:

```
USE AdventureWorks2008;
GO
CREATE TABLE DatabaseDDLAudit
(AuditID int IDENTITY(1,1) NOT NULL
,PostTime datetime NOT NULL
,LoginName nvarchar(128) NULL
,Command nvarchar(MAX) NULL
,EventData xml NULL);
```

2. Now that you have an audit table, you can create the DDL database trigger that will insert into the table and prevent any modifications to the database. To create the trigger, type and execute the following code:

```
USE AdventureWorks2008;
GO
CREATE TRIGGER NoDDLAllowed
ON DATABASE
FOR DDL_DATABASE_LEVEL_EVENTS
AS
SET NOCOUNT ON
DECLARE @data AS xml, @PostTime AS datetime, @HostName AS nvarchar(128)
DECLARE @LoginName AS nvarchar(128), @Command AS nvarchar(MAX)

SET @data = EVENTDATA()

SELECT
@PostTime =
  CAST(@Data.value(' (/EVENT_INSTANCE/PostTime)[1] ', 'nvarchar(25) ')AS
datetime)
,@HostName =
  @Data.value(' (/EVENT_INSTANCE/HostName)[1] ', 'nvarchar(25) ')
,@LoginName =
  @Data.value(' (/EVENT_INSTANCE/LoginName)[1] ', 'nvarchar(25) ')
,@Command =
  @Data.value(' (/EVENT_INSTANCE/TSQLCommand)[1] ', 'nvarchar(max) ')

RAISERROR ('What?! Are you nuts? Modifications to this database are not
allowed!
  You can expect a visit from human resources shortly.', 16, 1)
ROLLBACK
INSERT DatabaseDDLAudit
  (PostTime, LoginName, Command, EventData)
VALUES   (@PostTime, @LoginName, @Command, @Data)
RETURN;
```

3. To test the trigger and review the data collected, execute the following code:

```
USE AdventureWorks2008;
GO
ALTER TABLE Person.Person
ADD NewColumn varchar(10) NULL;
```

Your results should look like the following:

```
Msg 50000, Level 16, State 1, Procedure NoDDLAllowed, Line 21
What?! Are you nuts? Modifications to this database are not allowed!
    You can expect a visit from human resources shortly.
Msg 3609, Level 16, State 2, Line 1
The transaction ended in the trigger. The batch has been aborted.
```

4. Now, query the audit table to see the data collected by executing the following command:

```
USE AdventureWorks2008;
GO
SELECT * FROM DatabaseDDLAudit;
GO
```

When it comes time to make authorized changes to the database, the trigger will have to be disabled or dropped (preferably disabled). The following script demonstrates how to disable the DDL trigger, make changes, and re-enable the trigger when complete:

```
USE AdventureWorks2008;
GO
DISABLE TRIGGER NoDDLAllowed
ON DATABASE;
GO
CREATE TABLE TestTable
(Column1 int
,Column2 int);
GO
ENABLE TRIGGER NoDDLAllowed
ON DATABASE;
GO
```

Summary

As you can see, monitoring the database server can become a full-time job. This chapter only scratched the surface when it comes to the events that can be monitored and the methods you can use. However, this chapter should give you a very good start on designing a monitoring strategy and determining what is most important for your particular environment. Keep in mind that all monitoring will have a certain amount of impact on SQL Server's overall performance. The more you monitor, the more the cost. Monitor in small slices, but be sure to get the big picture by putting all the slices together. Then, when it comes to making changes to the system, make small changes and measure your results.

Monitoring and optimization are two sides of the same coin. Monitoring is commonly used to find areas in need of optimization, and after the optimizations are performed, monitoring is again used to test the effectiveness of the changes. The next chapter discusses several optimization methods and techniques that you can use to keep your server running smoothly.

Optimizing SQL Server

Webster's dictionary defines *optimization* as "an act, process, or methodology of making something as fully perfect, functional, or effective as possible." Looking at this definition in the context of SQL Server, one might say that *optimization* is making the best possible use of the Database Engine to minimize query response time, resource usage, and hardware stress. As you might imagine, this is not a trivial task, and in practice, it is as much art as it is science. There are so many choices, options, opinions, and techniques available that it is easy to get lost in all the rhetoric and lose sight of the goal.

My approach to optimization is not to try to tell you exactly what you need to do, but instead to share with you the knowledge and techniques that I have developed over many years as a successful database administrator and application designer. You may not agree with all of the ideas and methods that I will present, and it may well be that in your specific situation an alternative approach will yield better results. What follows is what I have found to work in the majority of cases.

In order to be successful at optimization, you need to have a clear understanding of any applications that are using your server and how they compete for limited resources. In this regard, the design of the application has a bigger long-term impact than any other factor. Time spent up front to properly design an application is more valuable than 10 times the effort spent later on to fix it. In fact, the best way to minimize performance issues is to make performance an ongoing and integral part of the life cycle of every database application.

One of the biggest challenges with optimization is in knowing where to target your efforts. It makes sense to focus on areas that will yield the biggest possible improvement over the widest range of situations. After design issues, the biggest opportunities for improvement can be found in the procedures and queries that are used by an application. Unfortunately, many databases, including those in commercial products, are delivered with a bare minimum of indexes and without consideration for the effect of long-term growth on query performance. Besides design, procedures, and queries, I will also cover hardware optimization. In some cases, this is the only viable option, and since the hardware forms the foundation of the server, it is also a good place to start.

Hardware Optimization

Improper hardware design and configuration is the source of many performance problems in SQL Server. This is understandable considering that the performance of SQL Server is dependent on all of the major hardware subsystems working together in concert, and any deficiencies in the CPU, memory, network, or storage subsystems can cause performance bottlenecks. The goal when designing the hardware is to maximize data throughput. In this context, *throughput* is simply the amount of data per unit of time that can be pushed through the processing pipeline.

The required hardware will also depend in part on the nature of the database you are implementing. Online Transactional Processing (OLTP) databases have different characteristics from Online Analytical Processing (OLAP) databases. OLTP databases are normally front-line operational business systems. They are characterized by small- to medium-sized databases (<100 GB) with large numbers of users running short transactions with a mix of Read and Write operations. OLAP databases are used for reporting and data warehousing. They tend to be much larger in size and have a smaller number of users performing long read/reporting operations. For best performance, try not to mix databases with different characteristics on the same server.

Using the monitoring techniques that you learned in Chapter 10, you can identify with reasonable certainty which, if any, hardware subsystems are causing throughput bottlenecks. However, before you run out and buy more hardware, it is worth considering alternative options (optimizations) to reduce the stress on the affected subsystems. For example, if your CPUs are overloaded, instead of buying more CPUs, it might be possible to achieve the same result by optimizing a poorly written or inefficient query. Similarly, if the disk storage system is straining to keep up, instead of buying an expensive new RAID, you might be able to eliminate the I/O bottleneck by moving the log files to a different physical volume or even to a separate drive controller.

Many DBAs are not hardware experts, and for this reason, it is very tempting to just "throw hardware" at any performance problems. I am generally not in favor of this approach for three reasons:

1.   It can be expensive, especially if you have not planned ahead to allow for future expansions. In most organizations, significant hardware purchases must be justified, budgeted, and approved, and management will then have a certain expectation that the proposed solution will resolve the problem.

2.   In cases in which the root cause of the performance problem is due to inefficient or poorly written applications, adding hardware will only provide a short-term fix. As the databases grow in size, it is not uncommon for the exact same problems to resurface a few short months later on the new hardware, which will definitely not improve anyone's credibility.

3.   The potential performance gains to be had when adding hardware are far less that the potential performance gains that can be achieved through optimization (in particular, the commonly used queries and procedures).

For these reasons, when faced with performance problems, it is generally prudent to first attempt optimization, and only fall back on additional hardware as a last resort.

That being said, there are occasions when adding hardware is justified and necessary, and when you reach this point, it is important to know where to focus your time and money. In addition, planning ahead when you initially purchase the hardware will allow you to react faster to, and reduce the costs associated with, future needs and changing conditions. The remainder of this section will cover several hardware-related considerations to help you when initially specifying your SQL Server hardware and when adding new hardware to address performance bottlenecks.

CPU Selection

The choice of processor is one decision that many DBAs agonize over unnecessarily. The fact is that internally the CPU is the fastest of the subsystems, making it more likely that the CPU will be waiting on itself rather than being waited on. A high-end dual-core processor can easily outpace the fastest currently available DDR3 memory. In many cases, I have found that CPU "pressure" is caused by excessive query plan compilations, missing indexes, and large sorting operations, all of which can be mitigated through optimizations.

For a "typical" dedicated server installation (if there is such a thing), hosting several moderately sized databases and averaging less than a few hundred concurrent connections, a single high-end dual or quad-core processor will probably be sufficient. Even so, it may make sense to buy a motherboard with more than one socket, just in case you decide to expand your server operations later on. Keep in mind that Microsoft's SQL Server "processor" license is by the physical socket rather than by the core, so a single quad-core CPU will only require a single processor license.

When selecting the specific type of CPU, the amount of L2 cache can have a significant impact on overall performance. A large L2 cache will keep data off the system bus and reduce memory transfers. For SQL Server, increasing the L2 cache from 512 KB to 2 MB can result in a 20–30 percent CPU performance boost.

All of the mainstream CPUs on the market today are 64-bit capable, and the 64-bit versions of Windows and SQL Server cost the same as the 32-bit versions. For SQL Server, it makes sense to go 64-bit unless you are faced with a compelling reason not to, such as driver issues or legacy co-resident software.

Hyperthreading

Hyperthreading presents two "logical" processors to the system for a single physical CPU, with the intention of helping the physical CPU to be more fully utilized by the OS. This is distinctly different from multi-core processors where each core is a distinct, separate physical processor (even though they may share a common L2 cache). SQL Server efficiently handles its own internal queuing and threading for the OS, and enabling hyperthreading tends to simply overload CPUs with already high utilization. For this reason, in most cases hyperthreading should be disabled.

One key indicator that hyperthreading is slowing down SQL Server is the "context switches/second" measurement for a processor. When SQL Server uses multiple schedulers to service requests, it is forced to context switch the threads between processors, whether they are physical or logical. If you measure more than 5,000 context switches/second per physical processor, then turning off hyperthreading may improve performance.

Memory

Memory is the single most important element for SQL Server to maintain consistent data throughput. While the fastest DDR3 memory is still only a fraction of the throughput of the CPUs, this same memory is still more than 10 times faster than the best fiber channel drives. All data must be transferred to memory before the processor can interact with it, so the more memory that you have available, the fewer round-trips the system will need to make to the storage layer. SQL Server uses its own advanced caching mechanism to keep commonly used data in memory for reuse.

The operating system and everything else on the server will require memory as well, so the best general rule is to get as much as you can, provided your operating system can support it. The 64-bit editions of Windows Server can support between 32 GB and 2 TB (terabytes) of directly accessible RAM. If you are still using a 32-bit server, then you will be limited to 4 GB of memory, except for the DataCenter and Enterprise editions, which can support up to 128 GB and 64 GB, respectively.

Storage Options

Disk I/O bottlenecks are very common because in many cases retrieving data from the disk is the slowest operation in the processing chain. Hard drives have a limited number of I/O operations per second (IOPS) that they can handle, which is directly related to the average seek time for the device. Storage arrays are a critical component of a well-designed server since they offer improvements to both the bandwidth and the IOPS over individual drives and provide redundancy as well.

Storage is the one area where there are so many options and recommendations that it is easy to get lost in the rhetoric. In fact, if you were to strictly follow Microsoft's guidelines, then for a typical installation, you would need to provide upwards of a dozen individual storage arrays to support the various logs, partitions, file groups, indexes, and data files. I have no doubt that the recommended configuration would provide outstanding disk I/O performance; however, for all but the largest installations, a more limited approach will suffice. A simpler approach will also be easier for you to manage.

In general, you will receive the largest performance benefit by placing the log files on their own RAID1 or RAID1+0 storage array. Log files are written sequentially, so moving them to their own array will reduce drive "thrashing," and for systems with high-transaction volumes may improve I/O performance by as much as 30 percent.

> **My typical chain of thought when designing SQL Server storage systems is to provision independent spindle sets for the OS, logs, and data as a starting point. This provides good performance and recoverability. After that it becomes a question of how many drives need to be in those spindle sets for performance and high availability. Then, if it's a high-demand server, I consider dedicated controllers for those spindle sets.**

Placing tempdb on its own storage volume is another option that can provide a significant performance boost. tempdb is not used just for temporary tables. It is also used as overflow storage for large sort operations, to hold intermediate objects when executing complex queries, as storage for queries that return large result sets, and as a workspace for several of the DBCC commands. In many cases, you can increase performance by placing tempdb on an additional local drive or a small local RAID1 array. One interesting new option for tempdb is to use a solid-state drive.

It is a good idea to test your configuration before placing it into production. Microsoft provides the free SQLIO Disk Subsystem Benchmark Tool for this purpose. For more information or to download this tool, search Microsoft's web site for "SQLIO."

Beyond moving the log files and `tempdb`, you can create additional SQL filegroups to distribute disk I/O loads to specific drives or arrays. Using filegroups, you can control the physical location of data files, indexes, text data, image data, and file streams. Using partitions, you can even split up a single table across multiple filegroups. Each of these options has the potential to improve disk I/O performance.

Write Caching

Write caching is a technique used by both drives and controllers that will queue several Writes in memory and then commit them to the drives in larger, more efficient batch operations. The danger with this is the potential for unwritten data in the cache to be lost during a power failure or unexpected shutdown.

Most drives that support Write caching rely on a capacitive mechanism that is not battery-backed. These drives can lose data during a power cycle or similar system failure. To guarantee data integrity, you should disable disk caching for any drives that will be used with SQL Server.

In contrast, caching controllers typically do provide a battery backup for their Write cache. These controllers disable on-disk caches and use their own caching memory instead. In the event of a system or power failure, these devices will store unwritten data until power is restored and will then flush the data to the disks before any further access is permitted. SQL Server is targeted to use these kinds of controllers for optimal I/O performance, and Write caching can be safely enabled in this environment.

> *Most caching controllers that I have worked with are configured from the factory for 100 percent Read caching. I believe that this is done because the manufacturers don't want to blindly enable Write caching on your behalf for safety reasons. In addition, the battery backing module is often optional and may not be installed in all cases.*

Solid-State Drives

A relatively new option in the storage realm is solid-state drives. Recent improvements in this technology have significantly boosted performance and at the same time reduced the cost. Solid-state drives have no moving parts and, as a result, can offer extremely fast average seek times and an impressive number of I/O operations per second (IOPS). On the downside, they are still considerably more expensive than traditional drives and do not provide as high a capacity. At this point, I would not consider them for primary storage; however, their excellent I/O characteristics make them an ideal option for `tempdb`.

Network Design

Network problems are rarely the cause of performance bottlenecks in a typical online transaction processing (OLTP) database, and in most cases, a single 100 Mbs/1 Gbs network card will be able to keep up with demand.

> *If you are using an iSCSI storage array, you should use a separate network card for the storage network. If your array can handle it, you might even consider teaming multiple network interfaces to improve performance even further.*

Be careful to confirm the speed and duplex setting when using auto-sensing 10/100 or 10/100/1000 network cards. It is not uncommon for these cards to auto-sense incorrectly, which can hurt your network performance. You can prevent this from happening by manually configuring the network card.

Finally, make sure that your network uses switches rather than hubs. Switches isolate non-broadcast communications and dramatically reduce data collisions. Replacing an old hub with a switch will often result in a dramatic performance improvement.

Virtualizing SQL Server

Recently I have started to receive a lot of questions regarding the effects of running SQL Server in a virtual machine. *Virtualization* decouples applications and data from the underlying hardware, allowing them to be more easily managed and moved from one server to another. Using virtualization, you can run several virtual servers on a single physical server. This is a fairly new concept and at this time is largely unproven territory with regard to production SQL Servers.

Virtualization has the potential of saving money by improving hardware utilization. This is based on the fact that many servers under-utilize their hardware. In these cases, virtualization can help you to achieve better overall hardware utilization by running several virtual servers on a single physical server. For example, if you have three physical servers, each averaging 20 percent utilization, then combining these onto a single similar physical server should provide similar performance while utilizing around 60 percent of the physical server's resources. The savings are realized by requiring only one physical server instead of three to achieve a similar result. Of course, the virtualization layer itself actually uses some resources, and this overhead tends to impact I/O performance the most.

When virtualizing SQL Server, a good rule of thumb is that, using similar hardware, you will take a 20 percent I/O performance hit. This may be acceptable for certain applications or specific uses, such as training or testbeds, but does not make sense for high-throughput applications. Provided that you have enough RAM, reasonably sized OLTP databases should not suffer too much in a virtualized environment. OLAP databases, on the other hand, are much more I/O-intensive and would probably take a much larger performance hit.

Design Considerations

An efficient database begins with an efficient implementation design. It is worth the effort to put in a little extra time up front to plan your implementation rather than waiting for any deficiencies to show up in production. Database and application design are complex and much debated topics, and no single approach can cover all possible scenarios.

When designing for integrity and performance, the idea is to work with SQL Server, not against it. SQL Server is a relational database, and you will reap the biggest rewards if you design normalized, relational solutions. Certain object constructs such as polymorphism and inheritance can be difficult to model, and newer application modes (offline clients) present new challenges for database designers and administrators. No solution is perfect, and there is always room for improvement in every design.

This section really just represents the tip of the iceberg as far as design theory goes. My goal is not to tell you exactly how to design your database. That is a decision that only you can make. Instead, in this section, I will share some guidelines that over the years I have found to work well in many different situations. My hope is that perhaps you will be able to take advantage of some of these recommendations to improve your own designs.

Database Recovery Model

One of the first decisions that must be made for every database is the choice of recovery model. The recovery model is used to determine what kinds of transactions are logged, and as such, this decision needs to be coordinated with your backup strategy. This choice also happens to have a significant impact on performance.

There are three choices for the recovery model:

❑ **Simple** — When using the *Simple recovery model*, the transaction log is truncated each time a checkpoint is issued, and log space is reclaimed. High-performance non-logged bulk-copy operations are permitted. This mode is ideal for test and development databases and should be considered for small production databases and data warehouses. Only Full or Differential backups are possible.

❑ **Bulk-Logged** — This recovery model allows high-performance non-logged bulk-copy operations but maintains the transaction log for all other changes. Consider using this model if you are willing to sacrifice some flexibility of point-in-time recovery. It is also possible to temporarily switch a database to this model to improve performance of large bulk operations like creating indexes or bulk copying.

❑ **Full** — This recovery model always logs every change. Using this model, you will not gain the performance benefits for bulk-copy operations like the other models provide; however, you will always be able to recover to any point in time. This mode is appropriate for most production databases.

If your database normally uses the Full recovery model, you can temporarily switch the recovery model to Bulk-Logged to increase the performance of certain bulk operations, including SELECT INTO, BCP, BULK INSERT, CREATE INDEX, and changes to TEXT and IMAGE fields. This can be accomplished using a T-SQL script as shown below:

```
USE AdventureWorks2008
GO


-- Switch the recovery mode to BULK_LOGGED
ALTER DATABASE AdventureWorks2008
SET RECOVERY BULK_LOGGED
GO


-- Run the bulk operation
CREATE NONCLUSTERED INDEX IX_ModifiedDate
ON Person.BusinessEntity(ModifiedDate)
GO


-- Assuming AdventureWorks2008 was using FULL recovery
-- Restore the recovery mode to FULL
ALTER DATABASE AdventureWorks2008
SET RECOVERY FULL
GO
```

If you want to review the currently configured recovery modes for your databases, you can use the following code:

```
SELECT [name],state_desc,recovery_model_desc
FROM sys.databases
```

Designing Efficient Tables

Tables are the heart and soul of every database. The choices that are made when designing the tables will have a bigger effect on the long-term performance of the database than any other factor. A good table design will be capable of adapting to future needs, scale well as the tables increase in size, guarantee the integrity of the data, minimize blocking and time-outs, and maintain high performance levels over time.

This is not an easy task. Almost every choice involves some kind of trade-off. A performance gain in one area is often accompanied by a performance loss in another. Under-normalized designs introduce the risk of data duplication and inconsistencies, while over-normalized designs reduce performance and increase complexity. Therefore, the best approach is to help you identify the key factors that will have the most impact, and then to let you be the final judge.

Consider the following general guidelines when designing tables:

❑ **Normalize to Third Normal Form** — Try to implement all of your tables using the third normal form (described later (p. 482–3)). This will maximize the ability of the query processor to optimize your queries and prevent data duplication, inconsistencies, and anomalies.

❑ **De-Normalize for Performance** — After normalizing the tables in a database, you should evaluate possible cases where intentionally de-normalizing specific attributes can significantly improve performance. In many cases, this involves saving the results of costly calculations over a range of child records in an associated parent table.

❑ **Always Define Primary and Cluster Keys** — Every table in a referential database should have both a primary key and a cluster key. In many cases, these may be the same key. Recommendations for selecting these keys are presented later in this chapter.

❑ **Enforce Referential Integrity** — Always use declarative referential integrity (DRI) and server-side constraints to enforce referential integrity. Never rely on an application to manage this in place of the database.

❑ **Limit the Number of Columns per Table** — If necessary, you can define up to 1,024 columns per table in SQL Server 2008 (and up to 100,000 additional "sparse" columns). Be aware, however, that the more columns that are defined, the wider the table will be, and the more work it will take to query and manage the data. In some cases, you may be able to separate a number of related fields into a 1:1 joined table and only create the related record when necessary. Typically large numbers of columns are an indication that your design is not normalized.

❑ **Use the Narrowest Data Types Possible** — Using smaller data types makes the tables narrower (fewer bytes per row), allowing more data to be saved in each storage range, which helps to minimize data I/O and improve query performance. Suggestions for appropriate data types are presented later in the section.

❑ **Consider Horizontal Partitioning for Very Large Tables** — Very large tables can severely degrade performance. One way of combating this is to partition very large tables into "current" and "archive" sections (perhaps using a transaction date). Assuming that the bulk of the queries are to retrieve current information, this will have a dramatic effect on query performance.

❑ **Use a Naming Convention** — This is good advice for any design project, and SQL Server is no exception. Using a naming convention helps to reduce the effort required to maintain and understand your design. For example, you might choose to prefix all views with a *v*, stored procedures with a *p*, unique constraints with a *UQ*, and so on.

The most important of these guidelines by far are the first two, so I will spend a little extra time covering them in more depth.

Normalization

Normalization is a technique for designing efficient tables in a relational structure and is all about reducing duplication of data and protecting data from logical inconsistencies and anomalies. In normalization theory, there are actually six normal forms, with each higher form making the table less and less vulnerable to inconsistencies. This also means that each additional form increases the complexity of the design, so in practical use, it is usually sufficient to stop at the third normal form. Normalizing beyond this point is often an exercise in diminishing returns, with the risk of the design becoming so complex that it significantly affects performance.

The best way to explain normalization is with an example. I will start with the following hypothetical employee table:

Employee Table (Zero Form)

Employee	Location	LocationAddress	Phone1	Phone2
Thierry Boillot	Main Office	123 Main Street	555-0001	555-0002
Brian Rawlings	Branch 1	456 Suburb Way	555-8877	555-6655

This is typically called a *zero form* because it does not follow any normalization rules. The first step is to convert this table into a first normal form. To do this, simply apply the following rules:

1. Eliminate repeating groups.

2. Provide a unique key.

Typically, the first normal form will increase the number of rows. Here is what it would look like:

Employee Table (First Form)

EmployeeId	Employee	Location	LocationAddress	Phone1
1	Thierry Boillot	Main Office	123 Main Street	555-0001
2	Thierry Boillot	Main Office	123 Main Street	555-0002
3	Brian Rawlings	Branch 1	456 Suburb Way	555-8877
4	Brian Rawlings	Branch 1	456 Suburb Way	555-6655

This is not very useful yet, so we will continue on to the second normal form. The second normal form requires that the following additional conditions be met:

1. Create separate tables for repeating sets of values.
2. Relate those tables together.

To represent the second normal form, the phone number needs to be separated from the Employee table. Here is a second normal representation of the data:

Employee Table (Second Form)

EmployeeId(Primary key)	Employee	Location	LocationAddress
1	Thierry Boillot	Main Office	123 Main Street
3	Brian Rawlings	Branch 1	456 Suburb Way

EmployeePhone Table

PhoneId(Primary Key)	EmployeeId (Foreign Key)	Phone
1	1	555-0001
2	1	555-0002
3	3	555-8877
4	3	555-6655

Notice that it requires two tables to represent the original data in this form, with a one-to-many relationship between the employee data and the phone data. This is much better, but it is still not quite good enough. The final step is to apply the rules for the third normal form. There is only one additional requirement:

❑ Eliminate fields that do not depend on the key.

In this case, the LocationAddress field clearly does not relate to the employee (it relates to the location), so it needs to be eliminated from the Employee table. So to reach the third normal form, an additional table is required for the Location as shown below (to conserve space, I will not repeat the phone table, which is unchanged):

Employee Table (Third Form)

EmployeeId (Primary Key)	Employee (Foreign Key)	LocationId
1	Thierry Boillot	1
3	Brian Rawlings	2

Location Table

LocationId (Primary Key)	Location	LocationAddress
1	Main Office	123 Main Street
2	Branch 1	456 Suburb Way

When implemented in SQL Server, tables in the third normal form will usually outperform those in zero form. In addition, the data is less subject to inconsistencies because each data attribute is stored in only one place.

For comparison, if you wanted to generate a query using the third normal form design that would output the equivalent of the original zero form, it would look like this:

```
select em.Employee,lc.Location,lc.LocationAddress,[1] 'Phone1',[2] 'Phone2'
FROM Employees em inner join Locations lc on em.LocationID=lc.LocationID
left join (select pvt.* from
   (select e.EmployeeID,e.Phone,
    DENSE_RANK() OVER (PARTITION BY e.EmployeeID ORDER BY e.Phone) denserank
    FROM EmployeePhones e) ep
  PIVOT (min(Phone) for denserank IN ([1],[2])) pvt) ea
   on em.EmployeeID=ea.EmployeeID
```

Notice how complicated it can be to simulate zero-form structures from a normalized design! To get the phone numbers requires a subquery that first ranks them and then pivots the top two ranks for each employee into a single output row. Normally you would probably never attempt something like this, because in a client application it makes more sense to view and edit child tables using a separate linked list.

In the real world, most database professionals intuitively design tables in the third normal form from the ground up. After a while, it becomes so second nature that when you do run across a de-normalized table, it looks *strange*, even if you don't see the anomaly right away.

Now that I have covered normalization and why it makes sense, I will turn right around and tear it down a bit by presenting some cases in which you might actually want to de-normalize a table.

De-Normalization

It has been said that there can be too much of a good thing, and optimization is no exception. Very few databases rigidly adhere to a fully normalized form. There are situations in which making a few small concessions in an otherwise normalized design can significantly improve performance. In these situations, most database professionals will choose to de-normalize and won't lose any sleep over it.

As with normalization, an example will serve better than words alone. Assume for a moment that in the AdventureWorks2008 application, it was a requirement that the business client display the date of the last order for a product whenever the product was viewed or used. This value could be retrieved from the fully normalized structure using the following query:

```
SELECT p.ProductID,p.Name,d.LastOrder
FROM Production.Product p left join
```

```
(SELECT sd.ProductId,MAX(sh.OrderDate) 'LastOrder'
      FROM Sales.SalesOrderDetail sd inner join Sales.SalesOrderHeader sh
  on sd.SalesOrderID=sh.SalesOrderID
  GROUP BY sd.ProductID) d on p.ProductID=d.ProductID
-- 221ms CPU time, 468ms elapsed time, 1931 logical reads
```

By itself, this query does not take all that long to run; however; if you had to run it 10,000 times a day, the cumulative effect might be considerable because of the overhead involved in reading and sorting all of the order history records to find the one value of interest. In this case, it might make sense to de-normalize the database a little bit and save the last order date for each product in the product record. Furthermore, to automatically maintain this calculation in real time, you should create a trigger or, if it is available, tap into the stored procedures used to update the sales order tables. After making these changes, you would be able to simplify the query above to look like the following:

```
SELECT ProductID,Name,LastOrder
FROM Production.Product
-- 0ms CPU time, 161ms elapsed time, 15 logical reads
```

The new query runs considerably faster than the original, and the biggest difference is in the number of reads required (15 vs. 1,931). The cost for this Read performance boost is the increased time to maintain the new value whenever a sales order is updated. If the usage pattern of the database suggests that product reads occur more often than product writes, then this would be a good optimization.

This optimization does introduce the possibility of inconsistent data, where the calculated last order date does not match the actual last order date. If you attempt something similar, you should create a validation procedure to check the calculated column and then run it regularly until you are confident that your calculation process is working correctly.

Another common scenario in which databases are de-normalized is when the business rules dictate that there will only be so many of a given element. For example, if your business rules limited a customer to only two phone numbers, then the overhead of creating a linked phone number list might outweigh any risks of data inconsistency. In this case, you might be better off by just creating a Phone1 and a Phone2 field in the customer table.

De-normalization is a difficult decision and should be carefully considered. Even so, as long as you make sure that you recognize the trade-offs involved, it is an optimization tool that you should consider.

Data Type Selection

When choosing the data types for columns in your tables, you should select the smallest data type that is capable of containing the possible range of values. Smaller data types will require less space to store, reduce I/O overhead, produce smaller indexes, and respond faster to searches. Consider the following when choosing a data type:

- ❏ Char **versus** Varchar — This seems to be one of the biggest problem areas. Char values are fixed width, and unless you are using compression, they will consume a byte of storage for every character position. Varchar values are variable length and will only use as many bytes of storage as there are characters; however, varchar fields do have a couple of bytes of overhead. In general, only use Char for fields that are less than 4 bytes in length, or where all the data is close to the same length.

❑ **Varchar versus Text** — This is an easy one: Use varchar! Microsoft intends to deprecate the Text, NText, and Image data types. In SQL Server 2005 and above, you can use the varchar(max) data type to hold up to 2^{31} bytes of text.

❑ **Unicode Strings** — Unicode strings are prefixed by an *N*. These strings consume twice as much space (2 bytes per character) as the non-Unicode equivalents. Only use the Unicode data types if your data will contain international characters.

❑ **Integer Options** — Sometimes I have to remind developers that there are other integer types besides int (Int32). For example, for small values between 0 and 255, you can use a tinyint (byte), and for values between −32,768 and 32,767, you can use a smallint (Int16).

❑ **Date/Time Options** — Data and time values can be difficult to deal with. Fortunately, SQL Server 2008 has addressed this by adding several new date and time data types. You can now choose between datetime, smalldatetime, date, time, datetime2, and datetimeoffset. Make sure that you understand the differences between these data types before deciding which to use.

❑ **Unique Identifiers** — Consider adding a GUID column if you want to support offline clients; however, you should avoid using a GUID as the primary or cluster key for the table.

❑ **Object Data** — If your object can be represented as XML, then use the XML data type. Otherwise, use the varbinary data types. Starting with SQL Server 2005, varbinary(max) columns can contain up to 2^{31} bytes of data!

❑ **Binary Data** — Pure binary data can be stored using the varbinary data type, but you might also want to consider the new filestream data type as well.

SQL Server supports several additional advanced data types. Refer to Books Online for the complete list.

Handling Complex Object Data

As business systems continue to evolve, complex data structures are becoming more and more common. Complex data presents a series of new challenges for database administrators because it often does not fit into a classical relational model.

Rather than trying to force the data into a rigid relational structure, SQL Server 2008 offers several other possibilities to store non-traditional data, such as the XML, FileStream, Spatial, Hierarchy, sql_variant, and varbinary data types. These options open up a host of new possibilities for using SQL Server.

Remember when planning for complex data that SQL Server is still a *relational* database (vs. an *object* database). If you want to be able to easily identify and search for your complex data, you should plan to extract one or more key *metadata* fields and save those in discrete columns along with your complex data blob. This will allow SQL Server to do what it does best and still support your complex data clients.

Declarative Referential Integrity (DRI)

Declarative referential integrity (DRI) is a feature of SQL Server that prevents inconsistent data, such as widowed or orphaned records. DRI is one of the best tools in the SQL arsenal, and I strongly encourage its use whenever possible. DRI not only provides guaranteed integrity for related data, but it also provides much better performance than trying to do the same thing using triggers or application code. The reason that DRI performs better is that it relies on constraints to enforce the data relationships, which prevents inconsistent changes up front rather than rolling them back after the fact (like triggers). DRI is also able to automatically cascade changes to related tables — all without having to write a single line of code.

If a DRI relationship is established between two tables, this allows you to confidently use a more efficient INNER JOIN when querying the tables together (discounting nullable fields). Without DRI, there is no guarantee that a matching record will exist in the other table, requiring the use of a less efficient OUTER JOIN to avoid excluding unmatched records. When designing queries, it is never safe to assume the validity of a relationship unless DRI is employed.

Consider the following example of how DRI can simplify a common task and protect your data:

In the AdventureWorks2008 database, the Person.BusinessEntity table contains a common underlying reference that identifies an *entity* that can be a person, store, or vendor (or all three at the same time) and can have an address and a list of associated contacts. Figure 11-1 shows the DRI relationships between these tables.

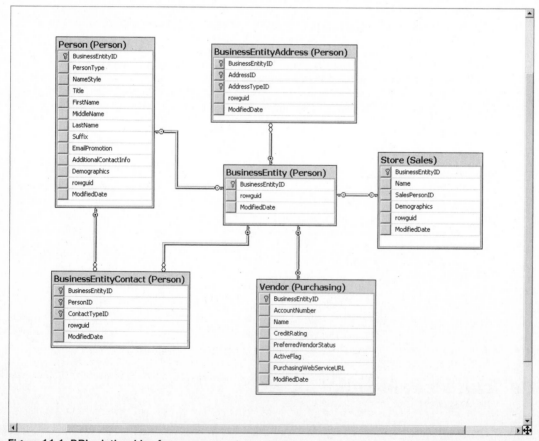

Figure 11-1: DRI relationships for Person.BusinessEntity.

It would not be prudent to delete the entity if any related records still existed in the database. This would "orphan" the related records and very likely break the application. In order to do this without DRI, you would need to do something like the following:

```
Use AdventureWorks2008
GO

BEGIN TRY

DECLARE @BEID int
SET @BEID=1

-- Has an Address?
IF EXISTS(SELECT * FROM Person.BusinessEntityAddress WHERE BusinessEntityID=@BEID)
  RAISERROR('In use in Person.BusinessEntityAddress table',16,0)
-- In use as a Person?
If EXISTS(SELECT * FROM Person.Person WHERE BusinessEntityID=@BEID)
  RAISERROR('In use in Person.Person table',16,0)
-- In use as a Contact?
IF EXISTS(SELECT * FROM Person.BusinessEntityContact WHERE BusinessEntityID=@BEID)
  RAISERROR('In use in Person.BusinessEntityContact table',16,0)
-- In use as a Store?
IF EXISTS(SELECT * FROM Sales.Store WHERE BusinessEntityID=@BEID)
  RAISERROR('In use in Sales.Store table',16,0)
-- In use as a Vendor?
IF EXISTS(SELECT * FROM Purchasing.Vendor WHERE BusinessEntityID=@BEID)
  RAISERROR('In use in Purchasing.Vendor table',16,0)

-- Everything is OK, delete the entity
DELETE FROM Person.BusinessEntity WHERE BusinessEntityID=1;

END TRY
BEGIN CATCH
  Print ERROR_MESSAGE()
END CATCH

-- RESULTS -
In use in Person.BusinessEntityAddress table
```

With DRI, you can accomplish the same thing (and more) in one line by simply attempting to delete the record as follows:

```
DELETE FROM Person.BusinessEntity WHERE BusinessEntityID=1;

-- RESULTS --
Msg 547, Level 16, State 0, Line 2
The DELETE statement conflicted with the REFERENCE constraint
 "FK_BusinessEntityAddress_BusinessEntity_BusinessEntityID". The conflict
  occurred in database "AdventureWorks2008", table "Person.BusinessEntityAddress",
  column 'BusinessEntityID'.
The statement has been terminated.
```

With DRI, maintaining data integrity is faster, easier, and more reliable than with other methods. DRI guarantees data integrity at all times, regardless of who or what is attempting to make the change.

DRI can also cascade updates and deletions to related tables or set related values to null, or to a default value. The bottom line is that DRI is the only way to absolutely ensure that your data remains consistent.

Constraints versus Triggers

Constraints and *triggers* are both means of using SQL Server to enforce conditions on data in tables. The difference between these two methods really boils down to flexibility versus performance. Triggers are more flexible, but they are much slower, require more overhead, and only fire after the rows have already been updated (forcing a rollback to undo changes). Constraints are more limited, leaner, and are applied before changes are made.

It is advantageous to use constraints in place of triggers whenever possible. In fact, SQL Server uses constraints internally to maintain primary key integrity and enforce DRI conditions. SQL Server supports several different kinds of constraints as listed below:

❑ **Primary Key** — Maintains unique entries for the defined primary key. This type of constraint is created automatically when you define a primary key.

❑ **Foreign Key** — Used to enforce DRI relationships to maintain data integrity. Foreign keys are created automatically when you define a DRI relationship between two tables.

❑ **Unique** — *Unique constraints* are used to guarantee that data values are unique across an entire table or a subset of a table (using a filtered index). Unique constraints are created when you define a unique index with a type of "unique key."

❑ **Check** — *Check constraints* are used to enforce data integrity by defining what data is valid in a table. Check constraints are enforced whenever data is inserted or updated. The most common type of check constraint is not allowing null values. Multiple check constraints can be applied to a given column.

❑ **Default** — *Default constraints* assign default values to columns that are not specified when inserting new records. This can help simplify insert statements by not requiring that a value be specified for every non-nullable field.

It is true that a trigger can do almost everything that a constraint can do; however, not taking advantage of constraints whenever possible would in a sense be using the wrong tool for the job. If you have to dig a hole, a shovel will work much better than a spoon. So why wouldn't you use the shovel?

The only time you should use triggers to enforce data integrity is when your business logic is too complex to represent as a constraint. Arguably, if this is the case, a better option for the business logic might be a middle-tier or an application server.

Deciding What to Index

The choice of what to index is probably the single biggest performance-related decision that you can make for a database. Indexes provide a context for locating and retrieving data rows in a table. They are used by SQL Server to identify specific records, speed up searches, optimize query plans, limit disk I/O, and even to physically order the raw data itself. Good index choices can improve query performance by several orders of magnitude, and poor choices can bring your database to its knees.

A basic overview of indexes is included in Chapter 5, and I won't attempt to repeat that information here. Instead, this section is devoted to providing you with a series of guidelines and recommendations that you can use to make better index decisions.

Primary Key Choice

The *primary key* is one of the two most important decisions that you will need to make for each table (the other is the cluster key choice). It is responsible for uniquely identifying rows in the table and prevents duplicate records from being created. Only one primary key can be declared per table, and all values must be unique and cannot be null. Every index that you create will implicitly include the primary key (or unique key) as a pointer in order to be able to look up the underlying records efficiently.

The choice of primary key is a hotly debated topic among database professionals. There are two main schools of thought on this subject: natural versus surrogate.

❑ **Natural Key** — A *natural key* is one that is based on a business element that represents the data entity. For example, a currency table might use a currency code as a natural key to uniquely identify the type of currency. In general, natural keys are easier to read and may reduce the complexity of queries, provided that the natural identifier is commonly understood. Simple lookup tables are ideal candidates for natural keys.

❑ **Surrogate Key** — A *surrogate key* is one that has nothing to do with any business requirements and is added simply to define a unique identifier. Identity columns are commonly used as surrogate keys, and you will find many examples of this throughout the AdventureWorks2008 database. Surrogate keys are preferred when a business entity (table) does not have a clearly identifiable natural key or when the natural key can frequently change.

A design that is largely based on surrogate keys will be extremely efficient since most of the joins between tables will be based on a single field. Using natural keys does not provide this advantage; instead, each level of child objects must define a composite primary key based on the parent's natural key and its own natural key. Take a look at Figure 11-2, which compares natural keys versus surrogate keys for a parent–child–grandchild structure.

> *The primary key in the natural key structure does not allow the same invoice number to be used more than once for the same vendor or the same line number to be used multiple times on the same invoice. To mirror these business rules in the surrogate version, you must create unique constraints for the* Invoice *and* InvoiceLine *tables as indicated.*

As you can see, using natural primary keys in an *n*-tier parent–child structure is not the best choice. Complex business systems commonly have parent–child hierarchies that are five or more levels deep. The fifth tier would end up having a five-part primary key! Smaller keys mean narrower (fewer bytes per row) tables, which improves performance by allowing more data and index pages to fit into the cache.

Consider what would happen in the example above if a vendor code was changed. In the natural key version, in addition to the vendor record itself, every related invoice and invoice line would have to be updated. In the surrogate version, the corresponding change would only require a single update to the vendor record. Now imagine the impact of changing the size of the vendor code. If the business decided that vendor codes needed to be extended by two characters, then the natural key approach would require a structural change to every table in the hierarchy, while the surrogate version would only require a change to a single table.

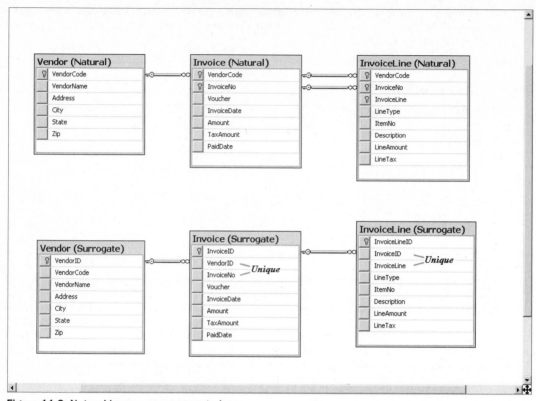

Figure 11-2: Natural keys versus surrogate keys.

So if surrogate keys are so good, why would you ever want to use a natural key? To put it simply, natural keys are more "natural." They make the tables easier for users to understand and manage. In fact, it is extremely uncommon to find a database that does not use some natural keys.

When choosing a primary key, consider the following:

- ❏ The primary key should not change.

- ❏ The data type should be an integer or a short, fixed-width character. Short character keys are often used for small lookup tables, such as currency, freight, commodity, group, or category codes. The narrower the primary key, the better the performance. This implies that an integer IDENTITY would be a better choice than a GUID.

- ❏ Avoid "smart" keys with embedded business codes. Using keys with embedded business meanings will require extensive data refactoring when the business requirements change. The meaning of the primary key should remain unchanged over time.

- ❏ Consider natural keys for simple lookup tables. Many lookup tables are perfectly suited to natural keys, such as lists of states, currencies, zip codes, freight carriers, or export commodities.

- ❏ Consider surrogate keys for hierarchical parent–child structures. As demonstrated previously, there are clear benefits for surrogate keys in parent–child structures, especially if they extend very many levels deep.

❑ Natural key searches must still be supported. Even if you use a surrogate primary key, you should still define an alternate unique natural key for lookup purposes. Humans prefer natural keys, and they look good on reports.

❑ Try to minimize the use of composite primary keys. Composite keys increase the width of the primary key, which, in turn, reduces performance. Even so, there are specific cases in which composite keys make sense. One such example is in many-to-many join tables, where the primary key is often a combination of the (surrogate) keys of the tables being joined.

Cluster Key Choice

The *cluster key* is what determines the physical order in which data is stored in pages on disk. The physical order of the data plays an important role in determining how many I/O operations must be done in order to find and retrieve records. Tables without a cluster key are basically an unorganized "heap" of data. A heap is not a very efficient way of storing information that you might actually need later on. Imagine that you had a collection of 10,000 baseball cards that were stored in no particular order in a big bin. If you wanted to locate your 1952 Mickey Mantle card, you would have to go through each card one-by-one. This is the equivalent of a "table scan" in SQL Server. If, instead, you had physically organized your cards in some way, then you would be able to find the one that you wanted much more quickly because you would have to "scan" fewer items. For example, if all the cards were in last name order, then you would be able to pull out just the "Mantle" cards and then scan through a much smaller set to find what you wanted. Scanning a subset of data based on its physical order is known as a *clustered index scan*.

Changing the cluster key on a production database can be a very resource-intensive task. This will lock the table while all of the existing data is physically moved and reordered, potentially causing downtime. For this reason, it is important to make the proper choice for the cluster key up front.

So what makes the best choice for physically ordering data in a table? This is actually a complex topic, and the easy out is to just say, "It depends," and leave it at that. Personally, I have never been satisfied with that answer, and my first response is usually "on what?" Looking at this from a performance perspective, I can provide a much better answer.

The choice of cluster key should have as many of the following characteristics as possible:

❑ **Highly Selective** — A highly selective key will result in fewer records that must be scanned per clustered range. In the baseball card example above, the last name is a highly selective value. A particular last name will limit a search to a small fraction of the whole collection. A weaker choice would be Year or Team, since these do not limit the results by nearly as much. Of course, the best choice would be a field with total selectivity — in other words, a unique value.

❑ **Rarely Changed** — Changing a cluster key value involves moving the record to a new page in order to maintain the physical order. Needless to say, this can be costly in terms of I/O performance, and it tends to cause fragmentation of the table, which slows down access even further. The best selection is a field with values that never change.

❑ **Ever Increasing Values** — When a table is clustered, records are stored in pages on disk, based on a range of cluster key values. As long as the key values are always increasing, new data will be efficiently added to the end of the cluster. This will eliminate fragmentation on the table and fill the data pages to capacity, which maximizes I/O throughput. If keys are inserted that fall into a prior range, then SQL Server may have to "split" a page to squeeze in the new value.

❑ **Narrow** — Keys with fewer bytes per record are preferable to wider keys. Not only does this allow for faster sorting and searching of the key values, it also has a hidden impact. In SQL Server, the cluster key is actually part of every non-clustered index as well! This makes sense when you consider that SQL Server has to have some way to look up the physical records associated with each index value. The best choice is a single column containing an `integer`, `datetime`, or small, fixed-length character value.

❑ **Commonly Filtered by Range** — Clustered indexes provide superior performance when you need to return a range of data. This includes using operators such as `BETWEEN`, `<`, `>`, `<=`, and `>=`.

❑ **Frequently Sorted or Grouped** — A clustered index on a column that is commonly used in `ORDER BY` or `GROUP BY` expressions can improve performance by eliminating the need for SQL Server to sort the data.

❑ **Often Used in Join Clauses** — In some cases, there is an advantage to clustering by a field that is often used to join tables, such as foreign key columns, especially when records are commonly retrieved using the foreign key as a filter. A common example of this is clustering a child table by the parent ID.

Considering the desirable characteristics defined above, there are three clear preferences for the cluster key choice. When selecting a cluster key, strongly consider one of the following:

❑ **The Primary Key** — This is the most commonly used cluster key, in part because SQL Server will automatically cluster the primary key when it is first created, provided that there is not a pre-defined cluster key on the table. This is normally a good choice because the primary key shares several of the characteristics that are desirable for a cluster key. In fact, if the primary key is a surrogate `IDENTITY` key, then this choice will be unique, unchanging, ever-increasing, and narrow. Depending on the specific business use for the table, the remaining criteria could be true as well, making this a nearly perfect choice.

❑ **A Transaction Date** — For transaction tables and archives, a compelling choice for the cluster key is the date of the transaction. Normally this is a stamped date that is ever-increasing. The `datetime` data type is accurate to within 3 ms (milliseconds), which is highly selective. Business rules normally dictate that transaction date stamps can never change, and the transaction date is commonly used to sort and limit query results.

❑ **A Foreign Key** — In certain cases, a foreign key can also make a good choice for a cluster key. This is particularly true for child tables in a hierarchical structure. Assuming that the database is using surrogate `IDENTITY` keys, choosing a parent ID as the cluster key provides an unchanging, narrow key that is often used in join clauses, and to filter and group results.

Of course, the final selection for the cluster key should be based on performance testing results gathered during a period of "typical" activity.

GUIDS as Cluster Keys

A common mistake made by database designers is to use a GUID as the cluster key. Don't do it!

First, take a look at the criteria for cluster keys as defined in the previous section. On the plus side, GUIDs are unique and do not change. On the minus side, they are wide, random, not used to sort or group, and not commonly filtered by range. This alone tips the scale against using a GUID as a cluster key, but there is an even bigger problem.

The fact that GUIDs are random is what makes them just about the worst possible choice for a cluster key. Clustering a GUID column will result in almost perfect fragmentation of the index ranges because SQL Server has no idea how to establish efficient ranges for random values. As records are added, additional page splits will occur as SQL Server moves data around to make room for the new values. Compounding the problem is that SQL Server includes the cluster key as a hidden part of every non-clustered index. Therefore, not only will the clustered index be fragmented, so will every non-clustered index!

If you are stuck with a table that uses a GUID cluster key and are unable to change the structure, consider generating the values using NEWSEQUENTIALID *instead of* NEWID. *This will generate GUIDs such that each new value will be greater than the prior values, which will considerably reduce fragmentation.*

When dealing with GUIDs, a better choice is to add a surrogate IDENTITY key for the table and to make that the primary and cluster key. Then create a unique constraint on the GUID column, allowing it to act as an alternate unique key.

Other Indexes

Beyond the primary and cluster keys, what else should be indexed? For most database administrators, this is a daunting question. I typically see two approaches: everything or nothing. Neither of these approaches is ideal. It is true that indexes are the single biggest factor in improving query performance; however, every index actually slows down insert and update operations and consumes storage space. In fact, for a heavily indexed table, it is not uncommon for the indexes to actually consume more storage space than the table itself! Therefore, what is needed is a way to find a compromise that balances data retrieval and data update performance.

Before continuing, it is worth pointing out that the benefits of *any* index will increase as the number of rows in the table increases. On a table with few rows (less than 1,000) the benefits of an index will be negligible. For small tables, the only indexes that you should consider are the primary/cluster keys and possibly a unique key.

The guidelines for *generic indexes* are a bit more relaxed than those for primary or cluster key indexes. In general, you will realize the biggest performance benefits if your indexes fall into one or more of the following categories:

- ❏ **Narrow** — Short, or "narrow," indexes will perform better than wider indexes, especially as the tables involved increase in size. Query operations on large tables (especially larger than the cache) are very disk I/O-intensive. A narrow index will require fewer disk reads and allow more values to be cached. In addition, indexes are commonly used for comparison operations, and smaller entries are easier to compare.

- ❏ **Selective** — The degree of selectivity is a critical factor for any index. This can range from perfectly selective (all values are unique) to all inclusive (all values are the same). It is pointless to index a column where all the values are the same! The higher the degree of selectivity, the more benefit an index will provide. SQL Server keeps track of the selectivity of each index and uses this when creating query plans.

- ❏ **Covering** — A *covering index* is a compound index that contains all of the columns required to produce the required results. This may seem contradictory to the *narrow* category described above, and, indeed, this type of index will be more I/O-intensive; however, it will be less intensive than having to look up the underlying row data. A good covering index can save a lot disk reads. To maximize the effectiveness of the index, order the columns from most selective to least selective.

❑   **Unique Constraints** — *Unique constraints* are used to enforce the uniqueness of the data in a column or a combination of columns. This is common when using a natural key as an alternative lookup value for a surrogate primary key.

Prime candidates for indexes are any columns that are used in DRI foreign key joins and any columns commonly used to limit query results. Each of these possibilities should be evaluated to determine if an index will be of benefit.

Indexed Views and Filtered Indexes

Indexed views and *filtered indexes* are more advanced indexing techniques that you can use to further refine and optimize your database. There is a certain amount of overlap in their functionality, and where this occurs, it makes sense to use the lighter-weight filtered indexes. I will briefly explain each of these index types and then present an example in which filtered indexes are a better choice.

An *indexed view* is really just an ordinary view that has a clustered index. This allows SQL Server to blur the line between tables and views by treating the view as a *virtual table*. As a result, indexed views inherit all the capabilities of views combined with the indexing benefits of tables. Traditionally, indexed views have been used to restrict users to a subset of data and to present data to users in a logical format, including pre-calculated data aggregations and transforms. When combined with schema binding, it is also possible to use indexed views to enforce constraints on subsets of the original table, and this approach provides a non-trigger-based option for enforcing unique values only for non-null entries in a column.

Another interesting use for indexed views is to virtually de-normalize a complex relational structure for consumption by an application. The indexed view will be automatically maintained by SQL Server when the source data changes and will have the side benefit of offloading I/O from the source tables. Placing an "instead of" trigger on the indexed view could even allow it be fully updateable by the client.

> I have often seen it stated that indexed views are an enterprise-only feature. This is not true. Indexed views can be created and used in any version of SQL Server. However, only in the Enterprise Edition will the Query Processor automatically consider the indexed view. In other versions, the indexed view will only be considered if you reference it by name and use the NOEXPAND hint. Filtered indexes, on the other hand, are automatically considered in all versions of SQL Server.

With SQL Server 2008, a new option has been introduced known as *filtered indexes*. A *filtered index* is simply a table index that only applies to a subset of data based on "simple" comparison logic (no *like* operators). Filtered indexes do not need to be unique, and since they are associated with the table directly, they are more likely to be used by the Query Optimizer for a wider range of queries than indexed views. Among other possibilities, filtered indexes offer a direct and easy solution for enforcing unique entries on a nullable column.

Owing to their performance advantage over indexed views, whenever possible you should use filtered indexes instead of indexed views. Filtered indexes must meet the following conditions:

- ❑ **Single Table** — All columns for a filtered index must be in the same table.
- ❑ **No Computed Columns** — No computed columns are permitted in filtered indexes.
- ❑ **Simple Comparison Logic** — The filter clause must be expressed using simple comparison operators (no *like* comparisons). Null evaluation is permitted using the IS NULL and IS NOT NULL operators.

Try It Out   Create a Filtered Index on a Nullable Column

In this example, assume that we need to establish a customer *alias* that can be used to uniquely identify a customer, but that not every customer will have an alias. There are three approaches that we could use to enforce this condition: a trigger, an indexed view, or a filtered index. You will need to evaluate each option and determine which one will work best:

1. You must create the alias column in the Sales.Customer table. You can do this either with SQL Server Management Studio or by executing the following in a new command window:

```
USE AdventureWorks2008
GO


ALTER TABLE Sales.Customer ADD Alias varchar(10) null
```

2. You need to update a couple of values in the new column. Enter the following into an SSMS command window and execute it:

```
USE AdventureWorks2008
GO


UPDATE Sales.Customer SET Alias='NJSP' WHERE CustomerID=1
UPDATE Sales.Customer SET Alias='DCJS' WHERE CustomerID=2
```

3. Now that the column has been defined and has a couple of data items, you need to evaluate the methods to enforce the business condition that non-null entries should be unique. A unique constraint is not possible in this case because more than one value might be null. Select an option below based on what you know about triggers, indexed views, and filtered indexes. Enter the code associated with your selection in a command window, and execute it within the AdventureWorks2008 database context.

```
-- OPTION 1, TRIGGER IMPLEMENTATION
CREATE TRIGGER Sales.trigUniqueAlias ON Sales.Customer FOR INSERT,UPDATE
AS
SET NOCOUNT ON;
IF (SELECT count(CustomerID) FROM inserted
   WHERE exists (SELECT CustomerID FROM Sales.Customer sc
       WHERE sc.Alias = inserted.Alias
       AND sc.CustomerID!= inserted.CustomerID)) > 0
```

```
        BEGIN;
          ROLLBACK TRANSACTION;
        END;
        GO
        --DROP TRIGGER Sales.trigUniqueAlias
        --GO

        -- OPTION 2, INDEXED VIEW IMPLEMENTATION
        CREATE VIEW Sales.vCustomerAlias WITH SCHEMABINDING
        AS
        SELECT CustomerID,Alias
        FROM Sales.Customer
        WHERE (Alias IS NOT NULL);
        GO
        CREATE UNIQUE CLUSTERED INDEX CK_vCustomerAlias ON
        Sales.vCustomerAlias(Alias);
        GO
        --DROP VIEW Sales.vCustomerAlias
        --GO

        -- OPTION 3, FILTERED INDEX IMPLEMENTATION
        CREATE UNIQUE NONCLUSTERED INDEX FICustomerAlias
            ON Sales.Customer (Alias)
        WHERE Alias IS NOT NULL;
        GO
        --DROP INDEX FICustomerAlias ON Sales.Customer
        --GO
```

4. Now you will need to evaluate your choice. You can use the built-in statistics-gathering ability of SQL Server to accomplish this inline. Enter the following code in a new command window and execute it:

```
        USE AdventureWorks2008
        GO

        SET STATISTICS IO ON;
        SET STATISTICS TIME ON;
        UPDATE Sales.Customer SET Alias='NJSP' WHERE CustomerID=2
```

The statement should generate an error and display the time and I/O statistics. Listing only the relevant time and statistics entries for each option, the output should be like one of the following:

```
    *** TRIGGER RESULTS ***
    Msg 3609, Level 16, State 1, Line 1
    The transaction ended in the trigger. The batch has been aborted.
    Table 'Customer'. Scan count 0, logical reads 2, physical reads 0,
     read-ahead reads 0, lob logical reads 0, lob physical reads 0,
     lob read-ahead reads 0.
    Table 'Customer'. Scan count 1, logical reads 3, physical reads 0,
     read-ahead reads 0, lob logical reads 0, lob physical reads 0,
     lob read-ahead reads 0.
    SQL Server Execution Times:
       CPU time = 10 ms,   elapsed time = 215 ms.

    *** INDEXED VIEW RESULTS ***
```

```
Msg 2601, Level 14, State 1, Line 1
Cannot insert duplicate key row in object 'Sales.vCustomerAlias'
 with unique index 'CK_vCustomerAlias'.
The statement has been terminated.
SQL Server Execution Times:
   CPU time = 10 ms,  elapsed time = 8 ms.

*** FILTERED INDEX RESULTS ***
Msg 2601, Level 14, State 1, Line 1
Cannot insert duplicate key row in object 'Sales.Customer'
 with unique index 'FICustomerAlias'.
The statement has been terminated.
SQL Server Execution Times:
   CPU time = 0 ms,  elapsed time = 2 ms.
```

Notice that the filtered index option is clearly superior when it comes to performance. In fact, the filtered index approach was four times faster than the indexed view approach and a whopping 100 times faster than using a trigger!

If you want, you can experiment with the other options by repeating the final update after first running the DROP code listed below each option and then running the code to activate a new option.

Minimizing Blocking

To support multiple concurrent users and updates, SQL Server implements a complex resource-locking system. Locks can occur at the row, index, page, extent, table, or database level, and are automatically escalated as needed during a transaction. Blocking occurs when multiple processes attempt to lock the same resources at the same time. The first process that requires a particular resource will lock it, and any other processes that require the same resource will be blocked until the first process releases the lock.

> *I am simplifying a bit here for the sake of brevity. In actuality, blocking is a bit more complex, in that there are multiple kinds of locks and only certain combinations will actually block.*

In addition to slowing down operations, there are two critical risks related to blocking — deadlocks and time-outs. Deadlocks occur when two processes become mutually locked, with each requiring a resource that is held by the other. When this happens, one connection is terminated by the server, which can cause application errors and data loss. Time-outs occur when a client has been blocked for so long that it simply gives up. By default, most connections will time-out after they have been blocked for 30 seconds. Again, depending on how the application is designed, in some cases time-outs can cause application exceptions that result in lost data.

Normally SQL Server is fairly good at handling locking and blocking issues; however, it always pays to help minimize these types of problems whenever possible. With that in mind, here are some tips that you can use to help minimize blocking issues:

❑ **Keep It Short** — The shorter the transaction, the less likely it is that it will block anything. When inside a transaction, try to avoid using loops (while, etc.) or cursors, and avoid statements that access large numbers of rows. Never ask for user input during a transaction.

❏ **Prepare, Then Transact** — Do all of your conditional evaluations, lookups, and other preparation before initiating the transaction. In addition, try to avoid interleaving reads and updates within the same transaction. One method that works well for this is to use table variables to store pre-calculated results and to determine affected records, and then update all necessary rows in a single operation.

❏ **Use Stored Procedures** — If possible, use stored procedures rather than direct table updates. Wrapping your transactions inside a stored procedure is more secure and provides better performance.

❏ **Use a Normalized Schema** — One of the nice side effects of normalization is that it automatically helps reduce blocking issues by separating tables into smaller logical units.

❏ **Separate Reporting from Transactions** — Gathering data for reports can access huge amounts of data at one time, especially when performing rollups or processing data cubes. Whenever possible, try to separate your analytical reporting (OLAP) databases from your transaction processing databases (OLTP).

In addition, you can affect blocking by adjusting the server transaction isolation level setting or by using a query or table hint to manually select a locking granularity level. Query and table hints are described in more detail in the "Query Optimization" section later in this chapter.

Hidden Dangers of Time-Outs

Locking leads to blocking, blocking leads to time-outs, and time-outs lead to trouble. At issue is the fact that a time-out is a *client-side* event, and when a client times out, SQL Server simply stops whatever it was doing on that connection. This can have some unanticipated results if the time-out occurs in the middle of a transaction, even if the transaction was initiated by the server inside a stored procedure!

Take a look at the following stored procedure. On the surface it appears solid, with no obvious way for the code to exit without closing out the transaction. If there are any errors, then the catch block will roll back the transaction; otherwise, the transaction will commit.

```
CREATE PROCEDURE up_UpdateInTrx
AS
BEGIN
  SET NOCOUNT ON;
  BEGIN TRY
    BEGIN TRAN

    UPDATE Production.Product
    SET SafetyStockLevel=55
    WHERE ProductID=1

    UPDATE Production.ProductInventory
    SET Bin=5
    WHERE ProductID=1

    COMMIT TRAN
    Return(0)
  END TRY
BEGIN CATCH
  ROLLBACK TRAN
```

```
        Return(1)
    END CATCH
  END
  GO
```

Looks can be deceiving. There is a subtle hole in this procedure that could let the code "escape" without rolling back or committing the transaction. You guessed it — a time-out. In particular, if any of the statements inside the transaction were blocked by another process for more than 30 seconds (by default), then the client would generate a time-out. When this occurs, the client tells the server to cancel whatever it is doing. SQL Server simply abandons the command, and no error is raised to trigger the catch block.

Because the time-out is initiated by the client, SQL Server expects the client to handle it and do any required cleanup. Part of this cleanup should be rolling back the open transaction; however, unless you were explicitly aware that the server initiated a transaction, it might not occur to you to check for this in your client exception-handling code. It is often overlooked.

There are a couple of possible outcomes. If the client closes the connection, then the open transaction will be automatically rolled back by SQL Server. On the other hand, if the client continues to use the connection for further transactions, then a serious problem develops. All of the additional transactions will occur inside the original uncommitted transaction. As more transactions are run on this connection, more and more resources will be locked, greatly increasing the chance of additional time-outs and even deadlocks. If this cycle continues long enough and locks enough resources, the server will become unresponsive. Eventually, the client application will be closed (or killed), or the server will be restarted, either of which will terminate the original connection and roll back every change that was made after the original time-out. Without understanding what is going on, it will appear that SQL Server "lost" data.

If you are using a connection pool, such as the ASP.NET default pool, then the problem can get even worse. Closing a pooled connection simply returns the connection to the pool rather than actually closing it. From there the connections will continue to lock resources on the server and may even be reused for additional transactions — which will also be uncommitted. Once the connection is ultimately closed, SQL Server will roll back every uncommitted change.

One way to avoid leaving open transactions after a time-out is to use the "SET XACT_ABORT ON" command in the stored procedure. By default, SQL Server leaves XACT_ABORT off, which means that it is the client's responsibility to clean up following a time-out. If you turn on XACT_ABORT at the beginning of your procedure, then SQL Server will take responsibility for cleaning up if there is a time-out.

Query Optimization

The Query Optimizer in SQL Server 2008 is responsible for handling the extremely difficult task of finding the most efficient way to execute a query. Every query has an intrinsic *search space* that represents the maximum possible number of operations that might be required to satisfy the search conditions. The Optimizer tries to order the execution steps in such as way as to reduce the search space as quickly as possible, thus limiting the overall number of operations required to generate a result.

Statistics are a critical factor in generating efficient query plans. They collect information on the cardinality (number of rows) and selectivity (distribution of data) for each table. Statistics are used by the Query Optimizer to weight the relative *costs* of the various methods for generating the same results. If the statistics are significantly out-of-date, or worse, non-existent, then the Optimizer will have to guess. Needless to say, if it guesses wrong, then your query performance will suffer. For example, if the statistics were out-of-date for a table and were reporting that it only had 10 rows of data, then the Optimizer might choose to do a table scan instead of an index lookup. If it turned out that the table actually had 100,000 rows, then the choice of a table scan would be very costly. Poor cardinality and selectivity estimates are the primary causes of inefficient query plans.

Indexes provide the Query Optimizer with additional options. Indexes on reasonably selective columns used in `where`, `join`, or `group by` clauses will typically be chosen by the Optimizer over a table scan. Indexes that contain all of the required output columns will even allow the Optimizer to avoid accessing the table data at all.

As you might have guessed, creating a plan for a complex query can consume a fair amount of CPU resources on its own. It would be a waste of resources to keep generating new plans over and over again, so in most cases SQL Server will only generate a plan once and then save it in memory in the *plan cache*. Subsequent executions will then use the cached plan until it ages out of memory or is invalidated.

Execution Plans

An *execution plan* describes the sequence of steps that the Query Optimizer has selected to process a query. Execution plans are a database administrator's primary means of troubleshooting poorly performing queries; therefore, it is very important to understand how to interpret them to identify and resolve problem areas and high-cost steps.

Execution plans come in two different flavors: estimated and actual. The *estimated plan* is what is generated by the Query Optimizer, and this plan is passed to the storage engine for processing. The *actual plan* is what the storage engine actually did. In the large majority of cases, the estimated and actual plans will be the same. The only time you are likely to see a difference is when the statistics are out-of-date or when the storage engine decides to try parallel processing in a multiple-CPU environment. In these cases, the storage engine may ignore the proposed plan and use its own.

Plan Caching

After the Query Optimizer submits the estimated execution plan, the storage engine compares it to any actual plans that are already in the plan cache. If a matching plan is found in the plan cache, then it will be reused, which saves the overhead of creating new actual plans every time a query is processed. Plans in the cache do not last forever; under normal circumstances, they are slowly "aged" out of memory (the lazywriter handles the aging, among other tasks).

There are other actions that can cause a plan to be discarded as well, which can generate a lot of CPU stress if it happens often enough. In particular, the following actions can cause a plan to be invalidated and recompiled:

❑   **Low Memory** — If the server runs low on memory, any plans not being referenced by a client connection may be cleared.

❑   **Table or Schema Changes** — Changes to any tables or schemas used in the plan will invalidate it. This includes any changes to the structure or schema of any temporary tables used in the query.

❑   **Index Changes** — Dropping or changing any of the indexes used by the plan will invalidate it.

- ❑ **Statistics Changes** — Any changes to the statistics used to develop the query plan will force the plan to be recompiled.

- ❑ **Significant Row Count Changes** — If enough inserts and deletes occur to any of the referenced tables, then the plan will be recompiled. This threshold can be adjusted by using the KEEP PLAN and KEEPFIXED PLAN query hints. Refer to the "Query Hints" section later in this chapter for more details.

- ❑ **Mixing DDL and DML** — Try to avoid interleaving DDL and DML within the same query, since this will always cause the plan to recompile.

- ❑ **Changing SET Options** — Changing any SET options inside the query will invalidate the plan. To avoid recompilation, make all of your SET changes at the beginning of the query rather than throughout the query.

> Sometimes during testing it can help to completely clear the procedure cache. This can be done by executing DBCC FREEPROCCACHE.

Viewing Execution Plans

Internally each query results in a single execution plan, but SQL Server provides you with several different options to view the plan:

- ❑ **Graphical** — SSMS will display graphical plans if you select to include either the estimated or actual execution plan when executing a query. The graphical plans are great for getting a quick feel for what is happening; however, only a limited of amount of detail is presented.

- ❑ **Text** — Text plans are a bit harder to understand but include more information. You can include text plans by adding one of the following SET statements in a query batch:

  - ❑ SHOWPLAN_ALL — Instructs SQL Server to return a detailed analysis of the estimated execution plan. The query will not actually be executed.

  - ❑ SHOWPLAN_TEXT — Similar to the previous option, this will return estimated execution information without actually executing the query; however, the output format is intended for use with command-line tools.

  - ❑ STATISTICS_PROFILE — Actually runs the query and then returns detailed information for each statement that was executed.

- ❑ **XML** — These are very complete data sets describing all of the details of the execution plan. XML plans can be included by using one of the following SET statements:

  - ❑ SHOWPLAN_XML — Returns estimated execution information in a well-formed XML document. This is the XML version of SHOWPLAN_ALL.

  - ❑ STATISTICS_XML — Runs the query and then returns detailed information for each statement in XML form. This is the XML equivalent of STATISTICS_PROFILE.

All of the SHOWPLAN options are also available as event classes in SQL Profiler; however, you are encouraged to use the XML versions. The non-XML versions have been deprecated and will be removed in a future release.

Analyzing Execution Plans

After you have captured and displayed an execution plan, you can analyze it to find potential changes that may improve performance. These changes may involve adding new indexes, changing sort options, partitioning, using query hints, or re-writing the original query in a new way. Figure 11-3 shows the graphical execution plan for the following query:

```
Select p.PersonType, p.LastName, p.FirstName, e.HireDate, e.JobTitle, ph.Cell,
    ph.Home, ph.Work
FROM Person.Person p left join HumanResources.Employee e on
    p.BusinessEntityID=e.BusinessEntityID
  left join (select BusinessEntityID, [1] 'Cell', [2] 'Home', [3] 'Work' FROM
  (select BusinessEntityID,PhoneNumberTypeID,PhoneNumber FROM Person.PersonPhone) p
  PIVOT (min(PhoneNumber) for PhoneNumberTypeID IN ([1],[2],[3])) pvt) ph
  on ph.BusinessEntityID=p.BusinessEntityID
WHERE PersonType='EM'
```

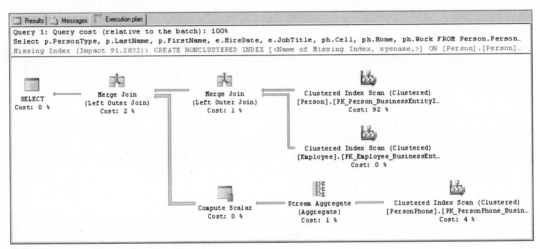

Figure 11-3: Graphical execution plan.

The first step in analyzing the plan is to look for certain specific operations that are commonly associated with performance issues. If you see any of the following operations, you should investigate them further to determine if there is a problem:

❑ **Clustered Index Scans or Table Scans** — Scans occur when SQL Server has to slog through the data record-by-record. When this occurs on large tables, it is often a sign that an additional index could be added to improve performance. If the Query Optimizer identifies any of these "missing" indexes, then it will display an index recommendation in green text at the top of the graphical plan.

❑ **Cross-Join** — This is almost always an error in the query design where a join was not defined between two tables. Cross-joins combine every record in the first table with every record in the second table, resulting in a table that contains the product of record counts of each table.

❑ **Key Lookup or RID Lookup** — These mean that the row data had to be retrieved in order to provide additional values required by the query. If you see a lot of these, you might be able to improve performance by reducing the number of output rows in the query, creating a covering index, or in some cases, changing the cluster key.

❑ **Filter** — This is another kind of scan operation, included where there is a complex expression that must be evaluated over all input rows. One place you will see this is if you use a function in the WHERE clause. In other cases, it may indicate the need for additional indexes.

❑ **Sort** — This indicates the presence of an ORDER BY clause. Sorting can be a very CPU-intensive task, so if you see this, make sure that the results really need to be sorted. In some cases, you may be able to create a covering index and avoid the sorting operation altogether.

When analyzing plans, you should focus on the most costly operations first. In the plan referenced above, notice that the most costly operation is a *Clustered Index Scan* on the Person.Person table to limit the rows based on the PersonType. Mousing over any of the operations in a graphical query plan will display a tooltip showing details of the operation. Figure 11-4 shows the operation details for the clustered index scan.

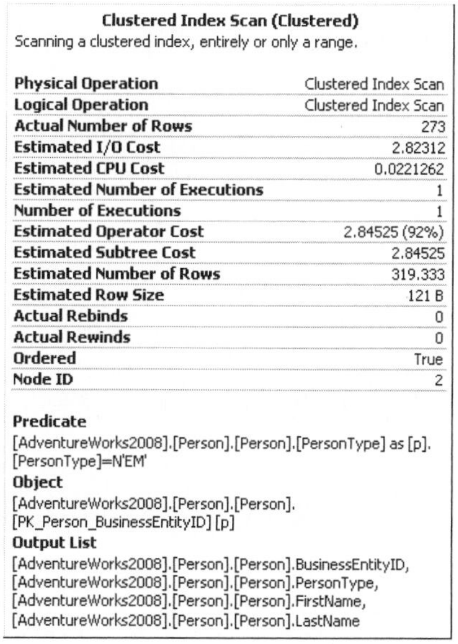

Clustered Index Scan (Clustered)	
Scanning a clustered index, entirely or only a range.	
Physical Operation	Clustered Index Scan
Logical Operation	Clustered Index Scan
Actual Number of Rows	273
Estimated I/O Cost	2.82312
Estimated CPU Cost	0.0221262
Estimated Number of Executions	1
Number of Executions	1
Estimated Operator Cost	2.84525 (92%)
Estimated Subtree Cost	2.84525
Estimated Number of Rows	319.333
Estimated Row Size	121 B
Actual Rebinds	0
Actual Rewinds	0
Ordered	True
Node ID	2

Predicate
[AdventureWorks2008].[Person].[Person].[PersonType] as [p].
[PersonType]=N'EM'
Object
[AdventureWorks2008].[Person].[Person].
[PK_Person_BusinessEntityID] [p]
Output List
[AdventureWorks2008].[Person].[Person].BusinessEntityID,
[AdventureWorks2008].[Person].[Person].PersonType,
[AdventureWorks2008].[Person].[Person].FirstName,
[AdventureWorks2008].[Person].[Person].LastName

Figure 11-4: Query plan operation details.

In the case of this particular query, the Optimizer has identified a missing index that might improve performance. Right-clicking on the screen and selecting Missing Index Details shows the following information:

```
/*
Missing Index Details from PlanTest.sql - AUGHTEIGHT.AdventureWorks2008
 (AUGHTEIGHT\Administrator (53))
The Query Processor estimates that implementing the following index could improve
 the query cost by 91.2832%.
*/

/*
```

```
USE [AdventureWorks2008]
GO
CREATE NONCLUSTERED INDEX [<Name of Missing Index, sysname,>]
ON [Person].[Person] ([PersonType])
INCLUDE ([BusinessEntityID],[FirstName],[LastName])
GO
*/
```

Notice that it recommends using the INCLUDE clause of the index, which includes additional columns in the index simply for covering purposes. The Query Optimizer is estimating a 91.3 percent increase in performance if we add the index that it recommends.

Very complex query plans can get a little confusing to navigate. Just remember that everything comes together at the top left of the screen. When following the query outward towards the right, you can use the estimated subtree cost to identify which path is the more costly. In addition, mousing over the connecting arrows between operations will display a tool tip showing the estimated number of rows and estimated data size that is being moved. Using these techniques, it is relatively easy to identify the most costly operations.

Updating Statistics

Statistics are used by the Query Processor to help determine optimal execution plans. By default, statistics are set to automatically create and update. In most cases, this provides an acceptable trade-off in that the time required to automatically compute statistics is more than compensated for by the gains in query performance.

If you choose to disable automatic statistics for a given table, then you will also need to periodically use the UPDATE STATISTICS command to manually update statistics. This should be done whenever the contents of the table have been significantly altered.

> *When using* UPDATE STATISTICS, *SQL Server will automatically re-enable automatic statistics unless you specify the* NORECOMPUTE *clause.*

If you want to make sure that statistics are current for every table in a given database, then you can use the sp_updatestats stored procedure. This procedure invokes UPDATE STATISTICS on every table in the target database that is out-of-date, as determined by the rowmodctr (row modification counter) column in the sys.sysindexes server view. The following example shows how to update statistics for the entire AdventureWorks2008 database:

```
USE AdventureWorks2008;
GO
EXEC sp_updatestats
```

Managing Indexes

Given the important role of indexes in the Query Optimizer, it is critical that they are properly managed in order to continue to provide optimal query results. Query statistics should be periodically analyzed to identify new potential indexes, and existing indexes need to be periodically de-fragmented and evaluated for effectiveness. Performing these relatively simple tasks will greatly assist the Query Optimizer and help maintain excellent query performance.

Identifying Missing Indexes

There are several different approaches that you can take to identify indexes that would potentially be of benefit. The first method is to use the "Missing Index" dynamic management views. SQL Server automatically maintains three DMVs that together can be used to view SQL Server's internal recommendations for new indexes as follows:

```
SELECT migs.user_seeks, migs.avg_total_user_cost, migs.avg_user_impact,
migs.last_user_seek, mid.[statement] 'database_schema_table',
mid.included_columns, mid.equality_columns, mid.inequality_columns,
migs.unique_compiles
FROM sys.dm_db_missing_index_group_stats migs WITH (NOLOCK)
INNER JOIN sys.dm_db_missing_index_groups mig WITH (NOLOCK)
ON migs.group_handle = mig.index_group_handle
INNER JOIN sys.dm_db_missing_index_details mid WITH (NOLOCK)
ON mig.index_handle = mid.index_handle
INNER JOIN sys.objects so on mid.[object_id]=so.[object_id]
INNER JOIN sys.databases sd on mid.[database_id]=sd.[database_id]
WHERE so.is_ms_shipped=0
-- and sd.name='AdventureWorks2008'  -- uncomment to limit to specific db
```

The information gathered by the three Missing Index views is cleared whenever you restart the server, so for best results, run the above query after the server has been operating for a while under normal load.

The Missing Indexes feature is a lightweight tool that has certain limitations. Make sure that you consider the following when using this feature:

❑   It is not intended to replace the Database Engine Tuning Advisor (covered later in this chapter). The Missing Indexes feature does not provide enough information for you to fine-tune your overall indexing configuration.

❑   It is limited to 500 missing index groups. After that point, no more missing index data will be gathered.

❑   It does not consider the optimal column order when suggesting covering indexes.

❑   It does not suggest filtered indexes, indexed views, or partitioning.

❑   It uses a simplistic model to generate cost information that may not be accurate. In addition, different costs may be returned for the same index group if multiple queries can benefit from the index in different ways.

❑   It does not consider trivial query plans.

To see an example of what the Missing Index views can do, enter the following into a new SQL Server Management Studio Query window and execute it:

```
USE AdventureWorks2008
GO

-- Run a query over some fields that are not indexed
```

```
SELECT sd.SalesOrderID,sd.ProductID,sd.OrderQty
FROM Sales.SalesOrderDetail sd
WHERE sd.LineTotal>1000
GO
```

Next, if you run the query using the three Missing Index views, you should see something like Figure 11-5:

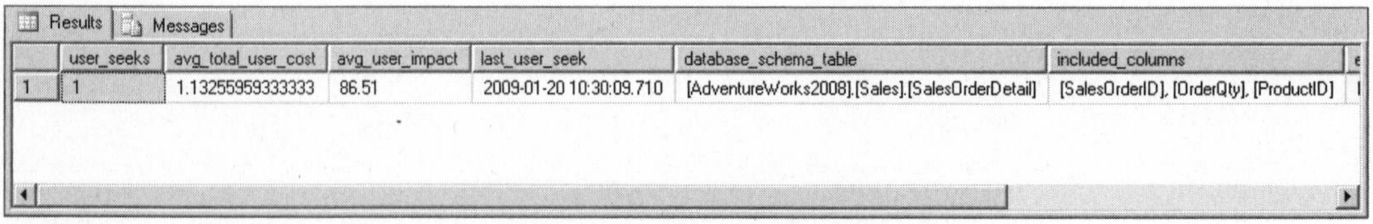

	user_seeks	avg_total_user_cost	avg_user_impact	last_user_seek	database_schema_table	included_columns	e
1	1	1.13255959333333	86.51	2009-01-20 10:30:09.710	[AdventureWorks2008].[Sales].[SalesOrderDetail]	[SalesOrderID], [OrderQty], [ProductID]	I

Figure 11-5: Identifying potential indexes using the Missing Index views.

Notice that SQL Server has identified a missing covering index that would benefit the sales order detail query.

Your results may include additional rows that correspond to previously executed queries for which SQL Server has identified a missing index. The result shown in Figure 11-5 is the only result that is directly related to the query in this example.

Using Automatic Statistics to Identify Missing Indexes

If auto-create and auto-update statistics are enabled, then SQL Server will automatically maintain statistics for all columns that are used to limit results in a query expression. If any of these columns do not have an index, then SQL Server creates a "placeholder" entry in its internal indexes table and calculates statistics on the column for the query processor to use. If SQL has created statistics for an un-indexed column, then the odds are that an index on the column will improve performance. Of course, the final determination should be made by testing the impact of any new queries in your particular environment.

Use the following query to display a list of non-indexed columns for which statistics have been generated. By adjusting the `WHERE` clause, this query can display information about all existing indexes as well.

```
SELECT so.name 'object_name', i.index_id,
  isnull(i.type_desc, '[Not Indexed]' ) 'index_type',
  stuff((SELECT ', ' + c.name FROM sys.stats_columns as sc
    INNER JOIN sys.columns as c on c.[object_id] = sc.[object_id]
      and c.column_id = sc.column_id
   WHERE ss.[object_id] = sc.[object_id] and ss.stats_id = sc.stats_id
   ORDER BY c.column_id FOR XML PATH('')), 1, 1, '') 'columns',
i.is_unique 'UQK',i.is_primary_key 'PK',i.is_unique_constraint 'UQC',
ss.auto_created 'auto',ss.user_created 'user',
ss.name as statsname,
CASE WHEN i.name is null then stats_date(t.[object_id], ss.stats_id)
 ELSE stats_date(t.[object_id], i.index_id)
 END 'stats_date'
FROM sys.stats as ss INNER JOIN sys.objects so on ss.[object_id]=so.[object_id]
 INNER JOIN sys.tables t on so.name = t.name
 LEFT OUTER JOIN sys.indexes as i on ss.name = i.name
```

```
WHERE t.is_ms_shipped = 0   -- filter out system tables
    and ss.auto_created=1          -- use this for just auto created stats
-- and i.type_desc='CLUSTERED'     -- use this to display just cluster keys
-- and i.is_primary_key=1          -- use this to display just primary keys
-- and so.name='Customer'          -- use this to display a specific table
ORDER BY t.name,i.index_id
```

Executing the above query just for the `Customer` object in the `AdventureWorks2008` database should return output similar to what is shown in Figure 11-6.

	object_name	index_id	index_type	columns	UQK	PK	UQC	auto	user	statsname	stats_date
1	Customer	NULL	[Not Indexed]	StoreID	NULL	NULL	NULL	1	0	_WA_Sys_00000003_2A4B4B5E	2008-08-06 09:18:36.277
2	Customer	NULL	[Not Indexed]	PersonID	NULL	NULL	NULL	1	0	_WA_Sys_00000002_2A4B4B5E	2008-08-06 09:18:36.293
3	Customer	1	CLUSTERED	CustomerID	1	1	0	0	0	PK_Customer_CustomerID	2008-08-06 09:18:18.623
4	Customer	2	NONCLUSTERED	rowguid	1	0	0	0	0	AK_Customer_rowguid	2008-08-06 09:18:22.677
5	Customer	3	NONCLUSTERED	AccountNumber	1	0	0	0	0	AK_Customer_AccountNumber	2008-08-06 09:18:23.067
6	Customer	5	NONCLUSTERED	TerritoryID	0	0	0	0	0	IX_Customer_TerritoryID	2008-08-06 09:18:23.237

Figure 11-6: Identifying potential indexes using automatic statistics.

Notice in Figure 11-6 that statistics have been automatically calculated for the `StoreID` and `PersonID` columns, but no index exists for these columns. This indicates that you might be able to improve performance for customer queries by adding these indexes.

Using XML ShowPlan to Identify Missing Indexes

It is also possible to display information about missing indexes directly in SSMS by using the XML ShowPlan feature. This method uses the same process as the Missing Index views, but displays the results immediately in XML format.

To see how this works, enter the following into a new SSMS Query window and execute it:

```
USE AdventureWorks2008
GO
SET STATISTICS XML ON
GO
-- Run a query over some fields that are not indexed
SELECT sd.SalesOrderID,sd.ProductID,sd.OrderQty
FROM Sales.SalesOrderDetail sd
WHERE sd.LineTotal>1000
GO
```

This will generate an extra XML result set with the query execution plan. Clicking on the ShowPlan XML will open the execution plan, and from there you can right-click and select "Missing Index Details" to view the Query Processor's recommendations. SQL Server generates the following recommendation for the previous query:

```
/*
Missing Index Details from ExecutionPlan1.sqlplan
The Query Processor estimates that implementing the following index could improve
 the query cost by 86.5124%.
*/

/*
```

```
USE [AdventureWorks2008]
GO
CREATE NONCLUSTERED INDEX [<Name of Missing Index, sysname,>]
ON [Sales].[SalesOrderDetail] ([LineTotal])
INCLUDE ([SalesOrderID],[OrderQty],[ProductID])
GO
*/
```

Notice that this is in code form, so if you want to take the recommendation, you can simply uncomment the code, give the index a name, and execute it. Nice!

Index De-Fragmentation

Indexes can become fragmented over time as changes are made to the underlying data. When indexes fragment, it leaves "gaps" in the data pages that are not filled with data. This, in turn, causes additional page reads to occur when doing table scans or partial table scans. If the fragmentation becomes bad enough, it can significantly degrade query performance. This is particularly true of the clustered index because it actually represents the physical order of the data on disk.

> For indexes that frequently become fragmented, you might be able to slow down the fragmentation process by using the "fill-factor" to reserve some extra space on each page. You will need to evaluate the trade-off between slowing down fragmentation and the extra disk reads caused by unfilled pages.

Beginning with SQL Server 2005, you can use the sys.dm_db_index_physical_stats management view to display information about the indexes, including their fragmentation level. The following query shows how to query detailed information for all indexes in the AdventureWorks2008 database with more than 10 percent fragmentation:

```
SELECT OBJECT_SCHEMA_NAME(ps.object_id) 'schemaname',
    OBJECT_NAME(ps.object_id) 'objectname', si.name 'indexname',ps.*
FROM sys.dm_db_index_physical_stats(DB_ID('AdventureWorks2008'),
    null,null,null,'DETAILED') ps
LEFT OUTER JOIN sys.indexes si on ps.[object_id]=si.[object_id] and
    ps.index_id=si.index_id
WHERE ps.avg_fragmentation_in_percent>10
```

The ALTER INDEX command, combined with the REORGANIZE or REBUILD directives, will attempt to de-fragment any clustered or non-clustered indexes. Reorganization is a bit lighter weight than rebuilding, in that it runs without doing any long-term locking, does not block running queries or updates, and does not update statistics. Rebuilding will lock the table for the duration of the operation (unless you use the ONLINE=ON option). Interestingly enough, the reorganization operation is always fully logged, regardless of the database recovery option selected, while the rebuild operation will honor the setting and minimally log if the recovery mode is set to Simple or Bulk-Logged.

The process for de-fragmenting a heap is a little different. Because a heap is, by definition, an unordered collection of rows, there actually is no index to rebuild. In order to de-fragment a heap, you will have to provide structure by creating a clustered key on the table, at least temporarily. If you don't want to keep the cluster key, you can drop it immediately after you create it and the heap will remain in its newly ordered state.

De-fragmentation is not always possible. Certain choices of cluster key, such as a GUID, will always result in a highly fragmented index.

The script below will automatically de-fragment every index in the AdventureWorks2008 database that is more than 10 percent fragmented. Heaps are ignored; the REORGANIZE option is used for mildly fragmented indexes, and the REBUILD option is used when there is heavy fragmentation.

```
USE AdventureWorks2008;
SET NOCOUNT ON;
GO

-- Get work table, all indexes >10% fragmented
DECLARE @work TABLE ([objid] int, idxid int, pnum int, avgfrag real);
INSERT @work ([objid],idxid,pnum,avgfrag)
SELECT [object_id],index_id,partition_number,avg_fragmentation_in_percent
FROM sys.dm_db_index_physical_stats(DB_ID('AdventureWorks2008'),
   null,null,null,'LIMITED')
WHERE avg_fragmentation_in_percent>10 and index_id>0;

-- loop through worklist
Declare @objfullname nvarchar(261), @indexname nvarchar(130), @pcount int,
   @cmd nvarchar(1000);
Declare @objid int, @idxid int, @pnum int, @avgfrag real
Declare worklist CURSOR FOR SELECT * from @work;
OPEN worklist
WHILE(1=1) BEGIN;
   FETCH NEXT FROM worklist into @objid,@idxid,@pnum,@avgfrag;
   IF @@FETCH_STATUS < 0 BREAK;

   -- Get the object full name, index name, and total partition count
   SELECT @objfullname=OBJECT_SCHEMA_NAME(@objid) + '.' + OBJECT_NAME(@objid);
   SELECT @pcount=(SELECT COUNT(*) FROM sys.partitions
      WHERE [object_id]=@objid and index_id=@idxid);
   SELECT @indexname=name FROM sys.indexes
      WHERE [object_id]=@objid and index_id=@idxid;

   -- Create the command, if fragmentation is over 25 then REBUILD
   SELECT @cmd=N'ALTER INDEX ' + @indexname + N' ON ' + @objfullname +
      case when @avgfrag>25 then N' REBUILD' else N' REORGANIZE' end

   -- Execute the command to defrag the index
   Exec (@cmd);
   Print 'Executed ' + @cmd;
END;

-- Clean up
CLOSE worklist;
DEALLOCATE worklist;
DELETE FROM @work;
```

Determining Index Effectiveness

Indexes do have a cost, and too many indexes on a table can seriously hurt the performance of inserts and updates. If an index is seldom or never used, then dropping the index will actually improve overall performance.

The `sys.dm_db_index_physical_stats` management view reports index usage information. The data that it collects is re-set every time the server is restarted, so before querying index usage information, make sure that you have been running a while during a period of typical system activity. The example below will display a list of all non-clustered, non-primary key indexes that have not been used by a user or by the system since the last restart:

```
SELECT DB_NAME([database_id]) 'dbname', so.name 'objname', si.name 'indexname',
    si.type_desc 'indextype', si.is_primary_key 'PK',
    ius.user_seeks+ius.user_scans+ius.user_lookups 'userusage',
    ius.system_seeks+ius.system_scans+ius.system_lookups 'sysusage'
FROM sys.dm_db_index_usage_stats ius
inner join sys.objects so on ius.[object_id]=so.[object_id]
inner join sys.indexes si on ius.[object_id]=si.[object_id]
    and ius.index_id=si.index_id
WHERE so.is_ms_shipped=0
-- comment out the following restrictions to see all indexes
    and ius.user_seeks+ius.user_scans+ius.user_lookups+
        ius.system_seeks+ius.system_scans+ius.system_lookups = 0
    and si.type <> 1 and si.is_primary_key = 0
```

Query Optimizer Hints

Hints allow you to give recommendations to the Query Optimizer to help it choose a better execution plan. When using query hints, be very careful to perform adequate testing. In most cases you will probably find that the Query Optimizer already has the best plan, and adding hints only serves to reduce performance. However, when used judiciously, hints have the potential to resolve some of the most difficult performance problems.

There are three types of hints supported in SQL Server 2008: Table, Join, and Query. I will briefly cover the most commonly used hints below.

Table Hints

Table hints apply only to a specific table or view. They are specified by using the `WITH` clause directly following the table name.

❑ NOEXPAND — This hint will prevent indexed views from being expanded to include their underlying tables. This forces the Query Optimizer to treat the indexed view as a table with a clustered index.

❑ FORCESEEK — This option will restrict the Query Optimizer to only use index seek operations to access data in the table. This is useful in cases in which the Query Optimizer incorrectly guesses the cardinality (number of rows) of the operation and opts to use a table scan. One example of where you might see this is in queries that use the LIKE or IN operators.

- ❑ INDEX(name) — This hint allows you to specify one or more indexes to use for the table. This can be useful in rare cases in which the Query Optimizer consistently chooses an inefficient index. There are two special forms of this hint to force table scans or seeks as follows:

  - ❑ INDEX(0) — Forces a clustered index scan or, if there is no clustered index, a table scan.

  - ❑ INDEX(1) — Forces a clustered index scan or seek. This option is not valid if the table does not have a clustered index.

- ❑ UPDLOCK — Specifies that update locks should be taken and held for the duration of the transaction. When combined with HOLDLOCK, you can use this to lock resources early on in a procedure that you will need to update later. This can help maintain integrity for procedures that update shared data.

- ❑ HOLDLOCK/SERIALIZABLE — Specifies that locks should be held for the duration of the transaction. Essentially this uses the "serializable" transaction isolation level for the specified table.

- ❑ NOLOCK/READUNCOMMITTED — This is a semicontroversial hint, but I find it very useful in situations in which dirty reads will not affect data integrity. This hint instructs the Query Processor to ignore exclusive locks on the data placed by other transactions (dirty reads) and to forego placing any shared locks on the data while reading. This introduces the possibility of reporting inconsistent data. Allowing dirty reads can greatly increase the performance of a query and will eliminate nearly all blocking issues. Schema locks are required for all queries, so even dirty reads will be blocked if another process has locked a required schema for modification.

Join Hints

Join hints allow you to specify a particular strategy to use when connecting two tables or views in a query. I very rarely use join hints, since in the vast majority of cases, I have found that SQL Server does an excellent job of identifying the best type of join to use. In the few cases in which I have seen join problems, more often than not the root problem turned out to be way the query was written.

If you ever do need to use a join hint, you can do so by specifying one of the following qualifiers directly in the ANSI-style join clause of the query:

- ❑ MERGE — Forces a merge operation for the join. Merging requires that both inputs be sorted on the join key, and then entries from each input are matched by comparing the values in a single pass through sorted lists. The merge join itself is very fast, but the sorting can be CPU-intensive.

- ❑ LOOP — Forces the join to use a loop operation. In a loop join, the inputs are labeled as the outer table and the inner table. Looping works by cycling through each entry in the outer table, and for each entry looking up a related entry in the inner table. This is efficient if the outer table is small and the inner table is pre-indexed and large.

- ❑ HASH — Forces a hash operation for the join. Hash joins are designed for set matching operations such as inner, left, right, and full outer joins; and for intersections, unions, duplicate removal, and grouping. They work by first building an intermediate hash table (preferably in memory) using the smaller input, and then using the hash table to look up related entries while scanning through the larger input (known as the *probe input*).

Query Hints

Query hints apply to the query statement as a whole. They are specified by using the OPTION clause at the end of a SELECT, INSERT, DELETE, UPDATE, or MERGE statement. I have found the query hints in this table to be particularly useful:

Hint	Description
FAST(rows)	Instructs the Query Processor to return the indicated number of rows as quickly as possible, then continue processing normally to retrieve the remaining rows.
MAXDOP(number)	Overrides the default "maximum degree of parallelism" server setting for a specific query. You can use this hint to reduce parallelism to a single CPU in cases in which the query generates an excessive number of context switches. This is particularly common with hyperthreaded processors but may occur on any multiple-CPU system.
OPTIMIZE FOR(@variable= constant)	Instructs the Query Optimizer to optimize the query using a specific value for a local variable. Using this option can protect the query from getting a query plan that is optimized for seldom used parameter values.
RECOMPILE	Tells the Query Processor to discard the execution plan rather than saving it in the plan cache. This will cause the query to be recompiled on every execution. This can improve performance for queries with large numbers of parameters, where the specific parameter values can make a significant difference in the execution plan.
KEEP PLAN	Extends the life of the plan in the plan cache by raising the threshold of the number of changes that can occur to the table before the query plan is recompiled. In some cases, reducing the recompile frequency may reduce CPU stress.
KEEPFIXED PLAN	This hint goes a bit further than KEEP PLAN and will preserve the plan regardless of changes to table statistics. Only a schema change or an explicit command will recompile a plan that uses this hint.
TABLE HINT(table,hint)	Allows you to specify a table hint at the query level. If the table is aliased, then the table reference must use the aliased name. This is useful when you need to modify the behavior of a specific table inside a query that you are otherwise unable to change.
USE PLAN(xml)	Forces the Query Optimizer to use an existing query plan. This option should always be used from within a plan guide rather than directly.

Plan Guides

Plan guides are used to optimize query performance in situations in which it is not practical to modify the query directly, as in an existing deployed application. As a side benefit, they can also be used to provide predictable performance by locking down query plans. Plan guides can even be transferred from server to server, allowing you to fine-tune the plan guide on a development system and then deploy it in production once you have perfected it.

Mainly owing to their complexity, plan guides have not been overly used; however, SQL Server 2008 has made several improvements that simplify and automate many of the most difficult tasks. New is the ability to pull plans directly from the plan cache, and plan forcing, which allows an XML execution plan to be explicitly specified.

Creating Plan Guides

Procedurally, plan guides are actually very easy to create. The difficulty lies in determining the correct values for the plan guide parameters. To create a plan guide, you can use the `sp_create_plan_guide` stored procedure or you can use SSMS by right-clicking on the Programmability ➤ Plan Guides node and selecting "New Plan Guide."

When creating a plan guide using SSMS, you will need to supply the following parameters:

Parameter	Description
Name	The name of the plan guide. You can select anything you want for this.
Statement	The statement to match. For SQL and Object plan guides, this can be tricky to properly define since it must exactly match the statement in the actual execution batch. Creating a plan guide from the plan cache is the best way to determine this value.
Scope Type	The context for the plan guide, which must be one of the following values:
	`Object` — Object plan guides apply to stored procedures, user-defined functions, and DML triggers.
	`SQL` — SQL plan guides apply to stand-alone statements and batches.
	`Template` — A variation of the SQL plan guide that is used to override the default parameterization setting.
Scope Batch	The `Scope Batch` is only valid for SQL plans, and even then it is optional. When not specified, this will default to the statement; otherwise, it must contain the batch text exactly as it was submitted to SQL Server.
Scope Schema Name	For object plans only, this is the schema name of the object.
Scope Object Name	For object plans only, this is the name of the object.
Parameters	For SQL and object plans, this is required and must be the exact parameters and data types as submitted to SQL Server. Note that this is the internalized parameterization, which is similar to `sp_executesql`.
Hints	Use this parameter to enter one or more query hints or to specify the query plan to force in XML format. The most commonly used hints for plan guides are `OPTIMIZE FOR`, `RECOMPILE`, `INDEX`, and `FORCESEEK`. When specifying hints, you must enter them in the following format: `OPTION(query_hint[, ... n])`.

As you can see, several of the required parameters are difficult to get right. If they do not match the actual submitted information, then the plan guide will not match and will not be used. This was the biggest problem with using plan guides prior to SQL Server 2008. Fortunately, now it is possible to create a plan guide directly from an execution plan in the plan cache, which takes care of all the tedious work for you.

Creating Plan Guides from the Plan Cache

The ability to create a plan guide directly from an execution plan in the cache is a huge improvement. This is still a two-step process, but it is easy and it does the bulk of the work for you. First, you need to query the plan cache using dynamic management views and locate the plan for which you want to create a plan guide. In most cases, it is easiest to find the plan by searching for a portion of the statement text as follows:

```
SELECT cp.plan_handle, sql_handle, st.text, objtype, qs.statement_start_offset
FROM sys.dm_exec_cached_plans AS cp
JOIN sys.dm_exec_query_stats AS qs ON cp.plan_handle = qs.plan_handle
CROSS APPLY sys.dm_exec_sql_text(sql_handle) AS st
WHERE st.text like '[enter start of statement to find]%';
```

Once you have the plan handle and the statement starting offset, you can create the plan guide using the `sp_create_plan_guide_from_handle` stored procedure. Hand entering plan handles is tedious, since they are `varbinary(64)` data types. It makes more sense to remember the value in a variable, as demonstrated in the example below:

```
-- Assume that this is the statement for which you want to create a guide
SELECT * FROM Person.Address WHERE StateProvinceID=1
GO

-- Using the management views, lookup the plan handle and offset
Declare @handle varbinary(64), @offset int
SELECT @handle=cp.plan_handle, @offset=qs.statement_start_offset
FROM sys.dm_exec_cached_plans AS cp
JOIN sys.dm_exec_query_stats AS qs ON cp.plan_handle = qs.plan_handle
CROSS APPLY sys.dm_exec_sql_text(sql_handle) AS st
WHERE st.text like 'select * from Person%';

-- Finally, use the plan handle and offset to create the guide
exec sp_create_plan_guide_from_handle
  @name = 'NewPlanGuide',
  @plan_handle = @handle,
  @statement_start_offset = @offset;
```

Notice that there is no option to specify any hints. When you create plans in this way, they are automatically created with the full query plan included. Finally, once the plan guide is created, you will be able to view it in SSMS and use SSMS to enable/disable or delete the plan guide as needed.

Plan Freezing

A query plan is considered *frozen* if there is a matching plan guide that specifies the actual execution plan. When you create plan guides from the cache (as shown previously), they include the XML execution plan, so whenever these queries are executed, the plan in the guide will be used instead of generating a new one.

Freezing plans can be helpful in a few specific circumstances:

❑ It can help to provide consistent query performance, even when the statistics are continually changing.

❑ You can use frozen plans to preserve application performance when you first upgrade to a new version of SQL Server.

❑ You can use a cloned test/development system to develop optimal execution plans and then use frozen plan guides to implement these optimizations on a production system.

Try It Out   Creating a Plan Guide

Assume that you have a deployed application that consistently runs a certain query that is causing performance problems by repeatedly context-switching threads between CPUs (parallelism problem). You do not have access to the source code to modify the query, and you also don't want to change the maximum degree of parallelism setting for the entire server. The solution to this problem is a plan guide.

1.   First, you will need to find the problem query in the plan cache. Of course, before that can happen, the query must actually be executed at least once so that it will exist in the plan cache. Enter the following into a new Query window in SSMS, then enable the Actual Execution Plan from the Query menu, and finally execute it:

```
USE AdventureWorks2008
GO
-- STEP 1, Run a query so that it will exist in the cache
-- Note: The following 'GO' is included to keep the comments seperate
-- from the statement in the cached text for the query plan.
GO
select top 5 pp.LastName,pp.FirstName,sum(sh.TotalDue) 'TotalSales'
from Sales.SalesOrderHeader sh join Person.Person pp on
  sh.SalesPersonID=pp.BusinessEntityID
group by pp.LastName,pp.FirstName
order by SUM(sh.totalDue) desc
GO
```

2.   Select the Execution Plan tab, and you should see a plan similar to the one shown in Figure 11-7.

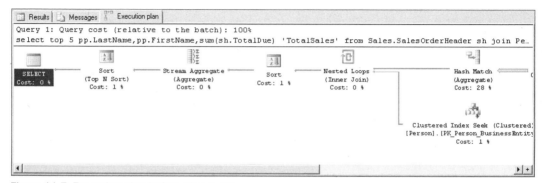

Figure 11-7: Execution plan before plan guide.

Notice that the plan is using a Nested Loop (Inner Join). This is significant only because this will be used as a marker later on to confirm that the plan guide is working.

3. You will need to create a plan guide for the problem query that uses the MAXDOP hint to limit parallelism and stop all of the context-switching. For testing purposes, you will also use the HASH JOIN hint to force the query to use a hash join. This change will show up on the execution plan and allow easy visual confirmation that the plan guide is working. Enter the following into a *new* Query window and execute it:

```
-- STEP 2, Create the Plan Guide
DECLARE @text nvarchar(max);
SELECT @text=st.[text]
FROM sys.dm_exec_query_stats AS qs
CROSS APPLY sys.dm_exec_sql_text([sql_handle]) AS st
CROSS APPLY sys.dm_exec_text_query_plan(qs.plan_handle,
    qs.statement_start_offset,
    qs.statement_end_offset) AS qp
WHERE text LIKE 'select top 5 pp.LastName,pp.FirstName%';

EXECUTE sp_create_plan_guide
    @name = 'HintGuide1',
    @stmt=@text,
    @type='SQL',
    @hints='OPTION(HASH JOIN,MAXDOP 1)';
GO
```

4. You should confirm that the plan guide was successfully created. This is easy to do using the sys.plan_guides system view.

```
-- STEP 3, Verify that the plan guide was created.
SELECT * FROM sys.plan_guides
WHERE scope_batch LIKE 'select top 5 pp.LastName,pp.FirstName%';
GO
```

You should see a row displayed that contains information about the plan guide. The content of the row is not important at this point, just the fact that it exists. You can also confirm that the plan exists by checking the Programmability ➤ Plan Guides node in SSMS. Expand this node, right-click HintGuide1, and select Properties. A dialog should appear that is similar to the one shown in Figure 11-8.

Notice that everything is grayed out. In this release of SQL Server you cannot directly edit plan guides in SSMS; however, you can script the plan guide to a new Query window and edit it there. Of course, if you do this, you will need to drop the original plan guide before you re-create a new one.

5. You need to confirm that the plan guide is actually going to be used for the problem query. Return to the original Query window and re-execute the problem query. After it completes, review the execution plan. It should look something like Figure 11-9.

6. Confirm that the query is now using a Hash Match (Inner Join). This confirms that the plan guide is, in fact, being used. Using this method, you were able to fix a problem in a deployed solution without modifying any source code. Neat!

If you want, you can use SSMS to enable or disable the plan guide. Whenever it is enabled, the problem query will use a hash match, and whenever it is disabled, a nested loop will be used.

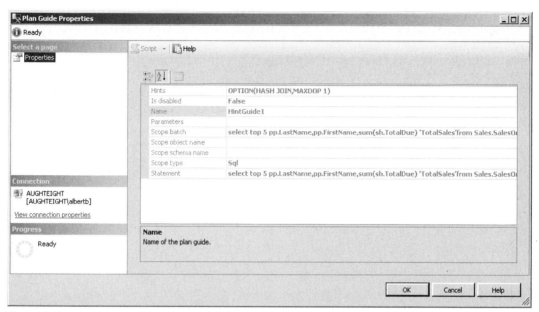

Figure 11-8: Plan Guide Properties in SSMS.

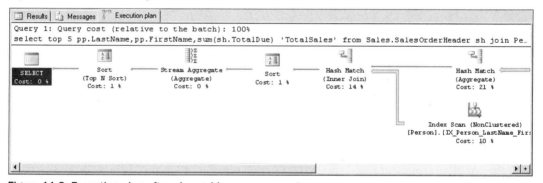

Figure 11-9: Execution plan after plan guide.

Database Engine Tuning Advisor

As described earlier, index usage can be analyzed with DMVs, but the analysis can be a bit tricky and take a great deal of time. Instead of spending hours analyzing index utilization and experimenting with various configurations, the Database Engine Tuning Advisor (DTA) can be used to analyze existing indexes. The DTA can return recommendations for the addition of indexes, indexed views, and table partitioning. It can also recommend the dropping of existing data structures where their existence is detrimental to performance.

> *The initial release of the Database Engine Tuning Advisor in SQL Server 2008 included a bug (KB#959790, Bug#50003717) that prevented the DTA from making any index creation recommendations when the database being analyzed included more than one default* FileGroup *(as is the case with*

AdventureWorks2008). This bug was fixed in Cumulative Update Package 2 for SQL Server 2008, released on November 19, 2008. Make sure to apply this update or a more recent service pack before continuing.

To try this out, start by creating three new tables to experiment with.

1.   Run the following script to create the `NewContact`, `NewSalesOrder`, and `NewTransactionHistory` tables with existing data:

```
USE AdventureWorks2008;
GO
SELECT * INTO dbo.NewContact
FROM Person.Person;

SELECT * INTO dbo.NewSalesOrder
FROM Sales.SalesOrderDetail;

SELECT * INTO dbo.NewTransactionHistory
FROM Production.TransactionHistory;
```

2.   These tables have no indexes on them, so any query against them will result in a full table scan, which is not the most efficient. You could analyze the queries that will be used to retrieve data from these tables manually and determine what indexes to create, or you can ask the DTA to give you some advice. The DTA can also give recommendations for dropping unneeded indexes, so you will create a non-clustered index on the `NewTransactionHistory` table's `rowguid` column to see what the Advisor thinks of it:

```
USE AdventureWorks2008;
GO
CREATE NONCLUSTERED INDEX ix_RowGUID ON dbo.NewSalesOrder (rowguid);
```

3.   Now that the tables and an index are in place, analyze a workload to see how queries perform against these tables. The following script flushes all dirty pages to disk, clears out the procedure cache, clears out the buffer cache, and sets `STATISTICS IO` on to capture I/O performance data. Finally, it then queries the three new tables. Write this query in the Query Editor and save it as `AWWorkLoad.SQL`:

```
CHECKPOINT;
DBCC FREEPROCCACHE;
DBCC DROPCLEANBUFFERS;

SET STATISTICS IO ON;
USE AdventureWorks2008;
GO

SELECT LastName FROM dbo.NewContact
WHERE LastName BETWEEN 'A' AND 'C';

SELECT LastName FROM dbo.NewContact
WHERE LastName LIKE 'M%';

SELECT ProductID, SUM(OrderQty) AS SumQty, SUM(UnitPrice) AS SumPrice
```

```
FROM dbo.NewSalesOrder GROUP BY ProductID;

SELECT ProductID, TransactionDate, SUM(Quantity) AS TotalQty
  , SUM(ActualCost) AS SumCost
FROM dbo.NewTransactionHistory
WHERE TransactionDate BETWEEN '2003-11-12' AND '2004-01-31'
GROUP BY ProductID, TransactionDate;
```

4. Before executing the query, select the "Include Actual Execution Plan" option to return the graphical query plan. The message results for this query show a large number of reads and the creation of work tables for the aggregations:

```
(2116 row(s) affected)
Table 'NewContact'. Scan count 1, logical reads 3808, physical reads 52,
 read-ahead reads 1630, lob logical reads 0, lob physical reads 0,
 lob read-ahead reads 0.

(1550 row(s) affected)
Table 'NewContact'. Scan count 1, logical reads 3808, physical reads 0,
 read-ahead reads 0, lob logical reads 0, lob physical reads 0,
 lob read-ahead reads 0.

(266 row(s) affected)
Table 'Worktable'. Scan count 0, logical reads 0, physical reads 0,
 read-ahead reads 0, lob logical reads 0, lob physical reads 0,
 lob read-ahead reads 0.
Table 'NewSalesOrder'. Scan count 1, logical reads 1495, physical reads 24,
 read-ahead reads 948, lob logical reads 0, lob physical reads 0,
 lob read-ahead reads 0.

(12849 row(s) affected)
Table 'Worktable'. Scan count 0, logical reads 0, physical reads 0,
 read-ahead reads 0, lob logical reads 0, lob physical reads 0,
 lob read-ahead reads 0.
Table 'NewTransactionHistory'. Scan count 1, logical reads 789, physical
reads 0,
 read-ahead reads 0, lob logical reads 0, lob physical reads 0,
 lob read-ahead reads 0.
```

The execution plan shows the table scans and creation of hash match working tables to perform the aggregations (see Figure 11-10).

5. To analyze this query batch, open the DTA (Tools ➢ Database Engine Tuning Advisor) and start a new session. In the "Session name" area, you can either leave the default value of the logged-in username with date, or type in a descriptive name. In Figure 11-11, the session is called **AWWorkLoad Analysis**.

6. Next, select the AWWorkLoad.SQL file as the workload file, set the starting database to AdventureWorks2008, and select just the three tables that are referenced in the file (see Figure 11-11).

7. On the Tuning Options tab, select the options to use indexes with no partitioning and don't keep existing structures, as shown in Figure 11-12.

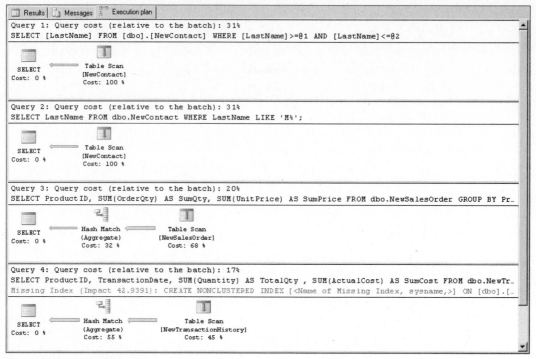

Figure 11-10: Execution plan.

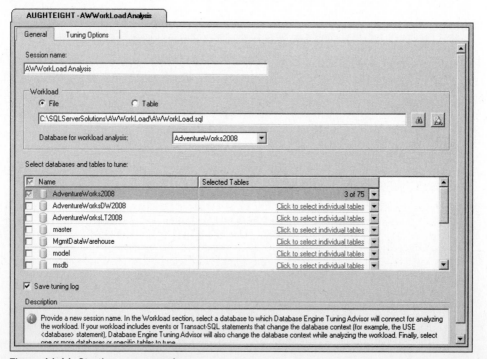

Figure 11-11: Starting a new session.

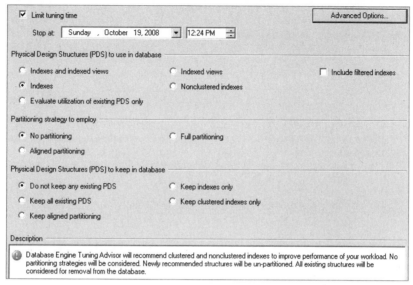

Figure 11-12: Selecting tuning options.

8. Click "Start Analysis" to analyze the AWWorkLoad.SQL file. The DTA will collect metadata about the objects and examine possible indexing strategies to improve the performance of the queries. When the analysis is complete, the DTA will return its recommendations. In this case, it shows that by dropping the index on the `rowguid` column and adding indexes to the three tables, it can improve performance by 85 percent, as shown in Figure 11-13.

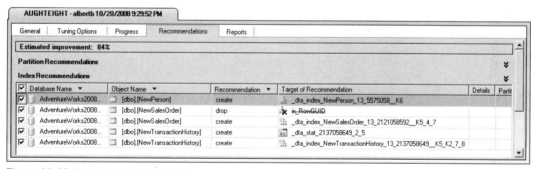

Figure 11-13: Improving performance.

9. The DTA's recommendations can be applied immediately by clicking on the "Apply Recommendations" option in the Actions menu, or they can be saved to a file by clicking on the "Save Recommendations" option. As you can see in Figure 11-13, the names the DTA gives to new objects are not exactly intuitive. I re-wrote the recommendations, as the following code illustrates:

```
USE [AdventureWorks2008]
GO
DROP INDEX [ix_RowGUID] ON [dbo].[NewSalesOrder] WITH ( ONLINE=OFF )

CREATE NONCLUSTERED INDEX _dta_ixProductID ON [dbo].[NewSalesOrder]
```

```
([ProductID] ASC) INCLUDE ( [OrderQty],[UnitPrice])
WITH (SORT_IN_TEMPDB=OFF, IGNORE_DUP_KEY=OFF, DROP_EXISTING=OFF, ONLINE=OFF)
ON [PRIMARY];

CREATE NONCLUSTERED INDEX _dta_ixTranDateProductID ON
    [dbo].[NewTransactionHistory]
([TransactionDate] ASC,[ProductID] ASC) INCLUDE ( [Quantity],[ActualCost])
WITH (SORT_IN_TEMPDB=OFF, IGNORE_DUP_KEY=OFF, DROP_EXISTING=OFF, ONLINE=OFF)
ON [PRIMARY];

CREATE NONCLUSTERED INDEX _dta_ixLastName ON [dbo].[NewContact]
([LastName] ASC)
WITH (SORT_IN_TEMPDB=OFF, IGNORE_DUP_KEY=OFF, DROP_EXISTING=OFF, ONLINE=OFF)
ON [PRIMARY];

CREATE STATISTICS _dta_statProductIDTranDate
ON [dbo].[NewTransactionHistory]([ProductID], [TransactionDate])
```

Take a closer look at the DTA's recommendations. The recommendation for the dropping of the rowguid column index is because that column was never referenced in the workload. Use caution with this behavior of the DTA. The index may be there for a very good reason, but the workload didn't use it.

The next recommendation is for the creation of an index on the ProductID column that includes the OrderQty and UnitPrice columns. This is because of the query that aggregates the two included columns and groups them by the ProductID column. By creating this index, the Query Optimizer can retrieve all the data to satisfy the query from the index, and no table access will be required. The same behavior is repeated with the NewTransactionHistory table, except that a composite index on the two group-by columns is created, and the aggregated columns are included. With the third index recommendation, it is simply a matter of speeding up the search for the LastName column. Finally, notice that the DTA recommends that statistics be maintained for the combination of the ProductID and TransactionDate columns in the NewTransactionHistory table. Statistics are used by the Query Optimizer when selecting an execution plan.

Either apply the recommendations, or execute the saved recommendation script to drop the unnecessary index and create the three new indexes. Next, return to the AWWorkLoad.SQL script and re-run it the same as before. Notice the difference in I/O.

```
(2116 row(s) affected)
Table 'NewPerson'. Scan count 1, logical reads 10, physical reads 2,
 read-ahead reads 8, lob logical reads 0, lob physical reads 0,
 lob read-ahead reads 0.

(1550 row(s) affected)
Table 'NewPerson'. Scan count 1, logical reads 9, physical reads 1,
 read-ahead reads 7, lob logical reads 0, lob physical reads 0,
 lob read-ahead reads 0.

(266 row(s) affected)
Table 'NewSalesOrder'. Scan count 1, logical reads 378, physical reads 3,
 read-ahead reads 376, lob logical reads 0, lob physical reads 0,
 lob read-ahead reads 0.

(12849 row(s) affected)
```

```
Table 'NewTransactionHistory'. Scan count 1, logical reads 118, physical reads 2,
  read-ahead reads 115, lob logical reads 0, lob physical reads 0,
  lob read-ahead reads 0.
```

The Read activity has indeed been reduced by a little more than 85 percent, resulting in a much more efficient query plan. Also notice that the work tables for aggregation were not created at a huge savings. An examination of the query plan shows that no table access was performed. All the data to satisfy the queries was returned from indexes. This, of course, is not always possible, but the DTA will lean toward creating these "Covering Indexes" unless there is a significant amount of data modification on those tables, as well as where the presence of the indexes may be detrimental to performance.

The bottom line is that the DTA can save you valuable time in analyzing table structures and recommend appropriate indexing strategies to improve performance. Just be sure that the activity that is being analyzed by the DTA is typical of the normal database activity. If the workload being analyzed contains large end-of-quarter analysis queries that are not the typical activity, the DTA may give some recommendations that would be detrimental to normal database operations.

Using the DTA with Profiler

The DTA can also analyze trace data collected by Profiler or the SQL Trace stored procedures to make recommendations. When creating a Profiler trace to use with the DTA, the Tuning template can be used, or you can configure your own event settings. However, in order for the DTA to analyze the trace file, performance data must be returned. The events that return data are the "Completed" events such as SP:Completed and SQL:Completed.

Correlating Database Activity with Performance Counters

Viewing performance counters with System Monitor or viewing SQL Server activity with Profiler can help monitor and detect high-cost activity. But until SQL Server 2005 was released, correlating data from the two tools was not possible except with third-party software. Profiler now has the capability to import and correlate performance data based on time. This is extraordinarily useful in finding out what processes are causing system bottlenecks.

Try It Out   Correlating Performance Data with Profiler Data

With the three tables created in the previous section and a new working script, try out this feature.

1.   Open a new Query window. Type the following code and save it as *AWPerformance.SQL*:

```
USE AdventureWorks2008;
GO
DECLARE @Iterations AS int;
SET @Iterations = 0;
WHILE @Iterations < 10
BEGIN
  SELECT ProductID, SUM(OrderQty) AS TotalProduct, SUM(UnitPrice)
  FROM dbo.NewSalesOrder GROUP BY ProductID
```

```
    WAITFOR DELAY '00:00:02'
  UPDATE dbo.NewSalesOrder SET UnitPrice = UnitPrice * 1.25
  WHERE ProductID % 2 = 0
  SET @Iterations = @Iterations + 1
END
  WAITFOR DELAY '00:00:02';

IF EXISTS (SELECT * FROM sys.indexes
WHERE name = 'ix_TransactionID')
DROP INDEX ix_TransactionID ON dbo.NewTransactionHistory
CREATE NONCLUSTERED INDEX ix_TransactionID ON dbo.NewTransactionHistory
(TransactionID);

SET @Iterations = 0;
WHILE @Iterations < 5
BEGIN
  INSERT dbo.NewTransactionHistory
  (ProductID, ReferenceOrderID, ReferenceOrderLineID, TransactionDate
  , TransactionType, Quantity, ActualCost, ModifiedDate)
  SELECT ProductID, ReferenceOrderID, ReferenceOrderLineID, TransactionDate
  , TransactionType, Quantity, ActualCost, ModifiedDate
  FROM dbo.NewTransactionHistory WHERE TransactionID % 21 = 1
    WAITFOR DELAY '00:00:02'
  UPDATE dbo.NewSalesOrder SET UnitPrice = UnitPrice / 1.25
  WHERE ProductID % 2 = 0
  SET @Iterations = @Iterations + 1
END
  WAITFOR DELAY '00:00:02';
ALTER INDEX ix_TransactionID
ON dbo.NewTransactionHistory REBUILD;
```

2. Now, open the Reliability and Performance Monitor and create a new Data Collector Set named *AwCollector* of type "Performance counter." For now, include a few counters to make it easier to see how to use the tools.

3. Add the Pages/sec, Avg. Disk Queue Length, %Processor Time, and Page Splits/sec counters to the counter log, and change the sampling interval to every 1 second, as shown in Figure 11-14. Click OK to save the Data Collector and start the sampling.

4. Open SQL Server Profiler and create a new trace called AWPerformance using the Blank template. Save the trace to a file called *AWPerformance.trc* with a maximum size of 15 MB. On the Events Selection tab, expand the TSQL events and select the SQL:BatchCompleted and SQL:StmtCompleted events. Click on the "Organize Columns" button, and move the Text Data column up just below Application Name; click OK, and then click Run.

5. Return to the AWPerformance script created earlier and run it. After the script completes (it will take a couple of minutes), stop the Profiler trace and the Data Collector.

6. In Profiler, open the AWPerformance.trc trace file that was created by Profiler. Then, import the Data Collector log by clicking File ➤ Import Performance Data. Notice that the Profiler events and Performance Monitor events are now time-correlated. By selecting a peak value in the performance data window, the corresponding trace event is highlighted in the trace window. Selecting a particular trace event will cause the associated performance data to be highlighted. Figure 11-15 shows the correlation between a spike in the Performance Counter Log and an INSERT operation in the Profiler results.

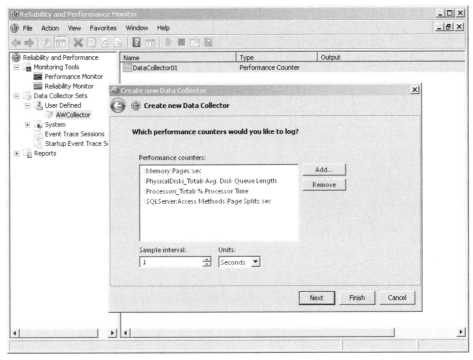

Figure 11-14: Changing the sampling interval.

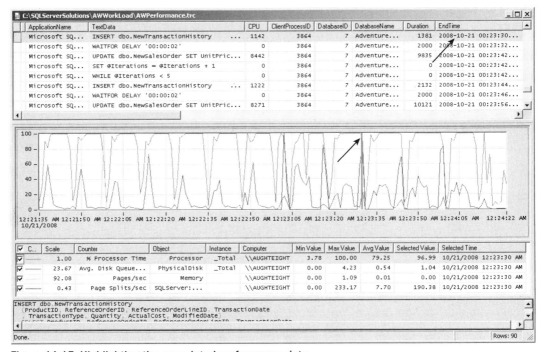

Figure 11-15: Highlighting the associated performance data.

T-SQL Optimization Tips

Transact-SQL optimization is perhaps the most complex and difficult topic that is covered in this chapter. This is simply because in T-SQL, as in any other high-level programming language, it is possible to express the same idea in a wide variety of ways. Programming languages are simply an expression of the ideas and methods conceived by a designer to solve a problem, and as such, each solution provides a glimpse into the mind of the person who created it. To a large degree this freedom of expression is what makes programming more of an art than a science. By the same token, it also makes optimizing these procedures that much more challenging.

Some database administrators prefer to stay out of the code and stop the optimization process after tuning the indexes. I can understand and respect this; however, it is important to consider that the potential benefits of optimizing the code itself far exceed any other form of optimization. Other database administrators are not hesitant to "get their feet wet," and identify and analyze particularly egregious procedures (even in commercial applications) and take steps to prevent them from having a negative impact on the rest of the server. This section is targeted directly at the later group, yet still has much to offer the former as well.

> **A few years ago I was called in to analyze a time-out problem that was plaguing a commercial timecard application. It turned out the procedure that retrieved an individual's timecard was so poorly written that it was unable to scale properly as the number of records in the database increased. By re-writing the procedure in a more efficient way, I was able to improve performance by more than 1,000 percent, reducing the execution time from more than 30 seconds to around 30 ms. The process has run flawlessly ever since.**

This section is not intended as a T-SQL programming guide. In fact, it is assumed that you have a basic working knowledge of T-SQL. My goal here is to examine several of the most common performance-related problem areas and to present you with alternatives and insights into how to make them more efficient. Keep in mind that your mileage may vary, and you should always thoroughly test your results when using these ideas to modify your own procedures.

Before moving on to cover the bigger areas, it is important to note that code optimizations are not always complex, and sometimes the little things can collectively have a big impact. The following tips are some of these little things that you should look for:

❑ SET NOCOUNT ON — Include this command at the top of every stored procedure to prevent SQL from reporting the number of affected rows after every operation. This will provide a small, but noticeable, performance boost.

❑ **Fully Qualify Object Names** — Include the schema name with every object name used. This will save a schema lookup and avoid potential problems if two objects have the same name in different schemas.

❑ **Avoid Using** DISTINCT — Adding the DISTINCT keyword when querying a result set will force SQL Server to build a temporary index to enforce this condition. In many cases, this is unnecessary, especially if any unique combinations of data are already included in the result set (such as a primary key value).

❑ **Use** UNION ALL **instead of** UNION — The UNION keyword will only include distinct rows and suffers from the same issue as described previously. Using UNION ALL includes all rows and thus avoids this overhead.

❑ **Avoid Unnecessary Sorting** — Don't arbitrarily include an ORDER BY clause if the calling procedure does not require it. Many client-side grid controls handle their own sorting anyway.

Each remaining topic in this section will discuss a specific area of concern in more detail. In many of the topics, you will notice that I include comments in the code samples that show I/O and time performance numbers. These metrics were all gathered using the SET STATISTICS IO ON and SET STATISTICS TIME ON commands. The first area that I will discuss also happens to be one of the biggest performance offenders.

Limiting Result Sets

One of the easiest ways to improve performance is to limit the data that gets returned from queries and procedures to just what is actually needed by the client. Limiting results in this way will reduce server I/O loads, minimize network congestion, and improve query response time. Unfortunately, over-inclusive results are one of the most common problems that I see, both in terms of rows and columns.

Including unnecessary columns is quite common because of over-use of the ubiquitous "select * from table" syntax. This is particularly egregious when multiple tables are included in the query, since the asterisk by itself will return all rows from all included tables. One problem that this causes is when any of the column names happen to be the same, which is fairly common in joined structures. This can wreak havoc with applications, causing unexpected exceptions, and even worse, causing the wrong field to get updated. Another problem with unnecessary columns shows up in the Query Optimizer. When you include all of the columns in the output, you will often see the Optimizer choose to use a clustered index scan on the entire table, even if other indexes exist. Finally, if the table happens to include any really big fields, then this could significantly increase the amount of data that would have to be retrieved from disk and pushed over the wire to the client. Take a look at the difference in performance of the following two queries:

```
SELECT sod.SalesOrderID, sod.SalesOrderDetailID FROM Sales.SalesOrderDetail sod
-- (121317 row(s) affected)
-- Table 'SalesOrderDetail'. Scan count 1, logical reads 228, physical reads 0.
-- CPU time = 40 ms,  elapsed time = 3777 ms.

SELECT * FROM Sales.SalesOrderDetail sod
-- (121317 row(s) affected)
-- Table 'SalesOrderDetail'. Scan count 1, logical reads 1240, physical reads 0.
-- CPU time = 250 ms,  elapsed time = 8398 ms.
```

If all we needed was the order and detail IDs, then the first query would provide the answer twice as fast, and only use one-sixth of the CPU time.

In a way, excessive row counts are an even bigger problem than extra columns because the filters used to limit rows often depend on parameters that are passed in by an application. Many applications even provide some level of ad hoc querying, which makes it nearly impossible for a DBA to guarantee performance levels. In general, try to define as many conditions as possible to limit the number of records returned, and wherever possible define indexes on any selective columns that are frequently used in the `where` clause. Even in cases in which it is not possible to define a sufficiently restrictive filter, you might still be able to limit the number of rows returned to a fixed maximum.

TOP N *and* SET ROWCOUNT

Using TOP N and SET ROWCOUNT are two ways to limit the number of rows returned even when the query itself would normally generate additional data. These techniques can be very effective in applications that only display a page of data at any one time, or when all you care about are the top results. For example, if a client application wanted to retrieve the five most expensive products from the AdventureWorks2008 database, it could just query the products list, sort it by ListPrice, and read the first five returned values. This would generate a query similar to the following:

```
SELECT ProductID,Name,ListPrice
FROM Production.Product
ORDER BY ListPrice desc
-- (504 row(s) affected)
-- Table 'Product'. Scan count 1, logical reads 15, physical reads 0.
-- CPU time = 0 ms,  elapsed time = 280 ms.
```

Instead of reading the first five values and throwing the rest away, the client could use TOP N or SET ROWCOUNT to tell the server to only return the first five values, thereby eliminating the waste. Here are examples of using these methods:

```
SELECT TOP 5 ProductID,Name,ListPrice
FROM Production.Product
ORDER BY ListPrice desc
-- (5 row(s) affected)
-- Table 'Product'. Scan count 1, logical reads 15, physical reads 0.
-- CPU time = 0 ms,  elapsed time = 6 ms.

SET ROWCOUNT 5
SELECT ProductID,Name,ListPrice
FROM Production.Product
ORDER BY ListPrice desc
SET ROWCOUNT 0
-- (5 row(s) affected)
-- Table 'Product'. Scan count 1, logical reads 15, physical reads 0.
-- CPU time = 0 ms,  elapsed time = 7 ms.
```

As you can see, TOP N and SET ROWCOUNT are roughly the same as far as performance goes, and either one will be many times faster than retrieving the full list.

In general, I prefer to use TOP (n) *over* SET ROWCOUNT. *The reason is that* SET ROWCOUNT *remains in effect for all statements until you execute a* SET ROWCOUNT 0, *while* TOP (n) *is limited to a single statement. Better isolation can help prevent unanticipated problems.*

HAVING *versus* WHERE

One of the most common questions that I have seen over the years is about the differences between the HAVING and WHERE clauses in a query. Specifically, which one is better? The answer is both, depending on what you need to accomplish!

The difference is in the timing. There are actually three different ways that you can filter a query in SQL Server. You can use joins, the WHERE clause, or the HAVING clause. Joins are processed first, followed by the WHERE clause, and then finally the HAVING clause. In general, the earlier in the process chain that a filter is applied, the better the results. Therefore, the only filters that must be placed in the HAVING clause are ones that are based on the calculation results themselves. In all other cases, the filter should be placed in the WHERE clause instead.

It is important to note that it will not always make a difference whether you place a filter in the HAVING clause or in the WHERE clause because the Query Optimizer in SQL Server 2008 is very smart about reordering the filters for you. For example, the following queries will actually result in the same execution plan:

```
SELECT pp.ProductLine, COUNT(pp.ProductID) 'Products'
FROM Production.Product pp
WHERE pp.ProductLine in ('R','M')
GROUP BY pp.ProductLine

SELECT pp.ProductLine, COUNT(pp.ProductID) 'Products'
FROM Production.Product pp
GROUP BY pp.ProductLine
HAVING pp.ProductLine in ('R','M')
```

Normally, you would expect the second filter to require a lot more work, because the aggregate would need to be calculated first, and only then would the HAVING filter be applied. However, in this case the Query Optimizer comes to the rescue by recognizing the improperly written query and moving the expression into the WHERE clause behind the scenes. Don't assume that the Query Optimizer will always be able to compensate for poorly written queries. You will experience more consistent results if you explicitly use the WHERE clause for filters that do not depend on an aggregate.

Functions in the WHERE Clause

A common mistake when constructing the WHERE clause is to wrap a table column in a function rather than using the function on a constant value. Performance in SQL Server depends heavily on the Query Optimizer's ability to use indexes. Wrapping the table column in a function tends to mask the column from the Query Optimizer, which forces a slower full table scan to be used instead of an index.

In most cases, it is easy to re-write these kinds of expressions in a way that will allow the Optimizer to use an index to help process the query. For example, take the following inefficient query:

```
SELECT Name
FROM Production.Product
WHERE substring(Name,1,2)='BE'
-- Index Scan
-- (1 row(s) affected)
-- Table 'Product'. Scan count 1, logical reads 5, physical reads 0.
-- CPU time = 10 ms,   elapsed time = 38 ms.

SELECT Name
FROM Production.Product
WHERE Name like 'BE%'
-- Index Seek
```

```
-- Table 'Product'. Scan count 1, logical reads 2, physical reads 0.
-- CPU time = 0 ms,  elapsed time = 2 ms.
```

The first query used a function (substring) that wrapped the Name column and effectively hid it from the Optimizer. This forced a more expensive scan operation to be used. Re-writing the query in a way that eliminated the function allowed the Query Optimizer to take advantage of the faster seek operation on the column. You will find this same behavior with *any* function that operates on the column that is being filtered. Whenever you notice this, try to find a way to isolate the data column and either eliminate the function or move the function to the constant side of the comparison.

ANSI-Style Join Syntax

The ANSI-style join syntax has been around for quite a while, and you are probably familiar with it already. ANSI join syntax basically requires that the join criteria for each joined table be explicitly declared when the tables are joined, rather than implicitly derived from a comparison in the WHERE clause. I have used the ANSI-style join syntax exclusively for many years and have found it to be superior to the older non-ANSI joins. Here are some of the reasons why I prefer ANSI-style joins:

❑ ANSI-style joins are easier to understand. Intermixing join expressions with your query filters in the WHERE clause can make it very difficult to understand and troubleshoot query problems.

❑ ANSI-style joins offer more join options, allowing you to more precisely specify the entity relationships, as well as permitting more advanced join types such as Full Outer, Star, and Merge joins.

❑ Non-ANSI joins are deprecated.

Starting with SQL Server 2008, the non-ANSI *= and =* join operators will no longer be accepted when using database compatibility level 90 or greater.

Even though you can still technically use the non-ANSI "=" join operator in the WHERE clause of a query, you should not do so. Besides the fact that this operator will also be deprecated at some point in the future, its use will make your queries less readable and harder to debug. Consider the following query, and see how long it takes you to spot the missing join:

```
-- SQL-style joins make it difficult to find problems
SELECT poh.PurchaseOrderID,poh.OrderDate,poh.EmployeeID,pod.ProductID,
  pp.Name 'ProductName',pv.Name 'VendorName'
FROM Purchasing.Vendor pv, Person.BusinessEntity pbe, Production.Product pp,
 Purchasing.PurchaseOrderHeader poh, Purchasing.PurchaseOrderDetail pod
WHERE pv.BusinessEntityID=poh.VendorID and poh.PurchaseOrderID<10
  and poh.PurchaseOrderID=pod.PurchaseOrderID   and poh.PurchaseOrderID>5
  and pp.ProductID=pod.ProductID
-- (290878 row(s) affected)
-- Table 'BusinessEntity'. Scan count 1, logical reads 62, physical reads 0.
-- Table 'Product'. Scan count 0, logical reads 28, physical reads 0.
-- Table 'PurchaseOrderDetail'. Scan count 4, logical reads 8, physical reads 0.
-- Table 'Vendor'. Scan count 0, logical reads 8, physical reads 0.
-- Table 'PurchaseOrderHeader'. Scan count 1, logical reads 2, physical reads 0.
-- CPU time = 871 ms,  elapsed time = 12919 ms.
```

Obviously something is wrong since the query is running very slowly and is returning hundreds of thousands of rows. This is a classic symptom of an accidental cross-product or *cross-join*, but where is it? Re-writing the query using the ANSI-style join syntax makes the problem obvious and easy to fix:

```
-- The problem is clear with the ANSI-sytle joins
SELECT poh.PurchaseOrderID,poh.OrderDate,poh.EmployeeID,pod.ProductID,
  pp.Name 'ProductName',
pv.Name 'VendorName'
FROM Purchasing.PurchaseOrderDetail pod
 inner join Purchasing.PurchaseOrderHeader poh on
          pod.PurchaseOrderID=poh.PurchaseOrderID
 inner join Production.Product pp on pod.ProductID=pp.ProductID
 inner join Purchasing.Vendor pv on pv.BusinessEntityID=poh.VendorID
 --,Person.BusinessEntity pbe  -- This table should not have been included
WHERE poh.PurchaseOrderID>5 and poh.PurchaseOrderID<10
-- (14 row(s) affected)
-- Table 'Product'. Scan count 0, logical reads 28, physical reads 0.
-- Table 'Vendor'. Scan count 0, logical reads 28, physical reads 0.
-- Table 'PurchaseOrderDetail'. Scan count 4, logical reads 8, physical reads 0.
-- Table 'PurchaseOrderHeader'. Scan count 1, logical reads 2, physical reads 0.
-- CPU time = 0 ms,  elapsed time = 2 ms.
```

When using the ANSI-style joins, the problem becomes obvious. The `Person.BusinessEntity` table was not explicitly joined to any other table, so it was being implicitly cross-joined with the rest of the query, which was inflating the row count.

Dealing with Null Values

Nulls are an unavoidable and important part of every database; however, most people have an incomplete view of what *null* actually means, and how and why it is used by SQL Server. The actual definition of *null* simply states that it is a "special value that represents the absence of any data value." There are a lot of misconceptions about what this really means, so first let's take a look at what null is not:

❑   Null is not zero. Zero is a value.

❑   Null is not an empty string. An empty string is actually a string value that is zero in length.

❑   Null is not a minimum date value, although many applications define it as such to avoid dealing with null dates.

❑   Null does not mean "not applicable." It is sometimes used in this capacity, but "no data" and "not applicable" are really different concepts.

❑   Null does not mean "unknown." A null value might be used to represent an unknown value during data entry, but the value might be missing for other reasons as well. As above, the concepts of "unknown" and "no data" are actually different.

So what does that leave? Well, nothing. . . .   And that is exactly what null actually is — *nothing*. It represents a missing or absent value. The presence of null values results in some interesting interactions when doing logical comparisons, as is done in the WHERE clause of a query. Figure 11-16 shows the logical truth tables when null values are taken into account.

Input A	Input B	AND	OR	NOT A
True	True	True	True	
True	False	False	True	False
True	NULL	NULL	True	
False	True	False	True	
False	False	False	False	True
False	NULL	False	NULL	
NULL	True	NULL	True	
NULL	False	False	NULL	NULL
NULL	NULL	NULL	NULL	

Figure 11-16: Logical truth tables including null values.

As you can see, several of the logical comparisons will result in a null value, and any rows for which the filter results in a null will be excluded from the output. With very few exceptions, an expression will result in null if any of its inputs are null. Looking at this from a logical perspective, most of the time it makes sense. For example, suppose that I asked for your birth date in order to calculate your age and you refused to provide it. I would then be unable to calculate your age because I was missing a key input. In this situation, in database terms, your birth date would be null. I think that most would agree that this makes sense, but there are some other implications of null that might make you scratch your head. Consider the following examples:

```
Declare @alive bit;
SET @alive=NULL;

if @alive=1 or @alive!=1
  Print 'Alive or Dead';
Else
  Print 'Huh? Neither alive nor dead';
-- Result: Huh? Neither alive nor dead

if @alive=@alive
  Print 'It must equal itself, right?'
else
  Print 'Not always. null does not equal null'
-- Result: Not always. null does not equal null
```

Since null is not actually a value, it cannot be equal to any value.

At this point, it is important to highlight the difference between "distinct" and "not equal." At first glance, it would seem that values that were not equal would also be distinct; however, in the context of nulls, this is not necessarily true. In SQL Server two null values are not considered distinct, and at the same time they are not equal. Confused? I don't doubt it. In SQL Server, grouping is based on distinct values rather than on unequal values, and as a consequence all of the null values are grouped together.

Another concession to the normal handling of nulls is in CHECK constraints on columns in a table. When evaluating CHECK constraints, SQL Server will accept data for which the condition evaluates to null. The exact same expression in a WHERE clause would exclude the data that evaluated to null.

Alternatives to Cursors

Too many times I have seen administrators and developers alike embark on crusades to eliminate cursors, just because they read an article somewhere that branded cursors as a problem. This is really disingenuous to the cursor, which does actually play an important role in T-SQL programming. I am not saying that eliminating cursors is not a good idea, because in many cases, there are alternatives that can actually improve performance. Rather, I am saying that it is important to understand why cursors can be a problem in the first place.

One of the first things that cursor crusaders will do is to arbitrarily replace the cursor with a while loop. This is not necessarily bad, but it really does not solve the problem either. The issue is the fact that cursors process data a single record at a time, rather than using a set-based approach. In some cases, this may be necessary, and, if so, then using a cursor may be the best solution. Perhaps each pass through the loop involves constructing a personalized e-mail message and then sending it to a particular recipient (like a vendor statement). In this case, it really is not going to make a lot of difference whether you use a cursor or a while loop.

In other cases, it might be possible to replace the cursor or while loop altogether, and this is where you can realize some really significant performance benefits. The real problem is in using a loop to do a job that could be done in a set operation. Here is an example that highlights this issue:

```
-- Generate a comma-delimited list of vendors that supply each product
DECLARE @results TABLE
  (ProductID int primary key,Vendors varchar(max))

DECLARE @pid int, @vname varchar(50), @vlist varchar(max)
DECLARE product_cursor CURSOR FOR SELECT ProductID FROM Production.Product pp
WHERE EXISTS(SELECT 1 FROM Purchasing.ProductVendor pv
   WHERE pv.ProductID=pp.ProductID)
OPEN product_cursor
FETCH NEXT FROM product_cursor INTO @pid
WHILE @@FETCH_STATUS = 0 BEGIN
  SET @vlist=''
  DECLARE vendor_cursor CURSOR FOR
    SELECT v.Name FROM Purchasing.ProductVendor pv
  inner join Purchasing.Vendor v on pv.BusinessEntityID=v.BusinessEntityID
  WHERE ProductID=@pid
  OPEN vendor_cursor
  FETCH NEXT FROM vendor_cursor into @vname
  WHILE @@FETCH_STATUS = 0 BEGIN
    SET @vlist = @vlist + '; ' + @vname
    FETCH NEXT FROM vendor_cursor into @vname
  END
  CLOSE vendor_cursor
  DEALLOCATE vendor_cursor

  INSERT @results (ProductID,Vendors)
  VALUES (@pid,substring(@vlist,3,datalength(@vlist)))
  FETCH NEXT FROM product_cursor INTO @pid
END
CLOSE product_cursor
DEALLOCATE product_cursor
```

```
SELECT * FROM @results
-- CPU time = 891 ms,  elapsed time = 4394 ms.
```

The cursor-based operation shown previously generates a table of product numbers, and for each product, it includes a semicolon-delimited list containing the name of every vendor that supplies the product. Somehow eliminating the cursor and replacing it with a `while` loop really would not accomplish very much. Instead, the process itself needs to be analyzed and then replaced with a set-based operation. The listing below shows a set-based replacement that generates exactly the same output:

```
-- The same operation using a set based approach
SELECT p.ProductID,
stuff((SELECT '; ' + v.name FROM Purchasing.Vendor v
  inner join Purchasing.ProductVendor pv
on v.BusinessEntityID=pv.BusinessEntityID
WHERE p.ProductID=pv.ProductID
ORDER BY pv.BusinessEntityID FOR XML PATH('')), 1, 1, '') 'vendors'
FROM Production.Product p
WHERE EXISTS(SELECT 1 FROM Purchasing.ProductVendor xv
    WHERE xv.ProductID=p.ProductID)
-- CPU time = 10 ms,  elapsed time = 503 ms.
```

In addition to being much more compact, the set-based operation runs nine times faster and uses 89 percent less CPU time! This is how to optimize a loop — by eliminating the sequential processing and replacing it with a set-based operation.

Merge Joins

The new merge join operator performs simultaneous insert, update, and delete operations on a single table. For the first time in SQL Server, it is possible to efficiently merge the contents of one table (or query) into another table in a single statement. Internally, the merge process has been optimized to minimize the number of necessary scans. This gives merge a clear performance advantage over the older method of using separate statements for each operation. As you can imagine, there are a lot of tasks that might benefit from this. It is particularly useful in maintaining data warehouse tables and when saving updated business objects from a client application.

The following example highlights many of the features of the merge join. First, the following code creates two matching tables, and then performs several updates to just one table.

```
USE AdventureWorks2008
GO

-- Setup a baseline to test from
SELECT TOP 10 BusinessEntityID 'ID',AccountNumber,Name
   INTO dbo.VendA FROM Purchasing.Vendor
   ORDER BY BusinessEntityID
SELECT * INTO dbo.VendB FROM dbo.VendA
GO

-- Make some changes to VendA
INSERT dbo.VendA (ID,AccountNumber,Name)
   VALUES (5000,'ACME0001','ACME Corporation')
```

```
UPDATE dbo.VendA SET Name='Zen Master' WHERE ID=1502
DELETE dbo.VendA WHERE ID=1510
GO
```

In order to implement the same changes to VendB that were done to VendA, we could use separate update statements or a merge join. Using separate update statements would require something like the following code:

```
-- Update VendB using separate statements, this must be wrapped in a
-- transaction to keep the operation atomic.
-- Don't actually run this, it is just here to show the alternative.
BEGIN TRY
  BEGIN TRAN
  -- UPDATE
  UPDATE VendB
  SET Name=VendA.Name, AccountNumber=VendA.AccountNumber
  FROM VendB inner join VendA on VendB.ID=VendA.ID
  -- INSERT
  INSERT VendB (ID,AccountNumber,Name)
  SELECT VendA.ID,VendA.AccountNumber,VendA.Name
  FROM VendA left join VendB on VendA.ID=VendB.ID
  WHERE VendB.ID is null
  -- DELETE
  DELETE VendB
  WHERE NOT EXISTS(SELECT * FROM VendA WHERE VendA.ID=VendB.ID)
  COMMIT TRAN
END TRY
BEGIN CATCH
  ROLLBACK TRAN
END CATCH
GO
-- Table 'VendB'. Scan count 3, logical reads 34, physical reads 0.
-- Table 'VendA'. Scan count 3, logical reads 43, physical reads 0.
-- Table 'Worktable'. Scan count 1, logical reads 5, physical reads 0.
-- CPU time = 0 ms,  elapsed time = 18 ms.
```

Now take a look at the same operation using a merge join:

```
-- Now use merge to populate VendB with the same data as VendA
MERGE INTO VendB
USING VendA
  ON VendA.ID=VendB.ID
WHEN MATCHED THEN
  UPDATE SET Name=VendA.Name, AccountNumber=VendA.AccountNumber
WHEN NOT MATCHED BY TARGET THEN
  INSERT (ID,AccountNumber,Name)
  VALUES (VendA.ID, VendA.AccountNumber, VendA.Name)
WHEN NOT MATCHED BY SOURCE THEN
  DELETE;
GO
-- Table 'VendB'. Scan count 2, logical reads 33, physical reads 0.
-- Table 'VendA'. Scan count 2, logical reads 22, physical reads 0.
-- CPU time = 0 ms,  elapsed time = 6 ms.
```

Much better! The merge join is easier to understand, performs fewer database reads, and runs faster than separate statements.

If you have ever worked with *n*-tier business objects, then you are familiar with the challenges in persisting object changes back to the database. Business objects are normally edited as a unit; for example, a purchase order and all of its lines will typically be edited and saved together. When it comes time to save the changes, depending on what the user has done, records might need to be deleted, inserted, or updated. It is now possible to use a `DataTable` client-side to create a list that contains just the changed rows, and then send the changes to SQL Server using a Table Valued Function (TVF). Then you can use the Table Valued Function with the merge operator to update the database table in a single statement. An example of this technique is beyond the scope of this book; however, if you are interested, a quick search online should yield several hits.

Grouping Sets

Grouping sets are another new feature of SQL Server 2008. They allow multiple field groupings to be aggregated at the same time, with all of the different results being returned together. Grouping sets provide a functional superset of the WITH CUBE and WITH ROLLUP grouping modifiers. They allow more flexibility in defining what groups to aggregate and offer a more compact and easy-to-understand syntax. A single grouping set operation can replace an entire collection of individual grouping statements.

With grouping sets, all of the different group values and subtotals are returned in a single result set, similar to what you would get if you calculated each group individually and then combined all of the results with a UNION ALL operator. For example, say that you wanted to return sales totals from the AdventureWorks2008 database by year, by customer, by territory, and overall. In prior versions of SQL Server, you could get all of these summaries by running four different queries and then combining them as follows:

```
-- Multiple groupings using individual queries
SELECT CustomerID,null 'TerritoryID',null 'Year',SUM(TotalDue) 'Total'
FROM Sales.SalesOrderHeader
GROUP BY CustomerID
UNION ALL
SELECT null,TerritoryID,null,SUM(TotalDue) 'Total'
FROM Sales.SalesOrderHeader
GROUP BY TerritoryID
UNION ALL
SELECT null,null,Year(OrderDate),SUM(TotalDue) 'Total'
FROM Sales.SalesOrderHeader
GROUP BY Year(OrderDate)
UNION ALL
SELECT null,null,null,SUM(TotalDue) 'Total'
FROM Sales.SalesOrderHeader
ORDER BY CustomerID desc,TerritoryID desc,[Year] desc
-- Table 'SalesOrderHeader'. Scan count 4, logical reads 2744, physical reads 0.
-- Table 'Worktable'. Scan count 0, logical reads 0, physical reads 0.
-- CPU time = 280 ms,   elapsed time = 1973 ms.
```

Using grouping sets, you can accomplish the same thing using a shorter and more easily understandable syntax:

```
-- Multiple groupings using grouping sets
SELECT CustomerID,TerritoryID,Year(OrderDate) 'Year',SUM(TotalDue) 'Total'
FROM Sales.SalesOrderHeader
GROUP BY GROUPING SETS ((CustomerID),(TerritoryID),(Year(OrderDate)),())
ORDER BY CustomerID desc,TerritoryID desc,Year(OrderDate) desc
-- Table 'Worktable'. Scan count 0, logical reads 0, physical reads 0.
-- Table 'SalesOrderHeader'. Scan count 3, logical reads 2058, physical reads 0.
-- CPU time = 301 ms,  elapsed time = 1845 ms.
```

Notice with the grouping sets solution that the conditions for each individual group are specified in parentheses after the `grouping sets` keyword. You can add as many different grouping sets as necessary, and you can even specify cube and rollup operations. There are many different possibilities, and I encourage you to experiment with this great new feature.

Distinct Aggregation

Distinct aggregation is where you use the `DISTINCT` keyword to calculate the number of unique values in the form `COUNT(DISTINCT field)`. SQL Server has trouble optimizing these kinds of statements, especially if more than one distinct count is used in a single query. It can be extremely frustrating to design an otherwise useful query and then have it slow to a crawl when you add a distinct aggregate.

The root of the problem is that in order for SQL Server 2008 to calculate a distinct aggregate, it has to create and read an intermediate result table based on the input data stream. For multiple distinct aggregates in the same query, SQL Server repeats this process, destroying and re-creating the data stream and generating new intermediate results for each total. This ends up being far more expensive than just calculating the totals in a subquery! As an example of this, consider the following query:

```
-- Counts using distinct aggregation
SELECT COUNT(distinct sd.SalesOrderID) 'Orders',
  COUNT(distinct sd.SalesOrderDetailID) 'Details',
  COUNT(distinct sh.CustomerID) 'Customers'
FROM Sales.SalesOrderDetail sd
  inner join Sales.SalesOrderHeader sh on sd.SalesOrderID=sh.SalesOrderID
GO
-- Table 'Worktable'. Scan count 3, logical reads 246112, physical reads 0.
-- Table 'SalesOrderDetail'. Scan count 1, logical reads 228, physical reads 2.
-- Table 'SalesOrderHeader'. Scan count 1, logical reads 45, physical reads 2.
-- CPU time = 1822 ms,  elapsed time = 2036 ms.
```

Notice the huge number of reads that were required in Worktable and the fact that it had to be scanned three times in order to generate the three distinct totals. Clearly, there must be a better way.

One alternative approach that I use in these kinds of situations is to leverage subqueries to group and count the unique values and then join the subqueries together into a final result set. The query below uses this technique to generate the same results, but using a fraction of the resources and time:

```
-- Distinct Counts using sub-queries
WITH OrderCounter (Orders,Details) AS
( SELECT COUNT(1) 'Orders',SUM(Lines) 'Details' FROM
  (SELECT SalesOrderID,COUNT(SalesOrderDetailID) 'Lines'
   FROM Sales.SalesOrderDetail GROUP BY SalesOrderID) s
),
CustomerCounter (Customers) AS
( SELECT COUNT(1) 'Customers' FROM
  (SELECT CustomerID FROM Sales.SalesOrderHeader GROUP BY CustomerID) c
)
SELECT Orders,Details,Customers
FROM OrderCounter,CustomerCounter
GO
-- Table 'SalesOrderHeader'. Scan count 1, logical reads 45, physical reads 0.
-- Table 'SalesOrderDetail'. Scan count 1, logical reads 1240, physical reads 16.
-- CPU time = 100 ms,  elapsed time = 250 ms
```

There are a couple of interesting aspects to this solution:

❑ The three distinct totals only required two subqueries because two of the totals were calculated at once.

❑ Notice that the final result uses an implicit cross-join because each intermediate result is guaranteed to return a single row. Of more importance, however, is the 95 percent reduction in the CPU time required and the 99 percent reduction in logical reads. The moral: Don't use distinct aggregates when you can use subqueries!

How Many Records Are in That Table?

There are many occasions when you might need to retrieve the total number of records that exist in a table. The typical way to do this is by using COUNT(*) as follows:

```
-- Get record count by physically counting the rows
SELECT Count(*) FROM Production.TransactionHistory
-- Table 'TransactionHistory'. Scan count 1, logical reads 157, physical reads 0.
-- CPU time = 40 ms,  elapsed time = 101 ms.
```

This approach works by physically counting the number of records in the table by performing an index scan on the primary key or by doing a full table scan if there is no primary key. For small tables this will happen very quickly, but for large tables it can take quite a while to count all of the records.

Fortunately, there is a much faster alternative that can also return the number of records in a table. There is a caveat, however, in that the record count is not guaranteed to be 100 percent accurate for tables that have recently had a lot of insertions or deletions. This alternative method takes advantage of the statistical information that SQL Server automatically keeps for every table and index (unless you have disabled auto-statistics). The following example uses statistics to return the record count:

```
-- Get record count using partition statistics
select sum(row_count) 'TotalRows'
FROM sys.dm_db_partition_stats
```

```
WHERE object_id=object_id('Production.TransactionHistory')
and index_id<=1
-- Table 'sysidxstats'. Scan count 1, logical reads 2, physical reads 0.
-- CPU time = 0 ms,  elapsed time = 0 ms.
```

Notice the execution time; this query completed so quickly that it didn't even register on the timer! Even better, this method will continue to operate nearly instantaneously regardless of how big the source table gets. Oh, and it also works with partitions as well. In fact, it can even be adapted to return the record counts for every table in the database in a single operation, as shown below:

```
-- Get Record counts for every user table in the current database
select so.name 'TableName', so.type, sum(row_count) 'TotalRows'
FROM sys.dm_db_partition_stats ps inner join sys.objects so
on ps.[object_id]=so.[object_id]
WHERE index_id<=1 and so.[type]='U'
GROUP BY so.name,so.type
ORDER BY SUM(row_count) DESC
-- Table 'sysschobjs'. Scan count 0, logical reads 294, physical reads 0.
-- Table 'sysidxstats'. Scan count 1, logical reads 11, physical reads 0.
-- CPU time = 10 ms,  elapsed time = 37 ms.
```

Amazingly, using partition statistics to return the record counts for every table in the database is faster than using COUNT(*) on a single medium-sized table. If you can live with the possibility that the record counts may be slightly off, then you can use statistics to save a lot of CPU time.

If necessary, you can manually update the statistical row totals by running the UPDATEUSAGE command, as shown below:

```
-- Update statistics for every table and index in the database
DBCC UPDATEUSAGE(0) WITH COUNT_ROWS

-- Update statistics for a single table
DBCC UPDATEUSAGE(0,'Production.TransactionHistory',1) WITH COUNT_ROWS
```

Temp Tables versus Table Variables

When writing stored procedures, there is often a need to temporarily store tabular data within the scope of the procedure. There are basically two ways of storing temporary data in SQL Server 2008: temporary tables and table variables. Temporary tables have been around for quite a while and generally well understood. Table variables, on the other hand, are a relatively new innovation, and there is still a lot of confusion about how best to use them.

Technically, there are two different types of temporary tables: local and global. However, for the purposes of this comparison, when I refer to temporary tables, I mean local temporary tables.

Temporary tables and table variables have a great deal of functional overlap, which gives rise to seemingly endless discussions as to which one is better to use. In fact, each was developed to solve a different set of problems, as becomes evident when looking at the differences and limitations of each option. Understanding these differences is the key to knowing which option is best suited for a given situation. So, when choosing between temporary tables and table variables, consider the following:

❑   Temporary tables are always created in tempdb, while table variables are created in memory. This is often cited as a reason to use table variables over temporary tables; however, there is not as much difference in this regard as you might first imagine. Temporary tables will be cached in memory for fast access, and table variables will use `tempdb` when subjected to memory pressure.

❑ Temporary tables have session scope, while table variables only have procedure/batch scope. Any object that goes "out of scope" is automatically cleaned up by SQL Server, so this difference has several interesting consequences:

❑ Table variables are not visible to the calling procedure, but temporary tables are.

❑ Table variables cannot be dropped, but temporary tables can.

❑ Table variables that are created inside of a dynamic SQL statement will not be visible outside the dynamic statement, but temporary tables will.

❑ Table variables cannot be generated dynamically, for example, via a SELECT INTO.

❑ You cannot use DDL on table variables. The structure of a table variable is fixed at the time of creation. The only indexes permitted are ones that can be declared directly in the DECLARE TABLE statement — a primary key and any number of additional unique keys. This implies that table variables will always be accessed via a scan operation. Temporary tables do allow DDL operations and allow any number of indexes to be added.

❑ Statistics are not calculated on table variables. The Query Optimizer always sees them with a cardinality of 1. This means that table variables will never force a recompile of the query plan. It also means that table variables will not take advantage of parallelism on multiple-CPU systems. For small tables, this can save time, but for medium to large tables with more than around 100,000 rows, a more relevant query plan will often save far more time than it takes to recompile.

❑ Table variables do not participate in transactions or locking and are not affected by rollbacks. A result of this is that table variables are logged only at the statement level, and these log entries are truncated as soon as the statement ends. Temporary tables will participate in transactions and locking and are logged normally. However, since they log to `tempdb`, the log will automatically be truncated at the next checkpoint (Simple recovery mode).

❑ Table variables can be created and accessed from within a user-defined function. Temporary tables cannot.

❑ Beginning in SQL Server 2008, table variables can be passed as parameters.

As you can see, table variables are more flexible, and, depending on the specific task you are trying to accomplish, they may be the only option. However, for large numbers of records, temporary tables gain a performance advantage due to their support for statistics and additional indexes. As always, make sure to test any given solution to see how it actually performs.

Resource Governor

The *Resource Governor* in SQL Server 2008 allows workloads to be differentiated and prioritized. This can be incredibly useful when you need to guarantee that certain critical processes have enough resources to operate efficiently, while still sharing resources with other less important jobs. It can also be used to insulate key processes from runaway queries and to prioritize queries. Prior to the Resource Governor, you could use multiple instances and a careful array of configuration values (such as affinity masks) to divide up resources. This solution was less than ideal because, in most cases, the resources used by one instance were reserved and could not be shared with other instances. The Resource Governor solves this problem by sharing resources when they are available and only kicking in to enforce limits when there is resource contention.

At this time, the Resource Governor is only available in the Enterprise, Developer, and Evaluation versions of SQL Server 2008.

The Resource Governor is comprised of three key components: a classifier function that differentiates workloads, resource pools that describe limits for shared server resources, and workload groups that are used to enforce policies for similar workloads. Figure 11-17 shows how these components work together.

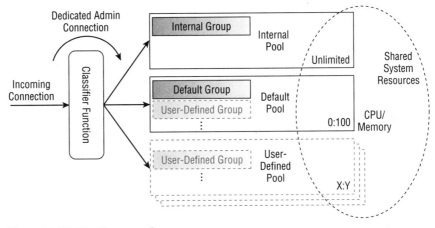

Figure 11-17: The Resource Governor.

Also included with the Resource Governor are several new database functions and events to support workload differentiation and resource monitoring. The following topics describe how to configure and monitor this new feature.

Configuring the Resource Governor

The Resource Governor must be configured before you can use it in a meaningful way. Configuration consists of the following four steps:

1. Configure resource pools.
2. Configure workload groups.
3. Create a classifier function.
4. Assign a classifier function and reconfigure.

Except for creating a classifier function, these steps can be performed using either SQL Server Management Studio or a command window using DDL statements. Oddly enough, when using SSMS, you must enable the Resource Governor before you can configure it. When using DDL statements, you can configure it before you enable it, which seems more natural to me. In any case, configuration is easy and reasonably straightforward. The following sections explain each step in more detail.

Configure Resource Pools

Resource pools are used to define logical boundaries for physical resources. It is helpful to think of a *resource pool* as a kind of virtual server instance. Each pool allows you to specify minimum and maximum utilization percentages for CPU and memory usage. The minimum values represent the minimum guaranteed resource availability, and the maximum values represent the shared resource limit.

> It is normal to see resource usage for a particular pool exceed the defined *maximum* value. If a resource is not required by another pool, then whatever is available to SQL Server as a whole is free to be used. The maximums are only enforced when the server has to divvy resources between competing pools.

Two resource pools are automatically created by SQL Server — the internal pool and the default pool. The *internal pool* is used by SQL Server itself for critical system tasks and cannot be altered in any way. It is an unrestricted pool and will consume resources as necessary, even if it means violating the limits established for the other pools. The *default pool* is used for everything else that has not been explicitly placed into a custom pool. The default pool cannot be created or deleted, but it can be re-configured to limit resource use.

Additional resource pools can be created as needed, but the total of all minimum values for a resource cannot exceed 100 percent, and the total of all maximum values for a resource must be between the total minimum and 100 percent. Resource pools can be created, altered, or dropped from SSMS, or by using DDL statements. For example, the following command will create a new resource pool that is limited to 50 percent of the total system memory and 25 percent of the total CPU resources:

```
CREATE RESOURCE POOL poolFinance
WITH
(
    MAX_CPU_PERCENT=25,
    MAX_MEMORY_PERCENT=50
);
```

Configure Workload Groups

Workload groups are used to define policies that apply to similar requests as determined by the classifier function. There are two built-in workload groups — the internal group and the default group — which are assigned to the internal pool and the default pool, respectively. The *internal group* is used by SQL Server itself for critical tasks and cannot be changed. The *default group* is used for everything else that has not been explicitly assigned to a user-defined group. The default group cannot be moved or deleted; however, you can configure it. Additional user-defined workload groups can be created as needed and assigned to either the default pool or to a user-defined pool. If necessary, user-defined workload groups can even be moved between pools.

The following policies (parameters) are available when creating a workload group:

❏ IMPORTANCE — This indicates the relative importance of tasks within a given resource pool. Valid values are HIGH, MEDIUM, and LOW. The default value is MEDIUM.

❑ REQUEST_MAX_MEMORY_GRANT_PERCENT — This is the maximum memory that a single request can use from the pool. If insufficient memory is available, then the request will be held until a memory grant becomes available or the request times out. The default value is 25 percent.

❑ REQUEST_MAX_CPU_TIME_SEC — This setting specifies the maximum CPU time that a request can use. Exceeding this value will not stop a request from processing; instead, a CPU Threshold Exceeded event will be raised, and the request will continue. The default is 0, which means unlimited.

❑ REQUEST_MEMORY_GRANT_TIMEOUT_SEC — This parameter sets the number of seconds that a request will wait for a memory grant before failing. The default is 0, which uses an internal calculation to determine the value based on the query cost.

❑ MAX_DOP — This sets the maximum degree of parallelism for requests. This setting overrides the server "max degree of parallelism" setting and sets an upper limit on the MAX_DOP query hint. The default is 0, which uses the system default setting.

❑ GROUP_MAX_REQUESTS — Sets the maximum number of simultaneous requests for the group. The default is 0, which means unlimited.

The following example will create a workload group and assign it to resource pool poolFinance:

```
CREATE WORKLOAD GROUP wrkgroupFinance
WITH
(
    IMPORTANCE = MEDIUM,
    REQUEST_MAX_MEMORY_GRANT_PERCENT = 50,
    REQUEST_MAX_CPU_TIME_SEC = 0,
    REQUEST_MEMORY_GRANT_TIMEOUT_SEC = 0,
    MAX_DOP = 4,
    GROUP_MAX_REQUESTS = 25
)
USING poolFinance;
```

Create a Classifier Function

The *classifier function* is used by the Resource Governor to decide which workload group to use for an incoming session. When the Resource Governor is enabled, this function will be executed after authentication and any logon triggers. It must return the name of the workload group to assign the incoming session to. If the classifier function fails for any reason or returns an invalid group name, then the session will be assigned to the "default group."

Make sure to test your classifier function before putting it into production. A poorly written classifier function can render the system unusable by causing all new sessions to time out. In addition, make sure to enable the Dedicated Administrator Connection. The DAC bypasses the classifier function and can be used to gain access to the server if there is a problem.

Classifier functions are subject to a few special conditions:

❑ They should always be created with server scope, meaning they should reside in the master database.

❑ Only one classifier function can be active at any point in time, and the active function cannot be dropped from the database.

❑ The classifier function must finish quickly to avoid causing connection time-outs.

The following table includes several functions that are useful in classifying workload groups. Included are a few functions that are new to SQL Server 2008 and are intended specifically for this task:

Function	Description
HOST_NAME	Returns the name of the workstation.
APP_NAME	Returns the name of the application; however, not every application sets this value.
SUSER_NAME	Returns the login name of the user in the syslogins table.
SUSER_SNAME	Returns the login name of the user based on their security identifier.
IS_SRVROLEMEMBER	Determines if the login is a member of a fixed server role.
IS_MEMBER	Determines if the login is a member of a Windows group or database role.
LOGONPROPERTY	Returns information about the login, including the default database.
CONNECTIONPROPERTY	Returns information about the connection that the request originated from, including the IP address and authentication mode.
ORIGINAL_DB_NAME	Returns the name of the database that was specified in the connection string.

The following example demonstrates how to create a classifier function:

```
USE master
GO

CREATE FUNCTION fnTestClassifier()RETURNS SYSNAME
WITH SCHEMABINDING
AS
BEGIN
  DECLARE @grpName SYSNAME
  IF (SUSER_SNAME() = 'sa')
    SET @grpName = 'wrkgroupAdmin'
  ELSE IF (APP_NAME() like '%Logistics%')
    SET @grpName = 'wrkgroupLogDep'
  ELSE IF (APP_NAME() like '%REPORT SERVER%')
    SET @grpName = 'wrkgroupReports'
```

```
      ELSE
        SET @grpName = 'default'
      RETURN @grpName
    END;
```

Assign the Classifier Function and Reconfigure

The final step in configuring the Resource Governor is to assign the classifier function. Before completing the configuration, make sure that you have thoroughly tested the function, and also make sure to enable the Dedicated Administrator Connection just in case something goes wrong. The following example shows how to complete the configuration:

```
ALTER RESOURCE GOVERNOR WITH (CLASSIFIER_FUNCTION = dbo.fnTestClassifier)
GO
ALTER RESOURCE GOVERNOR RECONFIGURE
```

The new configuration should take effect immediately.

Monitoring the Resource Governor

Monitoring the various workload groups and resource pools is a critical part of maintaining a smoothly running server. Monitoring will allow you to identify potential configuration issues and correct them before they affect critical business operations. There are three means of getting statistical information about the Resource Governor: performance counters, events, and system views.

Performance Counters

Performance counters are the preferred means of reporting Resource Governor performance statistics. There are two new counters that can be used for this purpose:

❑   SQLServer:Workload Group Stats — Reports workload group statistics, such as the number of active requests and how many are receiving less than optimal resources.

❑   SQLServer:Resource Pool Stats — Reports a variety of resource pool memory and CPU statistics, including overall CPU usage and the total memory in use by the pool.

Events

The Resource Governor also includes several new events that you can monitor using SQL Trace. These are listed below:

❑   CPU Threshold Exceeded — This event fires whenever the Resource Governor detects a query that exceeds the maximum CPU time configured for the workload group. This event is only guaranteed to fire if the threshold is exceeded for more than 5 seconds.

❑   PreConnect:Starting — This event is reported when a logon trigger or classifier function is executed.

❑   PreConnect:Completed — This event indicates that a logon trigger or classifier function has completed.

System Views

Rounding out the monitoring tools for the Resource Governor are several new catalog and management views that provide saved configuration information and current statistics:

❑   `sys.resource_governor_configuration` — Displays the saved Resource Governor configuration. This view only includes two columns that correspond to the classifier function name and whether or not the Resource Governor is enabled.

❑   `sys.resource_governor_resource_pools` — Displays the saved memory and CPU threshold values that have been configured for each resource pool.

❑   `sys.resource_governor_workload_groups` — Displays a list of defined workload groups, including the saved value of each configurable parameter, as described in the previous section on configuring workload groups.

❑   `sys.dm_resource_governor_configuration` — Shows the current in-memory configuration values for the Resource Governor, including whether or not a re-configuration is pending.

❑   `sys.dm_resource_governor_resource_pools` — This management view returns the in-memory configuration values of each resource pool, as well as accumulated statistics and current resource usage information.

❑   `sys.dm_resource_governor_workload_groups` — Returns the current configuration, accumulated statistics, and current resource usage information for each workload group.

The following code shows how to re-set the Resource Governor statistics that are reported by the resource pool and workload group management views. You may want to do this after making significant configuration changes to the Resource Governor.

```
DBCC TRACEON (8041, -1)
GO
ALTER RESOURCE GOVERNOR RECONFIGURE
```

Try It Out   Using the Resource Governor

Imagine that you are faced with the unenviable situation of permitting ad hoc query access to a few reporting users, while at the same time guaranteeing that business application users are not overly affected. This exercise will demonstrate how to use the Resource Governor to accomplish this goal. Before getting started, you will need a couple of users to simulate an ad hoc reporting user and a business application user.

1.   Open a new command window in SSMS, and execute the following code to create these users:

```
-- PREP Task 1, create test users
USE AdventureWorks2008
GO
CREATE LOGIN AdHocUser WITH password='P@ssw0rd',
    DEFAULT_DATABASE=AdventureWorks2008
exec sp_grantdbaccess 'AdHocUser'
```

```
exec sp_addrolemember 'db_datareader', 'AdHocUser'

GO
CREATE LOGIN FinanceUser WITH password='P@ssw0rd',
    DEFAULT_DATABASE=AdventureWorks2008
exec sp_grantdbaccess 'FinanceUser'
exec sp_addrolemember 'db_datareader', 'FinanceUser'
```

2. You must create a classifier function in the `master` database that will assign each user to a different workload group. The function can be created ahead of time and will not actually be used until you bind it to the Resource Governor. Enter the following code in a command window and execute it:

```
-- PREP Task 2, create a classifier function
USE master
GO
CREATE FUNCTION fnClassifier()
RETURNS sysname
WITH SCHEMABINDING
AS
BEGIN
  DECLARE @wrkGroup sysname

  IF SUSER_SNAME()='AdHocUser' BEGIN
    SET @wrkGroup='wrkgrpAdHoc'
  END ELSE IF SUSER_SNAME()='FinanceUser' BEGIN
    SET @wrkGroup='wrkgrpFinance'
  END ELSE BEGIN
    SET @wrkGroup='default'
  END
  RETURN @wrkGroup
END
GO
```

3. Now that you have a classifier function and a couple of test users, you are ready to configure the Resource Governor itself. Most of the configuration tasks can be done from one screen in SQL Server Management Studio. In Object Explorer, expand the Management tree, then right-click "Resource Governor" and select Properties.

4. Click on the "Enable Resource Governor" checkbox to enable editing, and then enter the configuration as described in the following table (see Figure 11-18). Most properties in the Resource Governor are case-sensitive, so be careful when entering the configuration.

Resource Pool	Associated Workload Group

poolAdHoc
  Maximum CPU % = 10
  Maximum Memory % = 25
	wrkgrpAdHoc
	  Maximum Requests = 15
	  Degree of Parallelism = 4

poolFinance
  (use default settings)
	wrkgrpFinance
	  (use default settings)

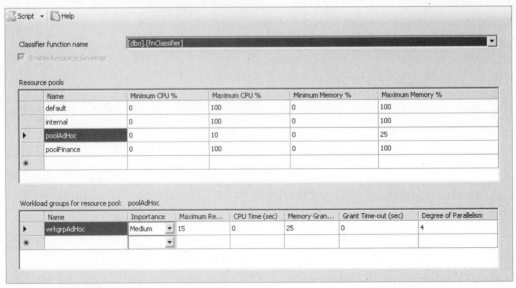

Figure 11-18: Resource Governor configuration.

5. Make sure to select the "Classifier function name" as shown in Figure 11-18, then click OK to save the configuration and enable the Resource Governor. The icon in Object Explorer should change to indicate that the Resource Governor is running.

6. Next, if you are running on a system with multiple CPUs, then you will need to limit the number of CPUs available to SQL Server to force the workloads to compete for the same CPU. There will never be any CPU resource contention as long as there are more CPUs available than there are requests. You can set the CPU affinity in SQL Server without restarting by executing the following code:

```
-- PREP Task 3, set CPU Affinity
sp_configure 'show advanced options', 1;
RECONFIGURE WITH OVERRIDE;
GO
sp_configure 'affinity mask', 1;  -- default value of 0 means use all CPUs
GO
sp_configure 'affinity i/o mask', 1;
RECONFIGURE WITH OVERRIDE;
```

7. Next, you will need to simulate two competing CPU-intensive workloads to confirm that the Resource Governor is functioning. You must open a separate query session for each of the two users that were created above. From SSMS, select File ➤ New ➤ Database Engine Query, then change the authentication mode to "SQL Server Authentication" and enter the username and password for AdHocUser. Then repeat this process for FinanceUser. Once the two query sessions have been created, you can confirm that they were assigned to the correct resource pools by running the following code in a new Query window. You should receive results similar to what is shown in Figure 11-19.

```
-- Confirm users are connected to the correct pools
select rp.name 'PoolName', wg.name 'WrkGrpName',xs.session_id,
xs.login_name,xs.login_time,xs.[program_name]
```

```
from sys.dm_exec_sessions xs
inner join sys.dm_resource_governor_workload_groups wg on
    xs.group_id=wg.group_id
inner join sys.dm_resource_governor_resource_pools rp on
    wg.pool_id=rp.pool_id
WHERE wg.pool_id>=256
```

	PoolName	WrkGrpName	session_id	login_name	login_time	program_name
1	poolAdHoc	wrkgrpAdHoc	62	AdHocUser	2008-10-28 15:46:22.507	Microsoft SQL Server Management Studio - Query
2	poolFinance	wrkgrpFinance	63	FinanceUser	2008-10-28 15:46:36.690	Microsoft SQL Server Management Studio - Query

Figure 11-19: Confirming resource pool assignment.

8. Assuming that the resource pool assignments are correct, all that remains is to monitor the pools while running some CPU-intensive workloads. To monitor the pools, you will use the Reliability and Performance Monitor. Open this tool from the control panel, and add counters to monitor the CPU usage percentage of each resource pool as shown in Figure 11-20. Start monitoring as soon as you finish entering the counters.

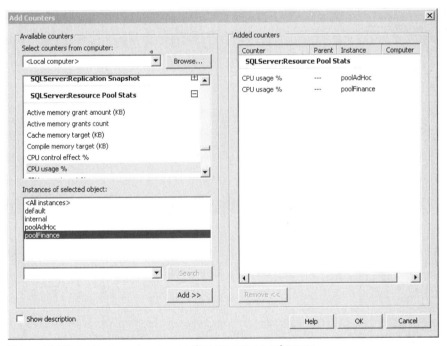

Figure 11-20: Adding counters to monitor resource pool usage.

9. Finally, enter the following code into the two Query windows that you opened for AdHocUser and FinanceUser, but wait to execute the code.

```
-- CPU Intensive Workload
USE AdventureWorks2008
GO

-- This query will peg the CPU at 100%
```

```
SELECT MAX(p1.r1 + p2.r2) mv FROM
 (SELECT ROW_NUMBER() OVER (ORDER BY ProductID) r1
  FROM Production.TransactionHistory) p1
CROSS JOIN
 (SELECT ROW_NUMBER() OVER (ORDER BY ProductID DESC) r2
  FROM Production.TransactionHistory) p2
OPTION (MAXDOP 1)
```

The code above will generate a *very* CPU-intensive workload. (It should peg the CPU at 100 percent for the duration of the query.) Execute the workload code for the AdHocUser first, then wait about 10 seconds and execute it for the FinanceUser. Both queries will continue running for a very long time. While they are running, switch over to the Performance Monitor screen and observe the results. You should observe something similar to what is shown in Figure 11-21.

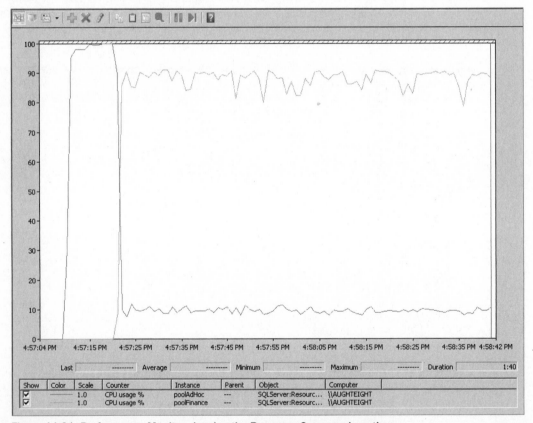

Figure 11-21: Performance Monitor showing the Resource Governor in action.

Notice that when the AdHocUser first started to run the query, they received all of the CPU resources because no other workloads were competing. However, once the FinanceUser started their query, then the Resource Governor kicked in and throttled the AdHocUser down to the configured CPU maximum of 10 percent.

If your results show both queries using 100 percent CPU, then you have a multi- CPU system and have not set the CPU affinity as described previously. When there are more CPUs than active queries, then every query will receive its own CPU resources.

When you are finished observing the results, you can stop both queries and close the associated Query windows. Once the Query windows are closed, you can use SSMS to disable the Resource Governor. Finally, if you configured SQL Server with a CPU affinity, then you can clear it by re-configuring 'affinity mask' and 'affinity i/o mask' as shown in step 6, but using a parameter of '0'.

Summary

I hope that this chapter has provided you with some insights into optimization that you will be able to put to use in your own databases. Remember that there is always more than one way to solve a problem, and no particular method that does the job is necessarily "right" or "wrong." When faced with a difficult situation, use your imagination and be creative in your solution.

I would like to reiterate the importance of a good design in maintaining high performance levels, especially as the database grows over time. Good designs will scale well, use a minimal amount of server resources, and rarely require administrative intervention. Poor designs, on the other hand, tend to result in ongoing performance issues. If you start with a solid design, it can make a world of difference.

Having a hot or warm standby server (or some other failover solution) is critical to maintaining a highly available server platform. Chapter 12 discusses how to use Windows Clustering, SQL Server Log-Shipping, and SQL Server Mirroring configurations to maximize the availability of your database.

SQL Server High Availability

It's that sinking feeling you get when your cell phone or pager goes off at 3:00 in the morning. No one ever calls to tell you that things are running smoothly (and if they did, they'd probably wait until a more appropriate time). No, the server has gone down . . . the database server . . . *your* server.

The problem could be any number of things. A failed disk, network problems, or power outages are among the many things that can plague you as a database administrator. However, with the right combination of hardware and software, many of these outages can be avoided.

This chapter should provide you with a basic understanding of the topic of high availability and the tools provided to help improve the availability of your databases. This chapter covers the following topics:

❑ Availability
❑ Clustering
❑ Log shipping
❑ Database mirroring

Introduction to High Availability

The definition of *high availability* is subjective. This is because you may have some applications that need to be available 24 hours a day, seven days a week; and you may have other database applications that only need to be available during business hours. High availability isn't always about full-time operations, but, rather, about services being accessible to your users when they need them.

High availability is also about being able to meet Service Level Agreements (SLAs) or Operating Level Agreements (OLAs), which define your requirements for maintaining application and service availability in order to meet user demand and keep services online. For example, there is a concept known as the *rule of nines*. The rule of nines is based on the realization that 100 percent availability is unattainable. There are too many variables that affect our networked systems to absolutely guarantee 100 percent uptime. These can be power outages, floods, fires, tornados, or human error. For example, I can remember a specific incident where a developer executed a query against a production database that managed to lock the database for more than an hour.

The *rule of nines* identifies a more realistic series of uptime requirements based on percentage values just shy of 100 percent. The following table lists the number of minutes per year based on the rule of nines:

Percentage of Uptime per Year	Downtime per Year in Minutes
99%	5,259.6
99.9%	525.96
99.99%	52.596
99.999%	5.2596

As you can see, the ultimate goal for any high-availability solution is the *five nines rule* — 99.999 percent — which provides you with a little more than 5 minutes of downtime per year. Again, you might not be supporting an application that needs to be running for all but an hour a year, so plan your availability solutions accordingly.

In Chapter 9, you learned about backup and recovery strategies as part of a disaster recovery plan. These days, the term *disaster recovery* has fallen out-of-favor. The more preferred term is *business continuity*. The idea is that you want to prevent your systems from becoming unavailable, or if a service does fail, its impact in your environment is minimal. The high-availability solutions identified in this chapter can help you maintain business continuity in the event of an outage.

High availability may also be dictated by your budget. To achieve the *five nines* of availability, you might have to maintain multiple data centers around the world, with redundancy built in at each location. While a full list of options for a true *five nines* environment is outside the scope of this book, this chapter will educate you about the features inherent to Microsoft SQL Server 2008 that allow you to improve your application availability.

Failover Clustering

When it comes to high availability with instant or near-instant failover, *clustering* provides an invaluable service. SQL Server Clustering is based on the Windows Clustering service and is only available in the Enterprise and Datacenter Editions of Windows Server. Clustering works by using two or more servers (referred to as *nodes*) to act as a single virtual server for your end-users. Windows Server 2003 supports a maximum of eight nodes in a cluster, while Windows Server 2008 supports up to 16 nodes.

Clustering is available in both the Enterprise and Standard Editions of SQL Server; however, a key difference is that the Standard Edition is limited to two nodes only.

When reviewing high-availability options for SQL Server, an understanding of how Windows Clustering works, as well as how SQL Server can use clustering, will help you make an informed decision. In this section, you'll learn about the basics of Windows Clustering and the pros and cons of how it works with SQL Server.

Windows Clustering — A Quick Primer

Microsoft offers two ways to introduce high availability into the Windows Server operating system: Network Load Balancing and Windows Clustering. *Network Load Balancing* (NLB) is based on the premise of several different servers operating somewhat independently but acting as a single unit. One of the best examples of an implementation of NLB is a Web farm. As you can see in Figure 12-1, each server that participates in a Web farm operates its own Web Services and usually has its own copy of the pages and applications that will be served to the public. The members of the Web farm appear to your clients as a single unified web site. For example, when UserA connects to www.yoursite.you, she might actually be connecting to server 37; but when UserB connects to www.yoursite.you, he might be connecting to server 42.

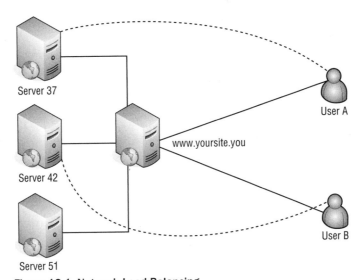

Server 37

Server 42

Server 51

User A

User B

www.yoursite.you

Figure 12-1: Network Load Balancing.

With *Windows Clustering* (shown in Figure 12-2), cluster-aware applications access data on a shared volume known as a *quorum*. The *quorum* is responsible for storing the shared data that will be accessed by the cluster nodes, as well as identifying which node is the primary node for the application. In many Windows Clustering scenarios, the *quorum device* is a single shared storage unit that requires each node to have a connection to it, using either Small Computer System Interface (SCSI) or Fibre Channel connectors. Unfortunately, this single storage model allows for a single point of failure should the quorum device no longer be available. Enhancements in the Windows Clustering service, however, can allow the quorum data to be replicated, so that each node can have a copy of the quorum data connected locally. This allows clusters to be used over wide area networks (WANs) or virtual private networks (VPNs). This is also referred to as a *majority node cluster*.

When building highly available applications, many organizations employ a model when NLB is used on the front-end, for firewall, proxy, and Web Services; and clustering is used on the back-end, for database applications.

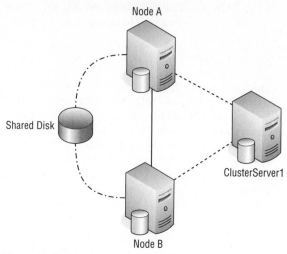

Figure 12-2: Windows Clustering.

Clustering Components

So, what do you need to begin clustering? Well, you'll need a couple of servers. Although having identical hardware in both servers is not required, at the very least, the hardware in both servers should be comparable (same processors, disk configuration, memory, etc.). I can remember a specific incident that happened years ago when two servers that had the same manufacturing defect were used in a cluster, and both servers failed at the same time. The likelihood of this happening again is rare, but it is something to consider when provisioning hardware. The platform, OS, service pack, and patch level must be the same on all nodes in the cluster.

You will also need a shared storage device. Serial Attached SCSI, Fibre Channel, and iSCSI are common interfaces for many cluster storage devices. If you are using iSCSI in your clustering solution, you will need to make sure you have a dedicated Network Interface Card (NIC) for the iSCSI connection that is separate from your Windows network adapter. If using Windows Server 2008, ensure that you are using a compatible storage device. On this device, you will create at least two volumes. One volume will be used as a witness disk, which holds the cluster configuration information. You will then need one or more data volumes for your applications.

Clustering works by defining a virtual server for the cluster. This virtual server appears to be a single server to your clients and end-user applications. It is given a unique name and IP address, and, as explained in Chapter 2, SQL Server can then be installed on it.

Active/Passive Clustering

Most applications (and SQL Server is no exception) use what is known as *active/passive clustering*. In the active/passive clustering model, for a single application, one node is designated as the *primary node*. All requests that come into the cluster virtual server are directed to this *primary cluster*. *Secondary nodes* are failover nodes and only become active when the primary node is unavailable and no heartbeat exists for that node. When this happens, a secondary node begins taking over the work for the cluster, allowing applications to continue running with little noticeable interruption. Figure 12-2 is an example of an active/passive cluster. Because your client applications always use the virtual server and not the primary server, they are oblivious to the work that goes on behind the scenes.

Active/Active Clustering

First of all, the term *active/active* can be a little misleading. You would think that unlike an active/passive cluster (in which one node does all the work, while the other nodes hang back and wait for something interesting to happen), an active/active cluster would ensure that everyone is playing an equal part in making this application highly available. This, however, is not the case. An *active/active cluster* usually describes a scenario in which more than one cluster-aware application is running, and each application has a different node configured as the primary node for that application. The primary reason for this is mainly because of the technical limitations of how databases and other application services work. Focusing just on SQL Server, for example, only one server can write to the active transaction log at a time. Because the other nodes are not able to write to the same transaction log, what else is there for them to do?

Well, you could configure a second virtual server using one of the existing standby nodes as the primary for this new server, and install another instance of SQL Server on that one. For example, suppose you have two servers, Node A and Node B, that are configured so that Node A is the primary node and Node B is the secondary node for ClusterServer1. You then decide to use these two servers to create a second virtual server named *ClusterServer2*, only this time Node B is the primary node, and Node A is the secondary node, as shown in Figure 12-3.

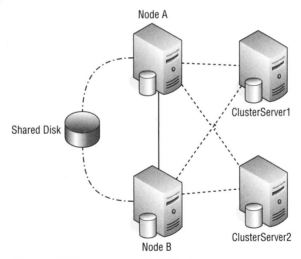

Figure 12-3: Active/active clustering.

In order for active/active clustering to work, the standby servers must be able to handle the combined workload for both virtual servers should they fail. So, if Server A comes to a screeching halt, Server B has to be able to respond to client requests for both virtual servers. Now, in a two-node environment, this may not be an optimal solution, but remember that with Windows Server 2008, you can have up to 16 nodes in a cluster.

Technically, this is really more of an (active/passive)/(active/passive) implementation, but that's just splitting hairs.

Considering Clustering

Now that you're familiar with how Windows Clustering works, you can see that it offers you some significant benefits. It can provide instant or near-instant failover with no client reconfiguration required, because they point to the cluster name, not individual nodes. It is also a high-availability solution that provides failover of the entire instance of SQL Server, not just a specific database. Cost may be a factor, though, when you consider the hardware and software requirements.

Log Shipping

Log shipping is another method by which you can maintain business continuity. Unlike failover clustering, log shipping is managed on a per-database basis. It provides you with the ability to designate one or more servers to hold a secondary copy of the database in question. It does this by making regular backups of the transaction log and then restoring the backups onto a secondary server. This section explains how to configure log shipping and how to perform failover for a database. Log shipping is also available in the Workgroup Edition of SQL Server 2008.

Preparing for Log Shipping

Before you can configure log shipping, you will want to ensure that a few things have been correctly configured. First of all, ensure that reliable network connectivity exists between the primary server and the standby server. When using the Wizard, you can make a full backup of the current server and restore that backup on the standby server. If your database is particularly large, a full backup from the Wizard may not be possible, so you may need to manually configure the backup and restore for the source database.

Next, ensure that your database is using the Full recovery model. This is required because the log shipping process must make regular backups of the transaction log. Using the Bulk-Logged recovery model prevents data entered at the primary server using a non-logged bulk operation from being applied to the secondary servers, as well.

You will also want to ensure that the target database doesn't already exist on the standby server. Typically, in production environments, this isn't a problem. However, sometimes a server that had been primarily used for testing gets "promoted" into the production environment. If this is the case, ensure that the server is clean, and if it does have a copy of the production database, it is from a recent backup.

Just a quick note about the examples you will see in this chapter: For the sake of (relative) simplicity, I am using two additional instances of SQL Server 2008 on the same server as my primary test environment. Keep in mind that in a production environment, you will likely be using separate physical servers for each of the roles.

Configuring Log Shipping with SQL Server Management Studio

You can configure log shipping for a database at any time by viewing the Properties sheet of the database or by right-clicking on the database and selecting Tasks ➤ Ship Transaction Logs from Object Explorer, as shown in Figure 12-4.

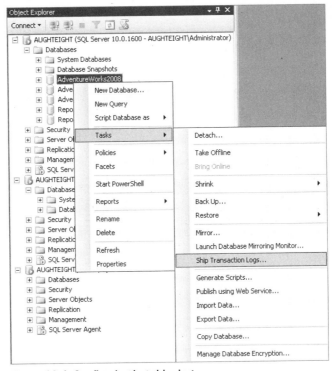

Figure 12-4: Configuring log shipping.

In the Transaction Log Shipping page, you can configure the required options for backing up the database, designating secondary servers, and a monitoring server. To begin, you will need to enable this database as the primary server for log shipping. Figure 12-5 shows a database that has already been configured for log shipping and monitoring. Notice the checkbox that indicates this server is the primary server.

If you click the "Backup Settings" button, a new window will appear that allows you to specify the location and frequency for the backup operations. Assuming that the secondary servers will be on different physical servers (which they should be — otherwise, you really don't gain much benefit from log shipping), you will need to provide a UNC path that the secondary servers can use to retrieve the backups generated by the log shipping process. The transaction logs will be copied from this location to a local file system path on each secondary server. You can also specify a local file system path where the initial full backup and subsequent Transaction Log backups will be located.

If you are going to have multiple secondary servers and you want to be able to continue using the alternate secondary servers after one of them has been promoted to the new primary server, consider placing the backup folder on a share that is accessible to all servers and will not be affected if there is a general server failure on the primary server.

Notice in Figure 12-6 that you can also specify automatic cleanup behavior for files generated by log shipping. The default configuration deletes files older than 72 hours and will generate an alert when a backup hasn't been performed for an hour. You can also specify the frequency of the backup operation and change the default name assigned to the backup job. You can also enable or disable backup compression from this window.

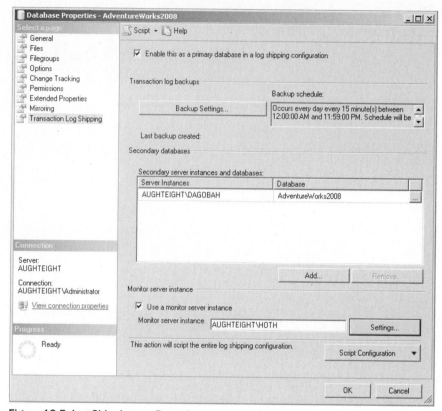

Figure 12-5: Log Shipping configuration page.

One thing you will want to be careful about, especially with environments that have a heavy transaction processing load, is how often the Transaction Log backup runs. A student of mine once ran into an issue where they had configured the backup job to run every 5 minutes because of the large number of transactions being processed. Unfortunately, at roughly the same time every week, another maintenance task would run that would cause the backup job to take longer than expected. This meant that the restore operation on the standby server was still waiting for the new log before the backup had been moved over. The remedy I suggested to this student was to specify a different schedule that would back up and restore the transaction log less frequently while this other maintenance task ran. It resulted in a larger file being copied over, but the backup and copy were able to complete before the next restore job.

Once you've configured the backup job settings, you can configure one or more secondary servers. Secondary servers can be configured as a hot standby that will sit in a NO RECOVERY state until failover is initiated, or they can also be configured as a Read Only copy of the database (which may be helpful for querying data for reporting and analysis services).

To configure a new secondary server, from the Transaction Log Shipping page, click Add. This also brings up a new window with three option screens. From the header section of the window, you can specify the name of the secondary server and the name of the standby database. If used for failover, the name of the secondary database should be the same as the primary to avoid re-configuring your client applications.

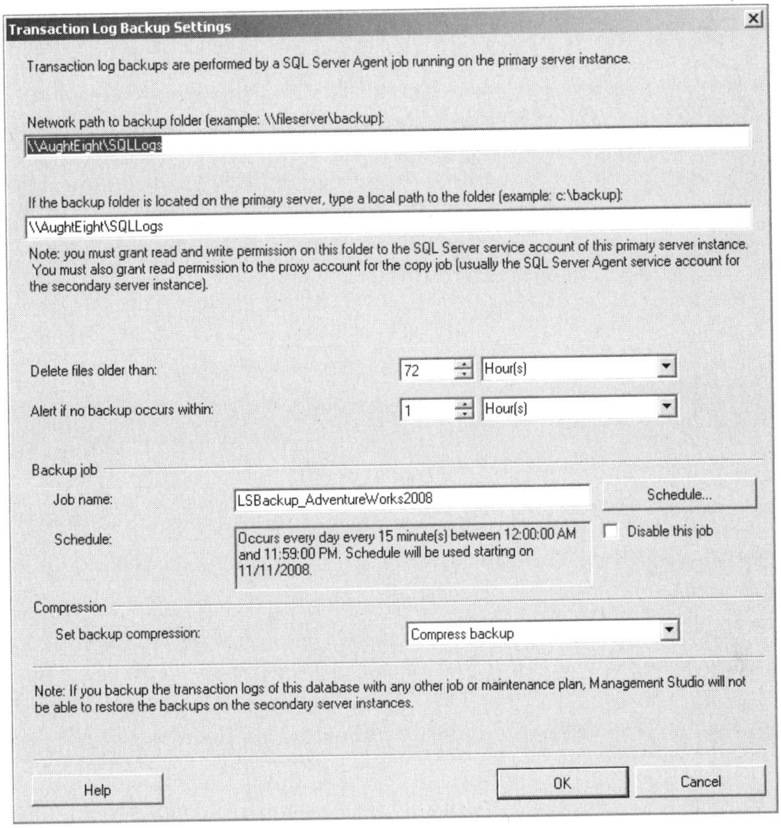

Figure 12-6: Backup options.

As you can see from Figure 12-7, you can configure the options for performing the initial restore of the database. You can have the restore begin immediately after configuring the log shipping options; you can specify an existing backup file to use for building a new standby server; or, if the standby server already has a restored copy of the database, you can use that database instead. If you have restored the database on a new standby server using existing backups, make sure you apply all Transaction Log backups to ensure that the database is in a consistent state.

The Copy Files tab allows you to configure options for the file copy task (see Figure 12-8). A new job will be created that copies the files created by the backup operation to the destination folder on the secondary server. As with the backup job, you can specify the frequency of this job and also the options for cleaning up older files.

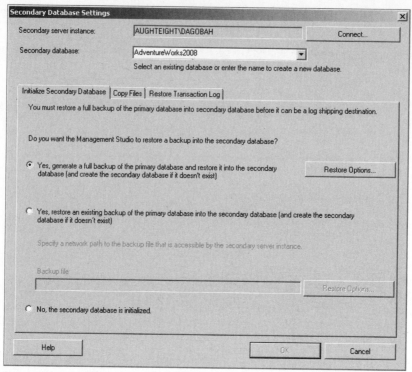

Figure 12-7: Configuring standby servers.

The Restore Transaction Log tab allows you to configure the restore operation. As you can see in Figure 12-9, you can choose to have the destination database use the NO RECOVERY mode (which prevents client access) or the STANDBY mode (which allows Read Only access to the database). Depending on the frequency of the restore operations and the tasks that will use the standby database, you may need to disconnect users when restoring the database backups. So, enable that checkbox if necessary. You can also configure the restore operation to be delayed to help guarantee that the backup and copy operations have a chance to complete, and specify how long the server should wait without performing a restore before an alert is fired. Finally, you can configure the appropriate schedule for the restore tasks. As with the other scheduled operations, the Transaction Log restore will run every 15 minutes.

Optionally, you can also configure a server to monitor log shipping operations. This server should be a SQL Server that doesn't directly participate in the log shipping process. Although you could potentially use the primary server or one of the secondary servers as the Log Shipping monitor, it may be counter-productive, because you want to be able to validate the status of the log shipping operation between the primary and standby servers. Because the purpose of log shipping is to create a standby server that could be used if the primary fails, it makes little sense to put the monitor on the server that is more likely to fail, or will be the one to handle the additional workload if the primary does fail.

The purpose of the Log Shipping monitor is simply to track the details of the log shipping process for that database. It will keep track of primary server backups, copy operations, and secondary server restore operations. It will also generate alert information for failed backups. Although this data is recorded on each of the respective servers, having a single repository for this data may make it easier to track and monitor the log shipping process.

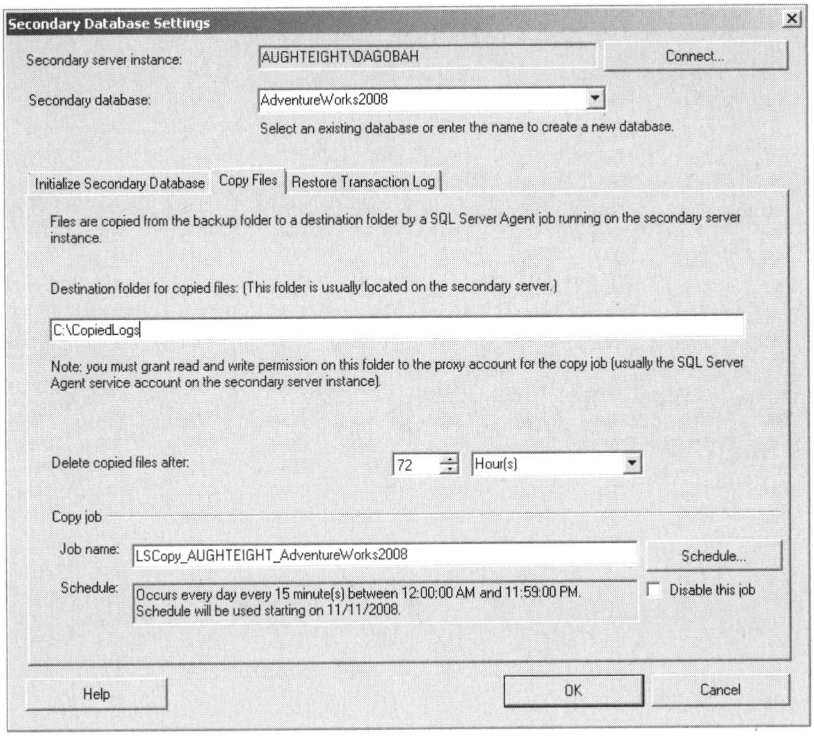

Figure 12-8: Copy Files options.

To add a monitor server, from the Transaction Log Shipping page, select "Use a monitor server instance," and then click Settings to add and configure the new server. As you can see in Figure 12-10, you can specify the server that will act as the monitoring server and the login that is used as the proxy account of the log shipping job. You can also configure the history retention value and the name for the job that will generate alerts if there is a problem with the backup, copy, or restore jobs.

Once the Log Shipping monitor is configured, you can also use it to view reports about any and all log shipping databases that this server monitors. Do this by right-clicking on the server name from Object Browser and then selecting Reports ➤ Standard Reports ➤ Transaction Log Shipping Status. Whereas the primary and secondary servers will let you view report information about the configuration on the servers themselves, using a monitoring server allows you to view the status of the primary and secondary servers from just the one report. You can also use this server to monitor multiple instances of log shipping for all your databases and keep track of them through this reporting tool.

Once you have your log shipping options configured, you can apply them to the database, and if everything is configured properly, the backups should begin right away. Unless you've changed the schedule for the jobs, the default has them run every 15 minutes.

Configuring Log Shipping with Transact-SQL

If you prefer, you can use a series of stored procedures to configure log shipping instead of Management Studio. This may make it easier for you to streamline the log shipping configuration process, especially if you will be configuring multiple secondary servers. Several stored procedures are available that will help automate the process of configuring log shipping.

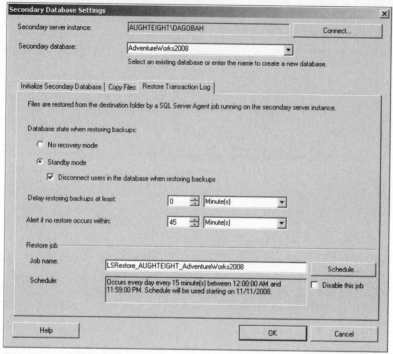

Figure 12-9: Restoring the logs.

The following table lists primary server-stored procedures:

Stored Procedure	Description
sp_add_log_shipping_primary_database	Use this to configure the primary database for log shipping.
sp_add_log_shipping_primary_secondary	This will add a secondary database to an existing primary.
sp_change_log_shipping_primary_database	This stored procedure changes the primary database settings.
sp_cleanup_log_shipping_history	You can use this to clean up local job history.
sp_delete_log_shipping_primary_database	When you want to stop log shipping, you can use this stored procedure.
sp_delete_log_shipping_primary_secondary	If you want to remove a secondary server from the primary, use this stored procedure.
sp_help_log_shipping_primary_database	This will display primary database settings for the local server.
sp_help_log_shipping_primary_secondary	This will display secondary server names for a specified primary database.
sp_refresh_log_shipping_monitor	This will update the monitor with the latest data.

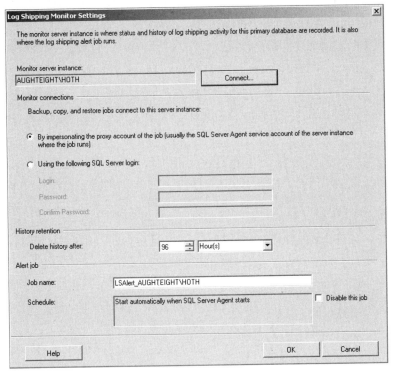

Figure 12-10: Log shipping monitor.

The following table lists secondary-server-stored procedures:

Stored Procedure	Description
sp_add_log_shipping_secondary_database	This will add a secondary database.
sp_add_log_shipping_secondary_primary	Use this to specify the primary server and database information for the secondary server.
sp_change_log_shipping_secondary_database	This allows you to change settings on the secondary database.
sp_change_log_shipping_secondary_primary	This allows you to change additional settings such as destination folder and file retention.
sp_cleanup_log_shipping_history	This will clean up local history.
sp_delete_log_shipping_secondary_database	Use this to remove a secondary database.
sp_delete_log_shipping_secondary_primary	This will remove information about the primary from the secondary server.

Continued

Stored Procedure	Description
sp_help_log_shipping_secondary_database	Use this to retrieve secondary database settings.
sp_help_log_shipping_secondary_primary	This allows you to view the settings for the primary database.
sp_refresh_log_shipping_monitor	Update the monitor with the latest information about the secondary database.

The following table lists monitor-server-stored procedures:

Stored Procedure	Description
sp_add_log_shipping_alert_job	Creates an alert job if one doesn't already exist.
sp_delete_log_shipping_alert_job	Removes the alert job if there are no primary databases listed.
sp_help_log_shipping_alert_job	This will return the job ID of the alert job.
sp_help_log_shipping_monitor_primary	Use this to display monitor records about the specified primary database.
sp_help_log_shipping_monitor_secondary	Use this to display monitor records about the specified secondary database.

If you want to see some of these stored procedures in action, rather than immediately applying the log shipping changes to the primary database, you can choose to script the commands to a file. You can then alter the file or copy its contents to automate the creation of multiple secondary databases. Following is the script that was generated from the example configuration presented earlier. Note that there are several elements that must be configured on both the primary and secondary servers. If you want to run the script to configure your servers, be sure to replace the server names AUGHTEIGHT, AUGHTEIGHT\DAGOBAH, and AUGHTEIGHT\HOTH with your server names as needed.

```
-- Execute the following statements at the Primary to configure Log Shipping
-- for the database [AUGHTEIGHT].[AdventureWorks2008],
-- The script needs to be run at the Primary in the context of the [msdb] database.
------------------------------------------------------------
Adding the Log Shipping configuration

-- ****** Begin: Script to be run at Primary: [AUGHTEIGHT] ******


DECLARE @LS_BackupJobId     AS uniqueidentifier
DECLARE @LS_PrimaryId       AS uniqueidentifier
```

```
DECLARE @SP_Add_RetCode        As int

EXEC @SP_Add_RetCode = master.dbo.sp_add_log_shipping_primary_database

@database = N'AdventureWorks2008'

,@backup_directory = N'\\AughtEight\SQLLogs'

,@backup_share = N'\\AughtEight\SQLLogs'

,@backup_job_name = N'LSBackup_AdventureWorks2008'

,@backup_retention_period = 4320

,@backup_compression = 1

,@monitor_server = N'AUGHTEIGHT\HOTH'

,@monitor_server_security_mode = 1

,@backup_threshold = 60

,@threshold_alert_enabled = 1

,@history_retention_period = 5760

,@backup_job_id = @LS_BackupJobId OUTPUT

,@primary_id = @LS_PrimaryId OUTPUT

,@overwrite = 1


IF (@@ERROR = 0 AND @SP_Add_RetCode = 0)
BEGIN

DECLARE @LS_BackUpScheduleUID     As uniqueidentifier
```

```
DECLARE @LS_BackUpScheduleID        AS int

EXEC msdb.dbo.sp_add_schedule

@schedule_name =N'LSBackupSchedule_AUGHTEIGHT1'

,@enabled = 1

,@freq_type = 4

,@freq_interval = 1

,@freq_subday_type = 4

,@freq_subday_interval = 15

,@freq_recurrence_factor = 0

,@active_start_date = 20081111

,@active_end_date = 99991231

,@active_start_time = 0

,@active_end_time = 235900

,@schedule_uid = @LS_BackUpScheduleUID OUTPUT

,@schedule_id = @LS_BackUpScheduleID OUTPUT

EXEC msdb.dbo.sp_attach_schedule

@job_id = @LS_BackupJobId

,@schedule_id = @LS_BackUpScheduleID

EXEC msdb.dbo.sp_update_job

@job_id = @LS_BackupJobId

,@enabled = 1

END

EXEC master.dbo.sp_add_log_shipping_primary_secondary

@primary_database = N'AdventureWorks2008'

,@secondary_server = N'AUGHTEIGHT\DAGOBAH'

,@secondary_database = N'AdventureWorks2008'
```

```
,@overwrite = 1

-- ****** End: Script to be run at Primary: [AUGHTEIGHT]  ******


-- Execute the following statements at the Secondary to configure Log Shipping
-- for the database [AUGHTEIGHT\DAGOBAH].[AdventureWorks2008],
-- the script needs to be run at the Secondary in the context of the
-- [msdb] database.
-------------------------------------------------------------------------
-- Adding the Log Shipping configuration

-- ****** Begin: Script to be run at Secondary: [AUGHTEIGHT\DAGOBAH] ******


DECLARE @LS_Secondary__CopyJobId  AS uniqueidentifier
DECLARE @LS_Secondary__RestoreJobId     AS uniqueidentifier
DECLARE @LS_Secondary__SecondaryId AS uniqueidentifier
DECLARE @LS_Add_RetCode      As int


EXEC @LS_Add_RetCode = master.dbo.sp_add_log_shipping_secondary_primary

@primary_server = N'AUGHTEIGHT'

,@primary_database = N'AdventureWorks2008'

,@backup_source_directory = N'\\AughtEight\SQLLogs'

,@backup_destination_directory = N'C:\CopiedLogs'

,@copy_job_name = N'LSCopy_AUGHTEIGHT_AdventureWorks2008'

,@restore_job_name = N'LSRestore_AUGHTEIGHT_AdventureWorks2008'

,@file_retention_period = 4320

,@monitor_server = N'AUGHTEIGHT\HOTH'

,@monitor_server_security_mode = 1

,@overwrite = 1

,@copy_job_id = @LS_Secondary__CopyJobId OUTPUT

,@restore_job_id = @LS_Secondary__RestoreJobId OUTPUT

,@secondary_id = @LS_Secondary__SecondaryId OUTPUT

IF (@@ERROR = 0 AND @LS_Add_RetCode = 0)
```

```
BEGIN

DECLARE @LS_SecondaryCopyJobScheduleUID  As uniqueidentifier
DECLARE @LS_SecondaryCopyJobScheduleID   AS int


EXEC msdb.dbo.sp_add_schedule

@schedule_name =N'DefaultCopyJobSchedule'

,@enabled = 1

,@freq_type = 4

,@freq_interval = 1

,@freq_subday_type = 4

,@freq_subday_interval = 15

,@freq_recurrence_factor = 0

,@active_start_date = 20081111

,@active_end_date = 99991231

,@active_start_time = 0

,@active_end_time = 235900

,@schedule_uid = @LS_SecondaryCopyJobScheduleUID OUTPUT

,@schedule_id = @LS_SecondaryCopyJobScheduleID OUTPUT

EXEC msdb.dbo.sp_attach_schedule

@job_id = @LS_Secondary__CopyJobId

,@schedule_id = @LS_SecondaryCopyJobScheduleID

DECLARE @LS_SecondaryRestoreJobScheduleUID       As uniqueidentifier
```

```
DECLARE @LS_SecondaryRestoreJobScheduleID          AS int

EXEC msdb.dbo.sp_add_schedule

@schedule_name =N'DefaultRestoreJobSchedule'

,@enabled = 1

,@freq_type = 4

,@freq_interval = 1

,@freq_subday_type = 4

,@freq_subday_interval = 15

,@freq_recurrence_factor = 0

,@active_start_date = 20081111

,@active_end_date = 99991231

,@active_start_time = 0

,@active_end_time = 235900

,@schedule_uid = @LS_SecondaryRestoreJobScheduleUID OUTPUT

,@schedule_id = @LS_SecondaryRestoreJobScheduleID OUTPUT

EXEC msdb.dbo.sp_attach_schedule

@job_id = @LS_Secondary__RestoreJobId

,@schedule_id = @LS_SecondaryRestoreJobScheduleID


END

DECLARE @LS_Add_RetCode2     As int


IF (@@ERROR = 0 AND @LS_Add_RetCode = 0)

BEGIN

EXEC @LS_Add_RetCode2 = master.dbo.sp_add_log_shipping_secondary_database

@secondary_database = N'AdventureWorks2008'

,@primary_server = N'AUGHTEIGHT'
```

```
    ,@primary_database = N'AdventureWorks2008'

    ,@restore_delay = 0

    ,@restore_mode = 1

    ,@disconnect_users    = 1

    ,@restore_threshold = 45

    ,@threshold_alert_enabled = 1

    ,@history_retention_period  = 5760

    ,@overwrite = 1

END


IF (@@error = 0 AND @LS_Add_RetCode = 0)
BEGIN

EXEC msdb.dbo.sp_update_job

@job_id = @LS_Secondary__CopyJobId

,@enabled = 1

EXEC msdb.dbo.sp_update_job

@job_id = @LS_Secondary__RestoreJobId

,@enabled = 1

END

-- ****** End: Script to be run at Secondary: [AUGHTEIGHT\DAGOBAH] ******
```

Configuring Failover

To configure failover between a primary and a secondary server, use the following procedure:

1. If there are any uncopied backup files from the backup share, copy them to the copy destination on each secondary server.

2. Apply all remaining transaction logs in sequence to each secondary database.

3. Perform a backup of the active transaction log on the primary database, if possible. Copy the backup and apply to each standby database.

4. If the primary server is still operational, you may be able to configure the primary database as a new secondary database once the failover has been completed. You can facilitate this by backing up the transaction log on the primary database using the NO RECOVERY option. This allows you to apply Transaction Log backups from the replacement database.

5. Select one of the secondary servers to host the new primary database by placing the database in recovery mode. As you learned in Chapter 9, this will bring the database to an operational state.

If you have additional secondary servers, you can configure the newly recovered database to act as the primary for additional secondary databases and make the original primary database a new secondary. Perform the following steps to swap roles:

1. Disable the backup job on the original primary server.

2. Disable the copy and restore jobs on the original secondary server.

3. Use the same share created for the original primary for backups of the new primary database.

4. Add the original database as a secondary database.

5. In the secondary database options on the original database, specify that the database is already initialized. This will save you from having to do a full restore.

Because log shipping is configured on a per-database basis, you may need to perform some additional tasks to ensure that your users can maintain consistent access to the database, even in the event of a failover. First of all, the applications your clients are using must be aware of the change. This may require that the application be manually configured to use the new primary server or that the old server name be reassigned as an alias for the new server. Also, to ensure consistent access to the database from your application, you will want to ensure that all associated metadata for that database is migrated over. This includes SQL Server Logins, jobs, and alerts, to name a few. Because of some of the limitations of log shipping, it is great for creating Read Only standby servers but is a moderate solution for failover considerations.

Database Mirroring

Database mirroring is a relatively new method for ensuring database availability. Database mirroring was first introduced in the earlier Community Technology Previews of SQL Server 2005; however, it was disabled when the product was released. After further testing and certification of database mirroring, it was re-enabled when SP1 was released. Database mirroring hasn't changed in SQL Server 2008, and the basic concept is very similar to log shipping in that transaction log records are sent from a source database (known as the *principal database*) to a destination database (known as the *mirror database*). However, instead of a transaction log being copied on a file basis, individual log records are sent on a transaction-by-transaction basis. While database mirroring is also a database-level redundancy solution, it relies on constant communication between servers to maintain transactional integrity. Database mirroring also offers the added advantage of automatic and almost instantaneous failover when configured with a third witness server.

Database mirroring is configured by establishing a partnership between the server hosting the principal database and the server hosting the mirror database. Rather than using the file system as the method of maintaining consistency between the two servers, communications are established and maintained using SQL Server endpoints. Another key difference between log shipping and database mirroring is that database mirroring restricts you to one principal and one mirror for each database.

Database mirroring requires the use of at least two instances of SQL Server. Although these instances could conceivably be on the same physical server, it makes much more sense to have them on separate servers to protect against server failure (see Figure 12-11).

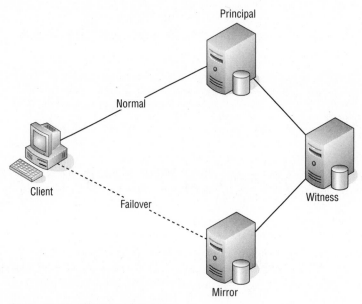

Figure 12-11: Database mirroring.

The three server roles in a database mirroring configuration are as follows:

❑   **Principal Server** — The *principal server* hosts the copy of the database that clients connect to and interact with. As transactions occur on the principal database, the transaction log records are forwarded to the mirror database.

❑   **Mirror Server** — The *mirror server* hosts a copy of the principal database and applies the transaction log records sent by the principal database to keep the mirrored database in sync with the principal database.

❑   **Witness Server** — The witness server is optional. It is only needed if automatic failover to the mirror server is required in the case of a principal database failure. The *witness server* monitors the status of the principal and mirror servers in a high-availability configuration, which is described in the section "Database Mirroring Modes," later in this chapter.

When using database mirroring, the mirror database is not directly accessible for client requests because it is in the constant state of recovering transaction log records. However, indirect access can be configured by creating a Database Snapshot of the mirrored database. Keep in mind that Database Snapshots are a point-in-time view of the database and will not reflect the ongoing modifications to the mirror.

It is also important to note that database mirroring cannot be used with databases that have FILESTREAM storage enabled.

Client Redirection

One of the big advantages of database mirroring is that clients can automatically be redirected to the mirror server in the case of a principal database failure. However, the automatic redirection is not a server-based feature. The connection string of clients is configured to work with a mirrored database by adding the `Failover Partner` attribute, as shown in the following example:

```
Server=AughtEight; Failover Partner=Dagobah; Database=AdventureWorks2008
```

If the client's attempt to connect to the server identified by the `Server` attribute fails, it will try the server identified by the `Failover Partner` attribute. The opposite is also true. If the client attempts to connect to the failover partner and it is not available, it will try the original server.

Database Mirroring Modes

When building a mirroring solution, you can choose between three operating modes. The database can be configured to use *high-performance mode*, *high-safety without automatic failover mode*, and *high-safety with automatic failover mode*. Each operating mode has its advantages and disadvantages. It is important to understand exactly what each mode provides and how it affects your high-availability solution.

High-Performance Mode

The *high-performance mode* uses asynchronous processing. In this mode, the principal server sends an acknowledgment to the client application of a successful transaction as soon as it sends the corresponding log record to the mirror server, but it does not wait for acknowledgment from the mirror server that the log record was received. Under normal workload conditions, the latency between the principal and the mirror is relatively small. However, if the principal server is under heavy workload, this can increase the gap between the two partners.

In high-performance mode, there is no automatic failover and no witness server is required. A witness server can be configured, but there is absolutely no advantage to this arrangement because a failure of the principal will still require a forcing of the database service on the mirror. Once the original principal is restored to service, it will configure itself as a mirror, but the mirroring session will remain in a SUSPENDED state until explicitly resumed by the administrator. Resuming and forcing the mirroring service are described later in this chapter.

High-Safety without Automatic Failover Mode

In the *high-safety without automatic failover mode*, the principal server does not send an acknowledgment to the client of a successful transaction until the mirror server acknowledges the receipt of the corresponding transaction log record. Although this helps protect against data loss in the case of a failure, it can add latency to your transaction processing. There is no automatic failover in this mode and no witness server. Failure of the principal database will require manually forcing the service on the witness server to promote its principal. The process of forcing the service is described later in this chapter. In the case of a mirror server failure, the principal will remain available to clients, but the mirroring session will be in a disconnected state.

High-Safety with Automatic Failover Mode

In the *high-safety with automatic failover mode*, a witness server is used to provide automatic failover. The witness server does not directly participate in the mirroring process but acts as an overseer between the two servers. As long as two of the three servers participating in this mode can vouch for connectivity, a database will be available to client requests. When two of the servers agree on the status of the mirroring session, it is called a *quorum*, similar to the idea of a quorum disk in a Windows Cluster.

If a quorum is lost by the mirror or principal server, the mirroring configuration will change. The following table describes some possible scenarios:

Mirror Configuration	Description
Loss of the principal server	If the mirror server and the witness server agree that the principal server is no longer available, the witness server will promote itself to principal and begin accepting client requests. Once the principal server is returned to service, it will contact the witness and original mirror server to discover the status of the mirror configuration, and then the witness server will demote itself to mirror status and synchronize with the new principal.
Loss of the mirror server	When the principal server and the witness server agree that the mirror server is no longer available, the principal server will remain online and service client requests, but the mirroring state will be changed to disconnected. Once the mirror server becomes available again, it will synchronize itself with the principal and the mirror session will continue.
Loss of the witness server	As long as the principal and mirror server can establish a quorum, the principal database will remain online and available to client requests. However, no automatic failover will be available as long as the witness server is out-of-commission.
Loss of the principal and witness servers	Without the possibility of a quorum, the mirror server will also be unavailable because it cannot verify the status of the principal or witness server. To restore the mirror database to service, it will be necessary to remove mirroring from the mirror and manually recover it.
Loss of the mirror and witness servers	If the principal server loses contact with both the witness and the mirror servers, it will take its database offline and change the database's status to RESTORING. This is to avoid the possibility that the mirror server and witness server have established a quorum and the mirror server is answering client requests, preventing a "dual brain" scenario where both the mirror and principal are responding to client requests. To bring the principal database back online, database mirroring must be removed and the principal manually restored.

Configuring Database Mirroring

This section explains how to configure database mirroring between two servers, with an optional witness server to monitor the mirror. I'll begin by showing you how to set up database mirroring from SQL Server Management Studio and then showing you the Transact-SQL alternative. Before you use either, though, you must perform a full backup of your database and restore it on the mirror server using the NO RECOVERY option. Refer to Chapter 9 for the backup-and-restore process.

Using SQL Server Management Studio

To set up mirroring, begin by opening the Mirroring page on the Properties sheet of the database. You can also get to this page by selecting Mirror from the Tasks menu of the database. As you can see in Figure 12-12, the first step you will need to execute is configuring security for database mirroring:

1. Clicking on the "Configure Security" button will launch a Wizard that will ask you to provide the connection options for the principal, mirror, and witness server endpoints.

2. The first page of the Wizard, like many other wizards, includes a summary of the tasks that will be completed when the Wizard is complete. Click Next to move to the next page, which will ask you if you will be configuring a witness server. While the witness is certainly optional, it's a good idea to have one for applications that need automatic failover.

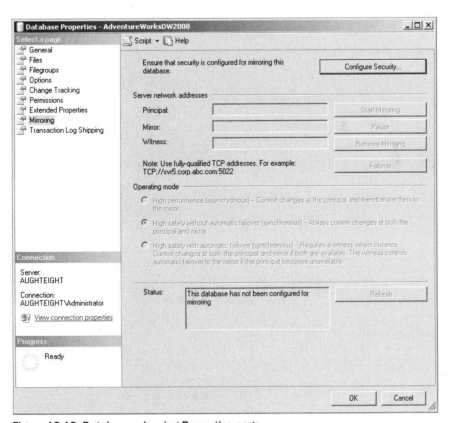

Figure 12-12: Database mirroring Properties page.

3. The next page of the Wizard asks you to identify which servers will be configured through this wizard. You will want to check all participating servers, including the witness server if one is being used.

4. Moving on to the next page of the Wizard, you can configure the options for the principal server, including the TCP port and name that will be used by the endpoint on the principal server. (Refer to Chapter 7 for a more detailed explanation of endpoints.) You can also specify whether or not the endpoint will use encryption. The default values for all endpoints use 5022 as the port number, *Mirroring* as the name, and encryption is enabled, but you can change these values as necessary. Figure 12-13 shows an example of the page you will see when configuring the endpoints. If you've already created an endpoint for mirroring, you will only be able to view the properties of this page.

5. Next, you will configure the same information for the mirror server. Note that when you are creating the endpoints on each of the servers, you must have the appropriate permissions to create and configure security on endpoints.

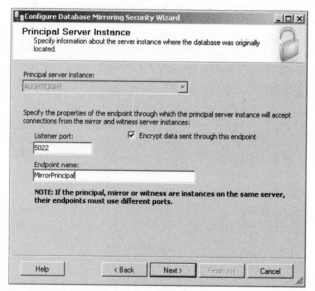

Figure 12-13: Configuring the mirror server.

6. If configuring a witness server, the next page will ask you to provide the server name and endpoint configuration for the witness. If you look at Figure 12-13, there is a note that specifies that if more than one role is on the same physical server, the port numbers must be different. For example, if you install another instance of SQL Server on the same server as your mirror database to act as the witness, when you create the witness endpoint, you will have to use a different port number.

> Note that if a SQL Server has more than one database that will participate in database mirroring, all databases will share the same endpoint. This prevents you from having to create five endpoints for the same purpose, but for five different databases. Make sure, however, that endpoint security is properly configured, especially if the databases are owned by different users.

7. Because database mirroring is designed to work without requiring that all machines be identically configured, or even members of the same domain, the Wizard then allows you to specify the account information for each server (see Figure 12-14). Note that the Wizard informs you that if the SQL Servers all use the same account, local accounts, or domain accounts in non-trusting domains, you should leave the values blank.

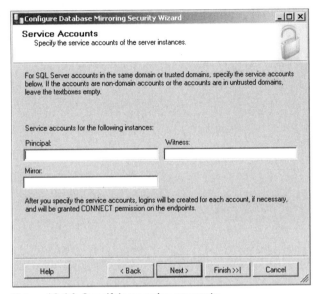

Figure 12-14: Specifying service accounts.

On my testbed, I have three instances defined: AUGHTEIGHT (principal), AUGHTEIGHT\DAGOBAH (mirror), and AUGHTEIGHT\HOTH (witness). I ensured that all servers were configured the same way (using the same service accounts and mixed mode authentication). I backed up and restored my sample database (for this example, I used the AdventureWorksDW2008 database) using both a Full database and a Transaction Log backup.

Once you have entered this information, the summary page of the Wizard allows you to review your configuration. If you are satisfied with your settings, click Finish to create the endpoints, and, if necessary, apply the appropriate permissions. Figure 12-15 shows a sample summary page. Note that the two endpoints that participate in the actual mirroring process have their roles identified as *partners*, whereas the witness server is simply identified as *witness*.

Now that you've completed the Wizard. SQL Server will prompt you to see if you want to start mirroring now or to delay mirroring. If you are satisfied that the configuration is correct and the mirror server is consistent with the principal server, then click on the button to begin mirroring.

Using Transact-SQL

The T-SQL commands for configuring database mirroring are easy to use and understand. Creating an endpoint for database mirroring is often a lot less complex than other endpoints you might create. Again, refer to Chapter 7 for a more detailed explanation on what endpoints are and how they work.

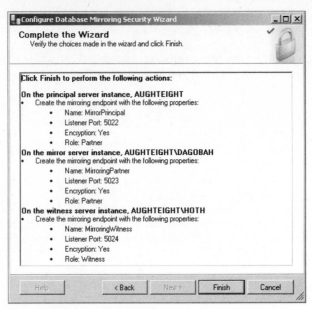

Figure 12-15: Wizard summary.

For database mirroring, execute the following to create an endpoint that does not use encryption:

```
USE Master;
GO
CREATE ENDPOINT MirroringEndPoint
    STATE = STARTED
    AS TCP ( LISTENER_PORT = 5022 )
    FOR DATABASE_MIRRORING (ROLE=PARTNER)
GO
```

Executing this statement on both the principal and mirrored servers creates identical endpoints that can be used for mirroring. If you are just testing mirroring for practice and don't have a separate physical server to use, installing another instance will allow you to mirror databases, as long as the endpoints use different port numbers.

Note that SQL Server will only let you configure one database mirroring endpoint per instance, so if a database mirroring endpoint already exists, the operation will fail.

When using a witness server, execute the following command on the witness instance to create the appropriate endpoint:

```
USE Master;
GO
CREATE ENDPOINT WitnessEndPoint
    STATE = STARTED
    AS TCP ( LISTENER_PORT = 5024 )
    FOR DATABASE_MIRRORING (ROLE=WITNESS)
GO
```

Note that the only things different are the endpoint name and the role, and of those two, only one is required to be different. (That would be the role; the name is irrelevant to the process.)

Additional options for creating database mirroring endpoints allow you to specify authentication and encryption options. Authentication allows you to choose from the following authentication methods:

- ❑   Windows NT LAN Manager (NTLM)
- ❑   Windows Kerberos
- ❑   Windows Negotiate (Use Kerberos if available; if not, fall back to NTLM.)
- ❑   Certificate certificate_name

You can also specify to try certificate authentication first, and failing that, use Windows authentication, or vice versa. Additionally, you can specify that encryption is disabled, supported, or required, and, if supported or required, which encryption algorithm to use, Advanced Encryption Standard (AES) or RC4. If you specify both AES and RC4, you can choose the preferred order for each. For more on encryption and certificates, refer to Chapter 6.

So, if you were to create a new endpoint that used Windows authentication and AES encryption, you might use the following code:

```
USE Master;
GO
CREATE ENDPOINT WitnessEndPoint
    STATE = STARTED
    AS TCP ( LISTENER_PORT = 5024 )
    FOR DATABASE_MIRRORING (AUTHENTICATION = WINDOWS NEGOTIATE,
    ENCRYPTION = REQUIRED ALGORITHM AES, ROLE = WITNESS);
GO
```

Now that you have your endpoints created; the next step is to establish the mirror. This is done simply by pointing the database on each server to the target partner. You will use an ALTER DATABASE statement to accomplish this, as in the following example (you may need to change the URLs to match your server names). In this example, I am reusing the endpoints I created through SSMS, but this time, I will be mirroring the AdventureWorksLT2008 database. (I've already backed up and restored it to my target server.)

```
-- Begin by configuring the Mirror database

USE Master;
GO
ALTER DATABASE AdventureWorksLT2008
SET PARTNER = 'TCP://AUGHTEIGHT:5022';

-- Execute this statement on the principal server
-- to specify the endpoint for the mirror

USE Master;
GO
ALTER DATABASE AdventureWorksLT2008
SET PARTNER = 'TCP://AUGHTEIGHT:5023';

-- Execute this statement on the principal server
```

```
-- to specify the endpoint for the witness

USE Master;
GO
ALTER DATABASE AdventureWorksLT2008
SET WITNESS = 'TCP://AUGHTEIGHT:5024';
```

When both the principal and mirror servers have been configured to recognize one another, the mirroring process begins. By default, database mirroring is configured to use the Synchronous mode, but you can change this after mirroring has begun by executing the following statement at the principal server:

```
USE Master;
GO
ALTER DATABASE AdventureWorksLT2008
SET PARTNER SAFETY OFF;
```

To turn the Synchronous mode back on, use the SET PARTNER SAFETY FULL option.

Monitoring Database Mirroring

Monitoring your mirrored database can give you an idea of how well your mirroring solution is working and whether or not there are latency or consistency issues that must be addressed. On both the principal and mirror servers, you can query the following system catalog views to view the status and configuration of all mirrors on that server:

❑   sys.database_mirroring

❑   sys.database_mirroring_endpoints

You can also query the sys.database_mirroring_witnesses on the witness server (if there is one) to view the witness server's summary of the mirrors that it is aware of. Microsoft also provides a nice UI tool that can be launched from the context menu of any user database on any SQL Server. You will need to provide the appropriate connection options to either the principal or the mirror to register a particular database, but the fact that you can launch the tool from anywhere makes it a handy resource. Just follow these steps:

1.   Choose the option to "Launch Database Mirroring Monitor" from the Tasks menu of a database (see Figure 12-16), and a new window appears.

2.   By default, you will be taken to the status page of the database from which you launched the tool (see Figure 12-17); however, you can also register additional mirrored sets by clicking on the Database Mirroring Monitor link in the tree navigation. As you can see in Figure 12-18, in the details pane you can click the link to register a new mirrored database that will be monitored by this tool.

3.   In the Registration page, click on the Connect button to connect to either the principal or the mirror server, using the appropriate authentication and connection options.

4.   You are then presented with a list of mirrored databases on that instance. Select the appropriate database(s) to register, and click OK.

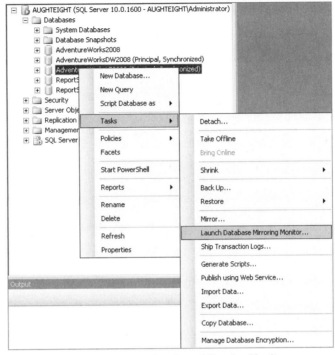

Figure 12-16: Launching the Database Mirroring Monitor.

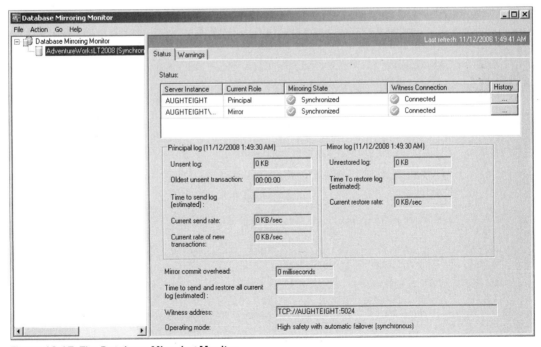

Figure 12-17: The Database Mirroring Monitor.

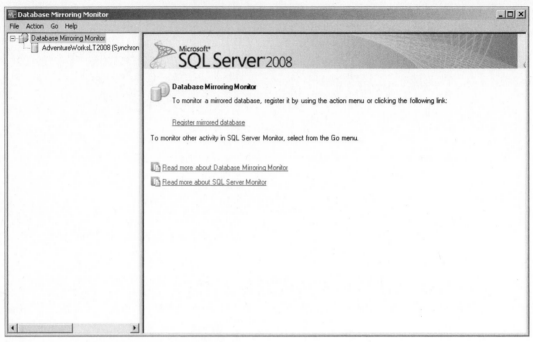

Figure 12-18: Monitoring the mirroring session.

5. If you need to use different authentication credentials between the principal and the mirror, you can also select the "Show the Manage Server Connections dialog box when I click OK" option to specify per-server connection options.

    Additional information is available that will help you identify potential latency properties by showing the stats for the principal and mirror logs.

6. Clicking on the Warnings tab allows you to view or configure the current settings for generating alerts based on mirroring conditions. The warnings can be generated on the following conditions:

    ❑   Threshold in kilobytes for the unsent log

    ❑   Threshold in kilobytes for the unrestored log

    ❑   Oldest unsent transaction in minutes

    ❑   Mirror commit overhead in milliseconds

As you can see from Figure 12-19, the thresholds can be defined on both the principal and the mirror, and you can, in fact, use different values on each. Your warning threshold should be based on known and expected performance values and may need to be adjusted to accommodate changes to your mirroring system. In any event, it's a good idea to make sure that you use consistent values between the principal and the mirror, so that you can respond appropriately to the alert.

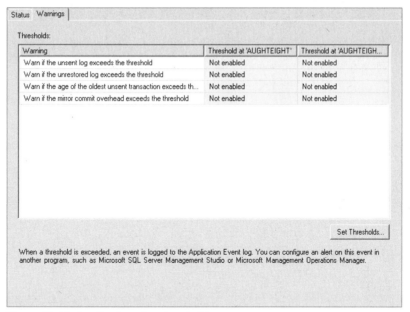

Figure 12-19: Configuring alert thresholds.

Managing Database Mirroring

Among the maintenance tasks associated with database mirroring are pausing a session, resuming a paused session, initiating mirror failover, forcing principal service, and removing mirroring for the database.

Pausing a Mirror Session

If there is a significant delay in database responsiveness that may be caused by the additional work of having to maintain constant communications between the principal and its mirror, you may want to consider temporarily suspending the communications. To pause the session using SQL Server Management Studio, navigate to the Mirroring page on the database Properties sheet, and simply click Pause (see Figure 12-20).

Using Transact-SQL, execute an `ALTER DATABASE` statement with the `SET PARTNER SUSPEND` option, as in the following example:

```
USE Master;
ALTER DATABASE AdventureWorksLT2008 SET PARTNER SUSPEND;
GO
```

Resuming a Mirror Session

Although pausing the session will allow you to resume the session later with no data loss, the transaction log cannot be truncated until the mirror has been resumed. For this reason, it is a good idea to resume the mirroring session as quickly as possible. To resume mirroring from SQL Server Management Studio, simply click on the Resume button, which replaced the Pause button when the session was suspended.

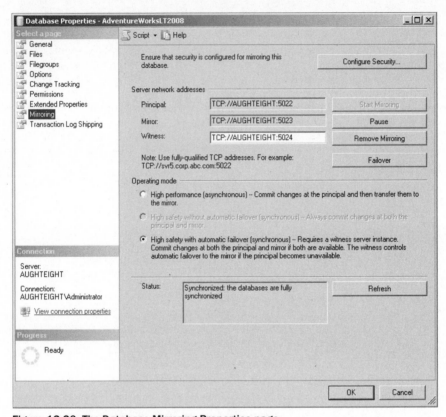

Figure 12-20: The Database Mirroring Properties page.

Use the SET PARTNER RESUME option for the ALTER DATABASE statement to resume the mirror from Transact-SQL, as in the following example:

```
USE Master;
ALTER DATABASE AdventureWorksLT2008 SET PARTNER RESUME;
GO
```

Manual Failover

Regardless of the operating mode of the mirror, you can manually initiate failover at any time from SQL Server Management Studio or T-SQL. When initiating failover, be aware that any clients that are connected to the original principal are immediately disconnected, and the mirror is brought online. The original principal, if online, is then converted to a mirror, and will remain in the NO RECOVERY state until failover is executed again.

Be aware of the effects that failover will have on your clients. Client applications that use the SQL Native Client or the .NET Framework Data Provider for SQL Server can be configured to use database mirroring, allowing clients to be re-directed to a mirror server in the event of a failover. Users may notice a slight delay or interruption after a failover, but, for the most part, operations should continue as normal, as long as a few precautions are in place.

Because database mirroring only copies the contents of a specific database, specific server-wide resources (such as logins) must be available on the mirror either prior to or immediately after the failover. For this reason, when using database mirroring, it's a good idea to create and schedule an Integration Services package, which will regularly copy additional objects. See Chapter 16 for an introduction to the Integration Services tools.

To initiate failover from SQL Server Management Studio, click on the Failover button in the Mirroring Properties page of the principal database. That's it. SQL handles the rest (see Figure 12-21). If you need to restore a former principal back to its "principalian" state, you must connect to the *new* principal, the original mirror, and click on the Failover button on that database's properties.

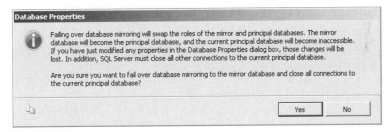

Figure 12-21: Manual failover.

To manually initiate failover using Transact-SQL, again, you must be connected to the principal server, then execute the following:

```
USE Master;
ALTER DATABASE AdventureWorksLT2008 SET PARTNER FAILOVER;
GO
```

This will immediately bring the principal down as a mirror and promote the original mirror to the principal database.

Forcing Service on the Mirror

As previously described, the mirror server is not automatically available in the case of a principal server failure when operating in high-performance or high-safety without automatic failover modes. To force the mirror server to promote itself and service client requests, the following command must be issued on the mirror server:

```
USE Master;
ALTER DATABASE AdventureWorksLT2008 SET PARTNER FAILOVER;
GO
```

Removing a Database Mirror

Once you no longer need a database mirroring session, you can "break the mirror." Breaking the mirror allows both participating servers to maintain a copy of the database. The principal will remain online, and the mirror will remain in Recovery mode.

Breaking the mirror will not delete, remove, or alter the endpoints, which is a very good thing, because they may still be used by other databases that are using database mirroring.

To break the mirror from SQL Server Management Studio, click on the "Remove Mirror" button on the Mirroring Properties page of the principal database. Using Transact-SQL, use the SET PARTNER OFF option for the ALTER DATABASE statement, as shown here:

```
USE Master;
ALTER DATABASE AdventureWorksLT2008 SET PARTNER OFF;
```

Optionally, you can then bring the mirror server online by using the RESTORE DATABASE AdventureWorksLT2008 WITH RECOVERY option. Just ensure that your clients know which one is the real database, and which one is the imposter!

Summary

There is no "magic bullet" for business continuity. In order to provide a highly available database environment for your users and applications, you will need to evaluate the different strategies and solutions that are available both out-of-the-box, as well as through after-market products. The best way to provide for a highly available and highly reliable solution is to use a combination of tools and techniques to allow your database to stay operational, even during the most serious outages.

This chapter introduced you to three options for keeping your data available to users. At the server level, you can leverage Windows Clustering services. At the database level, you can use log shipping or database mirroring as necessary. While I tend to prefer database mirroring as a rule, it works best when you have applications that leverage the Native SQL client.

If you've been reading this chapter in sequence, you will have already gotten a lot of good, detailed information that database administrators should know. The remaining chapters in this book introduce topics that may not be part of the daily maintenance of a SQL Server 2008 environment, but an understanding of the key components may be helpful.

In Chapter 13, you will be introduced to SQL Server replication. That chapter will cover the basics of replication topologies and strategies and familiarize you with the components of a replication implementation.

Introduction to Replication

As the amount of data we store increases, so does the need for making that data available. Many of us want to access our data from any place, at any time, and from any device. And we work for companies that have a global presence, or a mobile sales force. We can increase the accessibility of our data through *SQL Server Replication*.

This chapter is designed to provide you with a high-level understanding of SQL Server Replication. You will learn about the different replication methods and tools that are available in SQL Server 2008, including replication components and the physical and logical design options for replication.

Replication Overview

I may be dating myself by using the analogy, but *replication* is similar to how the print media operates. In fact, many of the terms used in replication are also used with newspaper and magazine distribution. Replication begins at the server known as the *publisher*. Just as a newspaper collects articles its readership is interested in, the publisher compiles and arranges data into *articles*, and one or more articles are included in a *publication*. To get data to *subscribers*, the newspaper needs to employ a *distributor*.

In SQL Server Replication, just as in the newspaper business, the subscribers can choose to have the distributor deliver the publication to them (although SQL distributors don't usually expect a tip during the holidays), or they can go to the distributor to pick up the publication — not unlike going to a newsstand or your favorite coffee shop and picking up a newspaper. In the SQL replication world, a publisher might also be a distributor. This is not unlike the newspaper hiring carriers directly versus outsourcing the work to a third party.

Here's a review of some of the key terms used in the last paragraph, and a preview of some of the terms used in the next section, to help provide a better understanding of the way replication works:

- ❑ **Publisher** — The server providing the source data that will be made available to subscribers
- ❑ **Article** — A collection of data that exists as part of a replication publication
- ❑ **Publication** — One or more articles that act as a unit of replication

❑ **Distributor** — The server that is responsible for providing data to subscribers

❑ **Subscriber** — A server or client that receives a publication

❑ **Push Replication** — A method of replication whereby the distributor delivers the data to the subscriber

❑ **Pull Replication** — A method of replication whereby the subscriber requests the data from the distributor

❑ **Publisher/Distributor** — A publishing server that acts as its own distributor

Replication has many uses. It can provide a copy of the production system data to another database for reporting, as well as allow remote users to enter data at a local server that will get aggregated or merged with data at a central office. It can also be used with client applications for offline or asynchronous use. When choosing a replication strategy, you must have a solid understanding of how the data will be used.

Consider the following:

❑ Do the users need access to up-to-the-minute data, or can they work with data that is provided on a regular schedule but may be several hours old (or older)?

❑ Do the users need to be able to make changes to the data, and should those changes be synchronized with the original source material?

❑ Will the data originate from a single source, or will multiple sources be used to provide data to a centralized database?

Finding answers to these questions (and more) can help you make the appropriate decisions about your replication topology. You can use this information to help build solutions to make your database applications more responsive and more useful to your users.

Also note that when replication is configured, a new system database named `distribution` is created. This database is used for storing metadata and historical information about your replication topology. In SQL Server 2008, you may elect to use a single `distribution` database for all replication tasks, or you may create additional `distribution` databases, each with a unique name, to handle distribution requests from multiple publishers.

SQL Server Replication Agents

Now that you've got the terminology down and have an idea of what your users' needs are, it's time to take a look at the mechanics behind replication. This section introduces the various replication agents that are available for your solution. *Replication agents* are programs that run certain tasks to control preparation and distribution of your data. The agents that are used depend on the type of replication used in your solution. Some of these agents are available to all replication types, and some are specific to just one type of replication.

Replication relies on the SQL Server Agent Service when the server is a publisher or distributor to automate the replication process. Although it is *possible* to execute the replication agents manually, it would be more work than it's probably worth. Ensure that your SQL Server Agent Service is running, and, in most cases, it should be configured to start when the server starts.

Snapshot Agent

With SQL Server Replication, the Snapshot Agent is used for almost all replication types. The Snapshot Agent is executed at the distributor and is responsible for preparing the initial data files and schema information about the articles that will be published. The data is written to a snapshot folder on the file system, and synchronization data is written to the distribution database. It often acts as the baseline for other replication agents. In this way, it's not unlike the way a Full backup works when using Differential or Transaction Log backups.

Log Reader Agent

The Log Reader Agent is used specifically with *transactional replication*. When a transaction that is part of a publication is written to the transaction log, the Log Reader Agent copies those transactions from the publisher to the distribution database on the distributor. This allows those transactions to be executed then, on the subscriber databases. Each database that participates in transactional replication has its own Log Reader Agent.

Distribution Agent

Used with both snapshot and transactional replication, the Distribution Agent applies snapshots to subscribers, and, in the case of transactional replication, moves the transactions to the subscribers. If *pull replication* is used, the Distribution Agent is executed at the subscriber. If *push replication* is used, it is run at the distributor.

Merge Agent

When *merge replication* is used, the Merge Agent provides the initial snapshot to the subscriber, not unlike the Distribution Agent. Each subscription has its own Merge Agent that handles the reconciliation of data between the publisher and the subscriber. Another similarity it shares with the Distribution Agent is that it runs at the distributor for push subscriptions and at the subscriber for pull subscriptions. When communicating between publishers and the subscribers, the Merge Agent typically *downloads* the changes to the subscriber and *uploads* changes to the publisher.

Queue Reader Agent

The Queue Reader Agent is used with a specific type of transactional replication that allows updatable subscriptions. When updates from the subscriber are provided to the publisher, these updates can be queued and then processed as a unit. This agent runs at the distributor, and only one instance is required for all publications in the distribution database.

SQL Server Replication Types

The term *replication type* refers to the logical model of a replication topology, and although there are only three main types (transactional, snapshot, and merge), each one offers additional configuration options that allow you to have more granular control over how data gets from source to destination and what happens to it when it gets there. Consideration for the different replication types is based on the way the data is going to be used and how important it is that the data be current.

Two key terms to remember when choosing a replication type are autonomy and latency. *Autonomy* refers to the amount of "hands-off-ness" of the data. *Latency* refers to the amount of time that elapses between when a change is made to the data and when the data is replicated to the subscriber. In the different replication types available, there is a direct correlation between autonomy and latency.

For example, let's say that AdventureWorks has a regional office that uses quarterly updates on sales figures for an employee incentive program. Because this program is only in place at the regional office, there's no need to provide updates back to the home office. Once the home office provides the data to the regional office, they don't do anything else with it. Any changes to the data will not be reflected back in the corporate database, much to the relief of the company's corporate auditors. In this scenario, a high amount of autonomy and latency is evident. The regional office gets the updated data once every three months; and once they get it, they own the data for their own needs.

Conversely, a retail chain requires real-time inventory tracking from their Point-of-Sale system that would not only update the local inventory database, but also ensure that each retail and warehouse location is aware of the product inventory at the other locations. This is an example of an application that requires very low latency. In this scenario, when a customer is looking for a DVD player that's out of stock at the Seattle location, a sales clerk can inform the customer of the availability of that model at the Bellevue and Tacoma locations.

Distributed Transactions

Although distributed transactions aren't part of SQL Server replication, per se, it's important to know how they fit into the distributed data model. First and foremost, any transaction that executes across more than one database, even if it is attached to the same instance, is considered a distributed transaction. This is because the scope of the transaction exists outside of the context of the current database.

For example, the following SQL script executes in the context of the AdventureWorks2008 database, but one of the tables is actually created in the tempdb database. Because both CREATE TABLE statements are wrapped in the BEGIN TRANSACTION and COMMIT TRANSACTION statements, they must both execute, or the entire transaction fails.

```
USE AdventureWorks2008;
GO
BEGIN TRANSACTION;
CREATE TABLE dbo.MyDTTable(col1 INT, col2 VARCHAR(10));
CREATE TABLE tempdb.dbo.MyOtherDTTable (col1 INT, col2 VARCHAR(10));
COMMIT TRANSACTION;
```

This is a very simplified example of how distributed transactions are designed to work, but you get the idea. When an application executes distributed transactions against multiple servers, an additional step may be taken in order to ensure the availability of the target servers. This is what's known as a *two-phase commit* (2 PC).

The first phase is the *preparation phase*. This step prepares the destination servers, known as *resource managers*, by sending out a command to inform them that a transaction is coming. The resource managers take every possible precaution to ensure that when the transaction is received, it can be processed without failure. This helps ensure the stability and reliability of the distributed transaction. The resource manager then informs the *transaction manager*, usually the Microsoft Distributed Transaction Coordinator (MSDTC), whether or not the preparations were successful.

The *second phase* is executed when all the resource managers have reported successful preparation. In this phase, the transaction manager expects to receive a successful commit from each of the resource managers. When it does, then it can report the transaction as having been committed to the application. If just one of the resource managers reports failure, the transaction must be rolled back from all resource managers, and the transaction manager reports the failure to the application.

Distributed transactions can also be executed directly from stored procedures or other Transact-SQL methods. You can use the BEGIN DISTRIBUTED TRANSACTION statement to explicitly invoke a distributed transaction.

Distributed transactions do not define a publisher, distributor, and subscriber the way replication does. Instead, they rely on the application design to control how data is processed across multiple servers. They do offer the least amount of autonomy and latency, because the transactions are immediately processed on destination servers.

Transactional Replication

Transactional replication has the lowest latency and autonomy of the three standard replication types. With transactional replication, you begin with a snapshot of the data that will be used as a baseline for further transactions to be applied against. As transactions are committed, those that apply to data that participates in transactional replication are copied to the distribution database on the distributor. Then the subscribers can receive the transactions and apply the changes to the copied data.

Standard Transactional Publication

Standard transactional publication replication is used when the subscriber accepts the publication for Read Only use. This prevents the subscriber from being able to update the data on the publisher, but does not prevent clients from updating data on the subscriber itself. For example, a remote server may use the replicated data in conjunction with SQL Reporting Services to provide access to historical and trend data, and modifications may be made locally, but no changes can be submitted at the remote server that will be accepted at the original publisher.

Transactional Publications with Updatable Subscriptions in a Hierarchical Topology

The *Transactional Publications with Updatable Subscriptions in a Hierarchical Topology* implementation of transactional replication allows a model in which you have a single publisher with multiple subscribers. Periodically, the subscribers may need to make changes to the replicated data, in which case, the update is sent back to the original publisher. The original publisher provides those updates (through the distributor) to all the subscribers. This can be helpful in an environment where a remote site receives corporate sales data but occasionally submits updates regarding its local sales department.

Updatable subscriptions in a hierarchical topology allow both immediate and queued updates to be submitted from the subscribers. Immediate updates are processed similarly to distributed transactions, in that a two-phase commit is used. If immediate updates are not necessary, subscriber updates can be stored in a queue and then applied asynchronously whenever the publisher is available.

Transactional Publications in a Peer-to-Peer Topology

Peer-to-peer transactional replication creates an environment where all participants are both publishers and subscribers. This implementation allows you to create a distributed database environment where all SQL Servers can provide and receive updates with low latency. This further lowers the autonomy previously offered by transactional replication, by allowing any data to be changed on any server, and all participating servers will receive the updates. When using peer-to-peer transactional replication, use SQL Server security features to take appropriate precautions to ensure that data can only be updated from approved locations. Peer-to-peer replication was first introduced in SQL Server 2005 and has been enhanced to include additional conflict resolution tools.

Snapshot Replication

Snapshot replication can be used in replication topologies where there can be significant latency between when changes are committed on the publisher and when they are received by the subscriber. Rather than providing updates on a transaction-by-transaction basis, snapshots of the entire article are taken at the publisher periodically and then applied to the subscriber as a unit.

When a snapshot is generated, it is saved as a file to a file system that must be accessible to the publisher, the distributor, and the subscriber. If one or more of these are on different physical servers, you should specify a Universal Naming Convention (UNC) path for the *snapshot* folder location. If all the components reside on the same server, which may sometimes be the case if you're using replication to populate a separate database on the same server, you can specify a local file system path for the snapshot location. The files generated by snapshot replication are files that can be easily applied to the subscriber using the Bulk Copy Program (BCP).

The obvious benefit of snapshot replication is for asynchronous environments where there can be a delay between the publisher and subscriber. However, because the snapshots are copied and applied each time replication occurs, it can be prohibitively resource-consuming for large amounts of data. There are options that can allow you to compress the snapshot files, as well as to help reduce disk usage and transfer times between the distributor and subscriber, though.

As with transactional replication, snapshot replication also supports the use of immediate or queued updating subscriptions.

Merge Replication

Merge replication is used in environments where data entry tasks may be performed independently of one another, and users or applications periodically need to connect to synchronize data. Merge replication is often used in client/server application environments. For example, if you have a mobile sales force where all members of the sales team need access to a Customer Relationship Management (CRM) application, but will not always have connectivity to your server, being able to synchronize customer data to a portable device such as a PDA or smartphone, will allow them to access information on the go. They can also use the application to submit orders, track invoices, and keep notes about their clients. When they are back in the office or can connect to the corporate network remotely, they can synchronize their changes with their home servers.

Merge replication introduces a number of changes to your publishing databases that are used for tracking and synchronization. This includes adding a column to published tables used for tracking, as well as additional tables and triggers that are used to store row history data for published rows. These elements are designed to be unobtrusive, and the triggers created by replication will not affect any user-defined triggers that you have created.

Merge replication offers both a blessing and a curse with its ability to handle synchronizations from multiple subscribers. Its blessings come from the ability to grant users offline access to data sets that are critical to their needs. Its curse comes from the fact that multiple offline subscribers may be trying to synchronize changes to the same data.

The Change Tracking mechanism used by merge replication allows you to define how conflicts are resolved between multiple subscribers. For example, a particular subscriber may be given more weight than others, and, therefore, its changes should be considered authoritative. There are also mechanisms to programmatically build more complex resolvers. This allows you to create more granular rules about conflict resolution, giving priority to certain subscribers only if specific criteria are met.

Oracle Replication

No, that's not a typo. Microsoft SQL Server 2008 supports replication of Oracle objects. Oracle replication requires at least SQL Server 2005 and Oracle 9i, but replication will support any Oracle publisher, regardless of the underlying platform.

Snapshot replication from an Oracle database operates similarly to SQL Server snapshots. The Snapshot Agent connects to the Oracle publication and retrieves rows and creates schema scripts for each published table. As with SQL snapshot replication, the entire data set is created each time the table is run.

Unlike homogeneous SQL Server transactional replication (which monitors the transaction log for changes), transactional replication for Oracle requires that changes be made to the Oracle database by creating tracking tables and triggers. When changes to a published Oracle table are made, the triggers fire and insert the changes into the tracking table. This is not unlike the behavior seen in merge replication. SQL Server, again acting as the distributor, executes the Log Reader Agent to move the changes from the tracking table to the distribution database. The distributor then provides the changes to the subscribers as would be expected.

SQL Server Replication Models

Now that you have an understanding of the different types of replication available, the next consideration in building your replication topology is to identify the model that will be used. Whereas the type defines the logical flow of data, the *model* defines the physical implementation of how the data will be distributed. Any of the aforementioned SQL Server Replication types can use any of the SQL Server Replication models. The overall design and topology for replication should be built around how the data is used, and the accessibility requirements for your users and your applications.

Another consideration when choosing an appropriate replication model is whether to have the publisher and the distributor on the same instance. Geographical distribution and network availability may influence your decision to use a local distributor versus a remote one.

Single Publisher/Multiple Subscribers

In cases in which the data should originate from one location only, a *single publisher/multiple subscriber model* can be used to provide access to data for remote locations. For example, our fictional company, AdventureWorks, has offices across the United States. The corporate office, headquartered in Tacoma, needs to make its sales data available to its remote offices in Omaha, Baton Rouge, and Rochester for a reporting application. In this case, the company may want to use a single distributor in the Tacoma office to provide updates using snapshot replication to each of the field offices.

In this scenario, the AdventureWorks field office will get sales data updates through an asynchronous delivery method. Because they will not be changing the data that is replicated, there is no need for updatable subscriptions, and each office will receive the same data.

Multiple Publishers/Single Subscriber

The *multiple publishers/single subscriber model* can be used when multiple servers will track and update data, but that data will need to be consolidated on a single server. Let's look at a retail chain as an example of how this can work.

An electronics retailer uses an inventory-tracking database to keep track of product stock at each location. Each store maintains its own inventory through its shipping department and point-of-sale application. Each location uses transactional replication to provide changes to its local stock to a regional warehouse, which holds the subscriber database. This helps the regional inventory manager keep track of when a specific store is running low on a certain product, and they can make arrangements to provide the items to the store. Because transactional replication is used in this topology, the inventory database at the regional warehouse gets updated with minimal delay.

Multiple Publishers/Multiple Subscribers

The *multiple publishers/multiple subscribers model* works well for environments where data must be shared among peers. This can be useful in applications in which the local database stores information about local and remote operations. Each publisher can provide updates made locally to all other replication partners that participate in this model and receive the updates, in turn.

For example, three friends decide to get into the fast-food business, and each buys several franchises within their cities. Each restaurant keeps track of its own inventory, as well as being able to see the inventory at the other locations. This is so that the local manager can call another store for spare ingredients, just in case the supplier cannot deliver in time. To prevent having a separate inventory table for each location, merge replication can be used. Each store updates its own inventory values daily and then synchronizes with the other locations so that each store is aware of the inventory at the other locations.

Replication Tools

When reviewing the options provided for designing the replication topology, additional considerations may be evaluated for determining what data is replicated and how. This section provides an overview of some of the available tools and procedures that can help provide a more robust replication architecture.

Filtering

It is not always appropriate to replicate entire tables from one server to another. You can, in fact, use *filtering* at the publisher to limit what will be available to the subscribers. Subscriptions can also use filters at the subscriber to ensure that only data relevant to that subscriber is received and processed. Four types of filters are available:

❑ Static row filters

❑ Column filters

❑ Parameterized row filters

❑ Join filters

Static Row Filters

Static row filters can be used with all types of replication. They are defined at the publisher and allow you to limit which rows will be made available in a publication by simply using a WHERE clause. For example, you could provide regional managers with Human Resources data about the employees at only their respective locations by using a static row filter based on the employee's city field, or another location-identifying column.

Column Filters

Column filtering can be used to remove certain columns from all rows in a publication. For example, if you have Human Resources data that will be made available to multiple databases for different applications, it may not always be appropriate to include confidential data such as salary information or the employees' Social Security numbers. In this case, you can create publications that eliminate the unnecessary data from the publication without removing it from the base table.

Column filtering can be used with all types of replication. However, certain types of columns may be excluded from filtering depending on which replication type you are using. You can use both column filters and static row filters in a single publication to narrow the scope of the published data.

Parameterized Row Filters

Parameterized row filters are available only with merge replication and are similar in concept to static row filters. In execution, though, they are significantly different. The purpose of parameterized row filters is to be able to create multiple data partitions that will be replicated without having to create multiple publications. For example, if you use the same base table and you have two different subscribers that each needs a different subset of that same table, using standard row filters would require you to create two publications, one for Subscriber A and the other for Subscriber B.

With parameterized row filters, you can specify that for Subscriber A, you are interested in rows that have the values WA, NE, and OK in the state field. For Subscriber B, you are interested in providing rows that contain the values CA, OR, and AK in the state field. Each of these data sets exists as part of the same publication.

The partitions created by parameterized row filters can also overlap. Using the preceding example, if a new subscriber wanted all the rows with the values WA, OR, NV, and TX in the state column, then that is an example of an *overlapping partition*. You can configure overlapping partitions to allow updates from the subscriber to any column, or only any non-shared column. *Non-overlapping partitions* can be made available to multiple subscribers, preventing the subscriber from updating the changes. If a non-overlapping partition is available to only one subscriber, then that subscriber can make changes to all columns in that partition.

Join Filters

Join filters are also limited to merge replication and are commonly used to extend the data in a publication that uses parameterized row filters. This operates similar to a JOIN statement in Transact-SQL to combine the data from one or more tables. The data in the related tables is published only if it meets the condition of the JOIN FILTER clause.

Replicating Partitioned Tables and Indexes

SQL Server 2008 includes several enhancements that make it easier to manage partitioned tables and indexes, and the replication tools are no exception. When configuring the properties of an article, you will have the ability to specify the schema options that determine whether or not partitioned objects are copied to the subscriber. This can be done through the New Publication Wizard (covered in the next section), the Publication Properties dialog, or through the schema_option parameter of the sp_addarticle, sp_addmergearticle, sp_changearticle, or sp_changemergearticle stored procedures.

In case that data needs to be moved between partitions, these changes can also be published using transactional replication. By default, SWITCH PARTITION operations are blocked when a table is enabled for replication, but partition switching can be manually enabled if it is needed.

New Publication Wizard

Once the design of your replication topology has been decided on and you know what type of replication you will be using, you can use the New Publication Wizard to create a new replication publication. To launch the Wizard, start SQL Server Management Studio and expand the Replication folder. Right-click on the Local Publications folder and choose "New Publication." Then follow these steps:

1. Click Next on the New Publication Wizard introduction page. On the next page, you can select which server will act as the distributor. As you can see in Figure 13-1, if you have not already configured a server to be the distributor, you can use the local server. In this case, it will create the distribution database and transaction log files. Click Next once you've selected your distributor.

2. On the next page, you must specify the location that will be used to store the snapshot files. Remember that if your subscriber is a remote client or server, you should specify a UNC path instead of a local file system path to enable pull subscriptions. In my example, I created a new folder called *C:\Snapshots*. This is because the SQL Server Agent account does not have permissions to write to the default location.

3. Next, choose the database that will be providing the publication. For this example, select the AdventureWorks2008 database from the list. After selecting the appropriate database, click Next to move on to the next page, which will ask you about the type of replication you will use.

4. When presented with the list of available replication options, note that a brief description of each replication type is available to help you review which type is the appropriate selection for your application. For this example, select "Transactional publication" and click Next.

5. On the next page, you can select which objects will be available for replication to the subscribers. Figure 13-2 shows an example in which the Sales.CreditCard table is selected. A

single publication can include multiple articles, which may be tables, views, or other SQL Server objects.

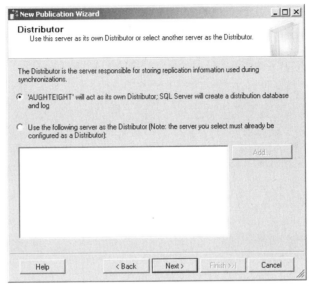

Figure 13-1: Choosing the distributor.

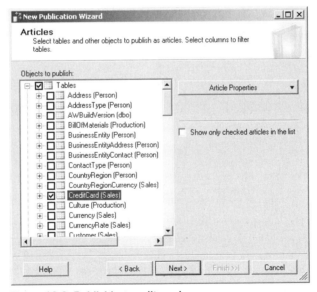

Figure 13-2: Publishing credit cards.

6. At this point, you can review or configure the article properties. The "Article Properties" button will allow you to configure the properties for a single (the currently highlighted article) or for all selected articles. From here, you can control or define what information will be copied to the subscriber.

7. The next page in the Wizard gives you the option of filtering the rows that will be included in the publication. Clicking on the Add button allows you to create a new filter. Note that the filter statement is prepared as a simple SELECT statement, where you can provide the value for the WHERE clause.

8. The Wizard will then ask you how to provide Snapshot Agent details. This will allow you to take a snapshot immediately, as well as define a schedule for managing the frequency of your snapshots. Based on the type of replication you will be implementing, you may only need the initial snapshot.

9. You can then select the accounts that the Snapshot Agent and Log Reader Agent will run as. Although you can use the SQL Server Agent account, it is generally not a best security practice, and the Wizard will warn you of that. You will also need to provide the credentials that will be used to connect to the publisher. The default option impersonates the process account, but you may also specify a SQL Server login and password.

10. Next, you can choose to create the publication immediately or simply generate a script that can be used to create the publication later. You can also enable both options, which would allow you to save the script information for reference, or to avoid having to rerun the Wizard if you are going to be performing the same task on multiple servers. If you choose to save the script, you will need to specify location and file format options before reaching the summary page of the Wizard.

11. Finally, on the summary page, give the new publication a name and click Finish to create the new publication. Figure 13-3 shows a summary of the options I selected in my example.

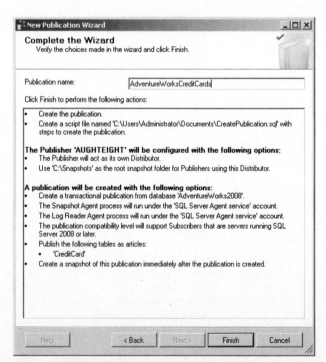

Figure 13-3: New Publication summary.

New Subscription Wizard

A newspaper is worthless if nobody reads it. Likewise, the purpose of publishing an article in SQL Server is to provide it for subscribers. In my example, I will need to create a target database that will act as the subscriber. If you're following along, you can execute the following code to create a new database called AWReplicationDemo. Because no options are specified when you create the target database, its configuration is based on your model database and should only contain system objects.

```
USE master
CREATE DATABASE AWReplicationDemo;
GO
```

Once the database has been created, you can create a new subscription:

1. Right-click on the "Local Subscriptions" folder and select "New Subscriptions." Once past the introduction page of the Wizard, you will see a dropdown list of Publishers, and publications that exist on the currently selected Publisher (see Figure 13-4). If your server is not listed, you can connect to another SQL or Oracle publisher.

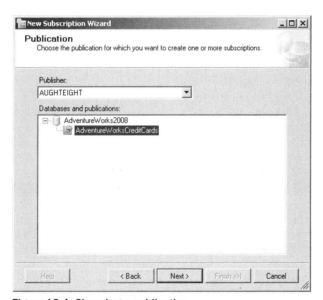

Figure 13-4: Choosing a publication.

2. Once you've selected your publisher, you can then specify whether this will be a push subscription or a pull subscription. (This example is a push subscription.) You will then be asked to specify the target subscription database. Choose the destination database from the list of databases on your server. If you look at Figure 13-5, note that you can also define other subscribers including non-SQL (Oracle, DB2) subscribers.

3. You must then choose the security context under which the Distributor Agent will run and connect to both the Distributor and Subscriber. You can specify a Windows account or use SQL Server logins. For demonstration purposes only, I have selected the SQL Server Agent account once again; however, in a production environment, I would want to use a Windows account that has limited permissions to allow me to read from the distribution source and write to the destination tables.

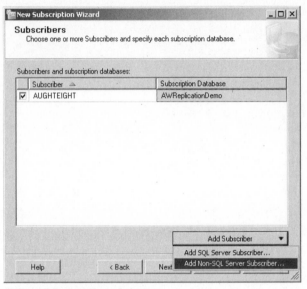

Figure 13-5: Defining subscribers.

4.   Next, specify an appropriate schedule for the Distribution Agent. You can have the synchronization run continuously, run when manually invoked, or create a job schedule that will be run by the SQL Server Agent Service. For this example, I have chosen to run continuously.

5.   Before finishing, you will be prompted to initialize subscriptions. This is optional, and if you enable initialization, you can choose to initialize immediately or at the first scheduled synchronization. Just as when creating a publication, you have the option of creating the subscription immediately, saving the Wizard steps as a SQL script, or both. Once you have completed the Wizard, you will see the summary page, as shown in Figure 13-6

Replication Monitor

SQL Server 2008 includes a Replication Monitor that can be used to track the status of your publications and subscriptions. It can provide information on latency, replication history, warnings, and alerts. You can view the Replication Monitor by right-clicking on the Replication folder and selecting "Launch Replication Monitor." Figure 13-7 shows you an example of the Subscription Watch List tab's interface for the Replication Monitor.

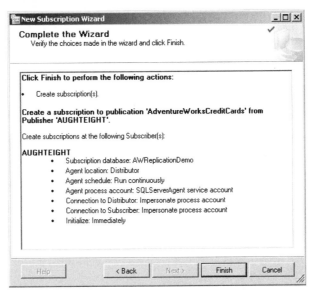

Figure 13-6: Creating the subscription.

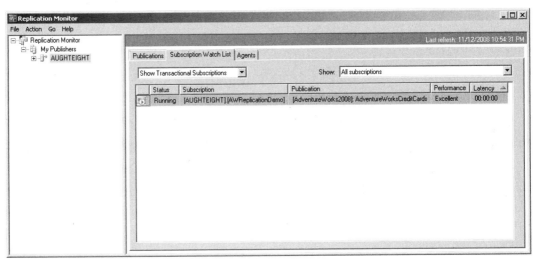

Figure 13-7: Replication Monitor.

If you double-click on a subscription, you can view the details of the subscription, including the history between the publication and distributor, and also between the distributor and subscriber. Figure 13-8 shows an example of the subscription details window. To test both the replication and see the Replication Monitor in action, begin by enabling Auto Refresh from the Action menu of the Subscription details window. Then, execute the following code to insert a new row in the `Sales.CreditCard` table on the `AdventureWorks2008` database, which should get replicated to the subscriber:

```
USE AdventureWorks2008;
GO
INSERT Sales.CreditCard (CardType, CardNumber, ExpMonth, ExpYear)
VALUES ('MisterClub','1234876510190210',12,2025);
```

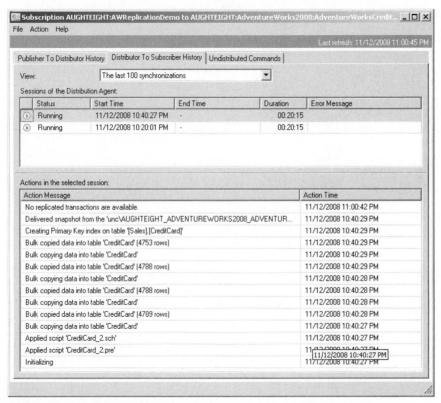

Figure 13-8: Subscription history details view.

Within a short period of time, you should see that the transaction was delivered from the publisher to the distributor and from the distributor to the subscriber. You can also verify this by running a select statement against `AWReplicationDemo.Sales.CreditCard`, and verify that the new entry appears.

Summary

Replication is a topic that every database administrator should be familiar with. This chapter should have helped you understand the different options that SQL Server Replication offers. This chapter looked at the following topics:

❑ An overview of how SQL Server Replication works

❑ The agents used by SQL Server Replication

❑ The different replication types

❑ The different physical replication models

❑ Some of the tools used in SQL Server Replication

In Chapter 14, you will learn about configuring and using the Common Language Runtime (CLR) for administering database objects through a .NET programming interface.

Introduction to the Common Language Runtime

In this chapter, we will look at how to manage the configuration and settings related to maintaining the security and stability of the SQL Common Language Runtime (CLR). Since this is not a programming book, I will use a short (but useful) code example, but it will certainly paint the picture of what is possible using the CLR. The main purpose of this chapter is to show you how to create and manage the CLR objects that developers have created for you.

Databases and Programming

If you're a career database administrator, then you probably know that I represent the contingent of unruly coders who often want to deploy precarious, custom-built applications on your servers. In the process of finding new and creative ways to solve problems with program code, programmers tend to break things. Because the administrator's job is to maintain a stable and secure server environment, it would naturally make sense to keep programmers (and their pesky program code) as far away from the servers as possible.

If you are a developer and you are reading this, you may think that I am making a great to-do about nothing, but most of the seasoned database administrators in the enterprise space (especially those with development skills) have learned to be very cautious of custom code and assemblies that could bring their servers down or cause hard-to-solve performance problems. I fully acknowledge the fact that many of you wear both a programming hat and an administrator hat from time to time, and, as you read this chapter, I may seem to present a single-minded view of the DBA role. This is to simply keep us focused on our purpose, which is database administration. Therefore, I ask that if you consider yourself to be a programmer/DBA, please place only your DBA hat squarely on your head and read on.

So, why in the world would you consider allowing new program code to run on your database server? I have good news. Managing custom code can now be completely secure, stable, and fully integrated into the SQL Server database server environment. Best of all, the control over these components is completely in the hands of our esteemed database administrators.

In past versions of SQL Server, database-programming objects (mainly stored procedures) could be extended using custom programming technologies. Even before Microsoft began to extend the original Sybase SQL Server product, extended stored procedures could be written using complex C and C++ programming. In later versions, a set of System Stored Procedures was added, allowing COM components to be called. Many production SQL Server–based applications use these procedures to send e-mail, automate Windows services, and to interact with the file system. Relying on extended stored procedures and custom-written COM objects can be risky business because these technologies provide no built-in protection from memory leaks, buffer overruns, and unstable operations. In contrast, the .NET Framework run time provides a rigid layer of protection of both stability and security.

Transact-SQL has been pushed to and beyond its limits for a long time now. Not too many years ago, the words *database* and *programming* were rarely used in the same sentence, especially when discussing work performed in a database, rather than in a separate application. However, these two words are commonly juxtaposed today and are often used to describe the day-to-day activities of a new breed of IT professionals who write stored procedures, user-defined functions, triggers, types, and aggregations for database solutions. The two isolated worlds of database management and programming began to collide about the time that the SQL Server product began to mature.

With the current state of the economy, many IT shops have been restructured with most technical professionals filling multiple roles. Although it's still true in larger companies that programmers are programmers and administrators are administrators, now it's not uncommon to find seasoned programmers who often build and configure development servers. It's also not uncommon to find administrators who write script and program code to perform automated administrative tasks. And in smaller shops, it's quite common to find one person who does both.

Is Transact-SQL Going Away?

Not even close! The Transact-SQL language is the most efficient way to retrieve and manipulate data stored in a relational database. The main purpose of SQL is to return results from one or more tables that are combined by using joins and unions. It is also the best way to insert new rows, update existing rows, and delete rows in a table. From the beginning, SQL was designed to operate on sets of data and was never really meant to perform procedural tasks. Although SQL may be used to efficiently perform common value comparisons, mathematical operations, numeric aggregation, string parsing, and concatenation, when it comes to processing complex business logic, SQL has its limits.

The capabilities to perform looping, enumeration, or conditional branching are very limited in the Transact-SQL language, and, even with structured error handling, exception handling is still a matter of failing gracefully, rather than recovering from and managing the program logic following an exception. Transact-SQL will remain for the foreseeable future the best language choice for standard data-retrieval and data-manipulation operations. However, for implementing complex business rule logic requiring row-by-row operations, loops and counters, decision structures, or including values from sources outside of SQL databases, extending database programming through the CLR may offer many advantages.

The SQL language has certainly been around longer than some modern-day object-oriented programming languages such as C# and Java, but for its purpose, SQL is by no means obsolete. It is definitely here to stay and should be used to perform the day-to-day administrative, management, and programming tasks in SQL Server. Many things in SQL Server 2008 have been enhanced, and the Transact-SQL language is one of them. It's lean and efficient and is the easiest way to get the best performance out of your SQL Server databases for most types of operations.

.NET and the CLR

Software developers know that the Microsoft .NET CLR is at the core of an entire application development platform. In simple terms, the CLR is really just a set of installed components that allow software and custom-built components to run on a computer. In addition to this capability, the CLR also provides a safety net to ensure that software runs safely and securely, and that it doesn't misuse or waste system resources. Because this book is designed for database administrators and not developers, I am making an assumption that you haven't had a lot of exposure to development terminology. In order to make it easier to talk about certain concepts later in the chapter, I am going to go ahead and hit a few high points. If you already feel comfortable in the development arena, then skip ahead to the next section.

Assemblies

A .NET *assembly* is the unit of deployment in the .NET world and contains various program objects. An assembly that contains SQL CLR objects is built as a class library with a .DLL file extension. A newly built assembly actually contains semicompiled Microsoft Intermediate Language (MSIL) code. An assembly is stored in this intermediate, semicompiled state so that it can be fully compiled into the most optimal form when it runs on the target computer, rather than the computer where it was developed.

SQL CLR object assemblies are fully manageable objects that are stored in the database rather than on the file system as DLL files, and just like any other object within the database, they can be secured and controlled. A single assembly can host many SQL Server objects such as functions, stored procedures, aggregates, or data types, each of which are defined programming objects organized into a simple hierarchy, consisting of namespaces, classes, and methods.

Namespaces

A *namespace* is an organizational structure used to group classes into manageable categories. A namespace may contain any number of subordinate namespaces that are used to group and manage similar object classes. The .NET Framework consists of scores of nested namespaces, which, in turn, contain thousands of classes. A namespace provides no inherent functionality other than to be a container for classes. In the case of SQL Server assemblies, the namespaces contained in the assemblies help organize the functionality of the assembly by using descriptive names to specify each embedded procedure or function contained in the assembly.

Classes

A *class* defines a programming object used to represent data and all functionality that can be performed on that data. For example, a `Customer` class can be used to encapsulate all data related to a customer such as name, address, phone number, and anything else you could think of. Classes are also used to define programming structures for collections and hierarchies of objects. A class provides the definition, or blueprint, for an object that is created by program code. If a programmer needed to represent a customer in memory, he would be able to create one by using the `Customer` class. Once created, it is known as an *instance* of the class. If you were learning to program with objects, this would be a very long and tedious, perhaps even philosophical, discourse about how you should use classes to implement object-oriented design patterns for designing software solutions. Luckily for you, as a database administrator using the SQL CLR, you won't be required to use classes at this level of depth. For our purposes, a *class* is merely a logical container for related program code.

Methods

Within classes, program code may define several things such as members, properties, structures, enumerations, events, and methods. For our purpose, the only thing really exposed to SQL Server is methods. In simple terms, a *method* is a function or procedure used to return values or structured data to its calling object. Just like a user-defined function in Transact-SQL, a method may accept any number of input parameters and return a value or some type of object.

SQL Server CLR Objects

We've survived for a long time without combining programming with databases. Business has driven technology (and, to some degree perhaps, technology has driven business) to the point where it's necessary to raise the bar. Business applications now require more than just the capability to put information into a database so that you can take it back out. Complex business processes require complex program logic, which goes beyond the scope of simple CRUD ("create, read, update, and delete") database operations.

For this reason, SQL Server 2008 allows five types of database objects (stored procedures, functions, triggers, aggregates, data types) that were traditionally defined either internally or in Transact-SQL code to now be created with .NET program code. This gives programmers and solution architects the ability to control the behavior of database operations and to provide advanced capabilities in the data storage layer of a solution.

SQL Server CLR objects are programming routines built into .NET assemblies that are stored and managed within a database. The execution of the objects occurs within the SQL Server process space, according to the rules and security context of the database and SQL Server. To behave well in this environment, certain restrictions apply:

❑ All assembly code must be type-safe. This means that all values exchanged between objects conform to standard data types and must be explicitly declared. The run time will not perform any implicit type conversion from one object to another if the types are not already compatible.

❑ Several class and method attributes have been added to support SQL CLR functionality, security, and features. Using unrelated attributes may render the assembly incompatible and not allow it to execute.

❑ All static (or shared) data members must be Read Only.

❑ SQL CLR doesn't support code with `Finalizer` methods. Assemblies containing this code will not be allowed to execute.

Only a subset of the .NET Framework is supported by the SQL CLR. Although unsupported assemblies can still be used by your code, you have to do a little extra work. All unsupported assemblies used must be imported into SQL Server. This makes using Visual Studio 2008 for deployment of your assembly a bit more difficult since it will only handle your assembly and not the unsupported assemblies. In fact, the Add Reference dialog will only show supported assemblies to prevent this problem. The following assemblies are the only supported assemblies for SQL CLR development:

❑ Microsoft.VisualBasic.dll

❑ Mscorlib.dll

- ❑ System.Data.dll
- ❑ System.dll
- ❑ System.Xml.dll
- ❑ Microsoft.VisualC.dll
- ❑ CustomMarshalers.dll
- ❑ System.Security.dll
- ❑ System.Web.Services.dll
- ❑ System.Data.SqlXml.dll
- ❑ System.Transactions.dll
- ❑ System.Data.OracleClient.dll
- ❑ Microsoft.SqlServer.Types.dll

Some Transact-SQL statements have been added to support new SQL CLR capabilities, and other statements have been updated. Generally, the CREATE and ALTER statements have been extended with provisions for the new programming paradigm. Some of these changes are noted in the following sections for the database objects supported by SQL CLR.

Enabling SQL CLR

The SQL CLR feature is disabled by default and must be explicitly enabled on the database server. This is done using the sp_configure System Stored Procedure. Pass the character value clr enabled in the first argument and the numeric value 1 (for True) in the second argument. The setting is then applied by executing the RECONFIGURE command after changing this setting. The following script demonstrates how this is done:

```
USE master
GO
sp_configure 'clr enabled', 1;
RECONFIGURE;
GO
```

The results of this command should look something like this:

```
Configuration option 'clr enabled' changed from 0 to 1.
Run the RECONFIGURE statement to install.
```

Creating a SQL CLR Assembly

To fully explore working with the SQL CLR, it would be helpful to have an assembly to work with. The following exercise guides you through the process of creating a simple function that will return the operating system version of the server when called from a T-SQL command:

1. To follow along with this exercise, you must have Visual Studio 2008 installed with C#. Open Visual Studio 2008, and create a new project by selecting New ➤ Project on the File menu (see Figure 14-1).

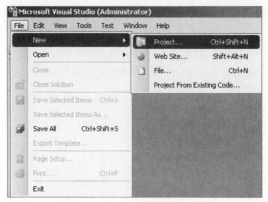

Figure 14-1: Starting a new project.

2. In the resulting New Project window (see Figure 14-2), expand the C# node, choose *Database* as the "Project type," and be sure the "SQL Server Project" is selected as the Template for the project. SQL Server projects are used to create all managed objects for SQL Server 2008 and can contain any combination of stored procedures, functions, aggregates, and triggers.

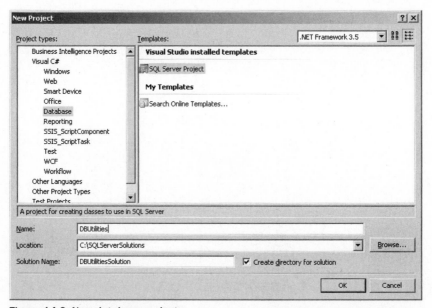

Figure 14-2: New database project.

3. By default, the solution has the same name as the project, but I changed it to make it a bit less redundant. Assign the project the name **DBUtilities**, the solution the name **DBUtilitiesSolution**, and click OK.

4. If connections have been created in Visual Studio from previous projects, you will be prompted to select one. If a connection object already exists for the `AdventureWorks2008` database (as shown in Figure 14-3), choose it. Otherwise, if a connection object does not exist for the needed database, you will need to create one by clicking on the "Add New Reference" button and supplying the appropriate values for a connection to the database, as shown in Figure 14-4.

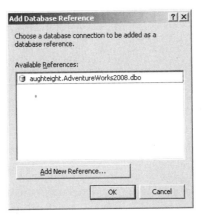

Figure 14-3: Add Database Reference.

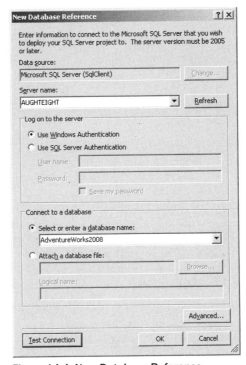

Figure 14-4: New Database Reference.

5. If this is a new connection or if SQL/CLR debugging has not been enabled previously on this connection, the message box shown in Figure 14-5 will appear. Click Yes to enable this feature.

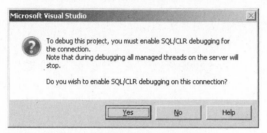

Figure 14-5: Enable SQL/CLR debugging.

6. If you didn't select a database connection during the creation of the project, don't fret. You can either select one or add one by clicking on the Browse button on the Database page of the Project Properties as shown in Figure 14-6. You can access this page by clicking Project ➤ DBUtilities Properties or by right-clicking DBUtilities in the Solution Explorer and selecting Properties. Again, if the connection hasn't been enabled for SQL/CLR debugging, you will be prompted to enable it.

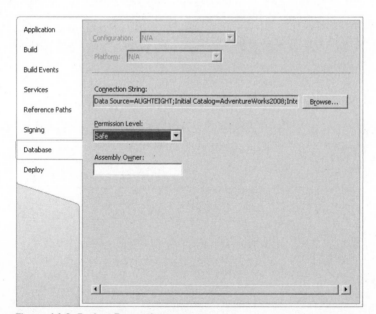

Figure 14-6: Project Properties page.

7. If you chose not to enable SQL/CLR debugging, you will not be able to use the debugging features of Visual Studio such as breakpoints and code step-through. You could later enable or disable SQL/CLR debugging on a connection by right-clicking on the connection in the Server Explorer window and selecting "Allow SQL/CLR Debugging," as shown in Figure 14-7.

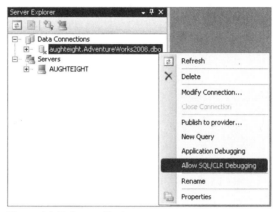

Figure 14-7: Server Explorer page.

8. You should now have an empty project with no objects. Database objects are added by either right-clicking on the project in Solution Explorer and choosing an object from the Add context menu, or by choosing an Add option from the Project menu (see Figure 14-8).

Figure 14-8: Adding a new item.

It really doesn't matter which approach you use, or for that matter which menu item you select. Clicking on any of the choices in the Project menu or the Add menu will launch the Add New Item dialog (see Figure 14-9). The only difference will be which template is initially selected. In this case, ensure that "User-Defined Function" is selected in the template pane, and give the function the name OSVersion.

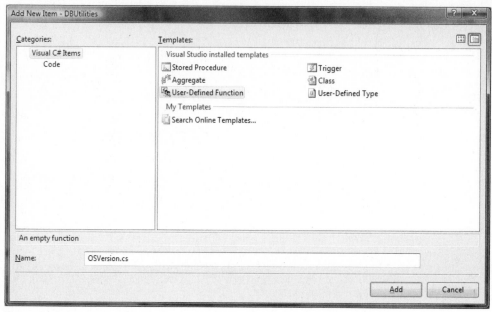

Figure 14-9: New Item dialog.

9. Creating any of the objects will generate the appropriate class or structure file in the Designer with a set of skeleton code to get you started. In the case of the function you just created, a simple class file will be added to the project. Figure 14-8 shows a new user-defined function code file added to a C# database project. Note the namespaces referenced in the using statements. These namespaces are either required or typically used in database projects. Also note the method attribute ([Microsoft.SqlServer.Server.SqlFunction]) that marks this function as a SQL CLR user-defined function.

10. To return the current version of the operating system, replace the code in the OSVersion method with the following code. Your screen should look like Figure 14-10 when completed.

```
return System.Environment.Version.ToString();
```

11. On the Build menu, click on the "Build DBUtilities" option to create the DLL that you will use in the following exercises. Note that another option is to "Deploy DBUtilities." Deploying the project will create the assembly and the function in the AdventureWorks2008 database. Because you want to explore this process more systematically, just build it for now.

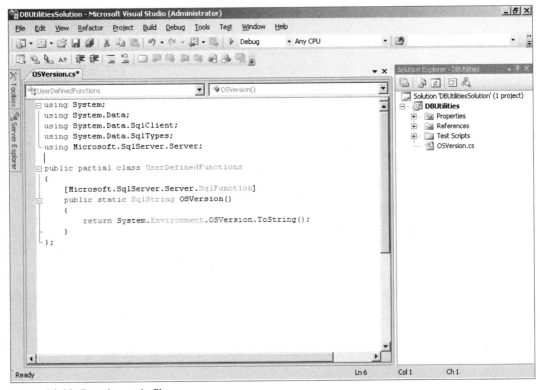

Figure 14-10: Function code file.

When I created the solution, I saved it to the C:\SQLServerSolutions folder and had Visual Studio create a new solution folder upon creation. As a result, the built DBUtilities.DLL file is now located in the C:\SQLServerSolutions\DBUtilitiesSolution\DBUtilities\bin\Debug folder. Next you'll explore how to add this assembly to the AdventureWorks2008 database and manage it.

Adding an Assembly

Prior to defining any SQL CLR object, the .NET assembly containing the executable code must be loaded into the database. This is performed with the CREATE ASSEMBLY statement. Note that the ALTER ASSEMBLY and DROP ASSEMBLY statements were also added for managing these objects. In its simplest form, the CREATE ASSEMBLY statement syntax is as follows:

```
CREATE ASSEMBLY <assembly name>
FROM <source file path>
WITH PERMISSION_SET = <permission set>
```

The following example shows this statement used to load the DBUtilities assembly file into the database. After this statement is executed, this file is no longer necessary because the executable code will be contained in a database object called ManagedUtilities.

```
USE AdventureWorks2008;
GO
CREATE ASSEMBLY DBUtilities
FROM
'C:\SQLServerSolutions\DBUtilitiesSolution\DBUtilities\bin\Debug\DBUtilities.dll'
WITH PERMISSION_SET = SAFE
```

The assembly contains only the code that will be executed; a SQL Server object is still needed to call from within T-SQL code. Once the assembly has been loaded into the database, you can create the T-SQL function that will be linked to the method within the assembly. Remember that assemblies can actually contain many objects, so one imported assembly can be referenced to create any number of new functions, stored procedures, aggregates, and types.

Compatible Data Types

As .NET programming procedures are defined and then integrated with SQL Server CLR objects, it is crucial that all data types be matched with compatible types. Most SQL Server data types have compatible equivalent native types in the .NET Framework. Note that variables, method arguments, and return values may be defined using either native .NET types or the data types defined within the System.Data.SqlTypes namespace. The types that are found in the System.Data.SqlTypes namespace are exact equivalents that map to each SQL Server type through internal wrapper code. Not all SQL Server types have compatible equivalents, though. If execution fails, reporting a type mismatch or invalid cast, you likely have an incompatible data type issue. The following table shows common SQL Server types with .NET equivalent types:

SQL Server Type	.NET Framework Type
bigint	Int64
binary	Byte[]
bit	Boolean
date	DateTime
datetime	DateTime
datetime2	DateTime2
datetimeoffset	DateTimeOffset
decimal	Decimal
float	Double
int	Int32
money	Decimal
nchar	String, Char[]
numeric	Decimal

SQL Server Type	.NET Framework Type
nvarchar	String, Char[]
real	Single
rowversion	Byte()
smalldatetime	DateTime
smallint	Int16
smallmoney	Decimal
sql_variant	Object
time	TimeSpan
tinyint	Byte
uniqueIdentifier	Guid
User-Defined Type	Same class that defines user-defined type
varbinary	Byte[]

User-Defined Functions

When a standard Transact-SQL user-defined function executes, SQL Server uses a work table to store intermediate values while a Table-Valued Function executes. In contrast, a SQL CLR function will use only available memory on the server to store intermediate rows and values. This doesn't necessarily mean that a SQL CLR function will always be faster because of the added overhead of calling into the .NET CLR. However, for complex operations and especially for larger result sets, using CLR-based functions may provide a significant performance edge over traditional functions.

To work with SQL CLR functions, the CREATE FUNCTION and ALTER FUNCTION statements have been extended. A SQL CLR function is created in the same manner as a traditional T-SQL function. The only real difference is that in place of the function body, there is a pointer to a method within an imported assembly. The following code creates the SQL CLR function for the OSVersion method in the assembly imported in the previous example:

```
USE AdventureWorks2008;
GO
CREATE FUNCTION dbo.GetOSVersion()
RETURNS nvarchar(255)
AS
EXTERNAL NAME DBUtilities.UserDefinedFunctions.OSVersion;
```

Scalar Functions

Outside of data access, there are some things that Transact-SQL just doesn't do very effectively. The mathematical, computational, and string-manipulation functions in Transact-SQL are limited and very basic when compared with classes in the .NET Framework.

Once the SQL CLR class has been loaded into memory and the necessary objects have been instantiated, the .NET function code should execute considerably faster than Transact-SQL. The performance improvement isn't as apparent in a simple demonstration because SQL CLR functions typically excel when used to perform complex operations on a large volume of data.

Table-Valued Functions

User-defined functions may be used to return table-valued result sets, much like a stored procedure or parameterized view. The implementation code for this type of function is quite a bit different from a standard .NET function or method routine. Because this is not a comprehensive programming reference, a simple example should serve to give you a starting point and introduce the concepts necessary to support this type of programming effort.

Two .NET methods are required to return a table-valued result set from a SQL CLR function. The first method is mapped to the SQL CLR function within the database, while the second method is used to populate each row of the result set. The first method, which is used to initialize the result set, must have a return type of IEnumerable. The [SqlFunction] attribute must set the FillRowMethodName property to the name of the second method and also define the table-valued result set with the TableDefinition property. Any discussion beyond this is out of the scope of this book. In other words, creating table-valued user-defined functions requires a bit of programming effort and must conform to a very specific pre-defined pattern to generate an appropriate table-valued result set. The following code is a simple example of a managed function that reads all entries from any event log on the system:

```
using System;
using System.Collections;
using System.Diagnostics;
using System.Data;
using System.Data.SqlClient;
using System.Data.SqlTypes;
using Microsoft.SqlServer.Server;

public partial class UserDefinedFunctions
{
    [Microsoft.SqlServer.Server.SqlFunction(
     FillRowMethodName = "FillRow",
     TableDefinition = "TimeWritten datetime,
                Message nvarchar(255),
                Category nvarchar(255),
                InstanceId bigint")]
    public static IEnumerable ReadEventLog(string logName)
    {
        return new EventLog(logName, Environment.MachineName).Entries;
    }

    public static void FillRow( object obj,
                                out DateTime timeWritten,
                                out string message,
                                out string category,
                                out long instanceId)
    {
```

```
        EventLogEntry eventLogEntry = (EventLogEntry)obj;
        timeWritten = eventLogEntry.TimeWritten;
        message = eventLogEntry.Message;
        category = eventLogEntry.Category;
        instanceId = eventLogEntry.InstanceId;
    }
}
```

Stored Procedures

Many of today's systems use a variety of extended stored procedures that call into COM components and other forms of unmanaged code. These are referred to as *extended stored procedures* and have been used for many years to perform operations that SQL Server doesn't provide out-of-the-box. The following are examples of operations that may have been performed using extended stored procedures and custom program code:

❑   Reading, writing, and manipulating files in the file system

❑   Interacting with the system event log

❑   Consuming data or services from a Web Service

❑   Interacting with the system registry

These extended stored procedures are great candidates for conversion to managed code. Aside from being a security risk and at times compromising system stability, some of these extended stored procedures may not be supported in future releases of SQL Server. Now, I don't suggest that you rush to replace all of your existing code, unless, of course, it's not working well or you have some other compelling reason to do so. However, you should make it a point to review these options and begin planning to make appropriate changes before it becomes a problem.

To create a SQL CLR stored procedure, simply add the `Microsoft.SqlServer.Server.SqlProcedure` attribute to any static method that returns either void or an int. The method used can accept any number of parameters. The following code is a simple method that is used to write an entry to the event log:

```
using System;
using System.Data;
using System.Diagnostics;
using System.Data.SqlClient;
using System.Data.SqlTypes;
using Microsoft.SqlServer.Server;

public partial class StoredProcedures
{
    [Microsoft.SqlServer.Server.SqlProcedure]
    public static void LogEvent(string message)
    {
        EventLog.WriteEntry("SQL Server 2008", message);
    }
};
```

Once the managed code is compiled and imported into the database, a T-SQL stored procedure must be created to point to the managed method. The syntax for creating a SQL CLR stored procedure from an assembly, in its simplest form, is as follows:

```
CREATE PROCEDURE <procedure name>
(<parameter list i.e. @Param1, @Param2...>)
AS EXTERNAL NAME <namespace.class.method>
```

The following example shows a stored procedure defined from a SQL CLR assembly called DBUtilities:

```
CREATE PROCEDURE LogInEventLog(@Message nvarchar(255))
AS EXTERNAL NAME DBUtilities.StoredProcedures.LogEvent
```

Triggers

Triggers are really just special stored procedures that instead of being executed by T-SQL code are executed automatically when certain database object actions occur. A trigger can be designated to execute for pretty much any action within SQL Server and for a variety of reasons. For tables, related triggers may execute when a record is inserted, updated, or deleted. Objects may have multiple triggers defined as well.

To create a SQL CLR trigger, the Microsoft.SqlServer.Server.SqlTrigger attribute simply needs to be applied to any static method. Because traditional triggers can't return any data or accept any parameters, the managed method should have a return type of void and require no arguments.

It is often useful to know the type of action the trigger is performing from the trigger code. The SqlTriggerContext class in the Microsoft.SqlServer.Server namespace can provide this type of information. This class provides a variety of useful metadata about the current trigger call. This object's properties include event data (such as the time, process ID, and event type), the trigger action (such as Insert, Update, or Delete), specific column update flags, and the count of affected columns.

The following is an example of a managed trigger that prevents the update of a record based on what the update value is:

```
using System;
using System.Data;
using System.Data.SqlClient;
using Microsoft.SqlServer.Server;
using System.Transactions;
using System.Text.RegularExpressions;

public partial class Triggers
{
    [Microsoft.SqlServer.Server.SqlTrigger(Name = "LogVendorModification",
            Target = "[Purchasing].[Vendor]",
            Event = "FOR UPDATE")]
    public static void LogVendorModification()
    {
        using (SqlConnection connection =
```

```
                        new SqlConnection(@"context connection=true"))
        {
            SqlCommand command;
            SqlDataReader reader;
            string emailAddress;

            // Open the connection.
            connection.Open();

            // Get the inserted value.
            command = new SqlCommand(@"SELECT PurchasingWebServiceURL
                                            FROM INSERTED", connection);
            reader = command.ExecuteReader();
            reader.Read();
            emailAddress = (string)reader[0];
            reader.Close();

            Regex regex =
                new Regex(@"\w+([-+.']\w+)*@\w+([-.]\w+)*\.\w+([-.]\w+)*");

            // Rollback transaction if invalid email address was inserted
            if (!regex.IsMatch(emailAddress))
                Transaction.Current.Rollback();

            // Close the connection.
            connection.Close();
        }
    }
```

Extensions have been made to the Transact-SQL standard for the CREATE and ALTER TRIGGER statements to support SQL CLR triggers. They are nearly identical to the traditional Transact-SQL counterparts, with the addition of the EXTERNAL NAME statement:

```
CREATE TRIGGER VendorAudit
ON Purchasing.Vendor
FOR UPDATE
AS EXTERNAL NAME DBUtilities.Triggers.LogVendorModification
```

User-Defined Types

User-defined types (UDTs) in Transact-SQL are not really user-defined data types — they are simply an alias for standard SQL Server data types. A UDT may be used to apply the correct data type and behaviors to many tables and columns in a database, but the Transact-SQL version of UDTs is very simple and extremely limited. User-defined types implemented through SQL CLR can be much more than just an aliased data type. They can enforce business logic rules and restrictions on data values. You can now apply a UDT to complex, structured data rather than just simple, scalar values.

In fact, Microsoft used SQL CLR UDTs when implementing many new features of SQL Server 2008. Both the Geography and Geometry data types in SQL Server 2008 are implemented using the SqlGeography and SqlGeometry data types, and the new HierarchyId data type uses the SqlHierarchyId data type, all of which are found in the Microsoft.SqlServer.Types assembly.

The most notable difference between a UDT and the previous database objects you have looked at is that a UDT is implemented as a structure or class, rather than as a method, in program code. The recommended technique is to use a .NET standard structure, rather than a class. Structures are similar to classes, but don't have to be instantiated in the same way that objects are. The following is the auto-generated C# code created by adding a new UDT called Point in a Visual Studio Database project:

```csharp
using System;
using System.Data;
using System.Data.SqlClient;
using System.Data.SqlTypes;
using Microsoft.SqlServer.Server;

[Serializable]
[Microsoft.SqlServer.Server.SqlUserDefinedType(Format.Native)]
public struct Point : INullable
{
    public override string ToString()
    {
        // Replace the following code with your code
        return "";
    }

    public bool IsNull
    {
        get
        {
            // Put your code here
            return m_Null;
        }
    }

    public static Point Null
    {
        get
        {
            Point h = new Point ();
            h.m_Null = true;
            return h;
        }
    }

    public static Point Parse(SqlString s)
    {
        if (s.IsNull)
            return Null;
        Point u = new Point();
        // Put your code here
        return u;
    }

    // This is a place-holder method
    public string Method1()
    {
```

```
        //Insert method code here
        return "Hello";
    }

    // This is a place-holder static method
    public static SqlString Method2()
    {
        //Insert method code here
        return new SqlString("Hello");
    }

    // This is a place-holder field member
    public int var1;
    // Private member
    private bool m_Null;
}
```

In this example, the Point type is used to manage the *x* and *y* coordinates within a coordinate system. A number of standard methods are used to provide common functionality. For example, the ToString(), IsNull(), and Parse() methods are common for most .NET types implemented as SQL CLR objects and provide the means for interrogating and returning a value.

Specific implementation code needs to be added to give this UDT its appropriate behavior. For example, the Parse() method is used when converting a string value to a UDT. In our Point UDT, this may include the validation of the value and breaking it up into its parts such as *x* and *y*. The ToString() method is called when the values need to be displayed to the user and can be used for formatting the value. The following is the final, working code for the Point UDT:

```
using System;
using System.Data;
using System.Data.SqlClient;
using System.Data.SqlTypes;
using Microsoft.SqlServer.Server;
using System.Text.RegularExpressions;

[Serializable]
[Microsoft.SqlServer.Server.SqlUserDefinedType(Format.Native)]
public struct Point : INullable
{
    private int x;
    private int y;
    private bool isNull;

    public override string ToString()
    {
        return string.Format("{0}, {1}", this.x, this.y);
    }

    public bool IsNull
    {
        get
```

```
            {
                return this.isNull;
            }
        }

        public static Point Null
        {
            get
            {
                Point point = new Point();
                point.isNull = true;

                return point;
            }
        }

        public static Point Parse(SqlString s)
        {
            string[] coordinates = s.ToString().Split(new char[] { ',' });

            Point point = new Point();
            point.x = Convert.ToInt32(coordinates[0]);
            point.y = Convert.ToInt32(coordinates[1]);

            return point;
        }

        public int X
        {
            get
            {
                return this.x;
            }
        }

        public int Y
        {
            get
            {
                return this.y;
            }
        }
    }
}
```

Once the assembly containing the UDT is imported into the database, you can create the SQL CLR object with the following T-SQL:

```
CREATE TYPE dbo.Point
EXTERNAL NAME DBUtilities.Point
```

It can now be used as any built-in data type is used. The following is an example of using the new Point data type:

```
DECLARE @p Point = '5,7'
SELECT @p.X AS X, @p.Y AS Y
```

Aggregates

Creating custom aggregations with managed code is a relatively complex process compared to what we have looked at so far. This is because multiple methods must be implemented that are called to build the aggregate value as the result set is populated. Throughout this process, the aggregate structure is initialized, values are added and may be merged with those previously collected, and then, finally, the resulting value is calculated and the structure is disposed of.

After the user-defined aggregate (UDA) assembly has been programmed, tested, and deployed to an external assembly, the database aggregation is defined using the following Transact-SQL syntax:

```
CREATE AGGREGATE [schema_name.]aggregate_name
        (@param_name <input_sqltype> )
RETURNS <return_sqltype>
EXTERNAL NAME assembly_name[.class_name]
```

Using the automated UDA feature in a Visual Studio SQL CLR project produces the following starting code:

```
using System;
using System.Data;
using System.Data.SqlClient;
using System.Data.SqlTypes;
using Microsoft.SqlServer.Server;

[Serializable]
[Microsoft.SqlServer.Server.SqlUserDefinedAggregate(Format.Native)]
public struct AverageWordCount
{
    public void Init()
    {
        // Put your code here
    }

    public void Accumulate(SqlString Value)
    {
        // Put your code here
    }

    public void Merge(AverageWordCount Group)
    {
        // Put your code here
    }

    public SqlString Terminate()
    {
        // Put your code here
        return new SqlString("");
    }

    // This is a place-holder member field
    private int var1;

}
```

As you see, four methods and one variable are defined by the template. Each of these methods has a specific purpose and may be called multiple times under certain conditions as a query is executed.

In SQL CLR UDAs, you define an initializing (Init) method that occurs on the start of a query's grouping (initiated by the SQL GROUP BY clause), an Accumulate method to aggregate new values within the grouping, and a Terminate method to return the final result. In addition, UDAs have a Merge method that the SQL Server engine may use when the optimizer chooses to implement the UDA with multiple threads. The Merge method combines the results of multiple instances of the UDA back into the parent thread to return a unified result. The ability to create custom aggregations allows you to add to a limited list of aggregation functions that are defined by the T-SQL language. This opens the possibility of making complex queries much easier to both write and understand. For example, imagine you require a list of CustomerIDs and the SalesOrderNumbers for each customer during a specific time frame. I know what you are thinking — that would be easy. But what I left out was that you need the SalesOrderNumbers returned as a semicolon-delimited string as shown in Figure 14-11. No longer is this a trivial query using just a T-SQL SELECT statement. Until user-defined aggregates, that is!

The following is a custom user-defined aggregate that produces the required output.

```
using System;
using System.Text;
using System.Data;
using System.Data.SqlClient;
using System.Data.SqlTypes;
using Microsoft.SqlServer.Server;

[Serializable]
[Microsoft.SqlServer.Server.SqlUserDefinedAggregate(Format.UserDefined,
MaxByteSize=4000)]
public struct Concatenate : IBinarySerialize
{
    private StringBuilder tempValue;

    public void Init()
    {
        this.tempValue = new StringBuilder();
    }

    public void Accumulate(SqlString inString)
    {
        if (inString.IsNull)
            return;

        this.tempValue.Append(inString.Value);
        this.tempValue.Append(";");
    }

    public void Merge(Concatenate group)
    {
        this.tempValue.Append(group.tempValue);
    }

    public SqlString Terminate()
    {
        if (this.tempValue != null && this.tempValue.Length != 0)
```

```
                return this.tempValue.ToString();
        else
                return new SqlString();
    }

    public void Read(System.IO.BinaryReader r)
    {
        this.tempValue = new StringBuilder(r.ReadString());
    }

    public void Write(System.IO.BinaryWriter w)
    {
        w.Write(this.tempValue.ToString());
    }
}
```

To use this custom user-defined aggregate, simply import the assembly and create the aggregate. The syntax for creating the SQL CLR aggregate for the previous example is as follows:

```
CREATE AGGREGATE dbo.Concatenate(@Value nvarchar(4000))
RETURNS nvarchar(4000)
EXTERNAL NAME DBUtilities.Concatenate;
```

It can then be used just as any built-in aggregate function is used. The following code uses the custom Concatenate aggregate function:

```
SELECT CustomerId, dbo.Concatenate(SalesOrderId) as SalesOrderNumbers
FROM Sales.SalesOrderHeader
GROUP BY CustomerId
```

	CustomerID	SalesOrderNumbers
1	13913	SO61756;
2	13914	SO56821;
3	13915	SO50532;SO53758;
4	13916	SO73071;
5	13917	SO50648;SO53706;
6	13918	SO73227;
7	13919	SO74353;
8	13920	SO55834;SO60980;SO62661;SO69590;
9	13921	SO67723;
10	13922	SO70780;
11	13923	SO55995;
12	13924	SO61059;

Figure 14-11: Results of using a custom aggregate.

Deployment with Visual Studio

In a previous exercise, you saw how to create a simple user-defined function using Visual Studio and how to add that assembly to SQL Server using the CREATE ASSEMBLY command. In the following sections, you will build on that exercise and explore additional features and capabilities of the Visual Studio Database Project.

Although it's important to understand how to import assemblies and create programming objects in SQL Server by referencing those assemblies, all of the SQL CLR objects can be developed, debugged, tested, and deployed from the Visual Studio development environment. I'll take you on a brief tour and step through this process. Once again, remember that this is not a book on programming, so I'm simply introducing the basic features. There are many elements to a complete solution, and considerations depend on the security restrictions and required access to external resources.

Follow these steps:

1. Drop the assembly and function created in earlier exercises. To do this, execute the following command:

```
USE AdventureWorks2008;
GO
DROP TYPE dbo.Point
DROP TRIGGER dbo.LogVendorModificationDROP PROCEDURE dbo.LogInEventLog;
DROP FUNCTION dbo.GetOSVersion;
DROP AGGREGATE dbo.Concatenate
DROP ASSEMBLY DBUtilities;
```

   If you created any of the other SQL CLR objects that we talked about, you will have to drop those as well before continuing.

2. Open the previous `DBUtilitiesSolution` solution.

3. You can set several optional properties for a project using the Project Property pages. For example, a digital signature can be added to the assembly. To view these tabbed dialogs, right-click on the DBUtilities project in the Solution Explorer tree, and select Properties. The Properties page has several tabs that enable the configuration of the project. The number of tabs will vary, depending on the installation of Visual Studio and add-ins such as Visual Source Safe 2005 or Visual Studio Team System. A fairly typical arrangement is shown in Figure 14-12.

4. To deploy the assembly directly to the database, you can right-click on the project in Solution Explorer and select Deploy from the menu or choose Deploy from the Build menu.

   This action saves the project, builds the assembly DLL file, adds the assembly to the database using the CREATE ASSEMBLY command, and executes the appropriate commands for all objects defined within the project. Visual Studio is actually using the attributes that we defined earlier on each method and class to determine what to execute. The attributes are not necessarily required by SQL Server but more so for Visual Studio to deploy the objects. After deploying the project, open SQL Server Management Studio to examine the newly created function and assembly.

5. Expand the `AdventureWorks2008` database, then the Programmability folder and Assemblies folder. Note that the `DBUtilities` assembly has been added. Expanding the Functions and "Scalar-valued Functions" folder in the Programmability folder will expose several functions, of which one is the `OSVersion` function just created by deploying the project with Visual Studio (see Figure 14-13).

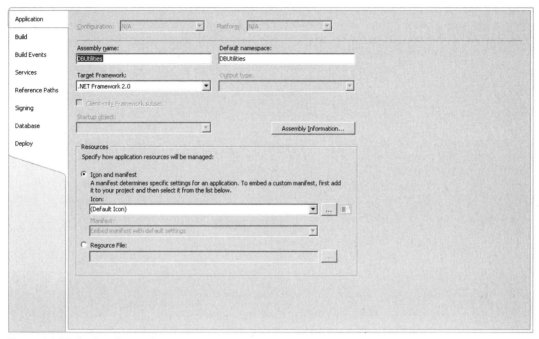

Figure 14-12: Project Properties page.

6. Test the function to make sure it works. Open a new Query window in Management Studio, and execute the following command:

```
USE AdventureWorks2008;
GO
SELECT dbo.OSVersion() AS OperatingSystemVersion;
```

You should see something similar to the following results:

```
OperatingSystemVersion---------------------
---------------------------------------
Microsoft Windows NT 6.0.6001 Service Pack 1
(1 row(s) affected)
```

Now, wasn't that easy! You will likely not have much use for an OSVersion function in your database, but it is not any more difficult to create very robust functions that execute complex mathematical calculations or complex string manipulation. Offloading these types of processes to the CLR will result in a great improvement over executing them with T-SQL.

As you can see, in an integrated environment where a developer has connectivity to the database server, Visual Studio can be used to manage the entire development, debugging, testing, and deployment cycle.

As an administrator, you will need to decide what level of access developers should have, which will determine just how simple and convenient this process may be for your development staff.

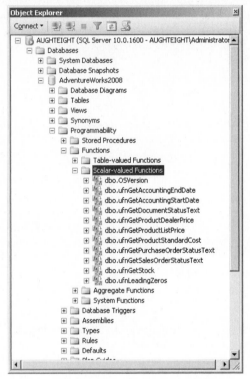

Figure 14-13: Deployed programming objects.

In a formal production environment, you may elect to set up a development database server and allow rights and connectivity for the developers to this machine. After objects have been properly tested and validated using the development server, you can either use these Visual Studio projects for deployment to production from the integrated development environment or execute Transact-SQL scripts manually. The object scripts can also be generated from the development server and then executed on the production server, saving you much of the manual scripting effort.

Now that you know how the SQL CLR object development process works, I'd like to spend the remainder of this chapter dealing with the common administrative tasks that you will need to understand to support these features in a production environment. I'll show you how to perform some of the same actions manually, and discuss some of the decisions you will need to make to maintain a safe and secure server to host SQL CLR objects and assemblies.

Programming Support

Taking database objects beyond the capabilities of Transact-SQL will require that your team understands the advantages afforded by using the .NET Framework and CLR. SQL Server already has strong features built in to take advantage of performance-enhancing features such as parallel code execution and explicit memory management. Solution designers and administrators see these capabilities as *black box features* and can do little to control the Database Engine's behavior. Programmers have the ability to work at a much lower level, and can determine how program code uses system resources under very specific conditions. The .NET CLR contains several security options. For example, program methods can be explicitly tagged to use external code known to be safe that might not otherwise be permitted to execute. Following are just a few common capabilities offered by custom code written for the .NET CLR.

Threading

The .NET Framework supports both implicit and explicit multi-threading. A *thread* is a distinct unit of execution that shares memory with the other threads in a process space. By spawning multiple threads of execution within an application, long-running code will not block the execution of another thread. Under the right conditions, this enables a component to perform multiple tasks in parallel with improved efficiency.

The SQL Server Database Engine is inherently multi-threaded, but threads are managed only by internal logic without input from the user or query designer. You can see evidence of this by viewing the execution plan for a complex query. Some steps in the plan will execute simultaneously. Buffers and in-memory tables may be used to synchronize the results of parallel operations. Again, this is a decision the Database Engine makes for you that may be influenced by the syntax of a query, but cannot be declared explicitly. In .NET program code, threads may be created either implicitly by using delegates, callbacks, and events, or explicitly by declaring and managing thread objects. Multi-thread programming can be a tricky business and often requires a high level of programming expertise.

Advanced programmers may use multi-threading to launch simultaneous operations. The results may be queued and then combined after all threads report completion. Because threads execute independently, some form of synchronization code must be used to determine when a threaded routine has completed. The overall effect, when used appropriately, may be a much faster set of coordinated operations.

Impersonation

Impersonation is the process of passing a security context from one area of execution to another, allowing access to multiple objects (which could exist in multiple components) having to authenticate only once. For example, say that a CLR stored procedure is executed (either interactively or by an automated process) and the procedure needs to write to the file system. Impersonation would copy the current user security context for the database object and apply it to the assembly and other related running code. SQL Server does not provide this for you, and it has to be done explicitly. In the context of this book, what is important to know is that when a SQL CLR object is executed, it will execute under the security context of the account that the SQL Server process is running unless programmed to impersonate the identity of the executing user.

Security Options

As a database system administrator, one of your primary concerns should be the safety and security of your server infrastructure. The very thought of allowing custom code to run on a production server may be enough to keep system administrators up at night. As an application developer, I've sat with many a database administrator, asking to have components installed, jobs scheduled, and script enabled to perform some task on a live server. In nearly every case, my code was viewed as a threat, and the administrator's job was to prevent *my* alien code from opening security holes on *his* server. I understand and fully embrace this as a working system of checks and balances. This works as long as coders understand the need for security restrictions and administrators appreciate the need to extend database and application functionality.

One of the first things you should know about .NET security from the beginning is that it is inherently designed to be safe right out-of-the-box and without additional configuration. Unlike many programming models in the past, default settings are restrictive and set to protect code from accessing volatile system resources and to prevent system invasion. That said, it is important that you understand what settings are necessary for program code to run and to have access to only the resources it needs to get the job done. You will likely be required to enable specific capabilities in order for CLR code to run on your servers. In addition to standard SQL Server permissions, there are two separate security measures that affect .NET code running within SQL CLR objects: one applied by SQL Server to restrict an assembly's freedom and one applied by the .NET run time itself.

.NET Security

Before any custom code can execute, the request must pass through many separate layers of authentication and permissions. First, any user request must be authenticated by Windows (assuming you are using Windows-integrated security in SQL Server), and then SQL Server must authenticate the user and grant object-level permission for the request. These measures apply to any database object and are not specific to an assembly. Next, the specific SQL CLR Permission Set, discussed in the next section, is checked to see whether SQL Server grants the assembly permission to use certain features of the .NET runtime classes and whether it can access any external resources. Finally, the assembly must satisfy the rules of Code Access Security (CAS), which is enforced by the .NET CLR. This security layer may also determine whether the assembly or certain class methods within the assembly can have access to external resources.

SQL CLR Permission Sets (managed by SQL Server) are applied to the assembly, which resides within the database and encapsulates SQL CLR database objects. These Permission Sets control what each object within the assembly is allowed to do (such as the file system, external data sources, and external managed or unmanaged components). This is the point of greatest potential risk and should be carefully planned and coordinated with application developers.

Securing SQL CLR

SQL CLR objects may be secured at different levels. After considering a user's access to the database server and permissions granted or denied within SQL Server to any objects, special execution permissions are set for SQL CLR objects. This gives an administrator a simple (but effective) blanket of control over each CLR object in the database. Without contending with the complexities of programming objects, SQL CLR Permission Sets simply allow you to enable varying levels of access to managed assemblies.

SQL Server CLR Permission Sets

To simplify the security model for assemblies added to a database, a set of three permission levels is defined within SQL Server. These are used to allow assemblies to have access to resources known to be safe. These settings are implemented by restricting the assembly's access to specific .NET Framework runtime system class libraries. The Permission Set is applied when a SQL CLR assembly is imported into the database. For example, the following code is used to import the DBUtilities assembly into the database and grant it the permission level of External Access:

```
USE AdventureWorks2008;
GO
CREATE ASSEMBLY DBUtilities
FROM
'C:\SQLServerSolutions\DBUtilitiesSolution\DBUtilities\bin\Debug\DBUtilities.dll'
WITH PERMISSION_SET = External_Access
```

The preceding command will fail with an "Assembly not authorized for PERMISSION_
SET = EXTERNAL_ACCESS" *error if certain criteria are not met, as described in the end of this section.*

SAFE *Permission*

This setting only allows safe .NET code to run in SQL CLR assemblies. You should use this setting when an assembly doesn't require the use of external data or components outside the SQL Server database server environment.

The SAFE Permission Set allows an assembly to execute with minimal permissions and to have access to only internal database resources and .NET classes that are known to be safe. Many of the .NET assemblies and even some classes have had some functionality disabled to prevent security work-arounds. In other words, the code can perform internal logic and access data from the local database server. The SAFE setting does not allow access to external data, nor to external resources (such as the file system, executables, or the system registry). Even though the use of this setting is fairly restrictive, this may be advantageous because the code has access to most of the .NET system classes and can process program logic beyond the capabilities of objects written in Transact-SQL. Beyond this, the SAFE permission setting will allow the code to perform most any task that would normally be granted to a SQL stored procedure or user-defined function. The SAFE Permission Set is the default Permission Set and is the recommended setting for SQL CLR assemblies.

External Access Permission

This setting is more permissive than the SAFE setting yet doesn't allow some of the more risky capabilities of the UNSAFE setting described later. Using the External_Access setting will allow an assembly to use .NET Framework class libraries to gain access to external system and network resources. These may include the local or remote file system, Active Directory, the system registry, logs, files, and external data sources. This setting will allow the code to send e-mail, use the Internet, and consume Web Services. The External_Access setting doesn't allow an assembly to call unmanaged code in any form, such as COM-based DLLs, ActiveX controls, and VBScript.

This is a useful and reasonably safe setting when used along with disciplined programming practices and thorough testing. Because the stability of .NET code is generally not a concern, an administrator's attention should be focused on ensuring that solution developers are accessing only essential resources, and that all code is tested and verified prior to being deployed to production servers.

UNSAFE *Permission*

The UNSAFE permission setting is at the opposite end of the permission spectrum and allows complete access to all of the .NET Framework classes. As such, code may access the file system, the system registry, network resources, and even the Internet. This setting also allows the assembly code to execute unmanaged components and executables.

Looking beyond security concerns for the moment, .NET code is generally stable because of the CLR's isolated process space and exception-handling model. Even if buggy code were to crash, the CLR would shut down the process gracefully without taking system processes with it. This built-in stability changes, however, when .NET code calls older, unmanaged code.

Before you get excited about using terms like *unsafe*, let's put this into perspective. We have had the capability to extend SQL Server's reach using external applications and components for several years in the form of command-line executables and extended stored procedures. Many trustworthy SQL Server solutions send e-mail messages using COM-based Collaboration Data Object (CDO) code or interact with the file system using external VBScript. Older custom, extended stored procedures are written in C++ and may use the MFC libraries. The point is that these are all examples of what is now called *unmanaged code* and fall into the category of *unsafe code* from the perspective of a SQL Server CLR object.

Using the UNSAFE setting to enable access to external resources isn't necessarily a bad thing. This just means that the .NET CLR can't guarantee that it's safe — you and your developers have to do that, just like many of us have been doing for the past 10 or 12 years. If you have existing components that your solution relies on that have been tested and verified to be safe, you can use the UNSAFE setting to call them from a CLR stored procedure, trigger, or user-defined function.

> *It is best practice to segregate code based on the required level of access. In other words, if one or two methods need the UNSAFE Permission Set, then they should be isolated into their own assembly. This prevents code from having a Permission Set that is not required just because another method within the assembly requires it.*

Enabling External Access and Unsafe Permissions

In order to set an assembly's permission level to External Access or UNSAFE, one of two conditions must be met. Either the database Trustworthy attribute must be True and the database owner has the EXTERNAL ACCESS ASSEMBLY or UNSAFE ASSEMBLY permission (the sa login does by default), or the assembly must be signed with a certificate or asymmetric key and that key is mapped to a login with the EXTERNAL ACCESS ASSEMBLY or UNSAFE ASSEMBLY permission. If either of these conditions is not met, any attempt to change the Permission Set of the assembly will fail with the error shown in Figure 14-14. Following the principle of least privilege, the recommended configuration is the use of a certificate or key and not to set the Trustworthy attribute to True if the only requirement is to allow CLR objects greater access. See Chapter 6 for more information on SQL Server certificates and asymmetric keys.

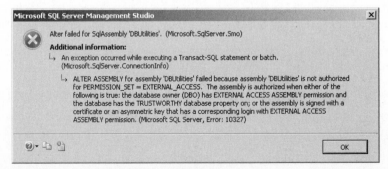

Figure 14-14: Unauthorized assembly error.

Summary

As a system administrator, you probably have your hands full with servers and databases that need to be stable and secure. Adding custom programming components to the mix has always been risky business, not to mention one more thing to worry about affecting your corporate infrastructure. Your task should be to minimize this risk and support only components that are easy to manage, and those that will play fairly with other applications. The .NET-managed Common Language Runtime (CLR) offers greater peace-of-mind with little risk of affecting anything else running on your servers.

Adding custom-programmed objects to your database opens a whole new world of opportunity for SQL Server users, developers, and administrators. SQL CLR takes database object security to the next level with a simple, integrated model. Executable assemblies reside in a SQL Server database rather than the file system. Database programming objects (such as stored procedures, triggers, types, user-defined functions, and aggregates) run as compiled .NET program code within the SQL Server processing space.

Applications developed with .NET-managed code are inherently secure and offer many choices for component configuration and flexibility, but along with these options comes a great deal of complexity. The SQL CLR security model makes security very simple by distilling the task of securing an object to three basic settings. As an administrator, you decide whether to allow an object to execute only code known to be absolutely safe to access external resources, or whether to let down your defenses to allow potentially unsafe code run. The latter choice allows you to depend on and trust the capable (but more complicated) features of .NET code access security. For most objects, trusting only safe code will be sufficient, and your task remains simple and uncomplicated. However, more sophisticated custom code objects may require a greater investment of knowledge and skill. In such cases, you will likely need to work closely with application developers to make appropriate trade-off decisions to provide the right functionality for your users, along with a manageable level of security for your peace-of-mind.

An Administrator's Guide to Business Intelligence

As I mentioned in Chapter 1, SQL Server 2008 is much more than a relational Database Engine. SQL Server 2008 is really a data platform that provides tools for collecting, manipulating, moving, analyzing, and presenting information. The next three chapters will introduce you to the specific services and technologies that compose SQL Server's Business Intelligence (BI) toolset.

If you're new to database administration or just new to SQL Server Administration, you might not have had much exposure to BI technologies and methods. Speaking from experience, my background has primarily been in Systems and Network Administration. Business Intelligence had never been part of my vocabulary until the last couple of years. I wanted to write this chapter for those of you who, like myself, had little exposure to BI, but are suddenly involved in a BI project or initiative.

This chapter will begin with an introduction to Business Intelligence, as well as define *Performance Management*. Then, you will learn how the different components in the Microsoft BI stack can be used to help business users get more from their data. In addition to talking about SQL Server, there are two other products that bear mentioning in this chapter, as well — Microsoft Office SharePoint Server (MOSS) 2007 and Microsoft Office PerformancePoint Server (PPS) 2007. Finally, this chapter will end with a summary of the database administrator's role in a BI initiative.

Understanding BI

Not everyone uses the same definition of *Business Intelligence*, but most of them agree on the basic concepts. *Business Intelligence* is defined as a set of tools, applications, and business practices for collecting data used in decision support systems, analytical processing, and reporting.

So what does that mean? Sometimes it's hard to talk about Business Intelligence without sounding like you're just mixing up "word salad." Business Intelligence is really about collecting data, and getting information from that data that can help you make better business decisions. For a finance department, that might include identifying where the company can afford to cut costs, increase revenue, or make better investment decisions. An IT or Operations Department might analyze information about their response time to customer requests, the amount of time it takes to complete a service request, and the level of customer satisfaction with the services delivered.

A misconception about Business Intelligence is that it's all about numbers. The truth is, it's all about facts. Facts may be measured or scored using numbers, but a number without context is just a number. Business Intelligence is about putting meaning behind these numbers and allowing that meaning to be shared and understood.

Performance Management

Performance Management is the process by which a set of objectives is defined, and actual performance is monitored, analyzed, and compared to these defined targets using a combination of management, methodologies, and information technology. Performance Management is often considered a subset of BI that can be used to measure progress toward clearly defined goals. In fact, it's not uncommon to see Performance Management objectives included as part of an overall BI initiative.

An effective Performance Management strategy will address five key questions that can be answered through planning, monitoring, and analysis. These key questions are:

- ❑ What has happened?
- ❑ What is happening?
- ❑ Why?
- ❑ What will happen?
- ❑ What do I want to happen?

Answering these questions can be done through monitoring, analysis, and planning, and although SQL Server includes several features that can help perform these tasks, Microsoft Office PerformancePoint Server is a product that is geared specifically to address these questions.

Business Intelligence Components

Now that you understand what Business Intelligence and Performance Management are, you should learn a little bit about the tools that are used to create and manage a BI solution. This section will provide you with a high-level overview of how the Microsoft BI components are used. This includes defining the roles of SQL Server Integration Services, SQL Server Analysis Services, and SQL Server Reporting Services, as well as how MOSS and PPS fit into the BI stack.

Data Goes In, Data Comes Out

OLTP databases are very good at writing and storing data. High transaction-processing applications such as point-of-sale systems need to be able to insert and update information very quickly. As you may have read in Chapter 11, OLTP databases are often *normalized*, meaning that duplication and redundancy of data are kept to a minimum. This makes it very easy to perform INSERT, UPDATE, and DELETE operations.

However, you might want to retrieve information that uses actual names, for example, you have to perform JOIN operations on several tables to be able to present the information in a readable fashion, not to mention additional operations that might need to be performed to ensure that only the relevant data is returned. In this case, data retrieval might be a costly operation that could cause bottlenecks in system performance, preventing Write operations from occurring.

The best plan of action would be to move data into another database designed for Read performance. This is where SQL Server Integration Services comes in. As you will read in Chapter 16, SSIS is an *Extract-Transform-Load* (ETL) service application. As the moniker suggests, you can use Integration Services to *extract* data from a data source. If the destination has specific requirements that the source data does not yet conform to, an ETL application will allow the data to be *transformed* prior to reaching its destination. Finally, once the data conforms to the target database requirements, the data is *loaded* into the destination database.

Analyze This!

While Chapter 17 will go into greater details about the tools and features of Analysis Services, this section will help you understand where SQL Server Analysis Services fits into the Microsoft BI Stack. As the name suggests, Analysis Services includes the ability to create and manage Online Analytical Processing (OLAP) databases. OLAP databases are used to create multi-dimensional storage objects, known as *cubes*, which allow data to be quickly retrieved using a variety of criteria. For example, if someone asked you to provide the sales revenue and total number of units of the BK-T18Y-62 Touring Bike sold by Linda Mitchell in Phoenix, AZ from October 2007 through December 2007, you would have to write one heck of a query. You'd have to join quite a few tables in your query to get that information, but it could be done. Of course, the minute you provide them with that information, they will then follow up with a request for the day-to-day sales numbers.

An easier way to provide access to this information is by building a *cube*, which allows data to be stored across a variety of hierarchically structured facets known as *dimensions*. Storing the data this way optimizes it for data retrieval, which makes it easier to analyze and report against. Also, the hierarchical nature of the dimensions makes it easier to break the data apart into smaller chunks through a process known as *slicing*. This allows a user who might be looking at monthly data to slice a month into smaller pieces like weeks or days.

Often, Analysis Services Databases are part of a corporate strategy to build a *data warehouse*. As the name suggests, data warehousing is about building an enterprise-wide data collection that can be used to get better insight into company performance. There are two competing schools of data warehousing methods. Ralph Kimball, a leading expert in data warehousing, favors a bottom-up approach that proposes building a warehouse by creating a series of smaller *data marts*. These data marts contain smaller subsets of multi-dimensional data that when grouped together help form the larger data warehouse. This is also (for obvious reasons) referred to as the *Kimball Method*.

The *Inmon Method*, named after Bill Inmon, one of the premier authors on data warehousing, favors a top-down approach. In this case, all data is built into a single data repository first, and that data can be provisioned into smaller data marts, which would be used for specific business processes. The "right" method for building a data warehouse is going to depend on the specific business needs of your organization.

For more information on applying the Kimball Method using Microsoft SQL Server, I recommend The Microsoft Data Warehouse Toolkit: With SQL Server 2005 and the Microsoft Business Intelligence Toolset *by Joy Mundy and Warren Thornthwaite (Wiley, 2006). If you're interested in the Inmon approach, check out* Building the Data Warehouse, *4th ed., by W.H. Inmon (Wiley, 2005).*

Did You Get the Memo about Cover Pages?

While Analysis Services provides a mechanism for being able retrieve business data quickly, there is no true Analysis Services "client tool" that is part of the SQL Server Product Suite. Technically, you could deploy SQL Server Management Studio and Business Intelligence Development Studio to your users' desktops and let them write their own ad hoc MDX queries against relational and multi-dimensional databases, respectively; however, that is far from a recommended solution. Microsoft Office Excel 2007 includes the ability to browse SSAS cubes as pivot tables and pivot charts, but that will have to be purchased and licensed separately, and it may not meet all of your business needs for performing analytics.

This is where SQL Server Reporting Services can come in handy. SSRS, covered in more detail in Chapter 18, allows you to create dynamic, interactive reports. The level of customization and flexibility is both a blessing and a curse. Using Visual Studio (or BIDS, if you prefer) is not something the average user will want to learn in order to create useful reports; however, developers have practically limitless design options for building reports that are both useful and aesthetically pleasing. SQL Server 2008's Reporting Services provide several new features for creating and managing reports.

If you find BIDS to be too intimidating for the average end-user who wants to build a simple report, you might find yourself in good company. Shortly after the release of SQL Server 2008, Microsoft released a new client tool for building reports, which they called *Report Builder 2.0*. The new Report Builder provides an easier-to-manage interface for creating a variety of reports.

Beyond SQL

One can't argue with the fact that SQL Server 2008 includes a rich set of tools for creating and managing a BI solution. If it has one failing, however, it is the fact that these tools are very developer-centric. While developers who are building a BI solution may find Business Intelligence Development Studio a very comfortable and familiar environment, it won't help the end-user who needs to perform ad hoc analysis or be able to generate interactive dashboards and scorecards. As a database administrator, it's important that you get at least a basic introduction to these tools, and the features that they offer, so that you can support them appropriately.

The BI Side of SharePoint

SharePoint is the product that just keeps on giving. You may already be familiar with some of the more heavily used features of SharePoint, such as its document management and collaboration tools. The Enterprise Edition of Microsoft Office SharePoint Server (MOSS) 2007 also includes a number of features for building dashboards and defining Key Performance Indicators (KPI).

MOSS 2007 also includes a SharePoint site template known as the *Report Center*. The Report Center is designed to be the intranet repository for creating and publishing dashboards, KPIs, and reports generated from SSRS or other applications. Another compelling feature of MOSS 2007 is Excel Web Services, which provides Read Only access to spreadsheets for clients that may not have the full Excel client installed. Because Excel Web Services is designed to look and feel like the rich Excel client, it includes the same `PivotTable` and `PivotChart` functions that users may already be using to browse and report against Analysis Services cubes.

ProClarity and PerformancePoint Server

In 2006, Microsoft acquired ProClarity Corp., makers of ProClarity Analytics Server and ProClarity Desktop Professional. ProClarity's product line includes tools for performing advanced analysis and visualizations of business data. Some of the more advanced visualization ProClarity offers are Performance Maps (also known as *Heat Maps*) and Decomposition Trees. One of the key benefits of the ProClarity tools is the benefit to publish these charts and graphs as interactive analytics that allow users to get more detailed information as they drill into the reports.

After the acquisition of ProClarity, Microsoft decided to integrate some of the features of ProClarity with its own Business Scorecard Manager (BSM), to create a new monitoring and analytics product known as *Microsoft Office PerformancePoint 2007*. PerformancePoint is actually several products in one. The first, the Monitoring Server, is centered around the creation and management of interactive dashboards that allow you to publish several reports, charts, and scorecards on one or more dashboard pages.

Although the PerformancePoint Monitoring Server includes several features that operate best when using a multi-dimensional data source like an Analysis Services cube, it also supports the use of SQL Server tables and views, Excel files, and SharePoint lists as additional data sources. PerformancePoint dashboards are designed to be published to a SharePoint document (or report) library. Because of its tight integration with SharePoint, it allows publishing reports from other applications as additional web parts in a dashboard page. For example, a PerformancePoint dashboard page might contain a scorecard, a ProClarity Performance Map, and a SQL Server Reporting Services Report that all provide information about a particular business unit or division.

In addition to the Monitoring Server, PerformancePoint includes another server component known as the *Planning Server*. The Planning Server is a unique offering from Microsoft that is designed to support building budgeting and forecasting scenarios. Although the use of the Planning Server is not limited to financial applications, it includes a number of Financial Intelligence (FI) features that support Generally Accepted Accounting Principles (GAAP) and International Financial Reporting Standards (IFRS).

The Planning Server is designed with the end-user in mind. Although there are some components that will require DBA or developer intervention, for the most part, the goal of a Planning Server implementation is to allow finance and other budget managers to have a tool they can use for building and managing their own data. What is somewhat unique about the Planning Server is the fact that it manages and maintains both the OLTP and OLAP databases that are used to store the data. Users can build their own data marts by defining the structure and properties of the models, which represent an Analysis Services cube.

The third component of the PerformancePoint Server is the PerformancePoint Management Reporter. As another offering in Microsoft's BIPM solution stack, the Management Reporter is designed to be a financial report-building tool. This includes templates and features for building some of the more common financial report types such as Cash Flow, Income Statement, and Balance Sheet reports. The Management Reporter is actually a re-design and re-branding of the Microsoft Dynamics and Microsoft FRx financial management reporting tool, which includes new features designed specifically to allow reporting against a PerformancePoint Planning Server data application.

Shortly before publication of this book, Microsoft had announced a new Microsoft BI roadmap, which unfortunately no longer includes PerformancePoint as a separate product; however, the Monitoring and Analytic components of PPS are expected to be added to the next version of SharePoint.

So Many Tools, So Little Time

It can be easy for a DBA, even a seasoned one, to be overwhelmed by the different BI offerings from Microsoft and other vendors. Quite often, I am asked by my clients what the best tool or solution is. Unfortunately, there is no absolutely right or wrong answer. The answer will vary based on what the business needs are, what the IT Department is capable of delivering, and what the total cost of ownership is for the applications and solutions that are being considered.

It is important to know that the role of a DBA can be, and sometimes is, more than just administering and maintaining a database server environment. A good DBA will also be able to understand the business needs being addressed by the applications their database server depends on. When you understand the data and understand the business value of the data, you can be more proactive about ensuring the integrity as well as the safety and security of said data.

Understanding Microsoft's BI offerings, and how they can meet the needs of your business, will also help you make the right decisions and provide good insight into which products have the lowest total cost of ownership and offer the greatest return on investment. It's also important to understand that Microsoft SQL Server 2008 is the foundation for all of these applications, which can help make the case for upgrading or migrating to SQL Server 2008.

If you're interested in learning more about Microsoft's Business Intelligence roadmap, you can find more information at www.microsoft.com/bi. There, you will also find a BI IT Solution Accelerator, to help IT departments use Business Intelligence to gain insight into their performance.

Summary

Business Intelligence is more than just a buzzword that gets thrown around by marketing people. It's about using a set of tools and practices to help add context to the data you already collect. BI tools can allow you to identify trends that you might have otherwise missed if you hadn't charted them in a line graph. Or it can help you identify which areas of your business need the most improvement, and where you're succeeding.

Database administrators play a key role in any Business Intelligence initiative because they will ultimately be responsible for the core services on top of which these application components run. Your role may be limited to just supporting the database. It may also include supporting and helping design solutions around analysis tools, reporting tools, and visualization tools.

This chapter sets the tone for the topics that you will be reading about in the next three chapters. You will begin by reading about SQL Server Integration Services in Chapter 16, and learn about the methods for moving and manipulating data. From there, you will learn more about Analysis Services and Reporting Services in the chapters following Chapter 16.

Introduction to SQL Server Integration Services

An important part of any Business Intelligence solution is moving the data from a source environment that isn't optimized for analysis into one that is. Sometimes this process can be straightforward; at other times, you will need to make structural or formatting changes to ensure that the data has value. This is known as the *ETL process*.

The *Extract, Transform, and Load (ETL) process* can be managed through a SQL Server service known as *SQL Server Integration Services*, or SSIS for short. This chapter will cover the basics of SSIS in SQL Server 2008. The following topics will be covered:

❑ A general introduction to SSIS and its features

❑ The import and export tools used to move data around

❑ The different options for transforming data using SSIS

About SSIS

Prior to SSIS in SQL Server 2005, SQL Server included a lightweight ETL product known as *Data Transformation Services* (DTS). Although DTS was a useful tool for moving data from one location to another, it was prohibitively difficult for many administrators who lacked significant programming or scripting skills to perform complex transformations. SSIS builds on the basic principles of DTS, but expands its capabilities to include additional, easier-to-manage, features.

Integration Services is part of a suite of tools included in the Business Intelligence Development Studio. As you may have read earlier, BIDS is simply an instance of Visual Studio, which includes add-ins for designing solutions for Integration Services, Analysis Services, and Reporting Services. One of the benefits of using BIDS is that it allows you to develop Integration Services solutions without having to maintain an active connection to an existing SQL Server. This gives you the flexibility to design solutions that can run on multiple servers or can be executed from a file system.

The ETL process, in its most simple definition, begins by defining a data source. From that data source, you define which data you are interested in copying to a new destination. As the data is being retrieved from the source, you may need to perform one or more transformations on the data to prepare it for its destination. For example, you may want to take a column that stores a string value that is either "True" or "False" into a Boolean value, "1" or "0," respectively. This allows you to match the current data type of the destination. Finally, the load sequence takes the transformed data and injects it into the appropriate destination.

SQL Server Integration Services is actually made up of four different components:

- ❑ Integration Services itself
- ❑ Integration Services object model
- ❑ Integrated Services run time
- ❑ Integrated Services data flow

Each of these components is used to create a robust experience for designing, managing, and executing packages built for SSIS. In the next few sections, you learn about each of these components.

Integration Services

Integration Services itself is actually managed through SQL Server Management Studio, not unlike many of the other SQL Server components. This component is used to handle the management and monitoring of both stored and running packages. Packages can be stored in the file system or they can be stored in the msdb database on a running instance of SQL Server 2008.

> Integration Services, when installed, assumes that the local default instance contains the msdb database that will be used for the package repository. However, because SQL Server 2008 can coexist with older versions of SQL Server installed on the same machine, it is possible that your default instance is running a legacy version of SQL Server. If this is the case, you must manually edit the <ServerName> element in the MSDtsSrvr.ini.xml file to reflect the correct instance name of your server. This file is in the 100\DTS\Binn directory of your SQL Server installation folder.

You can use SQL Server Management Studio to connect to an instance of SSIS, as shown in Figure 16-1. The following is a list of Integration Services features that can be managed through SQL Server Management Studio:

- ❑ Connect to multiple Integration Services servers.
- ❑ Manage package storage.
- ❑ Customize storage folders.
- ❑ Import and export packages.
- ❑ Start local and remote stored packages.
- ❑ Stop local and remote running packages.
- ❑ Monitor local and remote running packages.
- ❑ View the Windows Event log.

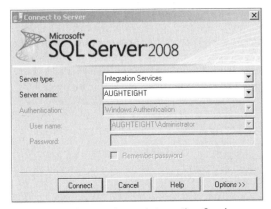

Figure 16-1: Connecting to Integration Services.

Once you've connected to Integration Services, you can manage packages using Object Explorer, as shown in Figure 16-2.

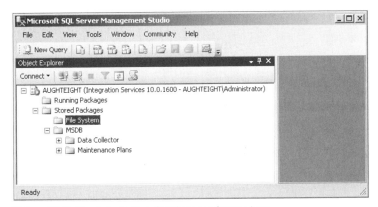

Figure 16-2: The Integration Services package store.

From Object Explorer, you can create additional folders for organizing your packages, import or export packages to the package stores, and execute packages or stop packages. You can also upgrade SQL Server 2005 packages to SQL Server 2008 using the SSIS Package Upgrade Wizard.

Integration Services Object Model

Integration Services includes a new object model for including both native and managed application programming interfaces (APIs) for customizing the behavior of your Integration Services solutions. You can use these APIs for accessing SSIS tools, command-line functions, or custom applications. You can also use the object model for executing SSIS tools and packages from within your own applications. The Integration Services object model will support any language that is compliant with the Common Language Runtime (CLR), described in Chapter 14.

Integration Services Run Time

The Integration Services runtime engine is responsible for saving the control flow logic and execution of SSIS packages. Integration Services runtime executables include packages, containers, pre-defined and custom tasks, and event handlers. The run time handles execution order, logging, variables, and event handling. Programming the Integration Services runtime engine allows you to automate the creation, configuration, and execution of packages through the object model.

Integration Services Packages

Packages are units of execution that are composed of a series of other elements, including containers, tasks, and event handlers. You can create and manage packages through Business Intelligence Development Studio or programmatically using the Integration Services object model. Each package contains a *control flow*, which is a series of tasks (related or not) that will execute as a unit. Similar to jobs in the SQL Server Agent Service (see Chapter 8), Integration Services packages use a customizable logic flow that controls the timed or constrained execution of individual tasks. An Integration Services project may contain multiple packages, and some packages may be instantiated by other packages in the same project or solution.

Integration Services Tasks

Tasks are the basic unit of work within an Integration Services package. Each task defines an action that will be taken as part of the execution of this package. Some of the basic task types include the Execute SQL task, in which a T-SQL script will be executed; a file system task, which interacts with a local or remote file system; and data flow tasks, which control how data is copied between a source and a destination. Many other types of tasks are discussed later in this chapter.

Integration Services Containers

Containers are objects that exist within the Integration Services environment to allow you to define one or more tasks as a unit of work. You can use containers to define parameters for the execution of these tasks. Four types of containers are available, and you learn more about them later in this chapter.

Integration Services Event Handlers

Event handlers are similar to packages, in that within them, you can define tasks and containers. One major difference, though, is that event handlers are reactionary. This means that the tasks defined within an event handler will only be executed when a specific event occurs. These events are defined on tasks, containers, or the package itself and include events that are fired before, during, and after the execution of the package.

Integration Services Data Flow

One of the most significant benefits of the SSIS features is the separation of the control flow from the *data flow*. Each package that contains a data flow task (such as an import or export) will identify that there is a data flow task to the runtime engine, but a separate data flow engine is invoked for that task. The data flow engine manages what is typically the whole point of an SSIS package, and that is extracting, transforming, and loading data. The data flow engine will extract data from data files or relational databases, manage any and all transforms that manipulate that data, and then provide that transformed data to the destination. A package may have more than one data flow task, and each task will execute its own data flow process for moving and manipulating data.

Importing and Exporting Data

One of the easiest ways to understand SSIS and to see it in action is through the Import/Export Wizard, which can be run from the Management Studio. The process is essentially the same for both operations. The primary difference between the import operation and the export operation is whether your SQL Server is the source or the destination. It should be noted, however, that SSIS doesn't need to use a SQL Server as either the source or the destination! You can use SSIS to import data from a flat-file source (such as a comma-separated value file) into a Microsoft Access database.

Using the Import Wizard

In this example, you use a simple comma-separated value (CSV) file that contains a list of additional promotions the AdventureWorks sales team will use for 2007. The contents of this file will then be imported into the `Sales.SpecialOffer` table. Begin by creating a folder on the root of your C: drive called *SSISDemos*. Create a new text file in this folder, and enter the following data into the text file:

```
Description,DiscountPct,Type,Category,StartDate,EndDate
President's Day Sale,0.1,Holiday Promotion,Customer,2/16/2007,2/19/2007
Memorial Day Madness,0.25,Holiday Promotion,Customer,5/28/2007,5/28/2007
Fourth of July Sale,0.05,Holiday Promotion,Customer,7/1/2007,7/7/2007
Seasonal Discount,0.075,Seasonal Discount,Reseller,10/1/2007,10/31/2007
```

Save the file as **Promos.csv**, and then follow these steps:

1. Start or open SQL Server Management Studio. Connect to the Database Engine.

2. In Object Explorer, select your server and expand Databases.

3. Right-click AdventureWorks2008 and select Tasks ➤ Import Data. This will launch the SQL Server Import and Export Wizard. As with many other wizards in SQL Server Management Studio, you can elect to not see the introductory page of the Wizard in the future.

4. Click Next to move to the Data Source selection page.

On this page, you can select the data source that will be used for the import process. Figure 16-3 shows the data source as you will configure it for this exercise. You should note that the options in the window will change to reflect the parameters of whichever data source you choose. Also note that several connection providers are already available out-of-the-box from SQL Server 2008, including the SQL Native Client, OLE DB providers for Analysis Services and Oracle, and Microsoft Office Excel and Access file formats, with support for the new Office 2007 XML-based file types.

Now, follow these steps to configure the data source:

1. Select "Flat File Source" as your data source.

2. In the "File name" box, you can enter the path to the file you created earlier (C:\SSISDemos\Promos.csv), or you can use the Browse button to find the file. Note that if you use the Browse button, it defaults to the .txt file extension, and you must select ".csv" from the dropdown list.

3. Based on the contents of the file, it should recognize the correct locale, code page, and format. You should select the "Column names in the first data row" checkbox because you have included the header row in your file.

4. Click Next on the Data Source selection page to take you to the Columns page.

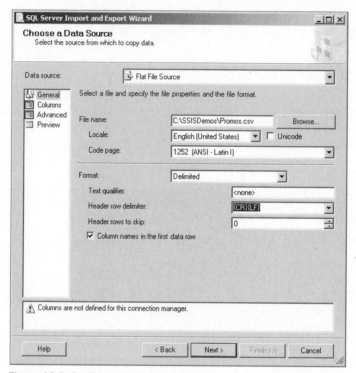

Figure 16-3: Configuring a flat-file data source.

This page, as shown in Figure 16-4, allows you to configure the row and column delimiters that are used in your flat file source. For example, if you used a pipe character (|) instead of a comma, you could enter that into the "Column delimiter" field.

This window also provides you with a columnized preview window of the data source, so that you can verify the configuration of the data source provider. If the columns appear to be misaligned or the data does not appear in the correct format, you may be using a different column or row delimiter and will need to adjust your settings accordingly.

Before clicking on the Next button, choose the Advanced window. This window, represented in Figure 16-5, allows you to view or configure the properties of each column. This can be helpful when preparing data for the destination and ensuring that it is in the correct format. You also have the ability to add or remove columns as needed and can use the "Suggest Types" button to evaluate the data in the file (Figure 16-6) and provide recommendations for the data types prior to importing the data.

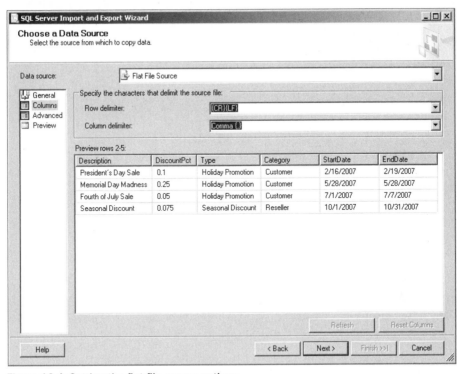

Figure 16-4: Setting the flat-file source options.

Click the "Suggest Types" button to have it change (or validate) the default data types for the DiscountPct, StartDate, and EndDate columns, then click on the Next button.

The next step in the Wizard asks you to provide configuration information for the data destination. As mentioned earlier, you can use any of the available providers for both source and destination, and neither of them has to be SQL Server. You could, in fact, use this Import Wizard to import the flat file into a Microsoft Excel spreadsheet, a Microsoft Access database, an Oracle database, or even another flat file. This functionality allows you to use SSIS to build complex packages that may have very distinct data migration paths before the execution can complete.

For this example, though, you're going to make it easy on yourself and choose the SQL Server Native Client 10.0 as your destination provider (this should be the default). When choosing the SQL Server Native Client 10.0, follow these steps:

1. Select your server name from the dropdown list if it is not already provided.

2. Choose "Windows Authentication."

3. Ensure that AdventureWorks2008 is selected as the target database.

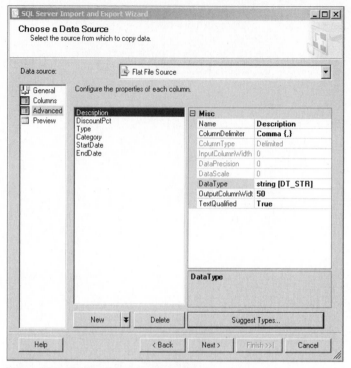

Figure 16-5: Setting the data type option.

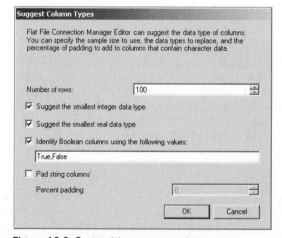

Figure 16-6: Suggest types parameters.

The New button on this screen allows you to create a new database on this server for your data import. Figure 16-7 displays the configuration information you should use.

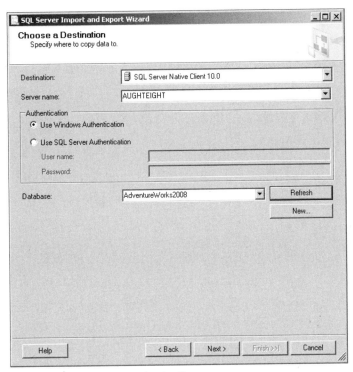

Figure 16-7: Choosing the destination.

The next page in the Wizard allows you to define the specific views or tables that will be used as the destination for the data in your file. The default behavior of the Wizard is to create a new table based on the name of the file, using the data types that were specified in the source configuration. You can use the dropdown list to select the correct table, as shown in Figure 16-8. Additionally, if the destination table does not yet exist in the database, you can type a new name in the Destination column, and the Wizard will create a new table for you.

Clicking on the "Edit Mappings" button, as seen in Figure 16-8, activates the Column Mappings window. This displays the column name in the data source and allows you to match it to a column name in the destination. Fortunately, the file you created earlier happens to use the exact same column names as the destination table, so there is no guesswork as to where the data will go. However, you can use this utility to specify that certain columns will be ignored, or simply mapped to a different target column.

You can also see in Figure 16-9 that there are options to delete or append rows in the destination table. In some cases, you may want to drop the table and then re-create it. This can be especially helpful if you want to completely purge the table and there are no foreign-key constraints on it.

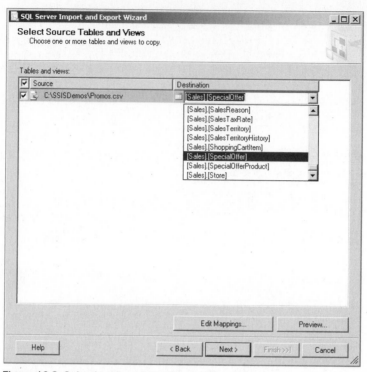

Figure 16-8: Selecting the destination table.

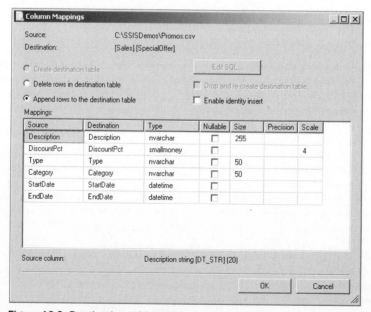

Figure 16-9: Destination table options.

Because the data types in the source and destination may not match, you have the option to review the data type mappings and specify whether or not the package should fail if there is an error or data needs to be truncated before reaching the destination. If you refer to Figure 16-10, you will note that several of the data types are inconsistent between the source and destination. In most cases, it's simply a matter of converting non-Unicode data into Unicode data. For the DiscountPct column, you need to convert it from a float to a smallmoney data type. For all columns, the convert option has been enabled. You can set the "On Error" or "On Truncation" behavior per column or use a global setting. In this example, I have specified to Ignore Truncate warnings.

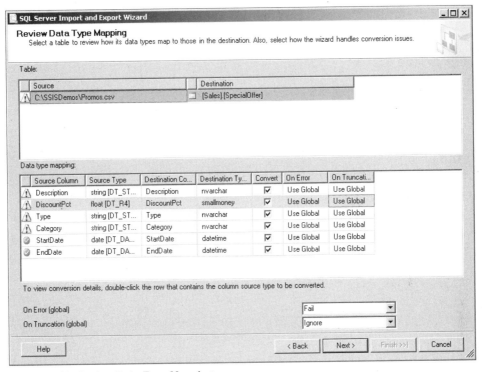

Figure 16-10: Review Data Type Mappings.

Once you have provided all the information about the source and destination, the Wizard will ask if you want to execute the package immediately and if you want to save your configuration as an SSIS package in either the msdb database or the file system (see Figure 16-11). For now, just choose to execute the package immediately, and don't worry about saving the package. You can either click Finish on this page to begin package execution, or you can click Next to view the summary information about the package before executing.

As long as all the steps have been followed as indicated, your data should now be imported successfully! You can execute a simple SELECT * FROM Sales.SpecialOffer query to see the imported data. If there was a problem with the execution of the package, use the error report information to pinpoint where the problem occurred and what could be done to resolve it.

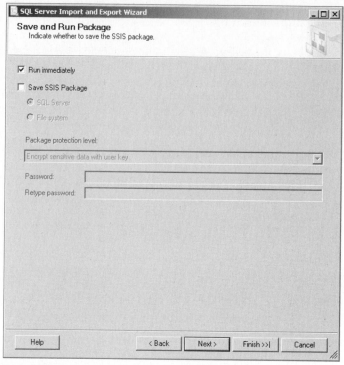

Figure 16-11: Execute the package without saving.

Using the Export Wizard

Now that you've had a chance to see the Import Wizard at work, you should see the Export Wizard in action! It's actually the exact same wizard. This time, however, you can export data using a query and save the results as a pipe-delimited file. Follow these steps:

1. Begin by right-clicking on the AdventureWorks2008 database and selecting Tasks ➤ Export Data.

2. In the "Choose a Data Source" page, ensure that the SQL Server Native Client 10.0 is specified as the Data Source, Windows Authentication is selected, and the database is AdventureWorks2008.

3. Once you've configured or confirmed as necessary, click Next.

4. In the "Choose a Destination" page, choose "Flat File Destination" as the destination.

5. Enter C:\SSISDemos\EmployeeData.txt as the filename. Leave the default locale and code page options.

6. Ensure that "Column names in the first data row" is selected, and click Next (see Figure 16-12 as a reference).

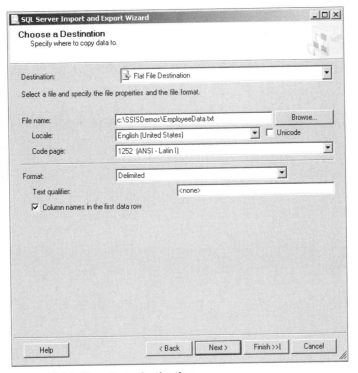

Figure 16-12: Choosing a destination.

7. In the next window, you will be asked if you want to select data from existing tables and views, or if you want to specify a query to find the data to transfer. Choose the second option, "Write a query to specify the data to transfer," and click Next.

8. In the Source Query window, enter the following query and click Next:

```
SELECT PC.FirstName, PC.LastName, PE.EmailAddress, HRE.MaritalStatus,
 HRE.Gender, HRE.VacationHours, HRE.SickLeaveHours, HRE.SalariedFlag,
HREP.Rate
FROM  Person.Person AS PC
INNER JOIN HumanResources.Employee AS HRE
  ON PC.BusinessEntityID = HRE.BusinessEntityID
INNER JOIN HumanResources.EmployeePayHistory AS HREP
  ON HRE.BusinessEntityID = HREP.BusinessEntityID
  INNER JOIN Person.EmailAddress AS PE
ON PC.BusinessEntityID = PE.BusinessEntityID
ORDER BY PC.LastName;
```

9. In the Configure Flat File Destination window, you can change the delimiter and column mapping options. Change the Column Delimiter to Vertical Bar { | } and click Next to continue. Feel free to explore the other options, but do not change them.

10. When asked to run or save the package, leave the defaults, and click Next, and then click Finish on the next page to execute the package immediately.

Your results should look something like Figure 16-13.

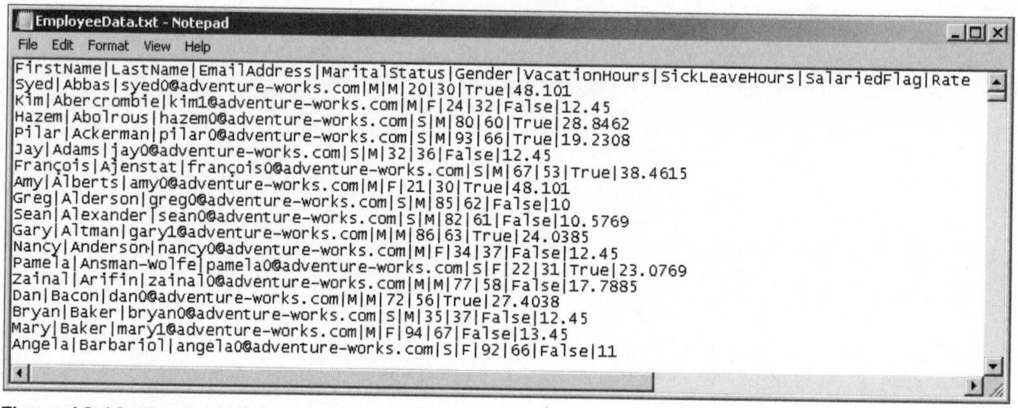

Figure 16-13: Viewing the exported text data.

Transforming Data with SSIS

Now the fun really begins. By now you should have a basic understanding of the concepts of how Integration Services can manage control and data flow, and you've seen a simple example of how to get data into and out of the SQL Server using the basic tools. In this section, you're going to see how those components can be expanded on to provide a more complete scenario for working with Integration Services.

You should first become familiar with the Integrated Development Environment (IDE). Integration Services, along with Analysis Services and Reporting Services, relies heavily on Business Intelligence Development Studio. BIDS is really just a fancy name for Visual Studio, and is, in fact, the Visual Studio 2008 IDE, but when installed by itself, it includes only add-ins for SQL Server BI components. If you install the full version of Visual Studio 2008 or the language compilers for Visual Basic and C#, you'll find that it starts the same environment. For the sake of simplicity, I will continue to refer to the IDE as *BIDS*.

To begin creating new SQL Server Integration Services packages, launch BIDS and create a new project. Of the types of projects available, the Integration Services Project is available under Business Intelligence Projects (see Figure 16-14). You may also notice another project type called *Integration Services Connection Project Wizard*. This template uses a wizard-based approach to creating an SSIS project, similar to what you did in the previous example. For this example, select "Integration Services Project."

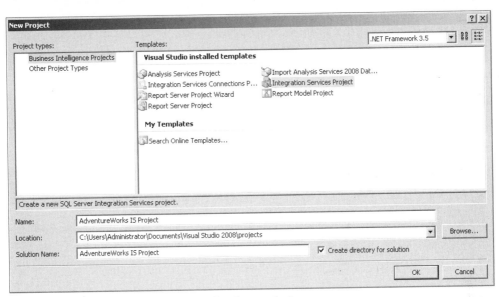

Figure 16-14: Creating a new Integration Services project.

Once you've created your new project, notice that as with other Visual Studio projects, you have a toolbox that contains controls and resources for your projects. The development environment is broken up into four different sections, each of which allows you to control different aspects of your project. These sections include a management area for the Control Flow, management of the Data Flow, Event Handlers, and a Package Explorer. During the execution or debugging of a package, a fifth tab appears, allowing you to view package execution progress. In the next few sections, you will learn about each of the different management areas, how they're used, and what options are available when working in those areas.

Understanding the Development Environment

As mentioned earlier, the development environment includes several tools and features that will allow you to have complete control over your Integration Services packages. In this section, you learn how to navigate your way through the different resources available to you. Chapter 3 covered the different tools and features of the SQL Server Management Studio development environment. The environment used by Integration Services is very similar. As with SQL Server Management Studio, you can pin and unpin different control boxes as needed to customize the look and feel of your workspace. Figure 16-15 shows an example of a typical development environment for Integration Services.

Toolbox

As with many other Visual Studio projects, the Toolbox is invaluable for finding the controls and features you need to make your project easy to design and configure. Integration Services packages are no exception and can provide you with a host of different elements. For the most part, you have two main toolboxes. The main Toolbox window contains Control Flow Items and Maintenance Plan Tasks and is your primary toolbox. The other contains data flow items such as sources, transforms, and destinations; it is only available while configuring a data flow task. The individual toolbox items are described later in this chapter.

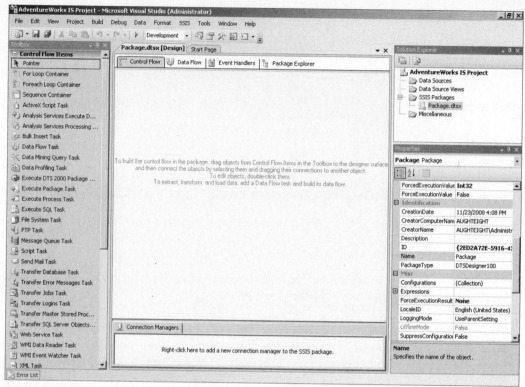

Figure 16-15: The Integration Services designer.

Solution Explorer

The Solution Explorer (shown on the right side of the screen in Figure 16-15) is a repository that allows you to manage multiple Integration Services packages and related resources. It is broken down into four main sections:

❑ **Data Sources** — These allow you to create Data Source objects that can be used by multiple packages in the same project. You can create a new data source using a wizard or choose an existing one.

❑ **Data Source Views (DSVs)** — These are objects that refer to a configurable subset of objects in your database and provide benefits such as caching metadata or defining relationships. These DSVs can also be used by multiple packages.

❑ **SSIS Packages** — You then have the SSIS Packages themselves.

❑ **Miscellaneous** — Finally, you have any Miscellaneous files that are used by your Integration Services packages.

Note that the package names end with a .dtsx file extension. This is the default extension for Integration Services packages that is kind of a holdover from when it was still called *Data Transformation Services*.

Properties

The Properties tab is a dynamically updating box that allows you to view or update the properties of the currently selected item. You can sort the list of property elements alphabetically or categorically.

Connection Managers

The Connection Managers tab (at the bottom of the screen of Figure 16-15) contains a list of connection objects specific to the package you are currently editing. Connections can be based on existing data sources, or you can create unique connections for only that package. Connections can use OLE DB, ADO.NET, Flat File, and other connection types. Connections can also be made on-the-fly, such as when defining a data flow task that uses a Microsoft Excel data source for an import operation. You will not need to create the connection to the Excel file beforehand, but once you define the source, it will be added to the list of connections.

Package Elements

When creating a new SSIS package, it's important that you be familiar with the different elements available. Familiarizing yourself with the variety of tools available will help you create more robust packages, which can execute a complex series of tasks. This section introduces you to these resources.

Control Flow

Your main environment is the Control Flow section, shown on the left side of Figure 16-15. The control flow environment allows you to define one or more tasks that will be executed for this Integration Services project and specify the order in which those tasks are executed (hence the term *Control Flow*). You can choose to define tasks that are serialized, meaning that one task must reach a completion state before the next task begins. You can also execute tasks in parallel, allowing multiple operations to be executed simultaneously. As long as there are no dependencies between these tasks, this can take advantage of your system resources and dramatically decrease the execution time of your packages with parallel execution.

To add items to your package's control flow, simply choose the appropriate item and drag it into the Control Flow pane. Once you've dragged an item into the Control Flow pane, you can then configure that item. Some tasks may display with an error symbol (the red circle with the white X) or a warning symbol (the yellow triangle with the black exclamation point) to indicate that further configuration is needed for that task to be able to execute properly. In many cases, simply configuring the task can "fix" the problem. You can also view the Error List (by pressing *[Ctrl]+E* or selecting View ➤ Error List) and review the available errors and warnings. You can also double-click on an error or warning to have BIDS take you straight to where you need to go to fix the event.

Control Flow Tasks

This section briefly identifies each of the control flow tasks that can be used to build your packages. Also listed are database maintenance plan tasks that may be useful to you as well. These items are listed in the order they appear in the Toolbox (refer to the left side of Figure 16-15).

Task	Description
For Loop Container	Containers are interesting in that they are both a task and a collection of tasks at the same time. In this case, the For Loop container allows you to execute one or more tasks that will continually execute until the result of the executed task returns a Boolean `false` value.
ForEach Loop Container	Similar to the For Loop container, ForEach Loop containers allow you to execute tasks for each instance of a type of object. The ForEachLoop includes enumerators for files, items, ADO record sets, ADO.NET schemas, variables, XML nodes, and SQL Management Objects.
Sequence Container	Allows you to define a series of tasks that will execute in sequence. It is similar in many regards to simply grouping tasks, which is covered later in this section, but allows additional functionality (such as limiting the scope of a variable to only the tasks within this container).

Each of the following tasks is also a container unto itself. This is referred to as the Task Host Container *and is not a container type you need to separately manage or add to your package.*

Task	Description
ActiveX Script Task	Allows you to run scripts that use VBScript or JavaScript as a step in your process flow. This has been largely superseded by the Script Task, which uses VisualBasic.Net scripts. ActiveX scripts are primarily used with older packages that have been upgraded from DTS 2000.
Analysis Services Execute DDL Task	Allows you to execute a Data Definition Language (DDL) statement in Analysis Services.
Analysis Services Processing Task	Contains configuration options for processing Analysis Services cubes and dimensions.
Bulk Insert Task	Used to import a large amount of data from a flat-file source.
Data Flow Task	Pretty much the bread and butter of Integration Services. It allows you to define how data is processed as it moves from source to destination.
Data Mining Query Task	Use the Data Mining Query task to run prediction queries using a Data Mining Extension (DMX) statement.

Task	Description
Data Profiling Task	Helps identify potential problems with your data, such as data that doesn't conform to an expected format (such as phone numbers) or computational problems with aggregate data.
Execute DTS 2000 Package Task	Executes packages created in DTS from SQL 2000, but that have not yet been upgraded or migrated to Integration Services.
Execute Package Task	Launches another Integration Services package.
Execute Process Task	Executes a Windows application or batch file.
Execute SQL Task	Executes a SQL script. Second only to the Data Flow Task, this is probably one of the more commonly used tasks.
File System Task	Used to interact with the file system, such as creating files and directories.
FTP Task	Use this to upload or download files to FTP servers.
Message Queue Task	Allows you to configure your package to interact with Microsoft Message Queuing (MSMQ) services.
Script Task	Executes a Microsoft Visual Basic.Net script.
Send Mail Task	Sends e-mail messages during the execution of a package.
Transfer Database Task	Transfers entire databases between different instances of SQL Server.
Transfer Error Messages Task	Allows you to copy user-defined error messages (with an error number above 50,000) between instances of SQL Server. The data is stored in the `sysmessages` table of the `master` database.
Transfer Jobs Task	Copies jobs between instances of SQL Server.
Transfer Logins Task	Copies logins between SQL Servers. This can be useful when creating a redundant server for fault-tolerance.
Transfer Master Stored Procedures Task	Use this task if you've created user-defined stored procedures in the `master` database that you want to copy to another instance of SQL Server.
Transfer SQL Server Object Task	Use this task to transfer other SQL objects such as tables, views, stored procedures, and triggers between instances.
Web Service Task	Initiates a connection to a web site, and can be used to return information to a variable or file.
WMI Data Reader Task	Used to query Windows Management Instrumentation (WMI) namespaces to return information about the computer system.
WMI Event Watcher Task	Used to query WMI for events relating to system behavior or performance.

Continued

Task	Description
XML Task	Adds XML tasks to work with XML files and data sets.
Back Up Database Task	Does exactly what the name suggests, and allows you to configure a database backup as part of a package.
Check Database Integrity Task	Checks the structural integrity and space allocation of all objects within a specified database.
Execute SQL Server Agent Job Task	You can also configure an Integration Services package to launch a SQL Server Agent Job as part of its process flow.
Execute T-SQL Statement Task	Similar to the Execute SQL task, this requires that you specifically use the Transact-SQL dialect of the SQL language.
History Cleanup Task	This task can be used to remove extemporaneous data from the `msdb` database, specifically historical information about backups, restores, jobs, and maintenance plans.
Maintenance Cleanup Task	Use this task to remove leftover data from maintenance plans, such as backup files or text reports.
Notify Operator Task	During the execution of a package, you may want to notify an operator that a certain step has completed or failed.
Rebuild Index Task	You can use this task to rebuild an index during the execution of your package.
Reorganize Index Task	Rather than rebuilding, you can also reorganize one or more indices from one or more databases.
Shrink Database Task	Use this task to shrink one or more databases.
Update Statistics Task	This task allows you to execute a controlled UPDATE STATISTICS task for one or more databases.

Precedence Constraints

Now that you've been introduced to the different tasks available for your control flow, you must understand how you can arrange or use these tasks together. When you add tasks to the control flow, you must specify how and when to execute these tasks. If you were to just add a bunch of tasks into the control flow and then run the package, all of the tasks would try to execute at the same time. That may be desirable in some instances, but in most cases, you want to ensure that there is a defined logic to how and when the different tasks will execute. In more complex packages, some steps may not be executed at all unless there is a problem.

Precedence constraints are used to control the order in which tasks are executed, and whether or not they are executed based on the prior task failing, succeeding, or either. Tasks may also have more than one precedence constraint defined. When defining multiple precedence constraints on a task, you can specify whether they are evaluated using the AND operator, which requires both constraints to evaluate to true; or the OR operator, which will execute the task as long as one of the constraints is met.

Remember that using multiple precedence constraints on a task could mean that either all conditions must be met, or just one condition must be satisfied. The conditions, however, could be completely different. For example, Task C has two precedence constraints defined. The first one requires that Task A succeeds, and the second one requires that Task B fails. If the AND operator is specified, then Task A *must* succeed, and Task B *must* fail. If Task B executes successfully, Task C will not run. If the OR operator is used, then Task C will run if Task A succeeds, regardless of the outcome of Task B, or if Task B fails, regardless of the outcome of Task A.

Figure 16-16 shows three tasks included in the control flow of a package. The first task will execute a SQL statement, and if it succeeds, the Data Flow task will execute. If the SQL Task fails, then the Send Mail Task will execute and notify the appropriate personnel. The solid line indicates that a logical AND condition is specified, meaning that *all* constraints must evaluate to TRUE, whereas the dotted line indicates an OR condition, requiring only one constraint to be met.

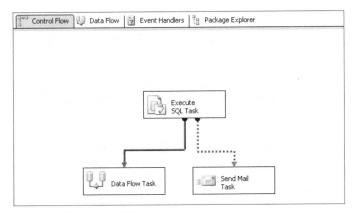

Figure 16-16: Control flow.

Task Grouping

There is also a feature in Integration Services that allows you to add multiple tasks and containers to a group (see Figure 16-17). Unlike containers, groups are not treated as a unit of execution, but they can help clean up the logic flow. As a UI enhancement more than anything else, when you group tasks together, you can "hide" the tasks from view by collapsing the group. This can be helpful when you have a complex package and want to simplify the view. Also, note that precedence constraints cannot be defined on a group, but are defined on the tasks within that group.

Data Flow

As mentioned earlier, one of the biggest improvements to managing Integration Services over DTS is removing the data flow logic from the control flow. This allows you to create more complex transformations that are easier to design and are more manageable. Data Flow Tasks appear as a single unit of execution in the control flow, but may have many complex steps in the data flow view.

When you switch to the data flow view, a dropdown list appears with all Data Flow Tasks in the package. Each Data Flow Task will allow you to configure at least a source and a destination. You can optionally apply one or more transforms that can modify or prepare the data before it reaches its destination.

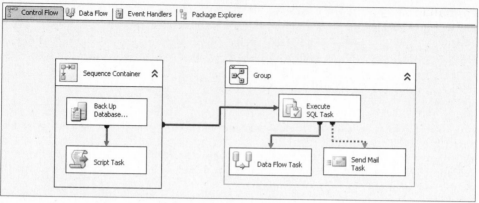

Figure 16-17: Control flow between a container and group.

Data Sources

Out-of-the-box, SQL Server 2008 includes six data sources you can use in your data flow. You can, in fact, use multiple data sources in any given Data Flow Task. This allows you to use a merge transformation to join the data sets before the data reaches the destination. The following data sources are available:

Source	Description
ADO.NET Source	Uses an Active Data Object connection manager to connect to a .NET provider. In SQL Server 2005, this was called the *DataReader Data Source*.
Excel Source	Use with Microsoft Excel workbooks.
Flat File Source	Allows you to import from a variety of flat-file formats (such as comma-separated, tab-separated, and fixed-length fields).
OLE DB Source	Use with any OLE DB data source.
Raw File Source	A specialized flat-file format that is optimized for quick use. This is typically created by Raw File destinations to allow fast processing of the data, because minimal translation is required.
XML Source	Allows you to use an XML file as a data source. You must ensure that elements within your XML file can be mapped to SQL fields. You can do this by creating a schema mapping file, using an inline schema within the file, or allowing Integration Services to try to create an XSD mapping file for this data source.

Transformations

Integration Services includes several built-in transforms to help modify or improve your data during the transfer process. With DTS 2000, many of these transforms had to be built programmatically, making the process of performing complex transformations burdensome. Although there are still programmatic options that let you build your own custom transforms, you can use the following transforms to create complex packages with minimal programming ability:

Transform	Description
Aggregate	Used to perform aggregate calculations, such as AVERAGE, GROUP BY, and COUNT.
Audit	Outputs additional data about the environment.
Cache Transform	Allows the creation of a cache (.caw) file managed through a Cache Connection Manager. This allows you to manage and transform data and metadata from the cache.
Character Map	Lets you transform string data. You can use this to convert uppercase to lowercase, and traditional Chinese to simplified Chinese, for example.
Conditional Split	Sends different data sets from the same source to different destinations.
Copy Column	As the name suggests, this copies a column and its associated properties to the destination. It is possible to change the properties of these columns as they reach the destination. For example, you might convert a non-Unicode column into a Unicode column.
Data Conversion	Use this when you need to change the data type between source and destination.
Data Mining Query	Performs prediction queries against data-mining models.
Derived Column	Modifies the data itself during transformation.
Export Column	This transform exports data into a file.
Fuzzy Grouping	Helps standardize your data. It allows you to look for string data that is similar, and replaces the variants with a standard value.
Fuzzy Lookup	Similar to the Lookup Transform, the Fuzzy Lookup uses values in a reference table, but accepts variants on the data.
Import Column	Reads data from a file and adds it to the data flow.

Continued

Transform	Description
Lookup	Existing data is joined to data being imported. This references values in a lookup table, but with an exact match.
Merge	As the name suggests, this merges data between two data sets. Use the Union All Transform to join more than two data sources.
Merge Join	Similar to the Merge Transform, this transform uses JOIN statements to combine the data.
Multicast	Allows the data to be sent to multiple destinations (or multiple transformation tasks).
OLE DB Command	Executes a SQL command for each row in the input flow.
Percentage Sampling	Returns a random sampling of data from the input. When using this transform, specify a percentage of the total rows that will be sent to the output.
Pivot	This can be used to denormalize data.
Row Count	Use this transform to return a count of the total number of rows passed through to a variable.
Row Sampling	Similar to Percentage Sampling, Row Sampling outputs random rows, but you specify the total number of rows to be returned.
Script Component	This transform allows you to execute a custom Script Task that will transform the data.
Slowly Changing Dimension	Used with dimension tables to perform changing attribute, historical attribute, fixed attribute, and inferred member changes.
Sort	This transform allows you to sort the data on one or more import columns.
Term Extraction	You can use this transform to extract English nouns or noun phrases and re-direct the terms to the output.
Term Lookup	This transform uses a reference table and returns a count of the items in the reference table that appear in the data flow.
Union All	This transform can be used to merge multiple data sets.
Unpivot	Use the Unpivot Transform to normalize data.

Data Destinations

Integration Services allows you to specify one or more destinations in a Data Flow Task. The following is a list of data flow destinations that are available with SQL Server out-of-the-box:

Destinations	Description
ADO.NET Destination	Similar to an ADO.NET Source, this allows connection to a variety of database types that use the Active Data Objects data provider.
Data Mining Model Training	Passes data through data-mining model algorithms to train the data-mining model.
DataReader Destination	Specifically uses the DataReader interface in ADO.NET.
Dimension Processing	Loads data into an Analysis Services dimension.
Excel Destination	Use this to output your data to a Microsoft Excel file.
Flat File Destination	Use to output the data to a comma-separated, tab-separated, or fixed-length file.
OLE DB Destination	Uses an OLE DB provider.
Partition Processing	Use to output the data to an Analysis Services partition.
Raw File Destination	Use as an intermediary output between data flow tasks; this format allows for quick processing as minimal formatting options need to be defined.
Recordset Destination	Outputs the data to an ADO recordset.
SQL Server Compact Edition Destination	Use for SQL Server Compact Edition clients.
SQL Server Destination	Inserts data into a Microsoft SQL Server destination.

Event Handling

Event handling is another feature of Integration Services that provides more granular control over the execution of your packages and the tasks within them. Frequently associated with error handling, event handling allows you to execute additional tasks before a task executes, during task execution, and after task execution.

Any well-designed package includes the ability to control or monitor the execution of the tasks within. Using efficient error handling and event handling is the cornerstone for creating packages that require minimal maintenance and hands-on execution. The Event Handling tab includes options for configuring tasks that execute for the following 12 packages — or task-level events:

❑ OnError
❑ OnExecStatusChanged

- ❑   OnInformation
- ❑   OnPostExecute
- ❑   OnPostValidate
- ❑   OnPreExecute
- ❑   OnPreValidate
- ❑   OnProgress
- ❑   OnQueryCancel
- ❑   OnTaskFailed
- ❑   OnVariableValueChanged
- ❑   OnWarning

Configuring additional tasks on these events can improve error handling and provide you with more precise control over execution of your packages. Be careful, though. Too much granularity can cause more administrative work than necessary.

Package Explorer

The Package Explorer is a useful utility that allows you to view the different elements of your package in an organized, hierarchical structure. Although this view isn't representative of the control or data flow, it can help you quickly find an element of either. You can view or modify the properties, or delete unused elements from your package.

Creating a Simple Package

So, now that you have a fairly good understanding of the different elements of an Integration Services package, it's time to put it to use. In this scenario, the employees at AdventureWorks have decided to pool some of their resources to keep a DVD library of titles in the office to share among themselves. Anyone is welcome to participate, but if you're going to borrow, you're going to contribute!

Up until now, the employees had been keeping track of their collection using an InfoPath form. However, over the last couple of months, the collection has grown significantly, and the core group who started the library wants a better way to manage it. They've decided to store the data in SQL, but rather than having to re-enter all the data by hand, they would prefer to import the XML file into the database.

For this example, you can download an XML file from http://p2p.wrox.com/ (search for the ISBN — 04700440919 — or title of this book), or you could build your own sample file. The one provided uses the following format:

```xml
<?xml version="1.0" standalone="yes"?>
<DVDs>
  <Table>
    <Title>Movie Title</Title>
    <Year>YYYY</Year>
    <Run-time>hh:MM</Run-time>
    <Rating>XX</Rating>
  </Table>
</DVDs>
```

Save the file as **C:\SSISDemos\DVDLib.xml**.

Creating the Connection

You'll begin by creating a new Integration Services project called *AdventureWorks IS Project*. When you create the project, a new package named *Package.dtsx* is created. Rename the package **XMLImport.dtsx**. A box will pop up, asking if you want to rename the package object as well — click Yes.

Follow these steps:

1. Although you'll only be creating one package in this exercise, create a new Data Source that will be available to all packages that are part of this project. Right-click Data Sources and select "New Data Source" to launch the Wizard.

2. In the Wizard, click Next on the introduction page. Then, on the next page, "Select how to define the connection," click New. In the Connection Manager dialog box, either enter your server name or select it from the dropdown list. Use Windows Authentication, and select AdventureWorks2008 as the database. Click OK when these options have been selected.

3. Click Next to go to the "Completing the Wizard" page, and leave the default Data Source name. Click Finish to complete the Wizard.

4. Now, below the Control Flow pane, you should see the Connection Managers pane. Right-click anywhere in the pane, then select "New Connection from Data Source."

5. Select AdventureWorks2008 and click OK.

Creating the Data Flow Task

Now it's time to put the package to work. Follow these steps:

1. Create a new Data Flow Task. From your Toolbox, drag the Data Flow Task into the Control Flow window, and rename it **XML Transfer**. This can be done from either the Properties window, or by pressing [F2] with the Data Flow Task selected.

2. Click the Data Flow tab. You should see "XML Transfer" in the dropdown list. If you had more than one Data Flow Task in your package, you could navigate through them without having to go back to the Control Flow Task to manage it.

3. Now, the next step to build the data flow is to specify the source. Drag the XML Source from the Toolbox into the Data Flow pane, and then double-click on it to open up the XML Source Editor.

4. For the Data Access mode, ensure that "XML file location" is selected. Type the path or browse to the DVDLib.xml file. Because there is no schema mapping file, you can have the SQL Server generate one. Click on the "Generate XSD" button, and use the default filename and location.

5. You can navigate to the Columns page to view the columns that will be imported into your database, but you should not need to change anything in there. You may also get a message that indicates that since no maximum field length was specified for the text columns, it will use a default of 255 characters. Click OK to accept the message. Click OK to exit the Editor.

6. Because the table you are going to create will store the Year and Run-Time columns as a smallint value, you can change the output of the XML file to use a 2-byte signed integer,

rather than the default of a 2-byte unsigned integer. This also gives you an opportunity to see the Advanced Editor. Right-click on the XML Source object and select "Show Advanced Editor."

7. Click on the "Input and Output Properties" tab and expand Output Columns. Select Year, and, in the right pane, under Data Type Properties, change the value 2-byte unsigned integer [DT_UI2] to 2-byte signed integer [DT_I2].

8. Next, change the value of the Run-Time column to a 2-byte signed integer [DT_I2] as well. See Figure 16-18 for an example.

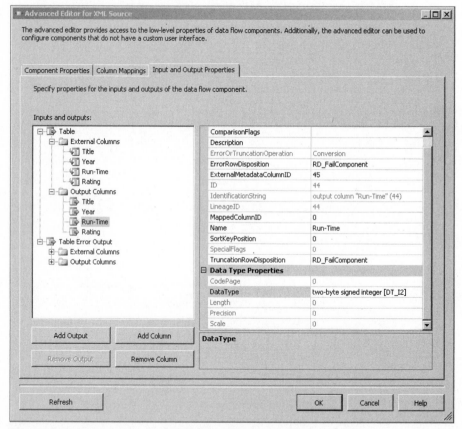

Figure 16-18: Using the Advanced Editor to change the output data type.

At this point, you could simply provide the data to a destination, but that wouldn't be much fun. To see how transforms work, you can apply a simple transform to your data before it reaches the destination. In this example, you'll use the Sort Transform to sort based on the title. Drag the Sort Transform from the Toolbox into the Data Flow pane.

Two things must happen next in order for the sort to work:

❏ You must configure the output of your XML Source to go to the Sort Transform. Select the XML Source, and then click and drag the green arrow to the Sort Transform.

❏ You must tell the transform which column or columns to sort on. Double-click on the Sort Transform to open the Editor.

In the Sort Transformation Editor, the top pane lists the available fields, and the bottom shows you which ones have been selected for sorting.. Your configuration should look like Figure 16-19.

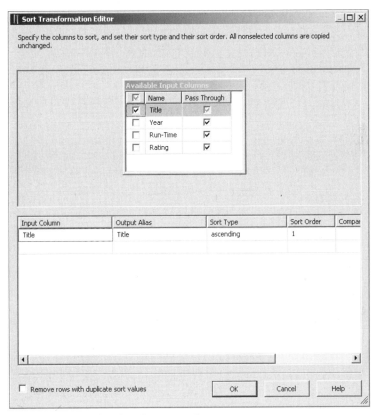

Figure 16-19: Configuring the sort options.

Defining the Destination

Now it's time to define the destination. Follow these steps:

1. Drag the SQL Server Destination object from the Toolbox into the Data Flow. Before you configure the destination options, select the Sort Transform, and drag the green output arrow to the SQL Server Destination object (see Figure 16-20).

673

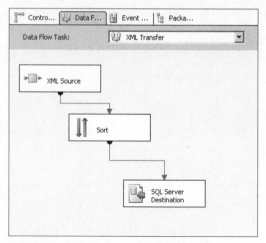

Figure 16-20: Data flow from XML to SQL.

2. Double-click on the SQL Server Destination to open the Editor. Because you've already defined a connection manager, Adventure Works should already be populated. Under "Use a table or view," click New, and replace the existing SQL code with the following:

```
CREATE TABLE [dbo].[Library] (
    [ID] int IDENTITY NOT NULL,
    [Title] NVARCHAR(255),
    [Year] SMALLINT,
    [Run-time] SMALLINT,
    [Rating] NVARCHAR(255)
)
```

3. Select the Mappings page and review the mapping, then click OK to close the Editor.

So That's It, Right? Applying Additional Transforms

You *could* save and execute the package now, and you'd have a new table with some movie data in it. But I'm not really happy with this data. The person who was adding the titles to the InfoPath form had no consideration for how to sort titles. When you execute this task, all of the movies that begin with articles like *The*, *An*, and *A* will be grouped together. For example, *The Black Hole* should be sorted alphabetically under *B*, not under *T*.

You could always fix this after the fact, but one of the requirements of being an effective database administrator is that you understand your data and how it will be used. So, before you can consider this package a success, you need to fix someone else's mistake:

1. Go back into the Control Flow Items list and drag an Execute SQL task into your Control Flow.

2. Define a precedence constraint (On Success) linking the Data Flow Task to the Execute SQL Task.

3. Double-click on the Execute SQL Task to open the Task Editor. On the General page, find the Connection parameter, and select `AdventureWorks2008` from the dropdown list.

4. Find the SQL Statement parameter and click on the " ... " button. Enter the following code in the SQL Query window:

```
Update dbo.Library
Set Title = CASE
    When Title like 'The %' THEN (SUBSTRING(Title, 5, 255) + ', The')
    When Title like 'An %' THEN (SUBSTRING(Title, 4, 255) + ', An')
    When Title like 'A %' THEN (SUBSTRING(Title, 3, 255) + ', A')
    Else Title
    END;
```

5. Click OK to exit the Query window, and then OK again to exit the Task Editor.

6. Save your package and then right-click on the package name from Solution Explorer. Select "Execute Package." All steps should execute successfully. When they do, select "Stop Debugging" from the Debug menu.

7. Open SQL Server Management Studio, and execute the following query:

```
USE AdventureWorks2008;
GO
SELECT * FROM dbo.Library
ORDER BY Title;
```

The query should return the data sorted by title, without articles like *The* being grouped together.

Summary

SQL Server Integration Services is a very powerful tool for controlling data transformation operations between SQL Servers and other data stores. It allows you to create very simple data flow models, or very complex ones. It is also extensible, allowing you to build additional transformations and controls programmatically. This chapter provided you with a high-level overview of how Integration Services works, how to use the Import and Export Wizards, and how to build simple packages using the SSIS designer. If you would like to learn more about Integration Services, check out *Professional Microsoft SQL Server 2008 Integration Services* by Brian Knight, Erik Veerman, Grant Dickinson, Douglas Hinson, and Darren Herbold (Wiley, 2008).

The next chapter continues with the BI toolset by introducing you to one of the most important components of a Business Intelligence solution — SQL Server Analysis Services.

Introduction to SQL Server Analysis Services

Analysis is at the heart of Business Intelligence; with it, you can put context to your data. SQL Server includes a very powerful engine for building multi-dimensional data structures that allow you to arrange, aggregate, and analyze your data, known as SQL Server Analysis Services. Collecting information for the sake of collecting it is a waste of time, money, and manpower. Using that information to discover trends, identify problems, and address shortfalls adds business value to the data.

SQL Server Analysis Services uses an Online Analytic Processing (OLAP) engine for building and storing multi-dimensional databases. In this chapter, you will learn about the basics of OLAP technology, the tools used to build OLAP databases, and the components used within.

Understanding OLAP

OLAP databases are built around the concept of the *cube*. *Cubes* are multi-dimensional objects whose structures are defined by hierarchical objects known as *dimensions*. An example of a commonly used dimension is *Date*. Units of time can be divided or combined as needed based on the level or depth of data that will be stored in the database. For example, the Date dimension might consist of a decade level, a year level, a quarter level, and so on, all the way down to the day (or lower, if necessary).

Another important concept when working with cubes is the understanding that most of the data being accessed is aggregated, or at least can be aggregated. This means that when building a cube, you don't need to store every possible calculation for data, but instead, you can define the way the lowest-level data is combined to provide you with the answer you need. For example, if I track my sales numbers daily, but I want to know what my total sales were for the last quarter, based on the way my cube is designed, it can automatically add the daily sales totals for the last 90 (or so) days together. Depending on how my Date dimension has been defined, I can also look at the same data broken up by month or by week without having to perform additional complex calculations.

OLAP cubes can also store summarized values as well as the lowest-level data. This makes it easier to retrieve information, such as the last 90 days of sales data, because that sum is already stored in the cube as a calculated value.

OLAP Terminology

You've already been introduced to a few key terms used in OLAP environments, but this section will present you with a more structured list of terms and definitions that are commonly used. Understanding the different components of an OLAP solution will better prepare you for managing OLAP databases (see the following table).

Key Term	Definition
OLAP Database	Essentially the container for different objects that are included in an Analysis Services solution. In addition to the dimensions and cubes mentioned in prior pages, this will also include other objects, such as data sources, which will be identified in this list.
Data Source	Data doesn't originate in an OLAP database, but instead uses another database, often a relational database as its source. Microsoft supports using the included OLE DB providers for connecting to Microsoft SQL Server 7.0 and later databases, as well as the SQL Native Client for SQL Server 2005 and 2008. Some third-party databases can be used as a data source, as long as you have an appropriate OLE DB driver.
Dimension	The structural building blocks of a cube. Dimensions are based on data source tables or views and will contain attributes that are based on the columns from those tables or views. Although dimensions are used to build cubes, the dimension definitions are not stored in the cube until they are added to a cube. The dimension definitions are also stored in the dimension collection of the OLAP database. This allows a single dimension to be used in one or more cubes.
Hierarchies	There are two types of hierarchies in SQL Server Analysis Services. *Attribute hierarchies* are built using the properties of the dimension to define a hierarchical structure. *User-defined hierarchies*, on the other hand, are built manually, by defining the method in which a cube can be *sliced* on a particular dimension. In addition to the example of the date hierarchy from the previous section, another example you might use is a geography dimension, which would allow you to analyze your data based on continent, country, state, province, county, parish or city, as necessary.
Level	Identifies a position within a hierarchy to which individual items (known as *members*) belong.
Member	Objects within a hierarchy that represent one or more instances of fact data. For example, the geography hierarchy might define the country level, which includes the United States, Canada, and Japan members. The city level would include Seattle, Vancouver, and Tokyo members.

Key Term	Definition
Measures	Measures represent quantifiable fact data in your database. Measures typically consist of numeric data that can be aggregated. A measure can also be calculated.
Measure Groups	Used to associate dimensions with the measures from underlying fact tables as well as when a distinct count is used as the aggregation behavior for the fact data. This allows aggregation processing to be optimized.
Cube	Primary objects created in an OLAP database. There are two main components to a cube: The *dimensions*, which are used to define the structure of the cube, and the *measures*, which contain the fact data that is referenced by the cube, are the essential building blocks of your OLAP databases.
Key Performance Indicator (KPI)	Calculations of measure group data that are used to compare actual performance against a defined target value. For example, the Sales Department might define two goals to help identify sales performance. The first goal would set a target value for the number of units sold, and the second would identify the projected revenue from all sales. Each of these goals could be tracked as a Key Performance Indicator, and you could compare your actual year-to-date sales against the defined targets.

Working with SSAS

As with other Business Intelligence services, you can use both the Business Intelligence Development Studio and SQL Server Management Studio to manage different aspects of SQL Server Analysis Services. BIDS is used primarily for creating and managing dimensions, building cubes, defining KPIs, and other tasks related to arranging and structuring the data, while SSMS will be used to manage the databases that are created from SSAS projects. Although database design is beyond the scope of this chapter, you will learn about using SSAS through a series of exercises that will allow you to gain an understanding of the tools used to build and manage multi-dimensional databases.

Creating the Project

Begin by creating a new Analysis Services Project. In BIDS, you will want to create a new project that uses the Analysis Services Project template. You may also note that there is an option to import an existing SSAS database into a new project. For my example, I will create a project called *AdventureWorks 2008 Data Warehouse*. See Figure 17-1 as a reference.

Defining a Data Source

Once you have created the project, the next step is to create a data source that will be used by the OLAP database. For this example, you will need the `AdventureWorks2008DW` database from Codeplex (`www.codeplex.com`). Follow these steps:

1. Begin by right-clicking on the Data Sources folder in Solution Explorer, and select "New Data Source." This launches the New Data Source Wizard. As with most SQL Wizards, the first page of the Wizard is introductory in nature and can be skipped without consequence.

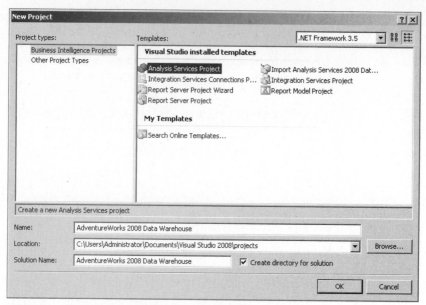

Figure 17-1: Creating an Analysis Services Project.

2. The next page of the Wizard allows you to define the data connection. You may already have data connections defined, but I would recommend for the purposes of this example to create a new data connection. Click on the New button (as seen in Figure 17-2) to create the new connection.

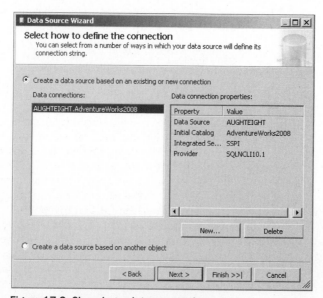

Figure 17-2: Choosing a data connection.

3.   As you can see in Figure 17-3, you can select the properties of the data connection, including the OLE DB provider (which in this example should be the SQL Server Native Client 10.0), the server name, and the database name. Although your server name may be different from the one I use in my examples, you will want to make sure that you are using the `AdventureWorks2008DW` database. Click OK to return to the Wizard.

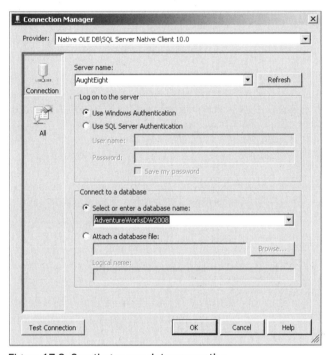

Figure 17-3: Creating a new data connection.

4.   Once you have the appropriate data connection, click Next to continue to the Wizard. The following page allows you to specify the login information used to connect to the data source. In this case, you can define a specific Windows or Active Directory account and password, use the SQL Server Analysis Services service account, use the credentials of the current user, or inherit the login information from the application. When building a data source for OLAP processing, it is not uncommon to use a shared account or the SSAS service account to build and process Analysis Services objects. Because this operation may be performed either manually by an administrator or as part of a scheduled job, using the current user credentials may not always be the best option. However, you should make sure that the account does have Read permissions to the objects in the source database that will be imported into the SSAS database. For data-mining operations, discussed later in this chapter, using the current user credentials is the preferred option since you do not want to expose any data that the current user doesn't currently have permissions to in the source database. For this exercise, choose the "Use the service account" option.

5. The last page of the Wizard allows you to configure a name for the data source, as well as shows you a preview of the connection string that will be used to connect to the source database. Click Finish to complete the Wizard and create the data source.

Creating the Data Source View

After you have created the initial data source, you will need to create a Data Source view before you can begin building your new cube. The Data Source view serves two purposes:

❑ It allows you to identify which tables and views from the data source will be used in your Analysis Services Project.

❑ It retrieves and stores the metadata about those objects, which allows you to build your cubes without having to maintain an active open connection to the data source.

A DSV can contain tables and views from multiple data sources, but it requires that one data source be first identified as the primary data source. Create the DSV as follows:

1. As you did when creating a data source, right-click on the Data Source Views folder, and select "New Data Source View."

2. After bypassing the informational page in the Wizard, the next page requires you to select the data source to use. Select the `AdventureWorks2008DW` data source created in the last section, and click Next to continue. Note that you can create a new data source from this Wizard, as well. The Advanced button allows you to restrict the Wizard to specific schemas in the relational database.

3. The next page in the Wizard allows you to specify which tables and views to include in your OLAP database. For the sake of simplicity, you will only use a subset of the available dimension and fact data in the relational database. Choose the following tables to add to your DSV:

   ❑ `DimDate`

   ❑ `DimGeography`

   ❑ `DimProduct`

   ❑ `DimProductCategory`

   ❑ `DimProductSubCategory`

   ❑ `DimReseller`

   ❑ `FactResellerSales`

   Once you have selected the required tables, click Next to give the DSV a name, and preview the list of objects that will be included in the DSV. As you can see from Figure 17-4, I have changed the default name of the DSV to *AW2008DW_DSV*.

Once you've finished the Wizard, the main workspace in your project will show you a diagram of the tables and views in your DSV. You can re-size the diagram and move the tables to better fit them within the available window. This operates not unlike the Database Diagramming tool in SQL Server Management Studio.

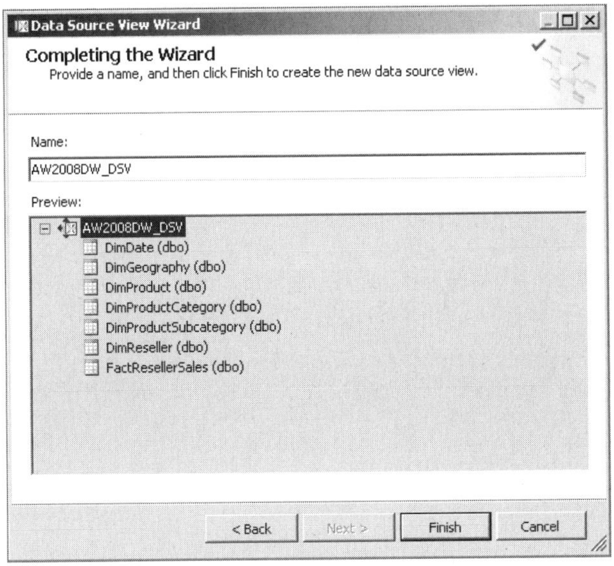

Figure 17-4: Creating a Data Source view.

Before you begin building the cube, you will want to rename the tables and views you added to your DSV in order to make them more user-friendly. Keep in mind that this just creates an alias that will be used by Analysis Services and will have no impact on the relational database at all. If you have the Properties window visible, you can simply select an object and change the FriendlyName attribute of the object. If the Properties window is not visible, you can enable it by pressing [F4], enabling it from the View menu of BIDS, or by right-clicking on a table and selecting Properties. Use the following list as a guide for renaming objects:

Object	Renamed Object
DimDate	→Date
DimGeography	→Geography
DimProduct	→Product
DimProductCategory	→Product Category
DimProductSubcategory	→Product Subcategory
DimReseller	→Reseller
FactResellerSales	→Reseller Sales

It's a good idea at this point to save your project, so click on the "Save All" button on the Toolbar, or choose "Save All" from the File menu.

Defining Dimensions

Before you can build a cube, you need to define the dimensions and hierarchies that will be used to define the structure of the cube. In this example, you will start by building the Date dimension with the Dimension Wizard:

1. Right-click on the Dimensions folder, and run the New Dimension Wizard. Read the informational text in the first page of the Wizard (opting to skip it in the future if you wish), and click Next. You will choose to create the dimension using an existing table, but you should review the options for creating time-based and non-time-based dimension tables in the data source, or a Time dimension on the server. Ensure that the first option is selected, and click Next to continue.

2. In the Specify Source Information page, ensure that your Data Source view is listed, and select the Date table from the Main Table dropdown list. DateKey should be listed as a column that will be included in the Key Columns list. Click Next to continue.

3. Now you will need to enable the following attributes and change the attribute types. Use the following table to find the appropriate attribute type for each dimension:

FullDateAlternateKey	Date →Calendar →Date
DayNumberOfMonth	Date→Calendar→Day of Month
MonthNumberOfYear	Date→Calendar→Month of Year
CalendarQuarter	Date→Calendar→Quarter of Year
CalendarYear	Date→Calendar→Year

4. Figure 17-5 should provide you with a reference for mapping the appropriate attributes. Click Next to review the Date dimension settings and change the dimension name if you wish. If you are satisfied with your options, click Finish.

Creating the Cube

You have manually created the Date dimension, but you're going to need more. Fortunately, you'll be able to create the required dimensions when you create the cube through the New Cube Wizard:

1. Right-click on the Cubes folder in Solution Explorer and choose "New Cube." Skip past the first page of the Wizard to get to the Select Creation Method screen. Review the different options for creating a new cube, but select the first option to "Use Existing tables," and click Next.

2. The next page of the Wizard requires you to specify a table that contains measure group information. Because the Reseller Sales table is the only one that contains fact data, select that, and click Next.

3. For the sake of simplicity, you're going to track only two measures in this cube. De-select all measures except Sales Amount and Reseller Sales Count (see Figure 17-6), and click Next.

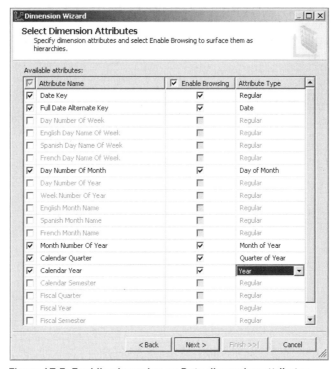

Figure 17-5: Enabling browsing on Date dimension attributes.

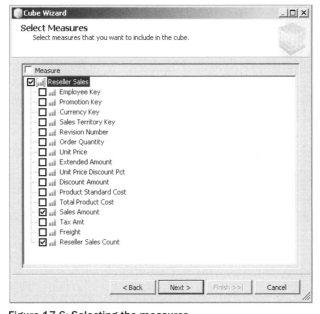

Figure 17-6: Selecting the measures.

4. You will now be asked to select existing dimensions; select the Date dimension and click Next. Based on the measures you selected, the Wizard will recommend additional dimensions that will be used with this cube. Select the Products and Reseller dimensions, if they're not already selected. Clear the check next to the Reseller Sales dimension, and click Next (see Figure 17-7).

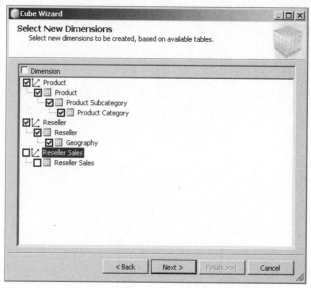

Figure 17-7: New dimensions.

5. Name the cube *AW2008 Reseller Sales* and then click Finish to generate the cube. Once the cube has been created, you will see a database diagram similar to the one you saw when you created the DSV, only with a subset of the available tables. Also note that the headers for fact tables are yellow, while dimensions are blue. Click "Save All" to save your changes. Note in Solution Explorer that you now have the two additional dimensions created from the Cube Wizard.

6. One other thing you may want to change, to help make the data a little more presentable, is the formatting of the measures, so that they're shown to the user in a friendlier way. For example, select the Sales Amount measure from the list of measures and, in the Properties window, change the FormatString value to "Currency" from the dropdown list. For the Reseller Sales Count measure, select the "Standard" value.

Create Hierarchies

Before you can use the cube, you need to define hierarchies that can be used for slicing and dicing the cube. Begin by creating hierarchies for the Product, Reseller, and Date dimensions. In one case, you will need to create two hierarchies in the same dimension. Use the following chart as a reference:

Dimension	Hierarchy	Level 1	Level 2	Level 3
Product	Products	Category	Subcategory	Product
Reseller	Resellers	Business Type	Reseller	
Reseller	Geographies	Country	State or Province	City
Date	Calendar	Year	Quarter	Month

Create the Products Hierarchy

To create the Products Hierarchy, follow these steps:

1. Double-click on the Product dimension in Solution Explorer to open it, or switch focus to it if it's already open. You should see a three-pane view that includes the list of available attributes, a Hierarchies pane, and a Data Source View pane that contains the table. Note that you have three attributes defined for the Product dimension. These are the Product Category Key, Product Key, and Product Subcategory Key attributes. Rename each of these to remove the word *Key* from each attribute.

2. Click on the Product Category attribute, and view its properties. Look for a property called Name Column. It will be under the Source section near the bottom of the list. Click on the ellipsis (...) button.

3. In the Name Column window, verify that "Column binding" is selected for the "Binding type," Product Category is selected as the "Source table," and select EnglishProductCategoryName as the "Source column." Your example should look like Figure 17-8. Click OK to continue.

    You may also wish to change the Order By property from Key to Name to allow the list of products to be sorted alphabetically.

4. Perform the same task for each of the remaining attributes, binding EnglishProductName to the Product attribute and EnglishProductSubcategoryName to the Product Subcategory attribute.

5. Next, you must build the hierarchy. Drag the Product Category attribute to the Hierarchies pane. It will create a new hierarchy called *Hierarchy*. Because that name isn't very helpful, you can right-click on Hierarchy and choose Rename to give it a new name. Name the new hierarchy *Products*.

6. Drag the remaining attributes into the Products hierarchy using Figure 17-9 as a reference.

7. Next, you will want to define the attribute relationships so that Analysis Services understands how the Categories, Subcategories, and Products are related. This helps optimize cube performance. Begin by selecting the Attribute Relationships tab (Figure 17-10).

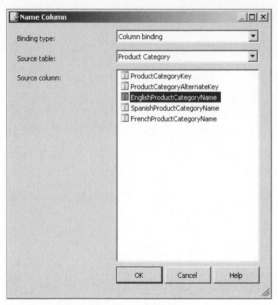

Figure 17-8: Name Column binding.

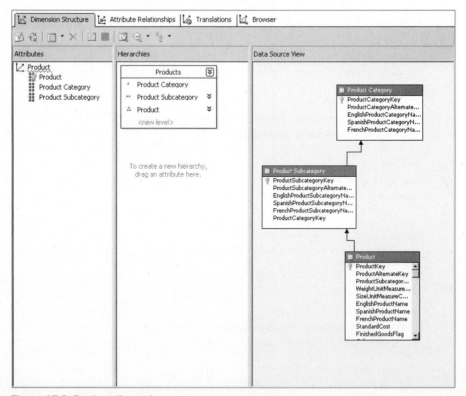

Figure 17-9: Product dimension.

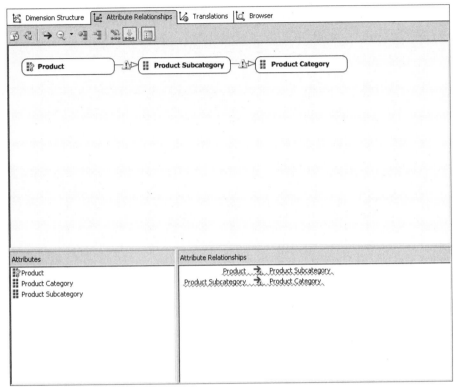

Figure 17-10: `Product` **attribute relationships (before).**

8.   Notice that an attribute relationship has already been defined based on the hierarchy you created. If you built the hierarchy before changing the name, there may be a couple of warnings that would need to be addressed. Select the arrow that points from the `Product` attribute to the `Product Subcategory` attribute. In the Properties window, change the `Name` value to just `Product Subcategory` (removing the word *Key*). This will remove the warning sign.

9.   Also in the Properties window, change the `RelationshipType` value to `Rigid`. This informs SSAS that the relationship will not change over time, meaning that a particular product will always be a member of the same subcategory. If a products subcategory will change over time, then the relationship should be `Flexible`.

10.   Perform the same task for the Product Subcategory to Category relationship, renaming the relationship to just *Product Category*, and changing the relationship type to `Rigid`. When finished, the Attribute Hierarchy should look like Figure 17-11. Click on the "Save All" button to save your changes.

Create the Resellers and Geographies Hierarchies

To create the Reseller and Geographies Hierarchies, follow these steps:

1.   Double-click on the Reseller dimension in Solution Explorer to open it, or switch focus to it if it's already open. You should see a three-pane view that includes the list of available

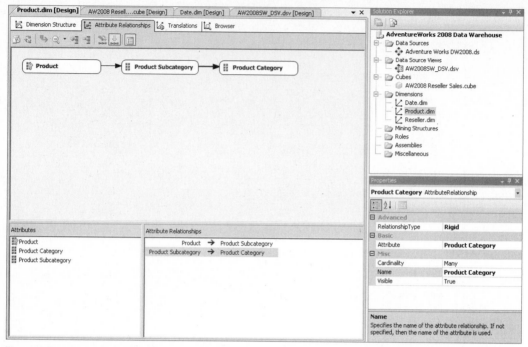

Figure 17-11: Product attribute relationships (after).

attributes, a Hierarchies pane, and a Data Source View pane that contains the table. Begin by renaming the Geography Key attribute to City and the Reseller Key attribute to Reseller.

2. Select the City attribute, and in the Properties pane, bind the City column using the NameColumn property.

3. For the Reseller attribute, bind the ResellerName column to the NameColumn property.

4. Drag the following attributes to the Attribute List, renaming and binding the NameColumn property as described in the following table:

Attribute	Source Table	New Name	NameColumn
BusinessType	Reseller	Business Type	<leave empty>
CountryRegionCode	Geography	Country	EnglishCountryRegionName
StateProvinceCode	Geography	State or Province	StateProvinceName

5. Create a new hierarchy called *Resellers* with the following attributes: Business Type→Reseller.

6. Create a new hierarchy called *Geographies* with the following attributes: Country→State or Province→City→Reseller.

7. When finished, your hierarchies should look like Figure 17-12. Note the warning for the Geographies hierarchy. You will fix this when you define the Attribute Relationships in the next step. Click "Save All."

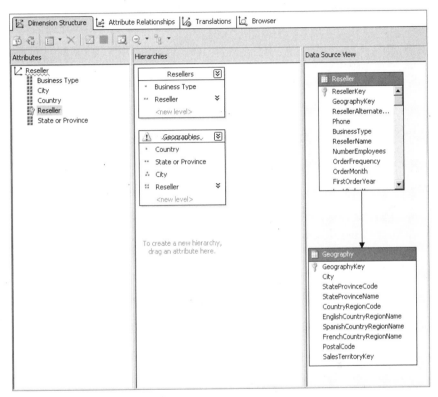

Figure 17-12: Reseller dimension.

Reseller Attribute Relationships

Now it's time to establish the Reseller Attribute Relationships. To do so, follow these steps:

1. Click the Attribute Relationships tab in the Reseller dimension. Notice that the Reseller attribute is linked to all the other attributes directly, but this isn't what you want. Begin by selecting the link to the City attribute.

2. Rename the attribute relationship to City (if not already so named), and change the RelationshipType to Rigid.

3. Delete the attribute relationships from Reseller to State or Province and Country.

4. Right-click on the City attribute and select "New Attribute Relationship."

5. As seen in Figure 17-13, define City as the "Source Attribute," State or Province as the "Related Attribute," and define the relationship type as Rigid.

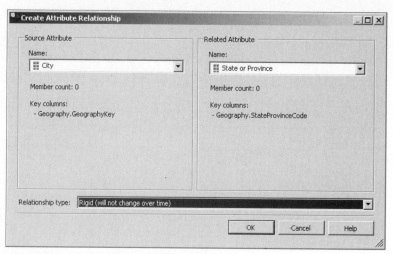

Figure 17-13: New attribute relationships.

6. Create a new attribute relationship with State or Province as the source, Country as the related attribute, and the type as Rigid.

7. Change the Business Type→Reseller attribute relationship to Rigid.

8. Ensure that your Attribute Relationships look like Figure 17-14, and click "Save All."

Build the Calendar Hierarchy

To build the Calendar Hierarchy, follow these steps:

1. Double-click on the Date dimension in Solution Explorer to open it, or switch focus to it if it's already open. You should see a three-pane view that includes the list of available attributes, a Hierarchies pane, and a Data Source View pane that contains the table.

2. You already have the attributes you want to use in the Date dimension, but you will need to rename the Month Number of Year column to Calendar Month.

3. With Calendar Month selected, in the Properties window, select the KeyColumns property, and click on the ellipsis (. . .) when it appears in the value field.

4. Add the Calendar Year column to the KeyColumns field. This will essentially create a composite key that includes the month number and year number to guarantee uniqueness. See Figure 17-15.

5. While still in the Calendar Month properties, bind the NameColumn property to the EnglishMonthName column.

6. Now add the Calendar Year column to the KeyColumns property of the Calendar Quarter attribute, just as you did with the Calendar Month attribute. Because attributes with composite keys must have a NameColumn defined, add Calendar Quarter as the NameColumn property.

7. Create a new hierarchy by dragging the Calendar Year attribute to the Hierarchies pane.

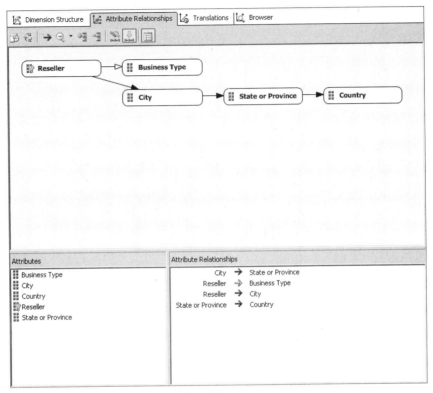

Figure 17-14: Reseller attribute relationships.

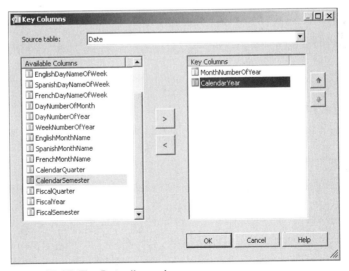

Figure 17-15: The Date dimension.

8. Change the name of the new hierarchy to *Calendar*.

9. Drag and drop Calendar Quarter below Calendar Year in the Time hierarchy to create a new level.

10. Finally, drag the Calendar Month into the Calendar hierarchy. When finished, your hierarchy should look like Figure 17-16.

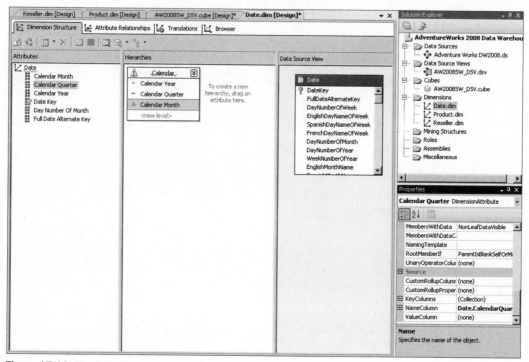

Figure 17-16: The Date dimension.

Calendar Attribute Relationships

To create the Calendar Attribute Relationships, follow these steps:

1. Select the Attribute Relationships tab in the Date dimension.

2. Right-click on the Calendar Month attribute, and select "New Attribute Relationship."

3. Ensure that Calendar Month is selected as the source, and, if necessary, select Calendar Quarter as the related attribute. Change the relationship type to Rigid. Note that once the new relationship is built, the relationship between Calendar Month and Calendar Quarter is automatically deleted.

4. Create a new attribute between Calendar Quarter and Calendar Year as Rigid.

5. Verify that your attribute relationships look similar to Figure 17-17, and click "Save All."

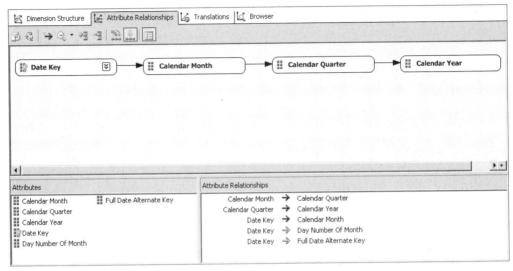

Figure 17-17: Date attribute relationships.

Deploying the Project

At this point, you cannot browse the cube because you have not actually built the cube. You've defined the structure for how data will be accessed, but the data is not available yet. You will need to deploy the cube to make the data available for browsing. In order to be able to deploy the cube, you will need to give the Analysis Services service account permissions to read from the source database. If you are using the same account for the OLTP and OLAP engines, which is not recommended, no further configuration should be necessary. In my case, I am running Analysis Services under a separate account called *ASService*. I will need to grant Read permissions to the dimension and fact tables that this project will be using. For demonstration purposes only, I will create a login for ASService, and grant it db_datareader permissions on the AdventureWorks2008DW database. For information on creating the logins, database users, and granting permissions, review Chapter 6.

To deploy the database and create the cube, select the Deploy option from the Build menu in Business Intelligence Development Studio (see Figure 17-18).

Figure 17-18: Deploying the
database.

A Deployment Progress window will appear while the database is being deployed. This will provide you with detailed information about the deployment process. As long as you get a "Deployment Completed Successfully" message (Figure 17-19), you're good to go! Often, deployment errors can be related to an invalid hierarchy or incorrect user permissions. Evaluate the error list to troubleshoot any problems.

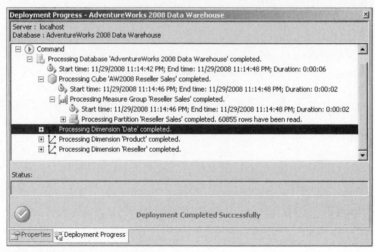

Figure 17-19: Deployment Progress.

Managing SSAS

Although you could use the Browse feature in BIDS to browse the cube, this is a good opportunity to step away from the development side of things and get into the administration side of things. Click "Save All" to save all your changes inside the AdventureWorks 2008 Data Warehouse project. Open SQL Server Management Studio, and create a new connection to Analysis Services (Figure 17-20). One thing you might notice about this connection window is that it does not allow you to choose an authentication method other than Windows Authentication. Unlike the relational Database Engine, the Analysis Services Database Engine can only use Windows or Active Directory logins. SQL Server logins cannot be created or used on Analysis Services databases.

Figure 17-20: Connecting to Analysis Services.

Unlike the relational engine, there are only two folders for organizing the components of SSAS in Object Explorer:

- ❑ **Databases** — You will only see those databases that have been deployed. In this case, you should see the AdventureWorks 2008 Data Warehouse. If you expand the database, you will see the same folders that you saw in the Solution Explorer in BIDS. In fact, you can perform many of the same tasks in BIDS that you can in SSMS, such as creating and managing roles. Unfortunately, the same cannot be said the other way around.

- ❑ **Assemblies** — Not unlike those that you would use in the relational database, Analysis Services has four assemblies that are pre-defined for being able to access the service and query the databases.

Browsing the Cube

In this exercise, you are going to use SQL Server Management Studio to browse the cube you just created. Follow these steps:

1. Expand the Cubes folder of your database.

2. Right-click on the AW2008 Reseller Sales cube, and select Browse. As you can see in Figure 17-21, you will have a list of measures and dimensions that you can drag into the totals, columns, rows, or filters section of the cube browser.

3. Expand the Measures folder.

4. Expand Reseller Sales.

5. Select and drag the Sales Amount measure into the "Drop Totals or Detail Fields Here" section of the browser. You should see the total sales amount in the browser window.

6. Expand the Reseller dimension.

7. Select the Geographies user hierarchy, and drag it to the Row Fields section. You should now see the Sales Amount based on Country, plus the Grand Total in the bottom row.

8. Expand the Order Date dimension.

9. Drag the Order Date.Calendar hierarchy into the Column Fields section. You will see the total for each country in a separate column for each year.

10. Click on the down arrow next to Calendar Year, and select only 2003 and 2004.

11. Expand the Product dimension.

12. Drag the Products hierarchy into the Filter Fields section.

13. Click on the down arrow next to Product, and select only Bikes.

Your matrix should now look like Figure 17-22. Feel free to expand the rows or columns to get more detailed information within the hierarchies.

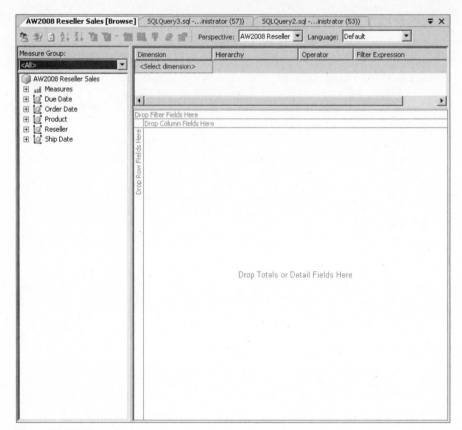

Figure 17-21: The cube browser.

SSAS Security

As mentioned earlier in this chapter, SQL Server Analysis Services relies solely on Windows-based authentication. One aspect of security is managing permissions through roles.

Roles operate similarly to the way they behave in the relational engine; however, because the structure of an OLAP database is significantly different from that of an OLTP database, it is important to introduce the concept of OLAP security. While this will not be an exhaustive review of SSAS security, this section should serve as a good introduction to the topic.

Creating a Role

Roles can be created in either SQL Server Management Studio or Business Intelligence Development Studio. Both tools will allow you to perform the same functions, but with a slightly different user interface for each. I personally tend to favor SSMS, but that's because it's a tool that I use more regularly than BIDS. You can create a role by right-clicking on the Roles folder in your SSAS database and selecting "New Role."

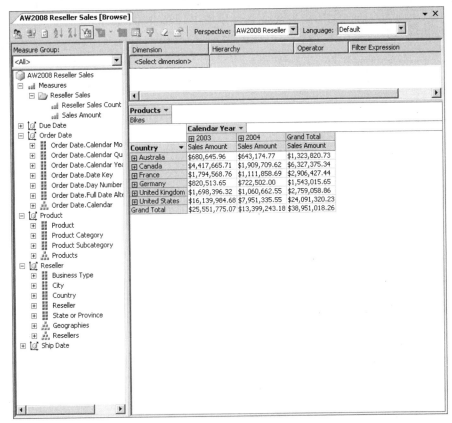

Figure 17-22: Bike reseller sales by country.

As seen in Figure 17-23, you can name the new role and provide a useful description. For this example, create a role called **NA Reseller**, which will have access only to the data for North American countries. Also note on this screen that you can define database-level permissions that would allow the user to have *Full Control*, the ability to process the entire database or read the metadata for objects in the database. For this role, do *not* select any of these options.

The next step is to add a user to the role. You can accomplish this by selecting the Membership page in the Create Role window and clicking on the Add button. In this case, I am going to use Bob, one of the Windows accounts I created in Chapter 6. For this exercise, you can use any non-administrative account or you can leave the role empty.

When creating the role, you can define what permissions this role will have on Data Sources, Cubes, Cell Data, Dimensions, Dimension Data, and Mining Structures. Feel free to browse through and review the different options for each. In this example, you are going to set permissions on specific dimension members by performing the following steps.

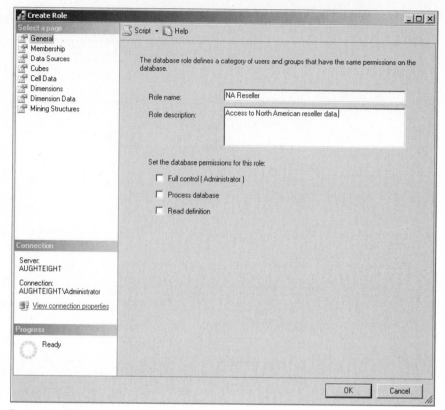

Figure 17-23: Creating the NA Reseller role.

First, you will need to grant Read permission on the AW2008 Reseller Sales cube:

1. Select the Cubes page in the Create Role window.

2. In the dropdown list in the Access column of the AW2008 Reseller Sales row, select Read.

3. Select the Dimension Data page in the Create Role window.

4. In the Dimension dropdown list, select the Reseller dimension from the AdventureWorks 2008 Data Warehouse.

5. Select the Country member set from the Attribute Hierarchy dropdown list.

6. Select the "Deselect All Members" radio button.

7. Check the boxes next to Canada and the United States. See Figure 17-24 as a guide.

8. Click on the Advanced tab. Note the MDX in the "Allowed member set" box. Click on the checkbox next to "Enable Visual Totals." This will allow the members of this role to see only the aggregate totals for the countries they have permissions to. Click OK to finish creating the role.

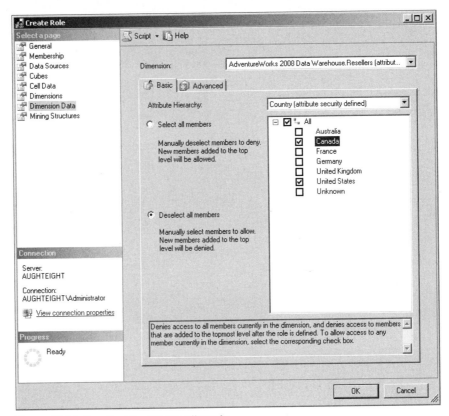

Figure 17-24: Creating the NA Reseller role.

Testing Security

SQL Server Analysis Services includes a great feature for testing security against one or more roles without having to log in as a different user:

1. Go back to your Cube Browser window, and click on the "Change User" button (Figure 17-25). You will see a Security Context window (Figure 17-26), which will allow you to select one or more roles to browse the cube as. This can be extremely handy when you want to test the permissions a particular user might have if he or she belongs to multiple roles, without having to log in as that user. Select the "NA Reseller" role, and click OK.

For example purposes, I have created another role called EU Sales. This role is only there to illustrate that multiple roles can be selected. You will not need this role.

Figure 17-25: "Change User" button.

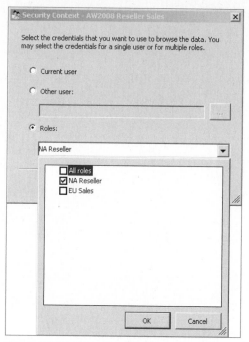

Figure 17-26: Selecting another role to browse as.

2. Note that the browser window has cleared all settings. Repeat the steps from earlier to add the OrderDate.Calendar hierarchy on columns, Reseller.Geographies on rows, and Product.Products on filter. Don't forget to add the Sales Amount measure to the body of the browser.

As you can see in Figure 17-27, the NA Reseller role can only access data that is applicable to the United States and Canada. Even the totals provided are limited to the totals of those two countries. Designing your security model can be one of the most critical steps of building a data warehouse. Understanding who needs access to which data will be the key to a successful SSAS deployment.

One very important thing to note when working with SQL Server Analysis Services is that you should avoid mixing and matching the management tools. Although this exercise showed you the option of creating a role in SQL Server Management Studio, that role will not be included as part of the project definition for the Analysis Services Project in BIDS. You can, however, open a new project in BIDS and select the "Import Analysis Services 2008 Database" template; this will allow you to "reverse engineer" the database as a new project that will include all the changes made via SSMS. If you're not careful, you can potentially overwrite an existing database with valid configuration performed through SSMS by re-deploying the project in BIDS.

Advanced SSAS Concepts

There are several other features and components of SSAS that simply can't be covered in detail in an introductory chapter. These topics are covered in greater detail in *Professional Microsoft SQL Server*

Analysis Services 2008 with MDX by Sivakumar Harinath, Robert Zare, Sethu Meenakshisundaram, Matt Carroll, and Denny Guang-Yeu Lee (Wiley, 2009); however, I just wanted to make mention of them here, so that you would be aware of them.

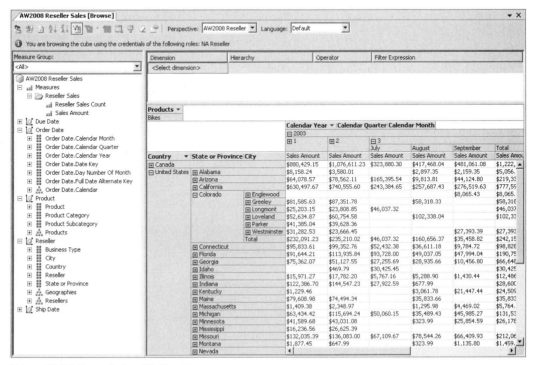

Figure 17-27: Browsing as NA Reseller.

MDX

SQL Server Analysis Services uses a query language known as *MultiDimensional eXpression* language, or MDX for short. MDX was developed by Microsoft, and although it is not an open standard, has been adopted by other vendors of OLAP database technology. MDX uses a different syntax from T-SQL, in that you will need to define what data appears in rows and columns, but the basic select concept is very similar. Below you will see a sample MDX query that returns the number of bikes sold in 2003 and 2004 in the United States and Canada:

```
Select ([Measures].[Reseller Sales Count],
{[Order Date].[Time].[Calendar Year].&[2003],
[Order Date].[Time].[Calendar Year].&[2004] })ON COLUMNS,
{[Resellers].[Geography].[Country].&[Canada],
[Resellers].[Geography].[Country].&[United States]} ON ROWS
FROM [AW2008 Reseller Sales]
WHERE ([Products].[Product].[Category].&[Bikes])
```

Note that the statement begins by selecting the Reseller Sales Count measure, and the years 2003 and 2004 in the columns. Canada and the United States will appear on rows. This query will be executed against the AW2008 Reseller Sales cube, using the Bikes product category as a filter.

This is just a simple example of how MDX works. Whole books have been written on the topic, and I personally only know a small handful of people who could be considered experts in the language. As your role as a database administrator expands beyond managing only the relational database, it may be in your best interest to learn MDX as well.

Data Mining

At the beginning of this chapter, I mentioned that having a whole bunch of data that you don't do anything with is just a waste of resources. The point of this chapter is to help you understand the tools that are used to put context to your data. The examples in this chapter focus on looking at historical information, and specifically looking at reseller performance based on geography, time, and product. This type of analysis helps provide insight into what has happened and will hopefully lead to better business decisions. Another type of analysis, however, can be used for getting a better idea of what is likely to happen.

This predictive analysis is known as *data mining*, and is part of the SQL Server Analysis Services tools. Since much of the data in a cube, data mart, or data warehouse is numeric fact data, it lends itself better to the proprietary data-mining algorithms that Microsoft has developed. Microsoft SQL Server 2008 supports building data-mining models that can be used for tasks such as targeting advertisements to customers based on their purchase history, identifying loss-leaders that will bring more customers into the store, and so on.

One of my favorite online retailers has kept track of my purchase history going back to prior to 2000. Because of this, they often offer me special deals and discounts on DVDs or electronics that they think that I might like. And it works. I often make impulse purchases based on their recommendations. Grocery stores do the same thing. Whenever I swipe my club card at the local food mart, not only am I saving 20 cents on milk, but they know how often I buy milk, and in what quantities. They can use this information to send me coupons tailored to my buying habits, or they can look at the sales data for all customers and decide how well a certain product line sells in my zip code.

Microsoft has a language that is separate from T-SQL or MDX for working with and building data-mining models called the *Data Mining eXtensions* language, or DMX for short. Similar to T-SQL, it includes Data Definition Language (DDL) and Data Manipulation Language (DML) statements, functions, and operators.

Data Mining Structures can be created in BIDS, as part of an existing Analysis Services Project, and can be built from either a relational data source or an existing OLAP cube. Microsoft supports the following proprietary data-mining techniques:

Technique	Short Description
Microsoft Association Rules	Builds rules that describe which items are most likely to appear together as part of the same transaction.
Microsoft Clustering	Iterative techniques that group records that share similar characteristics into a data set
Microsoft Decision Trees	Predictive modeling of discrete and continuous attributes

Technique	Short Description
Microsoft Linear Regression	Specific implementation of decision trees that disable splits and use a single root node for prediction of continuous attributes
Microsoft Logistic Regression	Regression-based implementation of Microsoft Neural Network that supports prediction of discrete and continuous attributes
Microsoft Naïve Bayes	Classification algorithm that uses discrete attributes and considers all input attributes as independent
Microsoft Neural Network	Allows the combination of each possible state of an input attribute with each possible state of a predictable attribute to calculate probabilities
Microsoft Sequence Clustering	Combination of sequence analysis and clustering that identifies clusters that are part of a similarly ordered sequence
Microsoft Time Series	Regression algorithms used to forecast continuous values over time

Each of the data-mining techniques will allow you to input specific parameters when building a data-mining model. You should take some time to experiment with the different techniques and options in the Mining Structures Wizard. Although data-mining functions are often outside the scope of a DBA's job, you should review some of the material in Books Online, specifically the "Special Considerations for Data Mining" section of the Security Overview (Analysis Services — Data Mining) topic.

Summary

In this chapter, you learned about the basic elements of an Analysis Services solution, including building a cube based on a relational data source. It is my hope that you walk away from this chapter with a basic understanding of some of the features that SQL Server Analysis Services brings to the table. As a database administrator, it is important that you understand more than just how your data is being stored, but also how it's being *used*.

The next chapter will introduce you to what is probably the most user-accessible portion of the Microsoft SQL Server 2008 BI stack — SQL Server Reporting Services.

Introduction to SQL Server Reporting Services

In today's business world, companies tend to collect massive amounts of information, from the products they sell to what the weather was like when it was sold. This often leads to accumulating many terabytes of information. Because companies collect vast amounts of information, it is often difficult to present that information in a useful way let alone gain insight into the health of their business to make effective business decisions. For the decision makers to make effective use of the information, they must have easy access to intuitive and useful reports that combine information from many different locations to provide a detailed account of business activity. Combining detailed information with a graphical representation aids in understanding and can provide a comprehensive view of various trends and comparisons. SQL Server Reporting Services has all of these capabilities and then some.

SQL Server Reporting Services Overview

SQL Server Reporting Services (SSRS) was first introduced in 2004 as an add-on product to SQL Server 2000 and was accepted with great fanfare. SQL Server 2005 didn't add all that much new functionality to Reporting Services but did fully integrate Reporting Services as part of the installation. By including Reporting Services as part of the product rather than just an add-on, SQL Server was able to provide a full Business Intelligence infrastructure. Reporting Services underwent a significant overhaul for the SQL 2008 release with many new features being added and the bulk of the architecture re-designed for added performance.

Reporting Services provides all the necessary tools and services to create, deploy, and manage reports in an enterprise environment. You can either use it right out-of-the-box or have developers extend it to fully customize the reporting experience. As a server-based platform, SSRS can provide reporting functionality that targets almost any relational, multi-dimensional, or XML data source. In addition to reports that developers create, Reporting Services also allows for more savvy users to create ad hoc reports based on report models. Report models provide an abstraction of the data in the form of entities so that users are not bothered with having to know the intricate details of the actual data sources.

Components and Tools

Reporting Services consists of a collection of components, tools, and APIs that you use to create and distribute rich reports for end-users. Each of these tools serves a specialized purpose in the reporting life cycle. There are tools designed to create the reports, configure and manage the reports and server instance, and for viewing the reports. The following sections discuss some of the common components and tools.

Report Server

The Report Server component is the heart of a SQL Server Reporting Services instance. It consists of three applications — Report Manager, Reporting Web Services, and Background Processing — all running within a single Windows Services, as shown in Figure 18-1. These applications use a combination of specialized processors to perform specific functions such as report processing, data processing, or report delivery. Two of these processors — the report processor and the scheduling and delivery processor — are considered the core processors, and they perform the initial processing of reports and all scheduling operations. The core processors maintain the integrity of the reporting system and supply an infrastructure that allows developers to add new functionality but cannot be extended themselves. These extensibility points are referred to as *extensions*, and Reporting Services provides default implementations for each of them.

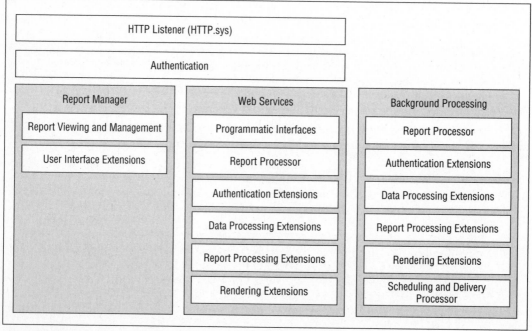

Figure 18-1: Report Server architecture.

Report Processor

The *report processor* is the component responsible for generating reports requested, either by an end-user or a scheduled process, and is considered one of the two core processors in a Reporting Services installation. The report processing happens in three distinct phases:

❑ **Report Definition Processing** — In this phase, the report processor retrieves the report definition from the Report Server database and prepares it to accept data. This includes the initialization of any parameters or variables that are used in expressions and all preliminary processing that is required by the report.

❑ **Data Processing** — By using the appropriate data processing extensions, the report processor retrieves any data required by the report and combines it with the report definition. The result does not produce an actual viewable report, but creates a report in an intermediate format.

❑ **Rendering** — The creation of an intermediate format allows the report processor to apply many rendering extensions to the same set of data to obtain different viewing formats.

Scheduling and Delivery Processor

The other core processor is the *scheduling and delivery processor*. This handles all scheduled operations and controls the delivery of reports to end-users. The scheduling and delivery processor works in conjunction with the SQL Server Agent to deliver reports to end-users. When a schedule is created, Reporting Services creates a corresponding SQL Server Agent job that executes on the schedule provided. The job executes the dbo.AddEvent stored procedure found in the ReportServer database, which adds an event to a queue maintained by Reporting Services. Reporting Services pools the queue at regular intervals to check for new events. The queue is checked every 10 seconds by default but can be adjusted by setting the PollingInterval setting in the RSReportServer.config file. When a new event is detected in the queue, the scheduling and delivery processor calls the report processor to handle the request in a background process. During the processing of the request, the report processor uses the delivery extension that is defined by the schedule to send the report to the proper destination. Delivery extensions are discussed later in this section.

To prevent users from gaining access to information they no longer have permission for, the scheduling and delivery processor performs an authentication step to verify the current permission set for the subscription owner prior to processing the report request. Later sections in this chapter discuss assigning permissions to users and creating scheduled events.

> Reporting Services depends on the SQL Server Agent Service to process schedules and must be running in order for events to be placed into the queue. If the SQL Server Agent Service is stopped, no events will be added to the queue, and any events that would have been generated will be lost.

Extensions

Reporting Services was designed using a very modular architecture allowing for maximum extensibility both by Microsoft and developers. In addition to the core set of processors discussed in the last section, Reporting Services provides many processes that can either be replaced or extended by developers to expand the processing capabilities of the server. The report processor then uses these extensions while processing reports. For example, imagine that you need to have a report faxed to one of your business partners every morning. This can be done by creating a custom delivery extension that faxes reports.

Reporting Services supports several types of extensions such as authentication, rendering, data processing, and delivery. Of these extensions, the Report Server requires at least one authentication, data processing, and rendering extension. The following table lists all of the default extensions that are included in a Report Server installation:

Extension	Included Extensions
Authentication	Windows Authentication, including impersonation and delegation features when enabled in the domain
Data Processing	SQL Server, Analysis Services, Oracle, Hyperion Essbase, Teradata, SAPBW, OLE DB, and ODBC data sources
Rendering	HTML, Excel, CSV, XML, Image, Word, and PDF
Delivery	e-mail and a file share (if configured for SharePoint integration, SharePoint library)

- ❑ **Security Extensions** — Used by Reporting Services for authentication and authorization of users and groups. A default extension based on Windows Authentication is included in Reporting Services, although it can be replaced with your own extension if you require a different authentication approach. However, only one security extension at a time is supported for each installation of Reporting Services. Using Windows Authentication is the recommended approach but is not always an option. For example, if you were exposing the reporting solution over the Internet or an extranet, using a custom security extension would eliminate the need to create user accounts in the Active Directory. In this situation, using Forms-based authentication allows you to fully integrate the reporting system with the rest of the site. Both the site and the reporting system can share a single authentication store.

- ❑ **Data Processing Extensions** — Reporting Services relies on data processing extensions to get information from a data store. Each type of data source has its own data processing extension. The data processing extension is responsible for such actions as opening a connection to the data source, passing any required parameter values to the query, running the query against the data source and returning a rowset, and iterating over the rowset to retrieve the data. The eight data processing extensions included with Reporting Services are SQL Server, Analysis Services, Oracle, SAP NetWeaver Business Intelligence, Hyperion Essbase, Teradata, OLE DB, and ODBC. In addition to these eight, any .NET data provider can be used from within Reporting Services.

❑ **Rendering Extensions** — These create viewable forms of the reports from the intermediate form of the report created by the report processor. Reporting Services provides seven rendering extensions, which are described in the following table:

Rendering Extension	Description
CSV	The Comma-Separated Value (CSV) rendering extension renders reports in comma-delimited text files containing no formatting instructions. The file can be opened with any application that has the capability of reading text files.
HTML	When a report is requested and viewed through a web browser, the report processor will use the HTML rendering extension to render the report in UTF-8 encoded HTML.
Image	When using the HTML rendering extension, the appearance of the report can vary depending on the version of the user's browser, browser settings, and available fonts. If you require that reports have a consistent look no matter what the browser, you may want to consider the image rendering extension, which renders the report on the server, so all users see the exact same image. Because the report is being rendered on the server, all fonts used in the report must also be installed on the server. By default, the extension will render the report as a TIFF image but can render it in the following formats: BMP, EMF, GIF, JPEG, PNG, TIFF, and WMF.
Microsoft Excel	This extension renders the report as an Excel spreadsheet that can be viewed or modified in Microsoft Excel 97 or later. The rendered report supports all the features available for any regular spreadsheet.
Microsoft Word	All I have to say is, finally! In every single Reporting Services class I have taught, there would be at least one student who would ask why they couldn't render in Microsoft Word, and honestly, I never had a good answer. Now I do: "You can in 2008." With this rendering extension, you can render a report as a Microsoft Word document that is compatible with Microsoft Office Word 2000 or later.
PDF	Renders reports in Portable Document Format (PDF) files that can be opened and viewed with Adobe Acrobat 6.0 or later.
XML	XML files provide a platform-independent view of the data, allowing you to send reports to a third party to be processed. You could also use an XSL Transformation to turn the report into another XML schema for use by another application. The XML generated by this extension is UTF-8 encoded.

❑ **Report Processing Extensions** — Can be added to provide custom report processing for report items that are not included with Reporting Services. By default, Reporting Services can process items such as tables, charts, matrices, lists, textboxes, and images. If you would like to host additional items within your reports, such as a Microsoft MapPoint map, you can create a report processing extension to do so.

❑ **Delivery Extensions** — As discussed before, the scheduling and delivery processor uses delivery extensions to deliver reports to various locations. Reporting Services includes three delivery extensions, which are discussed in the following table:

Delivery Extension	Description
File share	Allows you to place reports on a shared folder on your network. Users who want to view the report would then navigate to this location and open the report. The location of the shared folder, filename, rendering extension to use, and overwrite options are all configurable when using this extension. This approach is very useful for very large reports or if you need to keep copies for archival purposes.
e-mail	Uses Simple Mail Transfer Protocol (SMTP) to send a message to end-users. This message can contain the actual report or simply a URL to the report. It is recommended that the URL link to the report is sent rather than the report itself. There are two reasons for this. First, if you have several large reports sent to a large number of people, I can assure you that you will be getting a call from your mail server administrator. Second, when just the URL is sent, the user who is viewing the report will have to authenticate with the Report Server before seeing the information. This way if somebody other than the intended user gets the link, say through an accidently forwarded e-mail, they won't be able to see the information contained in the report unless they have permissions.
SharePoint Document Library	When using Reporting Services in SharePoint Integrated mode, there is also the option of having the report stored in a document library. This takes advantage of some of SharePoint's features such as versioning and workflow to create solutions for more complex scenarios.

Reporting Services Configuration Manager

The Reporting Services Configuration Manager (see Figure 18-2) is used to modify the configuration of a Reporting Services instance. Although it is mostly used to modify an already existing configuration, it is necessary to use this tool to complete the installation if you install Reporting Services using the Files-Only option. Until this has been completed, the instance will be unusable. Any of the following actions can be performed using the Reporting Services Configuration Manager:

❑ Configure the account that the Report Server service uses.

❑ Configure the account used for unattended report execution.

❑   Create and configure URLs that are used by the Report Server and Report Manager.

❑   Create and configure the Report Server database.

❑   Manage encryption keys that are used to protect stored connection strings and credentials.

❑   Configure e-mail settings for the Report Server.

Not all Reporting Services settings can be modified from the Reporting Services Configuration Manager. To configure certain server-level settings such as time-outs, logging, or security, SQL Server Management Studio is required.

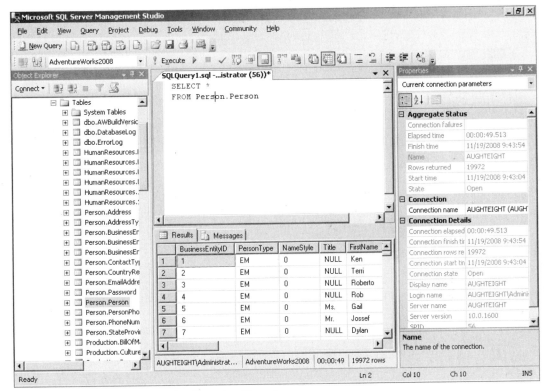

Figure 18-2: Reporting Services Configuration Manager.

SQL Server Management Studio

SQL Server Management Studio provides database administrators and developers with an integrated environment to manage and configure all aspects of SQL Server. Introduced in SQL Server 2005, Management Studio combines the features of Enterprise Manager, Analysis Manager, and Query Analyzer into a single application. This reduces the need to have multiple applications open and having to switch between them.

In SQL Server 2005, Management Studio was used to manage almost all aspects of Reporting Services, from creating roles and assigning permissions to managing reports that were deployed to the server. This has changed with SQL Server 2008. Although Management Studio is still used to control permissions and server settings, you can't use it to assign permissions, create folders, or manage the reports that are on the server. When you need to manage the content of a Report Server, such as reports or the creation of schedules, you must use Report Manager.

Business Intelligence Development Studio

Business Intelligence Development Studio (BIDS) (see Figure 18-3) really isn't part of SQL Server 2008; rather, it is an instance of Visual Studio 2008 that includes the required add-ins to work with SQL Server 2008. When SQL Server 2008 is installed, it checks to see if Visual Studio 2008 is installed on the machine. If found, the installation process installs a collection of project templates and designers that create the various SQL Server 2008 projects. If not found, the installation process installs the Visual Studio 2008 shell and then continues with the installation of the project templates and designers. Either way you end up with an instance of Visual Studio 2008.

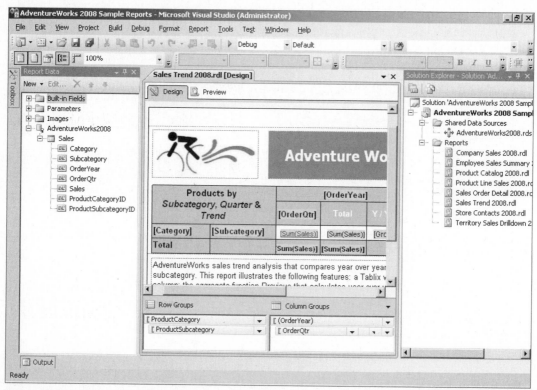

Figure 18-3: Business Intelligence Development Studio.

Business Intelligence Development Studio is used to create reports and report models for use in SQL Server 2008 Reporting Services. Report definitions use an XML-based schema called *Report Definition Language* (RDL). There were many changes made to the schema between the 2005 and 2008 versions of SQL Server. Because of this, BIDS can only be used to create reports for SQL Server 2008. If you open a SQL Server 2005 report, it will be upgraded to the 2008 RDL and will not be able to be deployed to a 2005 server.

Report Builder

Report Builder is a report authoring environment that can be used by business and power users to create ad hoc reports. There are actually two versions of Report Builder; version 1.0 is included with SQL Server 2008. One of the major downfalls of Report Builder 1.0 is that you have to build your report based on an already existing report model. Version 2.0 of Report Builder, which can be downloaded from the Microsoft web site, does not have this limitation. Version 2.0 is based on Microsoft Office (see Figure 18-4) and was designed for users advanced enough to create reports yet who do not need all the functionality of BIDS.

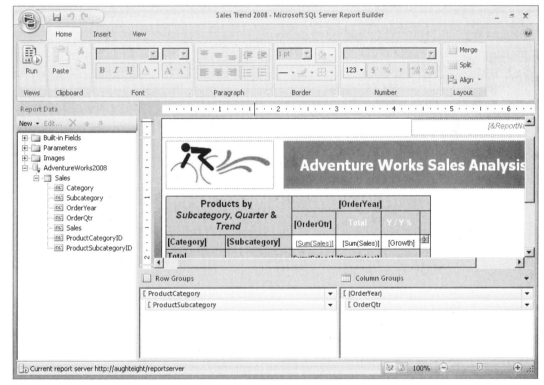

Figure 18-4: Report Builder 2.0.

Both BIDS and Report Builder generate RDL files, and reports can be modified in either tool regardless of where they were initially designed. This allows a more experienced report developer to use Business Intelligence Development Studio to initially create the report and then have users customize it using Report Builder to suit their needs.

Report Manager

Of all the tools used in Reporting Services, you'll likely use Report Manager the most. Report Manager is a web-based tool that performs actions such as deploying reports, viewing reports, creating schedules, and assigning permissions. Although you can use almost any web browser to view reports, only the Windows versions of Internet Explorer 6 with SP1 and Internet Explorer 7 guarantee all functionality.

Report Manager (see Figure 18-5) is only used if Reporting Services is configured to run in Native mode. When Reporting Services is installed in SharePoint Integrated mode, then the SharePoint itself is used to manage the reports.

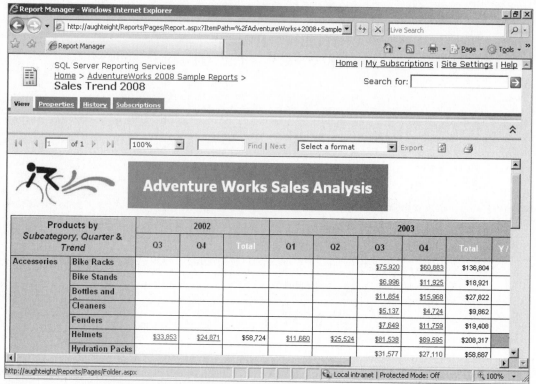

Figure 18-5: Report Manager in IE7.

Integrating Reporting Services with SharePoint is outside the scope of this book, and we will assume a Native mode installation from this point forward.

To open Report Manager, navigate to the Report Server URL using your web browser. The default URL is `http://<server_name>/reports`, but it can be changed either during or after installation. Using Report Manager, you can browse reports and folders, view reports, or even subscribe to a report to have it delivered to your inbox or shared folder on your computer. The actions you can perform will vary based on the permissions that have been assigned to you. We will visit security and permissions later in the chapter.

If you are installing Reporting Services on either Windows Vista or Windows Server 2008, you must configure the Report Server for local administration before you can use Report Manager to manage a local Report Server instance. This can be done by adding the Reporting Services URLs to the trusted sites zone within Internet Explorer.

Installation and Configuration

All components in SQL Server 2008 are installed through a single Setup application known as the SQL Server Installation Center. Using this application, you can select which features of Reporting Services you want installed (see Figure 18-6) so you don't have to install the client design tools like Business Intelligence Development Studio on your production report server.

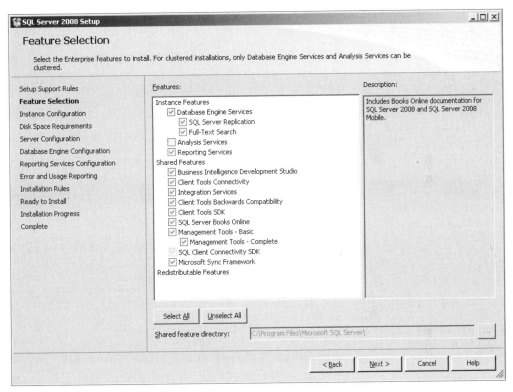

Figure 18-6: Feature Selection.

Hardware and Software Requirements

One of the biggest improvements in SQL Server 2008 Reporting Services is that it no longer depends on IIS. This is a huge step forward and allows companies that would not allow SQL Server Components installed on a Web Server to consider Reporting Services. Also, by removing the IIS dependency, it makes troubleshooting connectivity issues a bit easier because there is one less layer that needs to be configured.

Although IIS is no longer a required component, in order for Reporting Services to answer web requests using http.sys, a URL reservation needs to be made. To create a URL reservation, an IP address, TCP port, URL, and virtual directory are required. The installation program will use default values for these at installation, but you can change them afterwards on the Web Service URL page of the Reporting Services Configuration Manager tool.

Reporting Services has the same minimum requirements for processor and memory as the Database Engine. Please refer to Chapter 2, which goes into detail on what these requirements are for various scenarios. In addition to this, Reporting Services will require at least 120 MB of free disk space to install the core services and Report Manager.

Security Considerations

As discussed earlier in the chapter, all aspects of Reporting Services run within a single Windows Service. Because there is no default value, you will be required to select a user account for this service during installation, as shown in Figure 18-7. You can choose either a domain user account or one of the built-in accounts (Local System, Local Service, or Network Service). Honestly, the only good choices here are either a domain user account or the Network Service account. The Local Service does not have the appropriate permissions for Reporting Services, such as connecting to the Active Directory to authenticate users, and the Local System is a highly privileged account with far too many permissions. Best practice is to use a domain user account specifically created for Reporting Services. This allows you not only to have an account with a very low level of permissions, but also to audit the actions of the account, making it easier to detect if the account was compromised.

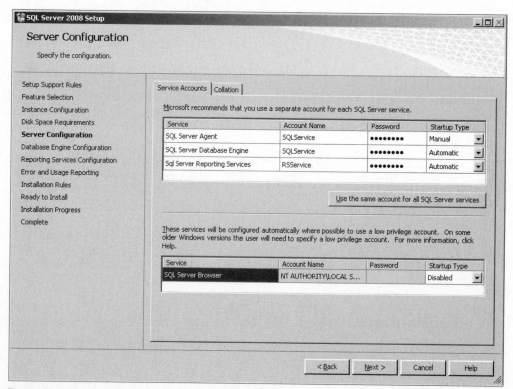

Figure 18-7: Specifying service accounts for SQL Server Reporting Services.

If you decide that you need to change the account that Reporting Services uses, you can only use the Reporting Services Configuration Manager tool after installation. Don't use the MMC service snap-in or you may get yourself into some trouble. The service account that is used is stored in many locations, and if you use the MMC snap-in, it will not be updated in all the locations necessary for Reporting Services to run correctly.

One important note to keep in mind is that although Report Manager is an ASP.NET application, it doesn't run under the context of the ASP.NET worker process defined in IIS. Reporting Services hosts its own copy of ASP.NET in the Windows Service that Report Manager is running in.

Installation Mode

When installing Reporting Services, you have the option to have it configured or not. During installation, Reporting Services will prompt you for how you would like to configure the newly installed instance, as shown in Figure 18-8. There are three options that you can choose from: Native mode, SharePoint Integrated mode, or Files-Only installation. Some of these options may or may not be available for selection based on what components are being installed or what is already installed. For example, the Native mode will only be available if you are installing Reporting Services and the Database Engine at the same time. Let's take a closer look at what each of these modes does:

❑ **Native Mode** — Of the three options, this is the easiest to use and will install the server with default values. In order for this option to be chosen, you will have to install Reporting Services and a local Database Engine at the same time. The option creates a fully functional server that can be used immediately after installation is complete.

❑ **SharePoint Integrated Mode** — This option requires a bit more work on your part. Like a Native mode installation, this option will only be available if you are installing Reporting Services and a local Database Engine at the same time. Setup will install Reporting Services with default values. This includes creating a database that has the necessary objects to work with SharePoint data storage such as a SOAP endpoint for communication with the SharePoint server. Once Reporting Services is installed, you will need to install the Microsoft SQL Server 2008 Reporting Services add-in for Microsoft SharePoint Technologies on the SharePoint server and make a few changes in SharePoint before the Report Server is fully functional.

❑ **Files-Only Installation Option** — If you need full control over the configuration of the Report Server, such as using an existing or remote Database Engine instance, then this is the option for you. This will also be your only choice if you are not installing both Reporting Services and the Database Engine at the same time. A Files-Only installation will only copy the program files to the server and register the Report Server WMI provider. You must configure the Report Server using the Reporting Services Configuration Manager tool before anything can be done with it.

Multiple Instances and Versions

As discussed in Chapter 2, it is possible to have multiple instances of SQL Server 2008 components installed on the same computer. Reporting Services is one of the instance-aware components and allows you to have a total of 50 instances running on the same computer. You can even run Reporting Services 2008 side-by-side with Reporting Services 2000 or 2005. Because the 2000 version of Reporting Services was not instance-aware, if you plan on having 2000 and 2008 on the same machine, you will need to install the 2008 version as a named instance leaving the default instance for Reporting Services 2000. You can install multiple instances by running the install on the same computer by running the setup program multiple times.

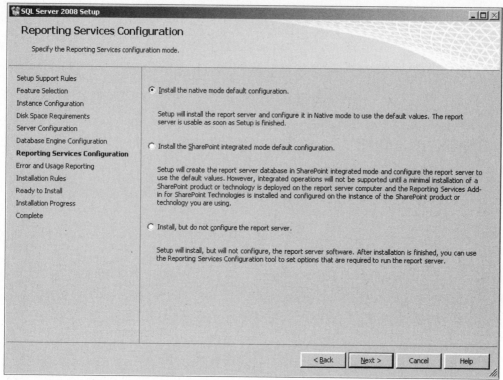

Figure 18-8: Choosing the installation mode.

When you are dealing with multiple instances of Reporting Services and they are different versions, be sure to install all the tools for each version. You can't use any of the Report Authoring, Configuration, or Management tools for one version on a different version.

Creating Reports

Now that you understand what makes up Reporting Services and how to install it, it is time to see Reporting Services in action and create some reports. In total, there are three tools that can be used to author reports in Reporting Services 2008: Report Designer, Report Builder 1.0, and Report Builder 2.0. Each of them provides ways to connect to a database, define report layouts, and deploy the reports. However, the amount of work on your part and the options that are available will differ between them. Let's take a look at each of these tools.

Report Designer

Report Designer is a developer-centric report authoring tool that is hosted within Business Intelligence Development Studio, which we saw earlier is really just Visual Studio 2008. It provides the report developer with all of the options you would expect in a full-featured report designer and is intended for use by more advanced designers who need to create or modify reports. BIDS has many features that make working with large reporting solutions easier and more productive such as the ability to integrate with source control systems and organization of reports into projects. Report Designer also provides many additional features on top of BIDS for more advanced reporting needs like free-form reports and graphs.

One really useful feature that the Report Designer brings to BIDS is the Report Wizard. This tool allows you to quickly create reports by providing some basic information making the initial report creation extremely easy; however, you cannot use it to modify an already-existing report. To create a report, you provide the Report Wizard with a data source, query, and layout and formatting information. Using this information, the Report Wizard generates a report that you can either deploy to the Report Server as is or use as a starting point to further customize with either Report Builder or Report Designer. You can access the Report Wizard tool one of two ways: Create a project using the Report Server Project Wizard template, or you could simply right-click on the project and choose "Add Report" from the context menu.

Report Builder

Although the Report Wizard is a quick way to create and deploy a report in minutes, it still requires the use of Business Intelligence Development Studio. For most users, this tool is overkill to create basic reports and is often a bit intimidating to non-developers. Report Builder was created for those business users who have the need to create reports yet do not require the full feature set of BIDS. As mentioned before, Report Builder comes in two versions, and the latest version is not installed as part of SQL Server 2008. Report Builder 1.0 shipped as part of SQL Server 2008, and if you would like to have the latest and greatest with Report Builder 2.0, you will have to download the Microsoft SQL Server 2008 Feature Pack. Report Builder 2.0 was designed after the familiar Office 2007 user interface, making it possible for anybody who regularly works in Microsoft Word 2007 to very quickly be able to create reports.

All existing reports can be opened and customized by either of these authoring tools; however, once customized by Report Designer 2008 or Report Builder 2.0, you will not be able to work with them in any of the older versions. Both tools convert the SQL Server 2000 or SQL Server 2005 reports' RDL to the new SQL Server 2008 RDL schema, thereby preventing any older tool from being able to work with it.

Let's work through creating a simple report using Report Builder 2.0 to see how this tool can be used by both report designers and also regular business users. Once you have downloaded and installed Report Builder 2.0, you can launch the application from the Start Menu, as shown in Figure 18-9.

Connecting to Data

Before you can start building your report, you must first define where the report will get its data from by creating a *data source*. *Data sources* contain metadata that describes how to connect to the underlying data. Reporting Services supports many types of data sources such as SQL Server databases, Oracle databases, ODBC databases, XML files, and many more. For the most part, a data source contains the server name, database name, provider, and credentials to use and can be either shared between reports or specific to a single report. Using Report Builder, you can create report specific data sources that are embedded in your report. However, if you would like to create a shared data source for use in many reports, you will have to use either BIDS or Report Manager. In an ideal world, the administrator of your Report Server — maybe this is you — creates several data sources that are stored on the server. This way the users only have to select the appropriate data source from a list rather than having to remember all of the connection details.

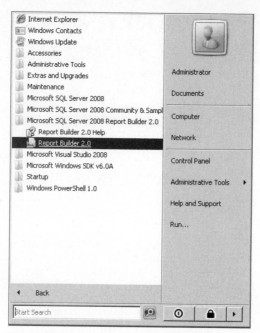

Figure 18-9: Launching Report Builder 2.0.

You can create a new data source by doing the following:

1. Click New ➤ Data Source from the toolbar in the Report Data pane. After connecting to the Report Server to download any shared data sources that are available, the Data Source Properties dialog, shown in Figure 18-10, will be displayed.

2. After providing a name for the data source, you can either specify a connection string to create an embedded data source, or you can select a shared data source that is stored on the server. Each report can contain multiple data sources, either embedded or shared, so the name that you choose for your data source must be unique within the scope of the report. For this example, complete the Data Source Properties dialog box as shown in Figure 18-10 and click OK.

Now that you have a data source that defines where to get the data from, you need to specify what data needs to be retrieved. You do this by creating a data set for the report. A *data set* contains a reference to a data source, a query that will be executed against that data source, parameters that specify values to the query, a collection of fields that is exposed to the report, and various other data options. Every non-trivial report requires at least one data set, but it is more likely that you will have multiple data sets defined.

Every data set is based on a single existing data source defined in the report. To create a data set, right-click on the data source that contains the data and choose `Add Dataset` from the context menu. This will display the Dataset Properties dialog (Figure 18-11), which is divided into five pages — Query, Parameters, Fields, Options, and Filters — allowing you to configure the data set. The type of data source that the data set is based on will determine some of the options that are available.

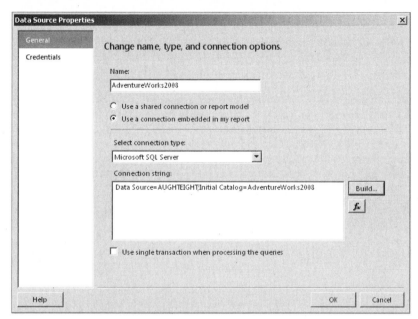

Figure 18-10: Creating a data source.

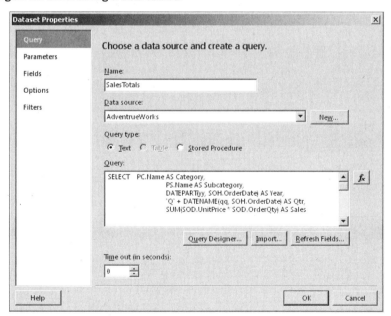

Figure 18-11: Creating a data set for the report.

❑ **Query** — The Query page is used to define the query type, such as text, table, or stored procedure, and the actual query itself. When defining the query, you can type it in directly, import the query from another report, or click on the Query Designer button and build the query graphically (as long as your data source supports it).

❑ **Parameters and Filters** — There are two ways that you can reduce the amount of data that is displayed to your users — parameters and filters. The difference between the two is when the filtering occurs, before or after the data is retrieved for the report. Parameters are used to pass values to the data source, and then the data source handles the filtering of the data — for example, a WHERE clause in a T-SQL statement or a FILTERS clause in a MDX query. Try describing parameters without using the word *filters* — it makes the distinction a bit easier to follow. This approach is often the best choice because less memory and network bandwidth is needed during the retrieval of the data; however, there are times when retrieving all the data is a better choice. You can alternatively create filters on the Filters page to have all of the data returned from the data source and the Report Server do the filtering. This approach may be a better choice if you have multiple data regions displaying subsets of the data. With filters the data is only retrieved once, and each data region applies the appropriate filters.

❑ **Fields** — Data sets are an abstraction of the data found in the data source, exposing the actual data through a collection of elements known as data set fields. Data set fields are used to populate items on the report such as tables and charts with the report data. The fields themselves can either be a direct link to a column returned by the query or a calculated field that you create in the data set. A customer's full name made up of the first and last name columns is an example of a calculated field. You can add and remove fields from the data set on the Fields page of the Dataset Properties window.

❑ **Options** — The Options page allows you to change how the data in the data set is treated and supports six settings that can be adjusted as shown in the following table:

Option	Description
Collation	Determines the collation that should be used when sorting data. By default, the server will try to use the collation used by the data source.
Case sensitivity	Specifies whether SQL Server distinguishes between uppercase and lowercase characters. If not selected, SQL Server considers them to be identical for sorting purposes. For example, *A* would be equal to *a*.
Accent sensitivity	Specifies whether SQL Server distinguishes between accented and unaccented characters. If not selected, SQL Server considers them to be identical for sorting purposes. For example, *a* would be equal to *â*.
Kanatype sensitivity	Specifies whether SQL Server distinguishes between the two types of Japanese kana characters: Hiragana and Katakana. If not selected, Hiragana and Katakana characters are considered equal.
Width sensitivity	Specifies whether SQL Server distinguishes between the single-byte representation and the double-byte representation of the same character. If not selected, the single-byte and double-byte representations of the same character are considered identical.
Interpret subtotals as detail rows	Indicates whether subtotal rows are to be treated as detail rows rather than aggregate rows.

If you are going to follow along with the example, you will need to create a data set for the sales data that we will be working with:

1. Right-click on the `AdventureWorks` data source and select "Add Dataset" from the context menu.

2. Set the Name property for the data set to `SalesTotals` and ensure that `AdventureWorks` is selected as the data source.

3. Use the following query to return the total quarterly sales for each Subcategory. Leave all other options set to their default values. Your screen should look similar to Figure 18-11:

```
SELECT → PC.Name AS Category,
PS.Name AS Subcategory,
DATEPART(yy, SOH.OrderDate) AS Year,
'Q' + DATENAME(qq, SOH.OrderDate) AS Qtr,
SUM(SOD.UnitPrice * SOD.OrderQty) AS Sales

FROM Sales.SalesOrderHeader SOH
INNER JOIN Sales.SalesOrderDetail SOD
ON SOH.SalesOrderID = SOD.SalesOrderID
INNER JOIN Production.Product P
ON SOD.ProductID = P.ProductID
INNER JOIN Production.ProductSubcategory PS
ON P.ProductSubcategoryID = PS.ProductSubcategoryID
INNER JOIN Production.ProductCategory PC
ON PS.ProductCategoryID = PC.ProductCategoryID

GROUP BY DATEPART(yy, SOH.OrderDate),
  PC.Name,
  PS.Name,
  'Q' + DATENAME(qq, SOH.OrderDate),
  PS.ProductSubcategoryID
```

Laying out Report Data

Once you have selected the data that you want to use in your report, it is time to define how the report will look. You do this by arranging the report data on the Designer surface using a combination of layout elements called *report items*. Report items give the report its structure; are bound to the data in the data sets; and include data regions, images, lines, rectangles, textboxes, and subreports. Each report item can have its individual properties, such as its font, color, and style set either by using the Ribbon in the Report Builder user interface or at run time by using an expression.

The report item that you will most likely use is a *data region*. *Data regions* allow you to group, sort, filter, and aggregate data from a single data set and come in five different flavors: Table, Matrix, List, Chart, and Gauge. The type of data region that you choose will largely depend on the type and volume of data that you have and what you are trying to communicate in your report. To make the best choice as to what data region to use, you must have a good understanding of your data and the purpose of the report. The following table breaks down the various types of data regions that are available in Report Builder 2.0:

Data Region	Description
Table	Displays the data grouped by row. Tables will dynamically expand down a page but have a fixed number of columns. Static rows can be added for labels or totals.
Matrix	Displays the data groups by row and column. A matrix must have at least one row group and one column group. Both rows and columns are dynamic and will expand both across the page for column groups and down the page for row groups. Static rows can be added for labels or totals.
List	Lists allow you to work with data in a free-form format. You define a *template* that is used for each value in the data set. For example, you may want to arrange textboxes in a vertical pattern alongside an image instead of having them in a single row. The template is then repeated for each row in the data set.
Chart	Helps to visualize summary data. Many chart types are available in Reporting Services 2008 such as pie charts and bar graphs.
Gauge	Gauges provide a visual representation of a value within a finite range of values. Gauges can be used either in a Table or List to show the relative strength of a value. Gauges can also be used individually to show an aggregated value.

Although you can add an empty table, matrix, list, gauge, or chart manually and configure its data source and properties, it is far easier to use the Table, Matrix, List, Gauge, or Chart Wizard, which can be found on the Insert tab of the Ribbon. The Wizard steps you through the process of creating the data region. For this example:

1. Click Insert ➤ Matrix ➤ Matrix Wizard. After selecting the data set containing the data, you need to specify how the data fields should be arranged in the report as shown in Figure 18-12. For this report, you want to display the total sales grouped by category and subcategory on rows, and by year and quarter on columns. In previous versions of Reporting Services, this type of report would have been extremely difficult, but the Wizard in Report Builder makes it as simple as drag-and-drop.

2. After dragging the appropriate data fields to the row groups, column groups, and values sections, your screen should look similar to Figure 18-12. Click Next and you will be prompted to select a pre-defined layout for your report (see Figure 18-13). This determines whether or not you want to display totals and subtotals for the groups and how you want them to be displayed. For our report, simply accept the defaults by clicking Next.

3. The final screen of the Wizard asks that you choose a style for the report, as shown in Figure 18-14. Choose any style that you want and click the Finish button to close the Wizard and have the matrix created for you.

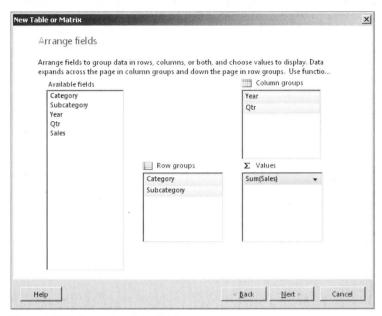

Figure 18-12: Arranging data fields.

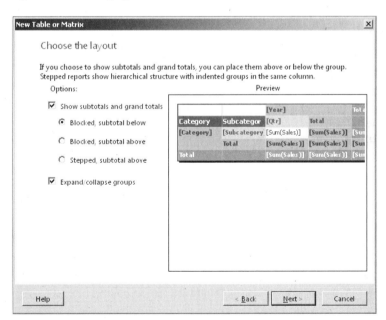

Figure 18-13: Choosing a layout for the report.

4. You could continue to fine-tune the layout and formatting of the report after the Wizard is complete; however, you will not be able to return to the Wizard for the data region. At this point you have a completed report that you can run. Test your report by clicking on the Run button on the Home tab of the Ribbon.

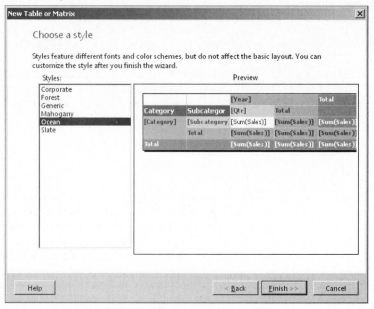

Figure 18-14: Choosing a style for the report.

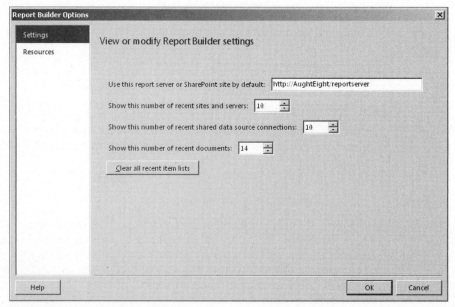

Figure 18-15: Report Builder Options.

Publishing Reports

After you have designed and tested a report, you will need to publish it to a Report Server instance before users can actually use it. This can be done by simply saving the report's RDL file to the Report Server. In order for you to do this, you will need to have permissions to add content to the Report Server. Report Builder tries to save reports to whatever Report Server is marked as the default. This can be changed in the Report Builder Options dialog, as shown in Figure 18-15. It is also important to note that when saving reports to your Report Server you will not be able to create folders. You will have to use Report Manager to create the folder before attempting to save your report.

Report Delivery

Now that we have our report published to the Report Server, there are two general ways end-users can gain access to the reports. Users could either execute a report on-demand (seeing the report immediately) or they could subscribe to a report (having it delivered on a regular basis). When using on-demand reports, the reports are essentially "refreshed" every time a user views them, thereby providing the user with the most current information. However, there will be times when this approach is not possible, such as when the report is resource-intensive, requiring some form of caching to meet the performance requirements. Alternatively, we could schedule the report to execute during idle times to reduce the load on the server and have the results delivered to the end-users. Let's take a closer look at caching and snapshots to increase server performance and subscriptions to have reports delivered to end-users.

Caching

Reporting Services can cache the results of a processed report to reduce the time required to retrieve it. This can be very handy if the report is large or frequently accessed; however, it is important to note that the content of the cache is extremely volatile. The cached reports are stored in memory only and therefore will not survive a server restart. The report is also not guaranteed to be present in the cache since reports may be removed from the cache as new reports are added or replaced. Also, not all reports have the ability to be cached. For instance, reports that are based on user-dependent data, use Windows Authentication, or need to prompt the user for credentials cannot be added to the cache. Use the Report Manager to configure caching for a report. The settings can be found on the Execution page on the Properties tab of the report.

Snapshots

Report caching can certainly improve performance, but can also be unpredictable because of the volatility of the cache. Report snapshots offer a much more predictable caching strategy. Snapshots can either be created at scheduled intervals or manually by a Report Server administrator. Just like the report cache, reports that are based on user-dependent data, use Windows Authentication, or need to prompt the user for credentials cannot have a snapshot generated for them.

When a snapshot is created, many elements besides the report snapshot are stored in the database. Everything that is needed to re-create the report as it existed when the snapshot was created is stored, including the report data, any parameter values used to obtain the report data, the report definition, and any embedded resources such as images. Use the Report Manager to configure snapshot settings for a report. The settings can be found on the Execution page on the Properties tab of the report.

Subscriptions

Subscriptions offer a way to have a report generated and delivered in a specified format either at a specific time or in response to a particular event. This provides an alternative to having to actively select the report each time you want to view it. Subscriptions are used to schedule the execution of reports and have the report ready for the users. For example, users may want to have the weekly report run every Friday at midnight and then delivered to their e-mail inbox so that it is ready when they come into work on Monday morning.

As mentioned earlier, the scheduling and delivery processor is responsible for all scheduled operations and controls the delivery of reports to end-users. The processor uses delivery extensions that are deployed on the Report Server to handle the actual delivery of the report after it is processed. Reporting Services provides three delivery extensions out-of-the-box: You can have a report delivered to a shared folder, an e-mail address, or a SharePoint document library. In order for subscriptions to be processed, the Report Server Events and Delivery feature must be enabled on the Report Server. This can be done by setting the `ScheduleEventsAndReportDeliveryEnabled` property on the Surface Area Configuration for Reporting Services facet to `true`. Also, to actually create subscriptions for a report, the report must use stored credentials, and the user creating the subscription must have permissions to view the report and to create subscriptions.

Two types of subscriptions are supported by Reporting Services — Standard subscriptions and Data-driven subscriptions. With a *Standard subscription*, an end-user configures a subscription for a single rendered report to be delivered to a single destination such as a file share or e-mail address. You can create a new Standard subscription when viewing the report you want to subscribe to and clicking on the "New Subscription" button in the toolbar. On the New Subscription page (Figure 18-16), you must select a delivery provider and schedule that the report will execute on.

Data-driven subscriptions work very much like Standard subscriptions with the exception that it is possible to have a single report delivered in multiple different formats to many destinations. A Data-driven subscription gets its subscription settings from an external database table that you create. This allows the subscription to be very dynamic because updates to the table affect how the subscription will format and deliver the report. Data-driven subscriptions become extremely useful when you have a large number of recipients who require the data in different formats. Creating Data-driven subscriptions requires a bit more work than standard subscriptions, requiring a database table to hold the subscription information and a query to return it. The results of the query are them mapped to the parameters of the subscription such as report format and destination. When the subscription is processed, each row is evaluated in the table and handled like an individual Standard subscription. Because it requires a bit more skill, Data-driven subscriptions are usually created and managed by the Report Server administrators.

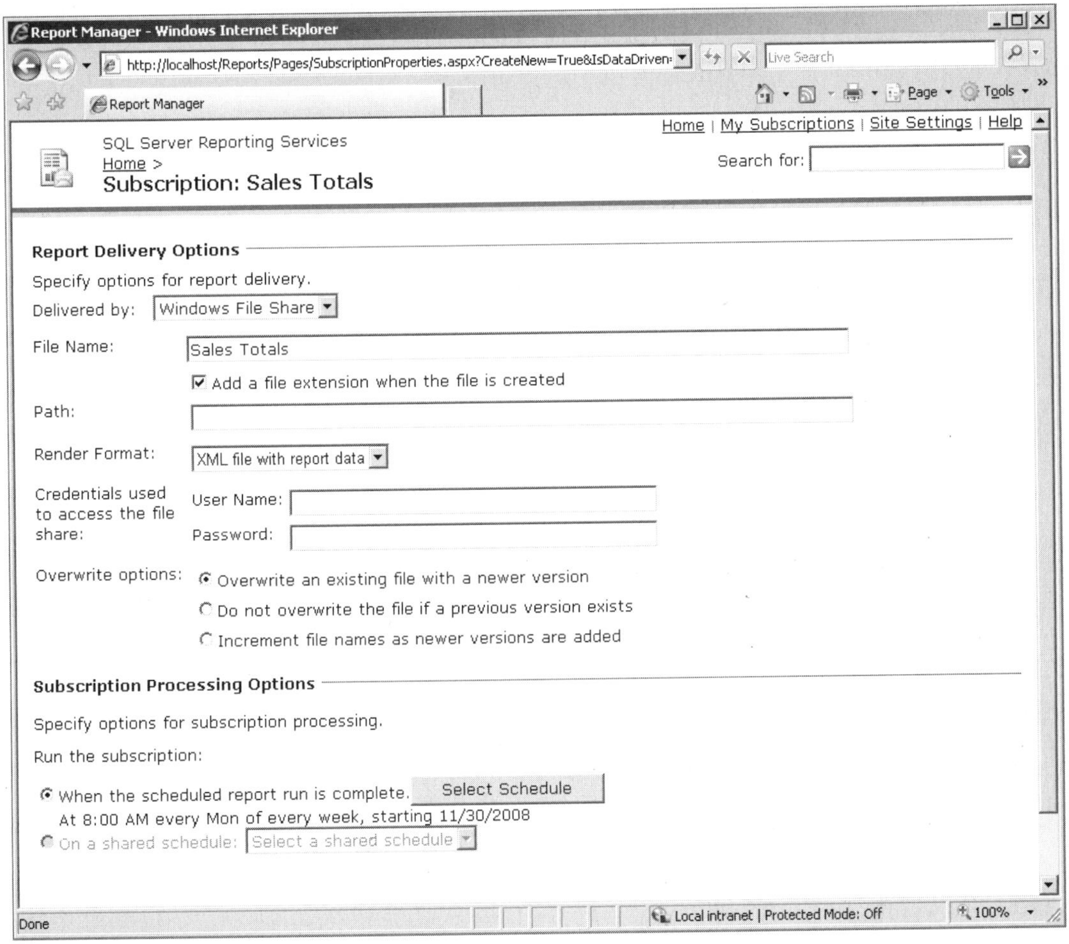

Figure 18-16: Creating a Standard subscription.

Summary

This chapter introduced you to Reporting Services for SQL Server 2008. You should be able to at least understand the different parts of Reporting Services, and be able to install a new Reporting Services instance if asked to do so. This chapter provided you with a brief introduction to Reporting Services architecture, described how to install a Reporting Services instance, and how to create and publish a basic report for users.

In Chapter 19, you will learn about using Service Broker in your applications to provide more accurate and reliable asynchronous message delivery.

Introduction to Service Broker

SQL Server 2005 introduced a new feature, known as *Service Broker*, that allows you to build more robust applications without having to rely on external technologies. Similar in concept to the Microsoft Message Queuing (MSMQ) service, Service Broker allows you to define services within one or more SQL Server databases that can all interact with one another and build communication paths for more complete end-to-end connectivity using native SQL Server features.

This chapter examines the basics of how the Service Broker features operate and how they can be leveraged to provide you with a mechanism for building inclusive application solutions. This chapter covers the following topics:

- ❏   Service-Oriented Architecture
- ❏   Service Broker overview
- ❏   Service Broker elements
- ❏   Service Broker security
- ❏   A sample Service Broker application

Service-Oriented Architecture

Service Broker employs a model that uses Service-Oriented Architecture (SOA) for defining how data is treated by the variety of applications that will interact with it. SOA is based on the idea of separating data from the different processes that will view or manipulate that data. This allows you to build applications that do one thing, and do it well, without having to format the data to fit the application.

A good example of SOA in action is e-mail. Many of us use e-mail every day without thinking about what happens behind the scenes when we send an electronic message to someone. When I open up my Microsoft Outlook client, I need to specify to whom the message will be delivered and what the message will say. I can also set other options, such as formatting the message with HTML or requiring that a read-receipt be sent.

Now, just because I've set these options in my client doesn't mean that the recipient has to conform to them. That person could be using another mail client that is configured to display all messages in plain text, regardless of source formatting. They can also explicitly specify not to return read-receipt messages to the originator.

Regardless of how we each have our respective clients configured, e-mail is doing exactly what it is supposed to, by providing an asynchronous message delivery that allows me to send information to an interested party, which can be read at their leisure.

Service Broker Overview

Service Broker operates similarly to the e-mail example I just described. Applications can use the features of Service Broker to create loosely coupled applications and services that provide asynchronous, ordered delivery of messages for efficient and appropriate processing. That sounds good, but what does it mean?

Well, it means that when your developers are building applications that use SQL, they can take advantage of features that allow them to submit updates without waiting for a response. It also means that when certain conditions are met, users can be notified that the data has changed or a process requires their attention. Service Broker provides you with the tools and the framework to build these types of solutions without having to purchase costly third-party products.

Because there are already external and third-party solutions that provide some (if not all) of the features that Service Broker offers, you may wonder why you would use Service Broker. The best advice is to weigh the benefits of Service Broker against your other options and decide which works best for you. One might argue in favor of using Service Broker because of its tight coupling with SQL Server and its ability to handle larger message sizes than MSMQ. At the same time, another person might argue that its integration with SQL might be considered a vulnerability, allowing for a single point of failure in your application design.

The decision to use Service Broker will be made by your application developers, but as a SQL Server 2008 database administrator, you will be responsible for knowing what this Service Broker is and how to manage it. Many of the features of Service Broker you learn about in this chapter build on an understanding of other topics covered elsewhere in this book. For example, you can refer to Chapter 6 for more information about creating certificates, and Chapter 7 to learn more about creating endpoints.

Service Broker Elements

Service Broker employs a framework that uses messages as a unit of work. However, the handling and processing of these messages are defined by a variety of elements, including the conversation architecture, delivery contracts, queues, and services. In this section, you learn about the components that are used in a Service Broker solution.

Conversations

Service Broker uses *conversations* to define a persistent communication architecture that is reliable and asynchronous. The conversation architecture uses messages, dialogs, and conversation groups to control the flow of data in a Service Broker application.

Messages

Messages are the unit of information in a conversation. When Service Broker applications communicate with one another, they must agree on what type of data will be passed between them and what formatting and data validation (if any) are required. Each message is tagged with the conversation identity, as well as a sequence number so that the messages can be processed in sequential order.

The content and formatting of the message are defined by the application. When a message is received by Service Broker, the message content is validated against the message type. Although the messages are stored as `varbinary(max)`, a *message type object* defines the message type and stores the type information as a database object. The message type object must be created on any SQL Server that will use that message type.

Creating a message type requires that you supply a validation parameter for the message to be considered correctly formatted. Message types are usually validated by using either well-formed XML or XML defined by a specific schema, but you can also define that the message type is empty, meaning that the message body is `NULL`. You can also choose to forgo message validation altogether. Validation is eschewed when Service Broker is using a data type other than XML.

Dialog Conversations

When messages are sent between two instances of Service Broker, a *dialog conversation* (or simply *dialog*) is established. Dialogs use message delivery that is defined as *exactly-once-in-order* (EOIO). The conversation identifier and sequence numbers for each message are used to identify related messages to ensure that they are delivered in the correct order. Dialogs, therefore, establish a long-running stream of messages that exist between two services.

For each dialog, one service acts as the *initiator*, which establishes the conversation. The *target* is the service that will accept the conversation. A *contract* for the conversation, described later in this chapter, determines the messages each participant can send.

Dialogs automatically generate *acknowledgments* when receiving a message to guarantee reliable delivery. Each outgoing message is stored in a transmission queue until the acknowledgment is received. Automating this process prevents the application from needing a separate, explicit acknowledgment mechanism for each message. These acknowledgment messages are part of the internal functions of Service Broker and are not part of the official application message stream.

Because Service Broker is designed for asynchronous communications, if a remote service is unavailable, the messages will be stored in a queue until the service is again available, or the lifetime for the dialog has ended.

The *lifetime of a dialog* is dependent on several factors. The dialog can be ended when an application either explicitly terminates it or receives an associated error message. Each participant is equally responsible for ending the dialog when one of those two conditions is met. Common scenarios for ending a dialog conversation require one of the participants to specify that the dialog will be ending without error and to notify the other participant.

When designing Service Broker applications, the application developer can also specify a maximum lifetime for the dialog. When this dialog lifetime is reached, a time-out error message is placed on the service queue, and new messages for that dialog are refused. Messages that were generated prior to the end of the conversation can still be received after the conversation has ended, but no new messages can be sent or received after the conversation has ended.

Conversation Groups

Conversation groups are used to identify conversations that are related and typically part of the same business logic. Conversation groups are associated with a specific service. Conversations that are members in a conversation group are either sent to or received from that particular service. For each service, SQL Server will associate the message with an appropriate conversation group, which guarantees that the messages received by the application for each conversation are processed exactly in order. This allows applications to receive messages from multiple sources but process related messages from those sources in the order that they are received by all services.

Conversation groups are subjective, meaning that the initiator may treat a message as belonging to Conversation Group A, whereas the target may treat the message as belonging to Conversation Group 24. This allows each participant to treat the message in a way that is appropriate for what it knows about the application.

For example, a sales tracking application may receive messages from a service that manages pricing information, as well as messages from an inventory service that tracks the availability of products in stock. This sales tracking application can tag messages from the independent conversations of the pricing and inventory services as being part of the same conversation group, which can be used to identify sales trends of products based on whether the price goes up or down. Neither the inventory service nor the pricing service is aware of this relationship because it is irrelevant to how they send messages to the sales tracking application.

Conversation Priorities

The ability to assign priority values to conversations is a feature that is new in SQL Server 2008. *Conversation priorities* are used to ensure that certain messages are treated differently based on whether the priority is higher or lower. The priority values range from 1 to 10, with 10 being the highest. If no priority value is set, the default value of 5 is applied. Note that when priorities are defined, they apply to the entire conversation from beginning to end, not just specific messages within a conversation.

Although it is common to set the same priority on both endpoints of a conversation, it is not a requirement. When the initiator and target have different priorities configured on them, the priority of the endpoint is applied to that conversation as the messages pass through it. So if I have an initiator configured with a conversation priority of 3 and the target has a priority of 9, messages are sent out from the initiator with a relatively low priority (meaning that other messages in the queue might be sent first), but received by the target with a high priority, which tells it to process those messages ahead of other, less preferred messages. Conversely, the target might respond by sending outgoing messages to that initiator before others, but the target would classify those messages received from that particular target as less important.

Another important trait to know about conversation priorities is how they affect conversation groups. Conversation groups are prioritized using the priority value of the highest active conversation with that group. For example, if a conversation has a priority of 7, as long as there are messages in the queue for that conversation, the whole group will inherit the higher priority. Once the conversation ends, though, the conversation group will fall back to either its default value or the next-highest priority conversation.

Contracts

Contracts are agreements between services about which messages each server will send to accomplish certain tasks. For each message type, a contract is defined to specify who can send that message type. Three types of contracts can be created:

- ❏ **Initiator Only** — Only the service initiator will be able to send messages of the type defined in this contract.
- ❏ **Target Only** — The service target will be the only one sending this type of message.
- ❏ **Any** — Allows either the target or the initiator to send this type of message.

In Service Broker, a default contract is created and configured to use the default message type. This contract uses the SENT BY ANY statement to allow either the initiator or target to send the default message type.

Queues

Queues are a major component in the Service Broker architecture. *Queues* are used to provide the asynchronous processing of data between applications and services as needed. Service Broker uses queues to store messages. When a message is sent or received by a service, the messages are inserted into the appropriate incoming or outgoing queue. Queues are managed by Service Broker, and the contents of the queues can be queried like a table or view object.

When viewing a queue, each row contains the content of the message, the message type, the target service, validation, contract, and conversation information for the message. Your application uses this information to identify and process the message as expected. Queues are also used to help guarantee that the messages are processed in the order they were sent, not the order they were received.

You can use stored procedures to process the messages in the queue when there is work to do. Service Broker also allows you to execute multiple instances of the same stored procedure to more efficiently process the messages in the queue.

Services

The term *service* when used in the Service Broker context refers to a software component that performs a specific business task or set of tasks. Conversations, as noted earlier, are defined between services. The service name is used as an addressable endpoint to deliver messages to the appropriate queue within the context of a database and to route messages to the appropriate service, as well as to enforce contracts and remote security requirements for a new conversation.

Services each use a specific queue for storing incoming messages, and the contracts used by the service define which tasks are accepted for new conversations.

Routes

Routes are used to indicate where messages should be delivered. When messages are sent by an initiator, Service Broker must be able to find the target service. Just as you might use a map to find the nearest

Italian restaurant, Service Broker must find a way to contact the target for a conversation. Routes are composed of three components to help uniquely identify the correct target:

❑ **Service Name** — The name must exactly match the target service.

❑ **Broker Instance Identifier** — A value of the GUID data type used to identify the database that holds the queue for the service

❑ **Network Address** — Usually a hostname or IP address of the system that hosts the target service. Optionally, this can instead be the address of a forwarding broker, which knows how to forward the message to the appropriate target.

When finding the appropriate route for a conversation, SQL Server must match the name and broker instance identifier specified in a BEGIN DIALOG CONVERSATION statement with the service name and broker instance identifier in the route. If the route does not provide a service name or broker identifier, any service name or broker identifier can be matched. SQL Server will choose the appropriate route based on a list defined in the sys.routes table of the database that contains the initiator service. If Service Broker cannot find the correct route for the message, the message is dropped.

Each database contains a route named AutoCreatedLocal, which will match any service name and broker instance. Message delivery is restricted to the current instance, however. Although this might be acceptable for applications that use services that are all stored in the same SQL Service instance, it is generally a good idea to manually create a route for each service to help guarantee the availability of the service. This also prevents the AutoCreatedLocal route from being modified to the point of being unusable for its intended purpose.

You can use the CREATE ROUTE statement to specify the connection option for the remote service. This is typically the address and port number used to connect to an endpoint on the target server.

Security Considerations for Service Broker

Security, of course, is a concern when building Service Broker solutions. Whether your application is completely localized to a single database or will span multiple databases on multiple servers, you need to have an understanding of the impact that security will have on your Service Broker applications.

Service Broker uses two security models to determine how to secure communications for Service Broker applications. Dialog security is used to handle encryption, remote authentication, and remote authorization for conversations. Transport security, on the other hand, handles security between two server instances.

Dialog Security

Dialog security focuses on securing individual conversations between services. If the initiator and target services exist in the same database, encryption is automatically enabled, and a session key is used to encrypt the communications. Encryption can also be turned off for intra-database service communications, but it's generally not recommended. Dialog security also provides two modes in which to operate when communicating between servers: Full security and Anonymous security.

Full Security

Full security requires that a mutual trust relationship be established between the initiator and target services. This is accomplished through the use of Public Key Certificates. When the target service resides on a remote server, a user with SEND permissions to the Service Broker service must own a certificate and the corresponding private key. The user and certificate information (but not the private key) must be defined on the database that holds the initiator service in a *remote service binding*. The remote service binding ties the username, certificate, and remote target service together to find and establish a trusted connection. The certificate that is used in the Full security model must have the options to begin Service Broker dialogs. This is done by using the ACTIVE FOR BEGIN_DIALOG = ON option in the CREATE CERTIFICATE statement.

Anonymous Security

Anonymous security authenticates the target service to the initiator, but not the other way around. Unlike the Full security model, this does not require a certificate mapping for the remote user, but the user specified in the remote service binding must be a member of the public role in the target database. This also requires that the public role in the target database be granted SEND permission on the target service. Messages using Anonymous security are encrypted using a session key generated by the database that contains the initiating service.

Transport Security

Transport security is managed by controlling access to the endpoints that are used to connect to a remote service. When creating the endpoint, you can specify the authentication options, using Kerberos, NTLM, or certificate-based authentication. You can also specify encryption options for the connection, using AES or RC4. Again, remember that transport security is defined for the entire server instance, which includes all services in all databases. Chapter 7 provides greater detail on creating endpoints.

Creating a Sample Application

This section provides some sample code that can help clarify some of the ambiguities in how Service Broker works. In this example, AWHelpDesk has a *helpdesk* application they use to allow users to submit trouble tickets using a web application. Service Broker will automate the process of inserting the data into a table used by the helpdesk application, as well as sending the user a confirmation that the support request has been received.

Figure 19-1 is a rough map of the sample application you will be using in this exercise. The intent is to allow you to follow the path the application will take.

It begins with the end-user submitting a service request through a Web Form. The request is then sent to the TicketInputService, which establishes a dialog with the TicketNotifyService. The message will be immediately delivered to the TicketNotifyService, which stores the information in the service queue until the HelpDesk.ProcessMessages stored procedure is executed. When the stored procedure executes, an e-mail is sent to the person who submitted the request, the message is logged to the HelpDesk.MessageLog table, and a response is automatically sent back to the TicketInputService. The response messages are held in the queue for the TicketInputService until the TroubleTicket.ProcessMessages stored procedure is executed, at which time the messages are logged and the queue is cleared.

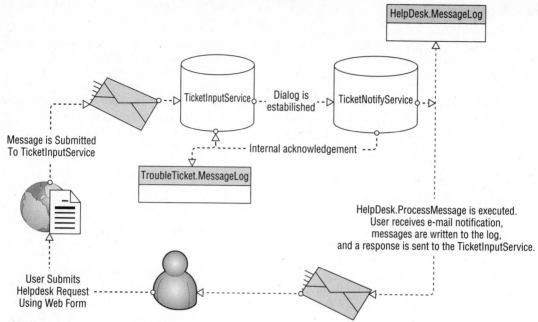

Figure 19-1: The sample application.

Creating and Preparing the Database

You need to begin by taking a couple of steps prior to building your Service Broker solution. In this case, I recommend beginning by creating a new database. If you use the sample AdventureWorks2008 database, you will have to execute an ALTER AUTHORIZATION ON DATABASE :: AdventureWorks2008 TO *[yourlogin]* statement in order for the samples to work. Create the AWHelpDesk database by doing the following:

1. Issue the following statement:

```
USE master
CREATE DATABASE AWHelpDesk;
GO
```

2. Create a database master key. There is actually one case in which you can get away without using a database master key, but it requires that your services all live in the same database and you explicitly set ENCRYPTION = OFF when starting a conversation. You can find more information about creating and using the database master key in Chapter 6. If you did not read through Chapter 6 and have not already created a database master key, you can use the following code to create one:

```
USE AWHelpDesk;
GO
CREATE MASTER KEY
ENCRYPTION BY PASSWORD = 'P@ssw0rd';
GO
```

3. Also, the sample scripts provided use a user-defined data type called `Name`, similar to the one in `AdventureWorks2008`. Create this data type with the following statement:

```
CREATE TYPE Name
FROM nvarchar(50) NULL;
GO
```

One interesting thing about Service Broker services and the database master key is that if encryption is enabled and no database master key exists, you can continue to submit messages to your services until you're blue in the face, and they never show up in the queue. However, if you later realize your mistake and *then* create the master key, the next time you submit a message, all of the previous messages that seemed to have disappeared into the ether will now be added to the service queue! I actually encountered this behavior several years ago when preparing some demonstrations using a beta build of SQL Server 2005. I had even deleted and re-created the queues and services several times before realizing my mistake. When I finally got the service to receive messages into the queue, I had 10 sample messages from previous attempts in addition to the one I had just submitted.

4. Ensure that the `ENABLE_BROKER` option has been set for the database. You can do this by using an `ALTER DATABASE` statement. Also, if your application will also be accessing services or resources outside the local database, you may need to set the `TRUSTWORTHY` setting to `ON`. The following example configures the database with both settings:

```
USE master;
GO
ALTER DATABASE AWHelpDesk SET ENABLE_BROKER, TRUSTWORTHY ON;
GO
```

with No-wait;
or
with Rollback imonediate

In SQL Server 2008, the `ENABLE_BROKER` is on by default; however, all databases except the `msdb` database have `TRUSTWORTHY` turned off. You can also enable or disable the Service Broker open from the Properties dialog box of the database, as seen in Figure 19-2. Note that you can see the status of the `TRUSTWORTHY` option, but you cannot change it.

Creating the Service Broker Objects

Now that you've prepared the `AWHelpDesk` database for your Service Broker application, it's time to begin creating the Service Broker objects. For this example, you are going to create two queues, two services, one message type, and one contract to use that message type between the services.

1. Begin by creating two new schemas for the objects you will create. Using different schemas helps define a separation of the resources used by each service. In this example, you are going to create a `Helpdesk` schema and a `TroubleTicket` schema. Use the following code to create the schemas:

```
USE AWHelpDesk;
GO

CREATE SCHEMA TroubleTicket;
GO
CREATE SCHEMA HelpDesk;
GO
```

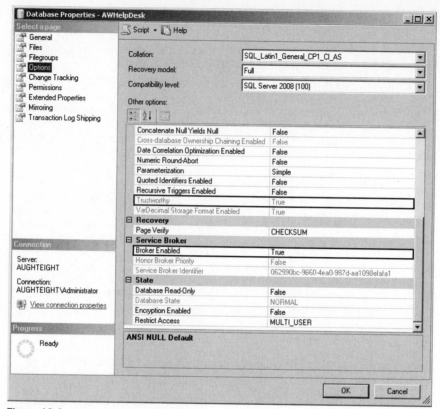

Figure 19-2: TRUSTWORTHY **and** ENABLE_BROKER **options.**

2. Create the message type and validation (if any) that will be used by the Service Broker application. Because both of the services you will create exist in the AWHelpDesk database, you will only need to define the message type once. Remember that if the initiator and target services exist in different databases, you will need to create the same message type in both databases. Use the CREATE MESSAGE TYPE statement to create a new message. This statement uses the following syntax:

```
CREATE MESSAGE TYPE message_type_name
    [ AUTHORIZATION owner_name ]
    [ VALIDATION = validation_method ]
```

The message_type_name value must be unique within the database and commonly uses a URL (or URL-like) convention that allows you to create a hierarchical namespace for creating multiple message types for different services. The AUTHORIZATION option allows the creator to specify a different database user as the owner of the message type, provided the creator has IMPERSONATE permissions, and the VALIDATION option can be one of the following choices:

❑ NONE — No validation of the data is performed by Service Broker.

❏   EMPTY — The message body contains no data.

❏   WELL_FORMED_XML — The message body must use well-formed XML.

❏   VALID_XML WITH SCHEMA COLLECTION schema_collection — The message body must contain XML data that conforms to a specific schema document, which must be supplied separately. You can create a new schema collection using the CREATE XML SCHEMA COLLECTION statement, providing the name and the schema definition.

For this example, you will create a new message type called //AdventureWorks.com/Helpdesk/SupportTicket that uses well-formed XML, as seen in the following code:

```
CREATE MESSAGE TYPE [//AdventureWorks.com/Helpdesk/SupportTicket]
    VALIDATION = WELL_FORMED_XML;
```

3. Create the contract that will call this message type and specify who can send messages of this type. The CREATE CONTRACT statement can contain multiple message types, each one having a different SENT BY clause. Because this example only defines one message type that will be sent by the initiator service (which you have yet to create), you can use the following example:

```
CREATE CONTRACT [//AdventureWorks.com/HelpDesk/SubmitSupportTicket]
(
    [//AdventureWorks.com/Helpdesk/SupportTicket]
    SENT BY INITIATOR
);
```

4. Create the queues that will be used by the services. The first queue will be used by the service that will receive the messages from the web application. This is the queue for the initiator service. The second queue, for the target service, will be used to receive the messages from the initiator and then automatically notify the end-user that the support ticket has been created. Use the following to create the queues:

```
CREATE QUEUE TroubleTicket.TicketInputQueue;
GO

CREATE QUEUE HelpDesk.UserNotifyQueue;
GO
```

5. The final step in this phase is to create the services. When creating a service, use the following syntax for the CREATE SERVICE statement:

```
CREATE SERVICE service_name [ AUTHORIZATION owner_name ]
    ON QUEUE [ schema_name. ]queue_name
    [ contract_name ]
```

When you create a new service, the required parameters are at least the service name and the queue for the service. If the service will be a target for an existing contract, you must specify the contract name.

For this demonstration, you will create two services. The first one, the initiator, will receive data from a web application, which calls a stored procedure to insert the required values. The second service, acting as the target, will be used to notify the end-user that the submission has been received. Execute the following code to create the required services:

```
-- Creating the Initiator Service
CREATE SERVICE [//AdventureWorks.com/HelpDesk/TicketInputService]
ON QUEUE TroubleTicket.TicketInputQueue;

-- Creating the Target Service
CREATE SERVICE [//AdventureWorks.com/Helpdesk/TicketNotifyService]
ON QUEUE HelpDesk.UserNotifyQueue
([//AdventureWorks.com/HelpDesk/SubmitSupportTicket]);
```

Creating Objects for the `TicketInputService`

In this section, you create several objects used by the `TicketInputService` to receive and process the messages, allowing them to move on to the next service. You will begin by creating a new table to store the incoming data, so that it can be used by the helpdesk application. This table will not actually be used by Service Broker, but will demonstrate how Service Broker can be implemented along with other features and objects in SQL Server.

1.   Use the following code to create the table that will store the data input by the user:

```
USE AWHelpDesk;
GO

-- Create a table to store Helpdesk Information

Create Table HelpDesk.TroubleTickets(
ID INT IDENTITY,
firstName Name,
lastName Name,
Issue nvarchar(max)
);
GO
```

Note that the `Name` data type is a user-defined data type that already exists in the `AWHelpDesk` database.

2.   Create a stored procedure that will take data from the Web Form. The stored procedure will then insert the data into the table you just created and will create a well-formed XML message with the same data that will be added to the queue for the `TicketInputService`. This stored procedure also establishes the dialog between the initiator and target services.

```
USE AWHelpDesk;
GO
-- stored procedure to send issues to the ticket submission Service
CREATE PROCEDURE TroubleTicket.AddNewTicket
@firstName Name,
@lastName Name,
@emailAddress Name,
@issue nvarchar(max)
AS
```

```
BEGIN

    Insert HelpDesk.TroubleTickets (firstname, lastname, issue)
VALUES (@firstname, @lastname, @issue)
    DECLARE @message NVARCHAR(MAX)
    SET @message = NCHAR(0xFEFF)
        + '<Customer>'
            + '<CustomerName>' + @firstName + ' ' + @lastName
    + '</CustomerName>'
            + '<EmailAddress>' + @emailAddress + '</EmailAddress>'
            + '<issue>' + @issue + '</issue>'
        + '</Customer>'

    DECLARE @conversationHandle UNIQUEIDENTIFIER

    BEGIN DIALOG CONVERSATION @conversationHandle
    FROM SERVICE [//AdventureWorks.com/HelpDesk/TicketInputService]
    TO SERVICE '//AdventureWorks.com/Helpdesk/TicketNotifyService',
'CURRENT DATABASE'
    ON CONTRACT [//AdventureWorks.com/HelpDesk/SubmitSupportTicket]

    ;SEND ON CONVERSATION @conversationHandle
    MESSAGE TYPE [//AdventureWorks.com/Helpdesk/SupportTicket]
    (@message)

END;
GO
```

Note that, in the BEGIN DIALOG CONVERSATION statement, the TO SERVICE parameter uses single quotes rather than brackets to encapsulate the target service. You should also provide routing information for the target service. As you can see, because this service exists within the same database as the initiator, you can use 'CURRENT SERVICE'. If the target service exists in another database, you can use the remote service's GUID.

3. Create a table that will log the activity of the TicketInputService. Do this by executing the following code:

```
USE AWHelpDesk;
GO
-- log table for received messages
CREATE TABLE TroubleTicket.MessageLog(
    messageID int IDENTITY PRIMARY KEY,
    queueName nvarchar(25),
    message nvarchar(max),
    conversationID uniqueidentifier);
GO
```

4. Create a stored procedure that will write to the TroubleTicket.MessageLog table:

```
USE AWHelpDesk;
GO
-- stored procedure to log messages
CREATE PROCEDURE TroubleTicket.LogMessage
```

```
(@queuename nvarchar(25), @message nvarchar(max),
 @conversation_id uniqueidentifier=NULL)
AS
     IF (@conversation_id IS NULL)
          PRINT 'Queue: ' + @queuename
               + ' Message: ' + @message
     ELSE
          PRINT 'Queue: ' + @queuename
               + ' Message: ' + @message
               + ' Conversation: ' + CAST(@conversation_id AS NVARCHAR(MAX))


     INSERT INTO TroubleTicket.MessageLog (queueName, message,
          conversationID)
     VALUES (@queuename, @message, @conversation_id);
GO
```

5. The final step in creating the objects for the `TicketInputService` is creating a stored procedure that will execute the stored procedure listed earlier, write the queued messages to the log (if any), and write a notice indicating that no further messages have been found once the queue has been cleared:

```
USE AWHelpDesk;
GO
-- stored procedure to read and process messages from queue
CREATE PROCEDURE TroubleTicket.ProcessMessages
AS
     WHILE (1 = 1)
     BEGIN
          DECLARE @conversationHandle UNIQUEIDENTIFIER,
                  @messageTypeName NVARCHAR(256)

          ;RECEIVE TOP(1)
               @conversationHandle = conversation_handle,
               @messageTypeName = message_type_name
          FROM TroubleTicket.TicketInputQueue

          IF @@ROWCOUNT = 0
          BEGIN
               EXEC TroubleTicket.LogMessage 'TicketInputQueue',
     'No further messages found.'
               RETURN
          END

          END CONVERSATION @conversationHandle
          EXEC TroubleTicket.LogMessage 'TicketInputQueue',
     @messageTypeName, @conversationHandle
     END;
GO
```

Creating Objects for the `TicketNotifyService`

Now, you need to create the supporting objects for the target service. Remember that this service will be used to notify the end-user that the submission has been received and a trouble ticket has been generated.

Your first object is a stored procedure that will extract the details of the message from the XML data so that it can be used in the notification message.

1. Create the stored procedure using the following code:

```
USE AWHelpDesk;
GO

CREATE PROCEDURE HelpDesk.ExtractXML
(@XMLstring NVARCHAR(MAX), @customerName Name OUTPUT,
        @emailAddress Name OUTPUT, @issue nvarchar(max) OUTPUT)
AS
    DECLARE @idoc int
    EXEC sp_xml_preparedocument @idoc OUTPUT, @XMLstring

    SELECT      @customerName = CustomerName,
                @emailAddress = EmailAddress,
                @issue = issue
    FROM OPENXML (@idoc, '/Customer',2)
    WITH (CustomerName Name, EmailAddress Name, issue nvarchar(max))

    EXEC sp_xml_removedocument @idoc;
GO
```

2. Just like you did with the last service, create a log table and a stored procedure that writes to the log table. The commands are essentially the same as for the TicketInputService, but these objects are located in the HelpDesk schema:

```
USE AWHelpDesk;
GO
CREATE TABLE HelpDesk.MessageLog(
    messageID int IDENTITY PRIMARY KEY,
    queueName nvarchar(25),
    message nvarchar(max),
    conversationID uniqueidentifier) ;
GO

-- stored procedure to log messages
CREATE PROCEDURE HelpDesk.LogMessage
(@queuename nvarchar(25), @message nvarchar(max),
 @conversation_id uniqueidentifier=NULL)
AS
    IF (@conversation_id IS NULL)
        PRINT 'Queue: ' + @queuename
            + ' Message: ' + @message
    ELSE
        PRINT 'Queue: ' + @queuename
            + ' Message: ' + @message
            + ' Conversation: ' + CAST(@conversation_id AS NVARCHAR(MAX))


        INSERT INTO HelpDesk.MessageLog (queueName, message, conversationID)
    VALUES (@queuename, @message, @conversation_id) ;
GO
```

3. Create a stored procedure that will read and process messages in the queue:

```
USE AWHelpDesk;
GO
CREATE PROCEDURE HelpDesk.ProcessMessages
AS
    WHILE (1 = 1)
    BEGIN
        DECLARE @conversationHandle UNIQUEIDENTIFIER,
            @messageTypeName NVARCHAR(256),
            @messageBody NVARCHAR(MAX);

        RECEIVE TOP(1)
            @conversationHandle = conversation_handle,
            @messageTypeName = message_type_name,
            @messageBody = message_body
        FROM UserNotifyQueue

        IF @@ROWCOUNT = 0
        BEGIN
            EXEC HelpDesk.LogMessage 'UserNotifyQueue',
                'No further messages found.'
            RETURN
        END

        IF
         @messageTypeName =
           'http://schemas.microsoft.com/SQL/ServiceBroker/Error'
        OR
         @messageTypeName =
           'http://schemas.microsoft.com/SQL/ServiceBroker/EndDialog'

        BEGIN
            END CONVERSATION @conversationHandle
            EXEC HelpDesk.LogMessage 'UserNotifyQueue',
            @messageTypeName, @conversationHandle
            CONTINUE
        END

        IF @messageTypeName <>
            '//AdventureWorks.com/Helpdesk/SupportTicket'
        BEGIN
            END CONVERSATION @conversationHandle
                WITH ERROR = 500
                DESCRIPTION = 'Invalid message type.'
            EXEC HelpDesk.LogMessage 'UserNotifyQueue',
            'Invalid message type found.', @conversationHandle
            CONTINUE
        END

        DECLARE @customerName Name, @emailAddress Name, @issue
          nvarchar(max)
        EXEC HelpDesk.ExtractXML @messageBody, @customerName OUTPUT,
```

```
                    @emailAddress OUTPUT, @issue OUTPUT

     /* Send an Email using Database Mail
        This section has been commented out so that the values may be
        substituted with your own, if you have a valid database mail
        profile, you can configure the stored proc to use it instead.
        Leaving these lines commented out will not impact the operation
        of the queues.

            EXEC msdb.dbo.sp_send_dbmail
                 @profile_name = 'HelpDesk',
                 @recipients= @emailAddress,
                 @subject='Trouble Ticket Issued',
                 @body='Your support call has been logged,
                 and someone will be contacting you soon.'
     */

            DECLARE @output NVARCHAR(MAX)
            SET @output = 'A HelpDesk support ticket has been created for '
                 + @customerName + '. '
                 + 'Email sent to ' + @emailAddress +
                 ', regarding ' + @issue + '.'

        EXEC HelpDesk.LogMessage 'UserNotifyQueue', @output,
          @conversationHandle

        END CONVERSATION @conversationHandle
     END;
GO
```

Testing the Application

Now it's time to see Service Broker in action. Because building a web-based front-end for your application falls well outside the scope of this book, you can just execute the stored procedures manually. The effect is still the same, and the results are no different.

1. So, begin by creating a couple of trouble tickets (from a couple of troublemakers):

```
USE AWHelpDesk;
GO
EXEC TroubleTicket.AddNewTicket
     'George',
     'Costanza',
     'George@adventureworks.com',
     'My monitor display is fuzzy';
GO

EXEC TroubleTicket.AddNewTicket
     'Comso',
     'Kramer',
     'Cosmo@adventureworks.com',
     'The nnnnnnnnn key onnnn my keyboard sticks';
GO
```

2. Because you have not configured the stored procedures that will process the messages to run automatically, or through any other invocation method, you will have to manually execute them as you step through this exercise. Before you process the messages, you can query the queue directly to see the messages that are queued up. Since the conversation is established when the `AddNewTicket` stored procedure is executed, the messages are delivered immediately to the queue for the `TicketNotifyService`. You can query its queue with the following statement:

```
SELECT * FROM HelpDesk.UserNotifyQueue;
```

3. This should result in output similar to Figure 19-3.

4. To process the messages and deliver notification to the end-user, execute the `Helpdesk.ProcessMessages` stored procedure:

```
EXEC HelpDesk.ProcessMessages;
```

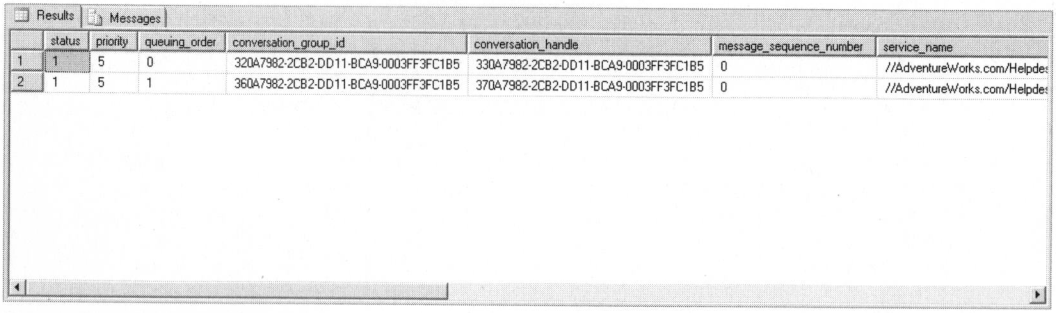

	status	priority	queuing_order	conversation_group_id	conversation_handle	message_sequence_number	service_name
1	1	5	0	320A7982-2CB2-DD11-BCA9-0003FF3FC1B5	330A7982-2CB2-DD11-BCA9-0003FF3FC1B5	0	//AdventureWorks.com/Helpde:
2	1	5	1	360A7982-2CB2-DD11-BCA9-0003FF3FC1B5	370A7982-2CB2-DD11-BCA9-0003FF3FC1B5	0	//AdventureWorks.com/Helpde:

Figure 19-3: The User Notify queue.

5. After executing this stored procedure, the following messages should be returned:

```
(1 row(s) affected)
Queue: UserNotifyQueue Message: A HelpDesk support ticket has been created
    for George Costanza. Email sent to George@adventureworks.com, regarding
    My monitor display is fuzzy. Conversation: 330A7982-2CB2-
    DD11-BCA9-0003FF3FC1B5

(1 row(s) affected)

(1 row(s) affected)
Queue: UserNotifyQueue Message: A HelpDesk support ticket has been created
    for Comso Kramer. Email sent to Cosmo@adventureworks.com, regarding The
    nnnnnnnnn key onnnn my keyboard sticks. Conversation: 330A7982-2CB2-
    DD11-BCA9-0003FF3FC1B5

(1 row(s) affected)
```

```
(0 row(s) affected)
Queue: UserNotifyQueue Message: No further messages found.

(1 row(s) affected)
```

This will generate the messages, as well as write to the message log you created in the last exercise. You can view the log contents by using the following query:

```
SELECT * FROM HelpDesk.MessageLog;
```

You should see results similar to Figure 19-4.

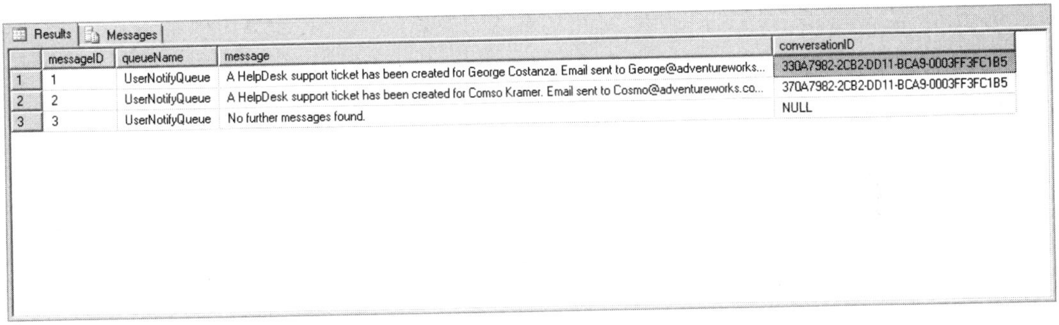

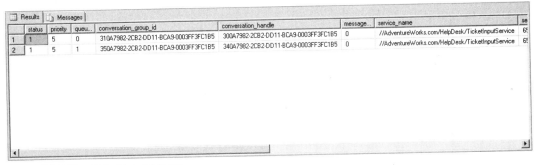

Figure 19-4: The `HelpDesk` **message log.**

Additionally, when the messages were processed by the `TicketNotifyService`, response messages were generated for the `TicketInputService`. You can view the queued messages for the `TicketInputService` by querying its queue, also:

```
SELECT * FROM TroubleTicket.TicketInputQueue;
```

This should return output similar to that shown in Figure 19-5.

Figure 19-5: The Ticket Input queue.

6. To write the queued responses to the log for the `TicketInputService`, execute the `TroubleTicket.ProcessMessages` stored procedure as listed here:

```
EXEC TroubleTicket.ProcessMessages;
```

As the messages get processed and logged, you should get messages similar to the following:

```
(1 row(s) affected)
  Queue: TicketInputQueue Message:
    http://schemas.microsoft.com/SQL/ServiceBroker/EndDialog
 Conversation: 300A7982-2CB2-DD11-BCA9-0003FF3FC1B5

(1 row(s) affected)

(1 row(s) affected)
  Queue: TicketInputQueue Message:
    http://schemas.microsoft.com/SQL/ServiceBroker/EndDialog
 Conversation: 300A7982-2CB2-DD11-BCA9-0003FF3FC1B5

(1 row(s) affected)

(0 row(s) affected)
Queue: TicketInputQueue Message: No further messages found.

(1 row(s) affected)
```

Now that the queue has been cleared, you can view the response messages in the log:

```
SELECT * FROM TroubleTicket.MessageLog;
```

The response messages confirm that the dialog for each message has ended, as shown in Figure 19-6.

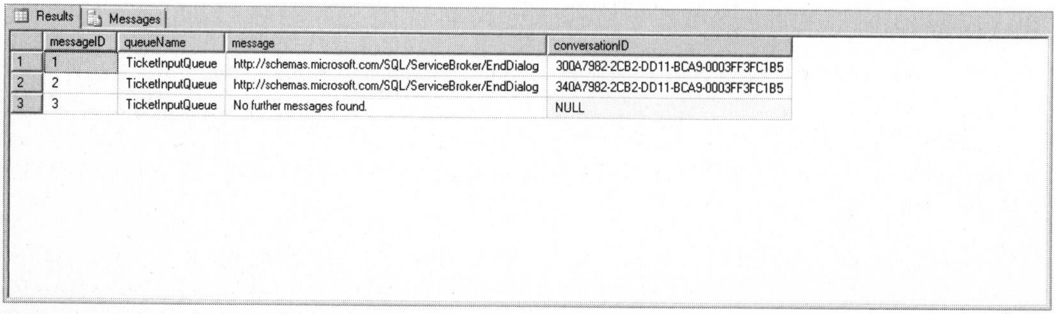

	messageID	queueName	message	conversationID
1	1	TicketInputQueue	http://schemas.microsoft.com/SQL/ServiceBroker/EndDialog	300A7982-2CB2-DD11-BCA9-0003FF3FC1B5
2	2	TicketInputQueue	http://schemas.microsoft.com/SQL/ServiceBroker/EndDialog	340A7982-2CB2-DD11-BCA9-0003FF3FC1B5
3	3	TicketInputQueue	No further messages found.	NULL

Figure 19-6: The `TroubleTicket` **message log.**

Managing Service Broker with SSMS

SQL Server 2008 expands the ability to browse and view the properties of Service Broker objects. While interaction with these components is limited to a Read Only state graphically, each object includes a "Create New or Modify" menu option that will open an object-specific CREATE or ALTER template in a new Query window. The ability to navigate and get the details of objects through Management Studio provides a significant benefit to those of us who prefer visual tools rather than text-based output. Figure 19-7 shows the expanded list of objects and their containers that you created in the previous example.

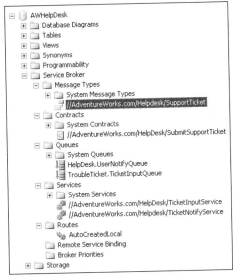

Figure 19-7: Service Broker objects in Management Studio.

Summary

Service Broker is a topic that can be intimidating to many DBAs, especially since it's still considered a fairly new feature. Hopefully, now that you've seen end-to-end delivery of messages using Service Broker, it should be easier for you to envision how it can be implemented with other applications. It is designed to create a more application-friendly architecture to meet the needs of many organizations, both large and small.

In this chapter, you learned about the concepts of SOA, what the Service Broker is, and what components are used in a Service Broker. You also had an opportunity to see Service Broker in action by building a simple application that shows you the process flow of Service Broker messages between services.

Index